VISITING COLLEGE
CAMPUSES

THE PRINCETON REVIEW

VISITING COLLEGE CAMPUSES

Sixth Edition

JANET SPENCER AND SANDRA MALESON

RANDOM HOUSE, INC.
NEW YORK
www.review.com

Princeton Review Publishing, L.L.C.
2315 Broadway
New York, NY 10024
E-mail: comments@review.com
© 1993, 1996, 1997, 2000, 2001 by Janet Spencer

This book was originally published by Citadel Press Books, an imprint of Carol
Publishing Group, New York, and was originally titled The Complete Guide to College
Visits.

ISBN 0-375-76208-6

Manufactured in the United States of America on partially recycled paper.

9   8   7   6   5   4   3   2   1

Sixth Edition

Dedicated to Leonard Maleson, in loving memory.

ACKNOWLEDGMENTS

Our special thanks to the Admissions Office staff members at each of the colleges and universities included in our guidebook. To our own research staff, Jennifer McCormick, Judy Farbman, Mickey Aronskind, Gabrielle Vitellio, and C.J. Rinaldi, we express our particular appreciation. Their thoroughness and persistence provided the details that will be so useful to our readers. We would like to thank the folks at The Princeton Review—Jennifer Fallon, Amy Kinney, Kevin McDonough, Julie Mandelbaum, Michael Palumbo, Nicole Kontolefa, Robert Franek, and Greta Englert— for their production, design, and editorial skills, and for keeping the book current. Thanks, too, to the many college alumni and students who gave us the student's perspective on schools included in this work and to the many parents, particularly Joan Powell and Helen Pomeroy, whose understanding of our mission and unstinting support and encouragement sustained us. We also thank college guidance counselors Laura Clark and Debra Ellman for sharing with us their expertise. And thanks to Martin Levin, former president of the Association of American Publishers, Inc., in the absence of whose initial enthusiasm this book would never have gotten off the ground.

Our own families receive our deepest gratitude. Thanks to Paul Maleson and Ron Spencer for their legal advice and moral support. Susannah and Stephen Maleson helped with various chores (physical and mental) and provided Sandy's initial experiences with college visiting. Amanda Spencer's college search and the prospect of George Spencer's college search were the real force that started the whole project.

This book has been fun to put together; we hope you have fun using it.

CONTENTS

INTRODUCTION

PARENTS, READ THIS

Planning the successful college trip can be a logistical nightmare. *Visiting College Campuses* will help you avoid this nightmare by simplifying the planning process. Since all the information you need is provided here, in one place, you can concentrate on making the college visiting experience pleasurable for you, your prospective college student, and the whole family. The college visit is a time to be together and to share the common goal of finding the environment in which your college student will thrive academically and socially for the next four (or five, or six) years.

If you are at all involved in your child's college application process, you will probably play a major role in planning these college visits. While you know these are supposed to be enjoyable, uplifting, informative experiences, you may be overwhelmed by the prospect of making them happen. Even the seasoned college visitor can feel this way, because each child has his or her own personalized list of possible colleges to visit and, guess what, even if you're visiting some schools for the second time, the information you gathered last time around may well be obsolete. Sure, the college is still in the same place, but don't assume the admissions office is.

You may be asking yourself "Where do I start?" or, more plaintively, "Why am I doing this?" Well, relax. We put this book together to help you, and we did so for three reasons. First, we think visiting colleges is important. Each trip will teach you and your child not only about the specific schools you visit, but about colleges in general. Your child will acquire a basis for comparison and will refine his or her ideas of what to look for in a college. Second, we think college visiting should be a great experience, a sort of mini-vacation. This country contains a wealth of universities and colleges that can stimulate the indifferent scholar and inspire the budding genius. Some of these schools will introduce you to intriguing spots you may not otherwise visit. The third reason is perhaps the most important. Even if your teenager is super-confident, you can't overlook the possibility that he might end up in a "safety" school. Anyone can suffer the disappointment of rejection from the first-choice school, and a visit to other colleges can turn up exciting second choices (and may even lead to a change in first choice). Help your child find these great places—**GO VISITING!**

STUDENTS, READ THIS (PARENTS TOO)

Visiting a college shouldn't be an awful experience, but it can be. Students and their families often start off on their college visiting trips without planning where to stay, what questions to ask, or what to do while they're there. You may be lucky; this "seat-of-the-pants" approach can sometimes work, but it's always best to have a plan.

That's why we wrote *Visiting College Campuses*. Whatever time you've allowed for visiting Dream College should be spent learning about the life you'll live if you go there, not rushing around looking for the admissions office, the nearest Ramada Inn, or the tour guide who left 15 minutes before you arrived.

SOME THINGS TO THINK ABOUT IN ADVANCE

The college visit, at a minimum, will consist of a tour and, typically, a group information session and/or individual interview. With the proper planning, this can be accomplished in two to three hours. Here are a few reasons for allowing more time.

If you have special interests, by all means, plan to explore what the college has to offer you in these areas. You may want to sit in on a lecture by some well-known professor. If so, you can check the sidebar information in each entry to see what kind of arrangements you need to make. If you plan on participating in inter-collegiate athletics, an interview with a coach will give you insight into the program offered, the requirements for participation, how your schedule will be affected, and what restrictions (athletes' tables, curfews, etc.) will affect your day-to-day life.

Just remember, you can't see everything in one visit. In fact, if you try to, you may have nothing left in your mind but a blur. It's more important for you to see those features you would actually make use of as a student. If you find that the tour still leaves some of your questions unanswered, by all means, speak up. Ideally, you will have allowed time to spend in the campus social centers, such as the student union. Plan on lunch in the cafeteria or a snack in the coffee shop. If school is in session, you'll be in the right place to get a feel for the students.

If the surrounding environment is important to you, take time to check it out. By exploring the nearby town, or discovering the lack thereof, you will avoid future surprises.

SOME SPECIFICS TO THINK ABOUT WHEN YOU VISIT

When visiting colleges, you will have certain questions in mind. The more colleges you visit, the more these questions will be refined and prioritized. The following list of questions isn't all-inclusive, but it does deal with some of the larger issues that could affect what you look for in a school.

HOW BIG IS THE PLACE?

If your list of college choices includes a mix of large and small schools, you'll want to find out which type of campus is best for you. If you're at a large school, think about whether you will feel overwhelmed. Sure, you'll have a wide choice of courses and professors, but will you enjoy being in a class of 300 or more students? On the other hand, the cozy, friendly feel of a small school might hold more appeal for you. Will you enjoy knowing everyone on campus by your sophomore year, or will you be chomping at the bit for a new face? Try to talk to the students you see. What do they think about the class size and the size of the student body?

WHAT IS THE SCHOOL'S CHARACTER?

Some schools are known as party schools, some as bastions of intense intellectualism. Usually the reality is somewhere in between. Talk to the students. Do they know and love their school's reputation, or do their comments paint a different picture? Do the students stay on campus on weekends? What do they do? Are social events campus-wide and do all students participate? What kinds of social events are there? Is the football (lacrosse, basketball) team the main focus of social life? Does one have to belong to a fraternity or sorority to be in the mainstream? As you listen to the students' answers to your questions, or even to their random remarks about life on campus, you will glean something of the school's character.

WHAT ARE THE STUDENTS LIKE?

Once again, talk to the students, and listen to their answers. Are they friendly? Arrogant? Competitive? Where do they come from? Do they like the school? Why? Do their reasons relate to your own concerns? Are the students unified, or is there divisiveness on campus? Does everyone look like you, or not like you? We're talking diversity here. Take a look at the bulletin boards and the school newspapers for clues.

A WORD ABOUT TOUR GUIDES . . .

We say "talk to students," but you might only have a chance to talk to the tour guide. By and large, the tour guide will be a wonderful advocate for the college. But, remember, tour guides are not chosen, nor do they volunteer, for the task of leading potential applicants around because they have complaints about the school. So expect their prepared remarks to be positive. They will answer your questions honestly, but you can assume that they will also put a positive gloss on their answers. Hence, our recommendation is that you keep your eyes and ears open and engage other students in conversation whenever possible.

Now, one very important point must be made here. You will have a natural tendency to like or dislike a school based on your feelings about the tour guide. Try to restrain this inclination, especially when you're not impressed by your guide. He might not always be your type of person, but that doesn't mean you won't find other folks on campus who are. Look around.

LIVING VS. LIFE

Beware of confusing the living situation with life on campus. You may be horrified when you see four students living in a room intended for two, or see long registration lines, large classes, and crowded cafeterias. This living situation results from a lot of people doing the same thing at the same time.

On the other hand, the life of the place is defined by how its students interact, and what people do with their time. We've already talked about ways of getting the feel for the college life. If you can't have a great living situation *and* a great student life, consider your priorities.

AFTER YOUR VISIT

Usually, only the odd or wacky things about a visit to a college stick out in your mind, so right after your visit, *write down* your impressions about the school. Many people believe in a grading system from 1 to 10 for categories like food, social life, academics, campus, student body. We think it's more helpful to write down the words that first come to mind after your experience. Describe as fully as you can the range of things that come into your head. Most often, these words will translate to a summary of your experience. Sometimes one word will pop up more than once. Pay attention to what you write; that will give you insight into what you feel about the college.

Remember that a college visit, done properly, can be the most useful tool you have in understanding what it is like to be student at a given school, and, eventually, deciding if you want to go there.

THE TEN-STEP PLAN
FOR SUCCESSFUL COLLEGE VISITS

Planning the college visiting trip can be daunting. At a minimum, it involves obtaining information and doing some logistical fancy footwork. This book contains all the information you need to make the planning easy and foolproof the trip's great fun. Following this step-by-step plan will make your life even easier.

To start, no doubt, you will have in mind some colleges you want to visit. Where do you begin, and when? Hint: Your child will get the best feel for a school when students are around—this means visiting during its regular session. Here's how you do this:

STEP 1

Figure out the days your child has off from school beginning in the spring semester of junior year. Obvious times will be spring break and Easter or Passover break. Also, if possible, leave the last week of August as well as early September free for visiting.

STEP 2

Once you have isolated a block of days, target a general geographical area to visit.

STEP 3

Determine that the colleges you are planning to visit in that area will be in session during your proposed trip.

Keep in mind that colleges have spring breaks at different times. Some begin as early as the first week of March, and some as late as the second week of April. Consult the College Calendars in this book or check with the admissions office of the school(s) you wish to see. If some of the schools in your targeted area are in session and some are not (and only one trip is feasible), you will have to make some hard choices. You may choose to plan around the more serious possibilities on your list or, alternatively, around the schools you know least about. Perhaps moving your trip a few days earlier or later will make a difference. Or consider going back to Step 2 for a different geographical area.

Also note that some, but not all, schools start the fall semester in late August rather than after Labor Day. You may wish to use the last days of summer for making an extended trip. (Some schools discourage visits while students are arriving, so double check with the admissions office as to if, and when, your visit might not be appreciated.) Columbus Day weekend is another option for a trip, as some colleges are in session on Monday when your child may be off. Consult the College Calendars in this book.

Saturday visits may be possible if your child is interested in a nearby school. Usually, though not always, the school's admissions office is open on Saturday morning during the regular academic year, and there may be morning classes. Check the entry in this book for the school you are considering visiting on Saturday. The campus will probably be quieter on Saturday than it is during the regular week.

STEP 4

Now, let's assume that you have targeted a particular geographical area for your tour and have made a list of the schools you would like to visit. Here's a suggestion: As long as you are in the area, think about expanding your itinerary to include some other colleges in the neighborhood. Get ideas by consulting the maps in this book. Some of these colleges may be unfamiliar to you; check them out with the college guidance counselor or in a college guidebook. You may be in for some pleasant surprises.

STEP 5

You are now going to plot your itinerary. If you are visiting two or more schools in one trip, you will want to make a nice, easy loop requiring as little backtracking as possible.

Determine the first college you want to visit in the area and how you will get there. Check the entry for car, plane, bus, or train information and maps showing the major cities and their distances from the schools.

Now, in order to plan out your loop, you are going to have to know where your target schools are located in relation to each other. Many of the schools will be in towns you have never heard of. Instead of undertaking serious map work, simply consult the regional and state maps in this book, where this information is provided.

Once you have laid out your loop, establishing the order in which you are going to visit your target schools, you will want to know how long it will take you to get from one school to another. Refer to the Mileage Matrices in this book for the mileage between schools on a state-wide and region-wide basis. With this information, you can estimate how long it will take you to get from one school to another by car.

STEP 6

Now estimate how much time you will spend at the school. This largely depends on what you want to do when you visit. Your options may include some or all of the following: a self-guided tour of the campus using a map supplied by the admissions office, a student-led tour of the campus, an on-campus interview with an admissions office staff member, an information session (a group meeting with a staff member, often in lieu of interviews), a visit to classes, a meeting with a faculty member or athletic coach, an overnight stay. Check the entries in this book for details on availability, schedules and how and when to make arrangements. You can also call the school for additional information.

The basic college visit will include a student-led tour and possibly an interview or information session. For this, you should plan on a minimum of two to three hours per visit and no more than two visits per day.

Once you have determined what you want to do on campus and how long it will take you to get to the next college in your loop, you can identify the optimum time for your campus visit. The accuracy of your calculations here becomes more important, of course, the tighter your schedule.

STEP 7

What about arrangements? If you wish simply to go on a tour, this will require a minimum of advance planning (although some schools request advance notice even for tours—check the entry in this book. Tours usually go out according to a schedule and you may want to time your visit accordingly. (Check the entries in this book or call the admissions office.)

At many colleges, (though not all—see the college entry in this book or call admissions), your child can be interviewed by a staff member of the admissions office at the time of your visit, even though an application has yet to be filed. If an interview is required as part of the admissions process, consider coordinating the interview with your campus visit.

Now, if you opt for the on-campus interview, you will have to do some advance planning. Call the admissions office far enough in advance so that a convenient time slot is still available (see the entries in this book, as schools vary as to how much advance notice is generally required). Hint: your child may be more comfortable touring the school before sitting down for the interview. Be sure to indicate your preference to the admissions office.

You may encounter a logistical hurdle if you are planning a spring trip. Some schools do not interview juniors until late spring (consult the entry in this book for details). In such an event, decide which is more important, seeing the school in session or having an on-campus interview.

Should your child schedule the interview? Some students may be up to this, but for others, merely talking about the interview and the college visit so far in advance will create unnecessary anxiety. It is okay for the parent to schedule the interview. In fact, ad hoc scheduling decisions may have to be made while conferring with the admissions office—decisions which are best made by the primary trip planner: you.

STEP 8

Now that you have the interview scheduled and know when the tour will depart, you can determine the precise time you should arrive at the admissions office. Hint: Plan to get there early so your child can relax before the tour and can look through student yearbooks and other publications.

Don't plan to rush off right after the interview either. During your 20- to 45-minute tour the guide will have taken you through the eating facilities and student union, but you may want to return on your own. Relax over lunch or coffee among the students.

STEP 9

Continue on! Consult your Step 5 itinerary to determine how long it will take to get to your next school. Allowing for adequate travel time, begin the planning process again at Step 6. Repeat this process for additional schools. Visiting more than two schools in one day is not advised.

STEP 10

Where to stay. Many college towns have great character. Why not stay in a local inn that has some special charm? Poke around in the shops or visit some of the local attractions. Or stay at a nearby resort, dude ranch, spa, campground, etc. and bring the whole family. In your free time, you can swim, play tennis, canoe, fish, or hike. Or splurge on a luxury hotel with an indoor pool and health club near shops and other amenities. Investigate what is within walking distance. There might be a delightful bed and breakfast with afternoon tea and homemade muffins in the morning, for example, right up the block. Sometimes the school itself has accommodations available. Check the entries in this book for all of the best, most convenient, and amusing accommodations near the colleges (as well as some budget options).

The key to the college trip is to make it fun and stress-free, as well as worthwhile. Advance planning will make things go smoothly and help you avoid disappointments. Good luck, and happy visiting.

PART I
How This Book Works

Visiting College Campuses helps you make sure you have everything planned in advance. To make it easier to find information about the schools of your choice, we've used the same format for every school. Look at the sample page below:

Office Hours

Highlights

The Rest of the Story

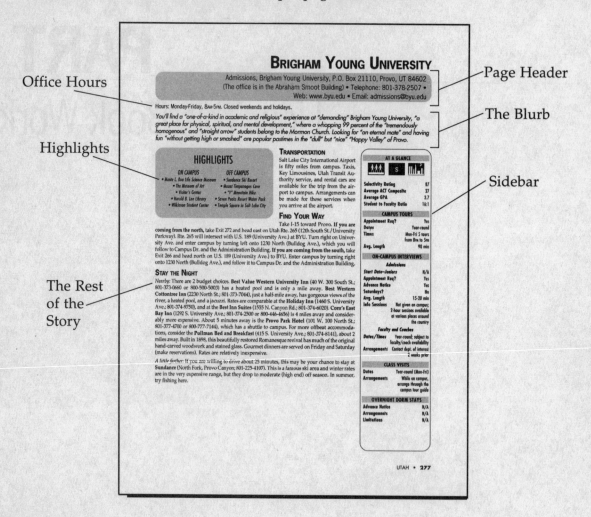

Page Header

The Blurb

Sidebar

Here's a rundown of the components you'll find on each page.

PAGE HEADER

The page header contains the college or university's admissions office address as well as the building it's in (which is not always included on the mailing address, but is very important to know once you're on campus). We've also included the admissions office phone number, fax number when possible, Web address, and e-mail address, so you can contact the school.

OFFICE HOURS

The header is followed by the admissions office's hours and vacation schedule. Use this information to start planning your college visit. Write or call them (or, even better, do both) to arrange for your information session, tour, etc.

"The Blurb"

The blurb is the *italicized* stuff near the top of each profile. The general idea behind every blurb is to give you some useful and interesting information about the school—where it's located, what students do for fun, school history, amusing trivia, etc. We've tried to make each blurb unique, practical, and (sometimes) even witty.

Sidebar

The At a Glance section that starts each sidebar relates some basic information that, like the blurb, is meant to give you a general sense of the school and the students who go there. The three icons at the top of each sidebar give the school's enrollment, tuition, and environment respectively.

Enrollment:

- Large (more than 10,000 undergraduates)
- Medium (4,000 to 10,000 undergraduates)
- Small (less than 4,000 undergraduates)

Tuition (for in-state students):

- $$$ Very Expensive (more than $15,000)
- $$ Expensive ($10,000 to $15,000)
- $ Moderate (less than $10,000)

Environment:

- Urban/City
- Suburban
- Rural/Small Town

The rest of the sidebar contains all sorts of information about the things you should do to learn about a school when visiting campus. This information will help you plan stuff like interviews (with admissions, faculty, and coaches), tours, information sessions, dorm stays, and class visits.

Highlights

Once you've survived that nerve-wracking interview and the thirty-minute campus tour in the rain (minus your umbrella), why not kick back and see the sights? In the highlights box, we have listed some of the attractions for which each college town is famous as well as some points of interest right on campus. These recommendations run the gamut from museums and art galleries to state parks and waterslides. We hope they make your good visits even more enjoyable, and your bad visits something less than disastrous.

The Rest of the Story

The remainder of the entry is about the part of your trip that happens off campus: how to get to the school and where to stay. You know, the fun stuff. It's divided into the following sections:

Transportation

This section starts out with the transportation available to campus; nothing makes a short couple of days seem like a long, horrible couple of days like getting stuck at the bus station, or taking a train when you could have flown. Once you decide on plane, train, or bus, we tell you the best way to get to campus from the airport, train station, or bus depot.

Find Your Way

If you are looking at schools in your general vicinity, you are probably driving. For you, the driver, we provide directions from the major highways to the front door of the admissions office.

Stay the Night

If you're going to stay overnight, *make reservations*. Do not get to the school and then decide where you are going to stay. Too often this puts you at the mercy of over-priced on-campus motels or last-resort hovels only too happy to take a tourist for a few extra bills. *Visiting College Campuses* gives you tons of choices—hotels, motels, resorts, bed-and-breakfasts—at each college we cover. We also let you know what prices to expect: cheap, moderate, or pricey. We even tell you when a subtle drop of a university's name will get you a special rate.

AND THERE'S MORE

To start off each new state, we provide a detailed road map and mileage matrix for the colleges and large cities in that state, so you know how far it is from, say, Dallas to the University of Texas at Austin, how far it is from school to school within the state, and how far it is from Dallas to San Antonio.

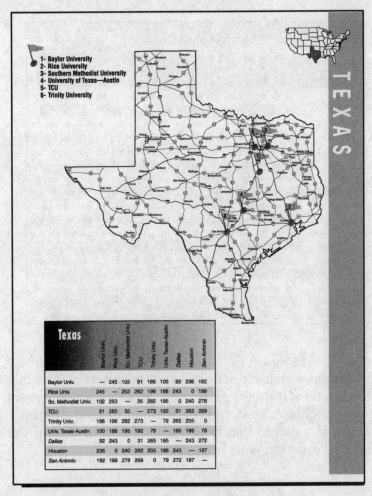

1- Baylor University
2- Rice University
3- Southern Methodist University
4- University of Texas—Austin
5- TCU
6- Trinity University

Texas	Baylor Univ.	Rice Univ.	So. Methodist Univ.	TCU	Trinity Univ.	Univ. Texas-Austin	Dallas	Houston	San Antonio
Baylor Univ.	—	245	102	91	186	100	92	236	182
Rice Univ.	245	—	253	282	196	186	243	0	189
So. Methodist Univ.	102	253	—	35	282	195	0	240	278
TCU	91	282	35	—	273	192	31	262	269
Trinity Univ.	186	196	282	273	—	79	265	205	0
Univ. Texas-Austin	100	186	195	192	79	—	195	186	79
Dallas	92	243	0	31	265	195	—	243	272
Houston	236	0	240	262	205	186	243	—	197
San Antonio	182	189	278	269	0	79	272	197	—

The road maps and mileage matrices will help you better plan a group of visits in a single state. Similarly, in Appendix One we have included mileage information for specific regions of the country. So, for example, if you are looking at schools in the South Atlantic region, you can find out how far it is from the University of Miami to the University of Georgia, and better plan your visit schedule.

South Atlantic	Atlanta	Baltimore	Charleston, SC	Clemson Univ.	Coll. William & Mary	Duke Univ.	Eckerd Coll.	Florida State Univ.	Orlando	Univ. of Delaware	Univ. of Florida	Univ. of Georgia	Univ. of Miami	Univ. S. Carolina	Univ. of Virginia	Wake Forest Univ.	West Virginia Univ.
Atlanta	—	654	291	117	591	374	484	267	426	796	333	66	668	215	575	350	654
Baltimore	654	—	568	609	195	296	968	895	892	58	824	615	1099	517	160	375	204
Charleston, SC	291	568	—	240	480	285	461	344	384	626	317	275	595	114	499	264	620
Clemson Univ.	117	609	240	—	478	261	561	364	517	667	418	85	747	118	395	207	566
Coll. William & Mary	591	195	480	478	—	204	899	781	822	253	755	548	1035	448	131	257	321
Duke Univ.	374	296	285	261	204	—	726	608	649	351	582	375	862	275	173	84	391
Eckerd Coll.	484	968	461	561	899	726	—	260	104	1026	166	580	278	513	899	693	1117
Florida State Univ.	267	895	344	364	781	608	260	—	254	953	158	279	494	358	728	538	936
Orlando	426	892	384	517	822	649	104	254	—	950	114	504	242	437	822	616	1040
Univ. of Delaware	796	58	626	667	253	351	1026	953	950	—	882	673	1157	575	218	433	262
Univ. of Florida	333	824	317	418	755	582	166	158	114	882	—	345	363	444	755	549	973
Univ. of Georgia	66	615	275	85	548	375	580	279	504	673	345	—	717	153	548	277	639
Univ. of Miami	688	1099	595	747	1035	862	278	494	242	1157	363	717	—	648	1035	829	1253
Univ. South Carolina	215	517	114	118	448	275	513	358	437	575	444	153	648	—	367	180	559
Univ. of Virginia	575	160	499	395	131	173	899	728	822	218	755	548	1035	367	—	190	190
Wake Forest Univ.	350	375	264	207	257	84	693	538	616	433	549	277	829	180	190	—	355
West Virginia Univ.	654	204	620	566	321	391	1117	936	1040	262	973	639	1253	559	190	355	—

Appendix Two contains a state-by-state guide to each school's academic calendar. The easy-to-reference format shows you exactly what's going on, month by month, at the schools of your choice. So if you're planning to visit Auburn University in March, you'll know at a glance that exams are scheduled during the second and third weeks, and you can plan your trip accordingly.

School	January	February	March	April	May
Alabama **AUBURN UNIVERSITY**	Winter session begins 2nd week. No classes MLK Day.	Classes continue.	Exams 2nd-3rd weeks.	Spring break 1st week.	Exams 2nd week. Summer session begins 3rd week.
TUSKEGEE UNIVERSITY	Spring session begins 3rd week.	Classes continue.	Spring break 2nd week. Classes resume 3rd week.	No classes Good Fri. through Easter Mon.	Exams 2nd week.

PART II

College Entries Arranged by State

1- University of Alabama
2- Auburn University
3- Tuskegee University

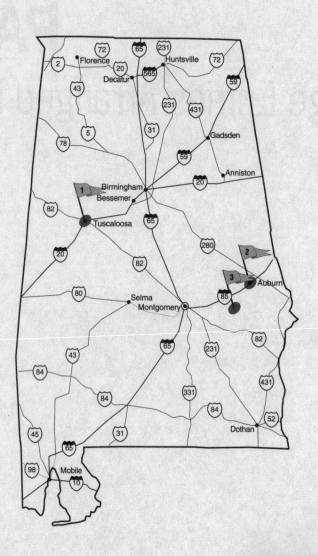

Alabama	Auburn Univ.	Tuskegee Univ.	Univ. of Alabama	Birmingham	Montgomery
Auburn Univ.	—	20	165	117	59
Tuskegee Univ.	20	—	149	136	39
Univ. of Alabama	165	149	—	49	104
Birmingham	117	136	49	—	93
Montgomery	59	39	104	93	—

AUBURN UNIVERSITY

Admissions Office, 202 Martin Hall, Auburn, AL 36849-5145
(Martin Hall is on Thach Ave.) • Telephone: 334-844-4080 • Web: www.auburn.edu •
Email: admissions@auburn.edu

Hours: Monday-Friday, 8AM-4:45PM. Closed weekends, July 4, Labor Day, Thanksgiving, and Christmas.

Auburn is a cost-effective school that offers a ton of majors and is especially strong in the sciences. Every student is required to complete a broad core curriculum during freshman and sophomore year that covers writing skills and all of the major arts and sciences. Much social life revolves around athletics, and there is plenty of school spirit, most notably for the football team.

HIGHLIGHTS

ON CAMPUS	OFF CAMPUS
• University Theatre	• Old Main and Church Street District
	• Chewacla State Park

TRANSPORTATION

Hartsfield International Airport in Atlanta, GA, is approximately 100 miles from campus. Dixie Excursions (334-887-6295) runs vans for 4 daily round trips between the airport and campus. Rental cars are available at the airport. The Columbus, GA, airport is 40 miles from campus, but is not as accessible as the Atlanta airport.

FIND YOUR WAY

From I-85 (which runs from Atlanta, GA, to Montgomery, AL), take Exit 51 onto U.S. Rte. 29 N. This becomes College St., which borders the campus. The campus is approximately 3 miles from I-85.

STAY THE NIGHT

Nearby: Across the street from the university is the **Auburn University Hotel and Conference Center** (241 S. College St.; 334-821-8200 or 800-2-AUBURN), where you can have a double room at a moderate rate. The hotel has a restaurant, lounge, gift shop, pool, weight room, and privileges at a tennis court. Also across the street is the inexpensive **Heart of Auburn Motel** (334-887-3462 or 800-843-5634). This large motel offers basic accommodations and has a pool. **The Crenshaw Guest House** (371 N. College St.; 334-821-1131) offers suites at a moderate rate and a carriage house in the garden at an inexpensive rate. It is a few blocks from the university and is on a historic block.

A little farther: One mile away is the **Quality Inn–University Center** (1577 S. College St.; 334-821-7001). It is inexpensive (tell them you're visiting the university), and you can enjoy a pool, game room, restaurant, lounge, gift shop, and bands on the premises Friday and Saturday nights. For additional lodging, see Web: www.auburn-opelika.com.

AT A GLANCE	
Selectivity Rating	78
Range SAT I Math	500-600
Average SAT I Math	551
Range SAT I Verbal	480-590
Average SAT I Verbal	541
Average ACT Composite	23
Average GPA	3.1
Student to Faculty Ratio	16:1

CAMPUS TOURS	
Appointment Req?	Recommended
Dates	Year-round
Times	Mon-Fri 8AM-4PM
Avg. Length	40-45 min

ON-CAMPUS INTERVIEWS	
Admissions	
Start Date–Juniors	Any time
Appointment Req?	Recommended
Advance Notice	Varies
Saturdays?	No
Avg. Length	40-45 min
Faculty and Coaches	
Dates/Times	Year-round, subject to faculty/coach availability
Arrangements	Contact the particular faculty/coach or admissions off.

CLASS VISITS	
Dates	Year-round (Mon-Fri)
Arrangements	Recommended

OVERNIGHT DORM STAYS	
Advance Notice	N/A
Limitations	N/A
Arrangements	N/A

TUSKEGEE UNIVERSITY

Admissions Office, Old Administration Building, Tuskegee University, Tuskegee Institute, AL 36088 • Telephone: 800-622-6531 or 334-727-8500 • Web: www.tusk.edu • Email: admis@acd.tusk.edu

Hours: Monday-Friday, 8AM-4:30PM; Saturday, by appointment only. Closed Sundays and holidays.

Despite several quality liberal arts departments and a great veterinary program (over 70 percent of the African American veterinarians in the world trained here), Tuskegee is proudest of its engineering programs, which enroll nearly a quarter of the students. It also produces the most African American military officers—including West Point and the Naval Academy. Alumni include 1980s pop phenom Lionel Richie.

AT A GLANCE

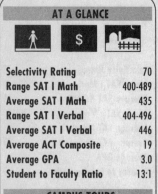

Selectivity Rating	70
Range SAT I Math	400-489
Average SAT I Math	435
Range SAT I Verbal	404-496
Average SAT I Verbal	446
Average ACT Composite	19
Average GPA	3.0
Student to Faculty Ratio	13:1

CAMPUS TOURS

Appointment Req?	Contact University Escorts at 800-622-6531
Dates	Year-round, except holidays
Times	7 days a week
Avg. Length	Varies

ON-CAMPUS INTERVIEWS

Admissions

Start Date—Juniors	N/A
Appointment Req?	N/A
Advance Notice	N/A
Saturdays?	N/A
Avg. Length	N/A
Info Sessions	Contact University Escorts

Faculty and Coaches

Dates/Times	Year-round; subject to availability
Arrangements	Contact University Escorts 1 week prior

CLASS VISITS

Dates	Year-round (Mon-Fri)
Arrangements	Contact University Escorts

OVERNIGHT DORM STAYS

Advance Notice	Yes
Arrangements	Contact University Escorts
Limitations	Subject to availability of an on-campus student

TRANSPORTATION

The Montgomery airport is approximately 50 miles from campus. Taxi and limousine services are available for the trip to campus. You can also take a taxi from the airport to the Montgomery bus station and then take a bus to the university.

FIND YOUR WAY

Take I-85 or U.S. Rte. 29 to Tuskegee.

STAY THE NIGHT

Nearby: You can't get nearer than the on-campus **Dorothy Hall Guesthouse** (334-727-8753). Breakfast is served in the café, except on Saturday and Sunday. The usual array of restaurants, many inexpensive, can be found 1 mile away in Tuskegee. The **Western Inn** (I-85 and Hwy. 81; 334-727-5400) costs only a little bit more. It's in a rural area 5 miles outside of Tuskegee and has a restaurant and a lounge.

A little farther: Auburn is 20 minutes from Tuskegee. See the Auburn University entry for places to stay in that area.

HIGHLIGHTS

ON CAMPUS
- George Washington Carver Museum
- Kellogg Conference Center
- Tuskegee Chapel
- The Tuskegee Cemetery
- General Daniel "Chappie" James Center

OFF CAMPUS
- Carver Museum
- Tuskegee National Forest

UNIVERSITY OF ALABAMA—TUSCALOOSA

Admissions Office, University of Alabama, P.O. Box 870132, Tuscaloosa, AL 35487-0132
(The office is in Rm. 151 of the Rose Administration Building, on University Blvd.) •
Telephone: 800-933-BAMA or 205-348-5666 • Web: www.ua.edu • Email: uaadmit@ua.edu

Hours: Monday-Friday, 8AM-4:45PM; Saturday, 8AM-noon. Closed Sundays and most holidays.

The Tuscaloosa campus of the University of Alabama offers a strong education program in areas from engineering to education to the arts and sciences to its nearly 15,000 students. Alabama's honors program allows motivated students opportunities for research not found in most undergraduate programs, and football here is practically a religion.

HIGHLIGHTS

ON CAMPUS
- University of Alabama Museum of Natural History
- Amelia Gayle Gorgas Library
- Bryant-Denny Stadium
- The Gorgas House Museum
- Paul W. Bryant Museum

OFF CAMPUS
- Holt Lake
- Lake Lurleen
- Lake Tuscaloosa

TRANSPORTATION

The Birmingham airport is a one-hour drive from campus. Rental cars are available at the airport. There is also a smaller airport (Van de Graff Field) in Tuscaloosa. Amtrak train service is available to Tuscaloosa from New York and New Orleans.

FIND YOUR WAY

I-20/59 is the main highway into Tuscaloosa. Take the McFarland Blvd. exit from I-59, turning onto McFarland (it's a right turn if you're coming from Birmingham). Stay on McFarland and take Exit 215 (University Blvd.); the Rose Administration Building will be on the left as you enter campus.

STAY THE NIGHT

Nearby: For convenience, you can't do better than the on-campus **Four Points Hotel** (320 Paul W. Bryant Dr.; 205-752-3200), whose moderate price includes passes to the health club and use of tennis courts. A number of Tuscaloosa motels are within a 15-minute drive. **The Holiday Inn** (3920 E. McFarland Blvd.; 205-553-1550), at the high end of the inexpensive range, is about 3.5 miles from the school and has a restaurant and pool. The standard room rate includes passes to the downtown YMCA. **Shoney's Inn** (3501 McFarland Blvd.; 205-556-7950) is also inexpensive and has a pool. It is about 15 minutes away. A **Best Western** (1780 McFarland Blvd. NE; 205-759-2511) is about 10 minutes away. It is inexpensive and has a pool.

A little farther: If you are willing to venture about 35 miles from the university, you might want to stay at the **Blue Shadows Bed and Breakfast Guesthouse** in Greensboro (a very interesting town). In a country setting on 320 acres, you will find a formal garden, nature trail, private fish pond, and bird sanctuary. Enjoy afternoon tea and a continental breakfast. The price is at the high end of the inexpensive range.

AT A GLANCE

Selectivity Rating	79
Range SAT I Math	480-600
Range SAT I Verbal	480-600
Average ACT Composite	24
Average GPA	3.3
Student to Faculty Ratio	17:1

CAMPUS TOURS

Appointment Req?	Yes
Dates	Year-round
Times	Mon-Fri 10AM-2PM; Sat 10AM
Avg. Length	1 hour

ON-CAMPUS INTERVIEWS

Admissions

Start Date—Juniors	Any time
Appointment Req?	Yes
Advance Notice	1 week
Saturdays?	No
Avg. Length	20 min
Info Sessions	Available on request

Faculty and Coaches

Dates/Times	Year-round; subject to faculty/coach availability
Arrangements	Contact admissions off. 1-2 weeks prior

CLASS VISITS

Dates	Year-round (Mon-Fri)
Arrangements	Contact admissions off.

OVERNIGHT DORM STAYS

Advance Notice	N/A
Arrangements	Contact admissions off.
Limitations	N/A

ARIZONA

1- University of Arizona
2- Arizona State University

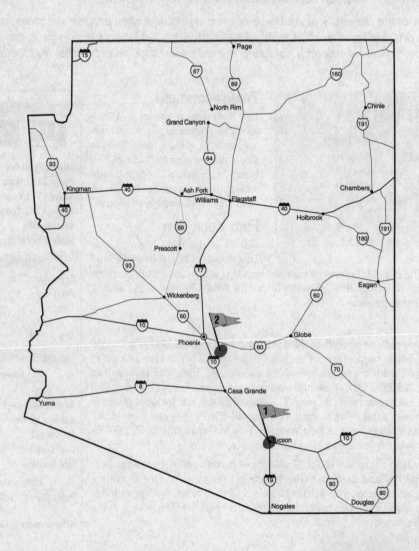

Arizona	Arizona State Univ.	Univ. Arizona	Phoenix	Tucson
Arizona State Univ.	—	103	4	113
Univ. Arizona	103	—	117	0
Phoenix	4	117	—	117
Tucson	113	0	117	—

ARIZONA STATE UNIVERSITY

Undergraduate Admissions Office, Arizona State University, P.O. Box 870112, Tempe, AZ 85287-0112 • Telephone: 480-965-7788 • Web: www.asu.edu • Email: ugradad@asuvm.inre.asu.edu

Hours: Monday-Friday, 8AM-5PM. Closed weekends and state holidays.

It's hard not to have a good time at ASU, what with year-round sun, warmth, fantastic sports and recreation facilities, and over 30,000 peers to accompany you as you strut the streets of Tempe.

HIGHLIGHTS

ON CAMPUS
- Campus Tour
- Grady Gammage Auditorium
- ASU Art Museum
- ASU Planetarium
- Computing Commons Gallery

OFF CAMPUS
- Tempe Town Lake
- Desert Botanical Gardens
- Baseball Spring Training
- Phoenix Zoo
- The Grand Canyon

TRANSPORTATION

Sky Harbor Airport in Phoenix is approximately 15 minutes from campus. Taxis, limousines, and shared rides are available at the airport, or you can call a local taxi company or Super Shuttle (800-331-3565 from outside Arizona or 602-244-9000 in Arizona). Amtrak train and Greyhound bus service is available to Phoenix. Taxis can take you to campus from the stations. Phoenix Transit System buses also travel between Phoenix and Tempe; call 602-257-8426 for information.

FIND YOUR WAY

From Sky Harbor Airport, take Highway 202 Loop east to Scottsdale/Rural Rd. Turn right (south) onto Rural Rd. to Apache Blvd. Turn right (west) onto Apache Blvd. to Forest Ave. Turn right (north) onto Forest Ave. The Student Services Building is located on the corner of Forest Ave. and Lemon St. (southwest corner of campus). Park in Visitor Parking Structure #1.

STAY THE NIGHT

Nearby: You have 3 convenient choices just across the street from the university. **Twin Palms Hotel** (225 E. Apache Blvd.; 480-967-9431) has moderate rates and a heated outdoor pool. The **Holiday Inn** (915 E. Apache Blvd.; 480-968-3451) is slightly more expensive but still moderate. It has a dining room, a heated outdoor pool, and an exercise room. The **Tempe Mission Palms Hotel** (60 E. 5th St.; 480-894-1400) is a bit more pricey, with most rooms in the expensive range, but some rooms are available at a moderate rate. It has an exercise room, a sauna, a jacuzzi, two tennis courts, a lounge, and a restaurant.

A little farther: The area is full of expensive resorts and hotels. To mention just two: **John Gardiner's Tennis Ranch** in Scottsdale (480-948-2100) is fantastic, and the **Arizona Biltmore** (480-955-6600) is the grand dame of Phoenix hotels. For more information call Tempe Chamber of Commerce at 480-967-7891.

AT A GLANCE

Selectivity Rating	75
Range SAT I Math	490-620
Average SAT I Math	559
Range SAT I Verbal	490-600
Average SAT I Verbal	548
Average ACT Composite	24
Average GPA	3.4
Student to Faculty Ratio	21:1

CAMPUS TOURS / INFORMATION SESSIONS

Appointment Req?	Yes
Dates	Year-round
Times	Contact admissions off. at 480-727-7013
Avg. Length	90 min

ON-CAMPUS APPOINTMENTS

Admissions

Start Date—Juniors	Any time
Appointment Req?	Yes
Advance Notice	A few weeks
Saturdays?	No
Avg. Length	30 min
Info Sessions	Contact admissions off.

Faculty and Coaches

Dates/Times	Year-round; subject to faculty/coach availability
Arrangements	Contact the dept. of interest 2-3 weeks prior

CLASS VISITS

Dates	Fall and spring semesters only (Mon-Fri)
Arrangements	Contact START (Student Admissions Relations Team) at 480-727-7013

UNIVERSITY OF ARIZONA

Admissions Office, Robert L. Nugent Building, University of Arizona, Tucson, AZ 85721 • Telephone: 520-621-3237 • Web: www.arizona.edu • Email: appinfo@arizona.edu

Hours: Monday-Friday, 8AM-5PM. Closed weekends and all holidays.

The University of Arizona in Tucson is a comprehensive institution with programs ranging from the liberal arts to technologically advanced engineering studies and about 25,000 highly satisfied and highly tanned students. Famous Chinese dissident and astrophysicist Fang Lizhi continues his groundbreaking research here, and he teaches undergraduate classes.

AT A GLANCE

Selectivity Rating	73
Range SAT I Math	490-610
Average SAT I Math	550
Range SAT I Verbal	480-600
Average SAT I Verbal	540
Average ACT Composite	23
Average GPA	3.3
Student to Faculty Ratio	19:1

CAMPUS TOURS

Appointment Req?	No
Dates	Year-round
Times	10AM and 2PM
Avg. Length	90 min

ON-CAMPUS INTERVIEWS

Admissions

Start Date–Juniors	Any time
Appointment Req?	No
Advance Notice	1 week
Saturdays?	No
Avg. Length	30 min
Info Sessions	N/A

Faculty and Coaches

Dates/Times	Year-round; subject to faculty/coach availability
Arrangements	Call 520-621-3641

CLASS VISITS

Dates	Year-round (Mon-Fri)
Arrangements	Call 520-621-3641

OVERNIGHT DORM STAYS

Advance Notice	N/A
Arrangements	N/A
Limitations	N/A

TRANSPORTATION

Tucson International is 10 miles from campus. For Stagecoach (van) service to campus, call 520-889-9681 at least 24 hours in advance; taxi service is also available. Amtrak trains and Greyhound/Trailways buses serve Tucson. Sun Tran is the public transportation system, which operates buses throughout the area.

FIND YOUR WAY

Take Speedway to Mountain Avenue. Turn right onto Mountain and get in the left-hand lane. At the stop sign at Second Street, turn left. Visitor parking is in the garage on your right.

STAY THE NIGHT

Nearby: **Plaza Hotel and Conference Center** (1900 E. Speedway; 520-327-7341 or 800-843-8052) is immediately across the street from the university and is a full-service, 7-story hotel with an outdoor pool. The rates are highest in January and February. **Marriot University Park Hotel** (880 East Second St.; 520-792-4100 or 800-228-9290) is one block from the University and is a 4-star, full service, 9-story atrium hotel with outdoor heated pool and jacuzzi, fitness center, business center, and full service restaurant. The **Lodge on the Desert** (306 N. Alvernon Way; 520-325-3366 or 800-456-5634), 4 miles from campus, is a moderately priced choice, with rates somewhat higher during the winter season (December–May). The lodge will remind you of a Mexican hacienda. The **Arizona Inn** (2200 E. Elm St.; 520-325-1541), just over 1 mile from the campus, has all the amenities of a grand hotel, including tennis courts, a swimming pool, and acres of lawns and gardens. Some less expensive choices are more convenient to the campus. **University Inn** (950 N. Stone Ave.; 520-791-7503 or 800-233-8466) has a midtown location close to shopping and to the campus, and you can have a double room in a relaxed atmosphere for an inexpensive rate. An even more basic and less expensive lodging can be had 3 miles from the campus at the **Discovery Inn** (1010 S. Freeway; 520-622-5871). The **La Quinta Motor Inn** (665 N. Freeway; 520-622-6491) is 6 miles from campus. One mile from campus (courtesy car to the campus) is the **Ramada Downtown** (1601 N. Oracle Rd.; 520-884-7422), with doubles in the moderate range, a peaceful garden, and a heated pool. A couple of nice bed-and-breakfasts are within walking distance of the university. **La Posada del Valle** (1640 N. Campbell Ave.; 520-795-3840) has a special rate in the moderate range for university visitors that drops down from June-September. **Peppertree's Bed and Breakfast** (724 E. University Blvd.; 520-622-7167) is a 1905 Territorial home offering a full gourmet breakfast and afternoon tea. Peppertree's has moderate rates for its 4 rooms.

A little farther: Consider **Tanque Verde** (14301 E. Speedway; 520-296-6275). This is a fabulous ranch with riding and tennis, indoor and outdoor pools, sauna, and exercise room. It's a very expensive choice, but the cost includes 3 full meals. Don't forget that the very expensive **Canyon Ranch Spa** (602-749-9000 or 800-742-9000) is in Tucson. You can enjoy a luxury spa and be only a 35-minute drive from the University of Arizona.

HIGHLIGHTS

ON CAMPUS
- Flandran Science Center
- Center for creative Photography
- UA Museum of Art
- Athletics Events
- Arizona State Museum

OFF CAMPUS
- Spring Training— Major League Baseball
- AZ/Sonora Desert Museum
- Old Tuscon
- Kartchner Caverns
- Sabino Canyon

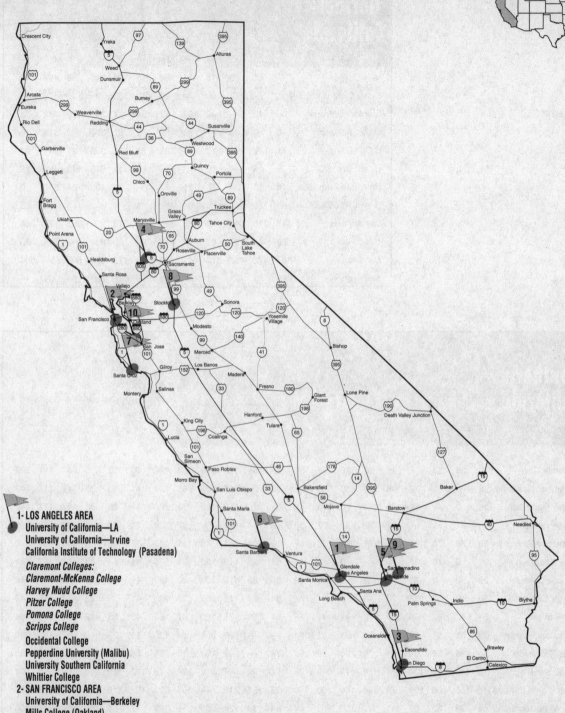

CALIFORNIA

Northern California

	Mills College	Santa Clara Univ.	Stanford University	U.Cal.-Berkeley	U.Cal.-Davis	U.Cal.-Santa Cruz	Univ. San Francisco	Univ. of the Pacific	Los Angeles	Sacramento	San Diego	San Francisco
Mills College	—	51	38	10	71	69	16	88	345	88	497	13
Santa Clara University	51	—	12	59	123	35	63	130	326	140	472	5
Stanford University	38	12	—	40	103	47	34	77	340	120	482	35
U.Cal.-Berkeley	10	59	40	—	70	80	15	81	367	87	513	11
U.Cal.-Davis	71	123	103	70	—	135	71	61	365	21	611	67
U.Cal.-Santa Cruz	69	35	47	80	135	—	87	110	323	149	484	75
Univ. San Francisco	16	63	34	15	71	87	—	94	403	84	516	0
Univ. of the Pacific	88	130	77	81	61	110	94	—	312	39	470	85
Los Angeles	345	326	340	367	365	323	403	312	—	382	122	384
Sacramento	88	140	120	87	21	149	84	39	382	—	509	95
San Diego	497	472	482	513	611	484	516	470	122	509	—	504
San Francisco	13	53	35	11	67	75	0	85	384	95	504	—

Southern California

	California Tech.	Claremont McKenna	Harvey Mudd Coll.	Occidental College	Pepperdine University	Pitzer College	Pomona College	Scripps College	U.Cal.-Irvine	U.Cal.-Los Angeles	U.Cal.-Riverside	U.Cal.-San Diego	U.Cal.-Santa Barbara	Univ. of Redlands	Univ. of San Diego	USC	Whittier College	Los Angeles	Sacramento	San Diego	San Francisco
California Tech.	—	26	26	6	38	26	26	26	51	23	55	118	116	58	127	15	18	5	387	117	392
Claremont McKenna	26	—	0	32	78	0	0	0	42	51	26	119	160	33	123	41	30	35	447	117	442
Harvey Mudd Coll.	26	0	—	32	78	0	0	0	42	51	26	119	160	33	123	41	30	35	447	117	442
Occidental College	6	32	32	—	34	32	32	32	56	18	64	130	106	67	139	11	26	0	380	130	379
Pepperdine University	38	78	78	34	—	78	78	78	62	18	104	134	78	111	143	32	46	8	368	134	370
Pitzer College	26	0	0	32	78	—	0	0	42	51	26	119	160	33	123	41	30	35	447	117	442
Pomona College	26	0	0	32	78	0	—	0	42	51	26	119	160	33	123	41	30	35	447	117	442
Scripps College	26	0	0	32	78	0	0	—	42	51	26	119	160	33	123	41	30	35	447	117	442
U.Cal.-Irvine	51	42	42	56	62	42	42	42	—	54	50	76	140	67	85	43	38	29	427	75	464
U.Cal.-Los Angeles	23	51	51	18	18	51	51	51	54	—	74	126	94	84	135	15	33	0	358	126	380
U.Cal.-Riverside	55	26	26	64	104	26	26	26	50	74	—	92	192	15	95	58	58	62	436	85	439
U.Cal.-San Diego	118	119	119	130	134	119	119	119	76	126	92	—	212	124	9	122	110	118	509	0	507
U.Cal.-Santa Barbara	116	160	160	106	78	160	160	160	140	96	192	212	—	203	221	101	116	87	371	212	312
Univ. of Redlands	58	33	33	67	111	33	33	33	67	84	15	124	203	—	127	77	61	69	537	117	466
Univ. of San Diego	127	123	123	139	143	123	123	123	85	135	95	9	221	127	—	129	119	127	518	0	516
USC	15	41	41	11	32	41	41	41	43	15	58	122	101	77	129	—	18	0	375	122	423
Whittier College	18	30	30	26	46	30	30	30	38	33	58	110	116	61	119	18	—	18	395	110	402
Los Angeles	5	35	35	0	8	35	35	35	29	0	62	118	87	69	127	0	18	—	382	123	384
Sacramento	387	447	447	380	380	447	447	447	427	358	436	509	371	537	518	375	395	382	—	509	95
San Diego	117	117	117	130	134	117	117	117	75	126	85	0	212	117	0	122	110	122	509	—	504
San Francisco	392	442	442	379	370	442	442	442	464	380	439	507	312	466	516	423	402	284	95	504	—

CALIFORNIA INSTITUTE OF TECHNOLOGY

Office of Undergraduate Admissions, California Institute of Technology, MC 55-63, Pasadena, CA 91125 (The office is at 515 S. Wilson) • Telephone: 800-568-8324 • Web: www.admissions.caltech.edu • Email: ugadmissions@caltech.edu

Hours: Monday-Friday, 8AM-5PM. Closed weekends, a few days around July 4, Thanksgiving, Christmas, and New Year's Day.

Arguably the best school in the country for science and technology, Caltech is an exceptional place. Students study more than four hours each day thanks to the intense courseload.

HIGHLIGHTS

ON CAMPUS	OFF CAMPUS
• Palomar Observatory	• Los Angeles
• Moore Laboratory	
• Mead Chemistry Laboratory	

TRANSPORTATION

Los Angeles International Airport is 40 miles away. Shuttle vans, taxis, and rental cars are available at the airport; contact the airport to make arrangements. Burbank Airport is 20 minutes from Caltech. Amtrak trains and Greyhound/Trailways buses serve Los Angeles.

FIND YOUR WAY

Take the 210 Freeway to the Lake Ave. off-ramp. Turn south on Lake Ave. to Del Mar Blvd., then left on Del Mar to Wilson. Turn right on Wilson to 515 S. Wilson. Use street parking.

STAY THE NIGHT

Nearby: The closest accommodations are at the **Holiday Inn** (303 E. Cordova St.; 818-449-4000). The special rate for college visitors is moderate, and the inn has lighted tennis courts and a heated outdoor pool. You have 2 inexpensive, basic options within 2.5 miles of Catech. One is **Comfort Inn** (2462 E. Colorado Blvd.; 818-405-0811). Ask for the special rate for college visitors. The other, the **Best Western Colorado Inn** (2156 E. Colorado Blvd.; 818-793-9339), is even less expensive than the Comfort Inn, and lodgings include a continental breakfast. A heated pool and jacuzzi and nearby eating spots are other assets. A special double rate in the moderate range is available at the **Pasadena Hilton**, only 1 mile from Caltech; it's described in the Occidental College entry. **Irish Inn** (119 N. Meredith Ave.; 818-440-0066). The rate for college visitors is moderate and includes a gourmet breakfast. The inn is in a quiet, residential area and has a country Irish decor. You will find flowers, fruit, and sherry in your room, and the inn can fix you lunch and dinner.

A little farther: See the University of California—Los Angeles entry for accommodations, particularly **Terrace Manor**, 20 minutes away.

AT A GLANCE

Selectivity Rating	97
Range SAT I Math	750-800
Average SAT I Math	771
Range SAT I Verbal	700-780
Average SAT I Verbal	729

CAMPUS TOURS

Appointment Req?	No
Dates	Year-round
Times	Mon-Fri 2PM
Avg. Length	1 hour

ON-CAMPUS INTERVIEWS

Admissions

Start Date–Juniors	N/A
Appointment Req?	N/A
Advance Notice	N/A
Saturdays?	N/A
Avg. Length	N/A
Info Sessions	3PM daily following campus tour

Faculty and Coaches

Arrangements	By prior arrangement

CLASS VISITS

Dates	Specific times of the year
Arrangements	Contact registrar

OVERNIGHT DORM STAYS

Advance Notice	N/A
Arrangements	N/A
Limitations	N/A

CLAREMONT MCKENNA COLLEGE

Office of Admission and Financial Aid, Claremont McKenna College, 890 Columbia Ave., Claremont, CA 91711 • Telephone: 909-621-8088 • Web: www.claremontmckenna.edu • Email: admission@mckenna.edu

Hours: Monday-Friday, 8AM-5PM. Closed weekends and holidays.

Truly exceptional Claremont McKenna College, in sunny Claremont, California, is one of the five Claremont Colleges and home to just over 1,000 mostly politically conservative and professionally oriented students.

AT A GLANCE

Selectivity Rating	96
Range SAT I Math	640-730
Average SAT I Math	690
Range SAT I Verbal	620-720
Average SAT I Verbal	690
Average ACT Composite	29
Average GPA	3.9
Student to Faculty Ratio	8:1

CAMPUS TOURS

Appointment Req?	Yes
Dates	Sept-May except holidays
Times	Mon-Fri 10AM and 2:30PM
Avg. Length	1 hour

ON-CAMPUS INTERVIEWS

Admissions

Start Date—Juniors	After May 1 of junior year
Appointment Req?	Yes
Advance Notice	2-3 weeks
Saturdays?	No
Avg. Length	30-45 min
Info Sessions	Yes

Faculty and Coaches

Dates/Times	Year-round; subject to faculty/coach availability
Arrangements	Contact admissions off.

CLASS VISITS

Dates	Aug-May (Mon-Fri)
Arrangements	Contact admissions off.

OVERNIGHT DORM STAYS

Advance Notice	2-3 weeks
Arrangements	Contact admissions off.
Limitations	1-night stay

TRANSPORTATION

Ontario International Airport is a 15-minute drive from campus. Taxis and limousines are available for the drive to campus from the airport; a shuttle also is available to the Claremont Inn near campus. Greyhound buses serve Claremont; the terminal is just south of I-10.

FIND YOUR WAY

From I-10 (San Bernardino Freeway), exit at Indian Hill Blvd. North. Proceed north to 10th St. and turn right (east). Go approximately a half mile to Columbia Ave. (a dead end). Turn right (south) onto Columbia and proceed to the admissions office on the southeast corner of Columbia and 9th St.

STAY THE NIGHT

The Claremont Graduate University, Pomona, Claremont McKenna, Harvey Mudd, Scripps, and Pitzer, known as the Claremont Colleges, are all located in Claremont, California, a charming little town not far from Los Angeles. The following choices are suitable for any of the schools. At **Faculty House** (703 N. College Way; 909-621-8109), on campus, the rates for college visitors are in the inexpensive range and include continental breakfast. Within walking distance, about half a mile from the schools, is **Claremont Inn** (555 W. Foothill Blvd.; 909-626-2411 or 800-854-5733). The moderate rate includes continental breakfast. An inexpensive choice a little farther away (10 minutes) is the **Ramada Inn** (840 S. Indian Hill Blvd.; 909-621-4831). There is a heated pool, a jacuzzi, lighted tennis courts, and a café with a Japanese-American menu. An even less expensive rate is available at the **Howard Johnson's Motor Hotel** (721 S. Indian Hill Blvd.; 909-628-2431), 10 minutes from the colleges.

HIGHLIGHTS

ON CAMPUS
• Marian Miner Cook Athenaeum
• Aquatics Center

OFF CAMPUS
• Disneyland
• Raymond M. Alf Museum
• Rancho Santa Ana Botanic Gardens

HARVEY MUDD COLLEGE

Admissions Office, Harvey Mudd College, 301 E. 12th St, Claremont, CA 91711
(The office is in Kingston Hall) • Telephone: 909-621-8000 •
Web: www.hmc.edu • Email: admission@hmc.edu

Hours: Monday-Friday, 8AM-5PM; Saturday, 9AM-noon (if counselors are available; usually Sept.-Dec.). Closed holidays.

Students study over four hours a day on average at Harvey Mudd College, the engineering branch of the five Claremont Colleges (Harvey Mudd, Claremont McKenna, Scripps, Pomona, and Pitzer). Outstanding academic programs are available here in engineering, biology, chemistry, physics, mathematics, and computer science and the school has tremendous facilities abound.

HIGHLIGHTS

ON CAMPUS	OFF CAMPUS
• Liquid Amber Mall	• Rancho Santa Ana Botanic Gardens
• Galileo Hall	• Mount Baldy
• Linde Activities Center	• Angeles National Forest
	• LA County Fairgrounds
	• California Speedway

TRANSPORTATION

Ontario International Airport is 5 miles from campus. The Claremont Inn (909-626-2411) shuttle takes passengers from the airport to the inn, which is just 5 blocks from campus. Taxis are also available at the airport for the ride to campus. Greyhound buses serve Claremont; the terminal is just south of I-10.

FIND YOUR WAY

From I-10, exit onto Indian Hill Blvd. North. Take Indian Hill N. for a few miles to 12th St. Turn right (east) on 12th St. for 5 blocks to the admissions office at 301 E. 12th (Kingston Hall).

STAY THE NIGHT

Call for an appointment 2 weeks in advance. College will help with arrangements and provide meal passes and guest passes.

AT A GLANCE

Selectivity Rating	94
Range SAT I Math	730-800
Average SAT I Math	760
Range SAT I Verbal	660-770
Average SAT I Verbal	710
Average GPA	3.8
Student to Faculty Ratio	9:1

CAMPUS TOURS

Appointment Req?	Yes
Dates	Year-round
Times	Sept-May: Mon-Fri 11AM, 1:30PM, and 3:30PM. June-Aug: Mon-Fri 10AM and 2PM.
Avg. Length	1 hour

ON-CAMPUS INTERVIEWS

Admissions

Start Date–Juniors	April 1
Appointment Req?	Yes
Advance Notice	1 week
Saturdays?	Yes, Sept-Jan; subject to counselor availability
Avg. Length	1 hour
Info Sessions	N/A

Faculty and Coaches

Dates/Times	Yes; subject to faculty/ coach availability
Arrangements	Contact admissions off. 1 week prior

CLASS VISITS

Dates	Year-round (Mon-Fri)
Arrangements	Contact admissions off.

OVERNIGHT DORM STAYS

Advance Notice	1 week prior
Arrangements	Contact admissions off.
Limitations	N/A

MILLS COLLEGE

Office of Undergraduate Admission, Mills College, 5000 MacArthur Blvd.,
Oakland, CA 94613 (The office is in Mills Hall) • Telephone: 510-430-2135 •
Web: www.mills.edu • Email: admission@mills.edu

Hours: Monday-Friday, 8:30AM-5PM. Closed weekends and holidays.

Mills College, located in Oakland, California, is a small women's liberal arts college. Mills boasts a very diverse campus, a stellar Bay Area location, and a wide array of extracurricular and recreational options, ranging from kayaking and horseback riding to rugby and yoga programs.

AT A GLANCE

Range SAT I Math	490-590
Range SAT I Verbal	540-670
Average ACT Composite	25
Average GPA	3.5
Student to Faculty Ratio	9:1

CAMPUS TOURS

Appointment Req?	Yes
Dates	Year-round
Times	During academic year: Mon-Fri 10AM and 2:30PM. During summer: 1 daily tour.
Avg. Length	1 hour

ON-CAMPUS INTERVIEWS

Admissions

Start Date–Juniors	Any time
Appointment Req?	Yes
Advance Notice	1 week
Saturdays?	No
Avg. Length	1 hour
Info Sessions	Yes

Faculty and Coaches

Dates/Times	Year-round; subject to faculty/coach availability
Arrangements	Contact admissions off. 1-2 weeks prior

CLASS VISITS

Dates	Academic year (Mon-Fri)
Arrangements	Contact admissions off.

OVERNIGHT DORM STAYS

Advance Notice	2 weeks
Arrangements	Contact admissions off.
Limitations	Mon-Thurs only; no stays during midterms and finals

TRANSPORTATION

The Oakland International Airport is a 20-minute drive from campus. Taxis are available at the airport for the drive to campus; no advance arrangements are necessary.

FIND YOUR WAY

From San Francisco, take I-80 (Bay Bridge) to I-580 (MacArthur Freeway). Take the second MacArthur Blvd. exit, which is on the right about 8.5 miles from the bridge. From the off ramp, turn right onto MacArthur Blvd.; the college gates are immediately ahead on the left. **From the east**, take I-580 W. to the MacArthur Blvd./High St. exit (just after the Hwy. 13 junction). Turn left at the stop sign and proceed under the overpass. Turn left at the stoplight. The college gates are immediately on the left. **From the south**, take I-880 N. (Nimitz Freeway) to Oakland. Exit at High St. (3 miles past the Oakland Airport exit). Turn right onto High St. and continue 3 miles to MacArthur Blvd. Turn right onto MacArthur, continue under the overpass and bear right. The college gates are immediately ahead on the left. **From the north**, take I-80 S. to I-580 E. at the Bay Bridge interchange. From there, follow the directions above from San Francisco.

STAY THE NIGHT

Nearby: Through the admissions office or by calling directly (510-430-2145), you can book a dormitory-style room at the **Alderwood Conference Center** on campus. Reservations are a must and are particularly difficult to come by during the summer. Bathrooms are dormitory style. Rates are very inexpensive and there are places to dine on campus. The **Oakland Marriott at City Center**, (1001 Broadway; 510-451-4000). **Jack London Inn**, (444 Embarcadero West; 510-444-2032). **Waterfront Plaza Hotel, Jack London Square,** (10 Washington St.; 510-836-3800). The **Washington Inn** (495 10th St.; 510-452-1776), opposite the Oakland Convention Center, is about 6 minutes away from the college. The rates are moderate (ask for the special rate for college visitors) and include a full breakfast and privileges at a health club nearby. A moderately priced motel about 15 minutes away is the **Best Western Thunderbird Inn** (233 Broadway at 3rd St.; 510-452-4565). It has a heated pool, a sauna, and an adjacent restaurant.

A little farther: If a resort appeals to you, the **Claremont Resort Hotel and Tennis Club** (Domingo and Ashby Ave.; 510-843-3000), about 15 minutes from the college, is great. There's tennis, swimming, and an exercise room. Rates run very high. Check the University of California–Berkeley and University of San Francisco entries for other possibilities.

HIGHLIGHTS

ON CAMPUS
- The Mills Museum
- Trefethen Aquatic Center
- Mills Hall
- Greek Theater
- 5,000 trees on campus

OFF CAMPUS
- Jack London Square
- Lake Merritt
- Paramount Theater
- Pacific Ocean and San Fransisco Bay
- San Fransisco

OCCIDENTAL COLLEGE

Admissions Office, Occidental College, 1600 Campus Rd., Los Angeles, CA 90041 •
Telephone: 800-825-5262 • Web: www.oxy.edu •
Email: admission@oxy.edu

Hours: Monday-Friday, 8AM-5PM; Saturday, 9AM-noon (only from October through January 15). Closed Sundays and New Year's Day, July 4, Labor Day, Thanksgiving, and Christmas.

Nearly one-third of Oxy's graduates proceed to professional programs within a year, and just as many go on to academic graduate programs. Oxy's program requires students to complete a demanding, two-year core curriculum that includes healthy doses of world culture, math, science, humanities, and a foreign language.

HIGHLIGHTS

ON CAMPUS
- Thorn Hall Auditorium
- Keck Theater
- Johnson Student Center
- Patterson Field
- Hillside Amphitheater

OFF CAMPUS
- The Getty Center
- Dodger Stadium
- Griffith Park Observatory
- Disneyland
- Rose Bowl

TRANSPORTATION

Burbank Airport is 10 miles from campus. Super Shuttle and taxi service is available from the airport to campus. Los Angeles International Airport is farther from campus, but close enough that buses run from the airport to hotels in the Pasadena area not too far from campus. Amtrak trains and Greyhound/Trailways buses serve Los Angeles. Rapid Transit District bus service (public transportation) to campus is available from downtown L.A.: take either line 83 (on York Blvd.) or line 84 (on Eagle Rock Blvd.). Call 213-626-4455 for bus information and schedules.

FIND YOUR WAY

From downtown L.A., take I-110 N. (Harbor Freeway). Follow signs for Pasadena. Take I-5 N. (Golden State Freeway) toward Bakersfield. Then take Rte. 2 (Glendale Freeway) going toward Glendale. Exit at Verdugo Rd.; turn left at the end of the off ramp onto Eagle Rock Blvd. Continue on Eagle Rock Blvd. for 5 traffic lights to Westdale Ave. Turn right onto Westdale and follow it until it ends at Campus Rd. **From the Ventura Freeway (Rte. 134) heading east**, go through Glendale to the Harvey Dr. exit. Turn right at the end of the off ramp and then left at the light onto Broadway. When Broadway merges with Colorado Blvd., continue on Colorado Blvd. to Eagle Rock Blvd. Turn right and continue for 4 traffic lights to Westdale Ave. Turn left onto Westdale and follow it to Campus Rd. **From the Ventura Freeway (Rte. 134) heading west**, exit at Colorado Blvd. Take Colorado Blvd. to Eagle Rock Blvd. (approximately one mile). Turn left onto Eagle Rock Blvd. and continue 4 traffic lights to Westdale Ave. Turn left onto Westdale and proceed to Campus Rd.

STAY THE NIGHT

In the moderate range, about 15 minutes away, is **Sheraton Pasadena** (303 East Cordove St.; 626-449-4000). It has a pool and exercise room. Ask for Occidental College's special rate. Also available, **Doubletree Hotel** (191 N. Los Robles; 626-792-2727), has a full health club, exercise room, pool, and Jacuzzi. The least expensive place we suggest is also the closest to campus: **Welcome Inn** (1840 West Colorado Blvd.; 323-256-1673). The California Institute of Technology entry also has suggestions for accommodations in Pasadena.

AT A GLANCE

Selectivity Rating	87
Range SAT I Math	550-660
Average SAT I Math	610
Range SAT I Verbal	550-660
Average SAT I Verbal	610
Average ACT Composite	27
Average GPA	3.8
Student to Faculty Ratio	11:1

CAMPUS TOURS

Appointment Req?	No
Dates	Oct-May (except during exam periods) and June 15-Sept 10
Times	Oct-May: Mon-Fri 10:30AM and 3PM; Sat 10AM and 11AM
Avg. Length	1 hour

ON-CAMPUS INTERVIEWS

Admissions

Start Date—Juniors	Spring break-Feb 1
Appointment Req?	Yes
Advance Notice	7-10 days
Saturdays?	Yes, Oct 1-Feb 1
Avg. Length	45 min
Info Sessions	Year-round

Faculty and Coaches

Dates/Times	Year-round; subject to faculty/coach availability
Arrangements	Contact admissions off. 7-10 days prior

CLASS VISITS

Dates	Year-round (Mon-Fri)
Arrangements	N/A

OVERNIGHT DORM STAYS

Advance Notice	2 weeks
Arrangements	Call admissions off.
Limitations	Mon-Thurs nights; except exam periods

PEPPERDINE UNIVERSITY

Office of Admissions, Seaver Admissions, 24255 Pacific Coast Hwy., Malibu, CA 90263 (2nd floor of the Thornton Administration Building) • Telephone: 310-456-4392 • Web: www.pepperdine.edu • Email: admission-seaver@pepperdine.com

Hours: Monday-Friday, 8AM-5PM. Closed weekends and holidays.

A truly stunning beach-front location in idyllic Malibu and a deep-seated affiliation with the Church of Christ set Pepperdine apart. A weekly assembly is mandatory, and the core curriculum contains three surveys in religion.

AT A GLANCE

Selectivity Rating	84
Range SAT I Math	627-680
Average SAT I Math	627
Range SAT I Verbal	621-670
Average SAT I Verbal	621
Average ACT Composite	27
Average GPA	3.8
Student to Faculty Ratio	13:1

CAMPUS TOURS

Appointment Req?	Yes
Dates	Year-round except University holidays
Times	Mon-Fri 9AM-3PM
Avg. Length	45 min

ON-CAMPUS INTERVIEWS

Admissions

Start Date–Juniors	June (of jr. year)
Appointment Req?	Yes
Advance Notice	1 week
Saturdays?	No
Avg. Length	45 min
Info Sessions	Year-round except university holidays

Faculty and Coaches

Dates/Times	Year-round; subject to faculty/coach availability
Arrangements	Contact admissions off. 1-2 weeks prior

CLASS VISITS

Dates	Sept 4-March 30 (Mon-Fri)
Arrangements	Contact admissions off.

OVERNIGHT DORM STAYS

Advance Notice	2 weeks
Arrangements	Contact admissions off.
Limitations	Completed applicants only; 2nd semester only; not during exams and holidays; 2-day, 1-night maximum stay

TRANSPORTATION

Los Angeles International Airport is 25 miles from campus. Rental cars, commercial shuttle service, and taxis are available at the airport. For Super Shuttle, call 213-338-1111; for Prime Time Shuttle, call 213-558-1606. Amtrak trains and Greyhound Trailways buses serve Los Angeles.

FIND YOUR WAY

Take **I-10 (Santa Monica Freeway)**
W. to the end, where it becomes the Pacific Coast Hwy. (California Rte. 1). Continue for 14 miles, turn right onto Malibu Canyon Rd., then turn left onto Seaver Dr., which is the campus entrance. **From the Ventura Freeway** (U.S. Rte. 101), take the Las Virgenes exit; turn south onto Las Virgenes, which becomes Malibu Canyon Rd., and follow it through the canyon. Turn right onto Seaver Dr., which is the campus entrance.

STAY THE NIGHT

Nearby: Enjoy sleeping to the sound of the pounding surf at **Casa Malibu** (22752 Pacific Coast Hwy.; 310-456-2219), a relatively small, moderately priced motel only a mile and a half from campus. The motel has a nice patio overlooking a private beach and rooms have refrigerators. **Malibu Beach Inn** (22878 Pacific Coast Hwy.; 310-456-6444) is a little closer, about a mile away, but a little more expensive. One budget choice, **Goodnight Inn** (26557 Agora Rd., Calabasas; 818-880-6000), is about 15 minutes away. A heated outdoor pool and jacuzzi are on the premises, and a restaurant is close by.

A little farther: 25 minutes away, in Santa Monica, is the quaint, inexpensive **Bay Side Hotel** (2001 Ocean Ave.; 310-396-6000). The hotel has 38 rooms, some with kitchens; the rooms that overlook the ocean are a bit more expensive than those overlooking the courtyard. There is a small additional charge for a kitchen. A French bakery and buffet are nearby. About 30 minutes away, also in Santa Monica, is the large, bustling **Sheraton Miramar** (101 Wilshire Blvd.; 310-576-7777). Rates are very expensive, but it is across from the beach. The Sheraton has a heated pool, bike rentals, and a shopping mall is adjacent to it. You can have privileges at the Santa Monica Athletic Club and its tennis courts. For more overnight options, you can check with Bed & Breakfast International at 800-872-4500.

HIGHLIGHTS

ON CAMPUS
- Eddy D. Field Stadium
- Payson Library
- Law Library
- Center for the Arts

OFF CAMPUS
- Getty Museum
- Santa Monica Pier
- 3rd Street Santa Monica
- Universal City Walk

PITZER COLLEGE

Admissions Office, Pitzer College, Broad Hall, Rm. 101, 1050 N. Mills Ave., Claremont, CA 91711-6312 • Telephone: 800-748-9371 • Web: www.pitzer.edu • Email: admission@pitzer.edu

Hours: Monday-Friday, 8AM-5PM; Saturday, 9AM-noon. Closed Sundays and holidays.

Pitzer is by far the most liberal of the five Claremont Colleges (Claremont McKenna, Harvey Mudd, Pitzer, Pomona, and Scripps). Students say the invigorating academic experience provides an ideal intellectual environment.

HIGHLIGHTS

ON CAMPUS
- The Arboretum
- Marquis Library
- Gloria and Peter Gold Student Center
- McConnell Center

OFF CAMPUS
- It's a short trip to Los Angeles
- Raymond M. Alf Museum
- Disneyland

TRANSPORTATION

Ontario International is 12 miles east of Claremont on I-10 (the San Bernardino Freeway). Direct or connecting flights are available from all parts of the country. Hotel shuttles (Claremont Inn, Sheradon Fairplex, and Ramada Inn), taxis, and rental cars are available for the ride to campus. Los Angeles International Airport is about 50 miles west of Claremont. Air and ground connections are available from there to Ontario International Airport. Greyhound buses serve Claremont; the terminal is just south of I-10.

FIND YOUR WAY

From any area except Pasadena, take I-10 to Indian Hill Blvd. (Exit 470) and travel north, toward the mountains, for 3 miles. At 12th St., turn right and continue on until the road ends. Turn right as 12th St. curves into N. Mills Ave. The admissions office is in Broad Hall, the building that faces N. Mills Ave. **From Pasadena and the San Fernando Valley**, take I-210 E. until it terminates at Foothill Blvd. Drive 4 miles on Foothill Blvd. and turn right on Claremont Blvd. Make the first right onto 9th St., and continue on until the road ends. Turn right onto N. Mills Ave. Broad Hall is on N. Mills Ave.

STAY THE NIGHT

See the Claremont McKenna College entry for suggestions about overnight accommodations.

AT A GLANCE

Selectivity Rating	81
Range SAT I Math	520-640
Average SAT I Math	584
Range SAT I Verbal	540-650
Average SAT I Verbal	601
Average ACT Composite	24
Average GPA	3.6
Student to Faculty Ratio	12:1

CAMPUS TOURS

Appointment Req?	Recommended
Dates	Year-round
Times	Mon-Fri and Sat mornings during the academic year
Avg. Length	30 min

ON-CAMPUS INTERVIEWS

Admissions

Start Date–Juniors	Summer before junior year
Appointment Req?	Recommended
Advance Notice	A few days
Saturdays?	Yes, 9AM-noon during the academic year
Avg. Length	30 min
Info Sessions	Available during interview

Faculty and Coaches

Dates/Times	Year-round; subject to faculty/coach availability
Arrangements	Contact admissions off. 1 week prior

CLASS VISITS

Dates	Year round (Mon-Fri morning)
Arrangements	Contact admissions off.

OVERNIGHT DORM STAYS

Advance Notice	2 weeks
Arrangements	Contact admissions off.
Limitations	Mon-Fri; 1-night stay; college covers all expenses

POMONA COLLEGE

Admissions Office, Pomona College, 333 N. College Way, Claremont, CA 91711 (The office is in Sumner Hall, Rm. 104, at the corner of College Way and Bonita Ave.) • Telephone: 909-621-8134 • Web: www.pomona.edu • Email: admissions@pomona.edu

Hours: Monday-Friday, 8AM-4:30PM; Saturday, 9AM-noon (late Sept to early December only). Closed Sundays and holidays.

Pomona College is the most distinguished school in the Claremont cluster—something of an academic paradise. The administration receives raves for spoiling its students.

AT A GLANCE

Selectivity Rating	94
Range SAT I Math	670-750
Average SAT I Math	710
Range SAT I Verbal	670-760
Average SAT I Verbal	720
Average ACT Composite	31
Student to Faculty Ratio	10:1

CAMPUS TOURS

Appointment Req?	No
Dates	Year-round, with occasional breaks
Times	Sept-May: Mon-Fri 10AM, noon, and 2:30PM. June-Aug: Mon-Fri, and Oct-Dec: Saturdays, please call for times.
Avg. Length	1 hour

ON-CAMPUS INTERVIEWS

Admissions

Start Date—Juniors	March 1
Appointment Req?	Yes
Advance Notice	2-3 weeks
Saturdays?	Yes, Oct-Dec
Avg. Length	45-60 min
Info Sessions	Year-round

Faculty and Coaches

Dates/Times	Year-round; subject to faculty/coach availability
Arrangements	Contact admissions off.

CLASS VISITS

Dates	Academic year (Mon-Fri)
Arrangements	Contact admissions off.

OVERNIGHT DORM STAYS

Advance Notice	2 weeks
Arrangements	Contact admissions off.
Limitations	Mid-Sept to end of semester and mid-Jan to April

TRANSPORTATION

Ontario International Airport is 10 miles from campus. Taxi, shuttle service, and rental cars are available at the airport. A 24-hour express shuttle to Claremont is available; for this service, call 800-554-6458 or, in California, 909-973-1100 or 310-338-1111. It is also possible to fly into Los Angeles International Airport (LAX), then take a commuter flight to Ontario, rent a car, or take a shuttle van to Claremont. Greyhound buses serve Claremont; the terminal is just south of I-10, approximately a mile and a half from campus. Metro link (train) serves Claremont from downtown L.A.

FIND YOUR WAY

From anywhere except Pasadena and the San Fernando Valley, take I-10 to Indian Hill Blvd. (Exit 47). Drive north approximately one mile to Bonita Ave.; turn right and go 4 blocks to the Sumner Hall parking lot. **From Pasadena and the San Fernando Valley**, take I-210 (Foothill Freeway) E. until it merges with Foothill Blvd. (Rte. 66). Continue east 5 miles to Indian Hill Blvd.; turn right and proceed south 10 blocks to Bonita Ave. Turn left on Bonita and go 4 blocks to the Sumner Hall parking lot.

STAY THE NIGHT

The **Pomona College Faculty House**, located on campus, offers a complimentary breakfast and inexpensive housing (703 N. College Way; 909-621-8109). The **Claremont Inn** (555 W. Foothill Blvd.; 909-626-2411) is within walking distance—about half a mile from Pomona. An alternative is the **Sheraton Suites Fairplex** (601 McKinley Ave.; 800-722-4055).

HIGHLIGHTS

ON CAMPUS
- Smith Campus Center
- Sontag Greek Theater
- Rains Center for Sports and Recreation
- Brakett Observatory

OFF CAMPUS
- Los Angeles and Pasadena
- J. Paul Getty Center, LA County Museum of Art
- Universal Studios
- Joshua Tree National Park
- Lakers, Dodgers, Angels, Galzxy, etc.

SANTA CLARA UNIVERSITY

Undergraduate Admissions, Santa Clara University, Santa Clara, CA 95053
(The office is on the 1st floor of Varsi Hall) • Telephone: 408-554-4700 •
Web: www.scu.edu • Email: ugadmissions@scv.edu

Hours: Monday-Friday, 8AM-5PM; Saturday, 9AM-noon (October-April by appointment). Closed Sundays and holidays.

Academic life at Catholic Santa Clara University is dictated by an academic calendar divided into three 10-week sessions that really keep the undergraduates here on their toes.

HIGHLIGHTS

ON CAMPUS
- Mission Church
- Pat Malley Fitness Center
- Mission Gardens
- Toso Pavillion
- Residential Learning Communities

OFF CAMPUS
- 3 miles to downtown San Jose
- Great America Theme Park
- Santa Cruz
- 45 miles to San Fransisco
- 4 hours to Lake Tahoe

TRANSPORTATION

San Jose International Airport is a 3-mile drive from campus. Rental cars, taxis, and public buses (Valley Transportation Authority #10) are available for the trip from airport to campus. San Francisco International Airport is 45 miles north of campus. From there, Airport Connection Shuttles take visitors to the San Jose airport; call 800-AIRPORT (from out of state) or 415-877-0903 (in California) for shuttle timetables and reservations. Amtrak trains serve San Jose; call 800-USA-RAIL for information. From the train station, take bus #81 westbound for the 3-mile trip to campus. Greyhound buses also serves San Jose. From the bus depot, walk one block north to W. Santa Clara St. and board a westbound bus #22; this bus makes several stops along the perimeter of the campus.

FIND YOUR WAY

From U.S. Rte. 101 (Bayshore Freeway), take the Santa Clara/De La Cruz Blvd. exit. Proceed south 2 miles. As the road forks, keep to the right and follow the signs to the university. **From I-880**, take the Alameda/Santa Clara exit. Travel north one mile to campus. **From I-280**, proceed to the interchange with I-880. Take I-880 N. toward Oakland and take the Alameda/Santa Clara exit. The university is 1 mile north of the exit.

STAY THE NIGHT

Nearby: The **Comfort Inn Airport South** (2118 The Alameda, San Jose; 408-243-2400) is only 4 blocks from the university and offers minisuites with refrigerators, a continental breakfast, and special moderate rates for college visitors. Some of the suites have jacuzzis. The inn has a heated outdoor pool and exercise room, and a cozy restaurant is across the street. Consider nearby **Days Inn Santa Clara** (859 El Camino Real; 408-244-2840) is located 5 blocks from the university. **Madison St. Inn** (1390 Madison St.; 408-249-5541), less than a mile from the school, is a Victorian bed-and-breakfast with 5 guest rooms and landscaped gardens. Its moderate rates include a full breakfast. The **Briar Rose** (897 Jackson St., San Jose; 408-279-5999) is also moderately priced (including a full breakfast) and is a 15-minute drive from the university. This classic, 115-year-old Victorian house is sumptuously decorated with antiques. It is 10 minutes from the airport, in a quiet, residential section of San Jose. **San Jose Fairmont Hotel,** (170 South Market St., San Jose; 408-998-1900), a 15-minute drive from campus. **San Jose Hilton and Towers,** (300 Almaden Blvd., San Jose; 408-287-2100), a 12-minute drive from campus.

A little farther: A **Marriott Hotel** (2700 Mission College Blvd.; 408-988-1500) is in Santa Clara, 20 minutes away. Rates range from moderate to very expensive. It has all the usual Marriott amenities, including indoor and outdoor pools and a lighted tennis court. Also see suggestions in the Stanford University entry.

SCRIPPS COLLEGE

Office of Admissions, Scripps College, Balch Hall, 1030 Columbia Ave., Claremont, CA 91711 • Telephone: 800-770-1333 • Web: www.scrippscol.edu • Email: admofc@ad.scrippscol.edu

Hours: Monday-Friday, 8AM-5PM. Closed weekends and holidays, except Saturday mornings in the fall.

Scripps College is the women's college in the Claremont Colleges cluster (Claremont McKenna, Harvey Mudd, Pitzer, Pomona, and Scripps). Overall, 2,500 courses are available to students here, and nearly all classes are small. Professors are accessible and receive high ratings for their teaching ability.

AT A GLANCE

Selectivity Rating	83
Range SAT I Math	560-670
Average SAT I Math	643
Range SAT I Verbal	600-690
Average SAT I Verbal	618
Average ACT Composite	27
Average GPA	3.7
Student to Faculty Ratio	11:1

CAMPUS TOURS

Appointment Req?	Yes
Dates	Year-round
Times	Mon-Fri 9AM, 10AM, and 2PM
Avg. Length	1 hour

ON-CAMPUS INTERVIEWS

Admissions

Start Date–Juniors	Any time
Appointment Req?	Yes
Advance Notice	2 weeks
Saturdays?	Yes, but only during fall semester
Avg. Length	30 min
Info Sessions	N/A

Faculty and Coaches

Dates/Times	Year-round; subject to faculty/coach availability
Arrangements	Contact admissions off.

CLASS VISITS

Dates	When classes are in session (Mon-Fri)
Arrangements	Contact admissions off.

OVERNIGHT DORM STAYS

Advance Notice	2 weeks
Arrangements	Contact admissions off.
Limitations	Student must arrive by 5PM and should bring a sleeping bag and a towel

TRANSPORTATION

Ontario International Airport is 15 miles from the campus. Taxis are available for the ride to campus (call from the courtesy phones at the airport). Greyhound buses serve Claremont (the terminal is just south of I-10). The Amtrak station is 5 miles from campus.

FIND YOUR WAY

From I-10 (San Bernardino Freeway), take Exit 47 (Indian Hill Blvd.) and proceed north on Indian Hill. Turn right on Tenth St. and proceed east to the corner of Tenth St. and Columbia Ave. **From Pasadena and the San Fernando Valley**, take I-210 E. until it terminates at Foothill Blvd. Drive 3 miles on Foothill and turn right on Dartmouth Ave., then left on Tenth St. to Columbia Ave.

STAY THE NIGHT

Only a 2-minute drive to campus, the **Claremont Inn** (555 W. Foothill Blvd.; 909-626-2411) is quite convenient and offers a special college rate. A couple of miles further and a bit more expensive is the **Sheraton Suites Fairplex** (601 W. McKinley Ave., Pomona; 800-325-3535 or 909-622-2220), which offers pleasant accommodations. Ask for the college rate here, too. There is also the **Marriott Hotel** (2200 E. Holt Blvd., Ontario; 909-986-8811), about 15 minutes from campus.

HIGHLIGHTS

ON CAMPUS
- Williamson Gallery
- Rare book room at Denison Library
- Margaret Fowler Garden
- Malott Commons
- Graffitti Wall

OFF CAMPUS
- Disneyland
- Beaches
- Hollywood
- Joshua Tree Monument
- Rodeo Drive

STANFORD UNIVERSITY

Undergraduate Admission, Stanford University, Old Union 232, Stanford, CA 94305-3005 • Telephone: 650-723-2091 • Web: www.stanford.edu • Email: undergrad.admissions@forsythe.stanford.edu

Hours: Monday-Friday, 8:30AM-5PM. Closed weekends, certain days for scheduled staff meetings, and holidays.

Stanford is an Ivy-caliber university with a California atmosphere. The engineering, physical sciences, and liberal arts programs are all nationally renowned. Sandra Day O'Connor and John Steinbeck are alums.

HIGHLIGHTS

ON CAMPUS
- Cantor Center for the Visual Arts
- Rodin Sculpture Garden
- Memorial Church
- Observation Deck at Hoover Tower
- New Guinea Sculpture Garden

TRANSPORTATION

San Francisco International Airport is 25 miles from campus, and San Jose International Airport is 16 miles from campus. Limousine and van service is available from the airport to campus. For service, call Airport Connection at 800-AIR-PORT or 650-363-1500. A Sam Trans Bus (650-871-2200) to campus is available at San Francisco airport's upper level near TWA; take the #7F bus, which leaves every 30 minutes and takes approximately 55 minutes to reach campus. Taxis are also available. Amtrak trains and Greyhound buses serve San Francisco. From San Francisco and San Jose you can take a commuter train, the CAL TRAIN, to Palo Alto. Disembark at the University Ave. Depot, Palo Alto, and take bus #24, bus #86, or the Marguerite (Stanford's red shuttle bus) to campus. For further information on the CAL TRAIN, call 800-558-8661.

FIND YOUR WAY

From Highway 101 North and South, take the Embarcadero Rd. exit west toward Stanford. At El Camino Real, Embarcadero turns into Galvez Rd. as it enters the university. Stay in the left lane and continue toward the center of campus. Galvez ends at Serra St., where there is metered parking. The visitor information center is in Memorial Hall, which is across from Hoover Tower on Serra St. **From Highway 280 North and South**, Exit Sand Hill Rd. east toward Stanford. Continue east, turning right at the traffic light on Santa Cruz Ave. Make an immediate left onto Junipero Serra Blvd. Turn left at the second stoplight, Campus Drive East. Turn left when you reach Serra St. at the gas station. Follow Serra St. until it ends at Galvez St. Turn right onto Galvez and look for the first parking lot on the right. The Visitor Center is in the front of Memorial Hall. Please note that parking is monitored Monday–Friday, 8AM–4PM

STAY THE NIGHT

Nearby: A small, very expensive place, the **Garden Court Hotel** (520 Cowper St.; 650-322-9000), is about a 5-minute drive away. In addition to the usual amenities, the hotel has a northern Italian restaurant, a charming bougainvillea-filled courtyard, and a shopping arcade. **Stanford Park Hotel** (100 El Camino Real, Menlo Park; 650-322-1234) is a fancy motor hotel, about half a mile away. This expensive hotel has a heated outdoor pool, jacuzzi, sauna, and exercise room. The rooms are large and furnished in French provincial decor. There are some more modest choices in the neighborhood. For a very inexpensive motel about 3 miles away, try **Country Inn Motel** (4345 El Camino Real, Palo Alto; 650-948-9154). Rolls and coffee are served in the morning, and there is an outdoor pool. **Best Western Riviera**, (15 El Camino; 650-321-8772) is 1.4 miles from campus. **Sheraton Palo Alto Hotel**, (625 El Camino; 650-328-2800) is .8 miles from campus.

A little farther: See suggestions in the University of Santa Clara entry. Santa Clara is just south of Palo Alto.

AT A GLANCE

Selectivity Rating	98
Range SAT I Math	690-780
Average SAT I Math	717
Range SAT I Verbal	670-770
Average SAT I Verbal	715
Average ACT Composite	31
Average GPA	3.9

CAMPUS TOURS

Appointment Req?	No
Dates	Year-round, except during exam periods, Christmas vacation, and spring break (mid-March)
Times	Mon-Sun 11AM and 3:15PM
Avg. Length	1 hour

ON-CAMPUS INTERVIEWS

Admissions

Start Date–Juniors	N/A
Appointment Req?	N/A
Advance Notice	N/A
Saturdays?	N/A
Avg. Length	N/A
Info Sessions	Spring, summer, and fall

Faculty and Coaches

Dates/Times	Year-round; subject to faculty/coach availability
Arrangements	Contact the dept. of interest or the particular faculty member or coach

CLASS VISITS

Dates	Fall, winter, spring (Mon-Fri)
Arrangements	Contact admission off.

OVERNIGHT DORM STAYS

Advance Notice	N/A
Arrangements	N/A
Limitations	Only during 3 days in April for accepted students

UNIVERSITY OF CALIFORNIA—BERKELEY

Office of Undergraduate Admissions and Relations with Schools, University of California, 110 Sproul Hall #5800, Berkeley, CA 94720-5800 • Telephone: 510-642-3175 • Web: www.berkeley.edu • Email: ouars@uclink.berkeley.edu

Hours: Monday-Friday, 10AM-noon and 1PM-4PM. Closed weekends and holidays.

The Berkeley campus of the University of California offers a tremendously diverse education in the liberal arts, natural sciences, and technology. The school enrolls about 22,000 students, many of whom advance to graduate studies. Berkeley is a hotbed for student activism and individual thinking, a cultural paradise, and the campus is home to 23 libraries.

AT A GLANCE

Selectivity Rating	94
Range SAT I Math	630-740
Average SAT I Math	685
Range SAT I Verbal	600-710
Average SAT I Verbal	655
Average GPA	3.9
Student to Faculty Ratio	17:1

CAMPUS TOURS

Appointment Req?	No
Dates	Year-round, except mid-Dec to mid-Jan
Times	Mon-Sat 10AM; Sun 1PM
Avg. Length	90 min

ON-CAMPUS INTERVIEWS

Admissions

Start Date–Juniors	N/A
Appointment Req?	N/A
Advance Notice	N/A
Saturdays?	N/A
Avg. Length	N/A
Info Sessions	Year-round, only for prospective freshmen

Faculty and Coaches

Dates/Times	Year-round; subject to faculty/coach availability
Arrangements	Contact the dept., faculty, or coach

CLASS VISITS

Dates	Year-round (Mon-Fri)
Arrangements	Secure prior approval from instructor

OVERNIGHT DORM STAYS

Advance Notice	N/A
Arrangements	N/A
Limitations	Only during the Cal Summer Orientation; limited to admitted students

TRANSPORTATION

Oakland International Airport is 20 miles from campus. The Airporter Shuttle provides transportation from the airport to campus; call 800-AIRPORT at least 24 hours in advance to arrange for it. Public transportation to campus is also available: from the airport, take the shuttle bus to the BART subway system at Richmond, then take the subway to Berkeley. Amtrak trains serve nearby Oakland. Greyhound/Trailways buses also serve the area.

FIND YOUR WAY

The best approaches to the university are from Rte. 24 or from I-80. For more detailed driving instructions, call the Visitor Center (510-642-5215). The visitor center is in Rm. 101 of University Hall, on Oxford St. north of Bancroft Way, across from the West Circle entrance to campus.

STAY THE NIGHT

Nearby: You have several choices within walking distance of campus. The least expensive is the **Berkeley Motel** (2001 Bancroft Way; 510-843-4043), a no-frills establishment. Moderately priced places include the **Shattuck Hotel** (2086 Allston Way; 510-845-7300), 1 block from the west end of campus, with special rates for college visitors and a continental breakfast and parking; and **Durant Hotel** (2600 Durant Ave.; 510-845-8981), 2 blocks from campus. It's near the small shops on the main strip. Nearby **Grandma's Rosegarden Inn** (2740 Telegraph Ave.; 510-549-2145) is a real charmer. Rates are moderate and include a full breakfast and wine and cheese. The inn is near restaurants and shops.

A little farther: Check the University of San Francisco entry for suggestions across the bay.

HIGHLIGHTS

ON CAMPUS
- Botanical Gardens
- Lawrence Hall of Science
- Museum of Anthropology
- Museum of Art

OFF CAMPUS
- Berkeley Marina
- Bistro Viola Restaurant

UNIVERSITY OF CALIFORNIA—DAVIS

Undergraduate Admissions and Outreach Services, University of California, 175 Mark Hall, One Shields Avenue (mailing only), Davis, CA 95616-8507 • Telephone: 530-752-2971 • Web: www.ucdavis.edu • Email: thinkucd@ucdavis.edu

Hours: Monday-Friday, 9AM-noon and 1PM-5PM. Closed weekends and holidays.

The Davis campus of the University of California is located in rural Davis, near Sacramento. The school's programs run the gamut from the arts and sciences to business and education, and students here give high marks to the school's technology resources. Campus life is reportedly laid back.

HIGHLIGHTS

ON CAMPUS	OFF CAMPUS
• Celeste Turner Wright Hall	• Napa Valley
• Peter J. Shields Library	• Old Sacramento
• The recreation hall	• Sutter's Fort
• The Walter A. Buehler Alumni & Visitors Center	• Sacramento River

TRANSPORTATION

Sacramento International Airport is 20 miles from campus. Davis Airporter Limousine Service (530-756-6715) is available to/from the airport; call at least one day in advance. Rental cars are also available at the airport.

FIND YOUR WAY

From Sacramento and from San Francisco, take I-80 to the UC Davis exit, which will lead you right to the campus. From the north, take Hwy. 113; exit at either the Russell Blvd. or UC Davis (Hutchison Dr.) exit and go east to campus.

STAY THE NIGHT

Nearby: The 18-room **Davis Bed and Breakfast Inn** (422 A St.; 530-753-9611) is just across the street from the university. The low price includes a full breakfast. **Best Western University Lodge** (123 B St.; 530-756-7890), just 2 blocks away, is another basic facility. A half block away is **Aggie Inn** (245 1st St.; 530-756-0352), with pretty rooms, a spa and sauna, continental breakfast, and moderate rates.

A little farther: At the university, you are only about 25 minutes west of Sacramento, where you might prefer to stay. Built in 1912, **Abigail's Bed and Breakfast** (2120 G St.; 530-441-5007) is a colonial revival mansion located in downtown Sacramento. It's within easy reach of many of the attractions of the city. Rates are in the moderate to expensive range and include a delicious breakfast. If you need twin beds, be careful to check in advance. **American Youth Hostel** (900 H St.; 530-443-1692) is a converted 100-year-old mansion within walking distance of Amtrak, Old Sacramento, and the Capitol, and 1 block away from the Yolo bus to Davis. The hostel is very affordable.

AT A GLANCE

Selectivity Rating	82
Range SAT I Math	540-660
Average SAT I Math	593
Range SAT I Verbal	500-620
Average SAT I Verbal	556
Average ACT Composite	24
Average GPA	3.7
Student to Faculty Ratio	19:1

CAMPUS TOURS

Appointment Req?	Yes, for Mon-Fri tours only
Dates	Year-round
Times	Mon-Fri 10AM and 2PM; Sat and Sun 11:30AM and 1:30PM
Avg. Length	90 min

ON-CAMPUS INTERVIEWS

Admissions

Appointment Req?	N/A
Advance Notice	N/A
Avg. Length	N/A
Info Sessions	No personal interviews; contact admissions off. for individual advising

Faculty and Coaches

Dates/Times	Call first; subject to faculty/coach availability
Arrangements	Contact faculty/coach

CLASS VISITS

Dates	Year-round (Mon-Fri)
Arrangements	Contact Tour Off. at 530-752-8111

OVERNIGHT DORM STAYS

Advance Notice	None
Arrangements	Contact Summer Housing Off./Conference Housing at 530-752-8000
Limitations	Only during summer sessions

UNIVERSITY OF CALIFORNIA—IRVINE

Admissions Office, University of California–Irvine, 240 Administration Building, Irvine, CA 92697 • Telephone: 949-824-6703 • Web: www.uci.edu • Email: oars@uci.edu

Hours: Monday-Friday, 8AM-5PM. Closed weekends, New Year's Day, Martin Luther King Day, Presidents' Day, Memorial Day, July 4, Labor Day, Thanksgiving, and Christmas.

The Irvine campus of the University of California is located about an hour from Los Angeles, and provides a research-oriented education in the arts and sciences. Irvine's programs in science are legendary. The campus is a mere five minutes from the beach and an hour from mountain skiing resorts.

AT A GLANCE

Selectivity Rating	76
Range SAT I Math	525-645
Range SAT I Verbal	475-585
Average GPA	3.7

CAMPUS TOURS

Appointment Req?	No
Dates	Year-round, except holidays
Times	Mon-Fri at noon
Avg. Length	75 min

ON-CAMPUS INTERVIEWS

Admissions

Start Date–Juniors	Any time
Appointment Req?	No
Advance Notice	None
Saturdays?	No
Avg. Length	N/A
Info Sessions	Yes

Faculty and Coaches

Dates/Times	Year-round; subject to faculty/coach availability
Arrangements	Contact Campus Tours Office

CLASS VISITS

Dates	Year-round (Mon-Fri)
Arrangements	Contact Campus Tours Office

OVERNIGHT DORM STAYS

Advance Notice	3 weeks
Arrangements	Contact Housing Off. at 949-824-5167
Limitations	Limited to prospective students who are high school juniors or seniors, and transfer students age 16-20; 1-night stay; Mon-Thurs nights; winter and spring quarter only; $25 fee

TRANSPORTATION

The John Wayne Airport (Orange County) is 5 miles from campus. Taxis are available at the airport.

FIND YOUR WAY

The campus is one mile south of the I-405 freeway. **From San Diego (south of Irvine)**, take I-405 to the Culver Rd. exit and proceed south to Campus Dr. Turn right on Campus Dr. to E. Peltason Dr. (the university entrance). Turn left on E. Peltason Dr. **From Los Angeles (north of Irvine)**, take I-405 to the Jamboree exit and proceed south to Campus Dr. Turn left on Campus Dr. and proceed to Bridge Rd. (the university entrance). Turn right on W. Peltason Dr.

STAY THE NIGHT

Nearby: The **Atrium Hotel** (18700 MacArthur Blvd.; 949-833-2770), 5 minutes away (and close to the airport), has a special moderate double-occupancy rate for university visitors. A shuttle bus will take you to the Irvine Racquet Club, where you can play squash and use the exercise room. The **Holiday Inn—Orange County Airport** (2726 S. Grand Ave., Santa Ana; 714-966-1955) is only 15 minutes from campus. Ask for the special inexpensive double-occupancy rate for university visitors. The Ramada has a fitness room and an outside pool and jacuzzi. You have a couple of interesting, moderately priced choices about 10 minutes from the university. The **Country Inn and Suites** (325 S. Bristol St., Costa Mesa; 714-549-0300) is a large hotel with a country inn atmosphere. It is located in a business district and has two pools, jacuzzis, and exercise facilities, as well as a French restaurant on the premises. Ask for the university rate (moderate) at the **Irvine Hyatt Regency** (17900 Jamboree Blvd.; 949-975-1234) which is 10 minutes away. There are lighted tennis courts, as well as a pool, jacuzzi, and exercise rooms. At the **Newport Beach Marriott Hotel and Tennis Club** (900 Newport Center Dr., Fashion Island; 949-640-4000) you can enjoy an ocean view in the lounge, lighted tennis courts, exercise rooms, pools, patios, balconies, and a band that plays Top 40 tunes. Golf privileges and a shopping center are additional pluses.

A little farther: For something different, consider Newport Beach, a half-hour's drive away. Prices are in the expensive range (full breakfast included) at the 10-room **Doryman's Inn** (2102 W. Oceanfront, Newport Beach; 949-675-7300), a historical landmark just across from Newport Pier. The inn, housed in a 1920s brick building, provides an elegant atmosphere with views of the Pacific from the roof deck.

HIGHLIGHTS

ON CAMPUS
- Amphitheater Recreation Center
- Zot Zone
- Science Library
- Aldrich Park
- Anthill Pub and Grill

OFF CAMPUS
- Irvine Spectrum
- The Block at Orange
- The beach
- Disneyland
- South Coast Plaza

UNIVERSITY OF CALIFORNIA—LOS ANGELES

Office of Undergraduate Admissions, University of California–Los Angeles, 405 Hilgard Ave., 1147 Murphy Hall, Los Angeles, CA 90095 • Telephone: 310-825-3101 • Web: www.ucla.edu • Email: ugadm@saonet.ucla.edu

Hours: Monday-Friday, 9AM-5PM. Closed weekends and holidays.

The distinguished Los Angeles campus of the University of California enrolls about 24,000 students and offers a wide range of programs including respected pre-med programs. The educational and extracurricular opportunities on campus are vast, but require student initiative, and the bustling city of Los Angeles does not lack for entertainment options.

HIGHLIGHTS

ON CAMPUS
- The UCLA Library
- UCLA Hammer Museum
- UCLA Fowler Museum of Cultural History
- Sunset Canyon Recreation Center

OFF CAMPUS
- Chinatown, Little Tokyo
- Parks, museums, sports
- Disneyland

TRANSPORTATION

Los Angeles International Airport (LAX) is 20 minutes from campus. Burbank Airport is 30 minutes from campus. Call the following numbers to arrange transportation from LAX: 818-556-6600 for Super Shuttle; 800-262-7433 for Prime Time Shuttle. Checker Cab Service (818-956-5959) also runs between campus and LAX. Amtrak trains and Greyhound/Trailways buses provide transportation to Los Angeles.

FIND YOUR WAY

From the I-405 freeway (north or south), take the Wilshire Blvd. exit and follow it east to Westwood Blvd. Turn left onto Westwood Blvd. and drive onto the campus. From downtown, take Wilshire Blvd. west and turn right onto Westwood Blvd.

STAY THE NIGHT

Many of the hotels and motels in the area offer special rates for campus visitors; make sure you tell them you are entitled to this discount.

Nearby: For convenience and price, the on-campus **UCLA Guest House** (330 Charles E. Young Dr. E.; 310-825-2923) is the place. The price is moderate (continental breakfast is extra). Your room key gives you access to various sports facilities on campus. One of the great Los Angeles hotels is located half a block from UCLA, the all-suite **Westwood Marquis** (930 Hilgard Ave.; 310-208-8765 or 800-421-2317). Charming but expensive, it has 2 pools, an exercise room, and a health spa. A moderately priced **Holiday Inn-Brentwood** (170 N. Church Lane, Brentwood; 213-476-6411) is two miles away. It has a pool and a small health club. About 6 miles from campus is another moderately priced hotel, the **Ramada Inn** (8585 Santa Monica Blvd., West Hollywood; 213-652-6400). See the Pepperdine University entry for information about bed-and-breakfasts in the area. **Bay Side Hotel** in Santa Monica, listed there, might be of interest. It is in the inexpensive range, and Santa Monica is only about 5 miles west of UCLA.

A little farther: **Mansion Inn** (327 Washington Blvd.; 310-821-2557), about 30 minutes away, is 1 block from the beach. It's a cozy, European-style hotel with moderate rates and a complimentary continental breakfast. The places listed below are in downtown L.A. and are suitable for a number of schools in the area. But be aware that each college recommends staying close by, since the traffic is horrendous. Of course, the **Hotel Bel Air** (701 Stone Canyon Rd.; 310-472-1211 or 800-648-4097) has to be mentioned, since it is "one of the 10 best in the world" according to *Travel and Leisure* magazine. **La Maida House** (11159 La Maida St., North Hollywood; 818-769-3857) is an inn very close to Universal City. Rates range from moderate to very expensive, including continental breakfast and afternoon refreshments.

UNIVERSITY OF CALIFORNIA—RIVERSIDE

Office of Relations with Schools, University of California–Riverside, 1120 Hinderaker Hall, Riverside, CA 92521 • Telephone: 909-787-4531 • Web: www.ucr.edu • Email: discover@pop.ucr.edu

Hours: Monday-Friday, 8AM-5PM. Closed weekends and all national holidays.

The Riverside campus of the University of California is located about an hour from Los Angeles. Riverside offers programs ranging from the liberal arts to business to a fast-track, seven-year MD program. For athletic excellence, check out the men's and women's karate teams, winners of six national championships.

AT A GLANCE

Selectivity Rating		78
Range SAT I Math		480-620
Average SAT I Math		554
Range SAT I Verbal		440-570
Average SAT I Verbal		512
Average ACT Composite		21
Average GPA		3.5
Student to Faculty Ratio		19:1

CAMPUS TOURS

Appointment Req?	Yes, call 909-787-5045
Dates	Year-round, call for reservations
Avg. Length	1 hour

ON-CAMPUS INTERVIEWS

Admissions

Start Date—Juniors	N/A
Appointment Req?	N/A
Advance Notice	N/A
Saturdays?	N/A
Avg. Length	N/A
Info Sessions	N/A

Faculty and Coaches

Dates/Times	Year-round; subject to faculty/coach availability
Arrangements	Contact Host Program

CLASS VISITS

Dates	Year-round (Mon-Fri)
Arrangements	Call 909-787-6350

OVERNIGHT DORM STAYS

Advance Notice	2.5 weeks
Arrangements	Call 909-787-6350
Limitations	1-night stay; student pays for own meals; no stays on weekends or during exam periods

TRANSPORTATION

Ontario International Airport is 20 miles from campus. Taxis and shuttles are available at the airport. The Riverside Transit Authority (RTA) provides convenient bus service throughout western Riverside County.

FIND YOUR WAY

From California Rte. 60/215 (Pomona Freeway), take the University Ave. exit. At the exit ramp, turn left (east) and proceed one block to the main entrance to the campus. Make a right turn into kiosk for parking instructions. Parking is $5/day.

STAY THE NIGHT

The Courtyard by Marriott (1510 University Ave.; 909-272-1200) is 5 blocks from campus and charges low rates. The **Comfort Inn** (1590 University Ave.; 909-683-6000) also gives special rates to university visitors. About 10 minutes away is the **Holiday Inn Riverside** (3400 Market St.; 909-784-8000), a multi-story hotel with a heated pool, jacuzzi, sauna, cafe, entertainment—the works. Rates vary from the high end of the moderate range to expensive. The **Historic Mission Inn** (3649 Mission Inn Ave.; 909-784-0300) is located approximately 5 miles from the campus.

HIGHLIGHTS

ON CAMPUS
- Botanic Gardens
- Sweeney Art Gallery
- University libraries
- Athletic events

OFF CAMPUS
- University Village
- Riverside Municipal Museum
- Riverside Art Museum
- California Museum of Photography

UNIVERSITY OF CALIFORNIA—SAN DIEGO

Office of Admissions and Outreach, University of California–San Diego, 9500 Gilman Dr., La Jolla, CA 92093-0337 • Telephone: 858-534-4831 • Web: www.ucsd.edu • Email: admissionsinfo@ucsd.edu

Hours: Monday-Friday, 8AM-4:30PM. Closed weekends and holidays.

The San Diego campus of the University of California is actually located in the quaint community of La Jolla. UCSD offers a solid liberal arts and sciences education, and its engineering and science programs are rated particularly high. For fun, students enjoy surfing and camping on the nearby beach.

HIGHLIGHTS

ON CAMPUS
- Geisel Library
- Stuart Art (sculpture) Gallery
- Sun God Statue
- Stephen Birch Aquarium and Museum

OFF CAMPUS
- San Diego Zoo
- Baboa Park
- Beaches
- Gaslamp Quarter
- Old Town

TRANSPORTATION

San Diego International Airport is 15 miles from campus. Taxis, shuttles and public buses are available for the ride to campus from the airport. Amtrak trains and Greyhound/Trailways buses serve downtown San Diego. The San Diego Metropolitan Transit System provides bus service in the area and the San Diego Trolley runs on 2 lines from the Amtrak depot.

FIND YOUR WAY

From I-5, exit to Gilman Dr. W. Follow it to the information kiosk, where you can get a parking permit, campus map, and directions. Parking is free on weekends.

STAY THE NIGHT

Nearby: The closest hotel to the university is the **Residence Inn by Marriott** (8901 Gilman Dr.; 858-587-1170). Another within walking distance is the **Radisson Hotel of La Jolla** (3299 Holiday Ct.; 858-453-5500).

A little farther: The **La Jolla Marriott Hotel** (4240 La Jolla Village Dr.; 858-587-1414), the **Hyatt Regency Hotel** (3777 La Jolla Village Dr.; 858-552-1234) and the **Embassy Suites** (4550 La Jolla Village Dr.; 858-453-0400) are all within 2 miles of campus.

AT A GLANCE

Selectivity Rating	81
Average SAT I Math	647
Average SAT I Verbal	609
Average ACT Composite	25
Average GPA	3.9
Student to Faculty Ratio	19:1

CAMPUS TOURS

Appointment Req?	Yes, recommended; call 858-534-1935 or email campustours@ucsd.edu
Dates	Year-round, except holidays
Times	Mon-Sat 11AM
Avg. Length	90 min

ON-CAMPUS INTERVIEWS

Admissions

Appointment Req?	N/A
Advance Notice	N/A
Info Sessions	Year-round Mon-Fri, 12:30PM, except holidays

Faculty and Coaches

Dates/Times	Year-round; subject to faculty/coach availability
Arrangements	For faculty, contact dept. of interest; for coach, contact Athletic Dept. 2-3 weeks prior

CLASS VISITS

Dates	Year-round (Mon-Fri)
Arrangements	Contact Office of Admissions and Outreach

OVERNIGHT DORM STAYS

Arrangements	N/A

UNIVERSITY OF CALIFORNIA—SANTA BARBARA

Undergraduate Admissions, University of California–Santa Barbara, 1210 Cheadle Hall, Santa Barbara, CA 93106 • Visitor Information: 805-893-8175 • Web: www.ucsb.edu • Email: appinfo@sa.ucsb.edu

Hours: Monday-Friday, 9AM-noon and 1PM-5PM. Closed Saturdays, Sundays, and holidays.

The laid-back University of California's Santa Barbara campus enrolls about 17,000 students in a variety of programs ranging from liberal arts and sciences to business and technology. Students claim the Santa Barbara campus has one of the nation's most active social scenes, and report that no UCSB experience is complete without a weekend party at the notorious Isla Vista area of student residences.

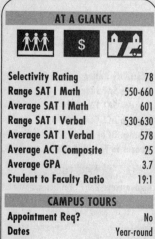

AT A GLANCE

Selectivity Rating	78
Range SAT I Math	550-660
Average SAT I Math	601
Range SAT I Verbal	530-630
Average SAT I Verbal	578
Average ACT Composite	25
Average GPA	3.7
Student to Faculty Ratio	19:1

CAMPUS TOURS

Appointment Req?	No
Dates	Year-round
Times	Mon-Fri 11AM and 2PM; Sat 11AM (fall and spring session only)
Avg. Length	2 hours

ON-CAMPUS INTERVIEWS

Admissions

Start Date–Juniors	N/A
Appointment Req?	N/A
Advance Notice	N/A
Saturdays?	N/A
Avg. Length	N/A
Info Sessions	N/A

Faculty and Coaches

Dates/Times	Year-round; subject to faculty/coach availability
Arrangements	For faculty, contact dept. of interest; for coach, contact coach directly

CLASS VISITS

Dates	Fall, winter, and spring quarters
Arrangements	Contact visitor center

OVERNIGHT DORM STAYS

Advance Notice	N/A
Arrangements	N/A
Limitations	N/A

TRANSPORTATION

The Santa Barbara Airport is a 5-minute drive from campus. Taxis are available at the airport. Amtrak trains and Greyhound buses serve downtown Santa Barbara. A direct express bus is available from downtown to campus. Taxis are also available for the ride from the stations to campus.

FIND YOUR WAY

From the north, take U.S. Highway 101 south to the Storke Road/Glen Annie Road exit, which is approximately 12 miles north of Santa Barbara. Turn right on Storke Road and proceed two miles to El Colegio Road. Turn left onto El Colegio Road and proceed to the campus entrance. **From the south**, take U.S. Highway 101 north to the Airport/UCSB exit (Route 217), which is approximately 8 miles north of Santa Barbara, then continue to the campus entrance. The daily parking fee at the campus is $5 Monday through Friday. There is no charge for weekend parking.

STAY THE NIGHT

Nearby: The campus is west of Santa Barbara, in Goleta, with no lodgings within walking distance. Two moderately priced motels are a short drive away; both have heated pools and complimentary van service to and from the airport. The least expensive and closest (about 2 miles away) is a **Holiday Inn** (5650 Calle Real, Goleta; 805-964-6241), with a restaurant. About 4 miles from campus is the **Ramada Limited** (4770 Calle Real, Santa Barbara; 805-964-3511 or 800-654-1965). Rates are only slightly more expensive than at the Holiday Inn, and the price includes a continental breakfast. Nearby beaches are a plus, and it is close to downtown shopping. If you need even more relaxation, watch the ducks on the freshwater pond.

A little farther: Santa Barbara has many small inns. You might consider **The Cheshire Cat** (36 W. Valerio St.; 805-569-1610), a 20-minute drive from campus. Prices range from moderate to expensive. All rooms have private baths and telephones. The inn is close to the Mission Santa Barbara and to the shops and restaurants of the town. The price includes a gourmet continental breakfast and afternoon wine. The famous, very expensive **San Ysidro Ranch** (900 San Ysidro Lane; 805-969-5046) is situated in the foothills of the Santa Ynez Mountains. It's 10 miles south of Santa Barbara and 25 minutes from campus. Hiking, and exercise room, swimming, golf, and tennis are available. **Circle Bar B Guest Ranch** is a more down-home guest ranch in Goleta (1800 Refugio Rd.; 805-968-1113), 30 minutes north of the university. This family-run, 1,000-acre ranch has 30 horses, hiking and riding trails, a swimming pool, and a jacuzzi. While its price is in the expensive range, it does include 3 meals a day. Comedy theater is presented on weekends. Also try the **Best Western South Coast Inn** (5620 Calle Real, Goleta; 805-967-3200) or the **Super 8** (6021 Hollister Ave, Goleta; 805-967-5591), or check the UCSB website at www.ucsb.edu for other Santa Barbara lodging.

HIGHLIGHTS

ON CAMPUS
- Storke Tower Plaza/University Center
- University Art Museum
- UCSB Davidson Library
- Recreation Center
- Career/Counseling Services Center

OFF CAMPUS
- Stearns Wharf
- Old Spanish Days/summer festivals
- Los Padres National Forest
- Santa Barbara Mission, Museum, Botanic Gardens, Zoo
- Santa Yenz/Solvang Danish Village

UNIVERSITY OF CALIFORNIA—SANTA CRUZ

Office of Admissions, Cook House, University of California–Santa Cruz, Santa Cruz, CA 95064
• Telephone: 831-459-4008 • Web: http://admissions.ucsc.edu •
Email: admissions@cats.ucsc.edu

Hours: Monday-Friday, 8AM-5PM. Closed weekends and holidays.

The Santa Cruz campus of the University of California enrolls about 10,000 students, the majority of whom have high praise for the school's educational programs, which include the liberal arts and sciences, as well as technology and engineering programs.

HIGHLIGHTS

ON CAMPUS
- Arboretum
- Farm and garden
- East Fieldhouse
- Pogonip Open Area Reserve
- Bay Tree Bookstore

OFF CAMPUS
- UCSC Long Marine Lab
- Natural Bridges and Lighthouse Beach
- State Parks
- Mystery Spot
- Boardwalk

TRANSPORTATION

San Jose International Airport is 35 miles from campus. Rental cars, buses, and limousines are available for the ride to Santa Cruz. Commercial bus service is available to Santa Cruz, and bus transportation within the county is convenient. The Metro Transit Center downtown serves Santa Cruz County; Rte. #1 loops through the campus.

FIND YOUR WAY

From U.S. Rte. 101 S. (from San Francisco), exit to I-880 S. Take I-880 to Rte. 17 S., then take Rte. 17 to Rte. 1 N. (toward Half Moon Bay). From Rte. 1, turn right on Bay St. in Santa Cruz and proceed to campus. **From Rte. 101 N.**, exit to I-880 S., then to Rte. 17 S. Follow the preceding directions from that point.

STAY THE NIGHT

You have a variety of choices within a few miles of campus. The least expensive and simplest is the **Ramada Limited** (130 W. Cliff Dr.; 831-423-7737), about 2 miles from campus on the boardwalk across from the beach. Some of the units have ocean views and balconies. **Mission Inn** (2250 Mission St., Hwy. 1; 831-425-5455), about 1 mile from the university, is equally well-priced. It's located in town, close to golf courses, and there is a covered hot tub in the courtyard. Two wonderful inns are within 5 minutes of the university. Both are moderately priced and include breakfast. **Darling House** (314 W. Cliff Dr.; 800-866-1131), is an elegant oceanside mansion set among orchards and palms. Each room has a theme or historical background. Rooms with a view are more expensive (but there's a discount for university visitors). **Babbling Brook Inn** (1025 Laurel St.; 800-866-1131) is an in-town inn with a country French ambience set in landscaped gardens among redwoods. You can stroll the garden walkways or play tennis and golf nearby. Wine, cheese, tea, and homemade cookies are served in the afternoon. **West Coast Santa Cruz Hotel** (175 W. Cliff Dr.; 831-426-4330) is a beachfront hotel 2 miles from the university. Its double rooms range from moderate to very expensive. All the rooms have ocean views and private balconies (and the views from the inn are fabulous). Relax in the heated pool, jacuzzi, or sauna. Another possibility is the Henry Cowell State Park Campgrounds, $17 per per night and reservation fee.

UNIVERSITY OF REDLANDS

Office of Admissions, University of Redlands, P.O. Box 3080, 1200 E. Colton Ave, Redlands, CA 92373-9999 (The office is in the Administration Building) • Telephone: 909-335-4073 or 909-335-4074 • Web: www.redlands.edu • Email: admissions@uor.edu

Hours: Monday-Friday, 8AM-5PM; Saturday by special appointment only. Closed Sundays, winter and Thanksgiving breaks, and July 4.

The primary reason to attend University of Redlands is the Johnston Center for Integrative Studies, in which students design their own majors in tandem with faculty members and, instead of grades, receive precise feedback from their collaborating professors.

AT A GLANCE

Selectivity Rating	73
Range SAT I Math	520-610
Average SAT I Math	553
Range SAT I Verbal	510-610
Average SAT I Verbal	558
Average ACT Composite	24
Average GPA	3.4
Student to Faculty Ratio	13:1

CAMPUS TOURS

Appointment Req?	No
Dates	Year-round, but not during exam periods
Times	Sept-May: Mon-Fri 10AM, 1PM, and 4PM; Sat 11AM. June-Aug: Mon-Fri 10AM and 2PM.
Avg. Length	1 hour

ON-CAMPUS INTERVIEWS

Admissions

Start Date—Juniors	Any time
Appointment Req?	Yes
Advance Notice	2 days
Saturdays?	Only by special appt.
Avg. Length	45 min
Info Sessions	Visitation days only

Faculty and Coaches

Dates/Times	Year-round; subject to faculty/coach availability
Arrangements	Contact admissions off. 2 days prior

CLASS VISITS

Dates	Year-round (Mon-Fri)
Arrangements	Contact visit coordinator at 909-335-4073 or 800-455-5064

OVERNIGHT DORM STAYS

Advance Notice	3 weeks
Arrangements	Contact visit coordinator
Limitations	Seniors and transfer students

TRANSPORTATION

Ontario International Airport is 28 miles west of the town of Redlands off I-10. It is 27 miles from campus. Taxi, Travelers Limousine, and Stagecoach service is available from the airport to campus; call at least two days in advance to arrange for these services (Travelers Limousine: 714-798-6674; Stagecoach: 714-877-9469). Bus transportation is available between Ontario and Los Angeles.

FIND YOUR WAY

From Los Angeles, take I-10 E. to the University St. exit in Redlands. Turn left and head north on University St. to Colton Ave.; turn right onto campus. **From the east**, take I-10 W. to the Redlands Blvd.-Ford St. exit; turn right (Ford becomes Judson). At Colton Ave., turn left and continue for a quarter mile to campus.

STAY THE NIGHT

Nearby: You have two inexpensive choices within a mile or two of campus. The **Goodnight Inn** (1675 Industrial Park Ave.; 909-793-3723) has a heated pool and spa. The **Best Western Sandman** (1120 W. Colton Ave.; 909-793-7001) is about a mile from the university. For a small additional charge, you may have a kitchen unit. There is a pool and a jacuzzi at the latter. Smack-dab in Redlands is a bed-and-breakfast called **Morey Mansion Bed and Breakfast** (190 Teracina Blvd.; 909-793-7970). This no-smoking landmark Victorian building offers moderate prices and a continental breakfast.

A little farther: In San Bernardino, **Inland Empire Hilton** (285 E. Hospitality Lane; 909-889-0133) is about 15 minutes from Redlands. Rates are at the high end of the moderate range. The motor hotel has a swimming pool, jacuzzi, and health club, and a public golf course is close by. See suggestions in the University of California–Riverside entry, particularly the **Sheraton Riverside**. It's about 30 minutes from the University of Redlands.

HIGHLIGHTS

ON CAMPUS
- Armacost Library
- Peppers Art Center
- Currier Gymnasium

OFF CAMPUS
- The University is right in between LA and Palm Springs

UNIVERSITY OF SAN DIEGO

Office of Undergraduate Admissions, University of San Diego, 5998 Alcala Park, San Diego, CA 92110 (The office is located in Serra Hall, Rm. 203) • Telephone: 619-260-4506 • Web: www.acusd.edu • Email: admissions@is.acusd.edu

Hours: Monday-Friday, 8:30AM-5PM; Saturday, 10AM-2PM (November-April only). Closed Sundays and holidays.

The ridiculously beautiful campus of the University of San Diego is home to Spanish-style architecture, almost 90 degree programs, and a strong Catholic heritage. Jenny Craig served on the USD Board of Trustees from 1990 to 1996 and contributed a whopping 7 million dollars for the student activities facility. USD also has one of the coolest names around for its sports teams: the Toreros.

HIGHLIGHTS

ON CAMPUS
- Copley Library

OFF CAMPUS
- San Diego Zoo
- Sea World
- San Diego Wild Animal Park

TRANSPORTATION

San Diego International Airport is 5 miles from campus. Taxi and shuttle services to campus are available; advance arrangements are not necessary. Amtrak trains serve San Diego from Los Angeles. Greyhound/Trailways buses also serve San Diego. The San Diego Metropolitan Transit System provides bus service in the area and the San Diego Trolley runs from the Amtrak depot.

FIND YOUR WAY

From I-5, exit at Sea World Dr.; turn east and follow signs to the university. **From I-8**, exit at Morena Blvd. and follow signs to the university.

STAY THE NIGHT

Nearby: We have a range of choices for you, but all of them are about 15 minutes away. The low-cost **Kings Inn** (1333 Hotel Circle S.; 619-297-2231 or 800-785-4647) has a coffee shop, heated pool, and jacuzzi, and you may use the health club at the Mission Valley Inn. A shopping mall is 5 minutes away. The other inexpensive choice is the **Quality Resorts** (875 Hotel Circle S.; 619-298-8281). Here you'll find a health club, tennis courts, lap pool, pool, exercise room, and aerobics on the premises. The inn is 5 minutes from a shopping mall. For both, ask for the special rate for university visitors. The **Hanalei Hotel** (2270 Hotel Circle N.; 619-297-1101), with its 4 outdoor pools, jacuzzi, gift shop, restaurants, tropical gardens, and health club with tennis and racquetball, is almost like a little city. Normally the double rooms are in the moderate-expensive range, but a special double-occupancy rate becomes available in a garden room if the occupancy drops below 76 percent. Be sure to ask if you can have one of these rooms. **Heritage Park Inn** (2470 Heritage Park Row; 619-295-7088) is located in the 7-acre Victorian preserve of Old Town in San Diego. The price includes a full breakfast, afternoon refreshments, and a classic film shown in the parlor in the evening.

A little farther: See also suggestions in the entry for University of California–San Diego, which is in La Jolla, a suburb of San Diego about a 20-minute drive north of downtown.

AT A GLANCE

Range SAT I Math	540-630
Range SAT I Verbal	520-610
Average GPA	3.6
Student to Faculty Ratio	17:1

CAMPUS TOURS

Appointment Req?	Suggested
Dates	Year-round
Times	Mon-Fri 10AM and 2PM
Avg. Length	1 hour

ON-CAMPUS INTERVIEWS

Admissions

Start Date—Juniors	N/A
Appointment Req?	N/A
Advance Notice	N/A
Saturdays?	N/A
Avg. Length	N/A
Info Sessions	Year-round

Faculty and Coaches

Dates/Times	Year-round; subject to faculty/coach availability
Arrangements	Contact admissions off. 2 weeks prior

CLASS VISITS

Dates	Year-round (Mon-Fri)
Arrangements	Contact admissions off. 2 weeks prior

OVERNIGHT DORM STAYS

Advance Notice	N/A
Arrangements	N/A
Limitations	Admitted students only

UNIVERSITY OF SAN FRANCISCO

Admissions Office, University of San Francisco, 2130 Fulton St., San Francisco, CA 94117 •
Telephone: 800-CALLUSF or 415-422-6563 • Web: www.usfca.edu •
Email: admission@usfca.edu

Hours: Monday-Friday, 8:30AM-5PM. Closed weekends and holidays.

The Jesuit University of San Francisco offers a wealth of excellent degree programs and a demanding core curriculum. The McLaren School of Business consistently ranks as one of the country's top international business schools, and you just can't beat college life in the heart of San Francisco.

AT A GLANCE

Selectivity Rating	80
Range SAT I Math	480-590
Range SAT I Verbal	480-590
Average GPA	3.3
Student to Faculty Ratio	15:1

CAMPUS TOURS

Appointment Req?	No
Dates	Year-round
Times	Mon-Fri 10AM and 2PM
Avg. Length	1 hour

ON-CAMPUS INTERVIEWS

Admissions

Start Date–Juniors	Any time
Appointment Req?	Yes
Advance Notice	1 week
Saturdays?	Yes
Avg. Length	1 hour
Info Sessions	Available as part of campus tour

Faculty and Coaches

Dates/Times	Year-round; subject to faculty/coach availability
Arrangements	Contact admissions off. 1 week prior

DAY VISITS

Dates	Mar 19-Apr 11
Arrangements	Contact admissions off.
Advance Notice	2 weeks

TRANSPORTATION

San Francisco International is a 20-minute drive from campus. Visitors can take the Shuttle Services at the airport without making advance arrangements. Amtrak trains serve nearby Oakland; Greyhound/Trailways buses bring passengers to San Francisco.

FIND YOUR WAY

If you enter the city from the airport or the Bay Bridge, follow the signs to the Golden Gate Bridge. Exit the Freeway on Fell St. and proceed for approximately 3 miles. Turn right at Masonic, and then left on Golden Gate Ave. The entrance to the university is on the left. **If you enter the city from the Golden Gate Bridge**, follow Park Presidio to Fulton St. Turn left and the university is at the top of the hill. From I-280, follow 9th Ave. for 3 miles. Go through Golden Gate Park and turn right on Fulton St. as you come out of the park.

STAY THE NIGHT

Nearby: The small, 36-room **Stanyan Park Hotel** (750 Stanyan St.; 415-751-1000) is about 6 blocks away. Rooms here are comfortable and romantic, and the moderate rate includes continental breakfast. The joggers among you will particularly appreciate being across from Golden Gate Park. The **Laurel Motor Inn** (444 Presidio Ave.; 415-567-8467), about 8 blocks away, is moderately priced (including continental breakfast) and convenient.

A little farther: Just blocks from Union Square (also 15 minutes from the university), is **The Petite Auberge** (863 Bush St.). This is a French-style country inn decorated in soft colors, antiques, and fresh flowers. The rates are in the expensive range and include full breakfast and afternoon tea. Of course, there are some fabulous and very expensive hotels in San Francisco. A few of them are the **Mandarin Oriental** (222 Sansome St.; 415-885-0999 or 800-622-0404), the **Huntington Hotel** (1075 California St.; 415-474-5400 or 800-227-4683), and the **Four Seasons Clift** (495 Geary St.; 415-775-4700 or 800-652-5438).

HIGHLIGHTS

ON CAMPUS
- Koret Health and Recreation Center
- War Memorial Gym
- St. Ignatius Church
- Geschke Learning Resource Center

OFF CAMPUS
- Golden Gate Bridge
- Alcatraz Island
- Union Square
- Pacific Bell Park
- Golden Gate Park

UNIVERSITY OF SOUTHERN CALIFORNIA

Office of Undergraduate Admissions, University of Southern California, 700 Childs Way, Los Angeles, CA 90089-0911 (The office is in TRO 101) • Telephone: 213-740-1111 • Web: www.usc.edu • Email: ugrd@usc.edu

Hours: Monday-Friday, 8:30AM-5PM. Closed weekends and most holidays.

If you are looking for a university with awesome facilities and a strong scholastic reputation, check out the University of Southern California, which, as an added bonus, is located near glitzy downtown Los Angeles. Alumni provide thousands of instant and permanent connections for job-hunting grads.

HIGHLIGHTS

ON CAMPUS
- Fisher Art Gallery
- School of Cinema and Television
- Leavey Library
- Heritage Hall
- Bing Theater

OFF CAMPUS
- Exposition Park
- Museum of Contemporary Art
- The Staples Center
- Los Angeles Music Center

TRANSPORTATION

Los Angeles International Airport is 15 miles from campus. Taxis (approximately $28) and the Super Shuttle (approximately $15) are available for the ride between airport and campus. Taxis can be picked up outside the airport terminal. The Super Shuttle is a minibus that will take you anywhere in Los Angeles and Orange counties; call 310-782-6600 a day or two in advance or when you arrive. Amtrak trains and Greyhound/Trailways buses provide transportation to Los Angeles.

FIND YOUR WAY

From I-110 (Harbor Freeway), exit onto Exposition Blvd. and go 1 block west. The campus will be on the right. From I-10 (Santa Monica Freeway), exit onto Hoover St. and go south approximately 1 mile to Jefferson Blvd. The campus will be directly ahead. **From the Los Angeles International Airport**, take the Glenn Anderson Freeway (105) east to the Harbor Freeway north (I-110). Exit on Exposition Blvd. and go 1 block west. The campus will be on your right.

STAY THE NIGHT

Across the street is the **Radisson Hotel** (3540 S. Figueroa St.; 213-748-4141), with a special double-occupancy rate in the moderate range. See the Pepperdine University entry for information about bed-and-breakfasts in the area. Also see suggestions for downtown Los Angeles in the University of California–Los Angeles, entry. USC is 2.5 miles south of downtown, right in the city.

AT A GLANCE

Selectivity Rating	82
Range SAT I Math	580-680
Average SAT I Math	636
Range SAT I Verbal	560-660
Average SAT I Verbal	607
Average ACT Composite	28
Average GPA	3.7
Student to Faculty Ratio	14:1

CAMPUS TOURS

Appointment Req?	Yes, call 213-740-6605
Dates	Year-round
Times	Mon-Fri 10AM, 11AM, 12PM, 1PM, 2PM, and 3PM
Avg. Length	50 min

ON-CAMPUS VISITS

Admissions

Start Date—Juniors	Any time
Appointment Req?	Yes, call 213-740-6616
Advance Notice	Varies
Saturdays?	Varies
Avg. Length	2.5 hours
Info Sessions	Yes

Faculty and Coaches

Dates/Times	Year-round; subject to faculty/coach availability
Arrangements	Contact dept. of interest or the particular faculty/coach 1 week prior

CLASS VISITS

Dates	Year-round (Mon-Fri)
Arrangements	Contact admissions off.

OVERNIGHT DORM STAYS

Arrangements	By invitation only
Limitations	Admitted students only; 1-night "Preview USC" programs

UNIVERSITY OF THE PACIFIC

> Admissions Office, University of the Pacific, 3601 Pacific Ave., Stockton, CA 95211
> (The office is in Knoles Hall) • Telephone: 800-959-2867 •
> Web: www.uop.edu • Email: admissions@uop.edu

Hours: Monday-Friday, 8:30AM-5PM; select Saturdays, 9AM-noon (by appointment only). Closed Sundays and holidays.

Students at University of the Pacific rave about their close relationship with professors. Health sciences are the school's strongest suit, although music, engineering, and business-related majors are also well-regarded.

AT A GLANCE

Selectivity Rating	74
Range SAT I Math	500-620
Average SAT I Math	568
Range SAT I Verbal	480-600
Average SAT I Verbal	544
Average ACT Composite	20
Average GPA	3.4
Student to Faculty Ratio	14:1

CAMPUS TOURS

Appointment Req?	Yes
Dates	Mon-Fri during academic year
Times	Call for times 800-959-2867
Avg. Length	1 hour

ON-CAMPUS INTERVIEWS

Admissions

Start Date–Juniors	Any time
Appointment Req?	Yes
Advance Notice	1 week
Saturdays?	Selected days by appointment
Avg. Length	1 hour
Info Sessions	N/A

Faculty and Coaches

Dates/Times	Year-round; subject to faculty/coach availability
Arrangements	Contact admissions off. 1 week prior

CLASS VISITS

Dates	Year-round (Mon-Fri)
Arrangements	Contact admissions off.

OVERNIGHT DORM STAYS

Advance Notice	2 weeks
Arrangements	Contact admissions off.
Limitations	Not available Fri-Sun

TRANSPORTATION

The Sacramento International Airport is an hour from campus, Oakland International and San Jose International are each about an hour and a half from campus, and San Francisco International is about 2 hours from campus. Limited transportation is available from these airports. For Super Shuttle Service from Sacramento International, call 800-BlueVan for a reservation. Greyhound provides direct and frequent service to Stockton. For fare and schedule information, call 800-843-2121. The bus station is approximately 3 miles from the University, so we recommend a taxi to campus. Amtrak trains (800-USA-RAIL) provide direct service to Stockton from almost everywhere in California. The Amtrak Station is approximately 5 miles south of campus, and taxi service is available.

FIND YOUR WAY

From I-5, exit at March Lane. Drive about 1.5 miles, turn right on Pacific Ave. The main campus entrance is less than a mile south of the intersection of March Lane and Pacific Ave. Turn right into campus at the traffic light. Guest parking is to your right. Permits are required weekdays 8AM to 5 PM anywhere on campus during the school year. Visitor permits may be obtained at the Office of Admissions or in Burns Tower lobby.

STAY THE NIGHT

Nearby: The university has 4 guest rooms in residence halls on campus that are incredible bargains, if you can get one. You must book well in advance by calling Housing at 209-946-2331. You can find breakfast on campus at the Summit. The nicest places to stay in Stockton are the **Stockton Radisson Hotel** (2323 Grand Canal Blvd.; 800-333-3333) and the **Marriott Courtyard** (3252 March Lane; 209-472-5700) and the **Marriott Residence Inn** (888-472-9801). **La Quinta Inn** (2710 W. March Lane; 800-531-5900) is less expensive. Even less expensive, is the **Red Roof Inn** (2654 W. March Lane; 209-478-4300), and the **Super 8 Motel** (209-477-5576). All of the above lodging is within 5 to 10 minutes from campus. Exit March Lane for all of them.

A little farther: Stockton is about 80 miles east from San Francisco. If you wish to stay there, check suggestions in the entry for University of San Francisco or, to the southwest, Stanford or Santa Clara University.

HIGHLIGHTS

ON CAMPUS
- Brubeck Institute for Jazz Studies
- John Muir Collection and Center
- Alex Spanos Center
- Reynolds Art Gallery
- 49ers Summer Training Camp

OFF CAMPUS
- Haggin Art Museum
- Stockton Civic Theater
- San Joaquin Delta Waterway
- World-famous Asparagus Festival
- Weber Point Events Center

WHITTIER COLLEGE

Office of Admissions, Whittier College, 13406 E. Philadelphia St., Whittier, CA 90608 (The office is in Weingart Hall at the southwest corner of Pacific Avenue and Philadelphia Street) • Telephone: 562-907-4238 (Fax: 562-907-4870) • Web: www.whittier.edu • Email: admission@whittier.edu

Hours: Monday-Friday, 8AM-5PM. Closed weekends, New Year's Day, Thanksgiving, Christmas, and Good Friday.

Only one school can claim Richard Nixon as an alumnus, and that school is Whittier College, a solid little liberal arts college not far from Los Angeles with a rich Quaker heritage. Students must choose between two courses of study: the Liberal Education Track (focused on the development of creative and analytical skills) or the Whittier Scholars Program (in which students work with advisors to design their own majors).

HIGHLIGHTS

ON CAMPUS
- Wardman Library
- Walter F. Dexter Student Center
- Harris Amphitheater
- Ruth B. Shannon Center for the Performing Arts

OFF CAMPUS
- Chinatown, Little Tokyo
- Parks, museums, sports
- Disneyland

TRANSPORTATION

The Los Angeles and Ontario airports are both 25 miles from campus. Super Shuttle service is available from both airports to campus. Call 818-556-6600 for Super Shuttle information. No particular advance arrangements are necessary for transportation from Los Angeles, but for transportation from Ontario, call 24 hours in advance. Amtrak trains and Greyhound/ Trailways bus lines provide transportation to and from Los Angeles. Taxis are available for the ride to campus from the terminals.

FIND YOUR WAY

From the 605 freeway, exit onto Beverly Blvd. East. Proceed east to Painter Blvd. and turn right. Take Painter to Philadelphia St. (the entrance to the college), turn right and park behind Weingart Hall.

STAY THE NIGHT

Pickings are slim in the immediate area, but some good choices are not too far away. The **Whittier Hilton Hotel** (7320 Greenleaf Ave.; 562-945-8511) is 6 blocks away. It has a pool, jacuzzi, and exercise room, and tennis is available. Rates are moderate, but don't forget to mention Whittier College to receive a special rate. About a mile away, also with an inexpensive rate for visitors (including continental breakfast), is the **Whittier Vagabond Hotel** (14125 E. Whittier Blvd.; 562-698-9701). A wide selection of restaurants is available in nearby Uptown Whittier Village. For bed-and-breakfasts, check the Pepperdine University entry for the bed-and-breakfast referral services.

AT A GLANCE

Selectivity Rating	74
Range SAT I Math	460-590
Average SAT I Math	528
Range SAT I Verbal	460-590
Average SAT I Verbal	536
Average ACT Composite	22
Average GPA	3.0
Student to Faculty Ratio	12:1

CAMPUS TOURS

Appointment Req?	Strongly recommended
Dates	During the summer and academic year
Times	Mon-Fri 9AM-4PM
Avg. Length	1 hour

ON-CAMPUS INTERVIEWS

Admissions

Start Date–Juniors	Any time
Appointment Req?	Recommended
Advance Notice	1 day
Saturdays?	No
Avg. Length	30 min
Info Sessions	Contact admissions off.

Faculty and Coaches

Dates/Times	Year-round; subject to faculty/coach availability
Arrangements	Contact admissions off. 2 weeks prior

CLASS VISITS

Dates	During the academic year (Mon-Fri)
Arrangements	Contact admissions off.

OVERNIGHT DORM STAYS

Advance Notice	2 weeks
Arrangements	Contact admissions off.
Limitations	1-night stays; Sun-Thurs nights only

COLORADO

1- Colorado College
2- Colorado School of Mines
3- University of Colorado—Boulder
4- University of Colorado—Denver

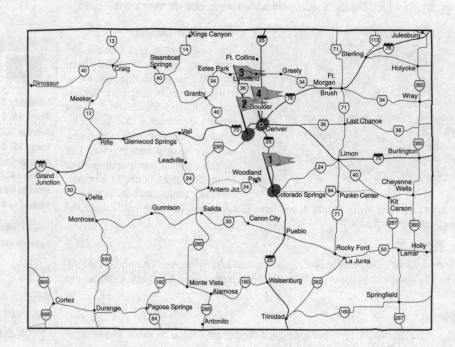

Colorado	Colorado Coll.	Colorado Sch. Mines	U. Colorado-Boulder	U. Colorado-Denver	Denver
Colorado Coll.	—	83	96	70	70
Colorado Sch. Mines	83	—	20	10	10
U.Colorado-Boulder	96	20	—	26	26
U. Colorado-Denver	70	10	26	—	0
Denver	70	10	26	0	—

COLORADO COLLEGE

Admissions Office, Colorado College, 14 E. Cache La Poudre, Colorado Springs, CO 80903 (The office is in Cutler Hall) • Telephone: 800-542-7214 or 719-389-6344 • Web: www.coloradocollege.edu • Email: admission@coloradocollege.edu

Hours: September-May: Monday-Friday, 8:30AM-5PM; Saturday, 10AM-noon. June-August: Monday-Friday, 8:30AM-5PM.

This small, unique liberal arts college breaks up its academic year into three-and-a-half-week blocks during which students concentrate on a single course. The workload can vary wildly, but students who stick around love the concept. Outside of class, skiing is big and the nationally ranked NCAA Division I hockey team enjoys rabid support.

HIGHLIGHTS

ON CAMPUS
- Worner Student Center
- Palmer Hall
- Shove Chapel
- Cutler Hall
- View of Pike's Peak

OFF CAMPUS
- Garden of the Gods
- Old Colorado City
- Pike's Peak
- U.S. Olympic Training Center
- Manitou Springs

TRANSPORTATION
Colorado Springs Airport is 10 miles southeast of campus. Taxis are available for the ride to campus.

FIND YOUR WAY
From I-25, take the Uintah St. exit and turn east. Proceed through 3 stoplights to Cascade Ave. Turn right and you are on campus. The admissions office is in Cutler Hall on the west side of Cascade Ave., about half a block north of Cache La Poudre.

STAY THE NIGHT
Nearby: You have quite an array of choices here, since the college is just north of the downtown section of Colorado Springs. If you are looking for a vacation with swimming, golf, tennis, ice skating, and hunting, the very expensive **Broadmoor** (800-634-7711), a 15-minute car ride from the college, is the place. Built in 1918, the Broadmoor is a staggeringly grand resort (especially the Main Building) with 3 championship golf courses. (Golfers should ask for the South Building, which is closest to the courses.) If you opt for the Main or South Building, ask for a mountain view—it is spectacular. Another candidate for upscale lodging is the **Antlers Adams Mark Hotel** (4 S. Cascade Ave.; 719-955-5600 or 800-528-0444) in downtown Colorado Springs. You're only minutes by car (1 mile) from campus here. The special rates available for college visitors are at the high end of the moderate range. An inexpensive choice around the corner from the admissions office is the **EconoLodge** (714 N. Nevada Ave.; 719-636-3385).

A little farther: Manitou Springs has loads of old-fashioned, inexpensive motels of the separate cabin variety. **Park Row Lodge** (54 Manitou Ave.; 719-685-5216) looks like nothing from the road, but in back and down the steps lie good, inexpensive, rustic cabins by a stream.

AT A GLANCE

Selectivity Rating	90
Range SAT I Math	590-680
Average SAT I Math	644
Range SAT I Verbal	590-680
Average SAT I Verbal	637
Average ACT Composite	28
Average GPA	3.8
Student to Faculty Ratio	11:1

CAMPUS TOURS
Appointment Req?	No
Dates	Year-round, except holidays
Times	Mon-Fri 1:15PM; Sat 11AM
Avg. Length	70 min

ON-CAMPUS INTERVIEWS

Admissions
Start Date—Juniors	Any time
Appointment Req?	Yes
Advance Notice	1 week
Avg. Length	20-30 min
Info Sessions	Year-round, except holidays

Faculty and Coaches
Dates/Times	Year-round; subject to faculty/coach availability
Arrangements	For faculty, contact admissions off.; contact coach directly

CLASS VISITS
Dates	Sept-May (Mon-Fri)
Arrangements	Contact admissions off.

OVERNIGHT DORM STAYS
Advance Notice	2 weeks
Arrangements	Contact admissions off.
Limitations	Sun-Thurs nights only; not during the last 3 days of any block or during breaks

COLORADO SCHOOL OF MINES

Admissions Office, Colorado School of Mines, Weaver Towers, 1811 Elm St.,
Golden, CO 80401 • Telephone: 800-446-9488 (outside Colorado) or 800-245-1060 (in Colorado) •
Web: www.mines.edu • Email: admit@mines.edu

Hours: Monday-Friday, 8AM-5PM. Closed weekends and holidays.

Colorado School of Mines is a small, but prestigious, engineering school where the students work hard and surf their idle hours away on the Internet, or dream about spending the big bonuses from the high-tech employers who are certain to hire them upon graduation.

AT A GLANCE

Selectivity Rating	84
Range SAT I Math	600-700
Average SAT I Math	650
Range SAT I Verbal	530-650
Average SAT I Verbal	590
Average ACT Composite	28
Average GPA	3.8
Student to Faculty Ratio	15:1

CAMPUS TOURS

Appointment Req?	Yes
Dates	During fall, spring, and summer sessions
Times	Mon-Fri 8AM-5PM
Avg. Length	1 hour

ON-CAMPUS INTERVIEWS

Admissions

Start Date–Juniors	Any time
Appointment Req?	Yes
Advance Notice	1 week
Saturdays?	Only by special request
Avg. Length	45 min
Info Sessions	Available as part of interview

Faculty and Coaches

Dates/Times	Year-round; subject to faculty/coach availability
Arrangements	Contact admissions off. 1 week prior

CLASS VISITS

Dates	Year-round (Mon-Fri)
Arrangements	Contact admissions off.

OVERNIGHT DORM STAYS

Advance Notice	N/A
Arrangements	N/A
Limitations	N/A

TRANSPORTATION

Stapleton International Airport in Denver is a 30-minute drive from campus. Taxis and airport shuttles are available for the drive from the airport to campus; the admissions office can provide details on these transportation services. Amtrak trains and Greyhound/Trailways buses serve Denver. Taxis are available for the ride to campus.

FIND YOUR WAY

From the east, take I-70 W. through Denver to Exit 265. Take Colorado Route 58 to Golden. Exit to Highway 93 (Washington Ave.) and head southeast (away from Boulder) to the campus. **From the west**, take I-70 E. past Idaho Springs to US Rte 6 E. Turn left on 19th St. to the campus.

STAY THE NIGHT

Nearby: The **Dove Inn** (711 14th St.; 303-278-2209) is only 2 blocks from campus. Rooms with private baths are available at an inexpensive rate, which includes a full breakfast. Built in 1889, this inn has lots of country charm. The **Holiday Inn Denver West** (14707 W. Colfax Ave.; 303-279-7611), 3 miles away from the school, offers a special rate for college visitors. The Holiday Inn has an indoor pool, an exercise room, ping-pong and pool tables, video games, and a singer during happy hour. The moderately priced **Denver-Marriott West** (1717 Denver W. Blvd.; 303-279-9100), 10 minutes from campus, has all the Marriott amenities, including an indoor pool, sauna, whirlpool, game room, exercise room, and restaurant. An inexpensive rate is available to school visitors at the **Day's Inn West** (15059 W. Colfax Ave.; 303-277-0200), 4.5 miles from campus.

A little farther: You're not far from Denver. Check the University of Colorado–Denver entry for some interesting suggestions there.

HIGHLIGHTS

ON CAMPUS
• Geology Museum
• National Earthquake Center

OFF CAMPUS
• Adolph Coors Brewery
• Colorado Railroad Museum
• Buffalo Bill's grave and museum

UNIVERSITY OF COLORADO—BOULDER

Admissions Office, University of Colorado–Boulder, Campus Box 30, Boulder, CO 80309-0007
(The office is in Regent Administrative Center Room 125) • Telephone: 303-492-6301 •
Web: www.colorado.edu • Email: apply@colorado.edu

Hours: Monday-Friday, 9AM-4PM. Closed weekends and holidays.

As the University of Colorado is situated right beside the Rocky Mountains, outdoor activities are popular. Academically, CU is a big-time research university with nationally renowned programs in music, psychology, the biological sciences, and a highly touted entrepreneurship program. Steve Wozniak, the founder of Apple Computers and one hell of an entrepreneur, is an alum.

HIGHLIGHTS

ON CAMPUS
- Fiske Planetarium
- Sommers-Baush Observatory
- University of Colorado Museum
- The Fine Arts Gallery
- University Memorial Center

OFF CAMPUS
- Chataqua (flatirons hiking trails)
- Pearl Street (galleries and shopping)
- The Hill (shopping and restaurants)
- Denver Broncos at Mile High Stadium
- Lake Eldora (ski resort)

TRANSPORTATION

Denver's Stapleton International Airport is 35 miles from campus. Public transportation (RTD buses), Airporter limousines, and taxis are available at the airport for the ride to campus; call airport information for pickup locations. Amtrak trains and Greyhound/Trailways buses serve Denver. Public transportation (RTD buses) and taxis are available from there to the Boulder campus.

FIND YOUR WAY

From U.S. Rte. 36, take the Baseline Rd. exit and turn left (west) on Baseline. At the second light, turn right (north) on Broadway. At the first light, turn right on Regent Dr. The Regent Administrative Center is on the left side of the street.

STAY THE NIGHT

You have a couple of options very close to the University of Colorado. The **Holiday Inn** (800 28th St.; 303-443-3322) is just across the street, with an exercise room, game room, indoor pool, and moderate rates. A cheaper choice, still with an outdoor pool, is the **University Inn Motel** (1632 Broadway; 303-442-3830), 3 blocks from campus. Restaurants are nearby, and the downtown mall is only 3 blocks away. The **Briar Rose** (2151 Arapahoe Ave.; 303-442-3007), half a mile from the university, includes a deluxe continental breakfast. Of its 11 rooms, 6 have private baths. If you're in the mood for luxury, try the **Pearl Street Inn** (1820 Pearl St.; 303-444-5584), a lovely Victorian inn with a brick-walled inner courtyard. The inn has 7 rooms, all with private baths, and the rates are expensive. A full breakfast is provided. Just a mile from the school is the **Hotel Boulderado** (2115 13th St.; 303-442-4344), a turn-of-the-century hotel with rooms at a high-moderate to expensive rate.

AT A GLANCE

 $

Selectivity Rating	83
Range SAT I Math	540-640
Average SAT I Math	587
Range SAT I Verbal	520-620
Average SAT I Verbal	573
Average ACT Composite	25
Average GPA	3.4
Student to Faculty Ratio	14:1

CAMPUS TOURS

Appointment Req?	Only for Sat tours
Dates	Year-round, except holidays
Times	Mon-Fri 10:30AM and 2:30PM
Avg. Length	1 hour

ON-CAMPUS INTERVIEWS

Admissions

Start Date—Juniors	N/A
Appointment Req?	N/A
Advance Notice	N/A
Saturdays?	N/A
Avg. Length	N/A
Info Sessions	Year-round, except holidays

Faculty and Coaches

Dates/Times	Year-round; subject to faculty/coach availability
Arrangements	Contact directory assistance at 303-492-1411

CLASS VISITS

Dates	Available only as part of special visiting programs
Arrangements	Contact admissions off.

OVERNIGHT DORM STAYS

Advance Notice	N/A
Arrangements	N/A
Limitations	N/A

UNIVERSITY OF COLORADO—DENVER

Office of Admissions, University of Colorado—Denver, P.O. Box 173364, Denver, CO 80217
(The office is in the North Classroom Building at 1200 Larimer St.) • Telephone: 303-556-3287 •
Web: www.cudenver.edu • Email: admissions@carbon.udenver.edu

Hours: Monday-Friday, 9AM-5PM. Closed weekends, July 4, Labor Day, and Thanksgiving and Christmas breaks.

The Denver campus of the University of Colorado educates a largely nontraditional student body of about 8,000 and offers large doses of hands-on, career-oriented education. All students can take advantage of on-campus daycare and recreational events held each day at noon.

AT A GLANCE

Range SAT I Math	470-595
Average SAT I Math	521
Range SAT I Verbal	460-570
Average SAT I Verbal	521
Average ACT Composite	22
Average GPA	3.3
Student to Faculty Ratio	14:1

CAMPUS TOURS

Appointment Req?	Yes
Dates	Year-round, except Christmas week
Times	Mon-Fri 9AM-5PM
Avg. Length	45-60 min

ON-CAMPUS INTERVIEWS

Admissions

Start Date—Juniors	N/A
Appointment Req?	N/A
Advance Notice	N/A
Saturdays?	N/A
Avg. Length	N/A
Info Sessions	N/A

Faculty and Coaches

Dates/Times	Year-round; subject to faculty availability
Arrangements	Contact dept. of interest

CLASS VISITS

Dates	Year-round (Mon-Fri)
Arrangements	Contact admissions off.

OVERNIGHT DORM STAYS

Advance Notice	N/A
Arrangements	N/A
Limitations	N/A

TRANSPORTATION

Stapleton International Airport is 6 miles from campus. Buses, taxis, and shuttles are available for the drive from airport to campus. For taxi information, call Yellow Cab at 303-777-7777. Amtrak trains and Greyhound/Trailways buses serve Denver. The terminals are a short ride (or long walk) from campus.

FIND YOUR WAY

From I-25/U.S. 87, exit to Speer Blvd. heading toward downtown Denver (southeast). Continue in the same direction when Speer splits for one-way traffic. Turn into the Auraria Campus at Larimer St. and proceed to the admissions office.

STAY THE NIGHT

Nearby: You have 3 great choices within 15 minutes of the university. The **Queen Anne Bed and Breakfast** (2147-51 Tremont Pl.; 303-296-6666), is in the heart of downtown Denver, 8 blocks from the university. The **Cambridge Club** (1560 Sherman St.; 303-831-1252) is a small, deluxe hotel offering chocolates at bedtime and continental breakfast in your room. Built in 1892, the renowned **Brown Palace Hotel** (321 17th St.; 303-297-3111) is listed on the National Register of Historic Places, and is 15 minutes away from the university. Rates are quite expensive. For more familiar accommodations close to school, try the **Comfort Inn** (401 17th St.; 303-296-0400) 1 mile away, where a double room and continental breakfast can be had at a moderate rate. Also consider the **Ramada Inn–Mile-High Stadium** (1975 Bryant St.; 303-433-8331), 5 minutes from the campus. It's a little bit more expensive than Comfort Inn, but still has low-to-moderate rates and offers an exercise room, outdoor pool, and rooftop café/lounge.

A little farther: Golden is only 12 miles to the west. Check the Colorado School of Mines entry for some less urban suggestions.

HIGHLIGHTS

ON CAMPUS	OFF CAMPUS
• PE/Events Center & Emmanuel Gallery	• Denver Zoo
• The Auraria Library	• The Denver Art Museum
• Tivoli Student Union	• Boulder mountains and parks
• St. Elizabeth's Church	• Denver Museum of Nature & Science
	• Denver Broncos at Mile High Stadium

1- University of Bridgeport
2- Connecticut College
3- University of Connecticut
4- Fairfield University
5- University of Hartford
   Trinity College
6- Wesleyan University
7- Yale University

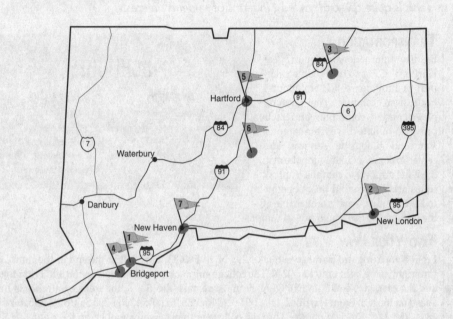

Connecticut	Connecticut Coll.	Fairfield Univ.	Trinity College	Univ. Bridgeport	Univ. Connecticut	Univ. Hartford	Wesleyan Univ.	Yale University	Hartford	New Haven
Connecticut Coll.	0	74	50	71	35	52	42	53	48	52
Fairfield Univ.	74	0	59	5	86	64	47	24	64	25
Trinity College	50	59	0	56	29	4	17	41	0	39
Univ. Bridgeport	71	5	56	0	83	61	43	21	61	20
Univ. Connecticut	35	86	29	83	0	29	38	66	27	64
Univ. Hartford	52	64	4	61	29	0	21	45	0	44
Wesleyan Univ.	42	47	17	43	38	21	0	26	15	25
Yale University	53	24	41	21	66	45	26	0	39	0
Hartford	48	64	0	61	27	0	15	39	0	42
New Haven	52	25	39	20	64	44	25	0	42	0

CONNECTICUT COLLEGE

Admissions Office, Connecticut College, Admissions Building, 270 Mohegan Ave., New London, CT 06320 • Telephone: 860-439-2200 • Web: www.conncoll.edu • Email: admit@conncoll.edu

Hours: Monday-Friday, 8:30AM-5PM (8:30AM-4PM during college vacations); Saturday 8:30AM-3:30PM (fall only). Closed Sundays and holidays.

Fine arts, drama, and dance are tremendous at Connecticut College; the liberal arts are excellent; and several NCAA Division III intercollegiate sports teams are quite competitive. As a result, the student population at this homey little college of about 2,000 students is quite diverse—at least in terms of students' interests.

AT A GLANCE

Selectivity Rating	91
Range SAT I Math	430-739
Average SAT I Math	670
Range SAT I Verbal	421-742
Average SAT I Verbal	680
Average ACT Composite	27
Student to Faculty Ratio	11:1

CAMPUS TOURS

Appointment Req?	No
Dates	Year-round,except school vacations and exam periods
Times	Mon-Fri hourly from 10:30AM to 3:30PM. Summer: Mon-Fri 10:30AM, 12:30PM, and 2:30PM.
Avg. Length	1 hour

ON-CAMPUS INTERVIEWS

Admissions

Start Date—Juniors	May 1
Appointment Req?	Yes
Advance Notice	Midsummer: a few days. Late summer/ fall: a few weeks.
Saturdays?	Yes, usually Sept-Nov
Avg. Length	45 min
Info Sessions	May-Dec

Faculty and Coaches

Dates/Times	Year-round; subject to faculty/coach availability
Arrangements	Contact admissions off.

CLASS VISITS

Dates	Year-round (Mon-Fri)
Arrangements	Contact admissions off.

OVERNIGHT DORM STAYS

Advance Notice	2 weeks
Arrangements	Contact admissions off.
Limitations	Sun-Thurs nights only; not during vacations and exam periods

TRANSPORTATION

Bradley International Airport near Hartford, CT, and T. F. Green Airport in Providence, RI, are about 1 hour from campus. The Groton/ New London commuter airport is only a 15-minute drive from campus. Van and limousine services and rental cars are available for the trip from the airports to campus. Amtrak trains and Greyhound buses operate to New London. Taxis are available at the stations for the 2-mile ride to campus.

FIND YOUR WAY

From New York and points west, take I-95 N. to Exit 83. Turn left at the end of the ramp, then turn right at the light onto Rte. 32 N. The college entrance is 1 mile ahead on the left. **From Boston and the east**, take I-95 S. to Exit 84 N. From there, take Rte. 32 N.; the college entrance is 1 mile ahead on the left. **From Hartford**, take I-91 S. to Rte. 2 S. Exit Rte. 2 at I-395 S.; from I-395, take Exit 78 to Rte. 32 S. Proceed on Rte. 32 to the college entrance, which will be on the right.

STAY THE NIGHT

Nearby: Close to the college (about 10 minutes away) is the **Lighthouse Inn** (6 Guthrie Pl.; 860-443-8411), a Victorian country place with 52 rooms and a restaurant. Prices are moderate, and higher in the summer than the winter. Almost a mile from campus is the **Queen Anne Inn** (265 Williams St., New London; 860-447-2600). Prices range from inexpensive to expensive, with private bath and full breakfast included. Guests may use the Waterford Health and Racquet Club. A few minutes away is the **Radisson Hotel** (35 Governor Winthrop Blvd., New London; 860-443-7000) with moderate prices (and special rates for college visitors), an indoor pool, and lighted tennis courts. Equally close is the **Holiday Inn** (I-95 and Frontage Rd., New London; 860-442-0631); it also offers a special rate for college visitors. The brand new **Spring Hill Suites by Marriot** (North Fontage Road, New London) is only minutes from the college (860-439-0151).

A little farther: You can have a seashore vacation while visiting Connecticut College. The **Shore Inne** (54 E. Shore Ave., Groton Long Point; 860-536-1180) is about 15 minutes from the campus. If you share a bath, it's very cheap. Guests have been coming here since the turn of the century to enjoy the wonderful views, beaches, tennis courts, and nearby fishing dock. The **Old Mystic Inn** (52 Main St., Old Mystic; 860-572-9422) was built in the 1800s when Mystic was a whaling, fishing, and shipbuilding town. The price, including breakfast, is in the moderate-to-expensive range. There's also a **Mystic Hilton** (20 Coogan Blvd.; 860-572-0731) right by Mystic's Aquarium and Seaport. Rates are in the expensive range. The **Inn at Mystic** (860-536-9604) is a moderate to expensive choice, with lower rates in the winter and early spring.

HIGHLIGHTS

ON CAMPUS
- Lynman Allyn Museum
- Connecticut College Arboretum

OFF CAMPUS
- Mystic Seaport
- Mystic Aquarium
- O'Neill Theatre
- Watch Hill
- Foxwoods Casino Resort

FAIRFIELD UNIVERSITY

Office of Admissions, Bellarmine, Rm. 114, Fairfield University, Fairfield, CT 06430 •
Telephone: 203-254-4100 • Web: www.fairfield.edu •
Email: admis@fair1.fairfield.edu

Hours: Monday-Friday, 8:30AM-4:30PM; Saturday, 10AM-3:30PM (October-December 9AM-12:30PM only). Closed Sundays and holidays except Martin Luther King Day and Columbus Day.

The professors are the highlight of this solid, Catholic, liberal arts school with a strong Jesuit tradition. Campus social life is reportedly excellent, and New Haven and New York City are both close by when students need a change of pace.

HIGHLIGHTS

ON CAMPUS
- Quick Center for the Arts (includes The Walsh Art Gallery, Kelley Theatre, and Wien Theatre)
- Egan/Loyola Chapel
- Nyselius Library

OFF CAMPUS
- New York City
- Fairfield Historical Society
- Long Island Sound
- Connecticut Audubon Center

TRANSPORTATION

La Guardia Airport in New York City is approximately 50 miles (a 75-minute drive) from campus. Metro North train service is available to Fairfield from New York City and from New Haven. Taxis are available at the Fairfield train station for the ride to campus.

FIND YOUR WAY

From New York on I-95 (Connecticut Tpke.), take Exit 22 and turn left onto Round Hill Rd. Turn right onto Barlow Rd. and then left into the university. **From New Haven on I-95,** take Exit 22 and turn right onto North Benson Rd. Turn left on Barlow Rd. and right into the university. **From New York Rte. 15 (Merritt Pkwy.),** take Exit 44 heading south, turn left off Exit 44 then left onto Black Rock Tpke. Proceed 2 miles and turn right on Stillson Rd. At the first light, bear left onto N. Benson Rd. The university entrance is ahead on the right.

STAY THE NIGHT

Accommodations in Fairfield are limited, but there are some good places to stay. The least expensive is the **Holiday Inn** (1070 Main St.; 203-334-1234), about 15 minutes away in Bridgeport, where a double is available at a moderate rate. A little bit more expensive, in the high-moderate range, is the **Westport Motor Inn** (1595 Boston Post Rd. E.; 203-259-5236), about 20 minutes away in Westport. It has a restaurant, fitness room, and heated pool. The **Marriott Hotel** (180 Hawley Ln., Trumbull; 203-378-1400) is 15 minutes away and slightly more expensive. It has a pool, exercise room, and a lounge with music. **The Seagrape Inn** (1160 Reef Road; 203-255-6808) is located in the beach section of Fairfield. For additional suggestions, see the University of Bridgeport entry.

AT A GLANCE

Selectivity Rating	78
Range SAT I Math	540-620
Average SAT I Math	584
Range SAT I Verbal	530-620
Average SAT I Verbal	575
Average ACT Composite	25
Average GPA	3.3
Student to Faculty Ratio	13:1

CAMPUS TOURS

Appointment Req?	Yes
Times	Mid-Sept to April: Mon-Fri 11:15AM, 12:15PM, 2:15PM. Oct-Dec: Sat 11:15AM. June-Aug: 11:15AM and 2:15PM.
Avg. Length	75 min

ON-CAMPUS INTERVIEWS

Admissions

Start Date—Juniors	April
Appointment Req?	Yes
Advance Notice	1 month
Saturdays?	Yes, Oct-Dec
Avg. Length	30 min
Info Sessions	Mon and Fri 10:30AM and 1:30PM. June-Aug: Mon-Fri 10:30AM and 1:30PM.

Faculty and Coaches

Dates/Times	Year-round; subject to faculty/coach availability
Arrangements	Contact faculty/coach directly 1 month prior

CLASS VISITS

Dates	Academic Year (Mon-Thurs)
Arrangements	Contact admissions off. 2 weeks prior

OVERNIGHT DORM STAYS

Arrangements	N/A

TRINITY COLLEGE

Admissions Office, Trinity College, 300 Summit St., Hartford, CT 06106-3100 •
Telephone: 860-297-2180 • Web: www.trincoll.edu •
Email: admissions.office@trincoll.edu

Hours: Monday-Friday, 8AM-4:30PM; Saturday, 9AM-noon (fall only). Closed Sundays, New Year's Day, Thanksgiving, and Christmas.

Trinity College is an excellent liberal arts college in Hartford, Connecticut. Beyond academics, students enjoy an active social scene and a beautiful campus. The College's library is custodian to Hartford's Mark Twain Memorial, an extensive collection of his work including much of his correspondence.

AT A GLANCE

Selectivity Rating	93
Range SAT I Math	590-680
Average SAT I Math	635
Range SAT I Verbal	590-680
Average SAT I Verbal	635
Average ACT Composite	28
Student to Faculty Ratio	10:1

CAMPUS TOURS

Appointment Req?	No
Dates	Year-round; irregular during exams and breaks
Times	Mon-Fri 9:30AM, 11:30AM, 1:30PM, 2:30PM, and 3:30PM; some Sat mornings
Avg. Length	1 hour

ON-CAMPUS INTERVIEWS

Admissions

Start Date–Juniors	June 1 (end of junior year)
Appointment Req?	Yes
Advance Notice	As much as possible
Saturdays?	Yes, most fall mornings
Avg. Length	30-45 min
Info Sessions	Year-round except as noted above

Faculty and Coaches

Dates/Times	Year-round; subject to faculty/coach availability
Arrangements	Contact admissions off. 1 week prior

CLASS VISITS

Dates	Academic year (Mon-Fri)
Arrangements	Contact admissions off.

OVERNIGHT DORM STAYS

Advance Notice	2 weeks
Arrangements	Contact admissions office
Limitations	1 non-weekend night

TRANSPORTATION

Bradley International Airport, north of Hartford, is 15 to 20 minutes from campus (except at rush hour). Limousine service is available from the airport to downtown hotels. From the hotels, take a taxi to campus. Amtrak trains and Greyhound buses serve Hartford. From the terminals, take a taxi to campus.

HIGHLIGHTS

ON CAMPUS
- The Learning Corridor
- Library
- The science/engineering labs
- Summit Suites (newest residence hall)
- The chapel

OFF CAMPUS
- Wadsworth Athenaeum
- Bushnell Theater
- Old State House
- Hartford Civic Center
- Mark Twain and Harriet Beecher Stowe Houses

FIND YOUR WAY

From the west, take I-84 E. to exit 48 (Capitol Ave.) At the traffic light at the end of the exit ramp turn left. Go to the first traffic light (Washington St.) and turn right. Proceed through 8 traffic lights (1.1 miles). Turn right at the eighth light onto New Britain Ave. Proceed on New Britain Ave. to the traffic light at Summit St. and turn right into the campus. **From the east,** take I-84 W. through Hartford to Exit 48 (Asylum Ave.). Turn left onto Asylum St. and follow the roadway to the right. Bear right through the brownstone arch onto Trinity St. Get in the left lane and proceed to the second traffic light (Washington St.). The Bushnell Memorial Hall will be on the left and the State Capitol on the right. Make a left onto Washington St., then follow the above directions to campus. **From the south,** take I-91 N. to I-84 W. Follow the preceding directions from the east. **From the north,** take I-91 S. to I-84 W. Follow the above directions from the east.

STAY THE NIGHT

Nearby: The **Hastings Hotel and Conference Center** (85 Sigourney Street; 860-727-4200) offers a Trinity rate and is less than 5 minutes from the campus and downtown. The **Hilton Hartford** (860-728-5151) offers reasonable rates and is located next to the Civic Center about 10 minutes from campus. The **Crowne Plaza** (50 Morgan St.; 860-549-2400) rate for a double is pretty expensive, but the hotel is nice with no surprises. In Glastonbury, 15 minutes from Hartford, is **Butternut Farm** (1654 Main St.; 860-633-7197), a moderately priced bed-and-breakfast (full breakfast included), 15 minutes from Wesleyan and the University of Hartford. Also consider **Chester Bulkeley House** bed-and-breakfast (184 Main St.; 860-563-4236), in historic Wethersfield, 10 minutes from Trinity and The University of Hartford, and 20 minutes from Wesleyan.

A little farther: To the east of Hartford, about 25 minutes from Trinity (an easy drive on I-84) are some places with character, including the **Old Babcock Tavern** (484 Mile Hill Rd., Tolland; 860-875-1239), a nice little bed-and-breakfast, and the **Tolland Inn** (63 Tolland Green; 860-872-0800), another quiet place. Moderate prices are the rule. If you are going to visit Sturbridge, keep in mind that it's only another 25 minutes up the road from Tolland. Check the University of Hartford entry for the Simsbury and Avon suggestions. Check the entry for the University of Connecticut for some good places to stay within a half-hour's drive of Hartford, due east toward Rhode Island.

UNIVERSITY OF BRIDGEPORT

Admissions Office, University of Bridgeport, 126 Park Ave., Bridgeport, CT 06601 •
Telephone: 800-Excel-UB (392-3582) • Web: www.bridgeport.edu •
Email: admit@bridgeport.edu

Hours: Monday-Thursday, 8:30AM-5:30PM; Friday 8:30AM-4:30PM; Saturdays, 9AM-12PM. Closed Sundays and holidays.

Located in Fairfield, Connecticut, just a short ride from New York City, the small University of Bridgeport combines a liberal arts education with scientific, legal, business, and professional programs. Bridgeport often sponsors trips into area cities and offers the use of a steam bath and sauna at the Wheeler Recreation Center.

HIGHLIGHTS

ON CAMPUS
- Arnold Bernhard Center
- Wheeler Recreation Center
- John J. Cox Student Center
- The University Gallery
- Hubbell Gymnasium

OFF CAMPUS
- Seaside Park
- The Maritime Aquarium
- South Norwalk (SoNo)
- Main Street, Westport
- Wooster Street

TRANSPORTATION

Sikorsky Airport in Bridgeport is 15 minutes from campus. Bradley International Airport near Hartford is 75 minutes from campus. La Guardia Airport and John F. Kennedy in New York City are an hour and a half from campus. Taxis and limousines are available for transportation from these airports to campus. Amtrak and Metro-North trains and Greyhound buses serve Bridgeport. Taxis are available for the ride from the train and bus stations to campus. Ferry service is also available from Port Jefferson, NY.

FIND YOUR WAY

From the north, take I-95 S.; take Exit 27. When exit forks, take left-hand fork marked University of Bridgeport. You are now on South Ave., parallel to I-95. Continue on South Ave. to the 4th light. Turn left on to Park Ave. Proceed south on Park Ave. approximately half a mile to the campus. **From south,** take I-95 N. and get off at Exit 26. At the bottom of the ramp continue straight on Pine St. Take a right onto Harbor St. and the next left onto Admiral St. Take a right onto Iranistan Ave. Proceed south on Iranistan Ave. to Waldemere Ave. Take a left onto Waldemere Ave., travel to Park Ave. (look for the Arch). Take a left onto Park Ave. **From the Merritt Parkway,** take Exit 52 (south fork) and bear left to route 8/25 Connector to Exit 1 (Prospect St./Myrtle Ave.). At the bottom of the ramp take a right onto Prospect St. to Park Ave. Take a left on Park Ave. Proceed south on Park Ave., approximately half a mile to the campus.

STAY THE NIGHT

Five minutes from the University, the **Bridgeport Holiday Inn** (1070 Main St.; 203-334-1234) has special rates and is relatively affordable. A bit further, the **Hampton Inn** in Milford (129 plains Rd.; 203-874-4400) is located 4 miles from the Sikorsky Airport. The **Stratford Ramada** (225 Lordship Blvd.; 800-2 Ramada) is about 20 minutes from campus. The **Trumbull Marriott** (180 Hawley Ln.; 800-221-9855), with its indoor-pool, up-to-date health club, 2 restaurants, and 2 lounges is the most expensive.

AT A GLANCE

Range SAT I Math	410-570
Average SAT I Math	494
Range SAT I Verbal	400-530
Average SAT I Verbal	471
Average ACT Composite	16
Average GPA	3.0
Student to Faculty Ratio	12:1

CAMPUS TOURS

Appointment Req?	Yes
Dates	Year-round
Times	Wed at 10:30AM and 2:30PM; first Sat of every month at 10:30AM
Avg. Length	45 min

ON-CAMPUS INTERVIEWS

Admissions

Start Date—Juniors	Year-round
Appointment Req?	Yes
Advance Notice	1 week
Saturdays?	By appointment
Avg. Length	45 min
Info Sessions	Year-round

Faculty and Coaches

Dates/Times	Year-round; subject to faculty/coach availability
Arrangements	Contact admissions off. 1 week prior

CLASS VISITS

Dates	Year-round (Mon-Fri)
Arrangements	Contact admissions off.

OVERNIGHT DORM STAYS

Advance Notice	1 week
Arrangements	Contact admissions off.
Limitations	Mon-Thurs nights Sept-April, except during exam periods

UNIVERSITY OF CONNECTICUT

Admissions Office, Taske Building, U88, University of Connecticut, Storrs, CT 06269 •
Telephone: 860-486-3137 • Web: www.uconn.edu •
Email: beahusky@uconn.edu

Hours: Monday-Friday, 8AM-5PM. Closed weekends and holidays.

The University of Connecticut is a public school with a well-deserved reputation for quality education in the arts and sciences. The UCONN 2000 plan aims to reconstruct school facilities (including the dorms) over the next few years. Until the plan is complete, the UConn campus will definitely look like a work in progress.

AT A GLANCE

Selectivity Rating	77
Range SAT I Math	510-620
Average SAT I Math	566
Range SAT I Verbal	500-610
Average SAT I Verbal	555
Student to Faculty Ratio	14:1

CAMPUS TOURS

Appointment Req?	Yes, call 860-486-4866
Dates	During academic year, except during breaks
Times	Mon-Fri 10AM and 2PM; call for Sundays
Avg. Length	2 hours

ON-CAMPUS INTERVIEWS

Admissions

Start Date—Juniors	January
Appointment Req?	Yes
Advance Notice	2 weeks
Saturdays?	No
Avg. Length	45 min
Info Sessions	Available as part of tour

Faculty and Coaches

Dates/Times	Year-round; subject to faculty/coach availability
Arrangements	Contact faculty and coaches directly

CLASS VISITS

Dates	Year-round (Mon-Fri)
Arrangements	Contact academic dept.

OVERNIGHT DORM STAYS

Advance Notice	3-4 weeks
Arrangements	Contact admissions off.
Limitations	Available during the spring semester only for students who have been admitted

TRANSPORTATION

Bradley International Airport in Windsor Locks, CT (north of Hartford) is approximately 40 miles from campus. Public transportation from the airport to campus is inconvenient and expensive. A rental car is a better alternative. Private limousine services include the Horizon Airport Shuttle (860-429-8002) and the Airport Shuttle (860-450- 2170). Call for rates and reservations.

FIND YOUR WAY

From the north and south, take I-91 to I-84 in Hartford. Take I-84 northeast to Exit 68, then take Connecticut Rte. 195 S. to Storrs and the campus. Turn right on North Eagleville Rd., and turn left onto N. Hillside Rd. Park in the North Paking Garage (fee charged). Tours begin in the visitor's center on the corner of N. Eagleville and N. Hillside Roads. The admissions office is located 1 block past the parking garage on Hillside Road. **From Boston**, take I-84 southwest to Exit 70; then take Connecticut Rte. 32 S. to Connecticut Rte. 195; take Rte. 195 S. to Storrs. From Providence, take U.S. 44 W. to Rte. 195, then 195 S. to Storrs.

STAY THE NIGHT

Nearby: Close to the campus (a mile and a half away) is **Altnaveigh Inn** (957 Storrs Rd.; 860-429-4490), a pleasant bed-and-breakfast that offers 6 rooms. **Tolland Inn** is about 7 miles from Storrs (see the Trinity College entry). If you prefer a standard motel, try the **Best Western Regent Inn** (Rtes. 195 and 6; 860-423-8451), 15 minutes from campus. Here you will find the usual amenities and, in addition, an adjacent shopping mall. Or consider the **Quality Inn and Conference Center** (51 Hartford Tpke., Vernon; 860-646-5700 or 1-800-228-5151), right off I-84 at Exits 63 and 64.

A little farther: See the listings in the University of Hartford and Trinity College entries for other possibilities.

HIGHLIGHTS

ON CAMPUS
- State Museum of Art
- Dairy Product Salesroom
- Puppetry Museum
- Greenhouses
- Jorgensen Auditorium and Connecticut Repertory Theater

OFF CAMPUS
- Caprilanos Herb Farm
- Connecticut State Museum of Natural History
- William Benton Museum of Art

UNIVERSITY OF HARTFORD

Admissions Office, University of Hartford, 200 Bloomfield Ave., West Hartford, CT 06117 (The office is in Bates House) • Telephone: 860-768-4296 or 800-947-4303 (Fax: 860-768-4961) • Web: www.hartford.edu • Email: admissions@uhavax.hartford.com

Hours: Monday-Friday, 8:30AM-4:30PM; selected Saturdays, 10AM-1PM. Closed Sundays and holidays.

The University of Hartford is located just two miles from downtown Hartford and offers a liberal arts education in areas from music to engineering to nursing. The school's 4,000 largely traditional students can join the ham radio club or play inner-tube water polo. Singer Dionne Warwick is a University of Hartford alum.

HIGHLIGHTS

ON CAMPUS
- Museum of American Political Life
- Art gallery

OFF CAMPUS
- Mark Twain House
- Hartford Civic Center (concerts)
- Meadows Music Theater (outdoor concerts)
- Bushnell Theater (Broadway tours)
- Minor league sports (baseball, hockey)

TRANSPORTATION

Bradley International Airport, which is north of Hartford, CT is 20 miles from campus. Taxis and airport shuttles are available for the trip to campus. Amtrak trains and Greyhound buses serve Hartford. Taxis are available at the stations for the trip to campus.

FIND YOUR WAY

From I-84 W., take Exit 44 and turn right onto Kane St. At the first light, turn left onto Prospect St. Proceed 2.5 miles to the end of the street, then turn right onto Albany Ave. Turn left at the first light onto Bloomfield Ave. and proceed half a mile to the university, which is on the right. **From I-84 E.,** take Exit 44. Proceed on Caya Ave. for a very short distance to the light at Prospect Ave. Turn left onto Prospect and follow the preceding directions from that point.

STAY THE NIGHT

Nearby: The most convenient place to stay is probably the **West Hartford Inn** (900 Farmington Ave.; 860-236-3221), about 8 minutes from the campus. This is a typical, bare-bones motel, but comfortable enough. The price is moderate.

A little farther: The **Goodwin Hotel** (1 Haynes St., Hartford; 860-246-7500 or 800-922-5006) is about 15 minutes from the campus. Doubles are moderate on weekends, but the rates are expensive during the week. This hotel definitely has character, but unless you have a reason to stay in Hartford, you might find it more enjoyable to head north to Simsbury. The **Simsbury 1820 House** (731 Hop Meadow St.; 860-658-7658 or 800-TRY-1820) is a lovely country inn with 34 rooms, a restaurant, and loads of charm. The rates are at the high end of the moderate range. The inn will help guests arrange golf, skiing, hiking, canoeing, and tubing outings. This is a good choice if you're arriving by plane, since it's only 15 minutes from Bradley Airport. Also try the **Avon Old Farms Hotel** (Rtes. 10 and 44; 800-677-1651 or 800-836-4000), 25 minutes from campus. Here, for a moderate to expensive rate, you can stay in an attractive country hotel that has an exercise room, sauna, and pool. Trinity College is also in the Hartford area, so you should check the Trinity entry for other possibilities.

AT A GLANCE

Range SAT I Math	470-590
Average SAT I Math	528
Range SAT I Verbal	470-580
Average SAT I Verbal	524
Average ACT Composite	22
Student to Faculty Ratio	13:1

CAMPUS TOURS

Appointment Req?	No
Dates	Year-round
Times	Sept-May: Mon, Wed, and Fri 9:30AM and 2:30PM; Tues and Thurs 11AM and 3PM. June-Aug: available on a limited schedule.
Avg. Length	1 hour

ON-CAMPUS INTERVIEWS

Admissions

Start Date—Juniors	Any time
Appointment Req?	Yes
Advance Notice	2 weeks
Saturdays?	No
Avg. Length	45 min
Info Sessions	Year-round

Faculty and Coaches

Dates/Times	Year-round; subject to faculty/coach availability
Arrangements	Contact admissions off.

CLASS VISITS

Dates	Year-round (Mon-Fri)
Arrangements	Contact admissions off.

OVERNIGHT DORM STAYS

Advance Notice	2-3 weeks
Arrangements	Call 800-947-4303
Limitations	Only on certain days of the week

WESLEYAN UNIVERSITY

The Stewart Reid House, Wesleyan University, Middletown, CT 06459-0265 •
Telephone: 860-685-3000 • Web: www.wesleyan.edu •
Email: admissions@wesleyan.edu

Hours: Sept.-May: Monday-Friday, 8:30AM-5PM; Saturday, 9AM-noon. June-Aug.: Monday-Friday, 8:30AM-5PM. Closed major holidays.

Students praise the academic reputation of Wesleyan University, a school of about 3,000 students that has resources and facilities beyond its size. Outstanding fine arts complement the uniformly strong curriculums in the humanities and sciences. Socially, the school is a haven for political correctness.

AT A GLANCE

Selectivity Rating	97
Range SAT I Math	640-720
Average SAT I Math	678
Range SAT I Verbal	640-730
Average SAT I Verbal	680
Average ACT Composite	29
Student to Faculty Ratio	9:1

CAMPUS TOURS

Appointment Req?	No
Dates	Year-round
Times	Mon-Fri 9AM, 11AM, 1PM, and 3PM; Sat-Sun 1PM during the academic year
Avg. Length	1 hour

ON-CAMPUS INTERVIEWS

Admissions

Start Date—Juniors	May of junior year
Appointment Req?	Yes
Advance Notice	2-3 weeks
Saturdays?	Yes, mid-Sept to early Dec
Avg. Length	30 min
Info Sessions	Year-round

Faculty and Coaches

Dates/Times	Year-round; subject to faculty/coach availability
Arrangements	Contact admissions off. 1 month prior

CLASS VISITS

Dates	Year-round (Mon-Fri)
Arrangements	Contact faculty teaching the classes of interest

OVERNIGHT DORM STAYS

Advance Notice	1 week
Arrangements	Contact admissions off.
Limitations	Limited to prospective seniors; 1-night stay; Sun-Thurs

TRANSPORTATION

Bradley International Airport near Hartford is 20 miles from campus. Taxi service is available from the airport to campus; the admissions office will give you the number to call for this service. Peter Pan and Greyhound bus service is available to Middletown from Boston, Hartford, New Haven, New York, Springfield, and other cities. Amtrak service from New York and Boston stops in Meriden, 10 miles west of Middletown.

FIND YOUR WAY

From the south, take I-91 to Exit 18; from there, follow Rte. 66 into Middletown, turning right onto High St. and right onto Wyllys Ave. **From the north**, take I-91 to Exit 22S; from there, take Rte. 9 to the Wesleyan exit (Washington St.). Follow Washington St. to the 4th light and turn left onto High St. and right onto Wyllys Ave.

STAY THE NIGHT

Nearby: **Radisson Hotel** (100 Berlin Rd., Cromwell; 203-635-2000), 5 minutes from the campus, has a special rate for college visitors, a health club, and glass-domed indoor pool. The **Holiday Inn** (4 Sebethe Dr., Cromwell; 203-635-1001) is a little bit farther from campus, but it's much less expensive if you get the college visitor rates. The **Ramada Inn** (275 Research Pkwy., Meriden; 203-238-2380) also offers a special rate for college visitors. The **Hampton Inn** (10 Bee St., Meriden; 203-235-5154), 15 minutes from campus, is another good low-priced alternative.

A little farther: Wesleyan is only about 15 miles from Hartford, so check the entries for Trinity, University of Hartford, and Yale University.

HIGHLIGHTS

ON CAMPUS	OFF CAMPUS
• Center for the Arts	• Gillette Castle and State Park
• Davison Arts Center	• Goodspeed Opera House
• Zilka Gallery	• Dinosaur State Park
• Olw Memorial Library	• Lyman Orchards
• Van Vuek Observatory	• Wadsworth Falls State Park

YALE UNIVERSITY

Office of Undergraduate Admissions, Yale University, P.O. Box 208234, New Haven, CT 06520 • Telephone: 203-432-9300 • Web: www.yale.edu • Email: undergraduate.admissions@yale.edu

Hours: Monday-Friday, 8:30AM-5PM.

What can you say about Yale University? The school has no core curriculum, instead requiring students to complete a broad range of general requirements. Actress Jodie Foster and conservative icon William F. Buckley are alums.

HIGHLIGHTS

ON CAMPUS
- Old Campus
- Sterling Memorial Library
- Yale British Art Center
- Beinecke Rare Book and Manuscript Library
- Payne-Whitney Gymnasium

OFF CAMPUS
- Long Wharf Theater
- Wooster Square
- Shubert Theater
- Amistad Memorial
- East Rock Park

TRANSPORTATION

Bradley International Airport near Hartford, is 50 miles from campus. Tweed Airport in New Haven has commuter service from most major East Coast cities. Amtrak trains serve New Haven from Boston or Washington, DC, via Penn Station in New York. There is hourly Metro-North train service between New Haven and Grand Central Station in New York; call 212-532-4900 for schedule details. Greyhound Bus Lines, the Arrow Line (800-231-2222), and Peter Pan Line (800-343-9999) provide intercity bus service to New Haven.

FIND YOUR WAY

From I-95, take Exit 47 to reach campus. From I-91, take Exit 3. Go past 3 lights and make the first right onto Hillhouse Avenue, where Yale is located.

STAY THE NIGHT

Nearby: Yale has several hotels and motels within walking distance. The **Colony Inn** (1157 Chapel St.; 203-776-1234) offers special moderate rates for Yale visitors. There is also the **Holiday Inn** (30 Whalley Ave.; 203-777-6221), the **New Haven Hotel** (229 George St.; 800-NH-HOTEL), **Three Chimneys Inn** (1201 Chapel St.; 800-443-1554) and the **OMNI New Haven Hotel** (155 Temple St.; 800-THE-OMNI).

A little farther: Inexpensive accommodations can be found at the **Quality Inn** (100 Pond Lily Ave.; 203-387-6651), 15 minutes away, with special rates for Yale visitors. A **Howard Johnson's** (400 Sargent Dr.; 203-562-1111) is 10 minutes away. Also check the **Nutmeg B&B Agency Host** (800-727-7592), which has a wide listing of bed-and-breakfasts in the area.

AT A GLANCE

Selectivity Rating	99
Range SAT I Math	680-760
Range SAT I Verbal	680-780

CAMPUS TOURS

Appointment Req?	No
Dates	Year-round
Times	Mon-Fri 10:30AM and 2PM; Sat and Sun 1:30PM
Avg. Length	1 hour

ON-CAMPUS INTERVIEWS

Admissions

Start Date—Seniors	July-Dec
Appointment Req?	Yes
Advance Notice	Several weeks
Saturdays?	No
Avg. Length	30 min
Info Sessions	Year-round

Faculty and Coaches

Dates/Times	Year-round; subject to faculty/coach availability
Arrangements	Self-initiated

CLASS VISITS

Dates	Academic year (Mon-Fri)
Arrangements	Contact admissions off. at 203-432-9386

OVERNIGHT DORM STAYS

Advance Notice	2 weeks
Arrangements	Contact admissions off.
Limitations	1-night stay; Mon-Thurs

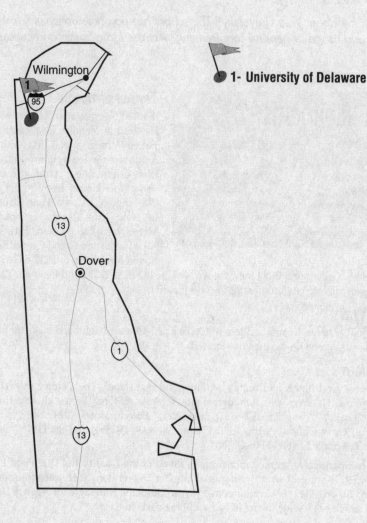

Wilmington

Dover

1- University of Delaware

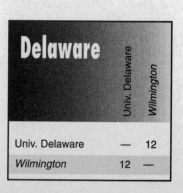

Delaware	Univ. Delaware	Wilmington
Univ. Delaware	—	12
Wilmington	12	—

UNIVERSITY OF DELAWARE

Admissions Office, University of Delaware, 116 Hullihen Hall, Newark, DE 19716 •
Telephone: 302-831-8123 • Web: www.udel.edu •
Email: admissions@udel.edu

Hours: Monday-Friday, 8AM-5PM. Closed weekends (Visitors' Center is open for campus tours on Saturday mornings), Martin Luther King Day, July 4, Election Day, and during Christmas break.

In-staters and students from all over the Northeast converge on the University of Delaware. Lively Main Street runs literally right through campus.

HIGHLIGHTS

ON CAMPUS	OFF CAMPUS
• Memorial Hall	• Hagley Museum
• Morris Library	• Winterthur
• Fred Rust Ice Arena	• Longwood Gardens
• Delaware Stadium	

TRANSPORTATION

Philadelphia International Airport is a 1-hour drive from campus. Transportation to and from campus is provided by Delaware Express (800-648-5466), Super Shuttle (302-655-8878), or taxi. Rental cars are also available at the airport. Amtrak trains that run between Florida and New England stop in Wilmington, a 20-minute ride from campus and Newark. Delaware Administration for Regional Transportation (DART) buses transport passengers between Wilmington and Newark; for schedules, contact DART (302-652-DART). SEPIA rail service is available to Newark from Wilmington and Philadelphia. Greyhound buses travel directly to the university from Baltimore, Philadelphia, Washington, DC, and New York City; for schedule information call 302-655-6111.

FIND YOUR WAY

From the north, take I-95 S. to Delaware Exit 1B, Rte 896 N. This takes you onto South College Ave.; continue past the stadium and fieldhouse until you reach the main campus. Turn into Visitor Parking Lot #41. **From the south,** take I-95 N. to Maryland Exit 109B, then take Rte 279 N. (also called Rte 2). Continue into Newark on this road, which becomes Elkton Rd. In Newark, turn right on West Park Pl., left onto South College Ave., and then left into Visitor Parking Lot #41. The gate leading to the admissions office in Hullihen Hall is on South College Ave. opposite Kent Way.

STAY THE NIGHT

Nearby: The University of Delaware has its very own University Guest Apartments (888-831-4UGA or Web: www.udel.edu/hcs/guestapt), which are located right on campus. Off I-95 in Newark, you will find the usual array of chain motels. In the inexpensive range are the **Comfort Inn** (1120 S. College Ave.; 302-368-8715), about half a mile from the university, and the **McIntosh Motor Inn** (100 McIntosh Plaza; 302-453-9100), about 3 miles away. Moderate choices include **Howard Johnson's** (1119 S. College Ave.; 302-368-8521) and **Best Western** (260 Chapman Rd; 302-738-3400). The latter is only a 10-minute drive away from the school and has a restaurant, fitness club, and outdoor pool. The **Hilton Inn Christiana** (100 Continental Dr.; 302-454-1500) is relatively expensive and offers tennis and golf nearby.

A little farther: A half-hour drive to the historic town of New Castle you will find two charming bed-and-breakfasts. Built around 1682, the **William Penn Guest House** (206 Delaware St., New Castle; 302-328-7736) is a lovely, antique-furnished, historical home located across from the courthouse on the square. The **Jefferson House Bed & Breakfast** (at the Strand at the Wharf; 302-325-1025), a 200-year-old hotel on the riverfront in the historic district, is a bit more expensive.

AT A GLANCE

Selectivity Rating	82
Range SAT I Math	520-630
Average SAT I Math	575
Range SAT I Verbal	510-610
Average SAT I Verbal	560
Average GPA	3.4
Student to Faculty Ratio	14:1

CAMPUS TOURS

Appointment Req?	No
Dates	Year-round
Times	Fall and spring semesters: Mon-Fri 10AM, 11:30AM, and 2PM; Sat, 10AM and 11:30AM. Winter and summer sessions: verify times.
Avg. Length	90 min

ON-CAMPUS INTERVIEWS

Admissions

Start Date–Juniors	Any time, but avoid late Sept and Oct
Appointment Req?	Yes
Advance Notice	7-10 days
Saturdays?	No
Avg. Length	30 min
Info Sessions	Begins a half hour before each campus tour

Faculty and Coaches

Dates/Times	Year-round; subject to faculty/coach availability
Arrangements	Contact particular faculty/coach

CLASS VISITS

Dates	Year-round (Mon-Fri)
Arrangements	Contact dept. of interest

OVERNIGHT DORM STAYS

Arrangements	Contact Honors Prog.
Limitations	Only for admitted Honors Prog. applicants

1- American University
2- Catholic University
3- Georgetown University
4- George Washington University
5- Howard University

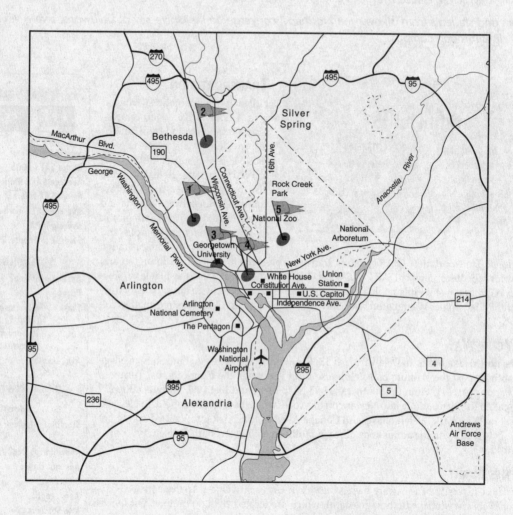

District of Columbia	American Univ.	Catholic Univ.	Geo. Washington U.	Georgetown Univ.	Howard Univ.
American Univ.	—	7	3	2	5
Catholic Univ.	7	—	3	5	2
Geo. Washington U.	3	3	—	1	3
Georgetown Univ.	2	5	1	—	3
Howard Univ.	5	2	3	3	—

AMERICAN UNIVERSITY

Admissions Office, American University, 4400 Massachusetts Ave N.W., Washington, DC 20016-8001
(The office is in the Hamilton Building) • Telephone: 202-885-6000 •
Web: www.american.edu • Email: afa@american.edu

Hours: Monday-Friday, 9AM-5PM; Saturday, 9AM-2PM (September-May only). Closed Sundays and holidays.

Located just inside the Beltway, AU has strong pre-law and international relations programs, as you might expect. Once reputed as a party school, it still has its fun-lovers, but most students head off campus nowadays, opting to spend their free time in the city.

HIGHLIGHTS

ON CAMPUS
- Watkins Gallery
- Faulkner Collection
- Weschler Theater
- Bender Arena
- Maori Statue

OFF CAMPUS
- Smithsonian Institution Museums
- National Zoo
- Kennedy Center for Performing Arts
- MCI Center (sports and concerts)
- U.S. Capitol

TRANSPORTATION

National Airport is 10 miles from campus. Taxis and rental cars are available at the airport for the ride to campus. Amtrak trains and Greyhound buses serve Washington, DC. The city has a fantastic public transportation system, but the university advises that it may be best to drive or take a cab if you are not familiar with the area. If you do plan to use public transportation (the Metro system), the subway station (Metro stop) nearest campus is Tenleytown on the Red Line. Take an AU Shuttle bus from the Metro stop to campus.

FIND YOUR WAY

From the northeast, take I-95 S. to I-495 (the Capitol Beltway); then take I-495 W. toward Silver Spring. Leave the Beltway at Exit 39 and carefully follow the signs for River Rd. east toward Washington. Continue east on River Rd. to the fifth traffic light. Turn right onto Goldsboro Rd. At the first traffic light, turn left onto Massachusetts Ave. Follow it directly through one traffic circle (Westmoreland Circle); continue 1 more mile into a second traffic circle (Ward Circle). Leave Ward Circle at the first right turn, onto Nebraska Ave. The campus will be on the right. **From the south or west**, take I-95 N. or I-66 E. to I-495 (Capitol Beltway). Follow I-495 north. Follow preceding directions from I-495 and River Rd.

STAY THE NIGHT

Nearby: The reasonably priced **Adams Inn** (1744 Lanier Pl. N.W.; 202-745-3600), is located near the zoo, 10 minutes from the university. Shops and restaurants are within walking distance. **Holiday Inn** (5520 Wisconsin Ave., Chevy Chase, MD; 301-656-1500) has moderate prices that drop on the weekends. Health club privileges are available, and there's good shopping nearby. Two glitzier choices are the **Hyatt Regency Bethesda** (7400 Wisconsin Ave., Bethesda, MD; 301-657-1234 or 800-228-9000), with a heated pool, exercise room, and spa, and the **Bethesda Marriott** (5151 Pooks Hill Rd., Bethesda, MD; 301-897-9400), which has an indoor pool, a health spa, lighted tennis courts, and golf privileges. Both are fairly expensive.

A little farther: The **Canterbury** (1733 N St. N.W.; 202-393-3000 or 800-424-2950), about a 10-minute drive, has an elegant charm, but is very expensive. Each accommodation is a suite. Health club privileges are available. The Canterbury is a 10-minute drive from American University and a 5-minute drive from George Washington University. The **Morrison Clark Inn** (11th St. and Massachusetts Ave. N.W.; 202-898-1200 or 800-332-7898) is about 15 minutes by car from Georgetown. Rates here are in the expensive to very expensive range (continental breakfast included), but this is a very charming choice. The inn is close to the Smithsonian and 25 minutes from American University.

AT A GLANCE

Selectivity Rating	81
Range SAT I Math	530-630
Average SAT I Math	586
Range SAT I Verbal	550-650
Average SAT I Verbal	605
Average ACT Composite	26
Average GPA	3.2
Student to Faculty Ratio	14:1

CAMPUS TOURS

Appointment Req?	Yes
Dates	Year-round
Times	Sept-May: Mon-Fri 10AM, 1PM, and 3PM; Sat 9:30AM and 11:30AM. June-Aug: Mon-Fri 10AM, 1PM, and 3PM.
Avg. Length	50 min

ON-CAMPUS INTERVIEWS

Admissions

Start Date—Juniors	May
Appointment Req?	Yes
Advance Notice	2 weeks
Saturdays?	Yes
Avg. Length	30 min
Info Sessions	Year-round

Faculty and Coaches

Dates/Times	Year-round; subject to faculty/coach availability
Arrangements	Contact admissions off. 2 weeks prior

CLASS VISITS

Dates	Year-round (Mon-Fri)
Arrangements	Contact admissions off. at least 7 days prior

OVERNIGHT DORM STAYS

Advance Notice	3 weeks
Arrangements	Contact admissions off. at least 7 days in advance
Limitations	1-night stay on specific dates

CATHOLIC UNIVERSITY OF AMERICA

Office of Undergraduate Admissions, Catholic University of America, 620 Michigan Avenue N.E., Washington, DC 20064 • Telephone: 800-673-2772 or 202-319-5305 • Web: www.cua.edu • Email: cua-admissions@cua.edu

Hours: Monday-Friday, 9AM-5PM. Closed Saturdays, Sundays, and holidays.

CUA is America's only Catholic university with a papal charter. Though some students complain about the number of compulsory philosophy and religion courses, most agree that Catholic's immense and required core curriculum is worthwile. CUA's breathtaking Basilica, the world's seventh largest church, dominates the campus.

AT A GLANCE

Selectivity Rating	85
Range SAT I Math	520-630
Range SAT I Verbal	530-640
Average GPA	3.3
Student to Faculty Ratio	10:1

CAMPUS TOURS

Appointment Req?	Yes
Dates	Year-round
Times	Mon, Wed, and Fri
	10:30AM and 2PM
Avg. Length	1 hour

ON-CAMPUS INTERVIEWS

Admissions

Start Date–Juniors	Any time
Appointment Req?	Yes
Advance Notice	7-10 days
Saturdays?	No
Avg. Length	30 min
Info Sessions	Year-round

Faculty and Coaches

Dates/Times	Year-round; subject to faculty/coach availability
Arrangements	Contact admissions off.

CLASS VISITS

Dates	Year-round (Mon-Fri)
Arrangements	Contact admissions off.

OVERNIGHT DORM STAYS

Advance Notice	2 weeks
Arrangements	Contact admissions off.
Limitations	Only for high school seniors who have applied to the University; only Sun or Thurs nights; visitors attend classes the following day

TRANSPORTATION

Washington National Airport is approximately 10 miles (a 30-minute drive) from campus. Taxis and Metro lines can bring you to campus from the airport; no advance arrangements are needed. The Metro Red Line Brookland/CUA stop is adjacent to campus. If you fly to Dulles International Airport, you can take the Washington Flyer limousine to many downtown hotels and then reach campus by Metro. Amtrak trains and Greyhound buses serve Washington. Taxis and Metro service can bring you to campus.

FIND YOUR WAY

From I-95 S., exit to the Capitol Beltway (I-495 W.). Take the Beltway to the first exit (New Hampshire Ave.); proceed south on New Hampshire to N. Capitol St. Turn left on N. Capitol to Michigan Ave., then turn left on Michigan to the campus. **From I-95 N.**, cross the Beltway to get on I-395 (the Shirley Hwy.). Stay on I-395; cross the bridge over the Potomac River into the District of Columbia, and follow I-395 to New York Ave. Turn right onto New York Ave., then left onto N. Capitol St., and then right onto Michigan Ave. to the campus.

STAY THE NIGHT

Days Inn (4400 Connecticut Ave.; 202-244-5600) offers easy access to the university by subway, and breakfast is included in the moderate rate. There is an inexpensive supersaver rate that must be booked 30 days in advance by calling 800-325-2525. The **Quality Inn-Capitol Hill** (415 New Jersey Ave. N.W.; 202-638-1616), with a rooftop pool, is a pricier alternative. So is the **Hyatt Regency** (400 New Jersey Ave. N.W.; 202-737-1234). Attention shoppers—the renovated Union Station, with its many stores, is close to both of these places. **Embassy Inn** (1627 Sixteenth St. N.W.; 202-234-7800) is a small, European, family-style establishment with moderate rates and a continental breakfast.

HIGHLIGHTS

ON CAMPUS
- Mullen Library
- St. Vincent de Paul Chapel
- Basilica of the National Shrine of the Immaculate Conception

OFF CAMPUS
- National Gallery
- Smithsonian Institution
- Library of Congress
- Washington Zoo
- Kennedy Center

GEORGE WASHINGTON UNIVERSITY

Office of Admissions, George Washington University, 2121 I St. N.W., Suite 201, Washington, DC 20052 • Telephone: 800-447-3765 • Web: www.gwu.edu • Email: gwadm@gwis2.circ.gwu.edu

Hours: Monday-Friday, 8:30AM-5PM. Closed weekends and holidays.

Nearly one-quarter of the students at George Washington University are engaged in international studies. Many others pursue government-related majors such as political science, political communication, and criminal justice.

HIGHLIGHTS

ON CAMPUS
- The Smith Center
- The Hippo
- "J" Street
- Kogan Plaza
- Gelman Library

OFF CAMPUS
- Vietnam Memorial
- Washington Monument
- Freer Gallery of Art
- Kennedy Center
- National Air and Space Museum

TRANSPORTATION

Washington National Airport is 5 miles from GW's Visitor Center. Taxis and Metro subways (the Foggy Bottom-GWU Metro station is on campus) can bring you to GW from the airport. Transportation to Washington is available from Dulles International and Baltimore International Airports. Amtrak trains come into Union Station, only a taxi or Metro ride from campus. Greyhound buses also serve Washington. From the Visitor Center, arrangements can be made to visit both the Foggy Bottom and Mount Vernon campuses.

FIND YOUR WAY

From the north, take I-95 S. to I-495 (Capital Beltway) toward Silver Spring/Northern Virginia. Take Exit 33 heading south on Connecticut Ave. for about 9 miles. Turn right onto Florida Ave. (just past the Washington Hilton) and turn left immediately onto 21st St. NW. Turn right on I Street. The visitor entrance to the parking garage is on 22nd St. between M and I Streets. **From the west,** take I-66 or Rte. 50 across the Theodore Roosevelt Bridge and exit at E Street, then turn again at Virginia Ave. Bear left, following signs for 23rd St. Turn right on 23rd St. and continue a few blocks to campus. Turn right on H Street and left onto 22nd St. to the parking garage. **From the south,** take I-395 to the Arlington Memorial Bridge exit. Cross the bridge and bear left at the Lincoln Memorial. Turn left onto 23rd St. NW, then right on 22nd St. to the parking garage.

STAY THE NIGHT

You have a number of choices within walking distance of GW's Visitor Center. A popular choice is **The George Washington University Inn** (824 New Hampshire Ave.; 800-426-4466), otherwise known as "The Official GW Hotel!" Other good choices are located on GW's website at www.gwu.edu.

AT A GLANCE

Selectivity Rating	89
Range SAT I Math	570-660
Average SAT I Math	620
Range SAT I Verbal	570-670
Average SAT I Verbal	620
Average ACT Composite	26
Student to Faculty Ratio	12:1

CAMPUS TOURS

Appointment Req?	Preferable
Dates	Year-round, refer to website
Times	Aug-April: Mon-Fri 10AM and 2PM; Sat 10AM and 1PM. May-July: Mon-Fri 10AM and 2PM.
Avg. Length	2 hours (includes the info session)

ON-CAMPUS INTERVIEWS

Admissions

Start Date–Juniors	May 1
Appointment Req?	Yes
Advance Notice	2 weeks
Avg. Length	30 min
Info Sessions	N/A

Faculty and Coaches

Dates/Times	Year-round; subject to faculty/coach availability
Arrangements	Contact Visitor Center at 202-994-6602

CLASS VISITS

Dates	Academic year (Mon-Fri)
Arrangements	Contact Visitor Center

OVERNIGHT DORM STAYS

Advance Notice	Yes
Arrangements	Call 202-994-0432
Limitations	Sun-Wed nights during academic year; applicants only

GEORGETOWN UNIVERSITY

Admissions Office, Georgetown University, 37th and O Sts. N.W., Washington, DC 20057-1002
(The office is in Rm. 103, White-Gravenor Building) • Telephone: 202-687-3600 •
Web: www.georgetown.edu • Email: guadmiss@gunet.georgetown.edu

Hours: Monday-Friday, 9AM-5PM; Saturday, 9AM-1PM. Closed Sundays and holidays.

Students at Georgetown University study from three to five hours per day. They still find time, however, for the myriad activities that Washington, D.C. has to offer, including countless internships for the many politics-minded students on campus. Speaking of politics, would you believe that Bill Clinton and Pat Buchanan can both call Georgetown their alma mater?

AT A GLANCE

Selectivity Rating	98
Range SAT I Math	630-720
Range SAT I Verbal	620-730
Student to Faculty Ratio	10:1

CAMPUS TOURS

Appointment Req?	Yes
Dates	Year-round
Times	Mon-Sat on a variable schedule
Avg. Length	1 hour

ON-CAMPUS INTERVIEWS

Admissions

Start Date–Juniors	N/A
Appointment Req?	N/A
Advance Notice	N/A
Saturdays?	N/A
Avg. Length	N/A
Info Sessions	Year-round

Faculty and Coaches

Dates/Times	Year-round; subject to faculty/coach availability
Arrangements	Contact particular faculty/coach a few weeks prior

CLASS VISITS

Dates	Fall/spring term only
Arrangements	Class lists available in admissions

OVERNIGHT DORM STAYS

Advance Notice	N/A
Arrangements	N/A
Limitations	N/A

TRANSPORTATION

Washington National Airport is 5 miles from campus. Taxis, buses, and Metro subways (the Rosslyn station on the Metro Blue Line is a half-hour walk) all travel to campus from the airport. If you fly to Dulles International Airport, you can take the Washington Flyer limousine to many downtown hotels and then reach campus by taxi. (Taxis all the way from Dulles to campus are very expensive.) Amtrak train service arrives at Union Station in Washington; from there, take a taxi or the Metro Red Line to DuPont Circle and transfer to the G-2 bus to campus (37th and O Sts. N.W.). Greyhound buses also serve Washington.

FIND YOUR WAY

From the north, take I-95 S. and exit to I-495 W. (the Capital Beltway). Follow I-495 W. to the George Washington Memorial Pkwy. Follow the parkway toward Washington and exit onto Key Bridge. Cross the bridge, and turn right on M St.; then turn left on 33rd St., and left again on Prospect St. Prospect ends at the entrance to the university's parking lot #3. **From the west**, take the Pennsylvania Tpke. east to Exit 12 (Breezewood). Follow I-70 S. to Frederick where Rte. 270 S. begins. Proceed on 270 toward Washington. When 270 intersects with I-495 (Capital Beltway), keep right and follow I-495 toward Northern Virginia and the George Washington Memorial Pkwy. Follow the preceding directions from that point. **From the south**, take I-95 N. to I-395 N. Exit I-395 to Virginia Rte. 27 (Washington Boulevard) headed north and east. Watch carefully for signs to Rosslyn and the Key Bridge. Cross the Key Bridge and follow the above directions from the north.

STAY THE NIGHT

Nearby: A very popular, convenient place is the on-campus **Georgetown University Guesthouse** (3800 Reservoir Rd.; 202-687-3200). Nearby **Georgetown Holiday Inn** (2101 Wisconsin Ave. N.W.; 202-338-4600) has special rates for students and their families (though they're not always available). Our choice is the **Georgetown Inn** (1310 Wisconsin Ave. N.W.; 202-333-8900 or 800-424-2979). Within walking distance (6 blocks) of campus, this moderately expensive place has a special countrified charm. A glitzy alternative is the **Marriott Key Bridge** (1401 Lee Hwy., Arlington, VA; 703-524-6400). Moderate prices, a pool and health club, and views that overlook the Potomac are its finer points. **Kalorama Guesthouse** (1854 Mintwood Pl.; 202-667-6369) is an interesting possibility. Rates range from inexpensive to moderate. The atmosphere is personal, and it's but a stone's throw to the Metro.

A little farther: Elegant, expensive **Canterbury** (1733 N St. N.W.; 202-393-3000 or 800-424-2950) is an all-suite hotel with health club privileges available. The Canterbury is a 15-minute drive from American University and a 5-minute drive from George Washington University. Charming **Morrison Clark Inn** is about 15 minutes by car from Georgetown (11th St. and Massachusetts Ave. N.W.; 202-898-1200 or 800-332-7898).

HIGHLIGHTS

ON CAMPUS	*OFF CAMPUS*
• Yates Field House	• Washington, D.C.
• The Leavey Center	• Smithsonian Institute
• The observatory	• National Mall and monuments
• The quadrangle	• Library of Congress
• Poulton Hall	• Arlington National Cemetery

HOWARD UNIVERSITY

Admissions Office, Howard University, 2400 6th St. N.W., Washington, DC 20059 (The office is in the Johnson Administration Building) • Telephone: 800-822-6363 or 202-806-2752 • Web: www.howard.edu • Email: admission@howard.edu

Hours: Monday-Friday, 8AM-5PM. Closed weekends and holidays

Most of the seriously ambitious students at traditionally African-American Howard University major in pre-professional areas such as international business, legal communications, political science, and pre-med. Howard's hometown of Washington, D.C., provides great opportunities for social activism as well as internships and future jobs.

HIGHLIGHTS

ON CAMPUS
- Founders Library
- Rankin Chapel

OFF CAMPUS
- Smithsonian Institute
- National Mall and monuments
- Library of Congress
- Arlington National Cemetery

TRANSPORTATION

Washington National Airport is approximately 8 miles from campus. Taxis and subways are available for the trip from the airport to campus. For public transportation information, as well as for Amtrak trains and Greyhound buses, call the Washington Metropolitan Area Transit Authority (202-637-7000) on arrival.

FIND YOUR WAY

From I-95 S. continue until it becomes the Capital Beltway E. Exit to the Baltimore-Washington Pkwy. South. At the intersection with U.S. Rte. 50, head west (toward the center of Washington). This becomes New York Ave. Turn right (north) on 6th St. until you reach the University. **From I-95 N.**, exit to I-395 N. (Shirley Memorial Hwy.) and cross the Potomac River. Exit to U.S. Rte. 1/50 N., which becomes 6th St. Leave Rte. 1/50 and stay on 6th St. until you reach the University.

STAY THE NIGHT

The **Howard Inn** (2225 Georgia Ave.; 800-368-5729) is on campus, but its rates are fairly expensive. A cheaper option is available 10 minutes away at the **Center City Travel Lodge** (1201 13th St. N.W.; 202-682-5300), with a special double rate for college visitors. If you're willing to pay for luxurious surroundings, consider the upscale **Park Terrace Hotel** (1515 Rhode Island Ave. N.W.; 202-232-7000 or 800-424-2461). See other entries for Washington, DC, particularly George Washington and Catholic Universities, which are the closest to Howard. If you want to stay in Georgetown, see the selections in the Georgetown University entry.

AT A GLANCE

Selectivity Rating	74
Range SAT I Math	410-680
Average SAT I Math	493
Range SAT I Verbal	430-640
Average SAT I Verbal	526
Student to Faculty Ratio	7:1

CAMPUS TOURS

Appointment Req?	Yes
Dates	Year-round, except holidays
Times	Mon-Fri 10AM-3PM
Avg. Length	1 hour

ON-CAMPUS INTERVIEWS

Admissions

Start Date—Juniors	N/A
Appointment Req?	N/A
Advance Notice	N/A
Saturdays?	N/A
Avg. Length	N/A
Info Sessions	Year-round

Faculty and Coaches

Dates/Times	Year-round; subject to faculty/coach availability
Arrangements	Contact your visit coordinator 2 weeks prior

CLASS VISITS

Dates	Year-round (Mon-Fri)
Arrangements	Contact your visit coordinator

OVERNIGHT DORM STAYS

Advance Notice	N/A
Arrangements	N/A
Limitations	N/A

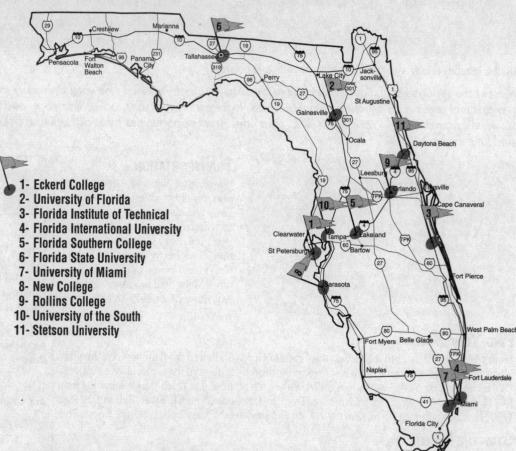

FLORIDA

1- Eckerd College
2- University of Florida
3- Florida Institute of Technical
4- Florida International University
5- Florida Southern College
6- Florida State University
7- University of Miami
8- New College
9- Rollins College
10- University of the South
11- Stetson University

Florida	Eckerd Coll.	Florida Inst. Tech.	Florida Int'l	Florida Southern	Florida State Univ.	New College	Rollins Coll.	Stetson Univ.	Univ. Florida	Univ. Miami	Univ. So. Florida	Miami	Orlando	St. Petersburg
Eckerd Coll.	—	168	258	65	260	40	92	124	166	278	32	253	104	0
Florida Inst. Tech.	168	—	165	106	326	199	72	119	178	185	143	178	60	165
Florida International	258	165	—	215	479	216	237	285	343	20	265	0	229	253
Florida Southern	65	106	215	—	261	88	76	109	132	230	36	222	54	70
Florida State Univ.	260	326	479	261	—	289	300	263	158	494	275	469	254	252
New College	40	199	216	88	289	—	152	187	194	256	63	216	132	39
Rollins Coll.	92	72	237	76	300	152	—	42	142	257	112	251	0	127
Stetson Univ.	124	119	285	109	263	187	42	—	105	294	124	290	31	149
Univ. Florida	166	178	343	132	158	194	142	105	—	363	134	333	114	173
Univ. Miami	278	185	20	230	494	256	257	294	363	—	267	4	242	256
Univ. So. Florida	32	143	265	36	275	63	112	124	134	267	—	260	89	32
Miami	253	178	0	222	469	216	251	290	333	4	260	—	221	253
Orlando	104	60	229	54	254	132	0	31	114	242	89	221	—	104
St. Petersburg	0	165	253	70	252	39	127	149	173	256	32	253	104	—

ECKERD COLLEGE

Admissions Office, Eckerd College, 4200 54th Ave S., St. Petersburg, FL 33711
(The office is in Franklin Templeton Hall) • Telephone: 727-864-8331 •
Web: www.eckerd.edu • Email: admissions@eckerd.edu

Hours: Monday-Friday, 8:30AM-5PM; Saturday, 9AM-noon. Closed Sundays and holidays.

Highlights of the excellent academic program at Eckerd include an intense core curriculum as well as extraordinary opportunities for undergraduate research.

HIGHLIGHTS

ON CAMPUS
- Waterfront Program
- Turley Athletic Complex
- Galbraith Marine Science Lab
- Marine Necropsy Lab
- Hough Campus Center

OFF CAMPUS
- Tampa Bay Devil Rays
- Florida International Museum
- Salvador Dali Museum
- St. Pete Beach
- Fort DeSoto Park

TRANSPORTATION

Tampa International Airport is 30 minutes from campus. Taxi and limousine services can be arranged for on arrival (follow ground transportation signs at the airport). Car rentals are also available at the airport. Greyhound/Trailways bus lines serve St. Petersburg. Amtrak trains serve Tampa and bus service is available from there to St. Petersburg.

FIND YOUR WAY

From the east and north, take I-4 W. or I-75 S. and I-275 S. to Tampa; continue on I-275 across Tampa Bay via the Howard Frankland Bridge to St. Petersburg. Continue south on I-275 (past the downtown St. Petersburg exits) and take Exit 4 (Pinellas Bayway/St. Petersburg Beach). Proceed around traffic circle (bearing left) to the first parking lot on the right, outside Franklin Templeton Hall. Additional parking is available across the street. **From the south**, take I-75 N. to I-275 and the Sunshine Skyway. After crossing the bridge and Tampa Bay, take the Pinellas Bayway-St. Petersburg Beach exit at 54th Ave. South. Proceed west on the Pinellas Bayway (54th Ave. S.) and turn left at the traffic light into the college's main entrance, just before the Bayway tollbooth. Follow preceding directions to the admissions office. **From the west** (and any other direction by sea), the college's Waterfront Complex is accessible from Egmont Lighthouse by way of Mullet Key Channel, the Skyway Channel, and Frenchman's Creek. Temporary docking is available for visitors.

STAY THE NIGHT

Nearby: Accommodations may be available on campus at the Continuing Education Center Lodge (727-864-8313; $50 single occupancy, $70 double occupancy). St. Pete Beach is approximately 4 miles from campus and offers affordable, scenic accommodations. **Howard Johnson's** (6100 Gulf Blvd.; 727-360-7041) and the **Trade Winds Resort** (5500 Gulf Blvd.; 800-237-0707) both offer discounts to College visitors. The **Holiday Inn SunSpree Marina Cove** (6800 Sunshine Skyway Lane; 800-227-8045) offers the closest off-campus accommodations. It has a tennis court, 2 pools, a children's playground, and a full-service restaurant.

A little farther: Check the University of South Florida entry for alternatives in nearby Tampa.

AT A GLANCE

Selectivity Rating	78
Range SAT I Math	520-640
Average SAT I Math	583
Range SAT I Verbal	520-630
Average SAT I Verbal	580
Average ACT Composite	26
Average GPA	3.2
Student to Faculty Ratio	14:1

CAMPUS TOURS

Appointment Req?	Yes
Dates	Year-round
Times	Arranged around scheduled interviews
Avg. Length	45-60 min

ON-CAMPUS INTERVIEWS

Admissions

Start Date–Juniors	Fall
Appointment Req?	Yes
Advance Notice	2 weeks
Saturdays?	Yes, Sept-May 9AM-noon
Avg. Length	45 min
Info Sessions	Sept-Nov

Faculty and Coaches

Dates/Times	Year-round; subject to faculty/coach availability
Arrangements	Contact admissions off. 2 weeks prior

CLASS VISITS

Dates	Academic year (Mon-Fri)
Arrangements	Contact admissions off.

OVERNIGHT DORM STAYS

Advance Notice	2 weeks
Arrangements	Contact admissions off.
Limitations	1-night stay preferred, 2-night stay maximum; not available during summer

FLORIDA INSTITUTE OF TECHNOLOGY

Admissions Office, Florida Institute of Technology, 150 W. University Blvd., Melbourne, FL 32901 (The office is in the Keuper Administration Building on Country Club Rd.) • Telephone: 800-888-4348 or 321-674-8030 • Web: www.fit.edu • Email: admissions@fit.edu

Hours: Monday-Friday, 8AM-5PM. Closed weekends and holidays.

Originally, Florida Institute of Technology had a limited set of majors and served nearby Cape Canaveral almost exclusively. Now, though technology is still at the forefront of Florida Tech's classes, the overwhelmingly male student body can also choose to major in business or even psychology. The importance of the space program is still evident on campus.

AT A GLANCE

Range SAT I Math	520-640
Average SAT I Math	584
Range SAT I Verbal	500-620
Average SAT I Verbal	559
Average ACT Composite	25
Average GPA	3.3
Student to Faculty Ratio	12:1

CAMPUS TOURS

Appointment Req?	Yes
Dates	Year-round, except on holidays
Times	Mon-Fri 10AM and 2PM
Avg. Length	1 hour

ON-CAMPUS INTERVIEWS

Admissions

Start Date–Juniors	Any time
Appointment Req?	Recommended
Advance Notice	1-2 weeks
Saturdays?	No
Avg. Length	30 min
Info Sessions	Mon-Fri 8:30AM-5PM

Faculty and Coaches

Dates/Times	Year-round; subject to faculty/coach availability
Arrangements	Contact admissions off. 1 week prior

CLASS VISITS

Dates	Year-round (Mon-Fri)
Arrangements	Contact admissions off. 1-2 weeks prior

OVERNIGHT DORM STAYS

Advance Notice	N/A
Arrangements	N/A
Limitations	N/A

TRANSPORTATION

Melbourne International Airport is about 2 miles from campus. Taxis are available at the airport.

FIND YOUR WAY

From I-95, take Exit 71 (U.S. Rte. 192). Take Rte. 192 E. for 5 miles to Country Club Rd. Turn right onto Country Club Rd. and proceed for 1 mile to the campus.

STAY THE NIGHT

Nearby: For lodgings in the immediate vicinity, you are limited to the well-known chains. The least expensive, offering a special rate for visitors to Florida Tech. is the **Melbourne Harbor Suites** (1207 E. New Haven Ave.; 321-723-4251), about 10 minutes from campus. Close to Florida Tech. and Melbourne Airport, the **Ramada Inn** (1881 Palm Bay Rd., NE, Palm Bay, FL; 321-723-8181), and **Melbourne Hilton** (200 Rialton Place; 800-437-8010) are both good options. **The Holiday Inn Beach Resort** (2605 North A1A, Melbourne; 321-777-4100) is 20 minutes away and has tennis courts, indoor and outdoor pools, a location on the beach, and a special rate for visitors. A little closer, 10 minutes away, is the **Hilton Melbourne Beach Oceanfront** (3003 North Hwy A1A, Melbourne; 321-777-5000). It offers an outdoor pool, health club, tennis and golf privileges, and a moderate special rate for Florida Tech visitors.

A little farther: Florida Institute of Technology is only about an hour's drive from Orlando, the home of Disney World. The same hotel chains have other locations convenient to Disney World, Sea World, Universal Studios and all of the major theme parks, as well as vacation packages that include one day at Kennedy Space Center.

HIGHLIGHTS

ON CAMPUS	OFF CAMPUS
• Botanical gardens	• Kennedy Space Center
• Evans Library	• Indian River Lagoon
• Clemente Center	• RonJon's Surf Shop at Cocoa Beach

FLORIDA INTERNATIONAL UNIVERSITY

Admissions Office, Florida International University, University Park Campus, PC 140, Miami, FL 33199 (The office is at S.W. 107th Ave. and 8th St. [Tamiami Trail]) • Telephone: 305-348-2363 • Web: www.fiu.edu • Email: admiss@fiu.edu

Hours: Monday-Thursday, 8AM-7PM, Friday, 8AM-5PM. Closed weekends and holidays.

Nearly 25,000 students attend classes on comprehensive, public FIU's two campuses, both of which are in the Miami area. Distractions include the Everglades, Miami nightlife, beaches, and the Bahamas, and the fact that Miami is a vacation destination draws hospitality management majors.

HIGHLIGHTS

ON CAMPUS
- Art museum
- Wolfsonia—A Museum of Art & Design
- North Campus Library
- Steven & Dorothea Green Library

OFF CAMPUS
- Hit the beach!
- Villa Viscaya Museum
- Historical Museum of South Florida
- Miami Seaquarium
- Parrot Jungle Theme Park

TRANSPORTATION

Miami International Airport is 8 miles (a 15-minute drive) from the University Park campus. Super Shuttles and taxis (305-444-4444 or 305-888-8888) are available for the ride from airport to the N. Miami and University Park campuses. Amtrak trains and Greyhound/Trailways buses serve Miami. Greyhound has several stations in the Miami area, including one in N. Miami Beach.

FIND YOUR WAY

To reach the University Park Campus from 826 (Palmetto Expressway), take 826 north or south to SW 8th St. exit (Tamiami Trail) and head west. Proceed on 8th St. to SW 112th Ave. Turn left. **From I-95**, take I-95 north or south to 836 (Dolphin Expressway) and head west. Continue on 836 west to the NW 107th Ave. South exit. Proceed on 107th Ave. to SW 8th St. (Tamiami Trail). Turn right proceed on 8th St. to SW 112th Ave. Turn left. **From the Florida Tpke.**, take the Florida Tpke. to SW 8th St. exit (Tamiami Trail) and head east. Proceed on SW 8th St. to SW 112th Ave. Turn right. **To reach North Campus, from Miami**, take I-95 north to 135th St. Head east to U.S. 1. Head north to 151st St. Turn right. From Ft. Lauderdale: Take I-95 south to 163rd St. Head east to U.S. 1. Head south to 151st St. Turn left.

STAY THE NIGHT

Florida International University has 2 campuses: one is in N. Miami and the other, the University Park campus, is in the southern part of Miami, just southwest of the airport. Since the primary admissions office is at the University Park campus, our nearby lodgings are focused there.

Nearby: **Best Western Miami Airport Inn** (1550 N.W. Lejeune Rd.; 305-871-2345) has special inexpensive rates for college visitors. **Days Inn** (3401 N.W. Lejeune Rd.; 305-871-4221), **Quality Inn Airport** (2373 N.W. 42nd Ave.; 305-871-3230), and **Crossway Inn—Howard Johnson's** (1850 N.W. 42nd Ave.; 305-871-4350), all with special rates for college visitors, are even less expensive. The **Holiday Inn—Airport South** (1101 N.W. 57th Ave.; 305-266-0000) has an inexpensive rate if booked 3 days in advance. Moderate rates are available at the **Sheraton River House** (3900 N.W. 21st St.; 305-871-3800), which has a pool, restaurant, tennis court, sauna, exercise room, jogging course, and golf. Similar amenities (plus water sports and lighted tennis courts) and rates can be found at the **Hilton Hotel** (Miami Airport, 5101 Blue Lagoon Dr.; 305-262-1000). If you're looking for bed-and-breakfasts contact the **Bed-and-Breakfast Company—Tropical Florida** (P.O. Box 262, South Miami, 33243; 305-661-3270).

A little farther: Coconut Grove is a cosmopolitan area of Miami. If you are willing to undertake the 25-minute drive in exchange for the fun, try **Double Tree at Coconut Grove** (2649 S. Bayshore Dr.; 305-858-2500). This is normally an expensive choice, but there are special rates available, depending on the time of year and availability of rooms. The University of Miami is in nearby Coral Gables, so check that entry if you're visiting both schools.

AT A GLANCE

Range SAT I Math	520-590
Average SAT I Math	555
Range SAT I Verbal	520-590
Average SAT I Verbal	558
Average ACT Composite	24
Average GPA	3.5
Student to Faculty Ratio	14:1

CAMPUS TOURS

Appointment Req?	Yes
Dates	Year-round (University Park)
Times	Mon and Wed 9:30AM; Fri 3PM
Avg. Length	50 min

ON-CAMPUS INTERVIEWS

Admissions

Start Date–Juniors	Any time
Appointment Req?	Yes
Advance Notice	A few days
Saturdays?	No
Avg. Length	Varies
Info Sessions	Year-round (University Park Campus)

Faculty and Coaches

Dates/Times	Year-round; subject to faculty/coach availability
Arrangements	Contact admissions off. or faculty/coach

CLASS VISITS

Dates/Times	Year-round (Mon-Fri)
Arrangements	Contact instructor

OVERNIGHT DORM STAYS

Advance Notice	Varies
Arrangements	Contact Housing Off. at 305-348-3982
Limitations	Subject to room availability; a small fee is charged

FLORIDA SOUTHERN COLLEGE

Office of Admissions, Florida Southern College, 111 Lake Hollingsworth Drive, Lakeland, FL 33801-5698 • Telephone: 800-274-4131 or 863-680-4111 • Web: www.flsouthern.edu • Email: fscadm@flsouthern.edu

Hours: Monday-Friday, 8AM-5PM. Closed weekends and major holidays.

Frank Lloyd Wright quite literally made his mark on this Methodist liberal arts college in Lakeland. Wright designed several campus buildings including the Anne Wright Chapel. Springtime here is a treat for baseball lovers thanks to the plethora of spring training baseball sites that dot the area.

AT A GLANCE

Range SAT I Math	460-590
Average SAT I Math	529
Range SAT I Verbal	470-590
Average SAT I Verbal	524
Average ACT Composite	23
Student to Faculty Ratio	17:1

CAMPUS TOURS

Appointment Req?	Preferred
Dates	Year-round
Times	Sept-May: Mon-Fri 10:15AM, 11AM, 2PM, and 3:30PM. June-Aug: as needed.
Avg. Length	1 hour

ON-CAMPUS INTERVIEWS

Admissions

Start Date–Juniors	Any time (even sophomores may be interviewed)
Appointment Req?	Preferred
Advance Notice	1-2 weeks
Saturdays?	Special arrangement
Avg. Length	Varies
Info Sessions	Group sessions available only as part of Day-on-Campus programs; interviews serve as individual sessions

Faculty and Coaches

Dates/Times	Year-round; subject to faculty/coach availability
Arrangements	Contact admissions off.

CLASS VISITS

Dates	Sept-May (Mon-Fri)
Arrangements	Contact admissions off.

OVERNIGHT DORM STAYS

Advance Notice	2 weeks
Arrangements	Contact admissions off.

TRANSPORTATION

Tampa International Airport is approximately 50 miles from Lakeland; Orlando International Airport is approximately 55 miles from Lakeland. Limousine service is available to Lakeland from both airports. Amtrak trains and Greyhound/Trailways buses both serve Lakeland.

FIND YOUR WAY

From I-4, exit to U.S. Rte. 98 S. This becomes Florida Ave. and State Rte. 37. Stay on Florida Ave. (do not turn off it to follow U.S. 98). **From the north**, take I-75 S. to the Sumterville Exit. Make a left at the light and drive east to Highway 301. Turn left onto Highway 301 and follow to Rte. 471. Proceed on Rte. 471 until it runs into Hwy. 98. Turn left on McDonald Ave., then right on Johnson Ave. This brings you to campus near the admissions office. **From the west**, take I-4 to Exit 16 (Memorial Blvd.). Continue on Memorial Blvd. to Ingraham Ave. Follow the preceding directions to campus. **From the east**, take I-95 S. to I-4 W. Stay on I-4 to Exit 19 and turn left. Continue on State Rd. 33, bearing right just past the overpass, where it becomes Massachusetts Ave. Proceed to Lake Morton Dr. and turn right. Proceed to Success Ave. and follow to Lake Hollingsworth Dr. Turn left, and then make another left onto Johnson Ave.

STAY THE NIGHT

Nearby: For convenience we recommend **The Terrace Hotel** (888-644-8400). Located in downtown Lakeland, less than a mile and a half from campus, The Terrace features 73 spacious rooms and 15 comfortable guest suites plus elegant conference and banquet facilities. **The Sheraton Four Points** (4141 S. Florida Ave.; 863-647-3000) is another option. Located a mile and a half away, it features a fitness room, swimming pool, and volleyball court. Both hotels offer special rates for visitors to Florida Southern. Nearby chain hotels include the **Holiday Inn South** (3405 S. Florida Ave.; 863-646-5731), **Amerisuites Studios and Suites** (863-413-1122), **La Quinta Inn and Suites** (1024 Crevasse St.; 863-859-2866), and the **Wellesley Inns and Suites** (3520 N. U.S. Hwy. 98 N.; 863-859-3399).

A little farther: If you're willing to drive 45 minutes and spend a few bucks, stay at **Chalet Suzanne** (U.S. Hwy. 27 S. and County Rd. 17A, Lake Wales; 800-433-6011), a European-type inn known for its gourmet dinners and atmosphere. Special rates include dinner and breakfast. Not far from Haunes City, about 25 miles to the east of Lakeland (a 1-hour drive), is a luxurious resort called **Grenelefe** (3200 State Rd. 546; 863-422-7511) with pools, lighted tennis courts, 54 holes of golf, an 18-hole miniature golf course, and a recreation director. Summer rates are moderate, but rates are otherwise very expensive. Also take a look at the accommodations listed for the University of South Florida.

HIGHLIGHTS

ON CAMPUS
- Frank Lloyd Wright buildings
- Festival of Fine Arts
- Roux Library
- The "Child of the Sun" Visitor Center
- Esplanade Gift Shop

OFF CAMPUS
- Spring training sites
- Polk Museum of Art
- Artisans Gallery at Peace Creek

FLORIDA STATE UNIVERSITY

Office of Admissions, Florida State University, A2500 University Center, Tallahassee, FL 32306-2400 • Telephone: 850-644-6200 • Web: www.fsu.edu • Email: admissions@admin.fsu.edu

Hours: Monday-Friday, 8AM-5PM. Closed weekends and holidays.

Florida State University offers a first-rate education at a bargain-basement price. Oodles of solid majors include business, meteorology, education, hotel/restaurant management, and the performing arts. Social life here is even better. To top it all off, Burt Reynolds himself is an FSU alum.

HIGHLIGHTS

ON CAMPUS
- Oglesby Union
- Strozier Library
- Bobby E. Leach Student Recreation Center

OFF CAMPUS
- Tallahassee's gardens, hills, and forests
- Maclay State Gardens

TRANSPORTATION

The Tallahassee airport is 5 miles from campus. Taxis and hotel limousines are available at the airport.

FIND YOUR WAY

From I-75, exit to I-10 W. Take I-10 to U.S. Rte. 90, the Florida State University exit. An alternate from the north is U.S. Rte. 319 to State Rd. 61 to U.S. Rte. 27S. Turn right at U.S. Rte. 90. An alternate from the south is U.S. Rte. 27 N.; turn left at U.S. Rte. 90. From the east and west, take I-10 to U.S. Rte. 90, the Florida State University exit.

STAY THE NIGHT

Nearby: Within walking distance of the university is the only 4-star lodging in town, **Governor's Inn** (209 S. Adams St.; 850-681-6855). Also nearby are the **Doubletree Hotel** (101 S. Adams St.; 850-224-5000), the **Radisson Hotel** (415 N. Monroe; 800-333-3333), and the **Courtyard by Marriott** (1018 Apalachee Pkwy.; 800-321-2211). Other options might include the **Cabot Lodge** (2735 N. Monroe; 850-386-8880 or 1653 Raymond Diehl Rd.; 850-386-7500), the **Ramada Inn** (2980 N. Monroe; 850-386-1027), and the **Shoneys Inn** (2801 N. Monroe; 850-386-8286). For inexpensive accommodations, your options include the **Travelodge Motel** (691 W. Tennessee; 850-224-8161), the **Hampton Inn** (3210 N. Monroe; 850-562-4300), and the **Days Inn** (2800 N. Monroe; 850-385-0136). For a complete listing of hotels and motels in the Tallahassee area, you can also call the Tallahassee Area Convention and Visitors Bureau at 850-413-9200.

A little farther: If you are willing to make the 30-minute drive south to Wakulla Springs State Park, you will find a fabulous old-fashioned lodge and nature preserve. Built in 1937 in Spanish mission style, the **Wakulla Springs Lodge and Conference Center** (1 Springs Dr., Wakulla Springs; 850-224-5950) features glass-bottom boat rides and nature walks. You may run into conference groups and, on summer weekends, day-trippers.

AT A GLANCE

Selectivity Rating	83
Range SAT I Math	530-630
Average SAT I Math	590
Range SAT I Verbal	520-620
Average SAT I Verbal	588
Average ACT Composite	25
Average GPA	3.6

CAMPUS TOURS

Appointment Req?	No
Dates	Year-round
Times	Mon-Fri 9:30AM, 11AM, 1PM, and 3PM; contact Visitor's Services at 850-644-3246
Avg. Length	1 hour

ON-CAMPUS INTERVIEWS

Admissions

Start Date—Juniors	N/A
Appointment Req?	N/A
Advance Notice	N/A
Saturdays?	N/A
Avg. Length	N/A
Info Sessions	Year-round

Faculty and Coaches

Dates/Times	Year-round; subject to faculty/coach availability
Arrangements	Contact Visitor's Services

CLASS VISITS

Dates	N/A
Arrangements	N/A

OVERNIGHT DORM STAYS

Advance Notice	N/A
Arrangements	N/A
Limitations	N/A

NEW COLLEGE OF UNIVERSITY OF S. FLORIDA

New College of USF Admissions, University of South Florida, 5700 N. Tamiami Trail, Sarasota, FL 34243-2197 (Office is in Robertson Hall to the right of College Hall on the Historic Bay Front Campus) • Telephone: 941-359-4269 • Web: www.newcollege.usf.edu • Email: ncadmissions@sar.usf.edu

Hours: Monday-Friday, 8AM-5PM; Saturday, 9AM-noon. Closed wekends and holidays.

New College is not your garden-variety state school. There aren't any large classes, nor are there grades. Instead, under a unique "contract" system, every class is pass/fail and students receive written evaluations. The academic environment is largely "devoid of structure" and self-motivation is crucial—along with the flexibility comes high expectations and rigorous workloads.

AT A GLANCE

Selectivity Rating	94
Range SAT I Math	580-660
Average SAT I Math	622
Range SAT I Verbal	630-730
Average SAT I Verbal	679
Average ACT Composite	27
Average GPA	3.8
Student to Faculty Ratio	11:1

CAMPUS TOURS

Appointment Req?	Yes
Dates	Year-round
Times	Mon 2PM; Tues-Fri 11AM and 2PM
Avg. Length	1 hour

ON-CAMPUS INTERVIEWS

Admissions

Start Date—Juniors	Year-round
Appointment Req?	Yes
Advance Notice	1 week
Saturdays?	No
Avg. Length	1 hour
Info Sessions	Year-round

Faculty

Dates/Times	Subject to faculty availability
Arrangements	Contact faculty or dept. of interest

CLASS VISITS

Dates	Sept-April (Mon-Fri)
Arrangements	Contact admissions off.

OVERNIGHT DORM STAYS

Advance Notice	2 weeks
Arrangements	Contact admissions off.
Limitations	1-night stay; application must be on file

TRANSPORTATION

The Sarasota/Bradenton Airport is across the street from campus; taxis and limousines are available for the ride to campus. Taxis are always stationed outside the baggage claim area. Greyhound and Trailways bus lines provide service to Sarasota.

FIND YOUR WAY

From I-75 S., take Exit 40 (University Pkwy.). Head west for about 7 miles on University Pkwy. to the end (in front of the Ringling Museum of Art.) Turn right onto Bayshore Rd., and proceed approximately three-tenths of a mile to the pink arch. Turn left through the arch, and continue going straight to the loop in front of College Hall. Park along the drive in designated areas. The New College office of admissions is located on the first floor of College Hall.

STAY THE NIGHT

Nearby: You have several inexpensive choices. Within walking distance is the very inexpensive **Knights Inn** (5340 N. Tamiami Trail; 800-843-5644). The **Days Inn** (4900 N. Tamiami Trail; 800-325-2525) is a mere half mile from the school. Both have outdoor pools. **Hampton Inn** (5000 W. Tamiami Trail; 800-Hampton), a quarter mile from the school, offers a continental breakfast and a special rate for college visitors. Hampton also has an outdoor pool and exercise room. **The Courtyard by Marriot** (850 University Pkwy.; 800-321-2211) is a newer facility directly across from the airport and only a quarter mile from school. In the moderate to expensive range is the **Hyatt Sarasota** (1000 Blvd. of the Arts; 941-366-9000), a 7-minute drive from the school. It has a heated pool and the usual Hyatt amenities. About 20 minutes north of the college is the town of Palmetto. The **Five Oaks Inn** (1102 Riverside Dr.; 941-723-1236), overlooking the Manatee River, has moderate prices and might provide you with an offbeat and pleasant alternative to the chain motels.

A little farther: **Colony Beach Resort** (1620 Gulf of Mexico Dr.; 813-383-6464 or 800-237-9443) on Long Boat Key, fairly close to Sarasota, is a great, family-oriented resort with tennis, beach, pool, spa, and activities for children. One- or two-bedroom apartments with kitchens are fairly expensive. The **Long Boat Key Club** (301 Gulf of Mexico Dr.; 813-383-8821 or 800-237-8821), up the road from Colony Beach Resort, is somewhat more formal in feeling. Rates are expensive..

HIGHLIGHTS

ON CAMPUS
- R.V. Heiser Natural Sciences Complex
- Rhoda and Jack Pritxker Marine Biology Research Center
- Caples Fine Arts Complex
- Historic bayfront mansions
- Jane Bancroft Cook Library

OFF CAMPUS
- Ringling Museum of Art
- Mote Marine Laboratory and Marine Mammal Hospital
- Marie Selby Botanical Gardens
- Free public beaches
- Myakka State Park

ROLLINS COLLEGE

Office of Admission, Rollins College, 1000 Holt Ave. 2720, Winter Park, FL 32789
(the office is in Carnegie Hall) • Telephone: 407-646-2161 •
Web: www.rollins.edu • Email: admissions@rollins.edu

Hours: Monday-Friday, 8:30AM-5PM; Saturday, 9AM-1PM (varies during the academic year). Closed Sundays and holidays.

Rollins College is a small liberal arts college that offers a variety of prospects to its graduates. Perpetually sunny Winter Park, Florida, and a dazzling Spanish-style campus are tough to beat as well.

HIGHLIGHTS

ON CAMPUS
- Olin Library
- Botanical Garden
- Art gallery, Cornell Fine Arts Museum
- Hauck Memorial Greenhouse

OFF CAMPUS
- Disney World
- Universal Studios
- Sea World

TRANSPORTATION

Orlando International Airport is 16 miles from campus. Taxis and limousines are available. Amtrak trains serve Winter Park; the station is on Park Ave. To get to campus, head south on Park Ave. about 6 blocks.

FIND YOUR WAY

From the north and east, take I-4 W. to Exit 45 (Fairbanks Ave.). Turn left onto Fairbanks. Turn right onto Park Ave., then left at the stop sign. **From the south and west,** take I-4 E. to Exit 45 (Fairbanks Ave.). Turn right onto Fairbanks and travel 3 miles to the campus.

STAY THE NIGHT

You have some nice choices in Winter Park, the home of Rollins, but you have to pay a little more to stay there. The **Fortnightly Inn** (377 E. Fairbanks Ave.; 407-645-4440) is across the street from the college and includes a full breakfast. Our favorite is the **Park Plaza Hotel** (307 Park Ave. S.; 407-647-1072). This European-style hotel, with antiques, a garden, and a delightful balcony, is a great place to relax after a long day on campus. A mile away is the moderately priced **Best Western Mount Vernon** (110 S. Orlando Ave.; 407-647-1166). It has a pool and restaurant and most of the rooms have refrigerators. For a change of pace, consider the 6-room **Courtyard at Lake Lucerne** (211 N. Lucerne Circle East; 407-648-5188), a short drive (5 minutes) from Rollins in Orlando. This inn, located in an old and picturesque part of Orlando, is the oldest house in town.

AT A GLANCE

Selectivity Rating	81
Range SAT I Math	540-630
Average SAT I Math	575
Range SAT I Verbal	540-630
Average SAT I Verbal	575
Average ACT Composite	25
Student to Faculty Ratio	12:1

CAMPUS TOURS

Appointment Req?	Yes, call 407-646-2161
Dates	Year-round
Times	Mon-Fri 10AM and 2PM; Sat 10AM
Avg. Length	1 hour

ON-CAMPUS INTERVIEWS

Admission

Start Date—Juniors	Any time
Appointment Req?	Yes
Advance Notice	2 weeks
Saturdays?	Yes, various Saturdays Nov-Apr
Avg. Length	45 min
Info Sessions	Year-round

Faculty and Coaches

Dates/Times	Year-round; subject to faculty/coach availability
Arrangements	Contact off. of admission

CLASS VISITS

Dates	Sept-May (Mon-Fri)
Arrangements	Contact off. of admission

OVERNIGHT DORM STAYS

Advance Notice	2 weeks
Arrangements	Contact off. of admission
Limitations	Accepted students only; certain weeknights in March and April

STETSON UNIVERSITY

Admissions Office, Stetson University, 421 North Woodland Blvd. Unit 8378, DeLand, FL 32720-3771 • Telephone: 800-688-0101 or 904-822-7100 • Web: www.stetson.edu • Email: admissions@stetson.edu

Hours: Monday-Friday, 8AM-5PM; Saturday, 8:30AM-noon (only from September-May). Closed Sundays and holidays.

Students on Stetson University's beautiful and historic palm tree-laden campus enjoy the multitude of majors and great facilities you'd find at a big university and the personal attention you only find at small colleges. The sunny Florida location is obviously a bonus.

AT A GLANCE

Selectivity Rating	80
Range SAT I Math	500-610
Average SAT I Math	557
Range SAT I Verbal	510-620
Average SAT I Verbal	561
Average ACT Composite	24
Average GPA	3.5
Student to Faculty Ratio	10:1

CAMPUS TOURS

Appointment Req?	No
Dates	Year-round
Times	Sept-May: Mon-Fri 10AM and 2PM; Sat 10AM
Avg. Length	45-60 min

ON-CAMPUS INTERVIEWS

Admissions

Start Date–Juniors	Any time
Appointment Req?	Yes
Advance Notice	Varies
Saturdays?	Yes, Sept-May
Avg. Length	45 min
Info Sessions	Year-round

Faculty and Coaches

Dates/Times	Year-round; subject to faculty/coach availability
Arrangements	Contact admissions off.

CLASS VISITS

Dates	Year-round (Mon-Fri)
Arrangements	Contact admissions off.

OVERNIGHT DORM STAYS

Advance Notice	As much as possible
Arrangements	Contact admissions off.
Limitations	1-night stay Mon-Wed nights only; only for high school seniors

TRANSPORTATION

The Daytona Beach International Airport is approximately 20 miles from campus. The Orlando International Airport is approximately 55 miles from campus. From either airport, DOTS shuttle service is available to campus; call 800-231-1965 (within Florida) or 800-223-1965 (from out of state). Amtrak train service is available to DeLand; take a taxi from the station to campus. Greyhound bus service is available, and the bus depot is within walking distance of campus.

FIND YOUR WAY

From I-4, take Exit 54 to Florida Rte. 472 (it heads in only one direction from the exit); proceed on Rte. 472 for 3 miles to Rte. 17/92 N. Proceed for 5 miles to campus. **From I-95**, take Exit 87 to U.S. Rte. 92 W. Proceed for 20 miles to the merger of Routes 92 and 17. Continue south (left) on Rte. 17/92 for 1.5 miles to campus. **From the northwest**, take I-75 S. to Exit 69 (Ocala). Take Florida Rte. 40 E. for approximately 45 miles to Barberville. Turn south on U.S. Rte. 17 for 14 miles to campus.

STAY THE NIGHT

University Inn (644 N. Woodland Blvd.; 904-734-5711) is within walking distance. It offers basic accommodations at an inexpensive rate (with a special rate for university visitors). There is a coffee maker in each room and an outdoor pool. The **Holiday Inn DeLand** (350 International Speedway Blvd.; 904-738-5200) is two miles away and for a moderate price you can enjoy the Hilton game room, restaurant, and outdoor pool. For a bed-and-breakfast option, try the **DeLand Country Inn** (228 W. Howry Ave.; 904-736-4244), just a few blocks from the school. The inexpensive-to-moderate rates include a full breakfast. This is a big 91-year-old Victorian house with a porch, two TV rooms, and 5 bedrooms. A courtesy car is available. **Clauser's Bed & Breakfast** (201 East Kicklighter Road, Lake Helen; 904-228-0310). Best Western Deltona Inn (487 Deltona Blvd, Deltona; 904-574-6693).

HIGHLIGHTS

ON CAMPUS
- Edmunds Center
- DuPont-Ball Library
- Duncan Art Gallery
- Gillespie Museum

OFF CAMPUS
- Daytona International Speedway
- Museum of Arts and Sciences
- Woodruff Wildlife Refuge
- Blue Lake State Park

UNIVERSITY OF FLORIDA

Admissions Office, University of Florida, 201 Criser Hall, Gainesville, FL 32611 (The main entrance is at the corner of S.W. 13th St. and S.W. 2nd Ave.) • Telephone: 352-392-1365 • Web: www.ufl.edu • Email: freshman@ufl.edu

Hours: Monday-Friday, 8PM-5PM. Closed weekends and state holidays.

The University of Florida in very hot and humid Gainesville is the most prestigious public university in the state, and its reputation, coupled with a very low in-state tuition, makes it the first choice of many Florida residents. Socially, students love the football team, and the Greek system is a very prominent mainstay of UF campus life.

HIGHLIGHTS

ON CAMPUS
- Center for Performing Arts
- Florida Museum of Natural History
- The Harn Museum of Art
- Brains Institute
- Lake Alice Wildlife Reserve

OFF CAMPUS
- Devil's Millhopper
- Gainesville
- State geological site

TRANSPORTATION

The Gainesville Regional Airport is approximately 7 miles from campus. Taxis and regional transit services are available from the airport.

FIND YOUR WAY

From I-75, exit to Archer Rd. and proceed east to U.S. Rte. 441 (13th St.). Head north (left) on 13th St. to the admissions office (corner of 13th St. and S.W. 2nd Ave.).

STAY THE NIGHT

Nearby: You have a choice of lodgings quite close by, including a motel on campus, **The Reitz Union** (352-392-1607). Slightly more expensive is the **Holiday Inn** (1250 W. University Ave; 352-376-1661), 1 block away. This facility has an indoor pool. Across the street is the **University Centre Hotel** (1535 S.W. Archer Rd.; 352-371-3333) more posh and moderately priced (ask for the special rate). A **Sheraton** (2900 S.W. 13th St.; 352-377-4000) is 3 miles away and has a special rate for visitors. It also has an outdoor pool and a nature walk.

A little farther: Try the **Herlong Mansion** (P.O. Box 667, Micanopy; 352-466-3322), 8 miles south of Gainesville. The mansion's moderate price includes a deluxe continental breakfast during the week and a full breakfast on the weekends.

AT A GLANCE

Selectivity Rating	87
Range SAT I Math	580-680
Range SAT I Verbal	560-670
Average GPA	3.5
Student to Faculty Ratio	17:1

CAMPUS TOURS

Appointment Req?	Yes
Dates	Year-round, except state holidays
Times	Mon-Fri 10AM and 2PM
Avg. Length	90 min

ON-CAMPUS INTERVIEWS

Admissions

Start Date–Juniors	No interviews, only info sessions
Appointment Req?	No
Advance Notice	None
Saturdays?	No
Avg. Length	10-15 min
Info Sessions	Year-round, except state holidays

Faculty and Coaches

Dates/Times	Year-round; subject to faculty/coach availability
Arrangements	Contact faculty/coach at least 2 weeks in advance

CLASS VISITS

Dates	Year-round (Mon-Fri)
Arrangements	Contact the department

OVERNIGHT DORM STAYS

Advance Notice	N/A
Arrangements	N/A
Limitations	Available only if you make your own arrangements to stay with a current student

UNIVERSITY OF MIAMI

Office of Admissions, University of Miami, P.O. Box 248025,
Coral Gables, FL 33124-4616 • Telephone: 305-284-4323 (Fax: 305-284-2507) •
Web: www.miami.edu • Email: admission@miami.edu

Hours: Monday-Friday, 8:30AM-5PM; by appointment on selected Saturdays. Closed Sundays and holidays.

Students say the University of Miami is what you make of it—you can find what you want here, if you look hard enough. Professors receive good marks for their instruction skills and especially for their accessibility (which is rare at a large school). The computer, recreational/athletic, lab, and library facilities are all excellent as well.

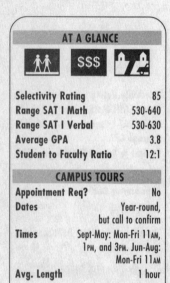

AT A GLANCE	
Selectivity Rating	85
Range SAT I Math	530-640
Range SAT I Verbal	530-630
Average GPA	3.8
Student to Faculty Ratio	12:1

CAMPUS TOURS	
Appointment Req?	No
Dates	Year-round, but call to confirm
Times	Sept-May: Mon-Fri 11AM, 1PM, and 3PM. Jun-Aug: Mon-Fri 11AM
Avg. Length	1 hour

ON-CAMPUS INTERVIEWS	
Admissions	
Start Date–Juniors	N/A
Appointment Req?	N/A
Advance Notice	N/A
Saturdays?	N/A
Avg. Length	30-45 min
Info Sessions	During academic year, information sessions follow the 11AM tour each day
Faculty and Coaches	
Dates/Times	Year-round; subject to faculty/coach availability
Arrangements	Contact faculty/coach well in advance

CLASS VISITS	
Dates	Year-round (Mon-Fri)
Arrangements	Contact admissions off.

OVERNIGHT DORM STAYS	
Advance Notice	N/A
Arrangements	N/A
Limitations	N/A

TRANSPORTATION

Miami International Airport is located in Coral Gables and is approximately 20 minutes from campus. Supershuttle (located on the downstairs level outside of baggage claim) and taxis are available for the ride to campus. Supershuttle is approximately $11 per person and taxis are in the neighborhood of $15 to $20.

FIND YOUR WAY

From the north, take I-95 S. to U.S. 1. Continue south for about 5 miles. Make a right on Red Rd. (S.W. 57th Ave.) and continue to the second light, which is at Miller Rd. (S.W. 56th St.). Make a right onto Miller Rd. and follow to the end. Make a left onto San Amato Dr. and follow the directory signs to the Ashe Building, then make a right onto Memorial Dr. (the main entrance). Ask the guard for directions to parking and the office of admission (located in the Ashe Building, Rm. 132). **From the west**, take I-75 to 826 S. Continue to the Miller Rd. exit. Make a left onto Miller Rd (S.W. 56th St.) and follow to the end. Follow the preceding directions to the office of admissions. **From Miami International Airport**, take Le Jeune Rd. south for about 5 miles through downtown Coral Gables. Make a right onto U.S. 1 and travel for about 1.5 miles. Turn right onto Red Rd. (S.W. 57th Ave.) and continue to the second light, which is at Miller Rd. (S.W. 56th St.). Make a right onto Miller Rd. and follow to the end. Follow the above directions to get to the office of admissions.

STAY THE NIGHT

Nearby: The **Holiday Inn—University of Miami** (1350 S. Dixie Hwy.; 305-667-5611) offers college visitors a special double-occupancy rate. No surprises here, but very convenient (it's across the street from the university). Our choice for character is the **Hotel Place St. Michel** (162 Alcazar Ave.; 305-444-1666), less than 5 minutes from the university and 3 blocks from the Miracle Mile shopping area. A bit farther away (10 minutes), you'll find the moderately priced **Marriott-Dadeland** (9090 S. Dadeland Dr.; 305-670-1035). Other hotels in the area include the **Biltmore Hotel** (1200 Anastasia Ave.; 305-445-1926); **The Holiday Inn—Coral Gables** (2051 Le Jeune Rd.; 305-443-2301); and the **Grand Bay Hotel** (2669 S. Bayshore Dr.; 305-858-9600). Check the **Bed and Breakfast Company—Tropical Florida** (P.O. Box 262, South Miami; 305-661-3270) for bed-and-breakfast accommodations in the area.

A little farther: If a resort beckons, **Sonesta Beach Hotel** (350 Ocean Dr.; 305-361-2021), about 25 minutes from the university in Key Biscayne, might be for you. Sonesta Beach has tennis courts, an Olympic pool, a fitness center, boat rentals, and 3 restaurants.

HIGHLIGHTS

ON CAMPUS	OFF CAMPUS
• Lowe Art Museum	• Everglades National Park
• Jerry Herman Ring Theater	• Coconut Grove
• Bill Cosford Cinema	• Miami Beach
• Mark Light Stadium	• South Beach
• Gusman Concert Hall	• Florida Keys

UNIVERSITY OF SOUTH FLORIDA

Office of Admission, University of South Florida, SVC 1036, 4202 E. Fowler Ave., Tampa, FL 33620-6900 (The office is in the Student Services Building, Rm. 1036) • Telephone: 813-974-3350 • Web: www.usfweb.usf.edu • Email: bullseye@admin.usf.edu

Hours: Monday-Friday, 9AM-5PM. Closed weekends and holidays.

The University of South Florida, which is located 10 miles north of downtown Tampa, is home to botanical gardens, a planetarium, and a weather station for research. There's also a championship golf course, swimming pools, art galleries, and the Sun Dome, which hosts concerts and the sporting events.

HIGHLIGHTS

ON CAMPUS
- Center Gallery
- The Tampa Campus Library
- Contemporary Art Museum
- Botanical Garden
- Sun Dome

OFF CAMPUS
- Busch Gardens (theme park)
- The Tampa Museum of Art
- Raymond James Stadium
- Tampa Buccaneers football

TRANSPORTATION

Tampa International Airport is 15 to 20 miles from campus. Buses, taxis, shuttles, and rental cars are available at the airport. Central Florida Limousine (813-276-3730) provides limousine service. During peak tourist seasons, you should make car rental reservations. Most hotels provide courtesy vans for airport transportation. Amtrak trains and Greyhound/Trailways buses provide service to Tampa. City and suburban bus service is provided by Hart Line (813-254-4278).

FIND YOUR WAY

I-275, I-75, and I-4 are the principal routes to Tampa. **From I-275**, take the Fowler Ave. exit (not Fletcher); turn east on Fowler to the university entrance, which is just past McKinley Blvd. **From I-75 (north or south)**, take the Fowler Ave. exit; turn west to the university entrance. **From the east on I-4**, take the Columbus Dr./50th St. exit and proceed north on 50th for approximately 7 miles. (Note that 50th becomes 56th after half a mile.) Turn west on Fowler Ave. to the university entrance. **From other routes**—U.S. Rte. 41 S., Florida Highway 60 S. and W., U.S. Rte. 92 N. and E.—take 40th or 50th St. or Nebraska or Florida Ave. to Fowler Ave. and the university's main entrance.

STAY THE NIGHT

There are a number of hotels in a 5-minute radius of the University that offer special rates to USF visitors, including **La Quinta Inn** (800-687-6667), **Wingate Inn** (813-979-2828) and the **Embassy Suites** (813-977-7066) located on Fowler Ave. In addition, located on Bruce B. Downs Blvd. are the **Amerisuites** (813-979-1922) and **Quality Suites** (813-971-8930).

AT A GLANCE

Range SAT I Math	490-590
Average SAT I Math	542
Range SAT I Verbal	480-590
Average SAT I Verbal	539
Average ACT Composite	22
Average GPA	3.5
Student to Faculty Ratio	16:1

CAMPUS TOURS

Appointment Req?	No
Dates	Whenever classes are in session
Times	Mon-Fri 11AM and 2PM; housing tours Mon-Fri 3:30PM and noon on Saturday
Avg. Length	2 hours

ON-CAMPUS INTERVIEWS

Admissions

Start Date—Juniors	N/A
Appointment Req?	N/A
Advance Notice	N/A
Saturdays?	N/A
Avg. Length	N/A
Info Sessions	N/A

Faculty and Coaches

Dates/Times	Year-round; subject to faculty/coach availability
Arrangements	Contact faculty/coach at least 2 weeks in advance

CLASS VISITS

Dates	During special visitation program
Arrangements	Contact admissions off.

OVERNIGHT DORM STAYS

Advance Notice	N/A
Arrangements	N/A
Limitations	N/A

GEORGIA

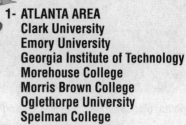

1- ATLANTA AREA
   Clark University
   Emory University
   Georgia Institute of Technology
   Morehouse College
   Morris Brown College
   Oglethorpe University
   Spelman College
2- Agnes Scott College
3- University of Georgia

Georgia	Agnes Scott Coll.	Clark Atlanta Univ.	Emory Univ.	Georgia Tech.	Morehouse College	Morris Brown Coll.	Oglethorpe Univ.	Spelman College	Univ. Georgia	Athens	Atlanta	Macon
Agnes Scott Coll.	—	9	4	5	9	9	14	9	68	65	1	91
Clark Atlanta Univ.	9	—	5	1	0	0	13	0	70	72	0	86
Emory Univ.	4	5	—	3	5	5	7	5	64	67	1	91
Georgia Tech.	5	1	3	—	1	1	9	1	68	72	0	87
Morehouse College	9	0	5	1	—	0	13	0	70	72	0	86
Morris Brown College	9	0	5	1	0	—	13	0	70	72	0	86
Oglethorpe Univ.	14	13	7	9	13	13	—	13	61	67	1	96
Spelman College	9	0	5	1	0	0	13	—	70	72	0	86
Univ. Georgia	68	70	64	68	70	70	61	70	—	0	66	90
Athens	65	72	67	72	72	72	67	72	0	—	66	90
Atlanta	1	0	1	0	0	0	1	0	66	66	—	82
Macon	91	86	91	87	86	86	96	86	90	90	82	—

AGNES SCOTT COLLEGE

Office of Admission, Agnes Scott College, 141 E. College Ave., Atlanta/Decatur, GA 30030 (The office is in Rebekah Scott Hall) • Telephone: 800-868-8602 or 404-471-6285 • Web: www.agnesscott.edu • Email: admission@agnesscott.edu

Hours: Monday-Friday, 8:30AM-4:30PM; open selected Saturdays during the academic year. Closed weekends and holidays.

Students at this college for women enjoy comfortable dorms and easy access to Atlanta with the rapid transit system a short jaunt away. Scotties laud their professors and say the education here is of the highest caliber. Weekend social life often entails seeking out fraternity parties at nearby Georgia Tech or Emory.

HIGHLIGHTS

ON CAMPUS
- Newly renovated Bradley Observatory
- Alston Campus Center
- McCain Library
- Six residence halls are on the
- National Register of Historic Places

OFF CAMPUS
- The Fox Theatre
- Atlanta History Center
- Martin Luther King, Jr.
- National Historic Site
- CNN
- The High Museum of Art

TRANSPORTATION

Hartsfield International Airport in Atlanta is 20 miles from campus. MARTA trains (public transportation) take to you to campus from the airport: Take the train from the airport to 5 Points station, then transfer to an eastbound train to the E6 station in Decatur; either take a taxi or the #15 bus the 2 blocks to campus. Taxi service is also available for the ride to campus from the airport. Amtrak trains and Greyhound buses serve Atlanta. MARTA provides buses and rapid-rail trains in the metropolitan area.

FIND YOUR WAY

From the north, take I-75 S. past I-285 to I-85 N. Take I-85 N. to the Clairmont Rd. exit. Turn right (signs will point to Decatur) and proceed for several miles until Clairmont ends at the square in Decatur. Turn right onto Ponce de Leon and at the first light (Commerce), turn left. At the second light (Trinity), turn left. At the first light, turn right onto McDonough; cross the train tracks and turn immediately to the left onto E. College Ave. Enter the campus by turning into the first driveway on the right. **From the north on I-85 S.**, pass I-285 and exit to Clairmont Rd. Turn left, then follow the preceding directions from Clairmont Rd. **From the south on I-75/85 N.**, exit to I-285 E. Follow I-285 to 33 (Covington Hwy.). Head west (left) toward Decatur. Covington becomes E. College Ave. The campus is on the left; enter the second driveway past Candler St. **From the east and west**, take I-20 to I-285 N. Follow the preceding directions from that point.

STAY THE NIGHT

Seniors are invited to stay overnight with a current student in a residence hall. Please schedule your visit with the office of admission 2 weeks in advance. The **Decatur Holiday Inn and Conference Center** (130 Clairmont Rd.; 404-371-0204) has moderate room rates, an indoor pool, and an exercise room. **University Inn** and the **Emory Conference Center Hotel** are conveniently located also.

AT A GLANCE

Selectivity Rating	79
Range SAT I Math	530-640
Average SAT I Math	582
Range SAT I Verbal	580-680
Average SAT I Verbal	627
Average ACT Composite	26
Average GPA	3.7

CAMPUS TOURS

Appointment Req?	Preferred
Dates	Year-round, except holidays
Times	Mon-Fri 8:30AM-4:30PM
Avg. Length	1 hour

ON-CAMPUS INTERVIEWS

Admissions

Start Date—Juniors	Any time
Appointment Req?	Preferred
Advance Notice	1 week
Saturdays?	No
Avg. Length	30 min
Info Sessions	Year-round

Faculty and Coaches

Dates/Times	Year-round; subject to faculty/coach availability
Arrangements	Contact admissions off. 2 weeks prior

CLASS VISITS

Dates	Year-round (Mon-Fri)
Arrangements	Contact admissions off.

OVERNIGHT DORM STAYS

Advance Notice	2 weeks
Arrangements	Contact admissions off.
Limitations	Not permitted on weekends or holidays

CLARK ATLANTA UNIVERSITY

Office of Admissions, Clark Atlanta University, James P. Brawley Dr. at Fair St. S.W., Atlanta, GA 30314 (The Office is in Rm. 101, Trevor Arnett Hall, at the corner of Brawley Dr. and Greensferry Ave.) • Telephone:404-880-8784 • Web: www.cau.edu • Email: pmeadows@cau.edu

Hours: Monday-Friday, 9AM-5PM. Closed weekends and holidays.

Clark Atlanta University is a historically African American University of about 6,000 students affiliated with the United Methodist Church. Clark Atlanta offers a diverse and comprehensive liberal arts and sciences education as well as vocational and pre-professional options. It also boasts a rich social life, as the campus is only minutes from downtown Atlanta.

AT A GLANCE

Average SAT I Math	444
Average SAT I Verbal	466
Average ACT Composite	19
Average GPA	2.8
Student to Faculty Ratio	16:1

CAMPUS TOURS

Appointment Req?	Yes
Dates	Year-round
Times	Mon-Fri 9AM-3PM
Avg. Length	30 min

ON-CAMPUS INTERVIEWS

Admissions

Start Date—Juniors	September
Appointment Req?	Yes
Advance Notice	7 days
Saturdays?	No
Avg. Length	30 min
Info Sessions	Year-round

Faculty and Coaches

Dates/Times	Year-round; subject to faculty/coach availability
Arrangements	Contact admissions off. 1 week prior

CLASS VISITS

Dates	Year-round (Mon-Fri)
Arrangements	Contact admissions off.; instructor's permission is required

OVERNIGHT DORM STAYS

Advance Notice	N/A
Arrangements	N/A
Limitations	N/A

TRANSPORTATION

Hartsfield International Airport in Atlanta is 12 miles from campus. Taxis, limousines, and MARTA trains (public transportation) are all available. Amtrak trains and Greyhound buses serve Atlanta. MARTA trains and buses (public transportation) are available for travel throughout the metropolitan area.

HIGHLIGHTS

ON CAMPUS
• Clark Atlanta University Art Galleries

OFF CAMPUS
• Woodruff Arts Center
• High Museum of Art
• The Atlanta Historical Society
• Stone Mountain Park

FIND YOUR WAY

From I-75/85 (N. and S.), take I-20 W. and exit at Ashby St. Turn right on Ashby and continue to Fair St. Turn right on Fair and continue to James P. Brawley Dr. The campus is on the right; several parking lots are on the left. **From I-20 E.**, exit at Ashby St. and turn left (north) to Fair St. From there follow the preceding directions. **From I-20 W.**, exit at Ashby St. and turn right to Fair St. From there follow the preceding directions. **From downtown**, take Peachtree St. south to Martin Luther King Dr. and turn right. Continue to James P. Brawley Dr. and turn left. Continue to the next traffic light, which is Fair St. The university is ahead on both sides of the street. Brawley Dr. is closed to vehicular traffic at this point; park on either side of the street.

STAY THE NIGHT

These suggestions also apply to Morehouse College, Morris Brown College, and Spelman College.

Nearby: Within a 10-minute walk is **Paschal's Motor Hotel** (830 Martin Luther King Dr. S.W.; 404-577-3150), with a pool and a restaurant. It offers a special inexpensive rate for visitors to any of the above colleges.

A little farther: See suggestions in the Emory University entry. The inns and bed-and-breakfasts listed there are within easy reach of Morehouse, Morris Brown, Spelman, and Clark Atlanta.

EMORY UNIVERSITY

Office of Admissions, Emory University, 200 Boisfeuillet Jones Ctr.,
Atlanta, GA 30322 • Telephone: 800-727-6036 • Web: www.emory.edu •
Email: admiss@emory.edu

Hours: Monday-Friday, 8AM-5PM; open various Saturdays. Closed Sundays and holidays.

Emory is one of the South's premier universities. Atlanta offers many opportunities for career advancement and virtually unlimited social options. The school's alumni list includes Newt Gingrich and reads like a Who's Who of the American South.

HIGHLIGHTS

ON CAMPUS
- Michael C. Carlos Museum
- Clifton Health Sciences Corridor
- Lullwater Park
- Top of Woodruff Library
- Cappucino Joe's Coffee House

OFF CAMPUS
- Carter Center
- CNN Center
- Coca-Cola Museum/Underground
- Virginia Highland
- Martin Luther King, Jr. Center for Nonviolent Social Change

TRANSPORTATION

Atlanta's Hartsfield International Airport is approximately 15 miles (a 30- to 40-minute drive) from campus. Airport limousines, rental cars, and public transportation (a combination of MARTA rapid-rail line and buses) provide transportation from the airport to campus. For public transportation from the airport, take the Northbound MARTA train to the Five Points rapid-rail station in downtown Atlanta. From there, take the train eastbound to the Candler Park station; then take the #6 Emory bus to campus. Amtrak trains and Greyhound/Trailways buses serve Atlanta. The city's MARTA public transportation system of rapid-rail lines and buses connects Emory to all parts of the city.

FIND YOUR WAY

From I-85, take the Clairmont Rd. exit (Exit #91). Turn east on Clairmont Rd. and follow it approximately 3 miles to N. Decatur Rd. Turn right and follow N. Decatur Rd. for approximately 1 mile to the Emory campus. Turn right in the Emory Village on Dowman Dr. at the main gates of the campus. The admissions office is the first building on the left, the B. Jones Center. **From I-20**, take the Moreland Ave. N. exit. Turn north on Moreland Ave. and follow it approximately 3 miles, at which point it becomes Briarcliff Rd. Continue straight on Briarcliff Rd. approximately 1 mile. At the large intersection with Oxford Rd., make a soft left onto campus on Dowman Dr., past the main gates of the campus. The admission office is the first building on the left, the B. Jones Center.

STAY THE NIGHT

Nearby: University-owned **Emory Inn** and more expensive **Emory Conference Center Hotel** (1641 Clifton Rd. NE; 800-933-6679 or 404-712-6700) are convenient and both boast swimming pool, spa, weight room, restaurant and lounge, and a shuttle service to the admission office. **Holiday Inn Select** (130 Clairemont Ave.; 800-225-6079 or 404-371-0204) in nearby quaint Decatur also offers a shuttle to the admission office. For nearby bed and breakfast listings, contact **Bed and Breakfast Atlanta** at 404-875-0525 or 875-9672.

A little farther: The stunning **Ritz-Carlton Buckhead** (3434 Peachtree Rd. NE; 404-237-2700) faces Atlanta's 2 best-known shopping centers. Attached to Lenox Square Mall is the **J. W. Marriot** (3300 Lenox Rd.; 800-228-9290 or 404-262-3344). In Midtown, **The Four Seasons** (75 14th St.; 800-332-3442 or 404-881-9898) offers luxury near Atlanta's Arts Center. Some less expensive options just a few miles from campus are the **Courtyard Marriot** (1236 Executive Park Dr.; 800-321-2211 or 404-728-0708) and the **Hampton Inn** (1975 N. Druid Hills Rd.; 800-426-7866 or 404-320-6600).

AT A GLANCE

Selectivity Rating	88
Range SAT I Math	645-715
Average SAT I Math	680
Range SAT I Verbal	620-700
Average SAT I Verbal	660
Average ACT Composite	29
Average GPA	3.7
Student to Faculty Ratio	7:1

CAMPUS TOURS

Appointment Req?	Yes
Dates	Year-round
Times	Mon-Fri, some Saturdays
Avg. Length	1 hour

ON-CAMPUS INFORMATION SESSIONS

Admissions

Appointment Req?	Yes
Advance Notice	Yes
Saturdays?	Yes
Avg. Length	1 hour
Info Sessions	Year-round, Mon-Fri, some Saturdays

Faculty and Coaches

Dates/Times	Year-round; subject to faculty/coach availability
Arrangements	Contact specific department 2 weeks prior

CLASS VISITS

Dates	Year-round (Mon-Fri)
Arrangements	Contact admissions off.

OVERNIGHT DORM STAYS

Advance Notice	2 weeks
Arrangements	Contact admissions off.
Limitations	Available only to high school seniors; scheduled only from Oct-April, but not on Fri or Sat nights

GEORGIA INSTITUTE OF TECHNOLOGY

Office of Undergraduate Admission, Georgia Institute of Technology, 225 North Ave., Atlanta, GA 30332-0320 • Telephone: 404-894-4154 • Web: www.gatech.edu • Email: admissions@success.gatech.edu

Hours: Monday-Friday, 8AM-5PM. Closed weekends and major holidays, including Thanksgiving weekend and Christmas week.

Georgia Tech is a world-class engineering school where difficult courses toughen the students and decrease the number of one's peers. For survivors, a well-paying job is the reward when you graduate from what is one of the best public schools in the state.

AT A GLANCE

Selectivity Rating		89
Range SAT I Math		630-725
Average SAT I Math		674
Range SAT I Verbal		590-690
Average SAT I Verbal		630
Average GPA		3.8
Student to Faculty Ratio		19:1

CAMPUS TOURS

Appointment Req?	No
Dates	Year-round, except holidays
Times	Mon-Fri 11AM and 2PM
Avg. Length	75 min

ON-CAMPUS INTERVIEWS

Admissions

Start Date–Juniors	N/A
Appointment Req?	N/A
Advance Notice	N/A
Saturdays?	N/A
Avg. Length	N/A
Info Sessions	Mon-Fri 10AM and 1PM

Faculty and Coaches

Dates/Times	Year-round; subject to faculty/coach availability
Arrangements	Contact faculty/coach

CLASS VISITS

Dates	Year-round (Mon-Fri)
Arrangements	Contact dept. of interest

OVERNIGHT DORM STAYS

Advance Notice	2 weeks
Arrangements	Contact Special Programs at 404-894-2691
Limitations	Only for accepted students and by invitation only

TRANSPORTATION

Hartsfield International Airport in Atlanta is approximately 11 miles from campus. To get to campus, take the MARTA (public transit) rail line from the airport baggage claim to the North Ave. station (about a 20-minute ride). Walk 3 blocks west to campus, or transfer to a bus on Route 13. Fare is $1.50 each way, and exact change is required (change machines are available at MARTA stations). At the intersection of North Ave. and Fowler St., ascend the stairs under the archway, and make an immediate right. Follow the path to the Student Success Center (which appears to be attached to the west stands of the football stadium). Amtrak trains and Greyhound/Trailways buses also offer service to Atlanta

FIND YOUR WAY

From I-75/85 S., take Exit 249D (North Ave.). Turn right onto North Ave. Cross Techwood Dr. (the first light), and continue on North Ave. approximately 1 block to Fowler St., which will be immediately before the cement walkway above the street. Turn left onto Fowler St. and park in the first level of the visitors' parking deck. **From I-75/85 N.**, take Exit 249D (Spring St./West Peachtree). Proceed through the first intersection to the next intersection (West Peachtree), and turn left. Continue for 1 block and turn left on North Ave. Cross over the interstate and Techwood Dr. Continue on North Ave. 1 block to Fowler St. and park in the first level of the visitors' parking deck.

STAY THE NIGHT

Nearby: Make reservations and obtain special rates at many local inns and hotels by calling **Connections** (800-262-9974). **Regency Suites** (975 W. Peachtree St.; 404-876-5003) offers moderate rates, kitchenettes, and a continental breakfast. The Regency also has a fitness room and offers pool privileges at an athletic club. The more expensive **Marriott Suites** (35 14th St.; 404-876-8888) offers a great breakfast, an indoor/outdoor pool, and a workout room. The nearby **Holiday Inn Express** (244 North Ave.; 404-881-0881) has moderately priced rooms and is located within walking distance of the campus.

A little farther: Morehouse, Agnes Scott, and Emory are not very far from Georgia Tech. Check the entries for these schools for additional suggestions.

HIGHLIGHTS

ON CAMPUS
- Olympic aquatic center/pool
- Georgia Tech Plaza
- The Hill/Tech Tower
- Bioengineering and Bioscience Bldg.
- Edge Intercollegiate Athletic Center

OFF CAMPUS
- Centennial Olympic Park
- World of Coca-Cola Museum
- Carter Presidential Library
- CNN Center
- Martin Luther King, Jr. Center for Nonviolent Social Change

MOREHOUSE COLLEGE

Admissions Office, Morehouse College, 830 Westview Dr. S.W., Atlanta, GA 30314 •
Telephone: 404-681-2800 • Web: www.morehouse.edu •
Email: apattillo@morehouse.edu

Hours: September-May: Monday-Friday, 9AM-5PM. June-August: Monday-Friday, 9AM-4PM. Closed weekends and holidays.

Morehouse College is an all-male, predominately African American liberal arts college in Atlanta with a solid core curriculum and a great national reputation. Half of all recent Morehouse graduates go on to pursue a graduate degree, and Martin Luther King, Jr. and Spike Lee head up a list of notables who received their undergraduate degrees from Morehouse.

HIGHLIGHTS

ON CAMPUS
- Olympic gymnasium
- Graves Hall
- Martin Luther King Chapel
- Mays Grave Site

OFF CAMPUS
- Woodruff Arts Center
- High Museum of Art
- The Atlanta Historical Society
- Stone Mountain Park

FIND YOUR WAY

From I-75/85, exit to I-20 W. Exit I-20 W. at Lee St. and turn right for 2 blocks until you reach campus. **From I-20 E.**, exit to Ashby St., and turn left for 3 blocks. Turn right on Westview and continue until you hit campus.

STAY THE NIGHT

These suggestions also apply to Morris Brown College, Spelman College, and Clark Atlanta University.

Nearby: Within a 10-minute walk is **Paschal's Motor Hotel** (830 Martin Luther King Dr. S.W.; 404-577-3150), with a pool and a restaurant. It offers a special inexpensive rate for visitors to any of the above colleges.

A little farther: The stunning **Ritz-Carlton Buckhead** (3434 Peachtree Rd.; 404-237-2700) is the essence of luxury. The hotel faces Atlanta's 2 best-known shopping centers. Prices are pretty high. For a complete change of scene, consider the **Evergreen Conference Center and Resort** in Stone Mountain Park (1 Lakeview Dr., Stone Mountain; 770-879-9900). You will find activities galore here, including golf, fishing, and boating.

TRANSPORTATION

Hartsfield International Airport in Atlanta is 10 miles from campus. Taxis, airport limousines, and MARTA (public transportation) trains and buses are available for the trip from the airport to campus and throughout the metropolitan area. Amtrak trains and Greyhound buses serve Atlanta.

AT A GLANCE

Selectivity Rating	85
Range SAT I Math	470-680
Average SAT I Math	530
Range SAT I Verbal	440-680
Average SAT I Verbal	526
Average ACT Composite	23
Average GPA	3.0
Student to Faculty Ratio	15:1

CAMPUS TOURS

Appointment Req?	Yes
Dates	Year-round, except during holidays and exam periods
Times	Mon-Fri 9AM-3PM
Avg. Length	90 min

ON-CAMPUS INTERVIEWS

Admissions

Start Date–Juniors	As soon as possible
Appointment Req?	Yes
Advance Notice	2 weeks
Saturdays?	No
Avg. Length	1 hour
Info Sessions	Year-round, except holidays and exam periods

Faculty and Coaches

Dates/Times	Year-round; subject to faculty/coach availability
Arrangements	Contact admissions off. 2 weeks prior

CLASS VISITS

Dates	Year-round (Mon-Fri)
Arrangements	Contact admissions off.

OVERNIGHT DORM STAYS

Advance Notice	2 weeks
Arrangements	Contact admissions off.
Limitations	None

MORRIS BROWN COLLEGE

Admissions Office, Morris Brown College, 643 Martin Luther King Dr. N.W., Atlanta, GA 30314 (The office is in Hickman Student Ctr. at the corner of Sunset Ave. and Martin Luther King Dr. N.W.) • Telephone: 404-220-0152 • Web: www.morrisbrown.edu

Hours: Monday-Friday, 9AM-5PM. Closed weekends and holidays.

Morris Brown College, home to about 2,100 students, is a historically African-American institution located in Atlanta. The school's programs are career-oriented and range from the liberal arts and sciences to education and psychology. Student recreational options range from a chess club to a baton-twirling team.

AT A GLANCE

Average SAT I Math	396
Average SAT I Verbal	407
Average ACT Composite	16
Student to Faculty Ratio	18:1

CAMPUS TOURS

Appointment Req?	Yes
Dates	During the academic year
Times	Mon-Fri 9AM-2PM
Avg. Length	1 hour

ON-CAMPUS INTERVIEWS

Admissions

Start Date—Juniors	September
Appointment Req?	Yes
Advance Notice	2 weeks
Saturdays?	No
Avg. Length	90 min
Info Sessions	Year-round

Faculty and Coaches

Dates/Times	Year-round; subject to faculty/coach availability
Arrangements	Contact admissions off. 2 weeks prior

CLASS VISITS

Dates	Year-round (Mon-Fri)
Arrangements	Contact admissions off.

OVERNIGHT DORM STAYS

Advance Notice	N/A
Arrangements	N/A
Limitations	N/A

TRANSPORTATION

Hartsfield International Airport in Atlanta is a 15-minute drive from campus. Public transportation (MARTA) trains and buses are available for the ride to campus from the airport; call 404-848-4711 for schedule information. Amtrak trains and Greyhound buses serve Atlanta, and MARTA is available from the stations to campus.

FIND YOUR WAY

From I-75/85, take Exit 93 to I-20 W. Exit I-20 at Exit 19 (West End) and head north on Ashby St. Turn right on Martin Luther King Dr. and proceed to the admissions office.

STAY THE NIGHT

These suggestions also apply to Morehouse College, Spelman College, and Clark Atlanta University.

Nearby: Within a 10-minute walk is **Paschal's Motor Hotel** (830 Martin Luther King Dr. S.W.; 404-577-3150), with a pool and a restaurant. It offers a special inexpensive rate for visitors to any of the above colleges.

A little farther: The stunning **Ritz-Carlton Buckhead** (3434 Peachtree Rd. N.E.; 404-237-2700) is the essence of luxury. The hotel faces Atlanta's 2 best-known shopping centers. Prices are pretty high. For a complete change of scene, consider the **Evergreen Conference Center and Resort** in Stone Mountain Park (1 Lakeview Dr., Stone Mountain; 770-879-9900). You will find activities galore here, including golf, fishing, and boating. The inns and bed-and-breakfasts listed here are within easy reach of Morehouse, Morris Brown, Spelman, and Clark Atlanta.

HIGHLIGHTS

OFF CAMPUS
- Woodruff Arts Center
- High Museum of Art
- The Atlanta Historical Society
- Stone Mountain Park

OGLETHORPE UNIVERSITY

Office of Admission, Oglethorpe University, 4484 Peachtree Rd., Atlanta, GA 30319 (The office is located on the main floor of Lupton Hall) • Telephone: 404-364-8307 or 800-428-4484 • Web: www.oglethorpe.edu • Email: admission@oglethorpe.edu

Hours: Monday-Friday, 8:30AM-5PM; Saturday, 9AM-noon (by appointment only). Closed Sundays and major holidays.

Oglethorpe University is a small liberal arts school on the outskirts of Atlanta with an unusually demanding, broad-based core curriculum.

HIGHLIGHTS

ON CAMPUS
- Phillip Weltner Library
- Oglethorpe University Museum
- Conant Performing Arts Center
- Hermance Stadium

OFF CAMPUS
- Lenox Square Mall/Phillips Plaza
- The High Museum of Art
- Stone Mountain Park
- The Fox Theater
- Martin Luther King, Jr. Center for Nonviolent Social Change

TRANSPORTATION

Hartsfield International Airport in Atlanta is located about 15 miles from campus. Rapid rail, airport shuttle, taxi, car rental, and limousine services are available. MARTA is the city's public transportation system and provides bus service in addition to rapid rail service. The Brookhaven/Oglethorpe University MARTA station is located 1 mile due south of campus on Peachtree Rd. and is served by the North Doraville MARTA line. Atlanta is also a major hub for both Greyhound Bus Lines and Amtrak.

FIND YOUR WAY

From I-85/75, take Exit 89 (N. Druid Hills Rd.). Proceed north/west on N. Druid Hills approximately 2.5 miles (make sure to veer right at Roxboro Rd., remaining on N. Druid Hills) until it dead-ends at Peachtree Rd. Turn right (north) onto Peachtree and proceed 1 mile. The campus is on the left. **From I-285,** take Exit 21 (Ashford-Dunwoody Rd.). Proceed south/east on Ashford-Dunwoody approximately 2.5 miles until it dead-ends at Peachtree Rd. Turn right (south) onto Peachtree and proceed approximately 1 block. The campus is on the right.

STAY THE NIGHT

There are countless hotels and inns located within a 5 mile radius of Oglethorpe's campus. One of the best bets is the **Sierra Suites-Brookhaven** (3967 Peachtree Rd.; 404-237-9100), a new hotel located directly next to the Brookhaven/Oglethorpe University MARTA station. It provides a discount for Oglethorpe University visitors. Also try the **Holiday Inn Select-Perimeter** (4386 Chamblee-Dunwoody Rd.; 770-457-6363), which features a weight room, a pool, a restaurant, and reasonable prices. **The Red Roof Inn-North Druid Hills** (1960 N. Druid Hills Rd.; 404-321-4174) offers nice accommodations at economy rates, and the **Swissotel Atlanta** (3391 Peachtree Rd.; 404-365-5500) is a world-class luxury hotel located in the Lenox/Buckhead area just south of Oglethorpe's campus.

AT A GLANCE

Selectivity Rating	84
Range SAT I Math	550-650
Average SAT I Math	603
Range SAT I Verbal	560-660
Average SAT I Verbal	617
Average ACT Composite	26
Average GPA	3.7
Student to Faculty Ratio	13:1

CAMPUS TOURS

Appointment Req?	Yes
Dates	Year-round
Times	Mon-Fri 11:30AM and 1:30PM
Avg. Length	90 min

ON-CAMPUS INTERVIEWS

Admissions

Start Date–Juniors	Any time
Appointment Req?	Yes
Advance Notice	2 weeks
Saturdays?	Yes
Avg. Length	90 min for interview and tour
Info Sessions	N/A

Faculty and Coaches

Dates/Times	Year-round; subject to faculty/coach availability
Arrangements	Contact Office of Admission 2 weeks prior

CLASS VISITS

Dates	Year-round (Mon-Fri)
Arrangements	Contact admissions off. 1 week prior

OVERNIGHT DORM STAYS

Advance Notice	2 weeks
Arrangements	Contact admissions off.
Limitations	No stays during summer or exams

SPELMAN COLLEGE

Admissions Office, Spelman College, 350 Spelman Lane, Atlanta, GA 30314
(The office is in Packard Hall) • Telephone: 800-241-3421 •
Web: www.spelman.edu • Email: admiss@spelman.edu

Hours: Monday-Friday, 9AM-5PM. Closed weekends and all holidays.

Spelman College is one of only two remaining all-female historically African American colleges in the country and one of the nation's pre-eminent historically African American institutions.

TRANSPORTATION

Hartsfield International Airport in Atlanta is a 20-minute drive from campus. Taxis, airport limousines (to some hotels), and MARTA (public transportation) trains are available for the trip between airport and campus. Amtrak trains and Greyhound buses provide service to Atlanta. MARTA trains and buses provide very good public transportation throughout the metropolitan area. The campus is accessible from #68 Ashby (West End station), #63 Atlanta University Ctr. (Vine City station), or #13 West Fair.

FIND YOUR WAY

From I-75 N. and S., take I-20 West and exit at Lee St. Turn right on to Lee St. and continue through the next traffic light (Westview Dr.). You will see a large parking lot on the right-hand side. Turn right into the first driveway and you will approach the gates of Spelman College. **From I-20 W.,** exit at Ashby St. Go across Ashby St. and continue on Oak St. to the next traffic light. Turn left onto Lee St. and cross the bridge over I-20. Continue through the next 2 traffic lights. You will see a large parking lot on the right-hand side. Turn right into the first driveway and you will approach the gates of Spelman College. **From I-20 E.,** exit at Lee St. Turn right onto Lee St. and continue through the next light (Westview Dr.). You will see a large parking lot on the right-hand side. Turn right into the first driveway and you will approach the gates of Spelman College. **From downtown Atlanta**, take Peachtree Streets south to Martin Luther King Jr. Dr. and turn right. Continue on M.L. King Jr. Dr. to Northside and turn left. Continue on Northside through next 3 traffic lights (passing Burger King on the right). Turn right at the 4th traffic light (Greensfery Ave.). Continue on Greensfery through the stop sign. Turn left into the gate of Spelman College.

STAY THE NIGHT

The **Sheraton Atlanta Hotel** is a full service hotel located in the heart of downtown Atlanta. This is a 765-room hotel with a 24-hour fitness center and indoor swimming pool. Three on-site restaurants allow for formal or casual dining. This hotel is conveniently located near the major highways and is a 7-minute drive from Spelman's campus. The **Regency Suites** is located in Midtown and is about a 10-minute drive from campus. There are several other resorts, hotels, and inns in the area. Please contact CONNECTIONS at 800-262-9974 for information and reservations on these and other properties. Please ask them about the Spelman Educational Rate offered by many of the hotels.

HIGHLIGHTS

ON CAMPUS
- Sister's Chapel
- The Spelman College Art Museum
- Camille Olivia Hanks-Cosby Academic Center
- State-of-the-art science center
- The Oval and Alumni Arch

OFF CAMPUS
- Historic Auburn Avenue
- Stone Mountain Park
- Six Flags, Georgia
- Centennial Olympic Park
- Martin Luther King, Jr.Center for Nonviolent Social Change

UNIVERSITY OF GEORGIA

Office of Undergraduate Admissions, University of Georgia, 212 Terrell Hall,
Athens, GA 30602 • Telephone: 706-542-2112 • Web: www.uga.edu •
Email: under2@admissions.uga.edu

Hours: Monday-Friday, 9AM-5PM. Closed weekends and national and state holidays.

The University of Georgia has made many efforts to better itself in recent years, and boasts an especially reward-ing and selective Honors Program.

HIGHLIGHTS

ON CAMPUS
- The Arch
- Sanford Stadium
- Ramsey Student Center for Physical Activities
- The Chapel
- Tate Student Center

OFF CAMPUS
- Downtown Athens
- Botanical Gardens
- Classic Center
- Milledge Avenue
- Bishop Park

TRANSPORTATION

Hartsfield International Airport in Atlanta is an hour and a half from campus. Athens has its own small commuter airport, which is served by USAir.

FIND YOUR WAY

From Atlanta, take I-85 to Highway 316 (University Pkwy.). This con-nects to the Athens Bypass, which leads to downtown Athens or call the Visitors Center at College Station Rd.

STAY THE NIGHT

Nearby: You can stay on campus at the **Center for Continuing Education** (706-548-1311). A double room is inexpensive and you can use the pool and weight room. Across the street, the **Holiday Inn** (Broad and Lumpkin St.; 706-549-4433) has moderate rates, an indoor pool, an exercise room, and a restaurant. A cheaper choice is the **Marriot Court Yard** (166 Finley St.; 706-369-7000), which serves a continental breakfast.

A little farther: Eight miles away is **Rivendell Bed & Breakfast** (3581 Barnett Shoals, Watkinsville; 706-769-4522) where, at an inexpensive rate, you can enjoy a very pleasant ambi-ence and a full southern breakfast. The house boasts beautiful walking trails and a picnic area, and is situated on the river.

AT A GLANCE

Selectivity Rating		83
Range SAT I Math		560-650
Average SAT I Math		597
Range SAT I Verbal		550-650
Average SAT I Verbal		598
Average GPA		3.6
Student to Faculty Ratio		15:1

CAMPUS TOURS

Appointment Req?	No
Dates	Year-round, except on holidays
Times	Mon-Fri 9AM, 1:15PM, and 3PM; Sat 10:30AM and 2:30PM; Sun 2:30PM
Avg. Length	90 min

ON-CAMPUS INTERVIEWS

Admissions

Start Date–Juniors	N/A
Appointment Req?	N/A
Advance Notice	N/A
Saturdays?	N/A
Avg. Length	N/A
Info Sessions	Year-round, Mon-Fri, except on holidays

Faculty and Coaches

Dates/Times	Year-round; subject to faculty/coach availability
Arrangements	Contact faculty/coach 2 weeks prior

CLASS VISITS

Dates	Year-round (Mon-Fri)
Arrangements	See professor prior to class

OVERNIGHT DORM STAYS

Advance Notice	N/A
Arrangements	N/A
Limitations	Available only through personal contact with current students

1- Idaho State University

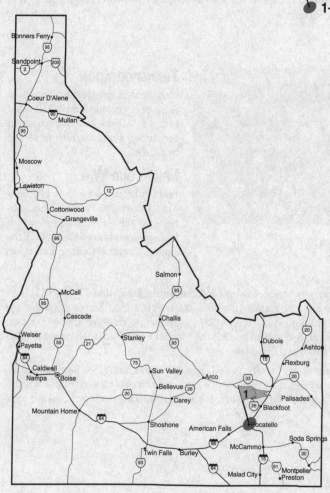

Idaho	Idaho State Univ.	Boise
Idaho State Univ.	—	234
Boise	234	—

IDAHO STATE UNIVERSITY

Office of Enrollment Planning and Academic Services, Idaho State University, P.O. Box 8054, Pocatello, ID 83209-8270 (The office is in the Administration Building) • Telephone: 208-282-3277 • Web: www.isu.edu • Email: echamike@isu.edu

Hours: Mon, Wed, Thurs, and Fri, 8AM-5PM; Tues, 8AM-7PM. Closed weekends and holidays.

Educating almost 12,000 traditional and nontraditional students, Idaho State provides a wide range of educational options, from traditional liberal arts programs to vocational and career offerings at its main campus location in Pocatello, Idaho. The Craft Shop in the student union offers everything from pottery and weaving to leatherworking classes.

HIGHLIGHTS

ON CAMPUS
- Idaho Museum of Natural History
- Rock Climbing Wall at Reed Gym
- Holt Arena
- Wilderness Center
- Particle Accelerator

OFF CAMPUS
- Ross Park Aquatic Center
- Pocatello Pump at Ross Park
- Mink Creek Recreation Area
- Justice Park Camping and Picnic Area
- Lava Hot Springs

TRANSPORTATION

Situated approximately 10 miles from campus is the Pocatello Regional Airport. Call the Office of Enrollment. Taxis are available for transportation from airport to campus; call 208-232-1115.

FIND YOUR WAY

From I-20, take the Clark St. exit and turn west into town on Clark St. to 8th Ave. Turn left on 8th Ave. and proceed to the stop light at 8th and Martin Luther King Jr. Way, then turn right.

STAY THE NIGHT

Accommodations in Pocatello offer convenience and value, but nothing out of the ordinary. Two very basic, quite inexpensive hotels are situated just across the street from the university. Frequented regularly by university visitors, the **Econolodge** (835 S. 5th Ave.; 208-233-0451) offer special rates. If you're craving hustle and bustle, you might try the **Cavanaughs** (2055 Pocatello Creek; 208-233-2200), a 5-minute drive away. It has restaurants, an indoor pool, a weight room, a sauna, and evening entertainment in the lounge. Rooms are only slightly more expensive than the 2 choices listed above. About 5 miles away is a **Holiday Inn** (1399 Bench Rd.; 208-237-1400) with an indoor pool, miniature golf, ping pong, a whirlpool and sauna, and fitness center privileges. **Ameritel** (1440 Bench Rd.; 208-234-7500) has a 24-hour pool, hot tub, and exercise room. It offers a deluxe continental breakfast and free HBO.

AT A GLANCE

Average ACT Composite	22
Student to Faculty Ratio	17:1

CAMPUS TOURS

Appointment Req?	Yes
Dates	Year-round, except on holidays
Times	Mon-Fri by appointment
Avg. Length	1 hour

ON-CAMPUS INTERVIEWS

Admissions

Start Date–Juniors	N/A
Appointment Req?	N/A
Advance Notice	N/A
Saturdays?	N/A
Avg. Length	N/A
Info Sessions	Contact admissions off.

Faculty and Coaches

Dates/Times	Year-round; subject to faculty/coach availability
Arrangements	Contact Enrollment Planning and Academic Services at 208-282-3277 7-10 days prior

CLASS VISITS

Dates	Year-round (Mon-Fri)
Arrangements	Contact Off. of Enrollment Planning and Academic Services at 208-282-3277

OVERNIGHT DORM STAYS

Advance Notice	7-10 days
Arrangements	Contact Off. of Enrollment Planning and Academic Services
Limitations	2-night maximum stay; up to 3 free meal tickets

ILLINOIS

1- University of Chicago
   Illinois Institute of Technology
2- University of Illinois—
   Champaign-Urbana
3- Knox College
4- Lake Forest College
5- Northwestern University
6- Wheaton College

Illinois	Illinois Inst. Tech.	Knox Coll.	Lake Forest Coll.	Northwestern Univ.	Univ. Chicago	Univ. Illinois-Champ.	Wheaton Coll.	Chicago	Peoria	Springfield
Illinois Inst. Tech.	—	198	32	17	3	143	34	0	152	198
Knox Coll.	198	—	221	206	196	139	183	184	53	106
Lake Forest Coll.	32	221	—	15	34	176	53	20	182	230
Northwestern Univ.	17	206	15	—	19	161	38	10	167	215
Univ. Chicago	3	196	34	19	—	140	37	0	155	195
Univ. Illinois-Champ.	143	139	176	161	140	—	158	135	92	198
Wheaton Coll.	34	183	53	38	37	158	—	16	143	182
Chicago	0	184	20	10	0	135	16	—	170	202
Peoria	152	53	182	167	155	92	143	170	—	74
Springfield	198	106	230	215	195	198	182	202	74	—

ILLINOIS INSTITUTE OF TECHNOLOGY

Office of Undergraduate Admissions, Illinois Institute of Technology, 10 W. 33rd St., Chicago, IL 60616 • Telephone: 800-448-2329 • Web: www.iit.edu • Email: admission@iit.edu

Hours: Monday-Friday, 8:30AM-5PM; also September-May: Saturday, 9AM-noon. Closed Sundays and holidays.

IIT—a demanding math and science–oriented school on the South Side of Chicago—requires students to complete two Interprofessional Projects before graduation. IPROs, as they're known, bring together undergrads and grad students from different academic disciplines to complete a task as a team. Recent IPROs have ranged from designing a new football stadium for the Chicago Bears to improving automated patient monitoring systems.

HIGHLIGHTS

ON CAMPUS
- S. R. Crown Hall
- McComick Tribune Center
- HUB rec center
- IIT Research Institute

OFF CAMPUS
- Comiskey Park
- Sears Tower
- Hancock Center
- Magnificent Mile
- Oprah Studios

TRANSPORTATION

Chicago's Midway Airport is 10 miles from campus; O'Hare International Airport is 25 miles from campus. CTA/Transit/Taxis are available at both airports. Take the Blue Line from O'Hare to the Green Line to campus. Take the Orange line from Midway, transfer to the Green Line to campus. Amtrak trains and Greyhound/Trailways buses provide service to Chicago's Loop area. For public transportation within Chicago, use either the CTA north-south subway or the CTA Lake/Dan Ryan rapid transit. On the CTA north-south subway, take the Englewood A train or the Jackson Park B train and get off at the ITT/Bronsville stop. Turn right onto State St. and walk 2 blocks north to the 33rd St. exit. Turn left onto 33rd St. to Perlstein Hall. On the CTA Lake/Dan Ryan rapid transit, take the A or B train and get off at ITT/Bronsville stop. Proceed north to the 33rd St. exit. Turn right onto 33rd St.

FIND YOUR WAY

From the Dan Ryan Expy./I-90/94, take the 31st St. exit. Go east on 31st about 1 block to State St. Turn right at State and proceed to 33rd St. and turn right. Perlstein Hall is on the NW corner of 33rd and State Sts. **From Lake Shore Dr.**, exit at 31st St.; turn right onto 31st and proceed west to State St. Turn left (south) on State for 2 blocks to 33rd St. and turn right to Perlstein Hall. **From Stevenson Expy./I-55 or Eisenhower Expy./I-290**, exit at the Dan Ryan Expy. (Indiana exit) and proceed south to the 31st St. ramp and exit the expressway. Go south to 33rd St. and turn left (east) to Perlstein Hall.

STAY THE NIGHT

Located on Chicago's famous "Magnificent Mile," in the heart of the city's business and shopping district, the **Hotel Intercontinental** (505 North Michigan Ave.; 312-321-8880) features a full fitness center and a junior Olympic-sized swimming pool. One block off "Magnificent Mile," **The Hyatt Regency Chicago** has a whopping 2,019 rooms and is attached to the 83-acre Illinois Center complex containing over 100 stores and 43 restaurants. For considerably less money, **The Days Inn** (644 North Lake Shore Dr.; 312-943-9200 or 800-541-3223 outside 312 and 708 area codes) is only 4 blocks from "Magnificent Mile" and offers views of Lake Michigan. There is also the **Best Western Grant Park Hotel** (1100 South Michigan Ave.; 312-922-2900), which offers safe, affordable, no frills lodging. To obtain a discounted rate at any of the above hotels, mention the Illinois Institute of Technology when making reservations. Also, airport to hotel and hotel to airport transportation can be arranged via Continental Air Transport. For schedule information call 312-454-7800; for reservations call 312-454-7799 or 800-654-7871.

AT A GLANCE

Selectivity Rating	83
Range SAT I Math	640-730
Average SAT I Math	676
Range SAT I Verbal	580-680
Average SAT I Verbal	630
Average ACT Composite	27
Average GPA	3.8
Student to Faculty Ratio	12:1

CAMPUS TOURS

Appointment Req?	No
Dates	Year-round
Times	Mon-Fri 12PM; Sat by appointment
Avg. Length	45-60 min

ON-CAMPUS INTERVIEWS

Admissions

Start Date–Juniors	Any time
Appointment Req?	Yes
Advance Notice	2 weeks
Saturdays?	Yes, but only during fall and spring semesters
Avg. Length	30 min
Info Sessions	Year round

Faculty and Coaches

Dates/Times	Year-round; subject to faculty/coach availability
Arrangements	Contact admissions off. 2 weeks prior

CLASS VISITS

Dates	Year-round (Mon-Fri)
Arrangements	Contact resident life office

OVERNIGHT DORM STAYS

Advance Notice	3 weeks
Arrangements	Contact admissions off.
Limitations	Subject to availability

KNOX COLLEGE

Office of Admission, Knox College, 2 E. South St., Galesburg, IL 61401-4999 (The office is on the 1st floor of the Center for the Fine Arts) • Telephone: 800-678-KNOX or 309-431-7100 • Web: www.knox.edu • Email: admission@knox.edu

Hours: September-May: Monday-Friday, 8AM-4PM; Saturday, 8AM-noon. June-August: Monday-Friday, 9AM-4PM.

Knox College, located in the rural reaches of central Illinois, places an emphasis on personal freedom. Knox students report receiving extremely generous financial aid packages and they praise the trimester system and take advantage of long breaks between sessions.

AT A GLANCE

Selectivity Rating	81
Range SAT I Math	550-650
Range SAT I Verbal	550-680
Student to Faculty Ratio	12:1

CAMPUS TOURS

Appointment Req?	Yes
Dates	Year-round
Times	Weekdays as needed year-round during regular admission off. hours; also Sat mornings during academic year
Avg. Length	60 min

ON-CAMPUS INTERVIEWS

Admissions

Start Date–Juniors	April 1
Appointment Req?	Yes
Advance Notice	1 week
Saturdays?	Yes, on a limited basis
Avg. Length	45 min
Info Sessions	Academic year

Faculty and Coaches

Dates/Times	Year-round; subject to faculty/coach availability
Arrangements	Contact admission off. 1 week prior

CLASS VISITS

Dates	Academic year (Mon, Wed, Fri)
Arrangements	Contact admission off.

OVERNIGHT DORM STAYS

Advance Notice	1 week
Arrangements	Contact admission off.
Limitations	1-night stay; seniors only

TRANSPORTATION

Greater Peoria Airport in Peoria and Quad Cities Airport in Moline are 40-minute drives from campus. The admissions office will send a representative to pick up visitors arriving at either airport; call 800-678-KNOX or 309-341-7100 at least 1 week in advance to make pickup arrangements. Amtrak trains provide daily service from Chicago and from the west to Galesburg train station. A college representative will pick you up at the station and escort you to campus. Call the admission office at least one week in advance to make pickup arrangements.

FIND YOUR WAY

From the north, take I-74 E. to Exit 46; take U.S. Rte. 34 W. to the Seminary St. exit. Turn left on Seminary St. and proceed to Main St. Turn left onto Main St. and proceed to Cherry St. Turn left on Cherry St. and cross South St. to the parking lot at the corner of Cherry and Berrien Streets. **From the south,** take I-74 W. to Exit 48A (Main St.). Take Main St. to Cherry St. Turn left on Cherry St. and cross South St. to the parking lot at the corner of Cherry and Berrien Streets.

STAY THE NIGHT

Galesburg offers a wide range of overnight accommodations, including some wonderful bed and breakfast options. **The Seacord House** (624 N. Cherry St.; 309-342-4107) is known for its hospitality and moderate prices. For a more upscale experience in Victorian luxury, try the **Fahnestock House** (591 N. Prairie St.; 309-344-0270) or the **Great House** (501 E. Losey St.; 309-342-8683). More conventional travelers will find comfortable, affordable accommodations with pool, breakfast, and other amenities at the **Country Inn and Suites** (907 W. Carl Sandburg Dr.; 309-344-4444), **Fairfield Inn** (905 W. Carl Sandburg Dr.; 309-344-1911), or **Holiday Inn Express** (East Main St. at I-74; 309-343-7100). You can also enjoy the Old World pleasures of a regional favorite, **Jumer's Continental Inn** (east Main St. at I-74; 309-343-7151), which offers Galesburg's only full-service hotel with fine dining, tavern, pool, and recreational facilities.

HIGHLIGHTS

ON CAMPUS
- Old Main (site of historic Lincoln-Douglas debates)
- Old Knox County Jail
- Seymour Library
- The Hard Knox Café
- T. Fleming Fieldhouse

OFF CAMPUS
- Carl Sandburg birthplace and state historic site
- Galesburg Railroad Museum
- Bishop Hill (national historic landmark)

LAKE FOREST COLLEGE

Admissions Office, Lake Forest College, 555 N. Sheridan Rd., Lake Forest, IL 60045
(The office is located in Patterson Lodge) • Telephone: 800-828-4751 or 847-735-5000 •
Web: www.lfc.edu • Email: admissions@lfc.edu

Hours: Monday-Friday, 8:30AM-5PM; Saturday, 9AM-noon (by appointment only in summer). Closed Sundays and major holidays.

Excellent academics, Division III sports, and financial aid set Lake Forest apart from the pack. The school also boasts an attractive campus, good grub, and a location on the well-to-do North Shore of Chicago.

HIGHLIGHTS

ON CAMPUS
- Donnelley Library
- Freeman Library
- Sonnenschein Gallery
- Sports center

OFF CAMPUS
- Bank Lane Bistro
- Chicago Botanic Garden
- Lake Region Historical Society
- Cuneo Museum and Gardens

TRANSPORTATION

Chicago's O'Hare International Airport is 25 miles from campus. Bus and limousine service are available from the airport. Call O'Hare Midway Limousine (847-234-4550) and ask for shared ride service a day in advance. Amtrak trains and Greyhound buses serve Chicago. The METRA/Chicago and North Western North Line commuter railroad serves Lake Forest.

FIND YOUR WAY

From the North, take I-94 S. from Milwaukee. Just past the Wisconsin-Illinois border, stay left to get onto U.S. Rte. 41. Continue south on U.S. 41 to Deerpath in Lake Forest. Exit and turn left (east) on Deerpath toward the town and the college. Proceed east through the Lake Forest business district and cross the railroad tracks. At the second stop sign beyond the tracks, you are at Sheridan Rd., facing the entrance to the college's North Campus. For Middle Campus and most college offices, turn right (south) onto Sheridan and go 1 block to College Rd. Turn left (east) into the college. The entrance to South Campus is at Maplewood and Sheridan. **From the West/Southwest,** take I-294 (Tri-State Tollway), which becomes I-94 N. to Illinois Rte. 60 (Town Line Rd.). Exit and turn right (east) on Rte. 60. At the first stop light, turn left (north) on Illinois 43 (Waukegan Rd.). At the first light, turn right (east) on Deerpath toward the town and the college. From Chicago, take I-94 N. (the Edens Expy) toward Waukegan. When I-94 splits off toward Milwaukee, stay on the Edens, which has become U.S. 41. Exit at Deerpath in Lake Forest and turn right (east) on Deerpath toward the town and the college.

STAY THE NIGHT

Our first choice for convenience and charm is the English-style **Deer Path Inn** (255 E. Illinois Rd.; 847-234-2280), a 10-minute walk from the college. Prices are expensive and include a full buffet breakfast. Less costly lodgings may be found at the **Highland Park Courtyard by Marriot** (2005 Lake Cook Rd., Highland Park; 847-831-3338), at the junction of U.S. 41 and I-94. Amenities include an indoor pool and an exercise room, and it's only 20 minutes from campus.

AT A GLANCE

Selectivity Rating	78
Range SAT I Math	510-620
Average SAT I Math	560
Range SAT I Verbal	510-620
Average SAT I Verbal	570
Average ACT Composite	25
Average GPA	3.4
Student to Faculty Ratio	13:1

CAMPUS TOURS

Appointment Req?	Yes
Dates	Year-round
Times	Mon-Sat
Avg. Length	1 hour

ON-CAMPUS INTERVIEWS

Admissions

Start Date—Juniors	Any time
Appointment Req?	Yes
Advance Notice	2-3 weeks
Saturdays?	Yes
Avg. Length	40 min
Info Sessions	N/A

Faculty and Coaches

Dates/Times	Year-round; subject to faculty/coach availability
Arrangements	Contact admissions off. 2-3 weeks prior

CLASS VISITS

Dates	Year-round (Mon-Fri)
Arrangements	Contact admissions off.

OVERNIGHT DORM STAYS

Advance Notice	3 weeks
Arrangements	Contact admissions off.
Limitations	1-night stay; not available on weekends

NORTHWESTERN UNIVERSITY

Admissions Office, Northwestern University, P.O. Box 3060, 1801 Hinman Ave., Evanston, IL 60204-3060 • Telephone: 847-491-7271 • Web: www.nwu.edu • Email: ug-admission@nwu.edu

Hours: Monday-Friday, 8:30AM-5PM; Saturday, 9AM-12:30PM (October-April only). Closed Sundays and holidays.

Located minutes from Chicago in Evanston, Illinois, academically tremendous Northwestern University provides a nationally respected, comprehensive, liberal arts education for about 8,000 largely traditional students.

AT A GLANCE

Selectivity Rating	98
Range SAT I Math	650-740
Average SAT I Math	700
Range SAT I Verbal	630-720
Average SAT I Verbal	680
Average ACT Composite	30
Student to Faculty Ratio	8:1

CAMPUS TOURS

Appointment Req?	No
Dates	Year-round, except Sundays & holidays
Times	Varies
Avg. Length	2 hours

ON-CAMPUS INTERVIEWS

Admissions

Start Date–Juniors	May 1
Appointment Req?	Yes
Advance Notice	4 weeks
Saturdays?	Yes, from Oct-Apr
Avg. Length	45 min
Info Sessions	Held in conjunction with campus tours

Faculty and Coaches

Dates/Times	Year-round; subject to faculty/coach availability
Arrangements	Contact faculty/coach 4-6 weeks prior

CLASS VISITS

Dates	Year-round (Mon-Fri)
Arrangements	Consult current class lists in admissions off.

OVERNIGHT DORM STAYS

Advance Notice	3 weeks
Arrangements	Contact director of on-campus programs in admissions off.
Limitations	Seniors only except for special programs; 1-night stay only Mon-Fri

TRANSPORTATION

O'Hare International Airport in Chicago is 18 miles from campus. Bus service is available from the airport to Northwestern's Foster Walker Complex (and to Evanston's Holiday Inn and Omni Orrington Hotel). Amtrak trains and Greyhound/Trailways buses provide service to Chicago. From there, take the CTA rapid-transit system to Howard St. and transfer to the Evanston train. Get off at the Davis St. stop and walk east on Davis St. to Orrington Ave.; walk north on Orrington to Clark St., then east on Clark to Hinman Ave. and the admissions office.

FIND YOUR WAY

From I-94 (Edens Expy.), take the Dempster St. east exit. From Dempster, head north on Hinman Ave. to the admissions office (at Clark St.).

STAY THE NIGHT

Nearby: There's a range of choices in Evanston. The **Omni Orrington Hotel** (1710 Orrington Ave.; 847-866-8700) is one block from the southern tip of the university. Its rates are expensive, although on the weekends you may be able to get a moderate rate. The **Margarita Inn** (2066 Oak Ave.; 847-869-2273), a Georgian-style inn close to Lake Michigan with reduced-fee access to the YMCA, is much more affordable. **Homestead** (1625 Hinman Ave.; 847-475-3300), just 2 blocks south of the campus and the lake, has 10 guest rooms and a French restaurant. Another bargain is **Holiday Inn** (2001 Sherman Ave.; 847-491-6400), just 4 blocks from campus. Its rates include a breakfast buffet. A **Howard Johnson's Motor Lodge** (9333 Skokie Blvd., Skokie; 847-679-4200) is about a 20-minute drive from school. Its rates also are in the moderate range, with a complimentary breakfast buffet. Other alternatives are the **Hampton Inn and Suites** (Old Orchard Rd.; 847-583-1111) and the **Best Western Hawthorne Terrace** (3434 N. Broadway Ave.; 888-675-BEST.)

A little farther: Check the University of Chicago entry for alternatives a little farther afield in Chicago. Winnetka, covered in the Lake Forest College entry, is not too far north of Evanston, and **Chateau Des Fleurs** listed there might interest you.

HIGHLIGHTS

ON CAMPUS
- Shakespeare Garden
- Deanborn Observatory
- Norris Student Center
- Henry Crown Sports Pavilion
- Lake Michigan

OFF CAMPUS
- The Charles Gates Dawes House Museum
- The Mitchell Museum of the American Indian
- Evanston Art Center
- Grosse Point Lighthouse

UNIVERSITY OF CHICAGO

Admissions Office, University of Chicago, 1116 E. 59th St., Chicago, IL 60637
(The office is in Harper Memorial Library Building) • Telephone: 312-702-8650 •
Web: www.uchicago.edu • Email: college-admissions@uchicago.edu

Hours: Monday-Friday, 8:30AM-5PM; also Oct.-Feb.: Saturday, 8:30AM-1PM. Closed Sundays and holidays.

A rigorous core curriculum consumes about one-third of the total credits required for graduation at the storied University of Chicago. Authors Kurt Vonnegut, Jr. and Susan Sontag are alums.

HIGHLIGHTS

ON CAMPUS	OFF CAMPUS
• Joseph Regenstein Library	• Art Institute of Chicago
• David & Alfred Smart Museum of Art	• Shedd Aquarium
• Bartlett Gymnasium	• Museum of Science & Industry
• Court Theatre	• Comiskey Park and the Chicago White Sox
	• Adler Planetarium & Astronomy Museum

TRANSPORTATION

Chicago's Midway Airport is 10 miles from campus. The C.W. Airport Service Bus (312-493-2700) provides service to Ida Noyes Hall on campus. Taxis also are available for the ride to campus. O'Hare is a 1-hour drive from campus. The C.W. Airport Service Bus also travels from O'Hare to campus regularly throughout the day and evening. From Palmer House, take a taxi or an Illinois Central train to campus (see below). Amtrak trains provide service to Chicago's Loop area. From there, take a taxi directly to campus or take the #207 bus or a taxi to a Metra commuter train station on Michigan Ave. Greyhound/Trailways buses also serve the Loop area. From the bus stations, walk east to Michigan Ave. and take the train. The train stops in the Loop area at Michigan Ave. and Randolph St. and at Michigan Ave. and Van Buren St. The station entrances are on the west side of the street and are well marked. Take a southbound train and get off at 59th St. Walk about 6 blocks west to the admissions office.

FIND YOUR WAY

From major routes near Chicago, take an expressway to I-55 N. (the Stevenson Expressway). Take I-55 N. to Lake Shore Dr. S. (U.S. Rte. 41). Follow Lake Shore Dr. S. to the 57th St. exit (Museum of Science and Industry). Follow the curve (Cornell Dr.) to the 4th right turn, the Midway Plaisance. Take the Midway approximately 6 blocks west to Woodlawn Ave.; turn right on Woodlawn for 1 block, then turn left on 59th St. at Rockefeller Chapel. Follow 59th St. for a block and a half to the admissions office.

STAY THE NIGHT

The **International House** (1414 E. 59th St.; 312-753-2270) has single rooms available in a dorm-style atmosphere on campus at a very inexpensive rate during the summer months (through mid-September). Rooms also may be available later in the academic year. Fairly close to campus is the **Ramada Inn Lake Shore** (4900 S. Lake Shore Dr.; 312-288-5800), with student rates in the moderate range (if available). Two reasonably priced hotels are located about 5 miles from campus. The **Blackstone Hotel** (636 S. Michigan Ave.; 312-427-4300) has an inexpensive student rate that includes a continental breakfast. The **Best Western Grant Park Hotel** (1100 S. Michigan Ave.; 312-922-2900) is within walking distance to most museums and shops. Rates are lower during the week and package specials are available—check for details.

AT A GLANCE

Selectivity Rating	94
Range SAT I Math	640-740
Range SAT I Verbal	650-750
Student to Faculty Ratio	4:1

CAMPUS TOURS

Appointment Req?	No
Dates	Year-round
Times	Through Dec 10: 10:30AM and 1:30PM. Dec 13-Feb 25: 10:30AM. Feb 28-June 2: 10:30AM and 1:30PM. Saturdays Sept 18-Nov 20: 9:30AM and 11:30AM.
Avg. Length	1 hour

ON-CAMPUS INTERVIEWS

Admissions

Start Date—Juniors	June
Appointment Req?	Yes
Advance Notice	1 week
Saturdays?	Sept 18-Nov 20
Avg. Length	45 min
Info Sessions	Year-round

Faculty and Coaches

Dates/Times	Year-round; subject to faculty/coach availability
Arrangements	Interviews usually are arranged on the day of visit; contact faculty/coach

CLASS VISITS

Dates	Oct-June
Arrangements	Set up visits when on campus

OVERNIGHT DORM STAYS

Advance Notice	2 weeks
Arrangements	Contact admissions off.
Limitations	Thurs and Fri nights; must arrive in admissions off. before 4:30PM

UNIVERSITY OF ILLINOIS—URBANA-CHAMPAIGN

Admissions Office, University of Illinois, 901 West Illinois, Urbana, IL 61801 • Telephone: 217-333-0302 • Web: www.uiuc.edu • Email: admissions@oar.uiuc.edu

Hours: Monday-Friday, 8:30AM-5PM. Closed weekends and holidays.

The University of Illinois is a very big state school with a very big Greek system that is a great bargain for in-state students (which is pretty much everybody). A good education is easily within reach here for students who don't need to be led by the hand to find it. Film critic Roger Ebert is an alum.

AT A GLANCE

Selectivity Rating	85
Range SAT I Math	590-710
Average SAT I Math	644
Range SAT I Verbal	550-650
Average SAT I Verbal	605
Average ACT Composite	27
Student to Faculty Ratio	16:1

CAMPUS TOURS

Appointment Req?	Yes, call 217-333-0824
Dates	Year-round
Times	Mon-Fri 10AM and 1PM
Avg. Length	1 hour

ON-CAMPUS INTERVIEWS

Admissions

Start Date—Juniors	N/A
Appointment Req?	N/A
Advance Notice	N/A
Saturdays?	N/A
Avg. Length	N/A
Info Sessions	Year-round

Faculty and Coaches

| Dates/Times | Year-round; subject to faculty/coach availability |
| Arrangements | Contact Campus Visitors Center at 217-333-0824 2 weeks prior |

CLASS VISITS

| Dates | During academic year (Mon-Fri) |
| Arrangements | Contact Campus Visitors Center |

OVERNIGHT DORM STAYS

Advance Notice	N/A
Arrangements	N/A
Limitations	N/A

TRANSPORTATION

Willard Airport, owned and operated by the University, is 5 miles from campus. Taxis, limousines, and rental cars are available at the airport for the trip to campus. Amtrak provides daily service to Champaign from Chicago and from the south (through Memphis). The Amtrak station is in downtown Champaign, approximately 1 mile from campus. Taxis and city bus services are available from the station. Greyhound/Trailways provide national and regional service to Champaign. The bus station is 1 mile from campus.

FIND YOUR WAY

From I-74 (E. and W.), take the Lincoln Ave. exit. Turn south on Lincoln Ave.; after 1.75 miles, turn right onto Illinois St. Proceed for 1 block to the Campus Visitors Center on the left in the Levis Faculty Center. **From the north**, head south on I-57 to I-74. Head east on I-74 to the Lincoln Ave. exit; then follow the preceding directions from that point. **From the south**, head north on I-57 to Exit 235, the junction with I-72. Head east; as you arrive in Champaign, I-72 becomes University Ave. Follow University Ave. east through Champaign, into Urbana, to Lincoln Ave. (approximately 3.5 miles). Turn right (south) on Lincoln; after the second light, turn right onto Illinois St. Proceed for 1 block to the Campus Visitors Center, which is on the left in the Levis Faculty Center.

STAY THE NIGHT

You have 2 choices right on campus. The **Quality Hotel** (302 John St., Champaign; 217-384-2100) offers a continental breakfast. Its sister hotel, the **Clarion** (2001 Neil St., Champaign; 217-352-7891), about a 10-minute drive from the admissions office, has an indoor pool, sauna, whirlpool, and weight room. Also on campus is **Illini Union** (1401 W. Green, Urbana; 217-333-1241), with rooms available at the low end of the moderate range. It's within walking distance of the campus tour, and has a bowling alley, eating facilities, and a game room. Several inexpensive choices are within 5 miles of the school. **Jumer's Castle Lodge** (Lincoln Square, Urbana; 217-384-8800) is less than 2 miles from the university and offers an indoor pool, sauna, and jacuzzi.

HIGHLIGHTS

ON CAMPUS
- The Krannert Art Museum
- The Krannert Center for Performing Arts
- Assembly hall
- The Beckman Institute
- The Japan House

OFF CAMPUS
- Lake of the Woods Park
- Allerton Park
- The Virginia Theater
- Tuscola Outlet Mall
- Jarlings Custard Cup

WHEATON COLLEGE

Admissions Office, Wheaton College, Student Services Building, Second Floor, North End, Suite 201, 501 E. College Ave., Wheaton, IL 60187 • Telephone: 800-222-2419 • Web: www.wheaton.edu • Email: admissions@wheaton.edu

Hours: Monday-Friday, 8AM-5PM; Saturday, 8:30AM-noon (only selected Saturdays). Closed Sundays and holidays.

Wheaton College is an ultra-religious school in the far-flung reaches of suburban Chicago.

HIGHLIGHTS

ON CAMPUS
- Billy Graham Center (archive, museum)
- Wade Center (collection of English authors, including C. S. Lewis)

OFF CAMPUS
- Ravinia Music Festival
- Art Institute
- Chicago Field Museum
- Wheaton is 25 miles outside of Chicago
- Sears Tower and Hancock Building

TRANSPORTATION

O'Hare International Airport in Chicago is 20 miles from campus. Call Airtran O'Hare (800-851-0200) to arrange for transportation from the airport to campus. Amtrak trains and Greyhound/Trailways buses also serve Chicago.

FIND YOUR WAY

From the east, take I-88 W. and exit at Naperville Rd. Go north to Roosevelt Rd. in Wheaton. Turn east and go 2 blocks to Chase St. Turn north and go 9 blocks to 418 Chase. **From the south**, take I-55 N. to I-355 N.; exit I-355 to Roosevelt Rd. (Rte. 38). Proceed west to Chase St. in Wheaton. Turn north and go 9 blocks to 418 Chase. **From the west**, take I-88, Rte. 56 (Butterfield Rd.) east to Naperville Rd., then go north to Roosevelt Rd. in Wheaton. Turn east 2 blocks to Chase St. Turn north to 418 Chase. **From the north**, take the Tri-state Tollway 294 S. to I-88. Go west on I-88 to the Naperville Road exit. Proceed north to Roosevelt Rd. in Wheaton. Turn east and go 2 blocks to Chase St. Turn north and go 9 blocks to 418 Chase.

STAY THE NIGHT

Nearby: The **Wheaton Inn** (301 W. Roosevelt Rd.; 630-690-2600), 1 mile from the college, is your closest and most expensive option. (All the rooms have telephones in the bathroom and down duvets.) You will find lower rates (with the special rate for college visitors) about 3 miles from the campus at the **Carol Stream Holiday Inn** (200 S. Gary Ave., Carol Stream; 630-665-3000). For a very small additional charge you can obtain a pass to the Wheaton Sports Center. You have several other choices about 5 miles to the south of campus. Two of these are the moderately priced **Hilton Inn** (3003 Corporate West Dr., Lyle/Naperville; 630-505-0900 or 800-HILTONS) and the less expensive **Courtyard By Marriott** (1205 E. Diehl Rd., Naperville; 630-505-0550 or 800-321-2211). Both have indoor pools and exercise rooms. A more basic and less expensive option is **Travel Lodge** (1617 N. Naperville-Wheaton Rd., Naperville; 630-505-0200 or 800-255-3050), also 5 miles away. Here the inexpensive rate (a special rate for college visitors) includes a continental breakfast.

A little farther: The **Harrison House Bed and Breakfast** (26 N. Eagle St., Naperville; 630-355-4665) is within walking distance of shops, restaurants, and the historic Naperville settlement. Harrison House has moderate rates that include a full breakfast. Golf courses and antique stores are in the area. Wheaton is due west of Chicago. If you want more urban alternatives, check the entries for the University of Chicago and Northwestern.

AT A GLANCE

Selectivity Rating	91
Range SAT I Math	600-700
Range SAT I Verbal	610-720
Average GPA	3.7
Student to Faculty Ratio	12:1

CAMPUS TOURS

Appointment Req?	No
Dates	Year-round
Times	Sept-May: Mon-Fri 3 tours daily; selected Saturdays 11:30AM
Avg. Length	1 hour

ON-CAMPUS INTERVIEWS

Admissions

Start Date–Juniors	Aug 15 before senior year
Appointment Req?	Yes
Advance Notice	2 weeks
Saturdays?	Only on selected mornings
Avg. Length	45 min
Info Sessions	Year-round

Faculty and Coaches

Dates/Times	Year-round; subject to faculty/coach availability
Arrangements	Contact admissions off. 2 weeks prior

CLASS VISITS

Dates	Year-round (Mon-Fri)
Arrangements	Contact admissions off.

OVERNIGHT DORM STAYS

Advance Notice	2 weeks
Arrangements	Contact admissions off.
Limitations	1 or 2 nights

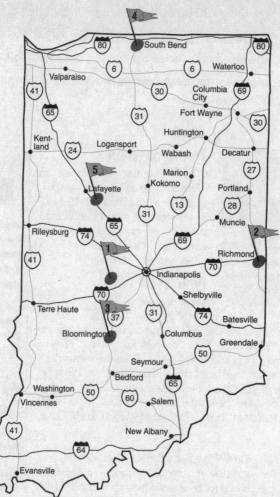

4
South Bend

80   80

6   6   Waterloo

Valparaiso

41

30   Columbia
                City   69

65

31   Fort Wayne

Huntington   30

Kent-   27
land   24   Logansport   Wabash   Decatur

5   Marion
                  Kokomo
Lafayette   Portland
                          13   28

31   Muncie
                    69

Rileysburg   74   2
                          Richmond
41   1
                              70
                    Indianapolis

              70   Shelbyville

Terre Haute   3   74   Batesville
              37   31

Bloomington   Columbus   Greendale

                          50
          Seymour
Washington   Bedford   65
          60   Salem
50
Vincennes

41

64

Evansville

1- DePauw University
2- Earlham College
3- Indiana University
4- University of Notre Dame
5- Purdue University

Indiana	DePauw Univ.	Earlham Coll.	Indiana Univ.	Purdue Univ.	Univ. Notre Dame	Fort Wayne	Gary	Indianapolis
DePauw Univ.	—	108	46	59	176	165	145	36
Earlham Coll.	108	—	122	135	173	94	226	73
Indiana Univ.	46	122	—	105	198	174	198	51
Purdue Univ.	59	135	105	—	110	117	90	55
Univ. Notre Dame	176	173	198	110	—	79	58	140
Fort Wayne	165	94	174	117	79	—	132	132
Gary	145	226	198	90	58	132	—	153
Indianapolis	36	73	51	55	140	132	153	—

DePauw University

Office of Admission, DePauw University, 101 East Seminary St., Greencastle, IN 46135 • Telephone: 800-447-2495 or 765-658-4006 • Web: www.depauw.edu • Email: admissions@depauw.edu

Hours: Sept.-May: Monday-Friday, 8AM-4:30PM; Saturday, 9AM-noon. June-Aug.: Monday-Friday, 8AM-4PM. Closed holidays.

DePauw's unique Winter Term and its excellent financial assistance separate this small liberal arts school from the pack (many students say they chose DePauw over the likes of Harvard and Vanderbilt because they couldn't pass up the bargain). A gargantuan Greek system provides most campus social life. Dan Quayle and Vernon Jordan are two of DePauw's prominent alums.

HIGHLIGHTS

ON CAMPUS
- DePauw University School of Music
- Roy O. West Library, music library, and the Prevo Science Library
- McKim Observatory

OFF CAMPUS
- Billie Creek Village
- Cagles Mill Lake
- Turkey Run State Park

TRANSPORTATION

Indianapolis International Airport is 45 miles from campus. The admissions office will provide transportation to campus for students traveling alone; call 800-447-2495 10 days to 2 weeks in advance to arrange for this service.

FIND YOUR WAY

From I-70, exit to State Road 231 N. and proceed 7.5 miles into Greencastle. Turn left on Seminary Street. Travel 3 city blocks. The admission office is located on the north side of the road with visitor parking to the east of the building.

STAY THE NIGHT

Nearby: The **Walden Inn** (2 Seminary Sq.; 317-653-2761) is a small hotel adjacent to DePauw's campus (within walking distance of the admissions office). Prices are moderate. Ask about the Gourmet Get-Away package, which includes dinner and champagne. You will also be able to use the university's athletic facilities, including an indoor swimming pool and tennis courts. The inn's dining room, the Different Drummer, is known throughout the state. Another lovely spot on campus is **Seminary Place Bed & Breakfast** (210 E. Seminary St.; 317-653-3177 or 317-653-9277). The moderate price includes a full breakfast with homemade breads and cakes. There is also a 2-room suite in the moderate range and a very elegant suite with a whirlpool for two at the low end of the expensive range.

A little farther: There are 3 motels in Cloverdale (8 miles south of Greencastle where I-70 meets Rte. 231), all with inexpensive rooms: the **Briana Inn** (R.R. 2; 317-795-3004); the **Dollar Inn** (R.R. 2; 317-795-6900); and the **Holiday Inn** (I-70 and Rte. 231; 317-795-3500 or 800-HOLIDAY). The Holiday Inn is a little more expensive than the others, but its price includes a buffet breakfast. **Days Inn** (Rte. 1; 317-795-6400), 9 miles south of the university, has very inexpensive rates. Its special rates for DePauw visitors include a continental breakfast.

AT A GLANCE

Selectivity Rating	85
Range SAT I Math	560-650
Range SAT I Verbal	550-650
Average GPA	3.7
Student to Faculty Ratio	11:1

CAMPUS TOURS

Appointment Req?	Yes
Dates	Year-round
Times	Academic year: Mon-Fri 9AM, 11AM, 1PM, 2PM, and 3PM; Sat 9AM, 10AM, 11AM, and 12PM
Avg. Length	Weekday 1 hr, Sat 45 min

ON-CAMPUS INTERVIEWS

Admissions

Start Date–Juniors	After April 1
Appointment Req?	Yes
Advance Notice	1 week
Saturdays?	Only during the academic year
Avg. Length	45 min
Info Sessions	Available, but interviews are encouraged

Faculty and Coaches

Dates/Times	Year-round; subject to faculty/coach availability
Arrangements	Contact admissions off. 1 week prior

CLASS VISITS

Dates	Academic year (Mon-Fri)
Arrangements	Contact admissions off. 1 week prior

OVERNIGHT DORM STAYS

Advance Notice	2 weeks
Arrangements	Contact admissions off.
Limitations	Available to high school seniors only; Mon-Thurs nights; not during exam periods

EARLHAM COLLEGE

Admissions Office, Earlham College, National Rd. W., Richmond, IN 47374
(The office is in Bolling House on the east side of Campus) • Telephone: 800-EARLHAM
or 765-983-1600 • Web: www.earlham.edu • Email: admission@earlham.edu

Hours: Monday-Friday, 8AM-5PM; Saturday, 9AM-noon (September-May only). Closed Sundays and some holidays.

Everybody from the president to the professors to the students knows each other at Earlham College, a tiny Quaker-affiliated liberal arts school in Indiana. Earlhamites like the fact that their opinions are important to the administration, and that their classes are stimulating.

AT A GLANCE

Selectivity Rating	80
Range SAT I Math	500-630
Average SAT I Math	565
Range SAT I Verbal	520-660
Average SAT I Verbal	594
Average ACT Composite	24
Average GPA	3.3
Student to Faculty Ratio	11:1

CAMPUS TOURS

Appointment Req?	Yes
Dates	Year-round
Times	Mon-Fri 11AM and 3PM; Sat 10AM and 11AM
Avg. Length	1 hour

ON-CAMPUS INTERVIEWS

Admissions

Start Date—Juniors	April 1
Appointment Req?	Yes
Advance Notice	1 week
Saturdays?	Yes, but not during the summer
Avg. Length	45-60 min
Info Sessions	Year-round

Faculty and Coaches

Dates/Times	Year-round; subject to faculty/coach availability
Arrangements	Contact admissions off. 2 weeks prior

CLASS VISITS

Dates	Academic year (Mon-Fri)
Arrangements	Contact admissions off.

OVERNIGHT DORM STAYS

Advance Notice	2 weeks
Arrangements	Contact admissions off.
Limitationsh	1-night stay; Sun-Thurs; offered on a first-call, first-served basis; student visitors receive 2 comp meal tickets

TRANSPORTATION

Dayton International Airport in Ohio is approximately 40 miles from campus. For visiting students, the college provides complimentary round-trip shuttles between the airport and campus. Call 800-EARLHAM in advance to arrange for this transportation. Shuttles leave from and return to the airport at 2PM and 8PM (Ohio time), and run only during the academic year. Taxi service is also available from Safeway Taxi Company (800-829-4747) in Richmond or from Yellow Cab (937-228-1205) in Dayton. Greyhound bus service is available to Richmond. The college provides complimentary transportation to and from the bus terminal; contact the admissions office to arrange for this service.

FIND YOUR WAY

The usual approach to Richmond is from I-70. Take exit 149A S. to U.S. Rte. 40 W. Turn right at the stoplight; Earlham is on the left, approximately 3 city blocks after this turn. On-campus signs will direct you to the admissions office.

STAY THE NIGHT

Nearby: If you can, try to stay at the on-campus **Norwich Lodge** (765-983-2075) reached via a pleasant walk through the woods. Guests have full use of college facilities and can eat at the campus coffee shop or drive to restaurants in town. Prospective students can get meal tickets for student dining facilities. A lovely bed and breakfast, **The Lantz House Inn**, is located in Centerville, just 4 miles west of Earlham. Call 800-495-2689 and ask for the special Earlham rate. **Lee's Inn** (6030 National Rd. E.; 765-966-6559), a 20-minute drive from the college, is a moderately priced (breakfast included) lodging. It offers a variety of amenities, including queen-size beds and jacuzzis. Ask for the special rate for Earlham visitors. The Richmond area has several inexpensive motels: **Ramada Inn** (4700 National Rd. E.; 765-962-5551), 4 miles from the school, and **Holiday Inn** (5501 National Rd. E.; 765-966-7511), about 6 miles from school. Ask for special school rates at both.

A little farther: Richmond is just west of the Ohio border. In Ohio, there are some interesting bed-and-breakfast choices that would make sense if you had reason to be in or near Dayton before or after your Earlham visit. In Dayton, 1 hour from Earlham, is **Price's Steamboat House Bed-and-Breakfast** (6 Josie St.; 937-223-2444), a 22-room Victorian mansion. Steamboat House is listed on the National Register of Historic Homes and is in a quiet, historical district near downtown Dayton.

HIGHLIGHTS

ON CAMPUS
- Athletics and wellness center
- Joseph Moore Natural History Museum
- The Swing
- Trails and rope courses
- Equestrian center

OFF CAMPUS
- Whitewater Gorge
- Hayes Arboretum
- Whitewater State Park
- Wayne County Historic Museum
- Cope Environmental Center

INDIANA UNIVERSITY—BLOOMINGTON

Office of Admissions, Indiana University, 300 N. Jordan Ave.,
Bloomington, IN 47405 • Telephone: 812-855-0661 •
Web: www.iub.edu • Email: iuadmit@indiana.edu

Hours: Monday-Friday, 8AM-5PM; Saturday, 8AM-noon (phone is not answered on Saturday). Closed Sundays and holidays.

Indiana University, is home to top-notch business and journalism schools as well as a competitive School of Music. Socially, the Greek system and Hoosier basketball predominate.

HIGHLIGHTS

ON CAMPUS
- Indiana Memorial Union
- Art museum
- Lilly Library
- Assembly hall
- Student recreational sports center

OFF CAMPUS
- Downtown Square
- Kirkwood Avenue
- Brown County State Park
- Chorten/Tibetan Culture Center
- Lake Monroe

TRANSPORTATION

Indianapolis International Airport is 50 miles from campus. For transportation between the airport and campus, call either the Bloomington Shuttle Service (800-589-6004) or limousine services (800-888-4639, 812-339-7269, 800-589-6004). Greyhound Bus Lines also stop in Bloomington.

FIND YOUR WAY

From the north, take Indiana Rte. 37 S. to the first Bloomington exit (College Ave.), then drive approximately 3.5 miles to the second stoplight. Turn left on State Rte. 45/46 and drive a mile to the second stoplight (Indiana State Police Post on the corner) and turn right. Proceed to the next traffic light (approximately half a mile) and turn left onto 17th St. As you reach the crest of the hill, turn right onto Jordan Ave. Proceed on Jordan through 2 traffic lights; then, proceed through the next stop sign. The admissions office is immediately on the left. **From the west and southwest**, take Indiana Rte. 45 or 48; then turn left onto Indiana Rte. 37 bypass. Continue north, then turn right onto the Rte. 46 bypass. At the 4th light (Indiana State Police Post on the right), turn right and follow the preceding directions from the Indiana State Police Post. **From the east**, follow Indiana Rte. 46, which becomes E. 3rd St. in Bloomington. Follow 3rd St. to Jordan Ave. and turn right on Jordan. The admissions office is on the right, just past the circular intersection.

STAY THE NIGHT

Nearby: The only place within walking distance is the on-campus **Indiana Memorial Union** (900 E. Seventh St.; 812-855-2536). **The Union**, with approximately 186 guest rooms, is a University-owned facility. Rates are moderate, but bookings are tight. If you are visiting on a football weekend or holiday, be sure to reserve a place early.

A little farther: There are several chain hotel/motels in the area and a number of bed and breakfast facilities. The Monroe County Convention and Visitors Bureau can provide up-to-date information on hotel availability and special event activities (800-800-0037). Also, Bloomington is located within 20 to 45 minutes of 3 state parks: Brown County in Nashville (812-988-6406), McCormick's Creek in Spencer (812-829-4881), and Spring Mill in Mitchell (812-849-4129), all with lodge facilities.

AT A GLANCE

Selectivity Rating	74
Range SAT I Math	490-610
Average SAT I Math	553
Range SAT I Verbal	490-600
Average SAT I Verbal	545
Average ACT Composite	24
Student to Faculty Ratio	19:1

CAMPUS TOURS

Appointment Req?	Yes
Dates	Academic year
Times	Mon-Fri 10AM, 1:30PM, and 2:30PM; Sat 9AM and noon (and 1:30PM in summer)
Avg. Length	1 hour

ON-CAMPUS APPOINTMENTS

Admissions

Start Date–Juniors	Any time
Appointment Req?	Yes
Advance Notice	2 weeks
Saturdays?	Yes, academic year
Avg. Length	45 min
Info Sessions	Year-round

Faculty and Coaches

Dates/Times	Year-round; subject to faculty/coach availability
Arrangements	Contact admissions off. for fall, winter, and spring interviews; contact dept. or coach for summer interviews 2 weeks prior

CLASS VISITS

Dates	Academic year (Mon-Fri)
Arrangements	Get list of classes from admissions off.

OVERNIGHT DORM STAYS

Advance Notice	3 weeks
Arrangements	Contact admissions
Limitations	Oct-Dec and Feb-April

PURDUE UNIVERSITY—WEST LAFAYETTE

Office of Admissions, Purdue University, 1080 Schleman Hall,
West Lafayette, IN 47907 • Telephone:765-494-1776 (Fax: 765-494-0544) •
Web: www.purdue.edu • Email: admissions@adms.purdue.edu

Hours: Monday-Friday, 8AM-5PM; Saturday, 9AM-noon (when classes are in session). Closed Sundays and holidays.

Purdue University in Indiana is one of the great buys of higher education, especially for Hoosiers, who make up the vast majority of the career-minded, math-oriented student population here. Great programs in business and engineering (one in five pursues an engineering degree) and a hopping Greek scene are other highlights. Neil Armstrong, the first person to walk on the moon, is an alum.

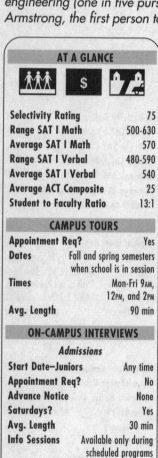

AT A GLANCE	
Selectivity Rating	75
Range SAT I Math	500-630
Average SAT I Math	570
Range SAT I Verbal	480-590
Average SAT I Verbal	540
Average ACT Composite	25
Student to Faculty Ratio	13:1

CAMPUS TOURS	
Appointment Req?	Yes
Dates	Fall and spring semesters when school is in session
Times	Mon-Fri 9AM, 12PM, and 2PM
Avg. Length	90 min

ON-CAMPUS INTERVIEWS	
Admissions	
Start Date—Juniors	Any time
Appointment Req?	No
Advance Notice	None
Saturdays?	Yes
Avg. Length	30 min
Info Sessions	Available only during scheduled programs
Faculty and Coaches	
Dates/Times	Year-round; subject to faculty/coach availability
Arrangements	Contact dept. of interest 1-2 weeks prior

CLASS VISITS	
Dates	Fall/spring semesters (Mon-Fri)
Arrangements	Contact admissions 2 weeks prior

OVERNIGHT DORM STAYS	
Advance Notice	N/A
Arrangements	N/A
Limitations	N/A

TRANSPORTATION

Indianapolis International is approximately 65 miles from campus. The Lafayette Limo Service, which is not affiliated with the university, provides round-trip shuttle service to and from campus for a fee; call 765-497-3828 to make arrangements. Purdue also has its own airport, serviced by commuter flights from Chicago and Indianapolis. Amtrak trains and major bus lines service Lafayette and W. Lafayette.

FIND YOUR WAY

Greater Lafayette can be reached by U.S. Rtes. 52 and 231, I-65, or Indiana Rtes. 25, 26, 38, and 43. The university is near the intersection of Indiana Rte. 26 (State St.) and Grant St. The Visitor Information Center is at 504 Northwestern Ave.

STAY THE NIGHT

The inexpensive **Union Club** (765-494-8900) is conveniently located on campus. The **Holiday Inn—North** (5600 State Rd.; 317-567-2131) is about 6 miles from campus. Rates are in the inexpensive range and the hotel has an indoor pool. The **University Inn** (3001 Northwestern Ave.; 317-463-5511) is a mile and a half away. Rates are at the low end of the moderate range and there is an indoor pool, sauna, jacuzzi, and exercise room.

HIGHLIGHTS

ON CAMPUS	OFF CAMPUS
• Purdue Memorial Union	• Wolf Park
• Sporting events	• Wabash Heritage Trail
• Horticulture park	• Fort Quiatenow
	• Various events in town

UNIVERSITY OF NOTRE DAME

Office of Undergraduate Admissions, University of Notre Dame, 220 Main Building, Notre Dame, IN 46556-5602• Telephone: 219-631-7505 • Web: www.nd.edu • Email: admissio.1@nd.edu

Hours: Monday-Friday, 8AM-5PM; Saturday, 8AM-noon (September-April). Closed Sundays and holidays.

The University of Notre Dame is the most famous Catholic university in the country, and with good reason: it's a great school with an almost mythical tradition. A definitely Catholic core curriculum includes the Freshman Year of Studies program, which prescribes the entire freshman curriculum.

HIGHLIGHTS

ON CAMPUS
- Grotto
- The Dome (main building)
- Basilica of the Sacred Heart
- Notre Dame Stadium
- Eck Center

OFF CAMPUS
- College Football Hall of Fame
- Morris Civic Auditorium
- Bendix Woods Park
- Studebaker National Museum
- East Race Waterway (whitewater rafting)

TRANSPORTATION

South Bend Regional Airport in South Bend, IN is 4 miles from campus. USAir and Northwest Airlines provide direct connecting flights into the airport; United Express and American Eagle Airlines have several daily shuttle flights in from Chicago's O'Hare International Airport. Other airlines fly to South Bend from other midwestern cities. Taxis are always available at the airport's terminal entrance for the ride to campus. Amtrak and South Shore railroads serve South Bend from Chicago. Taxis are available at the train station for the ride to campus. Bus transportation to the area is provided by Greyhound and United Limo bus lines through their terminals at the South Bend Regional Airport.

FIND YOUR WAY

Approach S. Bend on the Indiana Toll Rd. (I-80/I-90) and exit at Interchange 77. Proceed south on U.S. Rte. 31/33. Turn east on Angela Blvd., and at the next traffic light, turn north on Notre Dame Ave. As you approach the campus, turn right on the drive between the Hesburgh Center and the University Club. Follow the signs to the visitor parking area, which is located to the south of the stadium, near the Alumni-Senior Club.

STAY THE NIGHT

The on-campus **Morris Inn** (219-631-2000) has a restaurant and overlooks the golf course. You also enjoy athletic privileges, including racquetball, tennis, and golf. Prices are at the low end of the moderate range. Five minutes away is a small, charmingly decorated hotel, the **Jamison Inn** (1404 N. Ivy Rd.; 219-277-9682). Rates are moderate and include breakfast. For a traditional bed-and-breakfast, consider the **Queen Anne Inn** (420 W. Washington; 219-234-5959), about a mile from the school. The guest rooms (all with private baths) are named for birds in the area. (Why? We don't know.) The moderate price includes a wonderful full breakfast. Simple, inexpensive accommodations may be found at the **Signature Inn Hotel** (220 Dixie Way S.; 219-277-3211), 5 minutes from campus. There is an outdoor pool and a free breakfast. A **Marriott Hotel** (123 N. St. Joseph St.; 219-234-2000) is about 10 minutes from campus in downtown.

AT A GLANCE

Selectivity Rating	98
Range SAT I Math	640-720
Average SAT I Math	670
Range SAT I Verbal	620-710
Average SAT I Verbal	680
Average ACT Composite	31
Student to Faculty Ratio	12:1

CAMPUS TOURS
Appointment Req?	Yes, 2 weeks prior
Dates	Year-round
Time	Jan-Dec: Mon-Fri 11AM and 5PM; Sat 10AM and 11AM
Avg. Length	1 hour

ON-CAMPUS INTERVIEWS
Admissions
Start Date–Juniors	N/A
Appointment Req?	N/A
Advance Notice	N/A
Saturdays?	N/A
Avg. Length	N/A
Info Sessions	Jan-Dec

Faculty and Coaches
Dates/Times	Year-round; subject to faculty/coach availability
Arrangements	Contact particular faculty/coach

CLASS VISITS
Dates	During academic year
Arrangements	Contact admissions off.

OVERNIGHT DORM STAYS
Advance Notice	2 weeks prior
Arrangements	Contact admissions off.
Limitations	High school seniors only; 1-night stay; not during summer; bring sleeping bag; expenses paid by student

IOWA

1- Cornell College
2- Grinnell College
3- University of Iowa
4- Iowa State University

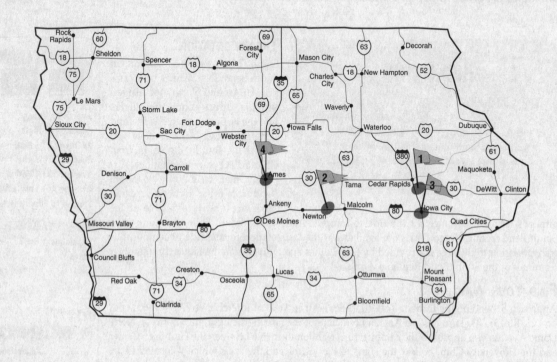

Iowa	Cornell College	Grinnell College	Iowa State Univ.	Univ. Iowa	Des Moines
Cornell College	—	79	113	19	130
Grinnell College	79	—	60	67	55
Iowa State Univ.	113	60	—	137	30
Univ. Iowa	19	67	137	—	112
Des Moines	130	55	30	112	—

CORNELL COLLEGE

Admissions Office, Cornell College, 600 1st St. West, Mount Vernon, IA 52314
(The office is in Wade House, across from the chapel) • Telephone: 800-747-1112 •
Web: www.cornell-iowa.edu • Email: admissions@cornell-iowa.edu

Hours: Sept.-May: Monday-Friday, 8AM-4:30PM; Saturday by appointment. June-Aug.: Monday-Friday, 8AM-4PM. Closed holidays.

Cornell College's unique and ultra-flexible One-Course-At-A-Time program offers one class for three and a half weeks, which is followed by a four-day break. Cornell University once asked Cornell College to change its name, but since Cornell College is actually two years older, perhaps the upstart University ought to just rename itself.

HIGHLIGHTS

ON CAMPUS
- Cole Library
- Norton Geology Center & Anderson Museum
- King Chapel

OFF CAMPUS
- Cedar Rapids
- Iowa City

TRANSPORTATION

Cedar Rapids Municipal Airport is 17 miles (a 20-minute drive) from campus. If you need transportation to campus from the airport, call the admissions office at least a week in advance. Bus service is available to the Ground Transportation Center in downtown Cedar Rapids; contact the admissions office a week in advance for transportation from there to campus too.

FIND YOUR WAY

From I-80 at Iowa City, take Iowa Rte. 1 N. for 20 miles; the college is at the intersection of Rte. 1 and U.S. Rte. 30. From I-380 at Cedar Rapids, go east on U.S. 30 for 20 miles; the college is at the intersection of U.S. 30 and Iowa Rte. 1.

STAY THE NIGHT

Nearby: The **College Guesthouse**, Brackett, circa 1877 is an antique-filled stately home that provides modern comfort and convenience at a moderate price (418 Second St. W.; 319-895-8845). The nearby city of Cedar Rapids is only 25 minutes from the school. The **Collins Plaza** (1200 Collins Rd. N.E.; 319-393-6600 or 800-541-1067) and **Stouffer Five Seasons** (350 1st Ave. N.E.; 319-363-8161) may not win any design awards, but they are fully equipped and moderately priced. **The Hampton Inn** (33rd Ave. and 6th St. S.W., Cedar Rapids, 319-364-8144). A little closer to the school in Cedar Rapids is the always-comfortable **Red Roof Inn** (3325 S. Gate Ct. S.W.; 319-366-7523).

A little farther: Between Cedar Rapids and Iowa City (to the south near the University of Iowa) are the historic Amana Colonies. In the little town of Homestead is **Die Heimat Country Inn** (Main St.; 319-622-3937), frequented by travelers in the 1850s as they crossed the plains. Later, it became one of the two communal kitchens serving Homestead. The inn offers reduced rates that include a continental breakfast and is 18 miles from the University of Iowa.

AT A GLANCE

Selectivity Rating	78
Range SAT I Math	530-630
Average SAT I Math	580
Range SAT I Verbal	520-650
Average SAT I Verbal	580
Average ACT Composite	25
Average GPA	3.4
Student to Faculty Ratio	15:1

CAMPUS TOURS

Appointment Req?	Yes
Dates	Year-round
Times	Mon-Fri 11AM and 3PM; Sat 10AM and 11AM by appt. only
Avg. Length	1 hour

ON-CAMPUS INTERVIEWS

Admissions

Start Date–Juniors	Any time
Appointment Req?	Yes
Advance Notice	1 week
Saturdays?	Yes, by appt., but only in the morning during the academic year
Avg. Length	1 hour
Info Sessions	Available only during special visit days

Faculty and Coaches

Dates/Times	Academic year; subject to faculty/coach availability
Arrangements	Contact admissions off. 1 week prior

CLASS VISITS

Dates	Academic year (Mon-Fri)
Arrangements	Contact admissions off.

OVERNIGHT DORM STAYS

Advance Notice	1 week
Arrangements	Contact admissions off.
Limitations	No stays Fri or Sat nights.

GRINNELL COLLEGE

Office of Admission, Grinnell College, Grinnell, IA 50112-1690 (The office is located in Mears Cottage, 1213 6th Avenue, at the corner of 6th Avenue and High Street.) • Telephone: 800-247-0113 or 641-269-3600 • Web: www.grinnell.edu • Email: askgrin@grinnell.edu

Hours: Monday-Friday 8AM-5PM; Saturday 9AM-noon. Closed Sundays and holidays. Summer hours are Monday-Friday, 8AM-4:30PM.

Small Grinnell College in Iowa offers its students many diverse opportunities and an open approach to a liberal arts education.

AT A GLANCE

Selectivity Rating	91
Range SAT I Math	610-710
Average SAT I Math	659
Range SAT I Verbal	620-730
Average SAT I Verbal	669
Average ACT Composite	29
Student to Faculty Ratio	10:1

CAMPUS TOURS

Appointment Req?	Preferred
Dates	Year-round except during breaks and exam periods
Times	Academic year: Mon-Fri 8AM-5PM; Sat 9AM-noon
Avg. Length	1 hour

ON-CAMPUS INTERVIEWS

Admissions

Appointment Req?	Yes
Advance Notice	10 days
Saturdays?	Fall semester only
Avg. Length	50 minutes
Info Sessions	Yes, average 30 minutes

Faculty and Coaches

Dates/Times	Academic year; subject to availability
Arrangements	Contact admissions off. 10 days prior

CLASS VISITS

Dates	Academic year (Mon-Fri)
Arrangements	Contact admissions off.

OVERNIGHT DORM STAYS

Advance Notice	10 days
Arrangements	Contact admissions off.
Limitations	Contact admissions off.

TRANSPORTATION

The Des Moines and Cedar Rapids airports are approximately 60 miles from campus. Transportation is available from both airports every day during the academic year, except during breaks, holidays, and exam periods. There is no charge for this service but reservations must be made at least 10 days in advance.

FIND YOUR WAY

From I-80, take Exit 182; drive north on Highway 146 for 3 miles to Grinnell. Turn right (east) on 6th Avenue and proceed 5 blocks. Mears Cottage, home to the Office of Admission, and visitor parking is located on the left at the corner of 6th Avenue and High Street.

STAY THE NIGHT

Nearby: Prospective students are welcome to spend an evening in the residence halls throughout the academic year. Contact the admissions office at least 10 days in advance. Within walking distance of campus you'll find the **Carriage House Bed and Breakfast** (641-236-7520) and the **Marsh House Bed and Breakfast** (641-236-0132 or 641-236-6782). Three hotels are located a short distance from campus on Highway 146, just off I-80: **Country Inn and Suites** (641-236-9600), **Super 8** (800-800-8000), and the **Days Inn** (800-325-2525).

A little farther: The city of Newton, 20 miles west of Grinnell, also offers a variety of motels including **Best Western Newton Inn** (800-528-1234), **Holiday Inn Express** (800-HOLIDAY), **Radisson Inn** (800-333-3333) and **La Corsette Maison Inn Bed and Breakfast** (641-792-6833). **The Amana Colonies**, one of Iowa's most well-known tourist attractions, can be found approximately 40 miles east of Grinnell with overnight accommodations available at the **Comfort Inn** (800-228-5200) or **Holiday Inn** (800-465-4349). The Office of Admission is happy to recommend additional accommodations if desired.

HIGHLIGHTS

ON CAMPUS
- Mears Cottage and Goodnow Hall (both on the National Register of Historic Places)
- Faulconer Gallery
- Burling Library

OFF CAMPUS
- Café Phoenix
- Rock Creek State Park
- The Grinnell Historic Museum

IOWA STATE UNIVERSITY

Office of Admissions, Iowa State University, 100 Alumni Hall, Ames, IA 50011-2010, •
Telephone: 800-262-3810 or 515-294-5836 • Web: www.iastate.edu •
Email: admissions@iastate.edu

Hours: Monday-Friday, 8AM-5PM; Saturday, 9AM-noon. Closed Sundays and holidays.

Strong programs in the sciences and a wealth of research resources set Iowa State University apart. The large number of older and otherwise nontraditional students on campus is well included in students life.

HIGHLIGHTS

ON CAMPUS	OFF CAMPUS
• C6 Virtual Reality Lab	• Downtown
• Reiman Gardens	• North Grand Mall
• Lied Recreation Center	• Numerous Parks
• Memorial Union	• Hickory Park
• Campanile	

TRANSPORTATION

Des Moines International Airport is 35 minutes from campus. Car rental, taxis, and commercial buses are available for the trip from the airport to the campus.

FIND YOUR WAY

Ames is centrally located and well served by ground transportation. North-south Interstate 35 passes Ames on the east, with east-west Highway 30 intersecting to bring visitors to campus. East-west Interstate 80 intersects with Interstate 35 just 25 miles south of Ames. Follow the Iowa State/Ames signs on interstates and Highway 30.

STAY THE NIGHT

The **Memorial Union** (2229 Lincoln Way; 520-292-1111), the student union building on campus, has a cafeteria open all day and a bowling alley in the building. Oh, you can sleep there too, and the rates are cheap. Within a few miles of the university you'll find the **Holiday Inn/Gateway Center** (U.S. 30 and Elmwood Dr.; 520-292-8600), with an indoor pool and all the usual Holiday Inn stuff like ice makers in the hall. This one also has jazz on the weekends. For more information contact the Ames Convention and Visitors Bureau at 800-288-7470.

AT A GLANCE

Selectivity Rating	75
Range SAT I Math	550-690
Average SAT I Math	610
Range SAT I Verbal	520-660
Average SAT I Verbal	590
Average ACT Composite	24
Average GPA	3.5
Student to Faculty Ratio	14:1

CAMPUS TOURS

Appointment Req?	Preferred
Dates	Year-round
Times	Mon-Fri 10AM and 2PM
Avg. Length	1 hour

ON-CAMPUS INTERVIEWS

Admissions

Start Date–Juniors	Any time
Appointment Req?	Preferred
Advance Notice	1 week
Saturdays?	Yes
Avg. Length	45 min
Info Sessions	Academic info sessions available daily from 1-2PM. "Open Houses" called "Experience Iowa State" held year-round. Contact admissions office for dates.

Faculty and Coaches

Dates/Times	Year-round; subject to faculty/coach availability
Arrangements	Contact admissions off. 1 week prior

CLASS VISITS

Dates	Available at "Open House" programs or arranged daily by request
Arrangements	Contact admissions off.

OVERNIGHT DORM STAYS

Advance Notice	N/A
Arrangements	N/A

UNIVERSITY OF IOWA

Admissions Office, University of Iowa, John G. Bowman House, Admissions Visitors Center, 230 N. Clinton St., Iowa City, IA 52242 • Telephone: 800-553-IOWA or 319-335-3847 • Web: www.uiowa.edu • Email: admissions@uiowa.edu

Hours: Monday-Friday, 8:30AM-4:30PM; Saturday, 9AM-11AM (only on selected Saturdays). Closed Sundays and holidays.

Surrounded by cornfields as far as the eye can see, Iowa City might not top the list of places you'd think of as an itellectual mecca. But this progressive midwestern berg is home to the University of Iowa, an educational institution of the highest caliber that offers world-class degree programs in just about every academic discipline imaginable.

AT A GLANCE

Selectivity Rating	78
Range SAT I Math	540-660
Range SAT I Verbal	520-660
Average GPA	3.5
Student to Faculty Ratio	14:1

CAMPUS TOURS

Appointment Req?	Strongly preferred
Dates	Year-round
Times	Mon-Fri 10:30AM and 2:30PM; selected Saturdays 10:30AM
Avg. Length	45-60 min

ON-CAMPUS INTERVIEWS

Admissions

Start Date—Juniors	Any time, but preferably in the last half of the junior year
Appointment Req?	Preferred
Advance Notice	2 weeks
Saturdays?	No
Avg. Length	30-60 min
Info Sessions	Year-round

Faculty and Coaches

Dates/Times	Year-round; subject to faculty/coach availability
Arrangements	Contact admissions off.

CLASS VISITS

Dates	Year-round (Mon-Fri)
Arrangements	Contact admissions off.

OVERNIGHT DORM STAYS

Advance Notice	N/A
Arrangements	N/A
Limitations	N/A

TRANSPORTATION

The Cedar Rapids Airport is 25 miles (a 35-minute drive on I-380) from campus. Van service to campus is supplied by Cedar Rapids Airport Transportation; call 319-365-0655 at least 1 day ahead to arrange for this service. Intercity bus service to Iowa City is provided by Greyhound and Missouri Transit buses; call the Union Bus Depot (319-337-2127) for information and schedules. Iowa City Transit (319-356-5151) and the University's Cambus (319-335-8633) provide local transportation throughout the Iowa City area.

FIND YOUR WAY

From I-80 (which connects Iowa City with Chicago, IL and Omaha, NE), turn south on the Dubuque St. exit, which leads to the downtown/campus area. The Admissions Visitors Center is 1 block west of Dubuque St. on N. Clinton St.

STAY THE NIGHT

You can't beat the **Iowa House** (319-335-3513), also known as the Student Union. The proximity to students, 3 restaurants, university bookstore, theater, recreation center, pool tables, video games, and the on-campus field house, which has badminton and basketball courts, a weight room, and an indoor track, make it hard to beat. Within walking distance is a **City Plaza Hotel** (210 S. Dubuque St.; 319-337-4058), moderately priced in downtown Iowa City. **The Golden Haug** (319-338-6452) is a bed and breakfast downtown near the university. Two motels are a convenient 10 minutes from the campus grounds. The **Radisson Highlander Plaza** (I-80 and Hwy. 1; 319-354-2000) has an indoor pool and coffee shop, and its well-liked restaurant, the Prime Grill, specializes in prime rib and seafood. Rates are moderate. Less expensive accommodations can be found at the **Hampton Inn** (1st Ave. N., Coralville; 800-962-0110). For additional suggestions peruse the Cornell College entry.

HIGHLIGHTS

ON CAMPUS
- The University of Iowa Museum of Art
- The University of Iowa Museum of Natural History
- Old Capitol Museum

OFF CAMPUS
- Arts Iowa City Center & Gallery
- Plum Grove Historic Home
- Heritage Museum of Johnson County
- Coral Ridge Mall Attractions

1- University of Kansas

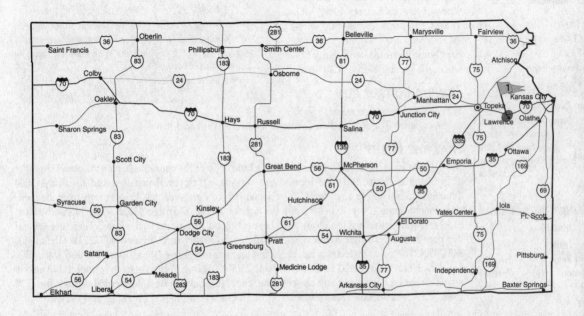

Kansas	Univ. Kansas	Kansas City	Wichita
Univ. Kansas	—	37	162
Kansas City	37	—	190
Wichita	162	190	—

UNIVERSITY OF KANSAS

Office of Admissions and Scholarships, University of Kansas, 1502 Iowa St., Lawrence, KS 66044 • Telephone: 785-864-3911 or 785-864-5135 • Web: www.ukans.edu • Email: adm@ukans.edu

Hours: Monday-Friday, 8AM-5PM; Saturday, 9AM-noon. Closed Sundays and most holidays.

The University of Kansas boasts first-rate pre-professional schools in architecture and engineering, and is also strong in pharmacy, nursing, journalism, and education. KU's library draws raves, and students rate the computer facilities very highly. Actor Don Johnson and basketball god Wilt Chamberlain are KU alums.

AT A GLANCE

Selectivity Rating	79
Average ACT Composite	24
Average GPA	3.4
Student to Faculty Ratio	15:1

CAMPUS TOURS

Appointment Req?	Preferred
Dates	During academic semesters, except exam periods
Times	Mon, Thurs, Fri 9:30AM and 1:30PM; Tues and Wed 10:30AM
Avg. Length	1 hour

ON-CAMPUS INTERVIEWS

Admissions

Start Date—Juniors	Any time
Appointment Req?	Preferred
Advance Notice	Preferred
Saturdays?	Yes
Avg. Length	30 min
Info Sessions	During regular school sessions

Faculty and Coaches

Dates/Times	Year-round; subject to faculty/coach availability
Arrangements	Contact visit coordinator in admissions off. 2-3 weeks prior

CLASS VISITS

Dates	Year-round (Mon-Fri)
Arrangements	Contact visit coordinator in admissions off.

OVERNIGHT DORM STAYS

Arrangements	Contact visit coordinator for alternative housing options
Limitations	None

TRANSPORTATION

Kansas City International Airport is 55 miles from campus. Amtrak trains and Greyhound buses provide service to Kansas City, MO. The KCI Express shuttle-bus operates from the airport to the Greyhound terminal and many hotels in the greater Kansas City area.

DRIVING INSTRUCTION

Take I-70 to Lawrence; take US 59 S. to the campus. The KU Visitor Center is located at 15th and Iowa.

STAY THE NIGHT

Nearby: You have a range of choices within a mile or so of the campus. Across the street from the girls' freshman dorm, and 4 or 5 blocks from campus, is **Halcyon House Bed-and-Breakfast** (1000 Ohio St.; 913-841-0314), a restored Victorian with 8 cozy guest rooms. Prices range from inexpensive to moderate. Nine blocks from the school is the **Eldridge Hotel** (701 Massachusetts; 913-749-5011). Prices are moderate and there is a good restaurant in the hotel. There are several inexpensive motels within a mile or so, including the **Quality Inn University** (2222 W. 6th St.; 913-842-7030). The price includes a full breakfast and the motel has an outdoor pool and free HBO. **Lawrence Travelodge** (801 Iowa St.; 913-842-5100) is about 15 blocks from school. HBO also is available here. Cheaper yet and closer to the school (8 blocks) is **Best Western Hallmark Inn** (730 Iowa St.; 913-841-6500). The inexpensive price includes continental breakfast and cable.

A little farther: Topeka is 22 miles to the west. Here you'll find **Heritage House** (3535 S.W. 6th Ave.; 913-233-3800), an inn listed on the National Register of Historic Places. Prices are moderate and include a full homemade breakfast. Each of the 13 rooms has been decorated by a local designer in connection with a designers' showcase.

HIGHLIGHTS

ON CAMPUS
- Spencer Museum of Art
- Memorial Stadium
- Spencer Research Library
- Watson Library
- Templin Hall & Visitor Center

OFF CAMPUS
- Old West Lawrence Historic District
- Oceans of Fun (water theme park)
- Worlds of Fun (amusement park)

1- Centre College
2- University of Kentucky

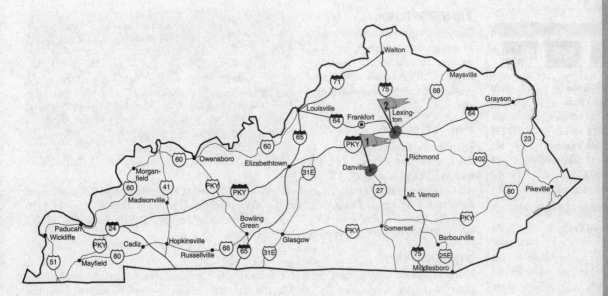

Kentucky	Centre Coll.	Univ. Kentucky	Louisville
Centre Coll.	—	36	92
Univ. Kentucky	36	—	74
Louisville	92	74	—

CENTRE COLLEGE

Admissions Office, Centre College, 600 West Walnut, Danville, KY 40422 (The office is in the Horky House at the corner of Maple and Main St.) • Telephone: 800-423-6236 • Web: www.centre.edu • Email: admission@centre.edu

Hours: Monday-Friday, 8:30AM-5PM; Saturday, 9AM-noon (September-May). Closed Sundays and holidays.

Greek life dominates at this small, challenging, liberal arts enclave in the heart of Kentucky Bluegrass country. While the surrounding town of Danville is certainly no Cambridge, it's no slouch, either, as Centre brings in lots of cultural events.

AT A GLANCE

Selectivity Rating	76
Range SAT I Math	580-680
Average SAT I Math	624
Range SAT I Verbal	570-690
Average SAT I Verbal	635
Average ACT Composite	27
Average GPA	3.7
Student to Faculty Ratio	10:1

CAMPUS TOURS

Appointment Req?	No
Dates	Year-round
Times	Sept-May: Mon-Fri 10AM, 1PM, and 3PM; Sat 10AM
Avg. Length	60 min

ON-CAMPUS INTERVIEWS

Admissions

Start Date—Juniors	No earlier than spring of junior year is recommended
Appointment Req?	Yes
Advance Notice	1 week prior
Saturdays?	Yes, Sept-May only
Avg. Length	45 min
Info Sessions	N/A

Faculty and Coaches

Dates/Times	Year-round; subject to faculty/coach availability
Arrangements	Contact admissions off. 1 week prior

CLASS VISITS

Dates	Year-round (Mon-Fri), but discouraged the first 2 days of a new term
Arrangements	Contact admissions off.

OVERNIGHT DORM STAYS

Advance Notice	2 weeks
Arrangements	Contact admissions off.
Limitations	Sun-Thurs only

TRANSPORTATION

Bluegrass Airport near Lexington is 40 miles from campus. The college provides transportation from the airport. Call the admissions office a week in advance to make arrangements.

FIND YOUR WAY

From the southwest, take I-65 N. to the Cumberland Pkwy. (Exit 43); take the Pkwy. east to US 127 N., which takes you to Danville. **From the north**, take I-75 S. exit to Kentucky Rte. 922 and follow signs to the Bluegrass Pkwy. W. Take the Pkwy. west to U.S. 127 S. Follow U.S. 127 S. to Danville. **From the southeast**, take I-75 N. to Exit 59. Take U.S. 150 N.W. (initially it is U.S. 25) to U.S. 127 N., which takes you into Danville.

STAY THE NIGHT

Nearby: There are several charming bed-and-breakfasts operating in the historic homes that line Danville's older streets. The best way to inquire about rooms in these homes is to call the Campus Visit Coordinator through the admissions office. We recomme5nd a beautifully restored pre–Civil War home, the **Twin Hollies** (406 Maple Ave.; 859-236-8954), a short one-and-a-half blocks from campus, and the **Elmwood Inn** (205 E. 4th St., Perryville; 859-332-2400) on the banks of the Chaplin River, 10 minutes from Centre. The Elmwood, an 1842 Greek Revival house listed on the National Register of Historic Places, has 2 rooms, and the moderate price includes a full breakfast with homemade muffins. Less expensive accommodations can be found within 5 miles of the school at the **Days Inn** (U.S. Rte. 127; 859-236-8600), or the **Super 8 Motel** (U.S. Rte. 150; 859-236-8881). The **Bright Leaf Resort and Motel** (U.S. Rte. 127 S., 1742 Danville Rd., Harrodsburg; 859-734-5481), about 5 miles from campus, is an inexpensive resort-type facility with a health club, outdoor pool, fishing lakes, and golf course. Special golf packages are available.

A little farther: About 15 miles from the college (two miles from Shakertown), is the **Canaan Land Farm Bed and Breakfast** (4355 Lexington Rd., Harrodsburg; 859-734-3984), an 18th-century brick building listed on the National Register of Historic Places as the Benjamin Daniel house. The house is filled with antiques, sheep and goats are raised on the farm, and there's a pool. Rates are inexpensive and include a full country breakfast. About 10 miles from the college is the **Beaumont Inn** (638 Beaumont Dr., Harrodsburg; 859-734-3381). This full-service hotel has tennis courts and a swimming pool, and offers golf privileges. See the University of Kentucky entry for other suggestions.

HIGHLIGHTS

ON CAMPUS	OFF CAMPUS
• Norton Center for the Arts	• Historic Shaker Village
• 2000's only vice-presidential debate	• Civil War Battle Field
• Great American Brass Band festival each summer	• Keeneland Racetrack (30 miles away in Lexington, KY)
• 21 campus buildings on National Register of Historic Places	• Constitution Square (historic site)

UNIVERSITY OF KENTUCKY

Office of Undergraduate Admission, University of Kentucky, 100 W. D. Funkhouser Building, Lexington, KY 40506-0054 (The University's Visitor Center is located in the Student Center on Euclid Ave.) • Telephone 859-257-2000 • Web: www.uky.edu • Email: admissio@pop.uky.edu

Hours: Monday-Friday, 9AM-4:30PM; open Saturdays September-April. Closed all University holidays.

Basketball is huge at the University of Kentucky, but students say the top-notch academics are the school's greatest asset. Profs are highly praised, and such pre-professional departments as business and management, communications, health sciences, education, and engineering are extremely popular.

HIGHLIGHTS

ON CAMPUS	OFF CAMPUS
• Arboretum	• Rupp Arena
• Commonwealth Stadium	• Henry Clay Estate
• Memorial Coliseum/Hall	• Kentucky Horse Park

TRANSPORTATION

Bluegrass Airport just outside Lexington is 5 miles (a 20-minute drive) from campus. Rental cars are available at the airport; the university has no shuttle service.

FIND YOUR WAY

From I-75/64 (which come into Lexington from the north, south, east, and west and merge briefly around the city), take Exit 113 (marked Paris/Lexington). Turn right off the exit ramp onto N. Broadway (U.S. 68). Follow through the downtown area for 3.5 miles. One block past the Hyatt Regency Lexington, turn left onto West Maxwell St. At the fourth light, turn right onto Martin Luther King Blvd. At the first list, turn left onto Avenue of Champions/Euclid Ave. Turn right into the Student Center parking lot. The Visitor Center is located on the first floor of the Student Center, across from the University Bookstore. *Please note that the Visitor Center is not located in the same building as the Office of Undergraduate Admissions.*

STAY THE NIGHT

The following are a list of hotels located near the University of Kentucky: **Best Western Regency** (2241 Elkhorn Rd.; 859-299-2613), **Hampton Inn** (Elkhorn Rd.; 859-299-2613), **Courtyard by Marriot** (775 Newtown Court; 859-253-4646), **Embassy Suites** (1801 Newtown Pike; 859-455-5000), **Marriot's Griffin Gate Resort and Gold Club** (1800 Newtown Pike; 859-231-5100), **Hyatt Regency Downtown** (401 West High St.; 859-253-1234), **Fairfield Inn** (3050 Lakecrest Circle; 859-224-3338), **The Springs Inn** (2020 Harrodsburg; 859-277-5751), **Shaker Village of Pleasant Hill** (3501 Lexington Rd., Harrodsburg; 859-734-5411).

AT A GLANCE

Selectivity Rating	79
Average ACT Composite	25
Average GPA	3.5
Student to Faculty Ratio	16:1

CAMPUS TOURS

Appointment Req?	Yes, call 406-257-3595
Dates	Year-round
Times	Sept-April: Mon-Fri 10AM and 2PM; Sat 11AM
Avg. Length	30 min

ON-CAMPUS INTERVIEWS

Admissions

Start Date–Juniors	Any time
Appointment Req?	Yes
Advance Notice	1-2 weeks
Saturdays?	Yes, Sept-April only
Avg. Length	30-45 min
Info Sessions	Only 1-on-1 sessions are available

Faculty and Coaches

Dates/Times	Year-round; subject to faculty/coach availability
Arrangements	Contact Visitor Center 2-3 weeks prior

CLASS VISITS

Dates	Year-round (Mon-Fri)
Arrangements	Contact Visitor Center

OVERNIGHT DORM STAYS

Advance Notice	N/A
Arrangements	N/A
Limitations	N/A

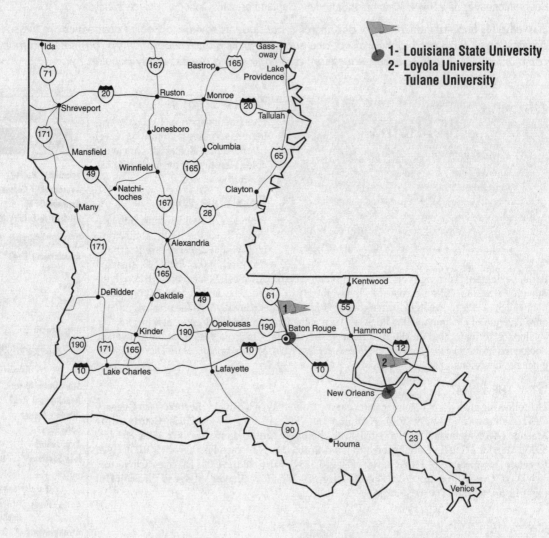

1- **Louisiana State University**
2- **Loyola University**
   Tulane University

	LSU	Loyola Univ.	Tulane Univ.	New Orleans	Shreveport
LSU	—	90	90	90	239
Loyola Univ.	90	—	0	0	329
Tulane Univ.	90	0	—	0	329
New Orleans	90	0	0	—	329
Shreveport	239	329	329	329	—

Louisiana

LOUISIANA STATE UNIVERSITY—BATON ROUGE

Admissions Office: Louisiana State University, Rm. 110 Thomas Boyd Hall, Baton Rouge, LA 70803 • Telephone: 225-388-1175 • Web: www.lsus.edu • Email: admissions@pilot.lsus.edu

Hours: Monday-Friday, 7:30AM-5PM. Closed weekends and holidays.

On the gorgeous campus of Louisiana State University, Fighting Bengal Tiger Football is an institution. A wide array of liberal arts and vocational educational options is available. LSU is one of the nation's few land- and sea-grant universities and is actively seeking space-grant status.

HIGHLIGHTS

ON CAMPUS	OFF CAMPUS
• Tiger Stadium	• Baton Rouge Zoo
• LSU Union	• Casino Rouge
• International Cultural Center	• Blue Bayou Water Park

TRANSPORTATION

Baton Rouge Metropolitan Airport is a 25-minute drive from campus. Taxis are available at the airport for the drive to campus.

FIND YOUR WAY

From New Orleans, take I-10 W. to the Dalrymple-LSU exit; follow Dalrymple Road south and west to the University. **From the west**, take I-10 E. and cross the Mississippi Bridge to the Highland Road exit. Follow Highland Road south to the University.

STAY THE NIGHT

Nearby: For convenience and price you can't improve upon **Pleasant Hall** (Dalrymple Dr.; 225-387-0297). About 20 minutes away is the **Plantation Inn** (10330 Airline Hwy.; 504-293-4100), with an outdoor pool and a dining room. If you're looking for pizzazz, try the **Courtyard by Marriott** (2421 S. Acadian Thruway; 225-924-6400) a 5-minute drive from the university. The moderate rate gets you a restaurant, exercise room, whirlpool, and outdoor pool. A few others include: **Best Western Richmond Suites Hotel** (5668 Hilton Ave.; 225-924-6500), **Comfort Inn University Center** (2445 S. Acadian Thruway; 225-927-5790), **Hampton Inn** (4646 Constitution Ave.; 225-926-9990), **Hilton Hotel** (5500 Hilton Ave.; 225-924-5000), **Holiday Inn** (9940 Airline Hwy.; 225-924-7021), and the **Embassy Suites Hotel** (4914 Constitution Ave.; 225-924-6566).

A little farther: If you're willing to shell out a few more dollars and drive a few more miles, check out the **Nottoway Plantation** (White Castle; 225-545-2730), 25 miles from LSU. This spectacular mansion is furnished in an opulent style and serves a full breakfast on the veranda. You can also tour some other plantation homes in your spare time.

AT A GLANCE

Selectivity Rating	76
Average ACT Composite	24
Average GPA	3.2
Student to Faculty Ratio	20:1

CAMPUS TOURS

Appointment Req?	Yes
Dates	Year-round, except on holidays
Times	Mon-Fri 10AM
Avg. Length	40 min

ON-CAMPUS INTERVIEWS

Admissions

Start Date–Juniors	Beginning of junior year
Appointment Req?	No
Advance Notice	None
Saturdays?	No
Avg. Length	30 min
Info Sessions	Year-round

Faculty and Coaches

Dates/Times	Year-round; subject to faculty/coach availability
Arrangements	Contact dept. of interest 1 week prior

CLASS VISITS

Dates	Year-round (Mon-Fri)
Arrangements	Contact undergraduate admissions off.

OVERNIGHT DORM STAYS

Advance Notice	N/A
Arrangements	N/A
Limitations	N/A

LOYOLA UNIVERSITY NEW ORLEANS

Admissions Office, Loyola University New Orleans, 6363 St. Charles Ave., Box 18, New Orleans, LA 70118 (The office is in Marquette Hall, Rm. 315) • Telephone: 800-4-LOYOLA or 504-865-3240 • Web: www.loyno.edu • Email: admit@loyno.edu

Hours: Monday-Friday, 8:30AM-4:45PM. Closed weekends and holidays.

Course work in religion and philosophy is mandatory at Loyola University New Orleans, but students may begin taking courses in their major their first semester. Outside of class, students love New Orleans.

AT A GLANCE

Selectivity Rating	76
Range SAT I Math	520-630
Average SAT I Math	575
Range SAT I Verbal	540-660
Average SAT I Verbal	598
Average ACT Composite	25
Average GPA	3.6
Student to Faculty Ratio	12:1

CAMPUS TOURS

Appointment Req?	Recommended
Dates	Year-round, except on weekends and major holidays
Times	Mon-Fri 11:30AM and 3:30PM
Avg. Length	1 hour

ON-CAMPUS INTERVIEWS

Admissions

Start Date–Juniors	Any time
Appointment Req?	Yes
Advance Notice	2 weeks
Saturdays?	No
Avg. Length	30 min
Info Sessions	Year-round

Faculty and Coaches

Dates/Times	Year-round; subject to faculty/coach availability
Arrangements	Contact admissions off. 2 weeks prior

CLASS VISITS

Dates	Fall and spring
Arrangements	Contact admissions off.

OVERNIGHT DORM STAYS

Advance Notice	2 weeks
Arrangements	Contact admissions off.
Limitations	Mon-Thurs nights; not during holidays, exam periods, or breaks

TRANSPORTATION

New Orleans International Airport is 15 miles from campus. Airport Shuttle Service and taxis are available at the baggage claim area. Amtrak trains and Greyhound/Trailways buses serve New Orleans. Taxis are available for the ride from the terminals to campus.

FIND YOUR WAY

From the west on I-10, take the Carrollton exit (Exit 232) and head south on Carrollton Ave. Follow South Carrollton until it ends in a sharp left hand turn and becomes St. Charles Ave. Loyola's main campus is on the left across from Audubon Park. **From I-10 East**, as you enter the downtown area, follow the signs to Hwy. 90 Business/West Bank. Exit at St. Charles Ave./Carondelet St. (do not cross bridge). At the second right, make a right onto St. Charles Ave. Continue down 4 miles until you see Loyola's main campus on the right.

STAY THE NIGHT

Because Loyola University is very close to Tulane, the places listed in the Tulane entry are equally suitable for visitors to Loyola. Please contact the office of admissions for suggested accommodations or call Roseanne at **Country Travel** (800-229-1060) for special discount rates for the **Avenue Plaza Suites, Le Pavillon Hotel**, the **Pontchartrain**, and the **Meridien Hotel**.

HIGHLIGHTS

ON CAMPUS
- J. Edgar & Louise S. Monroe Library

OFF CAMPUS
- Audubon Zoo
- City park
- St. Charles Avenue Street Car
- Aquarium of America
- French Quarter

TULANE UNIVERSITY

Office of Undergraduate Admission, Tulane University, 210 Gibson Hall, 6823 St. Charles Ave., New Orleans, LA 70118-5680 • Telephone: 504-865-5731 or 800-873-WAVE • Web: www.tulane.edu • Email: undergrad.admission@tulane.edu

Hours: Monday-Friday, 8:30AM-5PM. Closed weekends and holidays.

Everything old is new again at Tulane, where new buildings, facilities, and programs keep popping up with delirious swiftness. Tulane's largely traditional student body of approximately 7,000 benefits from an easy-going atmosphere and tremendous research programs. A visit to Tulane can be especially entertaining when coordinated with New Orleans's annual Mardi Gras celebration.

HIGHLIGHTS

ON CAMPUS
- Tulane Herbarium
- Cunningham Observatory
- Reily Recreation Center
- Howard Tilton Memorial Library

OFF CAMPUS
- Audubon Zoo
- City park
- St. Charles Avenue Street Car
- Aquarium of America
- French Quarter

TRANSPORTATION

New Orleans International Airport is 15 miles from campus. Airport Shuttle Service, taxis, and rental cars are available for the trip from airport to campus. Amtrak trains and Greyhound/Trailways buses serve New Orleans. Taxis are available for the ride from the terminal to campus.

FIND YOUR WAY

If you are heading east on I-10, follow signs to the Central Business District as you approach downtown New Orleans. When I-10 divides, do not bear left toward I-610 to Slidell. Just after this split, take the Carrollton Ave. exit. Remain on Carrollton to the end at St. Charles Ave. where you turn left, following the streetcar tracks. Continue on St. Charles to the admissions office. **If you are heading west on I-10,** follow the signs to Hwy. 90 Business. Exit at St. Charles Ave./Carondelet St. (do not cross the bridge). At the second traffic light, make a right onto St. Charles Ave. Follow St. Charles for 4 miles; Tulane and Gibson Hall will be on your right

STAY THE NIGHT

The **Tulane Travel Connection** (504-865-5673), which is on campus but not run by the university, can get special rates at several of the hotels and motels nearby. During certain times of the year, they offer even cheaper rates as part of special packages with some airlines.

Nearby: A number of hotels and motels are located on the St. Charles Ave. streetcar line that leads directly to the university. Of these, the least expensive is **Prytania Park** (1525 Prytania St.; 504-524-0427 or 800-862-1984), which is in the Garden District About 2 miles away in the Garden District is the **Ramada Hotel** (2203 St. Charles Ave.; 504-566-1200). Ask for its special double-occupancy rate for Tulane visitors. The 1927 **Pontchartrain** (2031 St. Charles Ave.; 504-524-0581), with a rooftop pool, is your choice for elegance and character. Make reservations through Tulane Travel Connection and you can get the special visitors' rate. The Pontchartrain also offers complimentary limousine service to the university. **Glimmer Inn Bed and Breakfast** (1631 7th St.; 504-897-1895) is a pleasant, inexpensive bed-and-breakfast with a delicious continental breakfast.

A little farther: There are hundreds of places to stay in the downtown and French Quarter areas. A couple that offer discounts to Tulane visitors are **Le Pavillon Hotel** (833 Poydras St.; 800-535-9095) and the **Meridien Hotel** (614 Canal St.; 504-525-6500 or 800-543-4300). The Meridien boasts Henri's, a fine French restaurant.

AT A GLANCE

Selectivity Rating	83
Range SAT I Math	591-690
Average SAT I Math	634
Range SAT I Verbal	600-703
Average SAT I Verbal	648
Student to Faculty Ratio	9:1

CAMPUS TOURS

Appointment Req?	Yes, 2 weeks prior
Dates	Year-round
Times	Mon-Fri 1 tour in the morning and 1 tour in the afternoon; Sat 1 tour in the morning (none held during the summer on Saturdays)
Avg. Length	90 min

ON-CAMPUS INTERVIEWS

Admissions

Start Date—Juniors	N/A
Appointment Req?	N/A
Advance Notice	N/A
Saturdays?	N/A
Avg. Length	N/A
Info Sessions	Year-round

Faculty and Coaches

Dates/Times	Year-round; subject to faculty/coach availability
Arrangements	Contact Athletic Off. 2 weeks prior

CLASS VISITS

Dates	Year-round (Mon-Fri)
Arrangements	Check list of available classes in admissions off.

OVERNIGHT DORM STAYS

Advance Notice	2 weeks
Arrangements	Contact admissions off.
Limitations	1-night stay; Mon-Thurs; not during holidays and exam periods; arrive by 4PM and bring a sleeping bag and towels

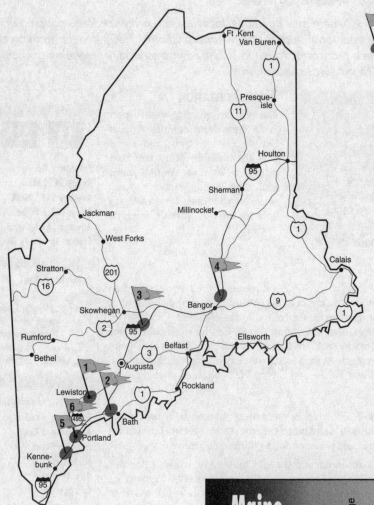

Ft .Kent
Van Buren
1
Presque-isle
11
Houlton
95
Sherman
Millinocket
Jackman
West Forks
201
Calais
Stratton
16
4
9
3
Skowhegan
Bangor
1
2
95
Rumford
Belfast
Ellsworth
Bethel
3
Augusta
1
1
Lewiston
2
Rockland
6
5
495
Bath
Portland
Kenne-bunk
95

1- Bates College
2- Bowdoin College
3- Colby College
4- University of Maine—Orono
5- University of New England
6- University of Southern Maine

Maine	Bates College	Bowdoin College	Colby College	Univ. Maine-Orono	Univ. New England	Univ. So. Maine	Augusta	Bangor	Portland
Bates College	—	22	51	109	53	42	28	105	40
Bowdoin College	22	—	56	110	48	28	31	108	26
Colby College	51	56	—	66	90	76	17	58	74
Univ. Maine-Orono	109	110	66	—	164	149	86	11	141
Univ. New England	53	48	90	164	—	18	74	154	15
Univ. So. Maine	42	28	76	149	18	—	58	136	0
Augusta	28	31	17	86	74	58	—	78	56
Bangor	105	108	58	11	154	136	78	—	134
Portland	40	26	74	141	15	0	56	134	—

BATES COLLEGE

Admissions Office, Bates College, Lindholm House, Lewiston, ME 04240 •
Telephone: 207-786-6000 • Web: www.bates.edu •
Email: admissions@bates.edu

Hours: Monday-Friday, 8AM-5PM (interviews scheduled 9AM-4PM); Saturday, 9AM-noon (fall only). Closed Sundays and holidays.

Bates College is a small liberal arts institution in Maine that follows a 4-4-1 calendar. There is a fall and a winter semester, then a shorter term in May, which provides students with opportunities to study less-traditional topics or to study or intern off campus. A heavy academic workload keeps the library full throughout the week.

HIGHLIGHTS

ON CAMPUS
- Bates College Museum of Art
- The George & Helen Ladd Library

OFF CAMPUS
- Bates-Morse Mountain Conservation Area

TRANSPORTATION

The Portland International Jetport is a 40-minute drive from campus. Shuttle van service is available at the airport for the ride to campus. Arrangements must be made in advance through the campus travel agency. Greyhound provides service to Lewiston.

FIND YOUR WAY

The College is located approximately 3 miles from Maine Tpke. Exit 13 (Lewiston Exit). **Northbound travelers**, take Exit 13 and turn left onto Alfred A. Plourde Pkwy. at the stop sign at the end of the off ramp. **Southbound travelers**, take Exit 13 and bear right onto Plourde Pkwy. Continue on Plourde straight to stoplight at intersection of Plourde and Pleasant; continue on Plourde .6 miles to stoplight at Webster Street. Turn left onto Webster and travel 1 mile to stoplight at Farwell Street. Turn right onto Farwell and follow .6 miles to stoplight. Continue straight across intersection onto Russell Street and follow for .9 miles to the third stoplight. Turn left onto College Street and follow to second blinking stoplight; turn left onto Campus Avenue. Take your first right onto Wood Street and turn right into the admissions parking lot. The admissions office (Lindholm House) is at 23 Campus Avenue.

STAY THE NIGHT

Nearby: **The Farnham House B&B** (520 Main St.; 207-782-9495) is right next door to campus. This old Victorian house offers 8 guest rooms, most with private bath. Also *Nearby:* **Ware Street Bed & Breakfast**, adjacent to campus (207-783-8171). If you're on a budget, there's the **Super 8 Motel** (1440 Lisbon St.; 207-784-8882) and **Motel 6** (207-782-6558), both about 10 minutes from campus. **The Ramada Inn** (490 Pleasant St.; 207-784-2331) has an indoor pool, an exercise room, and a live band with country rock every night in the lounge.

A little farther: See the University of Southern Maine entry for suggestions in Portland; Bowdoin College for suggestions in Brunswick and Freeport; and the University of New England for suggestions in the resort area of Kennebunkport.

AT A GLANCE

Selectivity Rating	97
Range SAT I Math	630-700
Average SAT I Math	660
Range SAT I Verbal	630-700
Average SAT I Verbal	660
Student to Faculty Ratio	10:1

CAMPUS TOURS

Appointment Req?	No
Dates	Year-round
Times	April 25-Nov 20: Mon-Fri 10AM-4PM. Nov 21-April 22: Mon-Fri 10AM, noon, and 2PM.
Avg. Length	1 hour

ON-CAMPUS INTERVIEWS

Admissions

Start Date—Juniors	May 1
Appointment Req?	Yes
Advance Notice	2 weeks
Saturdays?	Mornings in fall
Avg. Length	1 hour
Info Sessions	Aug and during the fall

Faculty and Coaches

Dates/Times	Year-round; subject to faculty/coach availability
Arrangements	Contact faculty/ coaches directly 2 weeks prior

CLASS VISITS

Dates	Year-round (Mon-Fri)
Arrangements	Contact admissions off.

OVERNIGHT DORM STAYS

Advance Notice	2 weeks
Arrangements	Contact admissions off.
Limitations	Not during reading weeks and exam periods

BOWDOIN COLLEGE

Office of Admissions, 5000 College Station, Bowdoin College, Brunswick, ME 04011 (The office is in Chamberlain Hall) • Telephone: 207-725-3100 (Fax: 207-725-3101) • Web: www.bowdoin.edu • Email: admissions-lit@polar.bowdoin.edu

Hours: Monday-Friday, 8:30AM-5PM; open many Saturday mornings in the fall and summer. Closed Sundays and holidays.

The alma mater of Nathaniel Hawthorne, Henry Wadsworth Longfellow, and Franklin Pierce has undergone significant changes in recent years. Bowdoin boasts two new, state-of-the-art science facilities and new residential halls, and it has bid a fond adieu to the traditional Greek system. Sports are a big deal here, and the Great Outdoors of Maine provide ample open-air opportunities.

AT A GLANCE

Selectivity Rating	95
Range SAT I Math	640-710
Average SAT I Math	680
Range SAT I Verbal	640-720
Average SAT I Verbal	680
Student to Faculty Ratio	11:1

CAMPUS TOURS

Appointment Req?	No
Dates	Year-round
Times	Mon-Fri 9:30AM, 11:30AM, 1:30PM, and 3:30PM; Sat 11:30AM
Avg. Length	1 hour

ON-CAMPUS INTERVIEWS

Admissions

Start Date—Juniors	May 1
Appointment Req?	Yes
Advance Notice	3-4 weeks
Saturdays?	Yes, during the fall
Avg. Length	30 min
Info Sessions	Sept-Dec and May-Aug

Faculty and Coaches

Dates/Times	Year-round; subject to faculty/coach availability
Arrangements	Contact faculty/coach as far in advance as possible

CLASS VISITS

Dates	Mon-Fri
Arrangements	Ask faculty a few minutes prior to class; class schedules available in admissions off.

OVERNIGHT DORM STAYS

Advance Notice	10-14 days
Arrangements	Contact admissions off.
Limitations	Seniors only; 1-night stay; not available on Fri or Sat nights or during exam periods

TRANSPORTATION

Portland International Jetport is about a 40-minute drive from campus. Mid Coast Limo (800-937-2424) is available for the trip from the airport to campus. Hertz (207-774-4544), Budget (800-527-0700), and other major rental car companies serve the airport. Arrange for limousine service or a rental car as early as possible.

FIND YOUR WAY

From the south, take the Maine Tpke. N. At Exit 6A (I-295, Portland), take I-295 N. Beyond Portland, I-295 rejoins I-95 N. Exit I-95 at Exit 22 (Bath-Brunswick/Coastal Rte. 1) and follow Rte. 1 into Brunswick, following signs for Maine St. At the intersection with Maine St., turn right; proceed straight (Bowdoin will be on the left), then turn left on College St., which takes you into the campus. **From the north**, take I-95 S. to the Topsham-Brunswick exit. Turn right onto Rte. 196; proceed to Maine St. in Brunswick and the College.

STAY THE NIGHT

Nearby: Down the main drag from the college is the **Captain Daniel Stone Inn** (10 Water St.; 207-725-9898). Rooms have color television, video cassette players (get movies from the desk), and phones. (Note: Rooms facing the highway are noisy.) **Brunswick B&B** (165 Park Row; 207-729-4914) is an appealing small bed-and-breakfast only a short walk from the college. Rates are moderate and include breakfast. For an indoor pool, exercise room, golf privileges, and game room, the best choice is **Atrium Inn and Convention Center** (U.S. 1; 207-729-5149, a mile north of campus). There is the **Comfort Inn** (800-221-2222), which isn't very far from the campus either.

A little farther: Many interesting, moderately priced bed and breakfasts are 10 to 20 minutes from campus. The **Captain York House** (207-833-6224) has the virtue of being on Bailey Island with spectacular ocean views. If closets are a must, this is not the place for you. **Harpswell Inn**, also on the water (141 Lookout Point Rd; 207-833-5509), is a rambling federal period house 12 minutes from campus, with charm, character, and a range of accommodations—plus a full breakfast. Your host is a Bowdoin grad. The **Tower Hill Bed and Breakfast** located on lovely Orr's Island (207-833-2311). For information on other accomodations please contact the Chamber of Commerce of the Bath-Brunswick Region (207-725-8797). See the University of New England entry for suggestions there. If you want to stay in Portland, see suggestions in the University of Southern Maine entry.

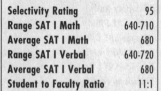

HIGHLIGHTS

ON CAMPUS
- Bowdoin College Museum of Art
- Peary-MacMillan Arctic Museum
- Hawthorne-Longfellow Library
- A 600-seat theater

OFF CAMPUS
- Pejepscot Historical Society
- Maine Maritime Museum
- Beautiful coastline and islands
- Plenty of seafood/ lobster restaurants

COLBY COLLEGE

Admissions and Financial Aid Office, Colby College, 4800 Mayflower Hill, Waterville, ME 04901 (The office is in the Lunder House, across the street from the Eustis Administration Building) • Telephone: 207-872-3168 or 800-723-3032 • Web: www.colby.edu • Email: admissions@colby.edu

Hours: Monday-Friday, 8:30AM-4:30PM; Saturday, 8:30AM-noon (only from September-January). Closed Sundays and holidays.

This small, selective college located in the center of Maine offers a great liberal arts education. The students at Colby College rarely leave campus when school is in session. A distinctive academic calendar allows students to study nontraditional subjects or intern during the month of January.

HIGHLIGHTS

ON CAMPUS
- Colby College Museum of Art
- Perkins Arboretum and Bird Sanctuary
- Johnson Pond
- Gravity Monument
- Bookstore

OFF CAMPUS
- Belgrade Lakes region
- Two-Cent Bridge
- Big-G's Sandwich Shop
- Waterville Opera House
- Railroad Square Cinema
  (Maine International Film Festival)

TRANSPORTATION

The Augusta State Airport is 20 miles from campus. Taxis are available for the ride from airport to campus. Most people fly to the Portland International Jetport, a 75-minute drive from Colby. Vermont Transit/Greyhound buses (800-231-2222) or Star Livery Shuttle (207-353-5244) can take you to Waterville from Portland.

FIND YOUR WAY

Take I-95 to Exit 33. Follow the signs off the exit ramp to get to Colby.

STAY THE NIGHT

Nearby: You have a number of motel choices in the area: **The Best Western** (356 Main St.; 207-873-3335), the **Holiday Inn** (375 Main St.; 207-873-0111), and **Econo Lodge** (455 Kennedy Memorial Dr.; 207-872-5577). For a Waterville bed and breakfast—**36 Burleigh Street** (207-873-6252).

A little farther: In Augusta, a 20-minute drive from Waterville, try **Best Western Senator Inn** (284 Western Ave.; 207-622-5804). Also, at Exit 31 from I-95, there are the **Comfort Inn** (Civic Center Dr.; 207-623-1000) and the **Holiday Inn** (Civic Center Dr.; 207-622-4751). Rates are moderate. See the Bates College entry for suggestions in and around Lewiston, and the University of Southern Maine entry for suggestions in Portland.

AT A GLANCE

Selectivity Rating	95
Range SAT I Math	610-700
Average SAT I Math	660
Range SAT I Verbal	610-690
Average SAT I Verbal	660
Average ACT Composite	28
Student to Faculty Ratio	10:1

CAMPUS TOURS

Appointment Req?	No
Dates	Year-round
Times	Call for times
Avg. Length	1 hour

ON-CAMPUS INTERVIEWS

Admissions

Start Date–Juniors	May 1
Appointment Req?	Yes
Advance Notice	2 weeks
Saturdays?	Yes, Sept to mid-Jan
Avg. Length	35 min
Info Sessions	Jan 16-April 30

Faculty and Coaches

Dates/Times	Year-round; subject to faculty/coach availability
Arrangements	Contact admissions off. 2 weeks prior

CLASS VISITS

Dates	Mon-Fri
Arrangements	Get class schedule at admissions off.

OVERNIGHT DORM STAYS

Advance Notice	2 weeks
Arrangements	Contact admissions off. at 207-872-3737
Limitations	Sun-Thurs in Oct, Nov, and April

THE UNIVERSTIY OF MAINE

Admissions Office, University of Maine, Chadbourne Hall, Orono, ME 04469 •
Telephone: 207-581-1561 • Web: www.umaine.edu •
Email: um-admit@maine.edu

Hours: Monday-Friday, 8AM-4:30PM. Closed weekends and holidays.

Engineering and forestry are both nationally esteemed at The University of Maine, but students say there is a wealth of excellent programs here. Social life features an abundance of outdoor activities and sports. Scary novelist extraordinaire Stephen King is an alum.

AT A GLANCE

Selectivity Rating	75
Range SAT I Math	480-600
Average SAT I Math	542
Range SAT I Verbal	480-590
Average SAT I Verbal	539
Average GPA	3.1
Student to Faculty Ratio	15:1

CAMPUS TOURS

Appointment Req?	Recommended
Dates	Year-round, excluding holidays
Times	Mon-Fri 9:15AM,11:15AM, and 1:15PM; Sat 11:15AM and 1:15PM
Avg. Length	75 min

ON-CAMPUS INTERVIEWS

Admissions

Start Date—Juniors	Any time
Appointment Req?	Preferred
Advance Notice	1 week
Saturdays?	No
Avg. Length	30-45 min
Info Sessions	Available as part of open house programs

Faculty and Coaches

Dates/Times	Year-round; subject to faculty/coach availability
Arrangements	Ask for professor's/ coach's permission

CLASS VISITS

Dates	Year-round (Mon-Fri)
Arrangements	With instructor's permission

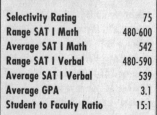

TRANSPORTATION

Bangor International Airport is 10 miles from campus. Taxis and rental cars are available at the airport.

FIND YOUR WAY

The university is located near Exit 51 from I-95. Follow the signs.

STAY THE NIGHT

Nearby: About a mile from campus is the **University Motor Inn** (5 College Ave.; 207-866-4921), with an outdoor pool and restaurant. While downtown, visit Margarita's for a taste of the border just off Main St. If Mexican doesn't sound just right, try the Bear Brew Pub or Pat's Pizza for some of the students' favorite foods. The **Best Western Black Bear Inn** (4 Godfrey Ave.; 207-866-7120) is only 2.5 miles from campus. It includes an exercise room and continental breakfast.

A little farther: Check out the **Ramada Inn** (357 Odlin Rd.; 207-947-6961) by the Bangor Airport, which has an indoor pool and is about 20 minutes from campus. **The Days Inn** (250 Odlin Rd.; 207-942-8272) also has an indoor pool. For a choice at the airport, try the **Budget Traveler Motor Lodge** (327 Odlin Rd.; 207-945-0110). For eating in Bangor, the Whig and Courier makes a great sandwich; and Bugaboo Creek Steak House provides a taste of the usual.

HIGHLIGHTS

ON CAMPUS
- Maine Center for the Arts
- Forest trails
- Art museum
- Planetarium
- Page Farm and Home Museum

OFF CAMPUS
- Acadia National Park
- Hermon Ski Mountain
- Lenard Mills
- Cole Transportation Museum
- Fort Knox

UNIVERSITY OF NEW ENGLAND

Admissions Office, University of New England, 11 Hills Beach Rd., Biddeford, ME 04005
(The office is in Decary Hall) • Telephone: 207-283-0171 or 800-477-4UNE •
Web: www.une.edu • Email: kberry@mailbox.une.edu

Hours: Monday-Friday, 9AM-4PM; open one Saturday a month. Closed Sundays and holidays.

Five-year programs in physical therapy and occupational therapy highlight the various health-related offerings at the University of New England, a small, independent college on the shores of the Atlantic Ocean in Biddeford, Maine. Practical experience is available at the University-run clinics of community health, physical therapy, and sports medicine.

HIGHLIGHTS

ON CAMPUS
- The Jack S. Ketchum Library
- The Campus Center
- The Point

OFF CAMPUS
- Maine Aquarium
- Dyer Library
- York Institute Museum

TRANSPORTATION

The Portland International Jetport is 17 miles from campus. Taxis and rental cars are available at the airport. Special transportation from the airport can be arranged for students by calling 207-283-0171, ext. 297, one week in advance. New England Transit and Maine Lines buses serve Biddeford.

FIND YOUR WAY

From I-95 (the Maine Tpke.), take Exit 4 (Biddeford) and turn left at the end of the toll gates onto Rte. 111. Follow Rte. 111 (Alfred St.) through the intersection with U.S. Rte. 1, and at the next light turn right onto Rte. 9/208 (Pool St.). Follow Pool St. approximately 4 miles to the university on the left.

STAY THE NIGHT

Nearby: You have 2 budget choices near the campus. **Sleepy Hollow** (297 Elm St. on U.S. Rte. 1; 207-282-0031) is an inexpensive motel in Biddeford, 4 miles from campus. **Beachwood Motel** (Rte. 9, Kennebunkport; 207-967-2483) is 7 miles away in nearby Kennebunkport (home of former president George Herbert Walker Bush) and is a little less expensive than Sleepy Hollow. **Captain Jefferds Inn** (Pearl and Pleasant Sts., Kennebunkport; 207-967-2311) is an early-19th-century former sea captain's home, now a delightful 15-room inn a half mile from the beach. Rates range from moderate to expensive and include a full breakfast in the dining room. **The Welby Inn** (92 Ocean Ave., Kennebunkport; 207-967-4655) is a comfortable bed-and-breakfast with 7 guest rooms, some with private baths. Rates are moderate and include a full breakfast. **The Captain Lord Mansion** (just off Ocean Ave., Kennebunkport; 207-967-3141) is listed on the National Register of Historic Places. The inn has 16 rooms and is a short walk to town. Midweek rates in May, June, November, and December are significantly lower than the normal, expensive rate. Ask about special packages. **Shawmut Inn** (Turbots Creek Rd., in Kennebunkport; 207-967-3931) is a 105-room motor hotel right on the ocean with pool, tennis courts, and golf privileges. There are supervised children's activities and live entertainment in the summer. Rates are expensive.

A little farther: See the University of Southern Maine entry for suggestions in Portland. See the Bowdoin College entry for suggestions in Brunswick and Freeport.

AT A GLANCE

Range SAT I Math	440-570
Average SAT I Math	540
Range SAT I Verbal	460-560
Average SAT I Verbal	530
Average GPA	3.2
Student to Faculty Ratio	9:1

CAMPUS TOURS

Appointment Req?	Preferred
Dates	Year-round
Times	Mon-Fri 10AM-1PM
Avg. Length	45-60 min

ON-CAMPUS INTERVIEWS

Admissions

Start Date—Juniors	Any time
Appointment Req?	Yes
Advance Notice	A few days
Saturdays?	No
Avg. Length	30-45 min
Info Sessions	Sept-March

Faculty and Coaches

Dates/Times	Year-round; subject to faculty/coach availability
Arrangements	Contact admissions off. for faculty and contact particular coach directly 1 week prior

CLASS VISITS

Dates	Year-round (Mon-Fri)
Arrangements	Contact admissions off.

OVERNIGHT DORM STAYS

Advance Notice	2 weeks
Arrangements	Contact admissions off.
Limitations	1-night stay; accepted students only

UNIVERSITY OF SOUTHERN MAINE

Admission Office, University of Southern Maine, 37 College Ave., Gorham, ME 04038 • Telephone: 207-780-5670 or 800-800-4876 • Web: www.usm.maine.edu • Email: usmadm@maine.maine.edu

Hours: Monday-Friday, 8AM-4:30PM; selected Saturdays 10AM-noon for campus tours and group information sessions.

The three cities of Lewiston, Portland, and Gorham host different branches of the University of Southern Maine. All the campuses build their degree offerings around a three-pronged, fancy-sounding core curriculum: Basic Competence; Methods of Inquiry/Ways of Knowing; and Interdisciplinary. Nearly 50 percent of the students here attend part time.

AT A GLANCE

Range SAT I Math	470-570
Average SAT I Math	520
Range SAT I Verbal	470-570
Average SAT I Verbal	523
Student to Faculty Ratio	13:1

CAMPUS TOURS

Appointment Req?	Yes
Dates	Sept-May and selected days in the summer
Times	Mon-Fri and selected Saturdays
Avg. Length	90 min; some tours include an information session

ON-CAMPUS INTERVIEWS

Admissions

Start Date–Juniors	N/A
Appointment Req?	Yes
Advance Notice	Yes
Saturdays?	Yes
Avg. Length	45 min
Info Sessions	Late Sept-early May and selected days in the summer

Faculty and Coaches

Dates/Times	Year-round; subject to faculty/coach availability
Arrangements	Contact particular faculty/coach several days to 1 week prior

CLASS VISITS

Dates	Late Sept-early May
Arrangements	Call 2 weeks prior

OVERNIGHT DORM STAYS

Advance Notice	N/A
Arrangements	N/A
Limitations	N/A

TRANSPORTATION

Portland International Jetport is approximately 5 miles from campus. Taxis or rental cars are available at the airport; call 207-774-3941 to make arrangements. New England Transit buses serve Portland.

FIND YOUR WAY

From the north, take Maine Tpke. to Exit 8. Follow Route 25 west to Gorham. At Gorham Center, stay straight on Route 25 west for approximately half a mile. Turn right onto Husky Drive. Admission House is immediately on left. **From the south**, take Maine Tpke. to Exit 6 and turn left after the tollbooth. At the second traffic light turn left onto Route 114 north; follow it to Gorham. At Gorham Center, take left to Route 25 west and follow for approximately half a mile. Take right onto Husky Drive. Admission House is immediately on left.

STAY THE NIGHT

Nearby: In the town of Gorham, there is **Pine Crest Bed and Breakfast** (207-839-5843), located on Route 114. This is a quaint old home within half a mile of the Gorham campus. The **Portland Regency** in the Old Port (20 Milk St.; 207-774-4200 or 800-727-3436) is a small hotel in the heart of the lively Old Port District. A 10-minute drive from the Portland campus, the Regency provides valet parking and has a well-equipped health club. Also located in the city of Portland, the **Eastland Hotel** (157 High St.; 207-775-5411 or 800-333-3333) is at Congress Square, near the Arts District. Nearby as well is the **Holiday Inn by the Bay** (88 Spring St.; 775-2311 or 800-HOLIDAY). Located beyond the downtown area, are the **Double Tree Hotel** (1230 Congress St.; 207-774-5611 or 800-222-TREE) and **Holiday Inn-Portland West** (81 Riverside St.; 207-774-5601 or 800-HOLIDAY).

A little farther: See the University of New England for suggestions in the Kennebunk area or Bowdoin College for suggestions in the Brunswick/Freeport area.

HIGHLIGHTS

ON CAMPUS
- Art Gallery
- Costello Sports Complex
- Russell Theater and Concert Hall
- Southworth Planetarium
- TV/radio station

OFF CAMPUS
- Minor league baseball and hockey
- Old Port/Caslo Bay Area
- Sebago Bay
- Portland Museum of Art
- Sunday River Ski Resort

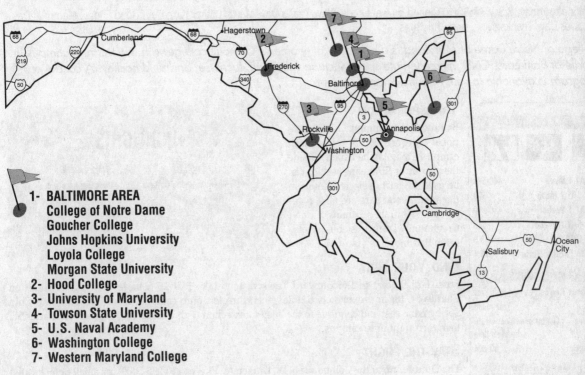

1- **BALTIMORE AREA**
   College of Notre Dame
   Goucher College
   Johns Hopkins University
   Loyola College
   Morgan State University
2- **Hood College**
3- **University of Maryland**
4- **Towson State University**
5- **U.S. Naval Academy**
6- **Washington College**
7- **Western Maryland College**

Maryland	Coll. Notre Dame	Goucher College	Hood College	Johns Hopkins	Loyola College	Morgan State	Towson State	U.S. Naval Acad.	Univ. Maryland-C.P.	Washington Coll.	Western Maryland	*Baltimore*
Coll. Notre Dame	—	3	52	6	3	4	3	25	37	70	27	0
Goucher College	3	—	51	6	3	4	1	25	39	71	26	0
Hood College	52	51	—	51	50	51	53	69	48	114	31	46
Johns Hopkins	6	6	51	—	1	3	4	25	37	70	30	0
Loyola College	3	3	50	1	—	1	3	25	38	69	30	0
Morgan State	4	4	51	3	1	—	4	25	39	68	31	0
Towson State	3	1	53	4	3	4	—	34	40	67	28	2
U.S. Naval Academy	25	25	69	25	25	25	34	—	30	49	54	25
Univ. Maryland-C.P.	37	39	48	37	38	39	40	30	—	92	61	28
Washington Coll.	70	71	114	70	69	68	67	49	92	—	97	67
Western Maryland	27	26	31	30	30	31	28	54	61	97	—	29
Baltimore	0	0	46	0	0	0	2	25	28	67	29	—

COLLEGE OF NOTRE DAME OF MARYLAND

Office of Admissions, College of Notre Dame of Maryland, 4701 N. Charles St., Baltimore, MD 21210 (The office is in Theresa Hall) • Telephone: 410-532-5330 • Web: www.ndm.edu • Email: admiss@ndm.edu

Hours: Monday-Friday, 8:30AM-4:30PM. Closed on weekends, New Year's Day, Martin Luther King Day, Good Friday, Memorial Day, July 4, Labor Day, Thanksgiving, and Christmas.

The College of Notre Dame of Maryland is a primarily all-women's Catholic college with a waterfront campus in the middle of Baltimore. CND intercollegiate sports include volleyball, lacrosse, and field hockey. A coed weekend program is available for busy nontraditional students.

AT A GLANCE

Range SAT I Math	440-540
Average SAT I Math	500
Range SAT I Verbal	480-590
Average SAT I Verbal	540
Average GPA	3.3
Student to Faculty Ratio	15:1

CAMPUS TOURS

Appointment Req?	Yes
Dates	Year-round
Times	Contact admissions off. to schedule a time
Avg. Length	50 min

ON-CAMPUS INTERVIEWS

Admissions

Start Date–Juniors	Any time
Appointment Req?	Yes
Advance Notice	1 week
Saturdays?	Regularly scheduled throughout the year
Avg. Length	20 min
Info Sessions	Regularly scheduled throughout the academic year

Faculty and Coaches

Dates/Times	Year round
Arrangements	Contact the admissions off. to schedule appointment

CLASS VISITS

Dates	Regularly scheduled throughout academic year
Arrangements	Contact admissions off. at 410-532-5330

OVERNIGHT DORM STAYS

Advance Notice	Yes
Arrangements	Contact admissions off.
Limitations	Regularly scheduled throughout the academic year

TRANSPORTATION

Baltimore-Washington International Airport is 18 miles from campus. Taxis can be hailed outside the airport or limousine service can be used to get to selected hotels in the area. Rental cars are also available. Amtrak trains and Greyhound/Trailways buses also serve Baltimore.

FIND YOUR WAY

From I-95 S., exit to I-695 toward Towson, then take Exit 25 (Charles St.). Travel south on Charles St. for approximately 5 miles, then turn left onto campus. From I-83, exit onto Cold Spring Lane east and continue to the busy intersection with Charles St. Turn left on Charles St., then turn right onto campus.

STAY THE NIGHT

The Double Inn at the Colonnade (4 W. University Pkwy.; 410-235-5400) is a small hotel located only minutes from campus. Also consider the Sheraton Baltimore (903 Dulaney Valley Rd., Towson; 410-321-7400). It has a pool, exercise room, sauna, jacuzzi, and two restaurants. Ask for the special college visitor rate. For Maryland bed-and-breakfasts, call The Traveler in Maryland (410-269-6232). Check the Johns Hopkins and Goucher entries for additional choices in the Baltimore area.

HIGHLIGHTS

ON CAMPUS
• Loyola/Notre Dame Library

OFF CAMPUS
• National Aquarium
• Inner Harbor
• Baltimore Museum of Art
• Oriole Park at Camden Yards
• Maryland Science Center

GOUCHER COLLEGE

Admissions Office, Goucher College, 1021 Dulaney Valley Rd., Baltimore, MD 21204 (The office is located in the College Center) • Telephone: 800-GOUCHER (outside Maryland) or 410-337-6100 • Web: www.goucher.edu • Email: admission@goucher.edu

Hours: Monday-Friday, 9AM-5PM. Open on six selected Saturdays in the fall for Information Days. Closed Sundays and holidays.

Once an all-women's bastion, this tiny liberal arts college took the great coed leap about a decade ago. Social life is laid back and the well-liked administration sponsors a number or events, including the Blind Date Ball and Goucherfest, an all-campus celebration.

HIGHLIGHTS

ON CAMPUS
- The Julia Rogers Library
- The Rosenberg Art Gallery
- Meyerhoff Art Center

OFF CAMPUS
- National Aquarium
- Inner Harbor
- Baltimore Museum of Art
- Oriole Park at Camden Yards
- Maryland Science Center

TRANSPORTATION

Baltimore-Washington International Airport (BWI) is 18 miles from campus. A hotel shuttle to the Towson Sheraton (which is adjacent to campus) is relatively cheap; reservations are not required. The hotel shuttle desk is located on the lower level at BWI near baggage carousel #4. Taxis are also available for the ride from the airport to campus; they are much more expensive than the hotel shuttle. Amtrak trains and Greyhound/Trailways buses serve Baltimore. Taxis are available from the stations to campus.

FIND YOUR WAY

From I-695 (Baltimore Beltway), take Exit 27A (Dulaney Valley Rd. S.). The entrance to the college is immediately on the left.

STAY THE NIGHT

Nearby: **The Sheraton Baltimore** (903 Dulaney Valley Rd., Towson; 410-321-7400) is within walking distance of Goucher. It has a pool, exercise room, sauna, jacuzzi, and 2 restaurants. Ask for the special rate for college visitors. A moderately priced **Holiday Inn** (1100 Cromwell Bridge Rd., Towson; 410-823-4410) with similar amenities is about 10 minutes away. For Maryland bed-and-breakfasts, call **The Traveler in Maryland** (410-269-6232).

A little farther: Goucher is actually in the suburb of Towson, 8 miles north of the center of Baltimore. If you prefer to stay in the center of town, see the Johns Hopkins University entry. It might be fun to explore historic Annapolis, 45 minutes away. See the U.S. Naval Academy entry for suggestions there.

AT A GLANCE

Selectivity Rating	79
Range SAT I Math	520-630
Average SAT I Math	570
Range SAT I Verbal	550-660
Average SAT I Verbal	610
Average ACT Composite	26
Average GPA	3.1
Student to Faculty Ratio	10:1

CAMPUS TOURS

Appointment Req?	Highly recommended
Dates	Year-round
Times	Sept-May: Mon-Fri 9:30AM, 10:30AM, 1:30PM, and 2:30PM. June-Aug: Mon-Fri 9:30AM, 10:30AM, and 12:30PM.
Avg. Length	1 hour

ON-CAMPUS INTERVIEWS

Admissions

Start Date–Juniors	April 1
Appointment Req?	Highly recommended
Advance Notice	1 week
Saturdays?	Selected days in the fall
Avg. Length	30-45 min
Info Sessions	Summer and fall

Faculty and Coaches

Dates/Times	Year-round; subject to faculty/coach availability
Arrangements	Contact admissions off. 1 week prior

CLASS VISITS

Dates	Year-round (Mon-Fri)
Arrangements	Contact admissions off.

OVERNIGHT DORM STAYS

Advance Notice	2 weeks
Arrangements	Contact admissions off.
Limitations	Mon-Thurs nights only

HOOD COLLEGE

Admissions Office, Hood College, 401 Rosemont Ave., Frederick, MD 21701
(The office is in Strawn Cottage) • Telephone: 800-922-1599 or 301-696-3400 •
Web: www.hood.edu • Email: admissions@hood.edu

Hours: Monday-Friday, 9AM-5PM; Saturday, 9AM-noon. Closed Sundays and holidays.

About 900 students take advantage of the dynamic liberal arts education at Hood College, a residential college for women (Hood also offers commuter and evening programs for male students). Located in historic Frederick, Maryland, the school's proximity to Washington, D.C., makes for phenomenal internship options, from the White House to the American Red Cross to CNN.

AT A GLANCE

Range SAT I Math	490-590
Average SAT I Math	544
Range SAT I Verbal	500-630
Average SAT I Verbal	572
Average ACT Composite	24
Average GPA	3.5
Student to Faculty Ratio	10:1

CAMPUS TOURS

Appointment Req?	Preferred
Dates	Year-round, except when officially closed
Times	Mon-Fri at 10AM; Sat at 10AM and 11AM
Avg. Length	1 hour

ON-CAMPUS INTERVIEWS

Admissions

Start Date–Juniors	Any time
Appointment Req?	Preferred
Advance Notice	2 days
Saturdays?	Yes, 9AM-noon
Avg. Length	35 min
Info Sessions	Available only as part of special programs

Faculty and Coaches

Dates/Times	Aug-May; subject to faculty/coach availability
Arrangements	Contact admissions off. 1 week prior

CLASS VISITS

Dates	Year-round (Mon-Fri)
Arrangements	Contact admissions off.

OVERNIGHT DORM STAYS

Advance Notice	1 week
Arrangements	Contact admissions off.
Limitations	2-night maximum stay; not permitted on Sat night

TRANSPORTATION

National Airport and Baltimore-Washington International Airport are 50 miles from campus. Dulles Airport is 40 miles from campus. Metro, taxi, and limousine services all serve the campus. Call the admissions office at 800-922-1599 to arrange for these services.

FIND YOUR WAY

From the north, follow I-95 S. to the Baltimore Beltway (I-695). Follow I-695 W. (toward Towson) to the exit for I-70 W. Proceed on I-70 W. to Frederick, and exit onto Rte. 15 N. At the Rosemont Ave. exit, turn left onto Rosemont for half a mile, then turn left at Hood's entrance. **From Washington,** follow I-270 N.W. to the junction with I-70 and Rte. 15. Take Rte. 15 N. and follow the preceding directions from that point. **From the west,** take I-70 E. from Hagerstown. At the first Frederick exit, take Rte. 40 E. to the junction with Rte. 15. Take Rte. 15 N. and follow the preceding directions from that point. **From the east,** take I-70 W. and follow the directions from the north from that point.

STAY THE NIGHT

Nearby: The **Tyler-Spite House** (112 W. Church St.; 301-831-4455) is a few blocks from campus. This historic 1814 mansion has 6 rooms with either queen or double beds. Rates are moderate on weekdays and expensive on weekends. The price includes breakfast, afternoon tea, and an evening carriage ride through the historic district to your choice of restaurant. The historic town of New Market (just off I-70 at Exit 62), about 6 miles from Hood, is the location of 2 great inns. **Strawberry Inn** (17 W. Main St.; 301-865-3318) is a serene, white clapboard built in the 1840s and restored by the present owners. Rates are moderate and a continental breakfast is included. **Turning Point Inn** (3406 Urbana Pike; 301-874-2421) is 6 miles to the south of campus. Rates are moderate. Also offering moderate rates are the **Marriott Courtyard** (5225 Westview Dr.; 301-631-9030) and a **Fairfield Inn** (5220 Westview Dr.; 301-631-2000) within 5 miles.

A little farther: Civil War buffs should stay at the **Inn at Antietam** (220 E. Main St., Sharpsburg; 301-432-6601), a Victorian inn on the Civil War battlefield. Rates are higher on weekends than during the week, and include a full breakfast.

HIGHLIGHTS

ON CAMPUS
- Whitaker Campus Center
- Beneficial Hodson Library and
- Information Technology Center
- Alumnae Hall
- Brodbeck Music Hall
- Coffman Chapel

OFF CAMPUS
- Historic Downtown Frederick
- Cunningham Falls State Park
- Antietam National Battlefield
- National Museum of Civil War Medicine
- Barbara Fritchie House and Museum

JOHNS HOPKINS UNIVERSITY

Office of Admissions, Johns Hopkins University, 3400 N. Charles St., Baltimore, MD 21218 (The office is in Rm. 140, Garland Hall) • Telephone: 410-516-8171 • Web: www.jhu.edu • Email: gotojhu@jhu.edu

Hours: Monday-Friday, 8:30AM-5PM; Saturday, 11AM-noon (in the fall). Closed Sundays (check with office about hours during holidays).

If you choose highly regarded and highly competitive Johns Hopkins University, be prepared for a tremendous workload and advanced course work. First-year students at this Baltimore school take their first semester pass/fail, which offers them a little more time to find their niches while staying afloat academically. Students say self-motivation is a requirement here.

HIGHLIGHTS

ON CAMPUS
- Arthur Friedheim Library
- Lacrosse Hall of Fame & Museum
- Homewood House
- Evergreen House

OFF CAMPUS
- Baltimore Museum of Art
- Maryland Science Center
- National Aquarium in Baltimore
- Oriole Park at Camden Yards
- B&O Railroad Museum

TRANSPORTATION

Baltimore-Washington International Airport is a 30-minute drive from campus. We recommend that you take a limousine to one of the downtown hotels, then take a taxi to Garland Hall on the university's Homewood Campus. Taxis also offer service to the campus from the airport. The Amtrak station is a 10-minute drive south of campus; the Greyhound bus terminal is in downtown Baltimore. From either station, take a taxi and be sure to ask to be driven to Garland Hall on the Homewood Campus of Johns Hopkins.

FIND YOUR WAY

From the north, take I-95 S. to Exit 64-B (695 W./Towson). (I-695 is the Baltimore Beltway.) Follow I-695 W. 9 miles to Exit 25 (Charles St., Rte. 139). Turn left at the stop sign, then left again onto Charles St. Follow Charles St. back over the Beltway, and proceed south 8 miles to University Pkwy. Johns Hopkins is on the right. Stay to the right and enter the service lane, which begins at the intersection of University Pkwy. and Charles St. Follow this lane to the third light and turn right onto Art Museum Dr. Proceed 1 block, and just beyond the Museum bear right onto Wyman Park Dr. for 100 feet to the southern entrance to the campus. Turn right at this brick-gated entrance; a visitor parking lot is on the left. Garland Hall is the first building on the left, beyond the grass field. **From the south**, take I-95 N. Do not take the Harbor Tunnel or Beltway exits. Follow signs for downtown Baltimore ("Inner Harbor/Memorial Stadium—Use 395 N." and "395 N., Right Lanes"). Take exits marked "395 N. Downtown" and "395 Downtown/Inner Harbor." Turn right at Conway St. (first traffic light). Proceed 2 blocks to Charles St. and turn left. Follow Charles St. north approximately 2.5 miles to 29th St. and turn left. Almost immediately ahead is a traffic light and beyond this is a fork in the road. Bear right, then merge onto Howard St. Immediately get into the center lane and at the triangular intersection turn left onto Wyman Park Dr. On the right just beyond this turn are the brick gates at the entrance to campus. Turn right into the entrance and look for visitor parking on the left. Garland Hall is the first building ahead on the left, beyond the grass field. **From U.S. Rte. 40 E. or W.**, drive through the city to Charles St. Turn north on Charles and follow the preceding directions (from the south) from Charles St. to campus.

STAY THE NIGHT

Across the street is the **Inn at the Colonnade** (4 W. University Pkwy.; 410-235-5400) with a special university-visitor rate. Another good choice is the **Hopkins Inn** (3404 St. Paul St.; 410-235-8600), only 2 blocks from campus. Rates are moderate. For more ideas in and around Baltimore, see the College of Notre Dame, Goucher, and Towson State entries.

LOYOLA COLLEGE

Admissions Office, Loyola College, 4501 N. Charles St., Baltimore, MD 21210
(The office is in the Humanities Building) • Telephone: 800-221-9107 ext. 5012
or 410-617-5012 • Web: www.loyola.edu

Hours: Monday-Friday, 9AM-5PM; Saturday, open only for special programs. Closed Sundays and holidays.

The course load is heavy at Loyola College in Baltimore, and the core curriculum allows few options the first two years, but classes are small, professors are concerned with helping students succeed, and the students here tell us they are challenged but satisfied. Novelist Tom Clancy is an alum.

AT A GLANCE

Selectivity Rating	81
Range SAT I Math	560-650
Average SAT I Math	603
Range SAT I Verbal	550-650
Average SAT I Verbal	602
Average GPA	3.4
Student to Faculty Ratio	14:1

CAMPUS TOURS

Appointment Req?	Preferred
Dates	Year-round
Times	Mon-Fri following the 10AM and 1:30PM info sessions
Avg. Length	1 hour

ON-CAMPUS INTERVIEWS

Admissions

Start Date–Juniors	Late April
Appointment Req?	Yes
Advance Notice	2 weeks
Saturdays?	No
Avg. Length	20 min
Info Sessions	Year-round

Faculty and Coaches

Dates/Times	Year-round; subject to faculty/coach availability
Arrangements	Contact dept. of interest or the particular coach 2 weeks prior

CLASS VISITS

Dates	Year-round (Mon-Fri)
Arrangements	Contact admissions off. at least 2 weeks prior

TRANSPORTATION

The Baltimore-Washington International Airport is 23 miles from campus. Taxis and rental cars are available at the airport, and limousine service is provided to area hotels. Amtrak trains and Greyhound buses also serve Baltimore.

FIND YOUR WAY

From I-695 (Baltimore Beltway), take Exit 25 (Charles St.). Proceed south on Charles St. approximately 7 miles. The college's main entrance is on North Charles St., just north of the Cold Spring Lane intersection.

STAY THE NIGHT

Check the College of Notre Dame, Goucher, and Johns Hopkins, and Loyola entries for places to stay in and around Baltimore. For Maryland bed-and-breakfasts, call **The Traveler in Maryland** (410-269-6232).

HIGHLIGHTS

ON CAMPUS
• Loyola/Notre Dame Library
• The Loyola College Art Gallery

OFF CAMPUS
• Baltimore's Inner Harbor
• National Aquarium
• Babe Ruth Museum
• Walters Art Gallery
• Oriole Park at Camden Yards

MORGAN STATE UNIVERSITY

Admissions Office, Morgan State University, 1700 East Cold Spring Lane and Hillen Rd., Baltimore, MD 21239 (The office is in Northwood Annex) • Telephone: 410-319-3000 • Web: www.morgan.edu • Email: tjenness@moac.morgan.edu

Hours: Monday-Friday, 9AM-5PM. Closed on weekends and holidays.

Morgan State is a primarily African American school that has gained national recognition in the past 10 years. Morgan boasts more than 30 specialized, nontraditional programs of study, including several for pre-college students.

HIGHLIGHTS

ON CAMPUS
- Morris A. Soper Library
- Murphy Fine Arts Center
- Armory

OFF CAMPUS
- National Aquarium
- Maryland Science Center
- Baltimore's Inner Harbor
- The Black Wax Museum
- Oriole Park at Camden Yards

TRANSPORTATION

The Baltimore-Washington International Airport is approximately 15 miles from campus. Taxis, limousines, and rental cars are available for the trip from the airport. Amtrak trains and Greyhound buses serve Baltimore.

FIND YOUR WAY

Take I-695 (the Baltimore Beltway) to Exit 30 S. (Perring Pkwy.). Take Perring Pkwy. for 5 miles to the campus at Cold Spring Lane and Hillen Rd. The admissions office is in Northwood Annex.

STAY THE NIGHT

The **Best Western** (5625 O'Donnell St.; 410-633-9500) has the advantage of an indoor pool. It also has a fitness center and restaurant on the premises. The price is moderate and it is a 20-minute drive from campus. A **Holiday Inn** (6510 Frankfurt Ave.; 410-485-7900) is closer (3 to 4 miles away), but more expensive (upper end of moderate range). For Maryland bed-and-breakfasts, call **The Traveler in Maryland** (410-269-6232). The colleges closest to Morgan State are College of Notre Dame and Towson State University. See these and the Goucher and Johns Hopkins entries for other accommodations.

AT A GLANCE

Student to Faculty Ratio	17:1

CAMPUS TOURS

Appointment Req?	Yes
Dates	Feb-April, June to mid-July, and Oct to early Dec; no tours during school breaks
Times	Mon-Fri 10AM-3PM for individuals and families; Mon-Fri 10AM-2PM for groups
Avg. Length	45 min

ON-CAMPUS INTERVIEWS

Admissions

Start Date–Juniors	Any time
Appointment Req?	Yes
Advance Notice	3 weeks
Saturdays?	No
Avg. Length	30 min
Info Sessions	Mon-Fri when school is in session; not available during school breaks and from mid-Dec to Feb

Faculty and Coaches

Dates/Times	Year-round; subject to faculty/coach availability
Arrangements	Contact admissions off.

CLASS VISITS

Dates	Year-round (Mon-Fri)
Arrangements	Contact admissions off.

OVERNIGHT DORM STAYS

Advance Notice	N/A
Arrangements	N/A
Limitations	N/A

TOWSON UNIVERSITY

Office of Admissions, Towson University, Towson, MD 21252 (The office is in the Enrollment Services Center at Osler Dr. & Towsontown Blvd.) • Telephone: 888-4TOWSON or 410-830-2113 • Web: www.towson.edu • Email: admissions@towson.edu

Hours: Monday-Friday, 8:30AM-5PM; Saturday, 10AM-1PM (fall and spring semesters only). Closed Sundays and holidays.

Located near Baltimore, Towson University is a comprehensive public institution with almost 15,000 students of both the traditional and nontraditional varieties. Towson boasts a perennially strong women's gymnastics team, and entertainment options abound in Baltimore—from the National Aquarium to Oriole Park at Camden Yards.

AT A GLANCE

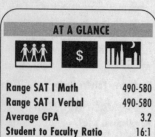

Range SAT I Math	490-580
Range SAT I Verbal	490-580
Average GPA	3.2
Student to Faculty Ratio	16:1

CAMPUS TOURS

Appointment Req?	Yes
Dates	Year-round
Times	Mon-Fri 11AM and 2:30PM (time may change when classes are not in session); Sat 11AM and noon
Avg. Length	90 min

ON-CAMPUS INTERVIEWS

Admissions

Start Date—Juniors	Any time
Appointment Req?	Yes
Advance Notice	3 weeks
Saturdays?	No
Avg. Length	45 min
Info Sessions	Available as part of the fall and spring Open Houses

Faculty and Coaches

Dates/Times	Year-round; subject to faculty/coach availability
Arrangements	Contact coach or academic dept. 2 weeks prior

CLASS VISITS

Dates	By appointment only

OVERNIGHT DORM STAYS

Advance Notice	N/A
Arrangements	N/A
Limitations	N/A

TRANSPORTATION

Baltimore-Washington International Airport is about 25 miles from campus. You can get a taxi at the airport or you can take an airport limousine to the Sheraton Towson, a short taxi ride to campus. Amtrak trains and Greyhound/Trailways buses serve Baltimore.

FIND YOUR WAY

From the Baltimore Beltway (I-695), take Exit 25 (Charles St.). Proceed south (toward Baltimore) on Charles St. to Towsontown Blvd. (the second traffic signal south of the Beltway on Charles St.); turn left on Towsontown Blvd. (a sign is posted at this intersection indicating the left turn to Towson University) and proceed to the campus.

STAY THE NIGHT

Nearby: If convenience and affordability are what you're into, check out the stylish **Burkshire Guest Suites and Conference Center**. Located on campus at York Rd. and Burke Ave., the Burkshire is minutes from shopping, theaters, fine dining, and all the recreational, cultural, and educational opportunities of a major metropolitan area. Be sure to mention TU's Open House for a discount. Call 410-324-8101 or 800-435-5986 for information and reservations.

A little farther: See the College of Notre Dame and Johns Hopkins University entries for some suggestions in Baltimore.

HIGHLIGHTS

ON CAMPUS
- Minegan Stadium
- Center for the arts
- University student union
- More than 100 clubs and organizations
- Honors Program

OFF CAMPUS
- National Aquarium
- Oriole Park at Camden Yards
- ESPN Zone
- Baltimore Zoo
- PSI Net Stadium

UNITED STATES NAVAL ACADEMY

Admission Office, United States Naval Academy, 117 Decatur Road, Annapolis, MD 21402-5018 • Telephone: 410-293-4361 or 800-638-9156 • Web: www.usna.edu • Email: webmail@qwmail.usna.com

Hours: Monday-Friday, 8AM-5PM; Saturday, 9AM-noon. Closed Sundays and all federal holidays.

The United States Naval Academy in Annapolis provides a stellar and rigorous education in the arts and sciences and, of course, training in military and naval service. The midshipmen eagerly anticipate the annual Army-Navy football game, perhaps the most historic of college gridiron contests.

HIGHLIGHTS

ON CAMPUS	OFF CAMPUS
• Dahlgren Hall	• Downtown Annapolis
• U.S. Naval Academy Museum	• The waterfront area and docks
• Armel-Leftwich Visitor Center	• Walking tours
• U.S. Naval Academy Chapel	• Boat cruises
• Lejeune Hall	• Beautifully preserved 18th-century buildings

TRANSPORTATION

Baltimore-Washington International Airport is 25 miles from the academy. Shuttle service is available from the airport.

FIND YOUR WAY

From I-95, take the Beltway to the east around Washington, DC (toward New Carrollton). Exit to U.S. Rte. 50/301 E. toward Annapolis. From U.S. 50/301, take Exit 24 Rowe Blvd. into Annapolis, then turn left onto College Ave. Proceed on College Avenue, and at the stoplight turn right onto King George Street. St. The Academy's entrance is at King George and Randall Streets.

STAY THE NIGHT

The Academy is at one end of the historic town of Annapolis. **Gibson's Lodgings** (110 Prince George St.; 410-268-5555) is adjacent to the academy and offers 20 rooms, some with private baths, in 3 houses. The moderate rate includes continental breakfast and parking. Rooms with shared baths are cheaper. Another moderately priced bed-and-breakfast near the Academy is the Victorian **Prince George Inn** (232 Prince George St.; 410-263-6418), with 4 guest rooms sharing 2 baths. Rooms are air-conditioned, and the price includes a large continental breakfast. There are 4 historic inns restored and run by **Historic Inns of Annapolis**, all close to the Academy. The **Maryland Inn**, the farthest away but the liveliest (44 rooms and a restaurant), is only a 10-minute walk from the Academy. All of these inns are booked through Historic Inns of Annapolis (410-263-2641 or 800-847-8882 outside of MD). Mail requests to 16 Church Circle, Annapolis, MD 21401. For an indoor pool, exercise room, restaurant, and weekend dancing, head for the **Wyandham Garden** (173 Jennifer Rd.; 410-266-3131), 5 miles away.

AT A GLANCE

Selectivity Rating	99
Range SAT I Math	630-720
Range SAT I Verbal	600-670
Student to Faculty Ratio	7:1

CAMPUS TOURS

Appointment Req?	No
Dates	Early March to late Nov
Times	Jun-Sept: Mon-Sat 9:30AM-3:30PM; Sun 12:30PM-3:30PM. Sept-Nov and March-Jun: Mon-Fri 10AM-3PM; Sat 10AM-3:30PM; Sun 12:30PM-3:30PM.
Avg. Length	1 hour

ON-CAMPUS INTERVIEWS

Admissions

Start Date–Juniors	Any time
Appointment Req?	No
Advance Notice	None
Saturdays?	Yes
Avg. Length	45 min
Info Sessions	Only admission briefs are available

Faculty and Coaches

Dates/Times	Year-round; subject to faculty/coach availability
Arrangements	Contact particular faculty/coach directly

CLASS VISITS

Dates	Only as part of an overnight visit
Arrangements	By invitation only

OVERNIGHT DORM STAYS

Advance Notice	1 month
Arrangements	Contact admissions off.
Limitations	Only candidates who have completed admissions packets and are judged by the academy to be competitive

UNIVERSITY OF MARYLAND—COLLEGE PARK

Office of Undergraduate Admissions, University of Maryland, College Park, Mitchell Building, College Park, MD 20742 • Telephone: 301-314-8385 or 800-422-5867 • Web: www.maryland.edu • Email: um-admit@uga.umd.edu

Hours: Monday-Friday, 8:30AM-4:30PM. Closed on weekends and holidays.

The very affordable University of Maryland is a major research university that offers a serious environment and, for those who qualify, an exemplary honors program. Maryland's core curriculum requires students to fulfill a wide range of distribution requirements and then, during senior year, take two seminars designed to help integrate these disparate courses into their majors. Newscaster Connie Chung and Muppet creator Jim Henson are graduates.

AT A GLANCE

Selectivity Rating	78
Range SAT I Math	580-680
Range SAT I Verbal	560-660
Average GPA	3.6
Student to Faculty Ratio	14:1

CAMPUS TOURS

Appointment Req?	No, but groups should call 800-422-5867 in advance
Dates	When classes are in session
Times	Call for times
Avg. Length	90 min

ON-CAMPUS INTERVIEWS

Admissions

Start Date—Juniors	N/A
Appointment Req?	N/A
Advance Notice	N/A
Saturdays?	N/A
Avg. Length	N/A
Info Sessions	Call in advance for current schedule

Faculty and Coaches

Dates/Times	Year-round; subject to faculty/coach availability
Arrangements	Contact dept. of interest or coach 2-4 weeks prior

CLASS VISITS

Dates	Year-round (Mon-Fri)
Arrangements	Contact Adopt-a-Student Program at 800-422-5867

OVERNIGHT DORM STAYS

Advance Notice	Yes
Arrangements	With current student
Limitations	Available only during open house programs; call 301-314-4255

TRANSPORTATION

Baltimore-Washington International Airport is 25 miles from campus. MARC trains (800-325-7245) and airport shuttles are available for the trip from the airport to the campus. Washington National Airport is 15 miles from campus. Metrorail trains (202-637-7000) are available for the trip from the airport to the campus. Amtrak and Greyhound are available to Washington, D.C. Switch to Metrorail at Union Station and take it to College Park. University shuttle buses (301-314-2255) provide transportation from the College Park MARC and Metrorail stations to campus.

FIND YOUR WAY

From Baltimore and the north, take I-95 S. to the Capital Beltway (I-495 around Washington, DC); follow signs to College Park. At Exit 25, take U.S. 1 S. for approximately 2 miles, then turn right into campus at the Visitor's Center. **From the west**, follow the preceding directions from the Capital Beltway (I-495). **From the east**, take U.S. 50 W. to the Capital Beltway (I-495); head north on I-495 to College Park. At Exit 25, take U.S. 1 S. for 2 miles and turn right into campus. **From Washington, DC**, take New Hampshire Ave. (U.S. 29) or Riggs Road (N. Capitol St. in DC, Maryland Rte. 212) north to the East-West Highway (Maryland Rte. 410); turn right onto Rte. 410 and proceed to U.S. 1 and turn left on it. Continue on U.S. 1 to the campus, turning left at the Visitor's Center.

STAY THE NIGHT

Nearby: The **Center of Adult Education** (301-985-7300), a conference center on campus, has moderately priced rooms. **The Quality Inn** (7200 Baltimore Ave.; 301-864-5829) is half a mile away. Slightly less expensive is **Econo Lodge** (9113 Baltimore Blvd.; 301-345-4900), 1 mile away. Your rock-bottom budget choice is **Comfort Inn** (9020 Baltimore Blvd.; 301-441-8110), a mile and a half away. For a more upscale chain motel, try the **Holiday Inn** (10000 Baltimore Blvd.; 301-345-6700), or **Courtyard by Marriott** (8330 Corporate Dr., Landover; 301-577-3373). There is an even fancier Marriott, the **Marriott Greenbelt** (6400 Ivy Lane, Greenbelt; 301-441-3700), 15 minutes away. Two bed-and-breakfast referral agencies with listings in the area are **The Traveller in Maryland** (410-269-6232), and **Amanda's B&B Reservation Service** (410-225-0001).

A little farther: College Park is 20 minutes from downtown Washington, DC. See entries for any of the Washington, DC schools for suggestions.

HIGHLIGHTS

ON CAMPUS
- Campus recreation center
- Adele H. Stamp Student Union
- Cole Student Activities Building
- Byrd Stadium
- Memorial Chapel

OFF CAMPUS
- Washington, D.C., attractions
- Baltimore's Inner Harbor

WASHINGTON COLLEGE

Admissions Office, Washington College, 300 Washington Ave., Chestertown, MD 21620-1197
(The office is located in the Casey Academic Center) • Telephone: 800-422-1782 or
410-778-7700 • Web: www.washcoll.edu • Email: adm.off@washcoll.edu

Hours: Monday-Friday, 8:30AM-4:30PM; Saturday, 8:30AM-noon (on selected dates only). Closed Sundays, New Year's Day, July 4, Thanksgiving, and Christmas.

About 1,000 students study at this, the nation's 10th oldest university, located in historic Chestertown, Maryland. In addition to offering a fine liberal arts education, the school boasts a creative writing program with exceptional resources at the O'Neill Literary House: a social haven, publishing house, and writer's think tank rolled into one.

HIGHLIGHTS

ON CAMPUS
- Miller Library
- Lifetime Fitness Center
- Gibson Center & Tawes Theater

OFF CAMPUS
- Chesapeake Bay Maritime Museum
- Chesapeake Bay
- The Historic District
- Eastern Neck Island National Wildlife Refuge

TRANSPORTATION

Baltimore-Washington and Philadelphia International airports are 75 miles from campus. Washington College students are available to transport visitors between the campus and either airport; call 410-778-7700 at least a week in advance to arrange for this service. Amtrak train and Greyhound bus service are available to Baltimore and Wilmington, DE. Contact the Washington College admissions office for more information on transportation available to campus from the bus and train stations.

FIND YOUR WAY

From the north, take I-95 S. to Rte. 896 S. in Newark, DE. Follow to Rte. 301 S. and exit at Galena. Proceed to Rte. 213. Take Rte. 213 S. to Chestertown. **From the south**, take I-95 N. to U.S. 50 and 301 (Exit 19). Take U.S. 50 and 301 E.; stay on U.S. 301 N. when it splits from U.S. 50. Continue on U.S. 301 to the intersection with Maryland Rte. 213; then take Rte. 213 N. into Chestertown.

STAY THE NIGHT

Nearby: **Comfort Suites** (160 Scheeler Rd.; 410-810-0555), a moderately priced motel, is just 5 blocks away. If you venture a little farther into historic Chestertown, you have a terrific choice of bed-and-breakfasts and inns. **Widow's Walk Bed and Breakfast** (402 High St.; 410-778-6864) is 6 blocks from campus and moderately priced. About 8 blocks from campus is the **White Swan Tavern** (231 High St.; 410-778-2300), a beautifully restored inn dating back to the 1700s with 6 rooms, private baths, and complimentary wine on arrival; bicycles are available for guests. Rates range from moderate to expensive. (Note: The inn does not take credit cards.) The **Imperial Hotel** (208 High St.; 410-778-5000) has 13 air-conditioned guest rooms with TVs and private baths. Rates are expensive. If you prefer a rural setting, consider **Brampton Bed and Breakfast** (Rte. 20; 410-778-1860), a wonderful brick house sitting on 35 lush acres 1 mile from campus (and from historic Chestertown).

A little farther: **Mears Great Oak Landing** (22170 Great Oak Landing Rd.; 410-778-2100) is a 70-acre yachting resort on a tributary of the Chesapeake Bay with a 9-hole golf course, tennis courts, pool, and private beach. The resort is 9 miles from campus and rates are moderate.

AT A GLANCE

Range SAT I Math	490-590
Average SAT I Math	545
Range SAT I Verbal	500-620
Average SAT I Verbal	562
Average GPA	3.2
Student to Faculty Ratio	12:1

CAMPUS TOURS

Appointment Req?	Yes
Dates	Year-round
Times	Mon-Fri 9AM-3PM
Avg. Length	40 min

ON-CAMPUS INTERVIEWS

Admissions

Start Date–Juniors	Any time
Appointment Req?	Yes
Advance Notice	At least 1 day
Saturdays?	Yes, but only on selected days
Avg. Length	40 min
Info Sessions	Available, but not regularly scheduled; sessions are 90 min

Faculty and Coaches

Dates/Times	Sept-May; subject to faculty/coach availability
Arrangements	Contact admissions off. 1 week prior

CLASS VISITS

Dates	Year-round (Mon-Fri)
Arrangements	Contact admissions off.

OVERNIGHT DORM STAYS

Advance Notice	1 week prior
Arrangements	Contact admissions off.
Limitations	1-night stay only

WESTERN MARYLAND COLLEGE

Admissions Office, Western Maryland College, 2 College Hill, Westminster, MD 21157-4390
(The office is in Carroll Hall) • Telephone: 410-857-2230 • Web: www.wmdc.edu •
Email: admission@wmdc.edu

Hours: Monday-Friday, 8:30AM-4:30PM; Saturday, 9AM-noon by arrangement only. Closed Sundays and holidays.

Situated between Chesapeake Bay and the Blue Ridge Mountains, in the Central Maryland community of Westminster, Western Maryland College is a private, liberal arts school with an enrollment of 1,500. Students rave about the exceptional scholarship offerings, as well as the breathtaking views available from most dorm windows.

AT A GLANCE

Range SAT I Math	500-610
Average SAT I Math	565
Range SAT I Verbal	500-620
Average SAT I Verbal	570
Average ACT Composite	24
Average GPA	3.4
Student to Faculty Ratio	13:1

CAMPUS TOURS

Appointment Req?	Yes
Dates	Oct-April
Times	Mon-Fri 10:15AM-2PM
Avg. Length	45 min

ON-CAMPUS INTERVIEWS

Admissions

Start Date–Juniors	Any time
Appointment Req?	Yes
Advance Notice	1-2 weeks
Saturdays?	Yes
Avg. Length	40 min
Info Sessions	Year-round

Faculty and Coaches

| Dates/Times | Year-round; subject to faculty/coach availability |
| Arrangements | Contact coach |

CLASS VISITS

| Dates | Oct-April (Mon-Fri) |
| Arrangements | Contact admissions off. |

OVERNIGHT DORM STAYS

Advance Notice	3 weeks
Arrangements	Contact admissions off.
Limitations	Students must attend classes

TRANSPORTATION

Baltimore-Washington International Airport is 45 minutes from campus.

FIND YOUR WAY

From I-95, exit to I-695 W. (Baltimore Beltway). From I-695, take Exit 19 to I-795 (the Northwest Expy.). Follow I-795 to its end, then follow signs to Westminster via Rte. 140 W. Proceed around Westminster and turn left onto Rte. 31. Continue for half a mile (with the Western Maryland College golf course on the left); at the second traffic light, turn left onto Uniontown Road. Proceed for a third of a mile and turn left into the college parking lot. **From I-495 (Washington Beltway)**, exit onto I-270 toward Frederick, then onto Rte. 27/Damascus. At the intersection of Rtes. 27 and 32, turn left and drive half a mile. Bear left at the fork; then make the first right into the college parking lot.

STAY THE NIGHT

Nearby: A **Best Western** (451 Western Maryland College Dr.; 410-876-0010) is across the street. Ask for the college visitor rate and you get tennis, golf, and health club privileges through the college. For something a little different, consider the **Winchester Country Inn** (430 Bishop St.; 410-876-7373), a 5-minute drive from campus. This 18th-century inn, with 5 guest rooms (some with private baths), is very close to the Carroll County Farm Museum and the Farmers Market. The moderate price includes a full breakfast and afternoon tea or sherry. The **Westminster Inn** (5 S. Center St.; 410-857-4445), half a mile away, is elegantly fitted with a jacuzzi and private bath in each room. Prices, which include a full breakfast, are fairly expensive. A good budget choice is **Boston Inn** (533 Baltimore Blvd.; 410-848-9095), 2 miles from campus.

A little farther: Westminster is 30 minutes from Gettysburg. See the Gettysburg College entry for suggestions in this historic area.

HIGHLIGHTS

ON CAMPUS
• The Hoover Library
• Peterson Hall

OFF CAMPUS
• Carroll Country Farm Museum
• Mills Homestead and House Museum
• Carroll County Historical Society

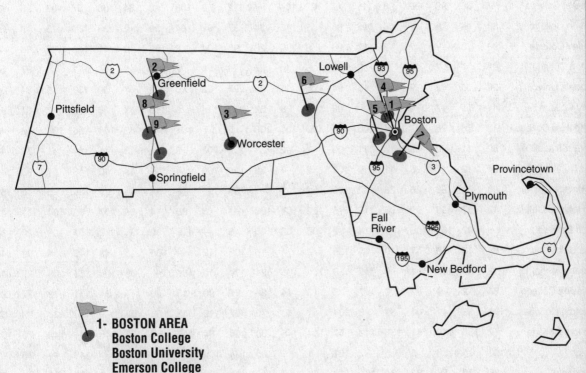

Pittsfield

Greenfield

2

2

Lowell

93 95

6

4

8

3

1

5 1

Boston

9

Worcester

90

7

Springfield

95

3

Provincetown

Plymouth

7

90

Fall
River

195

6

195

New Bedford

1- **BOSTON AREA**
Boston College
Boston University
Emerson College
Northeastern University
Simmons College
2- **AMHERST AREA**
Amherst College
Hampshire College
U. of Massachusetts-Amherst
3- **WORCESTER AREA**
Clark University
College of the Holy Cross
Worcester Polytechnic Inst.
4- **CAMBRIDGE AREA**
Harvard-Radcliffe Colleges
Massachusetts Inst. Tech.
Tufts University
5- **WELLESLEY AREA**
Babson College
Wellesley College
6- **WALTHAM AREA**
Bentley College
Brandeis University
7- **Curry College**
8- **Smith College**
9- **Mount Holyoke**

MASSACHUSETTS

Mass.

	Amherst College	Babson College	Bentley College	Boston College	Brandeis Univ.	Curry College	Hampshire College	Harvard-Radcliffe	M. I. T.	Merrimack Coll.	Mt. Holyoke Coll.	Smith College	Tufts University	U. Mass-Amherst	Wellesley College	Wheaton College	Williams College	Boston*	Springfield	Worcester**
Amherst College	—	88	98	99	96	111	7	102	104	96	12	8	108	2	84	106	57	103	25	47
Babson College	88	—	8	7	6	15	86	11	12	34	87	92	14	90	2	33	130	15	79	31
Bentley College	98	8	—	7	2	17	96	6	7	26	98	104	8	100	9	41	140	9	86	40
Boston College	99	7	7	—	9	9	97	6	5	25	99	105	7	101	9	41	141	6	87	38
Brandeis Univ.	96	6	2	9	—	16	94	8	11	28	97	102	10	98	7	39	138	6	84	38
Curry College	111	15	17	9	16	—	108	11	9	32	110	114	16	113	17	28	142	7	101	59
Hampshire College	7	86	96	97	94	108	—	100	101	100	5	7	105	9	82	104	56	101	18	45
Harvard-Radcliffe	102	11	6	6	8	11	100	—	2	21	102	108	2	104	13	41	144	1	89	44
M. I. T.	104	12	7	5	11	9	101	2	—	22	104	109	4	106	14	40	146	1	93	44
Merrimack Coll.	96	34	26	25	28	32	100	21	22	—	108	103	18	94	36	70	130	25	112	55
Mt. Holyoke Coll.	12	87	98	99	97	110	5	102	104	108	—	5	108	14	85	107	60	104	11	47
Smith College	8	92	104	105	102	114	7	108	109	103	5	—	112	10	90	112	54	109	20	53
Tufts University	108	14	8	7	10	16	105	2	4	18	108	112	—	106	15	43	146	4	91	46
U. Mass-Amherst	2	90	100	101	98	113	9	104	106	94	14	10	106	—	86	108	55	105	27	49
Wellesley College	84	2	9	9	7	17	82	13	14	36	85	90	15	86	—	34	131	12	77	29
Wheaton College	106	33	41	41	39	28	104	41	40	70	107	112	43	108	34	—	148	31	89	52
Williams College	57	130	140	141	138	142	56	144	146	130	60	54	146	55	131	148	—	143	70	100
Boston*	103	15	9	6	6	7	101	1	1	25	104	109	4	105	12	31	143	—	90	42
Springfield	25	79	86	87	84	101	18	89	93	112	11	20	91	27	77	89	70	90	—	53
Worcester**	47	31	40	38	38	59	45	44	44	55	47	53	46	49	29	52	100	42	53	—

*Use Boston mileage for Boston University, Emerson College, Northeastern University, and Simmons College.

**Use Worcester mileage for Clark University, College of the Holy Cross, and Worcester Polytechnic Institute.

AMHERST COLLEGE

Admissions Office, Amherst College, Box 2231, Amherst, MA 01002-5000 (The office is off Rte. 116) • Telephone: 413-542-2328 • Web: www.amherst.edu • Email: admissions@amherst.edu

Hours: Monday-Friday, 8:30AM-4:30PM; Saturday, 9AM-noon (fall only). Closed Sundays, Memorial Day, July 4, Labor Day, Thanksgiving, and Christmas.

Outstanding professors highlight the occasionally strenuous experience at this truly outstanding, small, liberal arts college. Campus life is often slow but there are numerous ways to get involved and, when students become claustrophobic, nearby UMass, Smith, Hampshire, and Mount Holyoke offer a nice change of pace.

HIGHLIGHTS

ON CAMPUS
- Mead Art Museum
- Pratt Museum of Natural History

OFF CAMPUS
- Emily Dickinson House
- Jones Library

TRANSPORTATION

Bradley International Airport near Hartford, CT is 45 miles from campus. Peter Pan bus line (800-237-8747), Valley Transporter limousines (800-237-8747 or 413-253-1350), rental cars, and taxis are available for the trip from the airport to campus. Amtrak trains provide regular service from New York City to Springfield, MA. Greyhound buses serve Springfield hourly from Boston and New York. Buses also run hourly from Springfield to Amherst. Taxis (and, during the academic year, the free Five College Bus Service) are available for the trip from town to campus.

FIND YOUR WAY

From the south, take I-91 N. to Exit 19. Take Rte. 9 E. for 7 miles. In the town of Amherst, turn right onto Rte. 116 S. Proceed a quarter mile to the admissions office on the left. **From the east**, take I-90 W. (Massachusetts Tpke.) to Exit 8 (Palmer-Amherst). Take Rte. 181 N. to Rte. 9 W. From Rte. 9, turn left onto Rte. 116 S. for a quarter mile to the admissions office. **From the west**, take I-90 E. to the W. Springfield exit. Head north on I-91 to Exit 19; then head east on Rte. 9 for 7 miles to the town of Amherst. Turn right onto Rte. 116 S. for a quarter mile to the admissions office. **From the north**, take I-91 S. to Exit 25 (Amherst). Take Rte. 116 S. to the admissions office.

STAY THE NIGHT

Lord Jeffery Inn (413-253-2576), on the Common in Amherst, is a popular place with Amherst visitors. It has character and is conveniently located within walking distance. Rates are moderate. **Howard Johnson Motor Lodge in Hadley** (413-586-0114). **Amherst Motel** (408 Northampton Rd.; 413-256-8122) is cheap and it has a pool, and a Friendly's is across the street. **Aqua Vitae Motel** (Bay Rd., Hadley; 413-586-0300) is even cheaper, and is only 5 miles away. No breakfast is served here, but there is a café nearby. A third choice is **Econo Lodge** (Rte. 9, Hadley; 413-584-9816), 10 minutes away. Just like the Aqua Vitae, no breakfast is served, but a café is nearby. Smith College, in Northampton, is only 15 minutes away. Check that entry. A couple of other motels convenient to Amherst are listed under the University of Massachusetts, which is only 2 miles to the north.

AT A GLANCE

Selectivity Rating	98
Range SAT I Math	650-740
Average SAT I Math	697
Range SAT I Verbal	650-760
Average SAT I Verbal	700
Average ACT Composite	30
Student to Faculty Ratio	9:1

CAMPUS TOURS

Appointment Req?	No
Dates	Year-round, except vacations, exam periods, and winter session; available only sporadically during the first 2 weeks of semester
Times	Sept-Dec: Mon-Fri 9AM, 11AM, 1PM, and 3PM; Sat and Sun 10AM, 12PM, and 2PM. Feb-May: Mon-Fri 9AM, 11AM, 1PM, and 3PM; Sat and Sun, 10AM, 12PM, and 2PM.
Avg. Length	1 hour

ON-CAMPUS INTERVIEWS

Admissions

Info Sessions	Late March to mid-Nov, mid-Dec to Jan

Faculty and Coaches

Dates/Times	Sept-Dec and Feb-May; subject to faculty/coach availability
Arrangements	Contact admissions off. as far in advance as possible

CLASS VISITS

Dates	Year-round (Mon-Fri)
Arrangements	Consult class schedule at the admissions off.

OVERNIGHT DORM STAYS

Advance Notice	2 weeks
Arrangements	Contact admissions off.
Limitations	Mon, Tues, and Wed nights only; late Sept-Nov, Feb-May 1

BABSON COLLEGE

Admission Office, Babson College, Babson Park, MA 02457 (The office is in Mustard Hall) • Telephone: 800-488-3696 or 781-239-5522 • Web: www.babson.edu • Email: ugradadmission@babson.edu

Hours: Monday-Friday, 8:30AM-4:30PM; open Saturdays in fall and January only. Closed Sundays and some holidays.

This small school in Massachusetts is touted by its students as the best business school in the country. A highly praised and compulsory entrepreneurship curriculum requires teams of students to start and operate their own actual businesses.

AT A GLANCE

Selectivity Rating	88
Range SAT I Math	590-670
Range SAT I Verbal	540-630
Student to Faculty Ratio	11:1

CAMPUS TOURS

Appointment Req?	No
Dates	Year-round
Times	Schedule varies; contact admissions off.
Avg. Length	45 min

ON-CAMPUS INTERVIEWS

Admissions

Start Date–Juniors	Preferably May 1 of junior year
Appointment Req?	Yes
Advance Notice	As far in advance as possible
Saturdays?	Yes, on selected days
Avg. Length	45 min
Info Sessions	Contact admissions off.

Faculty and Coaches

Dates/Times	Year-round; subject to faculty/coach availability
Arrangements	Contact admissions off. or athletic off.

CLASS VISITS

Dates	Year-round (Mon-Fri)
Arrangements	Contact admissions off.

OVERNIGHT DORM STAYS

Advance Notice	At least 2 weeks prior
Arrangements	Contact admissions off.
Limitations	Not Fri-Sun nights

TRANSPORTATION

Logan International Airport is approximately 12 miles from campus. Taxis are available for the ride to campus, but they are quite expensive. Public transportation by commuter rail line is convenient and more reasonably priced. Take the MBTA train from the Airport (Blue Line) inbound into Boston. Transfer at Government Center to the Green Line, and take the Riverside "D" train to Riverside Station. From there, you can take a taxi for the remaining 3-mile ride to the Babson campus. Amtrak trains and Greyhound buses also run to Boston.

FIND YOUR WAY

From I-90 (Massachusetts Tpke.), exit to I-95/Route 128 S. Follow I-95 to Exit 20B (Route 9W). Continue on Rte. 9 W for 1.9 miles and take the Rte. 16 exit. At the end of the exit ramp, turn left onto Rte. 16 W. (Washington St.). Follow Rte. 16 W. for half a mile and turn left at the traffic lights onto Forest St. Follow Forest St. for 1 mile to the stop sign. Proceed straight through the intersection for .2 miles. The main entrance to the Babson campus will be on your right.

STAY THE NIGHT

Nearby: **The Sheraton Needham** (100 Cabot St., Needham Heights; 781-444-1110) is located 10 minutes from Babson College. Rates vary from inexpensive to moderate, and the hotel has a health spa. The **Holiday Inn Newton** (399 Grove St., Newton; 617-969-5300), about 5 minutes away from the school, has a special moderate rate usually available for college visitors. Fancier motor hotels are also located in Newton, which is 15 minutes or so from Babson. The **Marriott Hotel** (2345 Commonwealth Ave.; 617-969-1000) has indoor and outdoor pools, a playground, an exercise room, and a game room. It is on the river, so you can go boating. Rates here are very expensive. See the Wellesley College entry for other suggestions in Wellesley and for bed-and-breakfast options. Be sure to check out the **Wellesley Inn** (576 Washington St.; 781-235-0180), 2 miles from Babson.

A little farther: See the Brandeis University entry for suggestions in Waltham (6 miles away) and in the historic Lexington-Concord area. See the Emerson College entry for accommodations in Boston center (about 15 miles away).

HIGHLIGHTS

ON CAMPUS
- Sorenson Arts Center
- Blank Center for Entrepreneurship
- Glavin Family Chapel
- The Gallery (Horn Library)

OFF CAMPUS
- Cultural and historic sites in Boston

BENTLEY COLLEGE

Undergraduate Admissions Office, Bentley College, 175 Forest St., Waltham, MA 02452-4705 (The office is on the 2nd floor of Rauch Administration Ctr.) • Telephone: 800-523-2354 or 781-891-2244 • Web: www.bentley.edu • Email: ugadmission@bentley.edu

Hours: Monday-Friday, 8:30AM-4:30PM; Saturday, 9AM for interviews and tours by appointment only. Closed Sundays and holidays.

Business-oriented Bentley College requires all students to take accounting, business law, computer information systems, finance, and marketing courses. The school is built on a mountain in Waltham, a Boston suburb only 15 minutes from Harvard Square.

HIGHLIGHTS

ON CAMPUS
- Financial trading room
- Smith Academic Technology Center
- Coffeehouse
- Center for Marketing Technology
- Dana Athletic Center

OFF CAMPUS
- Harvard Square
- Downtown Boston shopping
- Boston North End
- Boston's club scene
- Major league sports (Red Sox, Patriots, Bruins, Celtics)

TRANSPORTATION

Logan International Airport in Boston is 12 miles from Bentley College, with transportation to campus available by taxi, MBTA trains and buses, and rental car. Amtrak offer frequent passenger service to South Station in Boston from all points along the Northeast Corridor. Public transportation is available from South Station to campus.

FIND YOUR WAY

From the south, take Route 95/128 North to exit 28A (Trapelo Road). Turn right at the end of exit ramp and follow 2.6 miles toward Belmont. Turn right onto Forest Street. Approximately 1 mile on the left is the main entrance to the Bentley campus. **From the west,** take the Massachusetts Tpke. to exit 14 and follow signs to Route 95/128 N; proceed as directed in "from the south."

STAY THE NIGHT

There are several hotels located near the Bentley campus. These include: **Doubletree Guest Suites** (550 Winter St.; 781-890-6767), **The Westin Hotel** (70 Third Avenue; 781-290-5600), and **Wyndham Garden Hotel** (420 Totten Pond Road; 781-890-0100).

AT A GLANCE

Selectivity Rating	80
Range SAT I Math	520-610
Average SAT I Math	535
Range SAT I Verbal	490-580
Average SAT I Verbal	565
Student to Faculty Ratio	16:1

CAMPUS TOURS

Appointment Req?	Yes
Dates	Year-round
Times	Sept-May when class is in session: Mon-Fri 10AM-3PM on the hour; Sat by appt. only. When class is not in session: Mon-Fri 10AM and 2PM. June-Aug: Mon-Thurs 10AM and 2PM; Sat by appt. only.
Avg. Length	1 hour

ON-CAMPUS INTERVIEWS

Admissions

Start Date—Juniors	Any time
Appointment Req?	Yes
Advance Notice	2 weeks
Saturdays?	Yes
Avg. Length	45 min
Info Sessions	N/A

Faculty and Coaches

Dates/Times	Year-round; subject to faculty/coach availability
Arrangements	Contact admissions off. for faculty and contact coaches directly, several weeks prior

CLASS VISITS

Dates	Available only through the Day Visitation Program
Arrangements	Contact admissions off.

OVERNIGHT DORM STAYS

Advance Notice	N/A
Arrangements	N/A
Limitations	N/A

BOSTON COLLEGE

Office of Undergraduate Admission, Boston College, Devlin Hall 208,
Chestnut Hill, MA 02467-3809 • Telephone: 617-552-3100 (Fax: 617-552-0798) •
Web: www.bc.edu • Email: ugadmis@bc.edu

Hours: Monday-Friday, 9AM-4:45PM; some fall Saturdays and Columbus Day 9AM-3PM. Closed Sundays and holidays.

Boston College is neither a college (it's a university) nor in Boston (it's in Chestnut Hill). It is, however, a large Jesuit school with a rich Catholic tradition and nationally recognized schools of business, nursing, and education. Downtown Boston, with its vital, college-oriented nightlife, is only 20 minutes away by car or public transportation.

AT A GLANCE

Selectivity Rating	95
Range SAT I Math	610-690
Range SAT I Verbal	590-680
Student to Faculty Ratio	15:1

CAMPUS TOURS

Appointment Req?	No
Dates	Year-round, except Jan, spring break, May, end Aug to third weekend Sept, Thanksgiving break, and mid-Dec to Jan
Times	End of Sept to mid-Dec and Feb to April: Mon-Sat after Info Session. June to Aug: Mon-Fri 11AM,12PM, 1PM, and 3PM; Sat, 10AM and noon.
Avg. Length	1 hour

INFORMATION SESSIONS

Info Sessions	Year-round, except Jan, spring break, May, end Aug to third weekend of Sept, Thanksgiving break, and mid-Dec to Jan

Faculty and Coaches

Dates/Times	Year-round; subject to faculty/coach availability
Arrangements	Contact dept. 2 week prior

CLASS VISITS

Dates	Available through the Day Visitation Program
Arrangements	Contact Student Admissions Program at 617-552-3378

OVERNIGHT DORM STAYS

Advance Notice	N/A
Arrangements	N/A
Limitations	N/A

TRANSPORTATION

Logan International Airport in Boston is 7 miles from campus. Public transportation, rental cars, and taxis are available from the airport to campus. Amtrak trains and Greyhound buses provide service to Boston. Local public transportation to the College is provided by the Boston College branch of the Massachusetts Bay Transit Authority's Green Line. The Green Line ends at the Boston/Newton boundary on Commonwealth Ave. The walk up the hill brings you to the entrance of the Chestnut Hill campus.

FIND YOUR WAY

From **I-95 (also known as Rte. 128)**, take Exit 24 (Rte. 30). Proceed east on Rte. 30 (Commonwealth Ave.) for approximately 5 miles to the campus. **From the west**, take the Massachusetts Tpke. to Exit 17. At the first set of lights after the exit ramp, turn right onto Centre St. and follow it to the 4th set of lights. Turn left onto Commonwealth Ave. and proceed on it for a mile and a half to the campus.

STAY THE NIGHT

A conveniently located hotel is **Marriott-Newton** (2345 Commonwealth Ave.; 800-228-9290) priced moderately to expensive. Ten minutes away is a **Holiday Inn** (399 Grove St.; 800-HOLIDAY), which has a special BC rate. The **Best Western Terrace** (1650 Commonwealth Ave., Brighton; 800-528-1234) is 1.5 miles from campus and is inexpensive to moderately priced.

HIGHLIGHTS

ON CAMPUS
- McMullen Museum of Art
- Alumni Stadium
- Robsham Theater
- Bapst Library
- Higgins Biology and Physics Center

OFF CAMPUS
- Fenway Park
- Boston Commons
- Museum of Fine Arts
- Freedom Trail
- Walden Pond

BOSTON UNIVERSITY

Office of Admissions, Admissions Reception Center, 121 Bay State Rd., Boston, MA 02215 • Telephone: 617-353-2318 • Web: www.bu.edu/admissions/visit/campus • Email: visit@bu.edu

Hours: Monday-Friday, 8:30AM-5PM; designated Saturday mornings during the academic year (late September to mid-May). Closed Sundays and holidays. Please call the office or look online for the most current schedule.

Large, private Boston University offers an outstanding atmosphere for learning and a diverse student body. There's a lot of red tape, but the academic experience is excellent and the tremendous social life is second to none. Talk about prominent alumni: Martin Luther King, Jr. received his doctorate from BU.

HIGHLIGHTS

ON CAMPUS
- Marsh Chapel Plaza
- Special collections, Mugar Memorial Library
- DeWolfe Boathouse
- George Sherman Student Union
- The Photonics Center

OFF CAMPUS
- Museum of Fine Arts
- Boston Red Sox at Fenway Park
- Charles River Esplanade
- Newbury Street shopping district
- Symphony Hall

TRANSPORTATION

By the MBTA, the "T," take the Green Line train (Boston College B line, Cleveland Circle C line, or Riverside D line) to Kenmore Square Station. Walk west 1 block to Deerfield St. and turn right. Walk 1 block to Bay State Rd. and turn left. The Admissions Reception Center is located on the right side. From the airport, the T may take an hour and requires a transfer from the Blue Line to the Green Line at Government Center Station, and taxis may take approximately 30 minutes. For more information visit Logan International Airport online at www.massport.org/logan/toandfr. Amtrak service and major bus companies arrive at Boston's South Station. Taxis to Boston University take approximately 20 minutes, and the T may take 40 minutes and requires a transfer from the Red Line to the Green Line at Park St. Station.

FIND YOUR WAY

From west of Boston, take I-90 (Massachusetts Tpke.) to Exit 18 (Brighton/Cambridge). Pay toll, then follow signs for Cambridge down the ramp to the 2nd set of lights. Turn right at the lights (do not cross over the bridge/Charles River) and travel on Soldiers Field Rd./Storrow Dr. to the 2nd Boston University exit. Follow the local directions below. **From north of Boston,** take Route 93 south to the Storrow Dr. exit (Exit 26). Continue on Storrow Dr. to the Kenmore Square exit (left exit). Follow signs for Kenmore Square. Follow the local directions below. **From south of Boston,** take Interstate 93 N./Route 3 N. to Storrow Dr. exit (Exit 26). Go west on Storrow Dr. to Kenmore Square exit (left exit). Follow signs for Kenmore Square. Follow the local directions below. **Local Directions:** Turn right off the exit ramp at the traffic light (Beacon St.). Stay to the right to enter Bay State Rd. The Admissions Reception Center will be on the right, 121 Bay State Rd. Metered parking is available, and a campus parking lot, which offers parking for a flat fee, is located off Commonwealth Ave. just west of Kenmore Square.

STAY THE NIGHT

Boston University is located in the Back Bay/Fenway area of Boston. The University does not endorse any particular hotel establishment. The following list is provided to assist with travel planning.

Nearby: Within walking distance of the University are a number of hotels, including **Howard Johnson's Hotel** (575 Commonwealth Ave.; 617-267-3100), the **Eliot Suite Hotel** (320 Commonwealth Ave.; 800-44ELIOT), **Buckminster Hotel** (645 Beacon St.; 617-236-7050), **Beacon Townhouse Inn** (1047 Beacon St.; 800-872-7211), **Anthony's Townhouse Inn** (1085 Beacon St.; 617-566-0792), and the **Beacon Inn** (1087 Beacon St.; 617-566-0088).

A little farther: Within 10 to 15 minutes (by car or public transportation), there are a number of choices, including **Holiday Inn** in Brookline (617-277-1200), **Brookline Manor House** (800-535-5325), **Howard Johnson's Cambridge** (617-492-7777), **Westin Copley Place** (617-262-9200), **The Lenox** (800-471-1422), **Doubletree Guest Suites** (617-783-0090), **Best Western Terrace Inn** (617-566-6260), **Marriot Copley Place** (617-236-5800), **Sheraton Boston** (617-236-2000), and **The Park Plaza Hotel** (617-426-2000).

AT A GLANCE

Selectivity Rating	90
Range SAT I Math	590-680
Average SAT I Math	630
Range SAT I Verbal	590-680
Average SAT I Verbal	631
Average ACT Composite	27
Average GPA	3.5
Student to Faculty Ratio	13:1

CAMPUS TOURS

Appointment Req?	No
Dates	Year-round
Times	Mon-Fri and select Saturdays; check online for times
Avg. Length	1 hour

ON-CAMPUS INTERVIEWS

Admissions

Start Date—Juniors	Feb
Appointment Req?	Yes
Advance Notice	3-4 weeks
Saturdays?	No
Avg. Length	30-45 min
Info Sessions	Year-round

Faculty and Coaches

Dates/Times	Year-round; subject to faculty/coach availability
Arrangements	Contact admissions off. for information

CLASS VISITS

Dates	Year-round (Mon-Fri)
Arrangements	Contact admissions off. 3-4 weeks in advance

OVERNIGHT DORM STAYS

Advance Notice	N/A
Arrangements	N/A
Limitations	N/A

BRANDEIS UNIVERSITY

Shapiro Admissions Center, Brandeis University, Box 9110, Waltham, MA 02454-9110 •
Telephone: 800-622-0622 (outside MA) or 781-736-3500 • Web: www.brandeis.edu •
Email: sendinfo@brandeis.edu

Hours: Monday-Friday, 9AM-5PM; Saturday, limited schedule in October and April. Closed Sundays and holidays.

Relatively young Brandeis University (founded in 1948), is a liberal arts school in suburban Boston with world-class research opportunities and a host of great undergraduate programs. About 1 in 6 Brandeis grads goes on to law school and 1 in 11 to medical school.

AT A GLANCE

Selectivity Rating	90
Range SAT I Math	610-710
Average SAT I Math	660
Range SAT I Verbal	610-710
Average SAT I Verbal	660
Average GPA	3.5
Student to Faculty Ratio	8:1

CAMPUS TOURS

Appointment Req?	No
Dates	Year-round
Times	Mon-Fri 10AM, 11AM, 1PM, and 3PM; some on weekends, breaks, and in May
Avg. Length	1 hour

ON-CAMPUS INTERVIEWS

Admissions

Start Date—Juniors	May 15 jr. year to Feb 15 sr. year
Appointment Req?	Yes
Advance Notice	3 weeks
Saturdays?	No
Avg. Length	30 min
Info Sessions	June-Aug, some school vacation weeks, and Saturdays in Oct

Faculty and Coaches

Dates/Times	Year-round; subject to faculty/coach availability
Arrangements	Contact admissions off. 2-3 weeks prior

CLASS VISITS

Dates	Sept-April (Mon-Fri)
Arrangements	Contact admissions off.

OVERNIGHT DORM STAYS

Advance Notice	2 weeks
Arrangements	Contact admissions off.
Limitations	Seniors; 1-night stay; Mon-Thur; Oct-April

TRANSPORTATION

Logan International Airport in Boston is 15 miles from campus. To get to campus, you can take the U.S. Shuttle service to Brandeis (617-489-4701; about $20) or take a "Share-a-Cab," regular taxi, or airport shuttle and subway to campus from the airport. The admissions office will supply information on these transportation possibilities. Greyhound buses (and some other lines) serve the Riverside Terminal in Newton; from there you can take a taxi to campus. Amtrak trains and Greyhound and other bus lines serve Boston. Commuter trains from Boston bring you within walking distance of campus.

FIND YOUR WAY

From I-90 (Massachusetts Tpke.) eastbound, take Exit 14 for I-95/Rte. 128 and Rte. 30 exit in Weston. Follow the signs to Rte. 30 (exit 24); at the top of the ramp, turn left onto Rte. 30. Take the first right and continue to campus, which is 2 miles ahead on the left. **From I-90 westbound**, take exit 15 for I-95/Rte. 128 and Rte. 30. After the tollgate, go straight. At the top of the ramp, turn right; at the traffic light, turn right, and at the next traffic light, turn left. Campus is 2 miles ahead on the left. **From Rte. 128/I-95 northbound**, take Exit 24. At the top of the ramp, turn left onto Rte. 30; take the first right; campus is 2 miles ahead on the left. From **Rte. 128/I-95 southbound**, take Exit 24. At the traffic light, go straight; campus is 2 miles ahead—you guessed it—on the left.

STAY THE NIGHT

Nearby: A slightly expensive **Best Western TLC** (477 Totten Pond Rd.; 781-890-7800 or 800-424-2900) has an indoor pool and exercise room. For a bit more money, there is the newly renovated **Wyndham Garden Hotel** (420 Totten Pond Rd.; 781-890-0100 or 800-996-3426). **The Double Tree Guest Suites** (550 Winter St.; 781-890-6767), 10 minutes from campus, is cool but pricey. The **Westin Hotel** (70 3rd Ave.; 781-290-5600 or 800-332-3773) has an indoor pool and a health club and a special moderate rate for university visitors.

A little farther: For a dose of history, stay at the 18th-century **Longfellow's Wayside Inn** (508-443-8846), 15 miles west of campus. This charming spot was called Howe's Tavern when Longfellow wrote of it in *Tales of a Wayside Inn*. Rates are moderate. See the Harvard-Radcliffe entry for places to stay in Cambridge. See the Wellesley College entry for other suggestions in the western suburbs of Boston. Also see the Tufts, Boston University, and Massachusetts Institute of Technology entries for other suggestions in the Boston area.

HIGHLIGHTS

ON CAMPUS
• Volan Center for Complex Systems
• Spingold Theater

OFF CAMPUS
• Harvard Square
• Faneuil Hall/Quincy Market
• Freedom Trail
• Museum of Fine Arts
• Boston Common and Public Garden

CLARK UNIVERSITY

Admissions Office, Clark University, 950 Main St., Worcester, MA 01610
(The Admissions House is at 3 Maywood St.) • Telephone: 508-793-7431
or 800-GO-CLARK (Fax: 508-793-8821) • Web: www.clark.edu • Email: admissions@clarku.edu

Hours: Monday-Friday, 9AM-5PM; selected Saturdays, 10AM-2PM. Closed Sundays and holidays.

The social sciences and the natural sciences offer the strongest programs at this small research university in Worcester, Massachusetts. The school is a member of the Worcester Consortium, which allows undergraduates to take courses at any of nine other schools in the area.

HIGHLIGHTS

ON CAMPUS
- Larger-than-life statue of Freud
- Rare book room, Goddard Library

OFF CAMPUS
- Higgin's Armory
- Worcester Art Museum
- Sturbridge Village

TRANSPORTATION

Worcester Airport is 5 miles from campus. Continental and USAir serve the airport. Taxis are available for the trip from the airport to campus; call Arrow Cab at 508-756-5184, Yellow Cab at 508-754-3211, or Red Cab at 508-756-5000. You can also fly into Boston's Logan International Airport; shuttle-van and limousine service are available from there to campus. Worcester Airport Limousine provides service from Logan to the Worcester area; call 800-666-0992 (in Massachusetts), 800-343-1369 (outside Massachusetts), or 508-835-6936. Amtrak trains serve Worcester; the station is approximately 3 miles from campus. Greyhound/Trailways and Peter Pan Bus Lines also stop in Worcester.

FIND YOUR WAY

First, some advice. If you get lost, it's pronounced "Wuhstuh." **From points south,** take Rte. 290 east to Exit 17 (Rte. 9, Framingham/Ware). Stay in left lane. At the end of the ramp, take a left at the traffic lights. Go straight for about a mile, passing through 6 traffic lights. At the 7th traffic light, take a left onto Park Ave. At the 6th traffic light on Park Ave. (1.3 miles), take a left onto Maywood St. Go through 1 stop sign. The admissions house and visitors' parking are on the right. **From points north,** take Route 290 west to Exit 18 (Route 9, Framingham/Ware). Bear right at the end of the exit ramp. Go through the lights at the end of the ramp and get into the middle lane. Bear left, following signs to Lincoln Square. Take right at 2nd traffic light onto Highland St. At the 5th traffic light, turn left onto Maywood St. Go through 1 stop sign. The admissions house and visitors' parking are on the right.

STAY THE NIGHT

Clark University is southwest of the downtown area. Only 10 minutes away is the **Hampton Inn** (110 Summer St.; 508-757-0400 or 800-426-7866), which is located downtown. **Beechwood Inn** (363 Plantation St.; 508-754-5789) is 4 miles from Clark. Rooms are rather expensive, but you get passes to a local health club. Another hotel is the **Marriot Courtyard** (75 Grove St.; 508-363-0300). Right off the Massachusetts Tpke. (Exit 10), and at Exit 8 off I-290 (a 15-minute drive from school), is the **Ramada Yankee Drummer Motor Inn and Conference Center** (508-832-3221 or 800-528-5012). Rates are moderate, and there is an indoor pool. The **Baymont Inn** (444 Southbridge St.; 508-832-7000) is only 15 minutes from campus. If you are heading east toward Boston, or coming from that direction, try the **Courtyard by Marriott** (3 Technology Dr.; 508-836-4800).

AT A GLANCE

Selectivity Rating	81
Range SAT I Math	520-620
Average SAT I Math	561
Range SAT I Verbal	520-630
Average SAT I Verbal	564
Average ACT Composite	25
Average GPA	3.2
Student to Faculty Ratio	12:1

CAMPUS TOURS

Appointment Req?	No
Dates	Year-round
Times	When school is in session: Mon-Fri 10:30AM, 12PM, 2:30PM, and 3:30PM; Sat 12PM
Avg. Length	1 hour

ON-CAMPUS INTERVIEWS

Admissions

Start Date—Juniors	April
Appointment Req?	Yes
Advance Notice	2 weeks
Saturdays?	Some
Avg. Length	30-45 min
Info Sessions	July-late fall

Faculty and Coaches

Dates/Times	Year-round; subject to faculty/coach availability
Arrangements	Contact admissions off. 2 weeks prior

CLASS VISITS

Dates	Sept-Nov, Feb-April (Mon-Fri)
Arrangements	Contact admissions off.

OVERNIGHT DORM STAYS

Advance Notice	2-3 weeks
Arrangements	Contact admissions off.
Limitations	Scheduled only on a space-available basis

COLLEGE OF THE HOLY CROSS

Admissions Office, College of the Holy Cross, 1 College St.,
Worcester, MA 01610 (The office is in Fenwick, Rm. 106) • Telephone: 800-442-2421 •
Web: www.holycross.edu • Email: admissions@holycross.edu

Hours: Monday-Friday, 8:30AM-5PM. Closed weekends (with the exception of six Saturdays in the fall) and holidays.

Holy Cross is an excellent Catholic liberal arts college where tough grading and caring professors are the norm. Supreme Court Justice Clarence Thomas is an alum.

AT A GLANCE

Selectivity Rating	90
Range SAT I Math	550-670
Average SAT I Math	629
Range SAT I Verbal	550-670
Average SAT I Verbal	631
Student to Faculty Ratio	13:1

CAMPUS TOURS

Appointment Req?	No
Dates	Year-round, except during exams and registration
Times	Sept-Dec: Mon-Fri 9AM-4PM hourly. Jan-Aug: Mon-Fri 9AM, noon, and 3PM.
Avg. Length	1 hour

ON-CAMPUS INTERVIEWS

Admissions

Start Date–Juniors	May (April for students who travel long distances)
Appointment Req?	Yes
Advance Notice	2-4 weeks for spring interview; 4-6 weeks for summer; 2 months for fall
Saturdays?	Yes, 6 fall Saturdays for interview and tours
Avg. Length	45 min
Info Sessions	On scheduled visit days

Faculty and Coaches

Dates/Times	Year-round; subject to faculty/coach availability
Arrangements	Contact admissions off. 1 week prior

CLASS VISITS

Dates	Sept-Dec and Jan-May
Arrangements	Contact admissions off.

OVERNIGHT DORM STAYS

Advance Notice	2-4 weeks
Arrangements	Contact admissions office
Limitations	Sun-Thurs; Oct-Dec and April

TRANSPORTATION

Worcester Airport is a 15-minute drive from campus; taxis are available for the ride to campus. Logan International Airport in Boston is a 1-hour drive from campus. Worcester Airport Limousine provides service from Logan to the Worcester area; call 800-322-0298 (in Massachusetts), 800-343-1369 (outside Massachusetts), or 508-756-4834. (You can make advance reservations or call on arrival). Greyhound/Trailways and Peter Pan buses serve Worcester.

FIND YOUR WAY

(Note: See Clark University "Find Your Way" for important pronunciation tips.) From I-90 (Massachusetts Tpke.), take Exit 10 (Auburn/Worcester) to I-290 E. From I-290, take Exit 11 (College Square). To reach campus, make the first right turn after Howard Johnson's.

STAY THE NIGHT

Holy Cross is south of Worcester's downtown area, a couple of miles southeast of Clark University. See the Clark University entry for suggestions, which are equally suitable for Holy Cross. **Captain Samuel Eddy House Bed and Breakfast** is a 10-minute drive from Holy Cross, and **Beechwood Inn** is about 5 miles away.

HIGHLIGHTS

ON CAMPUS
- Bookstore
- Arboretum

OFF CAMPUS
- Boston
- Providence
- Tweeter Center for the Performing Arts

CURRY COLLEGE

Admissions Office, Curry College, 1071 Blue Hill Ave., Milton, MA 02186 •
Telephone: 617-333-2210 or 800-669-0686 • Web: www.curry.edu •
Email: curryadm@curry.edu

Hours: Monday-Friday, 8:30AM-4:30PM; Saturday, 10AM-3PM (but not every Saturday). Closed Sundays and some holidays.

Curry College is perhaps best known for its Program for Advancement of Learning , the first college-level program in the nation to help learning disabled students to achieve in college. Beyond PAL, this suburban liberal arts college of about 1,600 students located just seven miles from downtown Boston has satellite campuses in, among other places, Plymouth, Cambridge, Medford, and Peabody.

HIGHLIGHTS

ON CAMPUS	OFF CAMPUS
• Drapkin Student Center	• Quincy Market/Faneuil Hall in Boston
• Levin Library	• New England Aquarium
• WMLN campus radio station	• Museum of Fine Arts
• The Suites (new residence hall)	• Newbury Street in Boston
• Hafer Academic Center	• Blue Hills Nature Reservation

TRANSPORTATION

Logan International Airport in Boston is approximately 10 miles from campus. From the airport, you can take the MBTA (public transportation) and then the Curry College Shuttle to campus. Amtrak trains, Greyhound buses, and Vermont Transit (New England, New York, and Montreal) serve Boston. The MBTA (public transportation) combined with the Curry College Shuttle can bring you to campus.

FIND YOUR WAY

From I-90 (Massachusetts Tpke.), exit to Rte. 128 S. Proceed to Exit 2B and take Rte. 138 N. for 2.5 miles; the college will be on the left. **From Providence, RI**, take I-95 N. to Rte. 128 S. Proceed to Exit 2B and take Rte. 138 N. for 2.5 miles; the college will be on the left. **From Boston**, take I-93 S. to Rte. 128 N. Proceed to Exit 2B and take Rte. 138 N. for 2.5 miles; the college will be, yes, on the left.

STAY THE NIGHT

Nearby: Curry College is south of Boston, in the suburb of Milton. In the immediate area, choices include a number of chain motels and hotels. **Motel 6** (125 Union St., Braintree; 781-848-7890) offers basic accommodations 15 minutes from campus. Rates are reasonable. Three motels offer moderate rates: **Holiday Inn** (1374 N. Main St., Randolph; 781-961-1000), another **Holiday Inn** (55 Ariadne Rd., Dedham; 781-329-1000), and **Comfort Inn** (235 Elm St., Dedham; 781-326-6700). All are 15 minutes away from the campus. The more expensive options include the **Sheraton Tara** (South Shore Plaza, Braintree; 781-848-0600), which has an indoor pool, a health club, and 2 restaurants, and the **Hilton at Dedham Place** (95 Dedham Place, Dedham; 781-3297900). See the Wellesley College entry for bed-and-breakfast referral services. If you want to head west, check the Babson College and Wellesley College entries for suggestions in the Wellesley and Needham Heights areas.

A little farther: See entries for other Boston-area colleges; Emerson College has listings in the center of Boston. Boston University has guest house listings in the Back Bay and Brookline areas. If you're coming from the south, you might consider breaking up your trip in Attleboro. See the Wheaton College entry for **Colonel Blackinton Inn**, about a 40-minute drive from Curry.

AT A GLANCE

Average SAT I Math	420
Average SAT I Verbal	440
Average GPA	2.3
Student to Faculty Ratio	12:1

CAMPUS TOURS

Appointment Req?	Yes
Dates	During fall, spring, and summer sessions
Times	Mon-Fri: 9AM-3PM hourly; selected Saturdays: 10AM-2PM hourly
Avg. Length	45 min

ON-CAMPUS INTERVIEWS

Admissions

Start Date–Juniors	Spring
Appointment Req?	Yes
Advance Notice	2 weeks
Saturdays?	Yes, fall and winter only
Avg. Length	45 min
Info Sessions	N/A

Faculty and Coaches

Dates/Times	Year-round; subject to faculty/coach availability
Arrangements	Contact admissions off. or individual coach 1 week prior

CLASS VISITS

Dates	Year-round (Mon-Fri)
Arrangements	Contact admissions off.

OVERNIGHT DORM STAYS

Advance Notice	N/A
Arrangements	N/A
Limitations	Call to arrange visit; Sun-Thurs only

EMERSON COLLEGE

Admission Office, Emerson College, 120 Boylston St., Boston, MA 02116
(Admission office is located on the 3rd floor at 420 Boylston St.) • Telephone: 617-824-8600 •
Web: www.emerson.edu • Email: admission@emerson.edu

Hours: Monday-Friday, 9AM-5PM; Saturday, by appointment only. Closed Sundays and holidays.

An Emerson education is the ticket to getting a high-paying job in the entertainment industry, according to the students at this world-class school for communications and performing arts in Boston. Alums with the aforementioned high-paying jobs include Jay Leno.

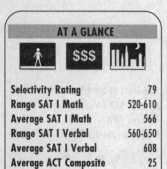

AT A GLANCE

Selectivity Rating	79
Range SAT I Math	520-610
Average SAT I Math	566
Range SAT I Verbal	560-650
Average SAT I Verbal	608
Average ACT Composite	25
Average GPA	3.2
Student to Faculty Ratio	14:1

CAMPUS TOURS

Appointment Req?	Yes
Dates	During class sessions
Times	Mon-Fri, some Saturdays
Avg. Length	90 min

ON-CAMPUS INTERVIEWS

Admissions

Start Date—Juniors	Any time
Appointment Req?	Yes
Advance Notice	2 weeks
Saturdays?	Rarely, and by appointment only
Avg. Length	30-40 min
Info Sessions	During class sessions

Faculty and Coaches

Dates/Times	Year-round; subject to faculty/coach availability
Arrangements	Contact admission off. 2 weeks prior

CLASS VISITS

Dates	Jan-April (Mon-Fri)
Arrangements	Contact admission off.

TRANSPORTATION

Emerson is conveniently located on Boston's subway/street trolley system, the "T" (Green Line). Transferring to the Green Line from the Red, Orange, or Blue Lines can be made at several downtown T stations (Park St., Haymarket, or Government Center). While most Emerson students use Boylston Station, visitors to the Admissions Office should exit at Arlington Station and walk 1 block west to 420 Boylston St. (The Berkeley Building). Logan International Airport is 5 miles from the Emerson campus. Taxis take about 30 minutes and cost approximately $20. Amtrak, the Commuter Rail, and major bus companies arrive at Boston's South Station, a 15-minute taxi ride from the campus.

FIND YOUR WAY

From the Massachusetts Tpke. (I-90), take Exit 18 Allston/Cambridge. After the toll booth, follow the signs for Cambridge, bearing right down the exit ramp. Keep to the right and make a right turn at the 2nd set of lights onto Storrow Dr. E. Proceed approximately 2 miles to the exit marked "Downtown." Follow the directions from Storrow Dr. below. **From Interstate I-93, Route 3, or U.S. Route 1,** take Exit 26 for Storrow Dr. W. and proceed 1 mile to the exit marked "Back Bay." Follow the directions from Storrow Dr. below. **From Storrow Dr.,** keep left and turn left onto Beacon St. Make an immediate right onto Arlington St. and proceed alongside the Public Gardens. At the 3rd traffic light turn right onto Berkeley St. and right again at the next light onto Boylston St. The Office of Undergraduate Admissions is located on the corner of Berkeley and Boylston Streets. Emerson does not have private parking facilities, and we urge visitors to use parking garages or public transportation. To reach the Boston Common Garage, continue on Boylston St. past the Admission Office and turn left at the 3rd light onto Charles.

STAY THE NIGHT

Nearby: Emerson is located in the heart of Boston's Theatre District. Close to the campus are the **Park Plaza Hotel** (64 Arlington St.; 800-225-2008), **Wyndham Tremont House Hotel** (275 Tremont St.; 800-331-9998), and the **Radisson Hotel-Boston** (200 Stuart St.; 617-482-1800). See the Northeastern University and Boston University entries for more hotel options.

A little farther: **The Lenox Hotel** (710 Boylston St.; 800-471-1422), **Westin** (10 Huntington Ave.; 617-262-9600), and **Marriot Copley** (110 Huntington Ave.; 617-236-5800) are located in the historic Copley Square neighborhood (4 blocks from campus). Less expensive hotels may be found in Boston's suburbs.

HIGHLIGHTS

ON CAMPUS
- The Apple Store
- The college library
- Emerson Majestic Theatre (Boston's second oldest theatre)
- WERS 88.9 FM (New England's oldest noncommercial radio station)

OFF CAMPUS
- Massachusetts State House
- Public Garden, swanboat rides
- Boston Red Sox at Fenway Park
- Freedom Trail
- Newbury Street shopping district

HAMPSHIRE COLLEGE

Admissions Office, Hampshire College, Amherst, MA 01002 (The office is on Rte. 116 S.—West St.) • Telephone: 413-559-5471 • Web: www.hampshire.com • Email: admissions@hampshire.edu

Hours: Monday-Friday, 8:30AM-4:30PM; Saturday 9AM-1PM (late September through January only). Closed Sundays and holidays.

Academic freedom is the name of the game at liberal Hampshire College. The school is part of the Five College Consortium (including Amherst, Mount Holyoke, Smith, and UMass—Amherst), which gives students abounding academic and social opportunities off campus.

HIGHLIGHTS

ON CAMPUS
- National Yiddish Book Center
- 650-acre working farm

OFF CAMPUS
- Old Deerfield historic village
- Skinner State Park (hiking, biking)

TRANSPORTATION

Bradley International Airport near Hartford, CT is 45 miles from campus. Peter Pan buses (800-343-9999), Valley Transporter limousines (413-253-1350), rental cars, and taxis are available for the trip from the airport to campus. Amtrak trains provide regular service from New York City to Springfield, MA. Greyhound buses serve Springfield hourly from Boston and New York. Buses also run hourly from Springfield to Amherst. The free Five College Bus Service is available for the trip from Amherst to Hampshire's campus, or call City Transportation (413-247-9000) for a taxi.

FIND YOUR WAY

From the south, take I-91 to Exit 19 (Northampton). Take Rte. 9 E. for 7 miles. In the town of Amherst, turn right onto Rte. 116 S. and proceed 3 miles to the campus. **From the east or west,** take I-90 (Massachusetts Tpke.) to Exit 4. Take I-91 N. to Exit 19 (Northampton). Take Rte. 9 E. for 7 miles to Amherst; then turn right onto Rte. 116 S. for 3 miles to campus. **From the north,** take I-91 S. to Exit 25 (Amherst). Take Rte. 116 S. to campus.

STAY THE NIGHT

See the Amherst College entry—Hampshire is just a 5-minute drive from Amherst. See the Smith College entry for suggestions in Northampton, which is a 10-minute drive from Hampshire.

AT A GLANCE	
Selectivity Rating	82
Range SAT I Math	550-650
Average SAT I Math	592
Range SAT I Verbal	610-720
Average SAT I Verbal	647
Average GPA	3.3
Student to Faculty Ratio	11:1

CAMPUS TOURS	
Appointment Req?	No
Dates	Year-round
Times	Mon-Fri 2-5 times daily; Sat late Sept-Jan call for times
Avg. Length	1 hour

ON-CAMPUS INTERVIEWS	
Admissions	
Start Date—Juniors	April
Appointment Req?	Yes
Advance Notice	1 week for Mon-Fri; 2-3 weeks for weekend
Saturdays?	Fall only
Avg. Length	30-45 min
Info Sessions	March-Aug
Faculty and Coaches	
Dates/Times	Not usually available
Arrangements	Contact admissions off.

CLASS VISITS	
Dates	Mon-Fri
Arrangements	Contact admissions off.

OVERNIGHT DORM STAYS	
Advance Notice	2 weeks
Arrangements	Contact admissions off.
Limitations	Oct 2-Nov 16 and Feb 25-April 19 except vacations; Sun-Thurs; limited availability

HARVARD COLLEGE

Harvard College Admissions, 8 Garden St., Cambridge, MA 02138
(The office is on the 1st floor of Byerly Hall) • Telephone: 617-495-1551 •
Web: www.fas.harvard.edu • Email: college@fas.harvard.edu

Hours: Monday-Friday, 9AM-5PM; nonholiday Saturday mornings in late September to November. Closed Sundays and holidays.

Home to a distinguished faculty and phenomenal, world-class research facilities, Harvard is perhaps the most prestigious hub of intellectual activity in America. The professors here are the college faculty equivalent of rock stars and the students are just as impressive.

AT A GLANCE

Selectivity Rating	99
Range SAT I Math	700-790
Range SAT I Verbal	700-800
Student to Faculty Ratio	8:1

CAMPUS TOURS

Appointment Req?	No
Dates	Year-round, except winter break, Intersession, and Commencement
Times	Dec-March: Mon-Fri 3PM; Sat 11AM. April-Nov: Mon-Fri 11AM and 3PM; Sat 11AM
Avg. Length	1 hour

ON-CAMPUS INTERVIEWS

Admissions

Start Date—Juniors	June
Appointment Req?	Yes
Advance Notice	Call from mid-May for Jun-Aug appt.; call from mid-July for Sept-Nov appt.
Saturdays?	No
Avg. Length	30 min
Info Sessions	Year-round

Faculty and Coaches

Dates/Times	Year-round; subject to faculty/coach availability
Arrangements	Contact dept./coach early after junior year

CLASS VISITS

Dates	Year-round (Mon-Fri)
Arrangements	Class list in Admissions

OVERNIGHT DORM STAYS

Advance Notice	3 weeks
Arrangements	Contact admissions off.
Limitations	Seniors only; 1-night stays; Mon-Thurs; mid-Oct to mid-March, except exams and breaks

TRANSPORTATION

Logan International Airport is 5 miles from campus. The least expensive way to get to campus from the airport is the subway—MBTA (the "T"). Taxis and rental cars are also available. Amtrak trains and Greyhound and Mass Transit buses serve Boston. From the train and Mass Transit bus stations, go to MBTA's South Station and take the Red Line subway toward Alewife. Go 6 stops to Harvard. The campus is a 3-minute walk from Harvard Square. From the Greyhound station, go to the Arlington MBTA station and take the Green Line subway inbound to Park St. (2 stops). Transfer to the Red Line outbound toward Alewife. Go 4 stops to Harvard. The campus is a 3-minute walk from Harvard Square.

FIND YOUR WAY

From I-90 (Massachusetts Tpke.), take the Cambridge exit and turn left immediately onto Storrow Dr. West. At the second light, cross the bridge (Anderson) and drive straight into Harvard Square. For Byerly Hall, turn left at the third traffic light onto Brattle St. and get into the right lane, bearing right immediately at the traffic island. The Radcliffe Yard is 2 blocks north on the right side of the street.

STAY THE NIGHT

Nearby: The **Harvard Square Hotel** (110 Mount Auburn St.; 617-864-5200) is a moderately priced, 72-room hotel within walking distance of the College. The price includes an informal continental breakfast. An old favorite with Harvard visitors is the **Sheraton Commander** (16 Garden St.; 617-547-4800), right on the Cambridge Common and a short walk from the university. Prices range from expensive during the week to moderate on weekends. The posh **Charles Hotel** (Harvard Sq.; 617-864-1200) is a short stroll from campus. **The Inn at Harvard** in Harvard Square, (1201 Massachusetts Ave.; 800-458-5886).

A little farther: Harvard is about 2 miles north of MIT, which is also in Cambridge. See suggestions in the MIT entry, especially the **Hyatt Regency**, which has hourly van service to Harvard Square. See the Boston University entry for guest houses and hotel suggestions in Back Bay and Brookline, across the river. See the Emerson College entry for suggestions in Boston center.

HIGHLIGHTS

ON CAMPUS
- Widener Library
- Harvard Yard
- Fogg Museum
- Annenburg/Memorial Hall
- Science center

OFF CAMPUS
- Harvard Square
- Faneuil Hall/Quincey Market
- Museum of Fine Arts
- Freedom Trail
- Boston Commons and Public Garden

MASSACHUSETTS INSTITUTE OF TECHNOLOGY

Admissions Office, Massachusetts Institute of Technology, 77 Massachusetts Ave., Rm. 3-108, Cambridge, MA 02139 (The office is in Building 10, Rm. 100) • Telephone: 617-258-5515 • Web: www.mit.edu • Email: admissions@mit.edu

Hours: Monday-Friday, 9AM-5PM. Closed weekends and national holidays.

Students at MIT study directly under Nobel Prize–winning professors and to work in some of the best research facilities in the universe. Freshmen here are graded on a pass/no credit basis, which takes a great deal of the pressure off.

HIGHLIGHTS

ON CAMPUS
- MIT Museum
- Killian Court
- Kresge Oral Media Lab
- Edgerton Center

OFF CAMPUS
- Museum of Science
- Museum of Fine Arts
- Freedom Trail
- Faneuil Hall
- Aquarium

TRANSPORTATION

Logan International Airport in Boston is 10 miles from campus. The subway (MBTA Red Line) and taxis are available for the trip from the airport to campus. Amtrak trains and Greyhound and Mass Transit buses serve Boston. From the stations, take a taxi or take the MBTA subway (Red Line) to the Kendall Square stop, which will bring you to the MIT Coop. Walk up Main St. away from Boston and take the second left (Ames St.). The first building on the right is the Ralph Landau Building (Building 66). Turn right into the building and walk to the end of the corridor. Go to the left and up a small set of stairs. Make the first right at the top of the stairs. Follow this long corridor to room 10-100 (for information sessions) or room 3-108 (the admissions office).

FIND YOUR WAY

From I-90 (Massachusetts Tpke.), take the Cambridge/Allston exit and follow the "Cambridge" signs over the River St. Bridge. Continue to the first large intersection, Central Square, and bear right onto Massachusetts Ave. Proceed for one-half mile to the main entrance, which will be on the left. **From Rtes. I-93, I-95, and the Expy.**, take the Storrow Dr., Back Bay Exit. Proceed to the 3rd exit on Storrow Drive, marked Massachusetts Avenue (on your left). When you get to the top of the exit, take a right across the Charles River. Once you cross the river you will be at MIT. The main entrance is at the 2nd light on your right.

STAY THE NIGHT

Nearby: There are a few places very close to MIT, which is in south Cambridge. **Howard Johnson's Motor Lodge** (Memorial Dr.; 617-492-7777) is within walking distance of MIT. It has balconies on the river, an indoor swimming pool, and a sundeck. Rates begin in the moderate range and rocket into the very expensive range. Nearby **Hyatt Regency** (575 Memorial Dr.; 617-492-1234) has all the amenities you would expect, including an exercise room and an indoor pool. It also offers free transportation to Boston. Rates are quite high. **Royal Sonesta** (5 Cambridge Pkwy.; 617-491-3600) is another solid choice—with an indoor swimming pool, a full health club, and jogging paths. For other Cambridge suggestions, see the entries for Harvard-Radcliffe and Tufts. The Wellesley entry lists bed-and-breakfast referral services. There are guest houses just across the river in the Brookline and Back Bay areas. See the Boston University entry for more information. **University Park Hotel**, very close to MIT, has 210 guest rooms (617-577-0200). Also very close is the **Cambridge Marriott**, Kendall Square (2 Cambridge Center; 617-494-6600).

A little farther: If you wish to stay in the center of Boston, see the Emerson College entry for suggestions.

AT A GLANCE

👥	$$$	🏙️

Selectivity Rating	99
Range SAT I Math	730-800
Average SAT I Math	752
Range SAT I Verbal	660-760
Average SAT I Verbal	702
Average ACT Composite	31

CAMPUS TOURS

Appointment Req?	No
Dates	Year-round, except holidays, weekends, and exam periods
Times	Mon-Fri 10AM and 2PM
Avg. Length	90 min

ON-CAMPUS INTERVIEWS

Admissions

Start Date–Juniors	N/A
Appointment Req?	N/A
Advance Notice	N/A
Saturdays?	N/A
Avg. Length	N/A
Info Sessions	Year-round, except holidays, weekends, and exam periods

Faculty and Coaches

Dates/Times	Year-round; subject to faculty/coach availability
Arrangements	Contact dept. of interest 1 week prior

CLASS VISITS

Dates	Year-round (Mon-Fri)
Arrangements	Obtain class schedule and campus map from admissions off.

OVERNIGHT DORM STAYS

Advance Notice	2 weeks
Arrangements	Call overnight coordinator at 617-253-4791

MERRIMACK COLLEGE

Admissions Office, Merrimack College, 315 Turnpike St., North Andover, MA 01845
(The office is in Austin Hall) • Telephone: 978-837-5100 • Web: www.merrimack.edu •
Email: admission@merrimack.edu

Hours: Monday-Friday, 8:30AM-4:30PM; Saturday, some mornings in fall. Closed Sundays and holidays.

Merrimack College is a small Roman Catholic institution about 25 miles from Boston in North Andover that offers programs in the liberal arts and sciences, business, education, and pre-professional and vocational programs. Red Sox legend Carl Yastrzemski is a Merrimack alum.

AT A GLANCE

Average SAT I Math	510
Average SAT I Verbal	510
Average ACT Composite	23
Average GPA	3.1
Student to Faculty Ratio	15:1

CAMPUS TOURS

Appointment Req?	Yes
Dates	When school is in session (including summer) and some vacation times
Times	Mon-Fri 10AM and 2PM; Sat in the fall; Mon and Thurs 11AM in the summer
Avg. Length	45-60 min

ON-CAMPUS INTERVIEWS

Admissions

Start Date–Juniors	Any time
Appointment Req?	Yes
Advance Notice	1 week
Saturdays?	Yes, but only on selected days
Avg. Length	25 min
Info Sessions	Only on selected dates in the fall

Faculty and Coaches

Dates/Times	Year-round; subject to faculty/coach availability
Arrangements	Contact admissions off.

CLASS VISITS

Dates	Year-round (Mon-Fri)
Arrangements	Contact admissions off.

OVERNIGHT DORM STAYS

Advance Notice	N/A
Arrangements	N/A
Limitations	N/A

TRANSPORTATION

Logan International Airport in Boston is 25 miles from campus. Taxi, limousine, and airport shuttle services are available; contact Flightline at 603-893-8254 or 800-245-2525. If you rent a car and drive to campus, take U.S. 1 N. toward Saugus/Peabody; then take Massachusetts Rte. 114 W. toward Middleton/N. Andover. The campus is at the intersection of Rtes. 114 and 125. Amtrak and Greyhound serve Boston.

FIND YOUR WAY

From Hartford, take I-84 N. to I-90 (Massachusetts Tpke.); take I-90 E. to the Auburn exit. Follow I-290 E. to I-495. Take I-495 N. to Exit 42A (Massachusetts Rte. 114). Take Rte. 114 E. toward Middleton, 1 mile to campus. **From Boston**, take I-93 N. to Exit 41; then take Massachusetts Rte. 125 (Andover Bypass) to Andover/N. Andover. The campus is on the left at the intersection of Rtes. 125 and 114. **From the north**, take I-95 S. to I-495 S. (from ME), or I-93 S. or I-3 S. to I-495 N. (from NH). Exit I-495 at Exit 42A and follow Massachusetts Rte. 114 toward Middleton for 1 mile to the campus (at the intersection of Rtes. 114 and 125).

STAY THE NIGHT

Nearby: Our favorite is **Andover Inn** (Rte. 28; 978-475-5903), 5 minutes away from the college on the grounds of the Phillips Academy in Andover. Rates are moderate. The following are inexpensive selections: **Hampton Inn** (224 Winthrop Ave., Lawrence; 978-975-4050), with an exercise room and breakfast in the lobby. **Wyndam Andover** (123 Old River Rd., Andover; 978-975-3600), with an indoor pool, health facilities, and evening entertainment. Other hotels are the **Marriott Courtyard** (978-794-0700) and the Tewksbury/Andover **Holiday Inn** (978-640-9000). All of the above are a few miles from the campus. A little more expensive and a little fancier is **Ramada Hotel Rolling Green** (311 Lowell St., Andover; 978-475-5400) at the junction of Rtes. 93 and 133 E. It boasts an indoor pool and health club, with tennis available.

A little farther: You might consider staying in historic Newburyport on the coast, northeast of Andover.

HIGHLIGHTS

ON CAMPUS
• The new Roger's Center for the Arts
• Deegan Residence Hall
• Campus Center
• McQuade Library
• Volpe Athletic Center

OFF CAMPUS
• Andover Center
• Addison Gallery of Art
• Boston Attractions
• North Shore beaches
• New Hampshire mountains

MOUNT HOLYOKE COLLEGE

The Board of Admissions, Mount Holyoke College, South Hadley, MA 01075
(The office is in Newhall Center on College St.—Rte. 116) • Telephone: 413-538-2023 •
Web: www.mtholyoke.edu • Email: admissions@mtholyoke.edu

Hours: Monday-Friday, 8:30AM-5PM; Saturday, 9AM-noon. Closed Sundays, New Year's Day, July 4, Labor Day, Thanksgiving Day, and December 24 and 25.

Mount Holyoke College was the nation's first all-women's college and it is still one of the most academically challenging and rewarding schools in the country. Students here enjoy a supportive atmosphere and a picturesque New England campus.

HIGHLIGHTS

ON CAMPUS
- The Williston Observatory
- The Mount Holyoke College Art Museum
- The Equestrian Center
- Wa-Shin An
- Williston Memorial Library

OFF CAMPUS
- Adelfia Restaurant & Banquets

TRANSPORTATION

Bradley International Airport near Hartford, CT is 34 miles south of campus by way of I-91. Bus service between the airport and campus (with a transfer in Springfield, MA) is offered by Peter Pan Express Service (413-781-3320). Limousine service to campus is easier and faster than bus service, but more expensive. The 2 limousine companies that service the college are Valley Transporter (800-872-8752) and Allard's College Limousine Service (413-539-9339). Amtrak trains serve Springfield; from there, take a bus, limousine, or taxi to campus.

FIND YOUR WAY

From the south, take I-91 N. to Exit 16 (Holyoke-S. Hadley/Rte. 202). Proceed north on Rte. 202 through the city of Holyoke and over the Connecticut River across the Muller Bridge. Take the exit marked "South Hadley Center-Amherst" to Rte. 116 N. The college is approximately 2 miles from the exit, on the right side of the road. The admissions office is in a white building marked "The Newhall Center," across the street from the college, just before the Village Commons. **From the north**, take I-91 S. to Exit 16 (Holyoke-South Hadley/Rte. 202). Proceed north on Rte. 202 through the city of Holyoke and follow the preceding directions from that point. **From east or west on I-90 (Massachusetts Tpke.)**, take Exit 5 (Holyoke-Chicopee) and bear right. At the end of the exit ramp, turn left on Rte. 33 for 5 miles to Rte. 116. Turn right on Rte. 116 and proceed approximately 2 miles north to the college.

STAY THE NIGHT

Nearby: **Willets-Hallowell Center** (413-538-2217), located on campus, offers moderately priced rooms for visitors with full breakfast included. Dinner is served to parties of 6 or more. The **Yankee Pedlar Inn** (1866 Northampton St., Holyoke; 413-532-9494) is an 18th-century country inn with private baths, TVs, and phones. Rates are moderate and include continental breakfast. And it's conveniently located 20 minutes from the college. For referrals to bed-and-breakfasts in the area, call **Pineapple Hospitality** at 508-990-1696.

A little farther: See the Smith College entry—the **Northampton Hilton** is 25 minutes from Mount Holyoke. Also see the Amherst College and University of Massachusetts entries. Suggestions there are approximately 30 minutes from Mount Holyoke. **Howard Johnson's Motor Lodge** in Hadley, detailed under the University of Massachusetts, is 20 minutes away.

AT A GLANCE

Selectivity Rating	85
Range SAT I Math	570-650
Average SAT I Math	602
Range SAT I Verbal	600-660
Average SAT I Verbal	626
Average ACT Composite	27
Average GPA	3.7
Student to Faculty Ratio	10:1

CAMPUS TOURS

Appointment Req?	No
Dates	Year-round
Times	Mon-Fri 9AM-3PM; Sat 10AM and 11AM
Avg. Length	45-60 min

ON-CAMPUS INTERVIEWS

Admissions

Start Date—Juniors	May
Appointment Req?	Yes
Advance Notice	2 weeks
Saturdays?	Yes, during the academic year only
Avg. Length	30-45 min
Info Sessions	July and August only

Faculty and Coaches

Dates/Times	Year-round; subject to faculty/coach availability
Arrangements	Contact admissions off. 1-2 weeks prior

CLASS VISITS

Dates	Year-round (Mon-Fri)
Arrangements	Contact admissions off. for a class schedule

OVERNIGHT DORM STAYS

Advance Notice	2 weeks
Arrangements	Contact admissions off.
Limitations	Sun-Thurs nights during regular academic sessions

NORTHEASTERN UNIVERSITY

Undergraduate Admissions, Northeastern University, 360 Huntington Ave.,
Boston, MA 02115 • Telephone: 617-373-2211 • Web: www.neu.edu •
Email: admissions@neu.edu

Hours: September-June: Monday-Friday, 8:30AM-4:30PM. Saturday, 8:30AM-1PM; July and August: Monday-Friday, 8AM-5PM. Closed Sundays and most Saturdays. Call for holiday hours.

Northeastern University's vaunted five-year co-op program—a tremendous hit with these business-oriented students—requires students to spend half of each year (after their first year) at work for one of thousands of employers. Jobs are predominantly in the New England area, although students do go across the country and even overseas.

AT A GLANCE

Selectivity Rating	75
Range SAT I Math	520-620
Average SAT I Math	572
Range SAT I Verbal	510-600
Average SAT I Verbal	553
Average ACT Composite	23
Average GPA	3.1
Student to Faculty Ratio	14:1

CAMPUS TOURS

Appointment Req?	No
Dates	Year-round
Times	Mon-Fri 9AM to 3PM; Sat 9AM, 10AM, and 11AM. Closed Saturdays during July and Aug.
Avg. Length	1 hour

ON-CAMPUS INTERVIEWS

Admissions

Start Date—Juniors	May 1
Appointment Req?	Yes, call 617-373-2211
Advance Notice	2 weeks
Saturdays?	No
Avg. Length	30 min
Info Sessions	Mon-Fri 10AM and 2PM; Sat 10AM and 11AM; closed July and Aug

Faculty and Coaches

Dates/Times	Year-round; subject to faculty/coach availability
Arrangements	Contact dept. of interest or the individual coach several weeks prior

CLASS VISITS

Dates	Year-round (Mon-Fri)
Arrangements	Contact admissions off. and the dept. of interest

TRANSPORTATION

Logan International Airport in Boston is 10 miles from campus. The MBTA subway (public transportation) and taxis are available for the trip from campus to the airport. Amtrak trains, private buses, and Mass Transit buses serve Boston. The MBTA subway (public transportation) can bring you to campus from the stations.

FIND YOUR WAY

From the Massachusetts Tpke. take Exit 22 (Copley Square), and bear right. Proceed to the traffic light, and turn right onto Dartmouth St. Then take the next right onto Columbus Ave. It is approximately 1 mile to the Northeastern University Parking Garage at 795 Columbus Avenue.

STAY THE NIGHT

The moderately priced **Midtown Hotel** (220 Huntington Avenue; 617-262-1000, 800-343-1177) is within walking distance. A few others include **Boston Back Bay Hilton** (40 Dalton Street; 617-236-1100, 800-445-8667), the **Boston Marriott Copley Place** (110 Huntington Avenue; 617-236-5800), **The Colonnade** (120 Huntington Avenue; 617-424-7000, 800-962-3030), and **Sheraton Boston Hotel and Towers** (39 Dalton Street; 617-236-2000, 800-325-3535).

HIGHLIGHTS

ON CAMPUS
- Marino Recreation Center
- Snell Library
- Curry Student Center
- Sculpture garden
- The Charles River

OFF CAMPUS
- Museum of Fine Arts
- Symphony Hall
- Boston Red Sox at Fenway Park
- Cultural District

SIMMONS COLLEGE

Admission Office, Simmons College, 300 The Fenway, Boston, MA 02115-5898
(The office is in Rm. C-116 of the Main Campus Building on the Fenway) •
Telephone: 800-345-8468 • Web: www.simmons.edu • Email: ugadm@simmons.edu

Hours: Monday-Friday, 8:30AM-4:30PM; Saturday, 8:30AM-noon. Closed Sundays and holidays.

Students at Simmons College, in the most excellent college town of Boston, enjoy small classes, a low student/ teacher ratio, a strong career-oriented emphasis, and a mind-boggling set of requirements are all intended to help graduates succeed in life.

HIGHLIGHTS

ON CAMPUS
- Trustman Art Gallery
- Beatley Library
- Park Science Center

OFF CAMPUS
- Museum of Fine Arts
- Isabella Stewart Gardner Museum
- Boston Red Sox at Fenway Park

TRANSPORTATION

Logan International Airport is approximately a 25-minute drive from campus, but the time varies with the amount of traffic. Taxis, local trains (see directions below), and rental cars are available for the trip to campus from the airport. Amtrak trains and Greyhound and Mass Transit buses serve Boston. From the Greyhound station, walk to the Arlington MBTA station. Take any Green Line "E" Huntington Ave. car outbound to the Museum/Ruggles stop. Walk to the right down Louis Prang St. to the Fenway. The college is on the Fenway just after the Gardner Museum. From the train or Mass Transit bus, walk to MBTA's South Statiohn and take the Red Line inbound to the Park St. station. Transfer to the Green Line "E" Huntington Ave. outbound and follow the preceding directions.

FIND YOUR WAY

From the south (Rte. 3) and from the north (Rtes. 1, I-93, or I-95), take Storrow Dr. W. to the Fenway, Rte. 1 S., overpass. Exit to the right onto Boylston St. outbound. Turn left at the next light onto Park Dr.; follow Park Dr., staying to the left. The first major intersection is Brookline Ave./Boylston St.; cross Brookline and bear left at the first opportunity, following the green sign pointing to the Fenway. (You will have made a U-turn.) Continue straight, again crossing Brookline, onto the Fenway. Immediately after Emmanuel College, take the first right onto Ave. Louis Pasteur. The college parking lot then is the first drive on the left. **From the west and Rte. 2**, take Storrow Dr. E. and follow the preceding directions.

STAY THE NIGHT

Nearby: There are a few places within walking distance of Simmons. The **Best Western Longwood** (342 Longwood Ave.; 617-731-4700) has a health club. Rates are impressively high. For a reasonable alternative consider tried-and-true **Howard Johnson's** (575 Commonwealth Ave.; 617-267-3100). The **Copley Square Hotel** is within walking distance; see the Northeastern University entry for details. See the Boston University entry for inn and hotel accommodations in nearby Brookline and Back Bay.

A little farther: See the Emerson College entry for more accommodations in Boston, and the MIT, Harvard-Radcliffe, and Tufts entries for accommodations in Cambridge.

AT A GLANCE

Selectivity Rating	76
Range SAT I Math	480-580
Average SAT I Math	529
Range SAT I Verbal	500-610
Average SAT I Verbal	540
Average ACT Composite	23
Student to Faculty Ratio	10:1

CAMPUS TOURS

Appointment Req?	No
Dates	Year-round
Times	Mon-Fri at 10AM, 11:30AM, 1PM, and 2:30PM (during semester break, only at 10AM and 2:30PM)
Avg. Length	1 hour

ON-CAMPUS INTERVIEWS

Admissions

Start Date—Juniors	Any time after sophomore year
Appointment Req?	Yes
Advance Notice	2 weeks
Saturdays?	Select Saturdays
Avg. Length	45 min
Info Sessions	Groups only

Faculty and Coaches

Dates/Times	Year-round; subject to faculty/coach availability
Arrangements	Contact admissions off. 2 weeks prior

CLASS VISITS

Dates	Academic year (Mon-Fri)
Arrangements	Contact admissions off.

OVERNIGHT DORM STAYS

Advance Notice	2 weeks
Arrangements	Contact admissions off.
Limitations	Academic year, Sun-Thurs; 1 night

SMITH COLLEGE

Office of Admission, 7 College Lane, Smith College, Northampton, MA 01063 • Telephone: 413-585-2500 • Web: www.smith.edu • Email: admissions@smith.edu

Hours: Monday-Friday, 8:30AM-4:30PM (8AM-4PM Memorial Day to Labor Day); Saturdays July 15 to the end of January, 9AM-1PM.

All-women's Smith College is a competetive school with a demanding workload, but the students here would have it no other way. Time permitting, there is a lot to do both on campus and in Northampton.

AT A GLANCE

Selectivity Rating	95
Range SAT I Math	580-670
Range SAT I Verbal	600-710
Average GPA	3.7
Student to Faculty Ratio	10:1

CAMPUS TOURS

Appointment Req?	No
Dates	Year-round
Times	Mon-Fri 10AM, 11AM, 1PM, 2PM, and 3PM
Avg. Length	1 hour

ON-CAMPUS INTERVIEWS

Admissions

Start Date—Juniors	Mid-March
Appointment Req?	Yes
Advance Notice	2 weeks
Saturdays?	Yes, first Sat after Labor Day to last Sat in Jan
Avg. Length	30 min
Info Sessions	Available only for large groups by request

Faculty and Coaches

Dates/Times	Year-round; subject to faculty/coach availability
Arrangements	Contact dept. of interest or coach several weeks prior

CLASS VISITS

Dates	Year-round (Mon-Fri)
Arrangements	Obtain class schedule in admissions off.

OVERNIGHT DORM STAYS

Advance Notice	1 month
Arrangements	Contact admissions off.
Limitations	Mon-Thurs; late Sept to early Dec and early Feb to late April

TRANSPORTATION

Bradley International Airport near Hartford, CT, is approximately 30 miles from campus. Shuttle-bus service is available from the airport to campus; call Valley Transporter at 800-872-8752 or 413-256-8484 as early as possible to arrange for this service. Amtrak train service is available to Springfield, MA. Valley Transporter also provides shuttle service from the train station to campus; call as early as possible.

FIND YOUR WAY

Take I-91 to Exit 18; then take U.S. 5 N. into the center of Northampton. Turn left on Massachusetts Rte. 9. Go straight through 4 traffic lights. Turn left on College Lane shortly after the 4th set. The Office of Admission is on your right, overlooking Paradise Pond.

STAY THE NIGHT

Nearby: A favorite with Smith visitors is **Hotel Northampton** (36 King St. N.; 413-584-3100), a restored 1926 building in the heart of Northampton within walking distance of the college. Also within walking distance is the **Autumn Inn** (259 Elm St.; 413-584-7660), a colonial-style, nicely appointed, moderately priced hostelry located on Rte. 9 adjacent to Smith. It has a swimming pool and provides parking.

A little farther: Sixteen miles north of Smith is historic Deerfield, a village of 12 museum houses. **The Deerfield Inn** (81 Old Main St., Deerfield, MA; 413-774-5581) is a great place, but prices are expensive. See the Mount Holyoke entry for **The Yankee Pedlar Inn** in Holyoke, about 25 minutes south of Smith. On the main drag in Stockbridge (an hour's drive away) is **The Red Lion Inn** (413-298-5545), a bustling old inn with moderate to expensive rates. Lenox is only a few miles away and has great shops and restaurants. (Try Cheesecake Charlie's.) **The Village Inn** (Church St.; 413-637-0020) is a charming and elegant place to stay the night. Rates are moderate; some rooms with shared baths are inexpensive.

HIGHLIGHTS

ON CAMPUS
- Lyman Plant House
- The Botanical Gardens
- Paradise Pond
- Mendenhall Center for Performing Arts
- Smith Art Museum

OFF CAMPUS
- The Summit House, Skinner State Park
- Old Deerfield
- Look Park
- Historic Northampton
- Yankee Candle

TUFTS UNIVERSITY

Office of Undergraduate Admissions, Tufts University, Medford, MA 02155
(The office is in Bendetson Hall) • Telephone: 617-627-3170 •
Web: www.tufts.edu • Email: uadmiss_inquiry@infonet.tufts.edu

Hours: Monday-Friday, 9AM-5PM; Saturday, most mornings from September to mid-December. Closed Sundays and holidays.

Many a student stuck on Ivy League waitlists has opted for Tufts, an academically rigorous liberal arts college in Boston. Few have been disappointed with their choice. A diverse group of alums includes singer Tracy Chapman, actor William Hurt, and Senator Patrick Moynihan.

HIGHLIGHTS

ON CAMPUS
- The Aidekman Arts Center
- Tisch Library, Edwin Ginn Library
- Cousens Gymnasium
- Ellis Oval

OFF CAMPUS
- Museum of Fine Arts
- Isabella Stewart
- Gardner Museum
- Boston Red Sox at Fenway Park

TRANSPORTATION

Logan International Airport in Boston is a 15-minute drive from campus. You can take a subway, bus, or taxi to campus from the airport. Amtrak trains and Greyhound buses serve Boston; public transportation and taxis can take you to Tufts from the bus and train stations.

FIND YOUR WAY

Take I-90 (Massachusetts Tpke.) to the Rte. 128 exit (exit also is to I-95, which coincides with Rte. 128 here). Take Rte. 128 (I-95) N. to Exit 29A (Massachusetts Rte. 2 E.). Take Rte. 2 E. (toward Cambridge) to Massachusetts Rte. 16 (this is at the end of Rte. 2). Turn left on Rte. 16 (marked 16 E.) and go through 2 full traffic lights (not counting blinking lights); after the second traffic light, take the next right turn, a sharp turn uphill, onto Powderhouse Blvd. Proceed to Packard Ave., the third left; turn onto Packard, which takes you to campus. Signs then will lead you to visitors' parking and the admissions office.

STAY THE NIGHT

Nearby: **A Cambridge House** (2218 Massachusetts Ave., Cambridge; 617-491-6300 or 800-232-9989) is an elegant turn-of-the-century colonial. Most, though not all, of the rooms share baths. Rates are moderate to very expensive and higher during the summer than during the rest of the year. The price includes a full breakfast and refreshments in the afternoon. Cambridge House also has a referral service to bed-and-breakfasts in the area. **Susse Chalet** (211 Concord Tpke., Cambridge; 617-661-7800) is inexpensive and a scant 2 miles from campus. **Days Inn** (19 Commerce Way, Woburn; 617-935-0039) is also close to campus, and has an indoor swimming pool and a restaurant. See the Harvard-Radcliffe entry for suggestions around Harvard Square— about 2 miles south—and the MIT entry for some posh hotel suggestions in southern Cambridge, about 4 miles south.

A little farther: You might want to go across the river into the Back Bay area of Boston. See the Boston University entry, which has some guest house and hotel suggestions. The **Lenox Hotel**, mentioned there, is about 20 minutes from Tufts. Brandeis University is 10 miles to the west, Boston College is 7 miles to the southwest, and Wellesley College is 15 miles to the southwest. See these entries if you wish to stay in the suburbs.

AT A GLANCE

Selectivity Rating	96
Range SAT I Math	640-720
Range SAT I Verbal	610-700
Student to Faculty Ratio	13:1

CAMPUS TOURS

Appointment Req?	No
Dates	Year-round, except exam periods and holidays
Times	Mon-Fri 9:30AM (occasionally), 11:30AM, and 2:30PM; Sat 10:30AM (fall only)
Avg. Length	1 hour

ON-CAMPUS INTERVIEWS

Admissions

Start Date—Juniors	N/A
Appointment Req?	N/A
Advance Notice	N/A
Saturdays?	N/A
Avg. Length	N/A
Info Sessions	April-Nov

Faculty and Coaches

Dates/Times	Year-round; subject to faculty/coach availability
Arrangements	Contact dept. of interest or athletics off. 1 week prior

CLASS VISITS

Dates	Year-round (Mon-Fri)
Arrangements	Obtain class visits list at front reception desk in Bendetson Hall

OVERNIGHT DORM STAYS

Advance Notice	2 weeks prior
Arrangements	Contact admissions off.
Limitations	Seniors only; fall visits are arranged but cannot be guaranteed; accepted students may visit during April Open House

UNIVERSITY OF MASSACHUSETTS—AMHERST

Undergraduate Admissions Office, University Admissions Center, University of Massachusetts–Amherst, University Box 30120, Amherst, MA 01003-0120 • Telephone: 413-545-0222 • Web: www.umass.edu • Email: mail@admissions.umass.edu

Hours: Monday-Friday, 8:30AM-5PM. Closed weekends and holidays.

From sports management to communications disorders to biochemistry to political science to landscape architecture, UMass—Amherst has much to offer.

AT A GLANCE

Selectivity Rating	74
Range SAT I Math	520-620
Average SAT I Math	570
Range SAT I Verbal	510-620
Average SAT I Verbal	564
Average GPA	3.3
Student to Faculty Ratio	18:1

CAMPUS TOURS

Appointment Req?	No
Dates	Year-round, except weekends in June and July, Christmas week, March break, and legal holidays
Times	7 days a week 11AM and 1:30PM
Avg. Length	50 min

ON-CAMPUS INTERVIEWS

Admissions

Start Date–Juniors	Any time
Appointment Req?	Yes
Advance Notice	2 weeks
Saturdays?	No
Avg. Length	30 min
Info Sessions	Same as campus tours

Faculty and Coaches

Dates/Times	Year-round; subject to faculty/coach availability
Arrangements	Contact dept. of interest or coach 2 weeks prior

CLASS VISITS

Dates	Year-round (Mon-Fri)
Arrangements	Contact dept. of interest

TRANSPORTATION

Bradley International Airport near Hartford, CT, is 45 miles south of the University. Logan International Airport in Boston is 90 miles to the east. Peter Pan Bus Lines (800-343-9999) links the campus to Bradley and Logan airports and to points throughout the region. Amtrak trains (800-872-7245) serve Springfield; the station is 2 blocks from the Springfield bus station, where you can get a bus to campus. Amtrak also serves Amherst.

FIND YOUR WAY

From New York, New Jersey, and points south, take I-95 N. to New Haven, CT. Head north on I-91 and get off at Exit 19. Make a right onto Rte. 9 E, proceed for 5 miles to Rte. 116 N. and turn left at the traffic lights. Take the University of Massachusetts exit, and bear right onto Massachusetts Ave. This will take you to the University. **From the east and northeast**, take I-90 W. (Massachusetts Tpke.) to Exit 4 (West Springfield). Proceed north on I-91 to exit 19. From here, follow the above directions for points south to the university. **From the west**, take I-90 to exit 4. Head north on I-91 and then follow the above directions for points south. From the north, take I-91 S. to Exit 25. Make a left and proceed to the intersection. Turn right onto Rtes. 5 and 10 S. Go 1 mile and turn left onto Rte. 116 S. Drive 8 miles to the University of Massachusetts exit. Turn left onto Massachusetts Ave. and follow to the University.

STAY THE NIGHT

Campus Center Hotel (413-549-6000) is on campus and its rates are moderate. The small **University Motor Lodge** (345 N. Pleasant St.; 413-256-8111) is within walking distance (a half-mile walk). Rates are inexpensive to moderate. **Howard Johnson's Motor Lodge** (401 Russell St, Hadley; 413-586-0114) is 2 miles away. It doesn't serve breakfast, but a Friendly's is nearby. Rates range from inexpensive to moderate. The University of Massachusetts is about 2 miles north of Amherst College. See the suggestions in the Amherst entry. You will find an inn listed here, as well as numerous budget choices. Northampton is about 15 minutes away. See the Smith College entry for suggestions there.

HIGHLIGHTS

ON CAMPUS
- The Mollins Center
- The Campus Center
- The Fine Arts Center
- The Visitors Center

OFF CAMPUS
- Downtown Amherst
- Northampton

WELLESLEY COLLEGE

Board of Admission, Wellesley College, 106 Central St., Wellesley, MA 02481-8203
(The office is in Green Hall, Rm. 240) • Telephone: 781-283-2270 (Fax: 617-283-3678) •
Web: www.wellesley.edu • Email: admission@wellesley.edu

Hours: Monday-Friday, 8:30AM-4:30PM; Saturday, 8:30AM-12:30PM (except late June to early Sept.). Closed holidays.

All-women's Wellesley College is home to 2,300 or so future leaders. Cross registration at MIT and cooperative education programs at Babson and Brandeis are available. Madeline Albright and Hillary Rodham Clinton are two of Wellesley's many prominent alums.

HIGHLIGHTS

ON CAMPUS
- Davis Museum and Cultural Center
- Whittin Observatory
- Science Center
- Betsy Wood Knapp Media and Technology Center
- Margaret C. Ferguson Greenhouses

OFF CAMPUS
- Harvard Square
- Faneuil Hall Marketplace
- Boston Public Garden/Boston Commons
- Museum of Fine Arts
- Symphony Hall

TRANSPORTATION

Logan International Airport in Boston is approximately 15 miles from campus; travel time to campus from the airport varies widely depending on traffic. Public transportation, taxis, and rental cars are available for the ride to campus. For public transportation, take the Logan Express bus to Framingham (call 800-23-LOGAN for schedules) and a taxi from Framingham to campus. If necessary, call Veteran's Taxi at 781-235-1600. It is also possible to take the subway: First take the free shuttle bus to the Airport MBTA stop; then take the inbound Blue Line 4 stops to Government Center. Go upstairs and change to the Green Line marked "Riverside-D." Get off at Woodland, the next-to-last stop. From Woodland take a taxi to campus. If necessary, call Veteran's Taxi at 781-235-1600. By public transportation, the trip from airport to campus takes approximately 2 hours. Have plenty of change—exact fares are required. Amtrak trains serve South Station in Boston. From there, take the Red Line (MBTA subway) 2 stops to Park St. Change to the Green Line marked "Riverside-D." Get off at Woodland, the next to last stop, and take a taxi to campus. If you travel by bus, take the Greyhound or Peter Pan bus to the Riverside Terminal at Route 128. From there, take a taxi to campus.

FIND YOUR WAY

From the west, take I-90 (Massachusetts Tpke.) to Exit 14 (Weston). Head south on I-95 (also called Rte. 128) for a half mile to the Rte. 16 exit. Follow Rte. 16 W. through the town of Wellesley for 4 miles to the college entrance, opposite the golf course. **From the east**, take the Massachusetts Tpke. to Exit 16 (West Newton). Take Rte. 16 W. and follow the preceding directions from that point. **From the north**, take I-95 (also called Rte. 128) S. to Exit 21B (Rte. 16 W.). Take Rte. 16 W. and follow the preceding directions from that point. **From the south**, take I-95 (also called Rte. 128) N. to Exit 21B (Rte. 16 W.). Take Rte. 16 W. and follow the preceding directions from that point.

STAY THE NIGHT

Nearby: The **College Club** (781-283-2700) is on campus. **Crowne Plaza** (508-653-8800) on nearby Route 9 in Natick. **Wellesley Inn** (Washington Street; 781-235-0180). **Holiday Inn in Newton** (Route 128 Exit 22, 617-969-5300).

A little farther: Waltham is readily accessible. For suggestions in that area, see the Brandeis University entry. See the Emerson College entry for accommodations in Boston.

AT A GLANCE	
Selectivity Rating	97
Range SAT I Math	630-720
Average SAT I Math	671
Range SAT I Verbal	630-720
Average SAT I Verbal	678
Average ACT Composite	29
Student to Faculty Ratio	10:1

CAMPUS TOURS	
Appointment Req?	No
Dates	Year-round
Times	Mon-Fri 9AM, 10AM, 11AM, 1PM, 2PM, and 3PM; Sat 9AM, 10AM, and 11AM (except June to Sept)
Avg. Length	1 hour

ON-CAMPUS INTERVIEWS	
Admissions	
Start Date—Juniors	May 1
Appointment Req?	Yes
Advance Notice	2 weeks
Saturdays?	Yes, second week in Sept to second week in June
Avg. Length	30-45 min
Info Sessions	June-Aug and Oct 10AM and 2PM
Faculty and Coaches	
Dates/Times	Year-round; subject to faculty/coach availability
Arrangements	Contact admissions off. or athletics dept.

CLASS VISITS	
Dates	Mid-Sept to Nov and mid-Feb to April
Arrangements	Contact admissions off.

OVERNIGHT DORM STAYS	
Advance Notice	2 weeks
Arrangements	Contact admissions off.
Limitations	Available Mon-Thurs nights when classes are in session; report to Admissions by 4PM

WHEATON COLLEGE

Admissions Office, Wheaton College, Norton, MA 02766 (The office is in the Admission Building, which is next to Cole Chapel and Balfour Hood Center) • Telephone: 800-394-6003 or 508-286-8251 ext. 251 • Web: www.wheatoncollege.edu • Email: admission@wheatonma.edu

Hours: Monday-Friday, 8:30AM-4:30PM; Saturday, 8:30AM-1PM (September-January only). Closed Sundays and holidays.

Wheaton College offers a rigorous liberal arts education and a challenging core curriculum. The school's pastoral campus is located in Norton, which is equidistant from Boston and Providence, Rhode Island.

TRANSPORTATION

Logan International Airport in Boston and Green State Airport in Providence, RI, are 45 minutes from campus. To get to campus from Logan, take a Bonanza bus to Foxfield Plaza in Foxboro and a taxi from the plaza to Wheaton. The Bonanza bus leaves hourly on the half hour from most terminals; call Bonanza at 800-556-3815 for bus information. Bonanza buses also run from downtown Providence to Foxboro. Taxis and rental cars are available at both airports. Amtrak provides rail service to Boston and Providence. From Boston's South Station, an MBTA commuter rail serves Mansfield and Attleboro, which are towns near campus; take a taxi from either town to Wheaton.

FIND YOUR WAY

From the west, take I-90 (Massachusetts Tpke.) East to Exit 11A; then take I-495 to Exit 11 and follow Route 140 S. for 2.5 miles. Turn left at the light onto Route 12B. **From Boston and northern New England,** take I-93 S. (the Southeast Expy.) to I-93 S./128 N. Continue to the junction with I-95 S. and take I-95 S. to I-495 S. At Exit 11 from I-495 follow Route 140 S. for 2.5 miles. Turn left at the light onto Route 12B. **From Providence and southern New England,** take I-95 N. to Exit 6A; then take I-495 S. to Exit 11 and follow Route 140 S. for 2.5 miles. Turn left at the light onto Route 12B.

STAY THE NIGHT

Nearby: Our first choice for charm is the **Colonel Blackinton Inn** (203 N. Main St. [Rte. 152], Attleboro; 508-222-6022), 6 miles from campus. This 19th-century inn is listed on the National Register of Historic Places and has an informal country atmosphere. Continental breakfast and afternoon tea are included in the moderate price. The **Holiday Inn** (700 Miles Standish Blvd., Taunton; 508-823-0430) is only 10 minutes away and has a health club, a restaurant, and a comedy club on the weekends. Rates vary between the inexpensive and moderate ranges. **Red Roof Inn** (60 Forbes Blvd., Mansfield; 508-339-2323) has inexpensive to moderate rates and is a 15-minute drive away. For an indoor pool and a health club, try the **Holiday Inn** (31 Hampshire St., Mansfield; 508-339-2200). Rates begin at the top end of the moderate range and go into the expensive range.

A little farther: Providence, RI, is less than half an hour to the south. See the Brown University entry for suggestions there.

WILLIAMS COLLEGE

Admissions Office, Williams College, 988 Main Street, Williamstown, MA 01267
(The office is in Mather House on Main St., Rte. 2) • Telephone: 413-597-2211 •
Web: www.williams.edu • Email: admissions@williams.edu

Hours: Monday-Friday, 8:30AM-4:30PM; Saturday, 9AM-noon (mid-September to mid-November only). Closed Sundays and holidays.

The knowledgeable and entertaining professors at Williams College truly make this challenging school worthwhile.

HIGHLIGHTS

ON CAMPUS
- Williams College Museum of Art
- Chapin Library of Rare Books
- Hopkins Forest
- Adams Memorial Theater
- Williamstown Theater Festival

OFF CAMPUS
- Clark Art Institute
- Tanglewood (summer only)
- Norman Rockwell Museum
- Images Theater
- Taconic Golf Course

TRANSPORTATION

The Albany, NY, airport is 50 miles from campus. Taxis and rental cars are available for the drive from the airport to campus.

FIND YOUR WAY

From the south, take the Taconic State Pkwy. (in New York) north to E. Chatham (the last exit before the toll). Take Rte. 295 E. to Rte. 22 N.; then take Rte. 22 N. to Rte. 43 E. (a sharp right turn). Proceed on Rte. 43 to U.S. Rte. 7 N., which takes you to Williamstown, where you turn right onto Rte. 2 E. The admissions office is on Rte. 2. **From the east and west**, take Rte. 2 to campus. **From the north**, take I-91 S. to Rte. 2; then take Rte. 2 W. to Williamstown.

STAY THE NIGHT

The Williams Inn (West Main St. on the green; 413-458-9371) is a big colonial-style inn within walking distance of campus. An indoor pool makes it very popular with college visitors. Rates are expensive. Two inexpensive motels are also within walking distance. **Northside Inn and Motel** (45 North St.; 413-458-8107) and **Maple Terrace Motel** (555 Main St.; 413-458-8101), both with outdoor pools, are worth checking out. There are many appealing bed-and-breakfast choices nearby. (You can get a long list from the admissions office.) Here are a few: **Field Farm Guest House B&B** (413-458-3135) is a bit farther out in a quiet rural setting on 247 acres with a tennis court, hiking trails, a pond, and cross-country skiing available on the property. Its 5 bedrooms have private baths. Rates are moderate. **River Bend Farm B&B** (413-458-5504) is an 18th-century colonial home. All 5 rooms share baths, and the inexpensive/moderate rates include a deluxe continental breakfast. **Steep Acres Farm B&B** (413-458-3774) also has inexpensive/moderate rates. It is on a working farm of 54 acres and its 4 rooms share two baths. Continental breakfast with homemade bread is included in the price. **The Orchards** (222 Adams Rd.; 413-458-9611) is a European-style country inn 1 mile from campus. Don't be put off by the location, which is on a busy commercial street across from a supermarket. Inside, it's gorgeous. Rates are expensive, and tennis and golf privileges are provided.

AT A GLANCE

Selectivity Rating	98
Range SAT I Math	660-750
Average SAT I Math	694
Range SAT I Verbal	650-760
Average SAT I Verbal	701
Average ACT Composite	30
Student to Faculty Ratio	11:1

CAMPUS TOURS

Appointment Req?	No
Dates	Year-round
Times	April to mid-Dec: Mon-Fri 10AM, 11:15AM, 1:15PM, and 3:30PM. Mid-Dec to March: Mon-Fri 10AM, 2:30PM; select Sat, 10AM and noon.
Avg. Length	1 hour

ON-CAMPUS INTERVIEWS

Admissions

Start Date–Juniors	June
Appointment Req?	Yes
Advance Notice	1 month
Saturdays?	No
Avg. Length	40 min
Info Sessions	June to mid-Dec: Mon-Fri 10AM and 2:30PM

Faculty and Coaches

Dates/Times	Year-round; subject to faculty/coach availability
Arrangements	Contact admissions off. 1 week prior

CLASS VISITS

Dates	Year-round (Mon-Fri)
Arrangements	Check with professor before class begins

OVERNIGHT DORM STAYS

Advance Notice	2 weeks
Arrangements	Contact College's Purple Key Society at 413-597-3148
Limitations	Seniors only

WORCESTER POLYTECHNIC INSTITUTE

Admissions Office, Worcester Polytechnic Institute, 100 Institute Rd.,
Worcester, MA 01609-2280 (The office is in Boynton Hall) • Telephone: 508-831-5286 •
Web: www.wpi.edu • Email: admissions@wpi.edu

Hours: Monday-Friday, 8:30AM-5PM; selected Saturdays, 9AM-noon. Summer: Monday-Friday, 8AM-4PM. Closed holidays.

The undergraduate experience at Worcester Polytechnic Institute centers around a series of required independent projects designed to build research ability and teamwork skills. Engineering and sciences are the name of the game here, and students gain a lot of lab experience under the guidance of dedicated professors.

AT A GLANCE

Selectivity Rating	82
Range SAT I Math	620-710
Average SAT I Math	660
Range SAT I Verbal	570-670
Average SAT I Verbal	620
Student to Faculty Ratio	14:1

CAMPUS TOURS

Appointment Req?	No
Dates	Year-round, except during student breaks
Times	Sept-Apr: Mon-Fri 9AM-4PM hourly; selected Saturdays 10:30AM and noon. May-August: 11AM and 2PM.
Avg. Length	1 hour

ON-CAMPUS INTERVIEWS

Admissions

Info Sessions	Year-round: 10AM and 2PM
Appointment Req?	Yes

Faculty and Coaches

Dates/Times	Year-round; subject to faculty/coach availability
Arrangements	Contact admissions off.

CLASS VISITS

Dates	Mon, Tues, Thurs, Fri when classes are in session
Arrangements	Contact admissions off.

OVERNIGHT DORM STAYS

Advance Notice	2 weeks
Arrangements	Contact admissions off.
Limitations	Available on Sun, Mon, Wed, and Thurs; only available to admitted students

TRANSPORTATION

Logan International Airport in Boston is a one-hour drive from campus. Buses, limousines, and rental cars are available at the airport for the trip to campus. For limousine service, call Worcester Airport Limousine at 800-660-0992 (Massachusetts), 800-343-1369 (outside Massachusetts), or 508-756-4834; reservations are recommended. Worcester Airport, a 10-minute ride from the Institute, is served by USAir and Delta; taxis are available for the ride to campus. Amtrak trains (800-872-7245) and Greyhound (508-754-3247) and Peter Pan (508-754-4600) buses provide regular service to Worcester. Train and bus stations are 5-minute taxi rides from campus.

FIND YOUR WAY

Remember: If you get lost, it's pronounced "Wuh-stuh." Okay, **from the south and west**, take I-90 (the Massachusetts Tpke.) to Exit 10 (Auburn). Proceed east on I-290 into Worcester. Take Exit 17 (Lincoln Square, Rte. 9), and follow Rte. 9 W. straight through Lincoln Square onto Highland St. Turn right at the traffic light onto West St. and proceed 2 blocks to campus. **From the east**, take I-90 to Exit 11A (Rte. I-495). Take I-495 N. to I-290, and take I-290 W. into Worcester. Take Exit 18 and turn right at the first traffic light; then make an immediate right before the next traffic light. At the third light, proceed straight through, then bear right onto Salisbury Street. Follow Salisbury to Boynton St. and turn left. Turn right at stop sign onto Institute Rd. Turn right at stop sign onto West St./entrance to visitor parking.

STAY THE NIGHT

The Holiday Inn Worcester (500 Lincoln St.; 508-852-4000) is only 10 minutes away and has an indoor pool, sauna, and fitness room. Rates are at the high end of the moderate range. **The Auburn Motel** (1 Buckley Drive, Auburn; 508-832-7003) is 5 miles from campus. **Crowne Plaza Motel** (10 Lincoln St.; 508-791-1600) is half a mile from campus and has recreational facilities, swimming pool, a baggage handling fee and handicap access. See the Clark University entry for other suggestions in Worcester.

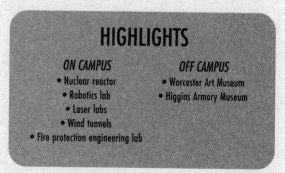

HIGHLIGHTS

ON CAMPUS
- Nuclear reactor
- Robotics lab
- Laser labs
- Wind tunnels
- Fire protection engineering lab

OFF CAMPUS
- Worcester Art Museum
- Higgins Armory Museum

1- Kalamazoo College
2- University of Michigan

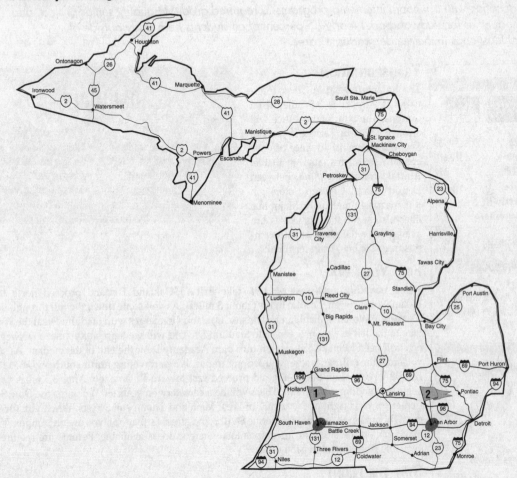

Michigan	Kalamazoo Coll.	Univ. Michigan	Detroit	Grand Rapids
Kalamazoo Coll.	—	97	140	52
Univ. Michigan	97	—	38	55
Detroit	140	38	—	156
Grand Rapids	52	55	156	—

KALAMAZOO COLLEGE

Admission Office, Kalamazoo College, 1200 Academy St., Kalamazoo, MI 49006
(The office is in Mandelle Hall) • Telephone: 800-253-3602 or 616-337-7166 •
Web: www.kzoo.edu • Email: admission@kzoo.edu

Hours: Monday-Friday, 8AM-5PM; Saturday, 9AM-noon (only when classes are in session). Closed Sundays and holidays.

Kalamazoo College's greatest asset is a unique program called the K Plan, which integrates a traditional liberal arts education with abundant internship programs, a required graduate-quality senior project, and excellent opportunities for study abroad. Nearly 85 percent of all students here study outside of Kalamazoo at least once in their undergraduate career.

AT A GLANCE

Selectivity Rating	80
Range SAT I Math	570-670
Average SAT I Math	622
Range SAT I Verbal	590-690
Average SAT I Verbal	640
Average ACT Composite	27
Average GPA	3.7
Student to Faculty Ratio	12:1

CAMPUS TOURS

Appointment Req?	Yes
Dates	Mon-Sat from Oct-May
Times	Call for times
Avg. Length	1 hour

ON-CAMPUS INTERVIEWS

Admissions

Start Date—Juniors	Weekdays
Appointment Req?	Yes
Advance Notice	10 working days
Saturdays?	Yes, Oct-May
Avg. Length	1 hour

Faculty and Coaches

Dates/Times	During academic year; subject to faculty/coach availability
Arrangements	Contact admissions off. 10 working days prior

CLASS VISITS

Dates	Oct-May (Mon-Fri)
Arrangements	Contact admissions off.

OVERNIGHT DORM STAYS

Advance Notice	2 weeks
Arrangements	Contact admissions off.
Limitations	1-night stay; Sun-Fri

TRANSPORTATION

The Kalamazoo-Battle Creek International Airport is 3.5 miles from campus. The admissions office will arrange a pick-up service if you call 5 working days in advance of your arrival. Taxis are also available. Amtrak trains traveling between Detroit and Chicago stop in Kalamazoo 4 times daily. Major bus lines also serve the city. Taxis are available for the short trip to campus from the bus/train terminal.

FIND YOUR WAY

When traveling east-west on I-94, take Exit 75/Oakland Dr. and proceed north toward Kalamazoo through 9 traffic lights (about 3 miles). As you come down the hill through the Old Campus of Western Michigan University, Oakland Dr. merges with Stadium Dr. at the 9th light. Stay to the left as you proceed onto Stadium Dr. You will see a green Kalamazoo College sign and will need to make a sharp left turn onto Academy St. at the end of the median. As soon as you cross the railroad tracks, you are on campus. **When traveling north-south on U.S. 131**, take Exit 38A West Main St. (M-43) and proceed east toward Kalamazoo. After 3.5 miles you will begin descending a steep hill. There will be a cemetery on your left. Look for the Dow Science Center on your right at the corner of West Main and Thompson Streets. When you turn right onto Thompson St. or onto Catherine St. (the 2nd street farther on), you are on campus. Visitors may park on the street or in campus lots where space is available. Permits are required and available from the admission office.

STAY THE NIGHT

Stuart Avenue Inn Bed and Breakfast (229 Stuart Ave.; 800-461-0621), across the street from the college, is an inn that consists of several lovingly restored Victorian mansions, each of which has a parlor and a concierge. One of the mansions, the **Bartlett Upjohn House**, is featured in the 1987 book *Daughters of Painted Ladies: America's Resplendent Victorians*. Rates run the gamut and include a continental breakfast with home-baked goods. **Hall House** (106 Thompson St.; 800-761-2525) is a Georgian Colonial Revival built in 1923, whose moderate rates and continental breakfast make it highly pleasing. Two lower priced motels: **Baymor Inn** (2203 S. Eleventh St.) and **Red Roof Inn—West** (5425 W. Michigan Ave.; 800-843-7663); both are about 3 miles from the campus. Upscale **Radisson Plaza Hotel** (100 Michigan Ave.; 800-333-3333) is 6 blocks from campus in downtown Kalamazoo with a health club, indoor pool, whirlpool, shops, and 3 restaurants.

HIGHLIGHTS

ON CAMPUS
- The bells of Statson Chapel
- Western Tennis Hall of Fame
- Upjohn Library
- Hicks Center

OFF CAMPUS
- Kalamazoo Institute of Arts
- Kalamazoo Air Zoo
- Kalamazoo Valley Museum
- Kellogg Biological Station
- Kal-Haven Trail

UNIVERSITY OF MICHIGAN—ANN ARBOR

Office of Undergraduate Admissions, University of Michigan, 1220 SAB, Ann Arbor, MI 48109-1316 (The office is in the Student Activities Building at Jefferson and Thompson Streets) • Telephone: 734-764-7433 • Web: www.umich.edu • Email: ugadmiss@umich.edu

Hours: Monday-Friday, 8AM-5PM; Saturday, 9AM-noon. Closed Sundays and holidays.

With several outstanding academic departments scattered among its 12 undergraduate schools, particularly the highly regarded engineering and business colleges, the University of Michigan offers a wealth of resources and opportunities to its students. The U of M is one of the very best public schools in all the land.

HIGHLIGHTS

ON CAMPUS
- Bentley Historic Library
- Gerald R. Ford Library
- Matthaes Botanical Gardens
- Museum of Art
- Margaret Dow Towsley Sports Museum

OFF CAMPUS
- Cobblestone Farm
- Hands-On Museum
- Leslie Science Center
- Kempf House
- Kerrytown

TRANSPORTATION

Detroit Metropolitan Airport is 28 miles east of campus. Hourly limousine service is available between the airport and the Michigan Union on campus (a short walk to Admissions in the Student Activities Building, the starting point for tours). The service leaves the airport on the hour; allow an hour to travel to campus. Tickets can be purchased at the airport. Taxis at the airport will take passengers to campus; rental cars are also available. Amtrak trains (those that run between Chicago and Detroit) and Greyhound buses serve Ann Arbor.

FIND YOUR WAY

From I-80/I-90 (Ohio Tpke.), exit to U.S. 23 N. (near Toledo, OH). Take U.S. 23 N. to I-94 W. Follow I-94 W. to State St. N. **From the Detroit Airport,** take I-94 W. to exit 177 (State St.). Take State St. north to campus.

STAY THE NIGHT

The **Michigan League** (911 N. University Ave.; 734-764-3177) and the **Oxford Conference Center** (627 Oxford St.; 734-764-5297) are University-owned facilities located on Central Campus. The **Campus Inn** (615 E. Huron St.; 800-666-8693) and the **Bell Tower Hotel** (300 S. Thayer St.; 800-562-3559) are hotels within walking distance of campus. Numerous hotel chains have locations near State St. (a short drive from Central Campus) and near Plymouth Rd. (a short drive from North Campus). For a complete list, call the Huetwell Visitors Center at 734-647-5692 or see the Visiting Campus section of the Admissions website at www.admissions.umich.edu.

AT A GLANCE

Selectivity Rating	90
Range SAT I Math	600-700
Average SAT I Math	655
Range SAT I Verbal	560-660
Average SAT I Verbal	615
Average ACT Composite	28
Average GPA	3.6
Student to Faculty Ratio	17:1

CAMPUS TOURS

Appointment Req?	Yes
Dates	Year-round, except on holidays, exam periods, and semester breaks
Times	Call 734-647-5692 for current times or check www.admissions.umich.edu
Avg. Length	1 hour

ON-CAMPUS INTERVIEWS

Admissions

Start Date–Juniors	N/A
Appointment Req?	N/A
Advance Notice	N/A
Saturdays?	N/A
Avg. Length	N/A
Info Sessions	Year-round

Faculty and Coaches

Dates/Times	Year-round; subject to faculty/coach availability
Arrangements	Contact dept. of interest 1 week prior

CLASS VISITS

Dates	Year-round (Mon-Fri)
Arrangements	Obtain class schedule in admissions off. and speak to instructor a few minutes prior to class

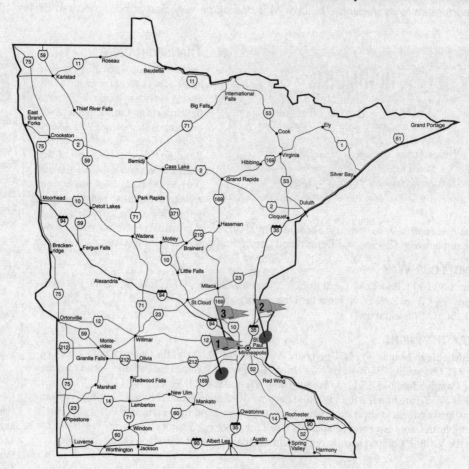

1- Carleton College
   St. Olaf College
2- Macalester College
3- University of Minnesota—Twin Cities

Minnesota	Carleton College	Macalester College	St. Olaf College	Univ. Minnesota-TC	Minneapolis
Carleton College	—	35	0	44	32
Macalester College	35	—	41	4	0
St. Olaf College	0	41	—	42	33
Univ. Minnesota-TC	44	4	42	—	0
Minneapolis	32	0	33	0	—

CARLETON COLLEGE

Admissions Office, Carleton College, 100 S. College St., Johnson House, Northfield, MN 55057 • Telephone: 800-995-CARL • Web: www.carleton.edu • Email: admissions@acs.carleton.edu

Hours: September-May: Monday-Friday, 8AM-5PM; Saturday, 8:30AM-noon. June-August: Monday-Friday, 8:30AM-4:30PM. Closed Sundays and holidays.

Carleton College is a little liberal arts school in a small, snowy, peaceful Minnesota town with 1,900 mostly happy students.

HIGHLIGHTS

ON CAMPUS
- Cowling Arboretum
- Art gallery
- Historic Goodsell Observatory

OFF CAMPUS
- Mall of America
- Science Museum of Minnesota
- Walker Outdoor Sculpture Garden
- Guthrie Theatre

TRANSPORTATION

The Minneapolis-St. Paul International Airport is 35 miles from campus. Carleton offers a co-op bus and drivers for the ride between the airport and campus; call the admissions office to make arrangements. Rental cars are also available at the airport. Amtrak trains serve Minneapolis/St. Paul. These trains generally arrive late at night; therefore, you should plan to stay overnight near the station and take a bus or taxi to Northfield the following day.

FIND YOUR WAY

From I-35, take Exit 69 to Minnesota Hwy. 19 and head east for 7 miles to Northfield. At the first stoplight (where Hwy. 19 merges with Hwy. 3), turn left. Proceed to the next stoplight (2nd St./Hwy. 19) and turn right onto 2nd St. You will come to a stop sign at Division St.; continue straight ahead up the hill on 2nd St. Turn left at College St., which takes you to campus and the admissions office.

STAY THE NIGHT

The **Archer House** (212 Division St.; 507-645-5661) is a restored turn-of-the-century inn just a couple of blocks from campus. Highlights are its convenient downtown location and gorgeous views of the Cannon River. Rates range all the way from inexpensive to expensive; special rates may be available during the week. The price includes continental breakfast. The **College City Motel** (Hwy. 3 N.; 507-645-4426) and **Country Inn** (300 Hwy. 3 S.; 800-456-4000) are both 1 mile from campus. **Super 8 Motel** (1420 Riverview Dr., Hwy. 3 S.; 507-663-0371) is a mere 3 miles from campus. **Amerielo** (1320 Ballenbach Dr.; 800-634-3444) is also in the area. See the University of Minnesota and Macalester College entries for suggestions in Minneapolis and St. Paul, about 45 miles away.

AT A GLANCE

Selectivity Rating	96
Range SAT I Math	640-720
Range SAT I Verbal	650-740
Student to Faculty Ratio	10:1

CAMPUS TOURS

Appointment Req?	Yes
Dates	Year-round
Times	Mon-Fri, varying times; Sat morning during the academic year
Avg. Length	1 hour

ON-CAMPUS INTERVIEWS

Admissions

Start Date–Juniors	Anytime
Appointment Req?	Yes
Advance Notice	2 weeks
Saturdays?	Yes, during the academic year
Avg. Length	40 min
Info Sessions	Year-round, except during Feb and March

Faculty and Coaches

Dates/Times	Year-round; subject to faculty/coach availability
Arrangements	Contact admissions off. 2 weeks prior

CLASS VISITS

Dates	Academic year (Mon-Fri)
Arrangements	Contact admissions off.

OVERNIGHT DORM STAYS

Advance Notice	2 weeks
Arrangements	Contact admissions off.
Limitations	1-night stay; bring a sleeping bag or reserve a rollaway bed; 3 complimentary meals in the dining halls are provided; April and May are for seniors only

MACALESTER COLLEGE

Office of Admissions, Macalester College, 1600 Grand Ave. St. Paul, MN 55105
(The office is at 62 Macalester St.) • Telephone: 800-231-7974 (outside MN) or 612-696-6357 •
Web: www.macalester.edu • Email: admissions@macalester.edu

Hours: September-May: Monday-Friday, 8AM-5:00PM; Saturday, 9AM-noon (fall only). Closed Sundays and holidays.

The facilities are exceptional and the academics at this demanding liberal arts college in the Twin Cities can't be beat. The dreary winters are a downer for some, but financial aid is good at Mac and the professors are often brilliant.

AT A GLANCE

Selectivity Rating	94
Range SAT I Math	610-700
Average SAT I Math	650
Range SAT I Verbal	630-720
Average SAT I Verbal	664
Average ACT Composite	29
Student to Faculty Ratio	11:1

CAMPUS TOURS

Appointment Req?	Strongly recommended
Dates	Year-round (Mon-Sat)
Times	Call for times
Avg. Length	1 hour

ON-CAMPUS INTERVIEWS

Admissions

Start Date—Juniors	April 1
Appointment Req?	Yes
Advance Notice	2 weeks
Saturdays?	Yes, during the fall
Avg. Length	45 min
Info Sessions	Year-round

Faculty and Coaches

Dates/Times	Year-round; subject to faculty/coach availability
Arrangements	Contact particular faculty/coach directly 2 weeks prior

CLASS VISITS

Dates	Mon-Fri check calendar of classes
Arrangements	Contact admissions off. 1 week prior

OVERNIGHT DORM STAYS

Advance Notice	2 weeks
Arrangements	Contact admissions off.
Limitations	Not available on Sat nights or during exams or holidays; not available to juniors during the fall or in April

TRANSPORTATION

The Minneapolis-St. Paul International Airport is 7 miles from campus. Amtrak trains and Greyhound buses serve St. Paul. If you are arriving in town by plane, bus, or train, we recommend that you come to campus by taxi. The campus is approximately 15 minutes from all terminals, and the fare should be $10-15.

FIND YOUR WAY

From I-95, take the Snelling Ave. exit and go south on Snelling to Grand Ave. Turn right (west) on Grand Ave. and go 1 block. Turn left (south) on Macalester St. **From the north on I-35**, take I-35E into St. Paul. Exit to I-94 westbound, and follow directions above. **From the south on I-35**, take 35 E into St. Paul. Exit at Randolph Ave. and proceed west on Randolph about 1 mile. Turn right (north) on Snelling and proceed to Grand Ave. and go 1 block. Turn left (south) on Macalester St. The admissions office is located at 62 Macalester St. Parking for visitors is available in a lot across the street.

STAY THE NIGHT

Nearby: Four rooms are available at the on-campus **Hugh S. Alexander Alumni House**. A double room is inexpensive and the rate includes breakfast. A 5-minute drive gets you to **Chatsworth Bed and Breakfast** (984 Ashland Ave.; 651-227-4288 or 877-978-4837), a peaceful, 1902 Victorian home near good restaurants and shops. The elegant **St. Paul Hotel** (350 Market St.; 651-292-9292 or 800-292-9292), Minnesota's only 4-star hotel, is a 10-minute drive from the school. Here's a quick list of lower-priced places accessible to Macalester: **Holiday Inn** (1010 W. Bandana Blvd.; 651-647-1637 or 800-465-4329), 2 miles away, and the **Sheraton-Midway** (400 Hamline Ave. N.; 651-642-1234 or 800-535-2339). The Sheraton has a pool, whirlpool, sauna, exercise room, restaurant, and bar.

A little farther: Stillwater is 30 minutes from Macalester. Try **River Town Inn** (306 W. Olive St., Stillwater; 651-430-2955). Its 9 guest rooms range in price from inexpensive to expensive, with full breakfast included. **Lowell Inn** (102 N. 2nd St.; 651-439-1100) offers nice rooms and high rates with no breakfast during the week. **The Holiday Inn International** (3 Appletree Square, Bloomington; 651-854-9000) is near the airport and Mall of America (20 minutes away by car).

HIGHLIGHTS

ON CAMPUS
- Stan Wagun Square Wheel Bicycle
- New Student Center
- The Macalester Art Gallery
- Ruminator Books

OFF CAMPUS
- Summit Avenue: Victorian Homes
- JJ Hill House at 240 Summit Avenue
- Science Museum of Minnesota
- St. Paul Cathedral at 239 Selby Avenue
- History Center of Minnesota

ST. OLAF COLLEGE

Office of Admissions, St. Olaf College, 1520 St. Olaf Ave., Northfield, MN 55057
(The office is in the Administration Building at the west entrance) • Telephone: 507-646-2222 •
Web: www.stolaf.edu • Email: admissions@stolaf.edu

Hours: Monday-Friday, 8AM-5PM; Saturday, 8:30AM-noon (except during the summer). Closed Sundays and holidays.

St. Olaf has a very good liberal arts program with strong curricula in economics and the sciences as well, and a demanding core curriculum.

HIGHLIGHTS

ON CAMPUS
- Buntrock Commons
- Beautiful 350-acre campus

OFF CAMPUS
- Mall of America
- Museum in Twin Cities
- Many Arts Activities in Twin Cities
- Historic downtown Northfield

STAY THE NIGHT

Please contact the admission office for a listing of accomodations or visit our website.

TRANSPORTATION

The Minneapolis-St. Paul Airport is 40 miles from campus.

FIND YOUR WAY

From **I-35 W.**, take Rte. 19 E. for 7 miles to the entrance to the college. **From I-90 near Rochester,** take U.S. 52 N. to Cannon Falls; then take Rte. 19 W. to the college.

AT A GLANCE

Selectivity Rating	85
Range SAT I Math	570-690
Average SAT I Math	627
Range SAT I Verbal	570-680
Average SAT I Verbal	624
Average ACT Composite	27
Average GPA	3.7
Student to Faculty Ratio	13:1

CAMPUS TOURS

Appointment Req?	Strongly recommended
Dates	Year-round
Times	Mon-Fri as needed; Sat mornings during academic year
Avg. Length	45-60 min

ON-CAMPUS INTERVIEWS

Admissions

Start Date–Juniors	Any time
Appointment Req?	Strongly encouraged
Advance Notice	1 week
Saturdays?	During academic year
Avg. Length	40-60 min
Info Sessions	Varies

Faculty and Coaches

Dates/Times	Year-round; subject to faculty/coach availability
Arrangements	Contact admissions off. 1 week prior

CLASS VISITS

Dates	Academic year
Arrangements	Contact admissions off. 1 week prior

OVERNIGHT DORM STAYS

Advance Notice	2 weeks
Arrangements	Contact admissions off.
Limitations	1-night stay

UNIVERSITY OF MINNESOTA—TWIN CITIES

Admissions Office, University of Minnesota–Twin Cities, 240 Williamson Hall, 231 Pillsbury Dr. S.E., Minneapolis, MN 55455 • Telephone: 800-752-1000 (outside the area) or 612-625-0000 • Web: www.umn.edu/tc/prospective • Email: admissions@tc.umn.edu

Hours: Monday, 8AM-6PM; Tuesday-Friday, 8AM-4:30PM; selected Saturdays September-May. Closed Sundays and holidays.

The University of Minnesota—located in the heart of the Twin Cities—boasts excellent programs to choose from across the board, including pre-professional majors like business and management, journalism, psychology, and engineering. The school is a big place that demands self-reliance, but offers many diverse opportunities.

AT A GLANCE

Selectivity Rating	80
Range SAT I Math	550-670
Average SAT I Math	572
Range SAT I Verbal	540-660
Average SAT I Verbal	583
Average ACT Composite	25
Student to Faculty Ratio	15:1

CAMPUS TOURS

Appointment Req?	Preferred
Dates	Year-round
Times	10:30AM and 2:15PM
Avg. Length	1 hour

ON-CAMPUS INTERVIEWS

Admissions

Start Date—Juniors	Fall
Appointment Req?	Preferred
Advance Notice	2-3 weeks
Saturdays?	Sept-May
Avg. Length	1 hour
Info Sessions	Mon-Fri 9:30AM and 1PM

Faculty and Coaches

Dates/Times	Year-round; subject to faculty/coach availability
Arrangements	Contact dept. of interest 2-3 weeks prior

CLASS VISITS

Dates	Year-round (Mon-Fri)
Arrangements	Contact Visiting Off. at 612-625-0000

OVERNIGHT DORM STAYS

Advance Notice	2-3 weeks
Arrangements	Contact University Housing Off. at 612-624-2994
Limitations	Available only mid-June to Aug

TRANSPORTATION

The Minneapolis-St. Paul International Airport is approximately 12 miles from campus. Two hotels on campus provide daytime limousine service from the airport. For details, call Radisson University Hotel (800-333-3333 or 612-379-8888) or Holiday Inn Metrodome (800-HOLIDAY or 612-333-4646). Amtrak trains and Greyhound buses serve the Minneapolis-St. Paul area. Taxis are available for the drive from the terminals to campus. Public transportation to campus is available: Metro Transit provides bus service to and from the Minneapolis-St. Paul airport. For more information, call 612-344-7000.

FIND YOUR WAY

From I-94 (east or west), take the Huron Blvd. exit (235B). From I-35 (east or west), take the University Ave. SE exit (18).

STAY THE NIGHT

Nearby: Dormitory housing is available on campus from mid-June through August. Call 612-624-2994 to book a spot. You can also purchase meal tickets and eat on campus. The **Radisson University Hotel** (615 Washington Ave. S.E.; 612-379-8888) has moderate rates and a good location on the East Bank Campus. The **Econo Lodge** (2500 University Ave. S.E.; 612-331-6000) is just 5 blocks away. It has an outdoor pool and the price includes a continental breakfast. The **Holiday Inn Metrodome** (1500 Washington Ave. S.; 612-333-4646), only 4 blocks away, has a special moderate double-occupancy rate, an indoor pool, sauna, whirlpool, exercise room, game room, and restaurant.

A little farther: A solid suggestion is **Hyatt Regency Minneapolis** (1300 Nicollet Mall; 612-370-1234 or 800-233-1234), which provides you the usual Hyatt amenities and activities. Rates are very expensive during the week, but drop on weekends. Ask for a special rate for University of Minnesota visitors.

HIGHLIGHTS

ON CAMPUS
- Weisman Art Museum
- McNamara Alumni Center
- Goldstein Gallery
- Northrup Memorial Auditorium
- University Theater, Rarig Center

OFF CAMPUS
- Science Museum
- Mall of America
- Walker Art Center
- Valleyfair Amusement Park
- Target Center Metrodome

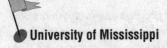

University of Mississippi

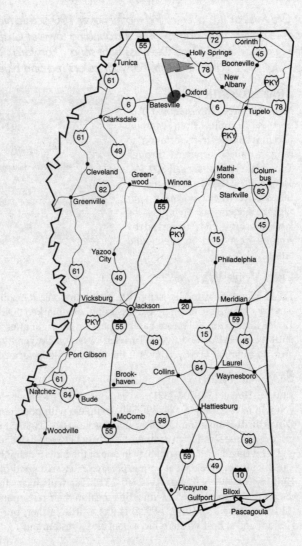

Mississippi	Univ. Mississippi	Jackson
Univ. Mississippi	—	157
Jackson	157	—

UNIVERSITY OF MISSISSIPPI

Admissions Office, University of Miss., Oxford, MS 38677 (The office is in Rm. 117 of the Lyceum; the Pre-admissions office, in Rm. 200 of the Lyceum, handles visits) • Telephone: 601-232-7226 (Admissions), 601-232-7378 (Pre-admissions) • Web: www.olemiss.edu • Email: admissions@olemiss.edu

Hours: Monday-Friday, 8AM-5PM; Saturday, 9AM-noon. Closed Sundays and holidays.

The University of Mississippi—or Ole Miss as it is often called—offers over 100 academic programs in everything from engineering to telecommunications to politics to pharmacy. The surrounding town of Oxford is a great college town as well. Impress administrators with your knowledge of the Ole Miss fight song: "Forward, Rebels, march to fame, Hit that line and win this game. We know that you'll fight it through, For your colors red and blue. Rah, rah, rah."

AT A GLANCE

Selectivity Rating	76
Average ACT Composite	23
Student to Faculty Ratio	19:1

CAMPUS TOURS

Appointment Req?	Strongly recommended
Dates	Year-round
Times	Mon-Fri 9AM-3PM; Sat 9AM-noon
Avg. Length	45 min

ON-CAMPUS INTERVIEWS

Admissions

Start Date—Juniors	Any time
Appointment Req?	Strongly recommended
Advance Notice	2 weeks prior
Saturdays?	Yes
Avg. Length	30 min
Info Sessions	Year-round

Faculty and Coaches

Dates/Times	Year-round; subject to faculty/coach availability
Arrangements	For faculty, call 601-232-7378; contact coach directly 2 weeks prior

CLASS VISITS

Dates	Year-round (Mon-Fri)
Arrangements	Contact pre-admissions

OVERNIGHT DORM STAYS

Advance Notice	2 weeks
Arrangements	Contact pre-admissions
Limitations	2-night maximum; only when school is in session and on a space-available basis; bring towels and bed linens

TRANSPORTATION

Memphis, TN, International Airport is 70 miles from campus. Ground shuttle transportation to campus can be arranged through Travel House Transit; call 800-844-4115 or 601-236-4115 to arrange for this service when you make your flight arrangements. Memphis (the largest nearby city) is served by Amtrak trains and by Greyhound buses.

FIND YOUR WAY

Take I-55 or U.S. 45 to Mississippi Rte. 6 and turn onto it heading toward Oxford. From the Rte. 6 bypass, take the University of Mississippi exit marked "Old Taylor Road." Go north on Old Taylor Road (you will pass a baseball park on the right after about a quarter mile), continuing until it ends at University Ave. Turn left (west) on University Ave. and you will soon be in the heart of campus. The Lyceum is at the top of the loop formed by University Ave.

STAY THE NIGHT

Alumni House (601-234-2331), on campus, is an excellent choice. Rates are inexpensive and you will have access to a health club, complete with pool, tennis courts, and all that jazz. The **Oliver Britt House Inn** (512 Van Buren Ave.; 601-234-8043) is a charming bed-and-breakfast just a 5-minute stroll from campus. Call them between 8AM and noon or between 4PM and 8PM—and let it ring. Don't give up! Stay in one of the inn's 5 delightfully decorated rooms and enjoy a full southern breakfast at an inexpensive rate. That good old inexpensively priced standby, **Holiday Inn** (400 N. Lamar Ave.; 601-232-7226), will always treat you right. Swim a few laps in the pool, and then recover with a fine meal in their restaurant. The **Best Western Oxford Inn** (1101 Frontage Rd.; 601-234-9500) is just a little farther, but rates here are competitive with Holiday Inn's. Best Western has a pool and a restaurant.

HIGHLIGHTS

ON CAMPUS
- University museums

OFF CAMPUS
- Kyle State Park
- Clear Creek Recreation Area
- Wall Doxey State Park
- Holly Springs National Forest

1- **University of Missouri**
2- **St. Louis University**
   Washington University

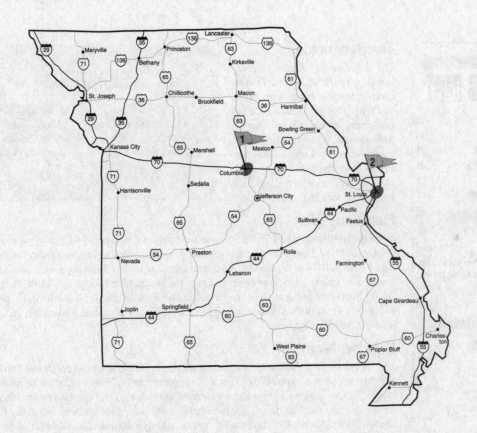

Missouri	St. Louis Univ.	Univ. Missouri	Washington Univ.	St. Louis	Springfield
St. Louis Univ.	—	132	5	0	215
Univ. Missouri	132	—	127	130	168
Washington Univ.	5	127	—	0	210
St. Louis	0	130	0	—	215
Springfield	215	168	210	215	—

SAINT LOUIS UNIVERSITY

Office of Undergraduate Admission, Saint Louis University, 221 N. Grand Blvd., St. Louis, MO 63103 (The office is in Rm. 119 of DuBourg Hall) • Telephone: 314-977-2500 or 800-SLU-FOR-U • Web: imagine.slu.edu • Email: admitme@slu.edu

Hours: Monday-Friday, 8:30AM-5PM; Saturday, 9AM-2PM. Closed Sundays and holidays.

Prestigious Saint Louis University is a small, private university with a strong Jesuit tradition that offers excellent academics at a very affordable price. Socially, students definitely party, but family values are reportedly very noticeable.

AT A GLANCE

Selectivity Rating	76
Average SAT I Math	580
Average SAT I Verbal	570
Average ACT Composite	26
Average GPA	3.5
Student to Faculty Ratio	14:1

CAMPUS TOURS

Appointment Req?	Yes
Dates	Year-round
Times	Mon and Fri 10AM, 12pm, 2PM, and 4PM; Sat at noon
Avg. Length	1 hour

ON-CAMPUS INTERVIEWS

Admissions

Start Date–Juniors	Any time
Appointment Req?	Yes
Advance Notice	10 days
Saturdays?	Yes
Avg. Length	1 hour
Info Sessions	N/A

Faculty and Coaches

Dates/Times	Year-round; subject to faculty/coach availability
Arrangements	Contact admissions off. 10 days prior

CLASS VISITS

Dates	During fall and spring semesters (except exam periods)
Arrangements	Contact admissions off.

OVERNIGHT DORM STAYS

Advance Notice	10 days
Arrangements	Contact admissions off.
Limitations	Fall and spring semesters; except exam periods

TRANSPORTATION

The Lambert-St. Louis International Airport is 13 miles from campus. Airport limousines, taxis, and rental cars are available for the ride from the airport to campus. Amtrak trains and Greyhound buses serve St. Louis. Taxis are available for the ride from the stations to campus. MetroLink also has a stop close to the University.

HIGHLIGHTS

ON CAMPUS
- St. Francis Xavier Church
- Cupples House Museum
- Museum of Contemporary Art

OFF CAMPUS
- Fox Theatre
- Art Powell Symphony Hall
- Forest Park

FIND YOUR WAY

From the northeast, take I-55/70 S. across the Poplar St. Bridge to I-64 W. Follow to the Grand Blvd. exit. Make a right on Grand Blvd. and proceed 1 block to campus. **From the northwest**, take I-70 E. to I-170 S. Proceed to I-64 E. and continue to the Grand Blvd. exit. Make a right on Grand and follow 1 block to campus. **From the south**, take I-55 N. to I-44 W. Follow to the Grand Blvd. exit. Make a left at the stop sign and then a right on Grand Blvd. Follow 2 miles to campus. **From the southwest**, take I-44 E. to the Grand Blvd. exit. Make a left on Grand and follow 2 miles to campus.

STAY THE NIGHT

Nearby: Located only half a mile from the university, the **Hampton Inn-Union Station** (22nd and Market Streets; 314-241-3200) is a convenient choice. Two blocks away from Historic Union Station, it offers a large indoor swimming pool, spa, and exercise room. Mention SLU for the special rate. Also quite close to the university is the **Best Western Inn at the Park** (4630 Lindell Blvd.; 314-367-7500) and the **Drury Inn at Union Station** (20th and Market Streets; 314-231-3900). Ask for the SLU rate at both. If you're looking for more luxurious accommodations, try the **Omni Majestic** (1019 Pine St.; 314-436-2355 or 800 451-2355). Listed on the National Register of Historic Buildings, this intimate, European-style hotel has been perfectly restored to its original beauty. It offers Joplin's Restaurant and Taproom, as well as a full-service concierge. Here, too, ask for the SLU rate.

UNIVERSITY OF MISSOURI—COLUMBIA

Admissions Office, University of Missouri, 230 Jesse Hall, Columbia, MO 65211 •
Telephone: 573-882-7786 or 800-225-6075 (in IL and MO) •
Web: www.missouri.edu • Email: admissions@missouri.edu

Hours: Monday-Friday, 8AM-5PM. Closed weekends and holidays.

The University of Missouri—Columbia offers as its crown jewel a nationally renowned journalism program. Greek life is big, and the men's basketball and football teams enjoy a great deal of popularity. Sam Walton, founder of Wal-Mart, is an alum.

HIGHLIGHTS

ON CAMPUS
- Francis Quadrangle, The Columns
- Jesse Hall
- Memorial Union
- Memorial Stadium/Faurot Field
- Brady Commons

OFF CAMPUS
- The Blue Note
- Columbia Downtown District
- Rock Bridge State Park
- Shelter Gardens
- MKT Fitness/Biking Trail

TRANSPORTATION

Columbia Regional Airport is 15 minutes from campus. Tiger Taxi is available for the ride from the airport to campus. Shuttles are also available to many of the hotels in town; check with the individual hotels/motels for such services.

FIND YOUR WAY

From east or west, take I-70 to Stadium Blvd.; then take Stadium Blvd. south to campus (approximately 4 miles). The campus is at the corner of Stadium and Providence Rd. **From north or south**, take U.S. Rte. 63 to Stadium Boulevard (State Rte. 740). Take Stadium Blvd. west to the campus, which is at the corner of Stadium and Providence Rd.

STAY THE NIGHT

Drury Inn (1000 Knipp St.; 573-445-1800) has 123 rooms and offers suites, has an indoor pool, and is located next to Columbia Mall and many nearby restaurants. The **Hampton Inn** (3410 Clark Lane; 573-449-2491) is another good option. The **Holiday Inn Select** (2200 I-70 Dr. SW; 573-449-4422) has 311 rooms, indoor and outdoor pools, and 2 restaurants. The **Ramada Inn** (1100 Vandiver Dr.; 573-449-0051) has 190 rooms, an outdoor pool, and restaurant.

AT A GLANCE

Average ACT Composite	25
Student to Faculty Ratio	11:1

CAMPUS TOURS

Appointment Req?	Yes
Dates	Year-round
Times	Mon-Fri almost hourly
Avg. Length	2 hours

ON-CAMPUS INTERVIEWS

Admissions

Start Date—Juniors	N/A
Appointment Req?	Yes
Advance Notice	2 weeks
Saturdays?	N/A
Avg. Length	45 min
Info Sessions	Year-round

Faculty and Coaches

Dates/Times	Year-round; subject to faculty/coach availability
Arrangements	Contact admissions off. 2 weeks prior

CLASS VISITS

Dates	Year-round (Mon-Fri)
Arrangements	Contact Off. of Admissions at 573-882-2456

OVERNIGHT DORM STAYS

Advance Notice	N/A
Arrangements	N/A
Limitations	N/A

WASHINGTON UNIVERSITY

Office of Undergraduate Admissions, Washington University, Campus Box 1089, 1 Brookings Dr., St. Louis, MO 63130-4899 (The office is in Rm. 135, South Brookings Hall) • Telephone: 800-638-0700 or 314-935-6000 • Web: www.wustl.edu • Email: admission@wustl.edu

Hours: Monday-Friday, 8:30AM-5PM; Saturday, 9AM-2PM (fall semester and April only). Closed Sundays and holidays.

Washington University in St. Louis is most widely known for being underrated. It's a great school, though, and a slew of students pursue graduate study, particularly in medicine (15 percent of all Wash U. grads head straight into med programs).

AT A GLANCE

Selectivity Rating	96
Range SAT I Math	650-730
Range SAT I Verbal	620-710
Student to Faculty Ratio	7:1

CAMPUS TOURS

Appointment Req?	Yes, call 800-676-2114
Dates	Year-round, limited during winter and spring breaks
Times	Sept-April: Mon-Fri 11AM and 2:30PM; Sat 10:30AM and noon (fall semester and April only). June-Aug: Mon-Fri 10AM.
Avg. Length	90 min

ON-CAMPUS INTERVIEWS

Admissions

Start Date—Juniors	N/A
Appointment Req?	N/A
Advance Notice	N/A
Saturdays?	N/A
Avg. Length	N/A
Info Sessions	Year-round

Faculty and Coaches

Dates/Times	During academic year; subject to faculty/coach availability
Arrangements	Contact admissions off. 1 week prior

CLASS VISITS

Dates	Year-round (Mon-Fri)
Arrangements	Ask prof. before class

OVERNIGHT DORM STAYS

Advance Notice	2-3 weeks
Arrangements	Contact Off. of Undergraduate Admissions
Limitations	1-night stay; Mon-Sun

TRANSPORTATION

Lambert-St. Louis International Airport is approximately 10 miles from campus. Limousines and taxis are available for the ride from the airport to campus. Call Airport Limousine (314-429-4940) one day in advance to arrange for a ride. County Cab (314-991-5300) should need only a few minutes' notice. Amtrak trains and Greyhound buses serve terminals in St. Louis. Taxis are available for the trip to campus.

HIGHLIGHTS

ON CAMPUS
- Gallery of Art
- Edison Theatre
- Olin Library
- Francis Gymnasium & Francis Field

OFF CAMPUS
- Fox Theatre
- Art Powell Symphony Hall
- Forest Park

FIND YOUR WAY

From I-55/70 south or west, exit to I-64 W. (U.S. 40/61). Exit I-64 at Skinker Blvd. and take Skinker north to campus. **From I-55 N.,** exit to I-270 W. and N. Exit I-270 to I-44 E. Take I-44 to Big Bend Blvd. and head north to campus. **From I-64 E.,** exit to Big Bend Blvd. and proceed north to campus. **From I-70 E.,** exit to I-170 S. Take I-170 S. to Forest Park Pkwy. E. and proceed to campus.

STAY THE NIGHT

A visit to Washington University is a good excuse to stay at the luxurious, European-style **Seven Gables Inn** (314-863-8400). Built in 1918 and inspired by Hawthorne's *House of the Seven Gables*, it has special moderate rates for university visitors, a French restaurant, and a lively café. **Cheshire Inn** (6300 Clayton Rd.; 314-647-7300 or 800-325-7378), a motor lodge done in Tudor style, has a free shuttle service for the 1-mile trek to school, an outdoor pool, and a well-equipped health club. Rates are quite reasonable. Serious shoppers should consider the **Ritz-Carlton**, (314-863-8100), about 10 minutes away from campus and close to the Galleria shopping center and the Plaza Frontenac. The Ritz has a beautiful health club with Nautilus machines, a masseuse, lap pool, jacuzzi, and sauna. Special rates for university visitors are actually not too bad (though still expensive), and complimentary upgrades may be available. Budget selections include the **Holiday Inn Clayton Plaza** (7730 Bonhomme Ave.; 314-863-0400), a mile from the university, with an indoor pool, weight room, sauna, and whirlpool, and the ever-popular **Red Roof Inn** (5823 Wilson Ave.; 314-645-0101), 15 minutes from WU. See the St. Louis University entry for some bed-and-breakfast suggestions. **Lafayette House**, listed there, is about 3 miles away from Washington University, and **Winter House** is about 5 miles away.

1- University of Nebraska—Lincoln
2- University of Nebraska—Omaha

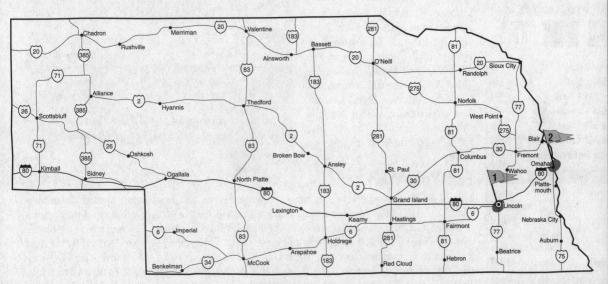

Nebraska	U. Nebraska-Lin.	U. Nebraska-Oma.	Omaha
U. Nebraska-Lin.	—	58	58
U. Nebraska-Oma.	58	—	0
Omaha	58	0	—

UNIVERSITY OF NEBRASKA—LINCOLN

Office of Admissions, University of Nebraska–Lincoln, 1410 Q. St., P.O. Box 880417, Lincoln, NE 68588-0417 • Telephone: 800-742-8800 • Web: www.unl.edu • Email: nuhusker@unl.edu

Hours: Monday-Friday, 8AM-5PM. Closed weekends and holidays.

The University of Nebraska provides the kinds of academic resources you would expect from a mammoth, world-class, state university along with a quality of life that can only be found in the Midwest. And, as if it needed any verification, Sports Illustrated listed UN among the Top 10 "best sports colleges" in the country. Johnny Carson, the original King of Late Night TV, is an alum.

AT A GLANCE

Selectivity Rating	90
Range SAT I Math	510-660
Average SAT I Math	584
Range SAT I Verbal	500-630
Average SAT I Verbal	566
Average ACT Composite	24
Student to Faculty Ratio	15:1

CAMPUS TOURS

Appointment Req?	Strongly recommended
Dates	Year-round
Times	Mon-Fri 9AM and 1PM; Sat by special appt.
Avg. Length	45-60 min

ON-CAMPUS INTERVIEWS

Admissions

Start Date–Juniors	N/A
Appointment Req?	N/A
Advance Notice	N/A
Saturdays?	N/A
Avg. Length	N/A
Info Sessions	Year-round

Faculty and Coaches

Dates/Times	Year-round; subject to faculty/coach availability
Arrangements	Contact Campus Visits 1 week prior

CLASS VISITS

Dates	Year-round (Mon-Fri)
Arrangements	Contact Campus Visits

OVERNIGHT DORM STAYS

Advance Notice	2 weeks
Arrangements	Contact Off. of University Housing at 800-742-8800, ext. 3561
Limitations	None

TRANSPORTATION

Lincoln Municipal Airport is 7 miles from campus. Taxis are available for the ride from airport to campus; call Capitol Cabs at 402-477-6074 or Husker Cabs at 402-477-4111. Amtrak trains and Greyhound buses serve Lincoln. The stations are within walking distance of campus. The city also has a good public transportation system.

FIND YOUR WAY

From I-80 (E. and W.), take the 9th St. downtown exit and head south toward downtown Lincoln. After 3 miles, you go over a viaduct and will see Memorial Stadium and the campus to the left. Continue south to the second stoplight (P St.). Turn left on P St. and proceed 8 blocks east to 17th St. Turn left on 17th St. and drive north 1 block to Q St. Turn left and travel west 2 blocks to the admissions office. **From U.S. Rte. 77 S.,** turn right onto Cornhusker Highway (the first major intersection when you get to Lincoln). Proceed west to 27th St. and turn left. Proceed south 3 miles to Q St. Turn right onto Q St. and continue west to 14th St. and the admissions office. **If you enter Lincoln from U.S. Rte. 77 N.,** turn right on Capital Parkway, proceed east into downtown Lincoln. Turn left on Q street and travel west 2 blocks to the admissions office.

STAY THE NIGHT

You have a few choices within walking distance. The larger **Holiday Inn** (141 N. 9th St.; 402-475-4011) has some special rates (depending on occupancy) in the inexpensive range. (Ask for the inexpensive student-faculty rate.) The hotel offers free parking and has an indoor pool and jacuzzi, a restaurant, and a coffee shop. Also consider the **Cornhusker Hotel** (333 S. 13th St.; 402-474-7474) or **Embassy Suites** (1040 P Street; 402-474-1111), which tend to run a bit higher. Lower rates are sometimes available on weekends. Both hotels have indoor pools and an exercise room. The Cornhusker Hotel also has 2 restaurants, one of which is reputed to be the only 4-star restaurant in the state. There is a small fee for parking.

HIGHLIGHTS

ON CAMPUS
- Center for Genetics and Biomaterials Research
- Art Gallery and Sculpture Garden
- Textiles Gallery and International Quilt Study Center
- Memorial Stadium and Hewitt Center

OFF CAMPUS
- Lincoln (state capital)
- Leid Center for Performing Arts
- Historic Haymarket
- Folsom Children's Zoo and Botanical Gardens
- Pioneers Park Nature Center and Golf Course

UNIVERSITY OF NEBRASKA—OMAHA

Office of Recruitment Services, 60th and Dodge Sts., Omaha, NE 68182-0559 (The office is located in Rm. 101 of the Eppley Administration Building) • Telephone: 402-554-MAV1 or 800-858-8648 • Web: www.unomaha.edu • Email: unoadm@unomaha.edu

Hours: Monday-Friday, 8AM-5PM. Closed weekends and major holidays.

The urban campus of the University of Nebraska at Omaha has a large percentage of part-timers among its 12,000 students, many of whom take advantage of weekend, evening, and summer programs. The school offers a wide range of majors as well as study abroad opportunities in Japan and Mexico. However, there is no on-campus housing.

HIGHLIGHTS

ON CAMPUS
- University library
- Strauss Performing Arts Center
- Caniglia Field Football Stadium

OFF CAMPUS
- Omaha's Children Museum
- Joslyn Art Museum
- Henry Doorly Zoo
- USS *Hazard* and USS *Marlin*

TRANSPORTATION
Eppley Airfield in Omaha is 8 miles from campus. Airport taxis are available for the ride to campus.

FIND YOUR WAY
From I-680, take Dodge St. eastbound for 4 miles to the campus at 60th St. From I-80, take the 72nd N. St. exit to Dodge St. East.

STAY THE NIGHT
You can stay 5 minutes from campus at **The Offutt House** (140 N. 39th St.; 402-553-0951), an 1894 mansion with fireplaces and antique-filled rooms. This renovated 7-room bed and breakfast is near museums and the old market. Rates vary from inexpensive to moderate, and include a breakfast. **Hampton Inn** (9720 W. Dodge Rd.; 402-391-5300) is 2 miles west of campus, near a shopping area in town. Rates are inexpensive (and lower on weekends) and include a continental breakfast. **The Embassy Suites Hotel** (555 S. 10th St.; 402-346-9000) in the Old Market area is another good place to stay. If an indoor pool is important, the **Holiday Inn** (3321 72nd St.; 402-393-3950), 5 miles from school, fills the bill. Moderate rates, a game room, exercise room, sauna, and whirlpool round out the experience. **Ramada Inn** (7007 Grover Street, 402-397-7030 or 800-228-5299) 5 miles from campus, it is at the 72nd Street exit of I-80.

AT A GLANCE

Average ACT Composite		22

CAMPUS TOURS
Appointment Req?	Yes
Dates	Year-round
Times	School year: Mon-Fri 9:30AM; Mon, Wed, Fri at 12:30PM. Summer: Mon and Fri 9:30AM.
Avg. Length	90 min

ON-CAMPUS INTERVIEWS
Admissions
Start Date–Juniors	Any time
Appointment Req?	Yes
Advance Notice	1 week
Saturdays?	No
Avg. Length	Varies
Info Sessions	Year-round

Faculty and Coaches
Dates/Times	Year-round; subject to faculty/coach availability
Arrangements	Contact Recruitment Services 1 week prior

CLASS VISITS
Dates	Year-round (Mon-Fri)
Arrangements	Contact Recruitment Services

OVERNIGHT DORM STAYS
Advance Notice	N/A
Arrangements	N/A
Limitations	N/A

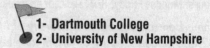

1- Dartmouth College
2- University of New Hampshire

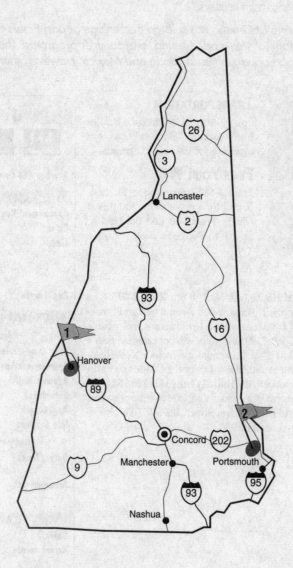

New Hampshire	Dartmouth College	U. New Hampshire	Manchester
Dartmouth College	—	114	86
U. New Hampshire	114	—	33
Manchester	86	33	—

DARTMOUTH COLLEGE

Office of Admissions, Dartmouth College, 6016 McNutt Hall, Hanover, NH 03755-3541 •
Telephone: 603-646-2875 • Web: www.dartmouth.edu •
Email: admissions.office@dartmouth.edu

Hours: Monday-Friday, 8AM-4:30PM; Saturday, 8AM-noon (September-November only; call for summer hours.)

Few schools offer the winning combination of caring, world-class professors and gorgeous setting that Dartmouth College does. Student life here has always revolved around frat parties and beer—the Greek scene here reputedly inspired the classic movie Animal House—but that may change thanks to the administration's recent prohibition of single-sex fraternities and sororities. Famous Dartmouth alums include Theodore Geisel, whom you may know better as Dr. Seuss.

HIGHLIGHTS

ON CAMPUS
- Hopkins Center for Creative and Performing Arts
- Hood Museum of Art
- Murals by Jose Clemente Orozco
- Ten-library system (all open to tourists)
- Ledyard Canoe Club (oldest in the country)

OFF CAMPUS
- Montshire Museum (hands-on science)
- Simon Pierce Glass Blowing
- Appalachian Trail
- Dartmouth Skiway
- Quechee Gorge

TRANSPORTATION

A commuter airport in Lebanon, a 15-minute ride from campus, is serviced by US Airways. Manchester Airport (75 minutes from campus) is serviced by several major airlines, and visitors can drive or take a Vermont Transit bus to campus. Logan Airport in Boston (2.5 hours to campus) is serviced by most major airlines. The Dartmouth Mini-Coach (603-448-2800) operates shuttles from Logan directly to Hanover several times a day. The Burlington, VT, airport (90 minutes from campus) is serviced by several major airlines, and visitors can drive or take a Vermont Transit bus to campus.

FIND YOUR WAY

From Boston (a 2.5-hour trip), take I-93 N. to I-89 N. Take Exit 18 (Rte. 120, Lebanon-Hanover). Turn right onto Rte. 120, then left onto Rte. 10 to campus. **From New York City** (a 5-hour trip), take I-95 to New Haven or I-684 and I-84 to Hartford. Pick up I-91 N. to Vermont. Take Exit 13 (Hanover-Norwich). Turn right off the ramp, cross the bridge, and drive straight to the campus (less than 1 mile from the I-91 exit).

STAY THE NIGHT

Located on campus next door to the Hood Museum is the **Hanover Inn** (Main and E. Wheelock Streets; 800-443-7024), and nightly entertainment. Sports facilities, including tennis and golf, are available at the College. Rates are expensive, but check for special deals. Also in Hanover (about 2 miles north of campus) is the **Chieftain Motel** (New Hampshire Rte. 10; 603-643-2550), featuring an outdoor pool and a view of the Connecticut River. Local hotels within a 10-minute drive of campus include the **Holiday Inn Express** (603-448-5070) and the **Residence Inn** (603-643-4511) in Lebanon, NH; the **Airport Economy Inn** (603-298-8888), **Fireside Inn and Suites** (603-298-5906), and the **Sunset Motel** (603-298-8721) in West Lebanon, NH; and the **Best Western** (802-295-3000), **Comfort Inn** (802-295-3051), **Hampton Inn** (802-296-2800), and **Ramada Inn** (802-295-3000) in White River Junction, VT. Local inns and bed and breakfasts within a 10-minute drive include the **Alden Inn** (603-795-2222) and **Dowd's Country Inn** (603-795-4712) in Lyme, NH; the **Norwich Inn** (802-649-1143) in Norwich, VT; and **Stonecrest Farm** (800-730-2425) in Wilder, VT. Additional accommodations exist in Quechee and Woodstock, VT (including the renowned **Woodstock Inn Resort**), 20 to 30 minutes from campus by car.

AT A GLANCE

Selectivity Rating	98
Range SAT I Math	680-760
Average SAT I Math	713
Range SAT I Verbal	670-770
Average SAT I Verbal	713
Student to Faculty Ratio	9:1

CAMPUS TOURS

Appointment Req?	No
Dates	Year-round
Times	Times vary depending on the season

ON-CAMPUS INTERVIEWS

Admissions

Start Date	June
Appointment Req?	Yes
Advance Notice	3 weeks
Saturdays?	Yes, Sept-Nov
Avg. Length	Varies
Info Sessions	Year-round

Faculty and Coaches

Dates/Times	Year-round; subject to faculty/coach availability
Arrangements	Contact admissions off.

CLASS VISITS

Dates	Year-round (Mon-Fri)
Arrangements	Consult class schedule in admissions off. and get prof's approval.

OVERNIGHT DORM STAYS

Advance Notice	3 weeks
Arrangements	Contact admissions off.
Limitations	During fall and winter terms only; contact admissions for more information

UNIVERSITY OF NEW HAMPSHIRE

Office of Admissions, University of New Hampshire, Grant House, 4 Garrison Ave., Durham, NH 03824-3510 • Telephone: 603-862-1360 (Fax: 603-862-0077) • Web: www.unh.edu • Email: admissions@unh.edu

Hours: Monday-Friday, 8AM-4:30PM. Closed weekends and holidays.

The affordable University of New Hampshire provides a variety of pre-professional and liberal arts majors—some of the more popular are occupational therapy, communications, nursing, and the pre-medical sciences. Life in Durham is generally easygoing and the Greek system dominates weekends at UNH.

AT A GLANCE

Selectivity Rating	77
Range SAT I Math	510-610
Average SAT I Math	560
Range SAT I Verbal	510-600
Average SAT I Verbal	550
Student to Faculty Ratio	14:1

CAMPUS TOURS

Appointment Req?	No
Dates	July-April (excluding holidays and breaks)
Times	Sept-May: Mon-Fri 10:30AM and 1:30PM; for info session on weekends contact admissions off.
Avg. Length	1 hour

ON-CAMPUS INTERVIEWS

Admissions

Start Date	Sept 28
Appointment Req?	Yes
Advance Notice	2-3 weeks
Saturdays?	No
Avg. Length	30 min
Info Sessions	Sept-Dec

Faculty and Coaches

Dates/Times	Year-round; subject to faculty/coach availability
Arrangements	Contact Athletics Office at 603-862-1850 2-3 weeks prior

CLASS VISITS

Dates	Year-round (Mon-Fri)
Arrangements	Contact admissions off.

OVERNIGHT DORM STAYS

Advance Notice	N/A
Arrangements	N/A
Limitations	Admitted students only

TRANSPORTATION

Boston's Logan International Airport is approximately 60 miles from Durham. The Manchester, NH, airport is approximately 40 miles from Durham. C & J Trailways bus lines has routes to the Seacoast area and the UNH campus from Logan Airport and South Station in Boston. For information and costs, call 742-5111 (from NH) or 800-258-7111 (from outside NH).

FIND YOUR WAY

From Boston, take I-95 N. to Exit 4 (New Hampshire Lakes and Mountains, Spaulding Tpke.). Continue to Exit 6 W. and take Rte. 4 W. past the UNH/Durham Rte. 108 exit. Exit at Rte. 155A and turn east toward Durham. Follow 155A through a short stretch of fields to the UNH campus. After passing through a blinking light and a traffic light, take the second left onto Garrison Ave. The office of admissions, Grant House, will be directly ahead on the right with parking behind. **From Portland**, take I-95 S. to Exit 5. Continue on the Spaulding Tpke. to Exit 6 W and follow Rte 4 W. Follow the preceding directions from Boston. **From Concord**, take Rte. 4 E. to the Rte. 155A exit. Follow the above directions from Boston. **From Manchester**, take Rte. 101 to Epping and exit onto Rte. 125 N. Continue to the Lee Traffic Circle and take Rte. 4 E. to the Rte. 155A exit. Follow the above directions from Boston.

STAY THE NIGHT

On campus is the **New England Center Hotel** (15 Strafford Ave., 800-590-4334). The rooms are in an unusual hexagonal tower (one side for each of the 6 New England states), and priced in the moderate range. It has a nice restaurant and a workout room, and you can use the pool, racquetball courts, tennis courts and indoor track on campus. Accommodations in Durham include: **Hickory Pond Inn** (603-659-2227**); Holly House** (603-868-7345); **The Pines Guest House** (603-868-3361); and **Three Chimney's Inn** (603-868-7800). In Portsmouth, accommodations include: **Holiday Inn** (603-431-8000); **Howard Johnson's** (603-436-7600); **Marriott Courtyard** (603-436-2121); **Sheraton Portsmouth** (603-431-2300); **Susse Chalet** (603-436-6363); and **Hampton Inn** (800-926-7866). In Dover, accommodations include **Days Inn** (603-742-0400) and **Holiday Inn Express** (603-742-4100).

HIGHLIGHTS

ON CAMPUS
- Diamond Library
- Whittemore
- Hamel Recreation Center
- Student Union
- College Woods

OFF CAMPUS
- Strawberry Banke
- Prescott Park
- Atlantic Ocean
- White Mountains
- Portsmouth

1- Drew University
2- Princeton University
3- Rutgers University

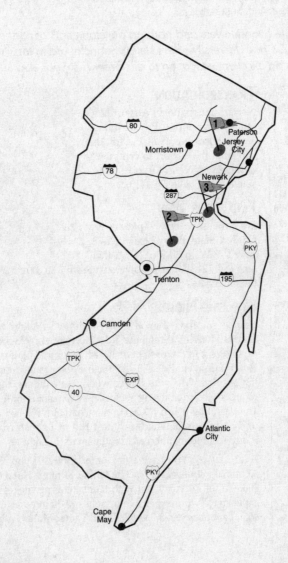

New Jersey	Drew University	Princeton Univ.	Rutgers Univ.	Trenton
Drew University	—	42	20	47
Princeton Univ.	42	—	18	11
Rutgers Univ.	20	18	—	26
Trenton	47	11	26	—

DREW UNIVERSITY

College Admissions, Drew University, 36 Madison Ave., Madison, NJ 07940 • Telephone: 973-408-DREW • Web: www.drew.edu • Email: cadm@drew.edu

Hours: September-May: Monday-Friday, 9AM-5PM; Saturday, 9AM-noon (October-February 1 only). June-August: Monday-Friday, 8:30AM-4:30PM. Closed Sundays and most holidays.

Located amid the corporate headquarters and housing developments of northern New Jersey, just a short distance from New York City, Drew University offers stellar financial aid to top-flight students who are willing to forgo the Ivies, and offers an excellent education to all. Every first-year student gets a laptop.

AT A GLANCE

Selectivity Rating	87
Range SAT I Math	550-660
Average SAT I Math	611
Range SAT I Verbal	550-670
Average SAT I Verbal	627
Student to Faculty Ratio	11:1

CAMPUS TOURS

Appointment Req?	Yes
Dates	Year-round during class sessions
Times	Post-interview
Avg. Length	1 hour

ON-CAMPUS INTERVIEWS

Admissions

Start Date—Juniors	April 15
Appointment Req?	Yes
Advance Notice	10 days
Saturdays?	Yes, Oct-Feb 1
Avg. Length	45 min
Info Sessions	Recommended, call for appointment

Faculty and Coaches

Dates/Times	Year-round; subject to faculty/coach availability
Arrangements	Contact admissions off. 2 weeks prior

CLASS VISITS

Dates	Year-round (Mon-Fri)
Arrangements	Contact admissions off.

OVERNIGHT DORM STAYS

Advance Notice	2 weeks
Arrangements	Contact admissions off.
Limitations	1-night stay; no additional friends may visit; not available during vacations, exam periods, or Jan term

TRANSPORTATION

Newark International Airport is 20 miles from campus. Private limousine services are available for the trip from the airport to campus; 1 of these services is Airport Limousine Express (800-624-4410).

FIND YOUR WAY

From the New Jersey Tpke. or the Garden State Pkwy., exit to I-78. Take I-78 W. to NJ Rte. 24 W., then take Rte. 124 W. to the university. **From I-80**, take I-287 S. to NJ Rte. 124 E. Take Rte. 124 E. to the university.

STAY THE NIGHT

Nearby: You have 2 good choices within 5 minutes of campus. One is the **Royce-Governor Morris Hotel** (2 Whippany Rd., Morristown; 973-539-7300). Rates range from moderate to expensive, and there is a pool, health room, and platform tennis court. The other is the **Madison Hotel** (1 Convent Rd.; 973-285-1800). Rooms range from moderate to very expensive. Furnished in Georgian style, with lots of wood and antiques, the hotel has an indoor pool and a health room. Rod's, an amusing Victorian-style restaurant featuring old rail cars, is on the premises. The **Parrot Mill Inn** (47 Main St., Chatham; 973-635-7722), about 10 minutes away from the university, is a bed-and-breakfast full of English charm. It has 11 moderately priced guest rooms—not to mention a complimentary breakfast.

A little farther: You have a few other choices if you are willing to go 20 to 30 minutes away. About 20 minutes away is **The Grand Summit Hotel** (570 Springfield Ave., Summit; 908-273-3000), a full-service hotel with tennis, golf privileges, exercise room, and masseur. Rates are expensive. Two inexpensive options are 30 minutes outside of town: the **Red Roof Inn** (Rte. 46E., Parsippany; 973-334-3737) and **Tamac Motor Lodge** (Rte. 10, Morris Plains; 973-539-7000).

HIGHLIGHTS

ON CAMPUS
- Wegard Photo Gallery
- Rose Memorial Library

OFF CAMPUS
- New Jersey Shakespeare Festival
- Museum of Early Trades and Crafts
- New York City is only 30 miles away

PRINCETON UNIVERSITY

Admissions Office, Princeton University, P.O. Box 430, Princeton, NJ 08544–0430
(The office is located in West College) • Telephone: 609-258-3060 •
Web: www.princeton.edu • Email: q3436@princeton.edu

Hours: September-June 15: Monday-Friday, 8:45AM-5PM. June 15-Labor Day: Monday-Friday, 8:30AM-4:30PM. Closed holidays.

Other prestigious institutions feature famous medical, law, and/or business schools, but Princeton has none of these: here, the focus is on the college student. Princeton's famous eating clubs (which are a lot like fraternities: they provide meals, host parties, and place students in a subcommunity) are the backbone of the social scene here.

HIGHLIGHTS

ON CAMPUS
- Nassau Hall
- Firestone Library
- McCarter Theater
- Princeton U. Art Museum
- University Chapel

OFF CAMPUS
- Washington's Crossing (Delaware River)
- Waterfront Park
- Jersey Shore
- Access to New York and Philadelphia
- Institute for Advanced Study

TRANSPORTATION

Newark and Philadelphia International Airports are an hour from campus. From the Newark Airport, A1 Limo or Princeton Airporter is available for the trip to campus. Princeton Airporter courtesy phones are located at the airport terminal's limousine counters. The vans take passengers to the Nassau Inn, one block from the university. From the Philadelphia Airport, take either a limousine or the airport shuttle train to Philadelphia's 30th St. Station; from there, take an Amtrak train to Princeton Junction. Rental cars are available at both airports. Amtrak train service to Princeton Junction is available through NYC and through Philadelphia. From Princeton Junction the Princeton Shuttle, a 1-car train (known as the Dinky), makes the 5-minute trip to Princeton. (Note: The Dinky does not meet every train; contact New Jersey Transit for a current schedule before making plans.) Bus service to Princeton is provided by New Jersey's Suburban Transit Corporation; every half hour throughout the day, buses leave NYC's Port Authority terminal for Princeton. The same schedule is followed for buses from Princeton to NYC.

FIND YOUR WAY

From north and south, take the New Jersey Tpke. to Exit 8 (Hightstown) and follow signs for Hightstown, then for Princeton. (Note that the NJ Tpke. is coincident with I-95 from central to northern New Jersey.) **From the Philadelphia area**, you also can take I-95 N. to U.S. 1 N. Follow U.S. 1 to the Hightstown/Princeton circle, and follow signs to Princeton. **From the west**, the Pennsylvania Tpke. (I-76, then I-276 E.) connects to the NJ Tpke.; take the NJ Tpke. north to Exit 8 (Hightstown) and follow signs for Hightstown, then for Princeton. For a recording of instructions to campus, call 609-258-2222.

STAY THE NIGHT

Nearby: The **Peacock Inn** (20 Bayard Lane, at the junction of Rte. 206 and Nassau St.; 609-924-1707) is a historic country inn with simple accommodations for overnight visitors. Rates for its 17 rooms range from moderate to expensive. **Nassau Inn** (10 Palmer Square; 609-921-7500) is within walking distance of the university, but it's expensive. The closest and cheapest motel is the **MacIntosh Inn** (3270 Brunswick Pike, Lawrenceville; 609-896-3700), 5 miles from campus. About the same distance away is **Red Roof Inn** (3203 Brunswick Pike, Lawrenceville; 609-896-3388). The **Hyatt Regency Princeton** (102 Carnegie Ctr.; 609-987-1234), only 4 miles away, has special rates for Princeton visitors.

A little farther: New Hope, PA, is near where George Washington crossed the Delaware River. If that's not reason enough to stay in New Hope, there are also lots of quaint shops and restaurants, as well as a theater. The **Centerbridge Inn** (2996 N. River Rd.; 215-862-2048) is a nice tranquil place by the river.

AT A GLANCE

Selectivity Rating	99
Range SAT I Math	710-780
Range SAT I Verbal	700-780
Student to Faculty Ratio	6:1

CAMPUS TOURS

Appointment Req?	No
Dates	Year-round, call 609-258-3603 for information
Times	Sept-May: Mon-Sat 10AM, 11AM, 1:30PM, and 3:30PM; Sun 1:30PM and 3:30PM. June-Aug: hours vary.
Avg. Length	1 hour

ON-CAMPUS INTERVIEWS

Admissions

Start Date–Juniors	May 1
Appointment Req?	Yes
Advance Notice	Several weeks
Saturdays?	Yes, but only on selected mornings in Oct or Nov
Avg. Length	45-60 min
Info Sessions	May 1-Dec 30

Faculty and Coaches

Dates/Times	Year-round; subject to faculty/coach availability
Arrangements	Contact faculty/coach

CLASS VISITS

Dates	Year-round (Mon-Fri)
Arrangements	Obtain class schedule in admissions off. and professor's approval

RUTGERS, THE STATE UNIVERSITY OF NEW JERSEY

Office of University Undergraduate Admissions, Rutgers, The State University of New Jersey, Administrative Services Bldg., P.O. Box 2101, New Brunswick, NJ 08903-2101 • Telephone: 732-932-INFO • Web: www.rutgers.edu • Email: admissions@asb-ugadm.rutgers.edu

Hours: Monday-Friday, 8:30AM-4:30PM; only Tour Office is open Saturday. Closed Sundays and holidays.

The University College of New Brunswick offers working and adult students a chance to complete one of a large number of degrees through day and/or evening courses. The school enrolls nearly 3,000 students, and offers courses designed to improve students' marketability in the professional world.

AT A GLANCE	
Student to Faculty Ratio	15:1
CAMPUS TOURS	
Appointment Req?	Yes
Dates	Oct-Dec (excluding holidays); Feb-April (excluding holidays and spring break); June-Aug
Times	Mon-Sat mornings after Info Sessions
Avg. Length	1 hour
ON-CAMPUS INTERVIEWS	
Admissions	
Start Date—Juniors	N/A
Appointment Req?	N/A
Advance Notice	N/A
Saturdays?	N/A
Avg. Length	N/A
Info Sessions	Oct-Dec (excluding holidays); Feb-April (excluding holidays and spring break); June-Aug
Faculty and Coaches	
Dates/Times	Year-round; subject to faculty/coach availability
Arrangements	Contact faculty/coach
CLASS VISITS	
Dates	Year-round (Mon-Fri)
Arrangements	Contact undergraduate admissions off.
OVERNIGHT DORM STAYS	
Advance Notice	N/A
Arrangements	Available only through a personal friend who is a current student
Limitations	N/A

TRANSPORTATION

The Newark International Airport is approximately 20 miles from campus. Taxis and rental cars are available at the airport. The Amtrak train and public bus station is 2 blocks from the Undergraduate admissions office.

FIND YOUR WAY

From the New Jersey Tpke., take Exit 9 and follow signs for Rte. 18 N./New Brunswick. To get to the College Ave. campus, proceed 2.5 miles along Route 18 N., past Rte. 27, to the second George St. exit, marked "George St.-Rutgers University." For visitors' parking, bear left on exit ramp, then turn left at the light onto George St. and proceed 3 blocks to Somerset St. Turn right through the entrance gate.

STAY THE NIGHT

A very expensive **Hyatt Regency** (2 Albany St.; 732-873-1234) is about 3 blocks from campus. It has a health center, a pool, a sauna, tennis courts, basketball, a jazz quartet on the weekends, and a pianist during the week. For a more reasonably priced option, try the **Quality Inn** (1850 Easton Ave., Somerset; 732-469-5050). It has a special inexpensive rate for university visitors. The inn, 3 miles from campus, has a full health club and Olympic-size pool. It is close to shopping and near bus service to Rutgers.

HIGHLIGHTS

ON CAMPUS
- Geology Museum
- Jane Voorhees Zimmereli Art Museum
- Rutgers Display Gardens and Heylar Woods
- Hutchenson Memorial Forest

OFF CAMPUS
- New York City (45 min.)

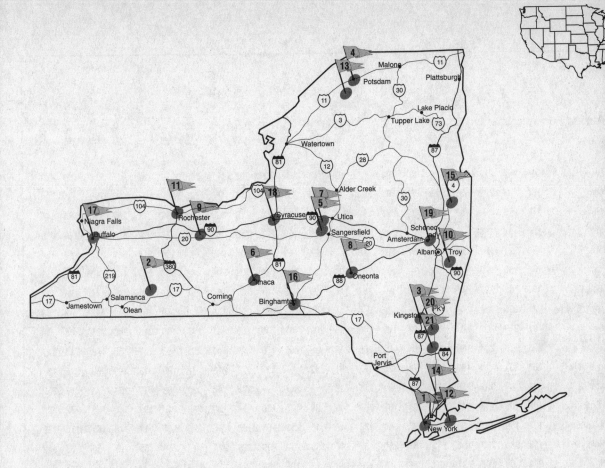

NEW YORK

1- **NEW YORK CITY AREA**
    Barnard College
    Columbia University
    Eugene Lang College
    Fordham University
    Julliard School
    New York University
2- **Alfred University**
3- **Bard College**
4- **Clarkson University**
5- **Colgate University**
6- **Cornell University**
    Ithaca College
7- **Hamilton College**
8- **Hartwick College**
9- **Hobart College**
    William Smith College
10- **Rensselaer Polytechnic Institute**
11- **University of Rochester**
    Rochester Institute of Technology
12- **St. John's University**
13- **St. Lawrence University**
14- **Sarah Lawrence College**
15- **Skidmore College**
16- **SUNY Binghamton**
17- **SUNY Buffalo**
18- **Syracuse University**
19- **Union College**
20- **U.S. Military Academy**
21- **Vassar College**

	Alfred Univ.	Bard College	Clarkson Univ.	Colgate Univ.	Cornell Univ.	Hamilton Coll.	Hartwick Coll.	Hobart & Wm Smith	Ithaca Coll.	RPI	St. Lawrence Univ.	Sarah Lawrence	Skidmore Coll.	SUNY Binghamton	SUNY Buffalo	Union Coll.	U.S. Military Acad.	Vassar Coll	New York City*	Rochester**	Syracuse***
Alfred Univ.	—	287	270	187	99	180	194	81	97	293	260	309	299	127	109	279	287	277	311	80	133
Bard College	287	—	299	51	221	158	101	295	219	78	301	67	108	169	385	98	51	27	90	328	235
Clarkson Univ.	270	299	—	197	199	172	223	192	201	203	10	355	173	223	282	197	311	287	357	225	140
Colgate Univ.	187	51	197	—	80	24	49	96	82	119	199	238	115	69	192	97	212	188	240	129	35
Cornell Univ.	99	221	199	80	—	92	118	48	2	206	189	235	204	49	149	184	218	202	237	90	54
Hamilton Coll.	180	158	172	24	92	—	66	95	94	104	174	238	109	96	185	89	205	181	242	128	39
Hartwick Coll.	194	101	223	49	118	66	—	187	116	90	225	181	107	64	250	73	141	117	179	195	97
Hobart & Wm. Smith	81	295	192	96	48	95	187	—	46	195	182	281	200	138	102	179	265	241	283	43	50
Ithaca Coll.	97	219	201	82	2	94	116	46	—	208	191	233	206	47	147	186	218	200	235	88	56
RPI	293	78	203	119	206	104	90	195	208	—	205	150	29	145	285	15	109	85	152	216	147
St. Lawrence Univ.	260	301	10	199	189	174	225	182	191	205	—	357	175	213	272	199	313	289	359	215	130
Sarah Lawrence	309	67	355	238	235	238	181	281	233	150	357	—	178	186	399	162	40	64	3	342	252
Skidmore Coll.	299	108	173	115	204	109	107	200	206	29	175	178	—	158	289	24	139	115	182	232	146
SUNY Binghamton	127	169	223	69	49	96	64	138	47	145	213	186	158	—	226	135	162	146	185	175	79
SUNY Buffalo	109	385	282	192	149	185	250	102	147	285	272	399	289	226	—	269	385	361	406	65	142
Union Coll.	279	98	197	97	184	89	73	179	186	15	199	162	24	135	269	—	128	104	156	212	130
U.S. Military Acad.	287	51	311	212	218	205	141	265	218	109	313	40	139	162	385	128	—	24	41	326	248
Vassar Coll	277	27	287	188	202	181	117	241	200	85	289	64	115	146	361	104	24	—	75	302	224
New York City*	311	90	357	240	237	242	179	283	235	152	359	3	182	185	406	156	41	75	—	365	265
Rochester**	80	328	225	129	90	128	195	43	88	216	215	342	232	175	65	212	326	302	365	—	83
Syracuse***	133	235	140	35	54	39	97	50	56	147	130	252	146	79	142	130	248	224	265	83	—

*   Use New York City mileage for Barnard College, Columbia College, Eugene Lang College, Fordham University, The Juilliard School, NewYork University, and St. John's University.
**   Use Rochester mileage for Rochester Institute of Technology and University of Rochester.
*** Use Syracuse mileage for Syracuse University.

ALFRED UNIVERSITY

Office of Admissions, Alfred University, Alumni Hall, Saxon Dr., Alfred, NY 14802 •
Telephone: 800-541-9229 • Web: www.alfred.edu •
Email: admwww@alfred.edu

Hours: Monday-Friday, 8:30AM-4:30PM; Saturday, 8:30AM-noon (by appointment only). Closed Sundays and holidays.

You can unearth one of the best ceramics programs on the planet at this small college named for Alfred the Great. Alfred U. is located in the Finger Lakes region of upstate New York, about two hours from Buffalo. Sledding down a snow-covered hill on a cafeteria tray is a favorite activity among the students during the long winters.

HIGHLIGHTS

ON CAMPUS
- Fosdick-Nelson Gallery
- Davis Memorial Carillon
- Museum of Ceramic Art
- John L. Stull Observatory
- Robert Turnes Student Gallery

OFF CAMPUS
- Corning Glass Museum (40 min.)
- Rockwell Museum (40 min.)
- Letchworth State Park (30 min.)
- Stony Brook State Park (25 min.)
- Glen H. Curtis Museum (30 min.)

TRANSPORTATION

Greater Rochester International Airport is 70 miles from campus. Corning-Elmira Regional Airport is 55 miles from campus. Bus lines serve Alfred and surrounding communities. New York Trailways Short Line buses provide service between Alfred and New York City with transfers to all major cities.

FIND YOUR WAY

From Rte. 17 E. (Rte. 17 is becoming I-86) or W. (the Southern Tier Expy.), take Exit 33 at Almond and follow signs for the university to Rte. 21 S. and to Rte. 244 into Alfred. **From Rochester,** take I-390 S. to Exit 4, the second Dansville exit. Turn right onto Rte. 36 S. and continue through Arkport. Turn onto Rte. 17 W. and follow the preceding directions from that point. **From the northeast,** take I-90 to Exit 42 at Geneva. Take Rte. 14 S.; near Dresden, turn right onto Rte. 54 and follow it through Penn Yan to Bath and Rte. 17 W. Follow the preceding directions from that point.

STAY THE NIGHT

Nearby: Luxurious accommodations are available on campus at **The Saxon Inn** (1 Park St.; 607-871-2600), located across the street from the admissions office. Continental breakfast is included and suites sleeping 5 people are available. Four options in Hornell (15 minutes away) are the **Comfort Inn** (1 Canisteo Square; 607-324-4300), the **Econo Lodge** (Rte. 36 N.; 607-324-0800), the **Williams Inn** bed and breakfast (607-324-2993), and **Hornell Super 8 Motel** (607-324-6222). Fifteen minutes southwest of campus in Wellsville are 2 inexpensive motels: **Wellsville Motel** (Rte. 417; 716-593-2494) and **Cook's Motel** (Rte. 417; 716-593-1747).

A little farther: Corning is about 45 minutes to the east of Alfred. The **Rosewood Inn** (134 E. 1st; 607-962-3253) is just off Rte. 17. A more expensive option is the **Radisson Corning Hotel** in downtown Corning (125 Denison Pkwy. East, 607-962-5000). Bath is about 35 minutes away offering 2 motels: **The Days Inn** (607-776-7644) and **Bath Super 8 Motel** (607-776-2187).

AT A GLANCE

Selectivity Rating	76
Range SAT I Math	490-610
Range SAT I Verbal	490-610
Student to Faculty Ratio	12:1

CAMPUS TOURS

Appointment Req?	Yes
Dates	Year-round
Times	Mon-Fri 9AM-4PM; Sat 9AM-12PM by appt. only
Avg. Length	1 hour

ON-CAMPUS INTERVIEWS

Admissions

Start Date–Juniors	Any time
Appointment Req?	Yes
Advance Notice	1 week
Saturdays?	Yes
Avg. Length	45-60 min
Info Sessions	Available on special visit days and Saturdays

Faculty and Coaches

Dates/Times	Year-round; subject to faculty/coach availability
Arrangements	Contact admissions off. 1 week prior

CLASS VISITS

Dates	During academic year (Mon-Fri)
Arrangements	Contact admissions off.

OVERNIGHT DORM STAYS

Advance Notice	1 week
Arrangements	Contact admissions off.
Limitations	Sun-Thurs; 1-night stay; not available during exam periods

BARD COLLEGE

Admissions Office, Bard College, Annandale-on-Hudson, NY 12504 (The office is located on the eastern edge of the campus—follow signs) • Telephone: 914-758-7472 (Fax: 914-758-5208) • Web: www.bard.edu • Email: admission@bard.edu

Hours: Monday-Friday, 9AM-5PM. Closed weekends, July 4, Thanksgiving, and the week between Christmas and New Year's Day.

The very unique students at Bard College are truly diverse in more ways than one would expect. Most definitely a "A place to think" (the school motto) Bard requires each of its students to complete a Senior Project. The progressive Excellence and Equal Cost Program makes Bard available to top students at a state-school price.

AT A GLANCE

Selectivity Rating	93
Range SAT I Math	550-670
Range SAT I Verbal	610-700
Average GPA	3.5
Student to Faculty Ratio	9:1

CAMPUS TOURS

Appointment Req?	Yes
Dates	Year-round
Times	10AM, 11AM, 12PM
Avg. Length	1 hour

ON-CAMPUS INTERVIEWS

Admissions

Start Date—Juniors	Any time; best after fall of junior year
Appointment Req?	Yes
Advance Notice	2 weeks
Saturdays?	No
Avg. Length	30 min
Info Sessions	No

Faculty and Coaches

Dates/Times	Year-round; subject to faculty/coach availability
Arrangements	Contact admissions off. 2 weeks prior

CLASS VISITS

Dates	Whenever classes are in session
Arrangements	Contact admissions off.

OVERNIGHT DORM STAYS

Advance Notice	2 weeks
Arrangements	Contact admissions off.
Limitations	Generally restricted to accepted candidates in April only

TRANSPORTATION

The closest airports are Albany and Stewart/Newburgh, both of which are about 50 miles from campus. In Albany visitors can get a taxi or ground transportation to the Albany/Rennselaer train station and take the Amtrak train south to Rhinecliff. Otherwise a rental car is necessary from both airports. All 3 New York City airports have ground transportation directly to Penn Station in Manhattan, and the Amtrak train goes regularly to Rhinecliff station. From there it is a short taxi or shuttle ride to campus. Bard shuttle schedules are on the Bard website at Web: www.bard.edu.

HIGHLIGHTS

ON CAMPUS
- Center for Curatorial Studies
- Woods Studio
- Bertelsmann Campus Center
- Chapel of the Holy Innocents
- Blithewood Mansion and Formal Gardens

OFF CAMPUS
- Montgomery Place
- Franklin Roosevelt House and Museum
- Eleanor Roosevelt House
- Mills Mansion
- Tivoli

FIND YOUR WAY

From the east side of the Hudson River, take the Taconic State Pkwy. to the Red Hook exit. Take Rte. 199 W. to Rte. 9G (this intersection is after the intersection with Rte. 9); turn right (north) onto 9G and proceed north 2 miles to campus. **From the west side of the Hudson**, take the New York State Thruway (I-87) to Exit 19 (Kingston). Follow signs to the Kingston-Rhinecliff Bridge. Cross the bridge and follow Rte. 199 to Rte. 96. Turn left onto Rte. 9G and proceed north 4 miles to the campus, which is on the left.

STAY THE NIGHT

Nearby: Pleasant and comfortable, the **Gaslight Inn** (Rt. 9N North, Red Hook; 917-758-1571) is about 3 miles east of campus. Bard is north of Rhinebeck in Annandale-on-Hudson. As long as you're in the area, don't pass up a chance to stay in the oldest inn in America, the **Beekman Arms Inn** (Rtes. 9 and 308; 914-876-7077), only 10 minutes from campus. The inn has a very popular restaurant, and the guestrooms are just above it, so it may be a little noisy. For more tranquility, you can stay 1 block north at the Victorian Delamater House. Call the Beekman Arms for reservations. Rates at both are moderate. Just south of Rhinebeck, about 15 minutes from the campus, lies the **Village Inn Motel** (Rte. 9 S.; 914-876-7000). Its normally inexpensive prices tend to climb a bit higher on the weekends. Or try the **Ramada Inn** (914-339-3900) also 15 minutes from campus, in Kingston (take Exit 19 off the thruway). The special double-occupancy rate is in the expensive range (high end). In the same location is a **Holiday Inn** (914-338-0400), with a special double-occupancy rate in the moderate range.

A little farther: See the Vassar College entry for suggestions in and around Poughkeepsie, to the south.

BARNARD COLLEGE

Admissions Office, Barnard College, 3009 Broadway, New York, NY 10027-6598 (The office is in Milbank Hall, Rm. 111) • Telephone: 212-854-2014 • Web: www.barnard.edu • Email: admissions@barnard.edu

Hours: Monday-Friday, 9AM-5PM; Saturday, 9AM-5PM (September-December only). Summer, call the office for hours of operation.

Barnard is an all-women's college located on the Upper West Side of Manhattan right across the street from the Ivy League's own Columbia University. Barnard's students enjoy the luxury of their own small classes, and they can take any course offered at Columbia as well. The one and only Martha Stewart is an alum.

HIGHLIGHTS

ON CAMPUS
- Milbank Hall-Minor Latham Playhouse
- Arthur Ross Greenhouse
- Held Auditorium
- Smart media classrooms
- Recently renovated environmental science center

OFF CAMPUS
- Riverside Church
- Central Park
- Metropolitan Museum of Art
- The Cloisters
- The Guggenheim Museum

TRANSPORTATION

Local area airports include La Guardia, Kennedy, and Newark. Taxi, bus, and subway service is available (in various combinations) to get you from airports to campus. The College recommends that you take a taxi from Kennedy and La Guardia; while expensive, it is efficient. Tell the driver that the most direct route to Barnard is the Triborough Bridge, not the Queens-Midtown Tunnel. Amtrak, Metro North, New Jersey Transit, and Long Island Railroad trains serve New York City; as do Greyhound and several local bus lines. Public transportation is available from Grand Central, Penn Station, and New York Port Authority. Four public bus lines (M4, M11, M5, and M104) and 2 subways (the Broadway IRT local, numbers 1 and 9) stop at 116th St./Columbia University.

FIND YOUR WAY

From the Henry Hudson Pkwy. (West Side Hwy.) in New York City, take the 95th/96th St. exit. Use the 95th St. off-ramp and drive 2 blocks east to Broadway. Turn left (uptown) to Barnard's main gate at 117th St. To reach the Henry Hudson Pkwy. **from the north**, take the NY State Thruway (I-87) or the New England Thruway (I-95) to the Cross-Bronx Expy., toward the George Washington Bridge. Bear right as you approach the bridge and take the exit for the Henry Hudson Pkwy. S. **From the east**, take the Grand Central Pkwy. or Long Island Expy. west to the Cross-Island Pkwy. north. Cross over the Throgs Neck Bridge to the Cross-Bronx Expy., toward the George Washington Bridge. Exit onto the Henry Hudson Pkwy. S. **From the south and west**, take I-95 N. or I-80 E. to the George Washington Bridge. Exit the bridge onto the Henry Hudson Pkwy. S.

STAY THE NIGHT

Barnard College, an affiliate of Columbia University, is on the Upper West Side of Manhattan at 116th St. and Broadway. We suggest that you arrange your accommodations as early as possible. When making reservations, ask if any special packages are being offered and be aware that rates change according to availability. For a reasonable price, visitors can stay at the **International House-Hostel** (500 Riverside Dr. at 122nd St.; 212-316-6300) or at the **Union Theological Seminary** (3041 Broadway; 212-280-1313). For a moderately priced hotel, visitors can stay at the **Radisson Empire Hotel** (44 W. 63rd St.; 212-265-7400)—Ask for the Columbia University rate—**The Excelsior** (45 W. 81st St.; 212-362-9200), and **The Lucerne** (201 W. 79th St.; 212-875-1000). At a slightly higher price, the **Doubletree Guest Suites** (800-362-2779) are located on West 47th and Broadway. Visitors should ask for the Columbia University rate.

AT A GLANCE

Selectivity Rating	95
Range SAT I Math	610-690
Average SAT I Math	652
Range SAT I Verbal	620-710
Average SAT I Verbal	671
Average ACT Composite	29
Average GPA	3.8
Student to Faculty Ratio	11:1

CAMPUS TOURS

Appointment Req?	No
Dates	Year-round except during winter intersession and spring break
Times	Mon-Thurs 10:30AM and 2:30PM; Fri-Sat (Sept-Dec) 10:30AM, 12:30PM, and 2:30PM
Avg. Length	1 hour

ON-CAMPUS INTERVIEWS

Admissions

Start Date—Juniors	May 1
Appointment Req?	Yes
Advance Notice	At least 2 weeks
Saturdays?	Yes, Sept to mid-Jan
Avg. Length	45 min
Info Sessions	N/A

Faculty and Coaches

Dates/Times	Year-round; subject to faculty/coach availability
Arrangements	At least 2 weeks prior

CLASS VISITS

Dates	During academic year
Arrangements	Schedules available in admissions off.

OVERNIGHT DORM STAYS

Advance Notice	At least 2 weeks prior
Arrangements	Contact admissions off.
Limitations	Mon-Thurs when school is in session

CLARKSON UNIVERSITY

Freshman Admission Office, Clarkson University, Holcroft House, Box 5605, Potsdam, NY 13699 • Telephone: 800-527-6577 or 315-268-6480 • Web: www.clarkson.edu • Email: admissions@clarkson.edu

Hours: Monday-Friday, 8AM-4:30PM; open Saturday by appointment only. Closed Sundays and holidays.

The faculty at Clarkson University is unusually helpful and approachable, especially for an engineering-intensive school. On campus, the Greek system is popular, as is the perennially powerful hockey team. Clarkson also boasts a student-run television station (WCKN-TV 31).

AT A GLANCE

Selectivity Rating	81
Range SAT I Math	560-660
Average SAT I Math	616
Range SAT I Verbal	520-620
Average SAT I Verbal	576
Average GPA	3.3
Student to Faculty Ratio	16:1

CAMPUS TOURS

Appointment Req?	Yes
Dates	When classes are in session and summer
Times	Mon-Sat 10AM, 12PM, and 1PM
Avg. Length	1 hour

ON-CAMPUS INTERVIEWS

Admissions

Start Date–Juniors	Any time
Appointment Req?	Yes
Advance Notice	1-2 weeks
Saturdays?	Yes, but by appt. only
Avg. Length	30-45 min
Info Sessions	Not available

Faculty and Coaches

Dates/Times	Year-round; subject to faculty/coach availability
Arrangements	Contact admissions off. 1-2 weeks prior

CLASS VISITS

Dates	When classes are in session
Arrangements	Contact admissions off.

OVERNIGHT DORM STAYS

Advance Notice	2-3 weeks
Arrangements	Contact admission off.
Limitations	1 night only; Mon-Thurs; accepted students only

TRANSPORTATION

The Massena airport is 21 miles from campus; the Ogdensburg airport is 35 miles from campus. Major airports include Syracuse (2.5 hours away), Montreal's Dorval Airport (2 hours away), and Montreal's Marabel International Airport (2.5 hours away). You can fly to Syracuse and rent a car or take a Greyhound bus from Syracuse to Potsdam; or you can fly from Syracuse to Massena on a commuter airline, and rent a car. Trailways bus lines (315-764-1331) and Greyhound buses (315-265-2270) serve Potsdam.

FIND YOUR WAY

From Syracuse, take I-81 N. to Exit 48 N. of Watertown. Proceed to U.S. Rte. 11, turning left (north) onto it. Continue for approximately 67 miles. Take the Sandstone entrance to campus on the right beyond the tennis courts as you enter the village of Potsdam. **From Albany**, take I-87 (the Northway) to Exit 23 (Warrensburg). From there, follow Rte. 28 to Indian Lake, where Rtes. 28 and 30 merge. Follow the combined Rtes. to Blue Mountain Lake; from there, take Rte. 30 N. to Tupper Lake; then head west on Rte. 3 for approximately 18 miles to Rte. 56. Proceed north on Rte. 56 to Potsdam. Turn left at the second traffic light in the village (onto U.S. Rte. 11 S.), and continue for three-quarters of a mile to the university. Driving time from Albany to Potsdam is approximately 4 hours.

STAY THE NIGHT

Nearby: **The Clarkson Inn** is a pretty brick building by the river in historic downtown Potsdam. It's within walking distance (2 blocks) of the campus, and rates are moderate. Two basic, inexpensive choices are close to campus. **Smalling Motel** (Rte. 56 N. ; 315-265-4640) is 2 miles from campus. It has a pool, picnic tables, and free coffee in the morning. **Smalling Motel South** (U.S. Rte. 11; 315-265-0700) is 1 mile from campus, and also has a pool.

A little farther: About 2 hours away is the exciting resort area of Lake Placid. A large **Lake Placid Hilton** (1 Mirror Lake Dr.; 518-523-4411) offers indoor and outdoor pools, game rooms, and all the winter and summer sports activities for which the area is known. Rates are moderate in the winter and expensive in the summer. If money is no object, you might consider the beautiful 10-room lakefront resort that was once the retreat of William Rockefeller. **The Point** (Star Rte., Saranac Lake; 518-891-5674 or 800-255-3530) is about the same distance from campus as Lake Placid, and all meals are included. Special winter rates are available. (Jacket and tie are required at dinner; black tie is suggested but not mandatory Wednesday and Saturday nights.) Contact the admissions office for a curent list of area Bed & Breakfast accomodations and other nearby hotels and motels.

HIGHLIGHTS

ON CAMPUS
- Bertrand H. Snell Hall (new academic building)
- The (new, outdoor) Lodge Cheel Campus Center
- CAMP Building
- Center for Health Sciences

OFF CAMPUS
- St. Lawrence River-Seaway
- Lake Placid, New York
- Thousand Island region
- Fredrick Remmington Museum
- Adirondack Mountains

COLGATE UNIVERSITY

Office of Admissions, Colgate University, 13 Oak Dr., Hamilton, NY 13346
(The office is in James B. Colgate Hall) • Telephone: 315-228-7401 •
Web: www.colgate.com • Email: admission@mail.colgate.edu

Hours: Sept.-May: Monday-Friday, 8:30AM-5PM; Saturday, 9AM-noon (Sept.-Dec. only). June-Aug.: Monday-Friday, 8AM-4PM.

Colgate University has a beautiful campus, a vibrant party scene, high quality academics, and professors that cause students to gush with joy. Great liberal arts programs are plentiful here, and a core curriculum is required of all students regardless of major.

HIGHLIGHTS

ON CAMPUS
- Picker Art Gallery
- Longyear Museum of Anthropology
- ALANA Culture Center
- Everett Needham Case Library
- Observatory

OFF CAMPUS
- Bouckville Antique Center
- Cooperstown
- Erie Canal Village
- Munson Williams Proctor Museum, Utica
- Museum of Science and Technology

TRANSPORTATION

The Syracuse-Hancock International Airport is approximately 40 miles from campus. Call the Town and Gown Limousine Service (315-824-1222) for transportation from the airport to campus. Rental cars are also available at the airport.

FIND YOUR WAY

From the New York City area, take the Tappan Zee Bridge and the NY State Thruway (I-87) to Exit 16; then take NY Rte. 17 W. to Exit 84 (Deposit). Turn right on NY Rte. 8 N. and follow that to New Berlin; then take NY Rte. 80 W. to Sherburne. Turn right on NY Rte. 12, then bear left for 12B to Hamilton. **From the north**, get to the NY State Thruway (I-87) and take it to Exit 24; then head west on U.S. 20. At Madison, head south on NY Rte. 12B to Hamilton. **From Philadelphia**, take the northeast extension of the PA Tpke. to I-81 at Scranton. Take I-81 N. to Exit 6 (Binghamton). Head north on NY Rte. 12 to Sherburne; then take 12B to Hamilton. **From the west**, take I-90 E. to Exit 34 (Canastota). Take NY Rte. 5 E. to Oneida, then take NY Rte. 46 S. across U.S. 20 to Rte. 12B S. Follow 12B S. to Hamilton and Colgate.

STAY THE NIGHT

Nearby: On Payne St., within walking distance of the university, is **Colgate Inn** (315-824-2300). Rates are moderate. Bed-and-breakfast options are within 3 miles of the school. The rates at **Hamilton Inn** (East Lake Rd.; 315-824-1245) range from moderate to expensive and include a continental breakfast. **Landmark Inn** (Rte. 20, Bouckville; 315-893-1810) is about 3.5 miles away. Its rooms are reasonably priced and comfortable. Breakfast is doled out on a raid-the-refrigerator basis.

A little farther: Twenty-three miles south of campus in Norwich is a **Howard Johnson's Lodge** (75 N. Broad St. on NY Rte. 12; 607-334-2200) with an indoor pool. Rates are at the low end of moderate. Cazenovia is an old resort town on a lake in one of the prettiest parts of the state. Only half an hour from Colgate, it offers two enticing inn choices: **Brewster Inn** (Rte. 20; 315-655-9232) is a restored old mansion built in the late 19th century in the style of an English manor house. Beautifully situated with a view of Cazenovia Lake, it has inexpensive to very expensive rates (continental breakfast included), and boasts a good restaurant too. **Brae Loch Inn**, (5 Albany St. Rte. 20; 315-655-3431), is a family-run Scottish inn with great charm. It's in town across from the lake. Rooms, including continental breakfast, range from moderate to expensive, and it too has a fine restaurant on the premises. See the Hamilton College entry for information on the **Horned Dorset**, which is not too far to the east of Colgate.

COLUMBIA UNIVERSITY

Office of Undergraduate Admissions, Columbia University, 212 Hamilton Hall,
New York, NY 10027 • Telephone: 212-854-2522 • Web: www.columbia.edu •
Email: ugrad-admiss@columbia.edu

Hours: Monday-Friday, 9AM-5PM; Saturday, 9AM-noon (mid-September to mid-December only).

Without the extensive, western civilization–focused core curriculum at this vaunted Ivy League bastion on Manhattan's Upper West Side, graduating might be easy. Socially, New York City offers, well, everything.

AT A GLANCE

Selectivity Rating		98
Range SAT I Math		640-740
Average SAT I Math		680
Range SAT I Verbal		650-750
Student to Faculty Ratio		6:1

CAMPUS TOURS

Appointment Req?	No
Dates	All year
Times	Group info sessions year-round Mon-Fri 10AM and 2PM
Avg. Length	1 hour

INFO SESSIONS

Admissions

Start Date–Juniors	June 1
Appointment Req?	Yes
Advance Notice	3 weeks
Saturdays?	Yes, mid-Nov to mid-Dec
Avg. Length	Varies
Info Sessions	All year: Mon-Fri at 11AM and 3PM; Sat 10AM and 11AM on 2nd Sat of the month (fall only)

Faculty and Coaches

Dates/Times	Year-round; subject to faculty/coach availability
Arrangements	Contact admissions off.

CLASS VISITS

Dates	Academic year (Mon-Thurs)
Arrangements	Contact Visitor's Center

OVERNIGHT DORM STAYS

Advance Notice	2 weeks
Arrangements	Contact admissions off.
Limitations	1 night; Mon-Thurs; during the regular academic year while classes are in session

TRANSPORTATION

La Guardia is the closest airport, and taxis are available for the ride to campus. Kennedy and Newark airports also serve the New York City area; bus service is available from all of these airports to the Port Authority Bus Terminal in the city. Public transportation is available from the bus terminal to the campus: Five local bus lines (M4, M11, M5, M60, and M104) and 1 subway (Broadway IRT locals 1 and 9) serve the Columbia/Morningside Heights area. Amtrak and commuter trains serve the city at Pennsylvania and Grand Central Stations. Long distance buses arrive at the Port Authority Bus Terminal.

FIND YOUR WAY

Columbia is best reached by taking the 95th/96th St. exit from the Henry Hudson Pkwy. (West Side Highway). Use the 95th St. off-ramp and turn left onto Riverside Dr. Proceed north to 116th St. A right turn at 116th St. leads you to the campus gate. Parking available on street or in local garage (120th between Claremont and Riverside).

STAY THE NIGHT

Columbia University is on the Upper West Side of Manhattan at 116th St. and Broadway. Located about 35 blocks to the south, between Central Park W. and Columbus Ave., on the West Side, is the **Excelsior Hotel** (45 W. 81st St.; 212-362-9200 or 800-368-4575). This is a very simple and clean hotel with moderate prices. A little farther south is the **Empire Hotel** (63rd St. and Broadway; 212-265-7400 or 888-822-3555). The hotel offers special rates for university visitors, but it is still fairly expensive. Other Upper West Side hotels that may have special rates for Columbia visitors are the **Lucerne** (79th St. and Amsterdam Ave.; 212-875-1000 or 800-492-8122), **On the Ave** (77th St. and Broadway; 212-362-1100 or 800-509-7598) and the **Beacon** (75th St. and Broadway; 212-787-1100 or 800-572-4969).

HIGHLIGHTS

ON CAMPUS
- Low Plaza
- Low Memorial Library
- Avery Hall
- St. Paul's Chapel
- Butler Library

OFF CAMPUS
- Statue of Liberty
- Central Park
- Metropolitan Museum of Art
- American Museum of Natural History
- Rockefeller Center

CORNELL UNIVERSITY

Admissions Office, Cornell University, 410 Thurston Ave., Ithaca, NY 14850 •
Telephone: 607-255-5241 • Web: www.cornell.edu •
Email: admissions@cornell.edu

Hours: Monday-Friday, 8AM-4:30PM. Closed weekends and holidays.

Cornell University is an Ivy League beast that offers over 4,000 undergraduate courses. Socially, the Greek system is big at Cornell, and the surrounding area, though often frigid, provides abundant opportunities for outdoor activities.

HIGHLIGHTS

ON CAMPUS
- Johnson Art Museum
- College Town
- Center for Theater Arts
- Cornell Plantations
- Fuertes Observatory

OFF CAMPUS
- Treman State Park
- Buttermilk Falls State Park
- Ithaca Falls
- Stewart Park/Cayuga Lake
- Ithaca Commons (shopping)

TRANSPORTATION

The Ithaca-Tompkins County Airport is 5 miles (a ten-minute drive) from campus. Taxis and limousine service are available for the ride from the airport to campus. Greyhound Bus and short Line serve Ithaca; from the bus station you can take a taxi (607-277-8294) or a Tompkins Consolidated Area Transit (TCAT) Bus Routes to campus.

FIND YOUR WAY

From Binghamton, take NY Rte. 17 W. to Oswego (Exit 64); then take NY Rte. 96 N. At Candor, take NY Rte. 96B N. into Ithaca. **From Syracuse**, take I-81 S. to NY Rte. 13 S. and W. Rte. 13 takes you into Ithaca.

STAY THE NIGHT

Nearby: If you're willing to shell out some cash, our choice would be **Statler Hotel** (800-541-2501), a fine campus hotel run by students of Cornell's hotel management school. **Peregrine House Inn** (140 College Ave.; 607-272-0919) is an 8-room bed-and-breakfast within walking distance of campus. This old, 3-story brick house with Victorian furnishings offers moderate rates. For a convenient budget choice, try **Hillside Inn** (518 Stewart Ave.; 607-273-6864), just 3 blocks from campus. About a mile away from the university is **Best Western University Inn** (East Hill Plaza; 607-272-6100). Reasonable rates, a pool, a health club, and nearby golf privileges are all parts of its appeal. A no-frills **Super 8** (400 S. Meadow St., Rte. 13; 607-273-8088) is also just 2 miles away.

A little farther: **Buttermilk Falls B&B** (110 E. Buttermilk Falls Rd.; 607-273-3947) is a 6-room bed-and-breakfast set at the foot of a waterfall. It's just gorgeous. The inn is furnished with Early American antiques and Persian carpets. Rates are moderate, and all the rooms have private baths. Or consider **Rose Inn** (813 Auburn Rd., NY Rte. 34 N.; 607-533-4202). This 1851 Italianate mansion with a cupola features a wonderful mahogany staircase and antique furniture. Nine miles north of Cornell, this luxurious inn overlooks Lake Cayuga (and is convenient to it for sailing, fishing, and swimming). Prices begin on the moderate end and go up from there. For more information, visit the Welcome website for Ithaca and Tompkins County: www.ithaca.com.

AT A GLANCE

Selectivity Rating	97
Range SAT I Math	650-750
Average SAT I Math	700
Range SAT I Verbal	620-710
Average SAT I Verbal	660
Average ACT Composite	29
Student to Faculty Ratio	11:1

CAMPUS TOURS

Appointment Req?	No
Dates	Year-round
Times	April-Nov: Mon-Fri 9AM, 11AM, 1PM, and 3PM; Sat 9AM and 11AM; Sun 1PM. Dec-Mar: Mon-Sun 1PM.
Avg. Length	75-90 min

ON-CAMPUS INTERVIEWS

Admissions

Start Date–Juniors	Contact admissions
Appointment Req?	Yes
Advance Notice	Far in advance
Saturdays?	No
Avg. Length	45 min
Info Sessions	Year-round; contact admissions off. for info.

Faculty and Coaches

Dates/Times	Year-round; subject to faculty/coach availability
Arrangements	Contact admissions off.

CLASS VISITS

Dates	During class sessions
Arrangements	Contact admissions off.

OVERNIGHT DORM STAYS

Advance Notice	2 weeks
Arrangements	Contact the Red Carpet Society at 607-255-3447
Limitations	Available during fall and spring sessions

EUGENE LANG COLLEGE

Admissions Office, Eugene Lang College, The New School for Social Research, 65 W. 11th St., New York, NY 10011 (The office is on the 3rd floor) • Telephone: 212-229-5665 • Web: www.lang.edu • Email: lang@newschool.edu

Hours: Monday-Friday, 9AM-5PM. Closed weekends and major holidays; open during March break.

Eugene Lang, the undergraduate division of the New School for Social Research, is an ideal choice if you are a left-leaning, self-reliant student with an interest in the humanities and social sciences and know what you want to do in life.

AT A GLANCE	
Selectivity Rating	76
Average SAT I Math	570
Average SAT I Verbal	610
Average ACT Composite	27
Average GPA	3.4
Student to Faculty Ratio	10:1

CAMPUS TOURS	
Appointment Req?	Yes
Dates	Year-round
Times	Mon, Wed, Fri 1PM
Avg. Length	1 hour

ON-CAMPUS INTERVIEWS	
Admissions	
Start Date—Juniors	Winter
Appointment Req?	Yes
Advance Notice	1 week
Saturdays?	No
Avg. Length	30 min
Info Sessions	Not available
Faculty and Coaches	
Dates/Times	N/A
Arrangements	N/A

CLASS VISITS	
Dates	When classes are in session
Arrangements	Contact admissions off.

OVERNIGHT DORM STAYS	
Advance Notice	N/A
Arrangements	By advance request only
Limitations	N/A

TRANSPORTATION

Kennedy International, La Guardia, and Newark airports all serve New York City. At Kennedy and La Guardia, Carey bus service provides group rides into the city at regular intervals; check with your airline for details. Taxis are also available, though expensive. From Newark, Carey Bus brings passengers into the Port Authority Bus Terminal, which is a subway ride away from the college. Amtrak, Metro-North, New Jersey Transit, and Long Island Railroad trains all serve New York City. Greyhound and several local bus lines also come into the city. Public transportation is available from the terminals to the college. New Jersey's PATH train stops at 14th St. and 6th Ave., only 2 blocks from campus. The BMT, IND, and IRT subway lines all have stops within walking distance of the school.

FIND YOUR WAY

From north of New York City, take the Saw Mill River Pkwy. to the Henry Hudson Pkwy. S. (Rte. 9A) and continue to the West Side Highway (which becomes 12th Ave./West St.). Exit at 14th St. and continue east on 14th. Turn right onto 7th Ave., then left onto 12th St. The college is one-and-a-quarter blocks ahead. **From west of New York City**, take the George Washington Bridge to the Henry Hudson Pkwy. S. and proceed according to the previous directions. From the Lincoln Tunnel, follow signs to 39th or 40th Street and head east (1 block) to 9th Ave. Proceed south on 9th Ave. to 14th St. Turn left onto 14th St. and continue east to 7th Ave. Turn right onto 7th Ave., then left onto West 12th St. The college is one-and-a-quarter blocks ahead. **From east of New York City**, take the Long Island Expressway (I-495) west to the Midtown Tunnel. Follow signs to 34th St. and the F.D.R. Dr. Take the F.D.R. south to the 15th St. exit and continue south to 14th St. Proceed west on 14th, then turn left onto 7th Ave. Turn left again on 12th St. and proceed to the college.

STAY THE NIGHT

Nearby: Eugene Lang College is in Greenwich Village, just north of New York University, so see the NYU entry for suggestions. Note that the **Hotel Chelsea** (with the coolest lobby you are ever going to see, though the rooms are a bit shabby) and the **Gramercy Park Hotel** are both within walking distance of Eugene Lang. Another possibility, about a 40-block bus ride from Eugene Lang, is the **Hotel Elysee** (60 E. 54th St.; 212-753-1066). Rates here are expensive but quite reasonable for New York City.

A little farther: Check the Columbia and Juilliard entries for suggestions uptown and near Lincoln Center.

FORDHAM UNIVERSITY

Office of Undergraduate Admissions, Fordham University, Dealy Hall 115, Bronx, NY 10458
(The office is in Thebaud Hall) • Telephone: 800-FORDHAM •
Web: www.fordham.edu • Email: enroll@fordham.edu

Hours: Monday-Friday, 9AM-5PM. Closed weekends and national holidays.

Fordham University has two campuses, a traditional campus in the Bronx and an urban one near Lincoln Center in Manhattan. The Bronx campus remains a traditional liberal arts and sciences institution, while Lincoln Center offers a wide range of courses but focuses on media studies, visual arts, and theater. At both campuses, students must complete a core curriculum.

HIGHLIGHTS

ON CAMPUS
- Millennium Hall (Rose Hill Campus)
- William D. Walsh Family Library
- Keating Hall/Edwards Parade
- McMahon Hall (Lincoln Center)
- Pope Auditorium

OFF CAMPUS
- Bronx Zoo
- NY Botanical Gardens
- Arthur Avenue/Little Italy (Rose Hill Campus)
- Central Park
- Broadway (Lincoln Center Campus)

TRANSPORTATION

La Guardia, Kennedy International, Newark, and West-chester County airports all serve New York City. The closest to Fordham's Rose Hill Campus (on E. Fordham Rd. at 190th St. in the Bronx), is La Guardia, which is a 20-minute drive from campus. Taxis and limousine service (call Riverdale Jitney, 718-884-9400) are available for the ride from airport to campus. The other area airports are also served by shuttle and taxi service. Amtrak, Long Island Railroad, and New Jersey Transit trains all serve New York City. Greyhound buses come into the Port Authority Terminal. Several local train and subway lines offer access to campus: the Metro-North commuter railroad (Fordham station), the Woodlawn-Jerome IRT subway (#4 to the Fordham Rd. station), and the IND subway (Concourse "D" line). A number of local bus lines pass the campus along Fordham Rd.

FIND YOUR WAY

New York City can be approached on many highways. After you are in the city area, any of the following roads and exits will get you close to Fordham: Bronx River Pkwy. (Fordham Rd. westbound exit), Saw Mill River Pkwy. (Mosholu Pkwy. exit), and the Cross-Bronx Expy. (Bronx River Pkwy. W. exit). Ample parking facilities are available on campus.

STAY THE NIGHT

Fordham University is in the Bronx, the borough of New York City that is north of Manhattan. The closest place to stay is in Yonkers at **Holiday Inn** (125 Tuckahoe Rd.; 914-476-3800) only 15 minutes away. Rates are moderate. **Days Inn** (Tarrytown Rd., Elmsford; 914-592-5680), 25 minutes away, is always a reliable, inexpensive choice. It also has an outdoor pool and health club privileges. For an indoor pool, pick the **Ramada Inn** (540 Saw Mill River Rd., Elmsford; 914-592-3300). Rates range from moderate to expensive. See the Columbia University and Juilliard School entries for options in upper Manhattan. See the New York University and Eugene Lang College entries for options in midtown and downtown Manhattan. See the Sarah Lawrence College entry for options in Westchester County, just north of the Bronx. Be sure to check the **Westchester Marriott** in Tarrytown and the **Ramada Hotel** in New Rochelle.

HAMILTON COLLEGE

Admissions Office, Hamilton College, 198 College Hill Rd., Clinton, NY 13323 •
Telephone: 800-843-2655 or 315-859-4421 • Web: www.hamilton.edu •
Email: admission@hamilton.edu

Hours: Monday-Friday, 8:30AM-4:30PM; Saturday, 8:30AM-12:30PM (mid-September to mid-February). Closed Sundays and holidays.

Hamilton College is a small liberal arts school with a close-knit community. Though Hamilton enjoys its beautiful and secluded campus, modern amenities are close by.

AT A GLANCE	
Selectivity Rating	91
Range SAT I Math	580-670
Range SAT I Verbal	580-670
Student to Faculty Ratio	9:1

CAMPUS TOURS	
Appointment Req?	No
Dates	Year-round
Times	Tour times are subject to change; contact admissions off.
Avg. Length	1 hour

ON-CAMPUS INTERVIEWS	
Admissions	
Start Date–Juniors	April 1
Appointment Req?	Yes
Advance Notice	2 weeks
Saturdays?	Yes, Sept-Dec
Avg. Length	45 min
Info Sessions	Times vary
Faculty and Coaches	
Dates/Times	Year-round; subject to faculty/coach availability
Arrangements	Contact admissions off. 2 weeks prior

CLASS VISITS	
Dates	Consult class schedule in admissions off.

OVERNIGHT DORM STAYS	
Advance Notice	2 weeks
Arrangements	Contact admissions off.
Limitations	Sun-Thurs, after Oct 1 during academic year

TRANSPORTATION

Oneida County Airport (served by USAir) is 8 miles from campus. Taxis and limousine service are available at the airport for the ride to campus. (Note that taxis are approximately twice as expensive as the limousines.) Syracuse Airport is 45 miles from campus. Limousine service to campus is available, but must be arranged in advance by calling 315-736-9601 or 315-736-5221. Amtrak trains are available to Union Station in Utica, a 20-minute drive to campus. Taxis are available for the drive to campus.

FIND YOUR WAY

From the NY State Thruway (I-90), take Exit 32 (Westmoreland). After the exit, bear right, then turn left onto Rte. 233 S. Proceed for approximately 5 miles into Clinton (crossing Rte. 5). At the blinking light at the foot of a steep hill (look for the Hamilton College sign on the right), turn right up the hill onto College Hill Rd. The admissions office is a yellow house on the left of College Hill Rd. **From the south**, take I-81 N. through Binghamton to Exit 6 (sign says "Rt. 12, Norwich"). Follow Rte. 12 N. for approximately 50 miles; in the village of Sherburne, bear left onto Rte. 12B. Follow 12B N. for approximately 35 miles. Approximately 3 miles north of the village of Deansboro, turn left onto Rte. 233. Follow Rte. 233 to the flashing red light. Turn left and follow signs to campus.

STAY THE NIGHT

Nearby: On campus, the newly renovated 4th floor of the **Bristol Campus Center** (315-859-4194) has moderately priced rooms available. During the academic year, a snack bar is open for breakfast. Bed and breakfasts in the area are **The Hedges** (180 Sanford Ave.; 800-883-5883 or 315-859-5909) and **The Artful Lodger** (7 East Park Row; 315-853-3672), both about a mile from campus. The recently remodeled **Alexander Hamilton Inn** (21 West Park Row; 315-853-2061) offers exquisitely appointed guest rooms and fine dining in a centuries-old building on the Village Green.

A little farther: The moderately priced **Comfort Suites** (800-221-2222) in Vernon, NY, is 15 minutes away. **The Utica Radisson** (315-797-8010) has an indoor swimming pool, game room, Jacuzzi, weight room, a restaurant, and a nightly band (except Sunday). A special dining experience can be found at **La Petite Maison** in Waterville (315-841-8030), 20 minutes south of campus. See the Colgate entry for more suggestions in the area (a 25-minute drive away).

HIGHLIGHTS

ON CAMPUS	OFF CAMPUS
• Emerson Gallery	• Adirondack Park
• Root Glen	• Stanley Performing Arts Center
• Hamilton College Jazz Archive	• Glimmerglass Opera
	• Munson-Williams Proctor Art Institute
	• National Baseball Hall of Fame

HARTWICK COLLEGE

Admissions Office, Hartwick College, Hartwick Dr., Bresee Hall,
Oneonta, NY 13820 • Telephone: 888-Hartwick or 607-431-4150 •
Web: www.hartwick.edu • Email: admissions@hartwick.edu

Hours: Monday-Friday, 9AM-5PM; Saturday, 11AM-2PM (most Saturdays). Closed Sundays, and from noon on Wednesday before Thanksgiving through the weekend, and December 22 to January 1.

Hartwick College is a traditional liberal arts school in the upstate village of Oneonta, New York, with about 1,400 students. The upstate campus is near a variety of attractions, including the Boxing Hall of Fame, and Hartwick boasts "Dilbert" creator Scott Adams as an alum.

HIGHLIGHTS

ON CAMPUS
- Yagen Museum
- Stevens-German Library
- Shineman Chapel

OFF CAMPUS
- National Soccer Hall of Fame
- Baseball Hall of Fame
- Catskills Park

TRANSPORTATION

Oneonta has a small airport that can handle private planes. Albany and Binghamton have larger airports, which are 75 miles (an hour to an hour-and-a-half drive) from Oneonta. Greyhound buses are available from these airports to Oneonta. Greyhound also provides service into Oneonta. Taxis to campus are available at the station.

FIND YOUR WAY

From the New York City area, take the NY State Thruway N. (I-87) to Exit 19 (Kingston), then take Rte. 28 W. to Shandaken. Turn right onto Rte. 42 to Lexington. Turn left at Lexington to Rte. 23A, which becomes Rte. 23 W. Follow this into Oneonta. **From the south**, get onto I-81 N. through Scranton, PA, into Binghamton, NY. Take I-88 E. to Oneonta. Use Oneonta Exit 15, marked "Colleges, Airport."

STAY THE NIGHT

Nearby: Three motels are within 10 minutes of the college. From least expensive to most expensive, they are the **Christopher's Country Lodge**, (Rt. 28; 607-432-2444), **Cathedral Farms Country Inn** (Rt. 205; 607-432-7483), and **Holiday Inn** (NY Rte. 23; 607-443-2250) 10 minutes away with a restaurant and a video game room.

A little farther: From May to October, you can stay in Cooperstown (home of the Baseball Hall of Fame) at the **Otesaga Hotel** (60 Lake St.; 607-547-9931), situated on beautiful Lake Otesaga. There's a groovy porch and a formal dining room with music and all-American cuisine. There is also an annex to the Otesaga, **Cooper Inn**, a wonderful old building a block or so closer to the Baseball Hall of Fame. You can use all the facilities of the Otesaga, which include a golf course and a heated swimming pool. Lunch is served buffet-style by the pool. Rates at the Otesaga are very expensive but include breakfast and dinner. Rates at the Cooper Inn are at the low end of the expensive range but do not include meals.

AT A GLANCE

Range SAT I Math	500-600
Average SAT I Math	554
Range SAT I Verbal	500-610
Average SAT I Verbal	558
Average ACT Composite	23
Student to Faculty Ratio	11:1

CAMPUS TOURS

Appointment Req?	No
Dates	Year-round
Times	Mon-Fri 9:45AM-3:30PM hourly; Sat 11:30AM, 12PM, and 1PM
Avg. Length	1 hour

ON-CAMPUS INTERVIEWS

Admissions

Start Date–Juniors	None during March
Appointment Req?	Strongly preferred
Advance Notice	1 week
Saturdays?	Yes
Avg. Length	1 hour
Info Sessions	Yes

Faculty and Coaches

Dates/Times	Year-round; subject to faculty/coach availability
Arrangements	Contact admissions off. 1 week prior

CLASS VISITS

Dates	Year-round (Mon-Fri)
Arrangements	Contact admissions off.

OVERNIGHT DORM STAYS

Advance Notice	2 weeks
Arrangements	Contact admissions off.
Limitations	Available Mon-Thurs nights; bring a sleeping bag

HOBART AND WILLIAM SMITH COLLEGES

Admissions Office, Hobart and William Smith Colleges, Pulteney St., Geneva, NY 14456-3385 • Telephone: 800-852-2256 or 315-781-3623 • Web: www.hws.edu • Email: admissions@hws.edu

Hours: Monday-Friday, 8:30AM-5PM; Saturday, 9AM-noon (September-May only). Closed Sundays and holidays.

Hobart and William Smith Colleges are separate, single-sex institutions sharing the same scenic campus in the Finger Lakes region of upstate New York. In an effort to combine the best aspects of single-sex and coeducational instruction, the schools share classes and even a common faculty, yet maintain separate traditions and curricular priorities.

AT A GLANCE

Selectivity Rating	83
Range SAT I Math	530-620
Average SAT I Math	600
Range SAT I Verbal	530-620
Average SAT I Verbal	550
Average GPA	3.3
Student to Faculty Ratio	13:1

CAMPUS TOURS

Appointment Req?	Preferred
Dates	Year-round
Times	Academic Year: Mon-Fri 9AM, 10AM, 11AM, 1PM, 2PM, and 3PM; Sat 9AM, 10AM, and 11AM
Avg. Length	1 hour

ON-CAMPUS INTERVIEWS

Admissions

Start Date—Juniors	April
Appointment Req?	Yes
Advance Notice	1 week
Saturdays?	Yes, during academic year
Avg. Length	45 min
Info Sessions	Spring, summer, fall

Faculty and Coaches

Dates/Times	Year-round; subject to faculty/coach availability
Arrangements	Contact admissions off.

CLASS VISITS

Dates	Academic year (Mon-Fri)
Arrangements	Contact admissions off.

OVERNIGHT DORM STAYS

Advance Notice	2 weeks
Arrangements	Contact admissions off.
Limitations	Available on weeknights, except during vacations and exam periods

TRANSPORTATION

The Syracuse, Rochester, and Ithaca airports are all approximately a one-hour drive from campus. Amtrak trains serve Syracuse and Rochester; Greyhound buses serve Geneva.

FIND YOUR WAY

From I-90, take Exit 42. Take Rte. 14 S. to the first light (approximately 5.5 miles). Turn right on North St.; pass Geneva General Hospital and take the next left turn onto Main St. The admissions offices are located in 629 and 639 South Main Street. **From downstate**, take I-81 N. to Binghamton; then take Rte. 17 W. to Rte. 96, and follow 96 through Ithaca to Rte. 96A at Ovid. Follow 96A to Rtes. 5 and 20 W., and take them into Geneva. Enter campus by turning left at Pulteney St. Proceed to St. Clair St. and turn left to S. Main St. Turn left again onto S. Main to the admissions offices.

STAY THE NIGHT

Nearby: Seneca Lake is home to a couple of great choices. The **Inn at Bellhurst Castle** (Rte. 14 S.; 315-781-0201) is a grand, heavily paneled Victorian mansion with grounds that run down to the lake. Rates are moderate to expensive. **Geneva on the Lake** (10001 Lochland Rd.; 315-789-7190) is a handsome, all-suite resort with a pool, boating, and access to many sporting activities. Rates are very expensive. Two low-priced motels are within half a mile of campus: **Chanticleer Motor Lodge** (473 Hamilton St.; 315-789-7600) and **Motel 6** (485 Hamilton St.; 315-789-4050). More moderately priced is the **Ramada Geneva Lake Front** (315-789-0400), with 148 rooms on the shore of Seneca Lake.

A little farther: A **Holiday Inn** is 9 miles from campus (Rtes. 414, 5, and 20 E. in Waterloo; 315-539-5011). Rates are moderate, and there is a restaurant and weekend entertainment. See also the University of Rochester and Rochester Institute of Technology entries (Rochester is 35 miles to the northwest), the Syracuse University entry (Syracuse is 50 miles to the northeast), and the Cornell University entry (Ithaca is 45 miles to the southeast).

HIGHLIGHTS

ON CAMPUS
- Warren Hunting Smith Library
- St. John's Chapel
- Seneca Lake

OFF CAMPUS
- Seneca Lake
- Women's Hall of Fame
- Women's Rights National Historic Park

ITHACA COLLEGE

Admission Office, Ithaca College, 100 Job Hall, Ithaca, NY 14850-7020 •
Telephone: 607-274-3124 or 800-429-4274 • Web: www.ithaca.edu •
Email: admission@ithaca.edu

Hours: Monday-Friday, 8:30AM-5PM; most Saturdays, 8:30AM-1PM (please call to confirm). Closed Sundays and major holidays.

The other college in Ithaca is Ithaca College, an institution that originated as a Conservatory of Music and has grown into a nationally renowned pre-professional college with a broad range of courses and an eminent physical therapy program.

HIGHLIGHTS

ON CAMPUS
- New Academic Facilities
- Art gallery
- Music and theater performances
- The Tower Club Restaurant
- Division III intercollegiate sports

OFF CAMPUS
- Ithaca Commons
- Numerous gorges and parks
- Finger Lakes–area wineries
- Ithaca Farmer's Market
- Fine dining and unique shops

TRANSPORTATION

Ithaca is served by US Airways at the Tompkins County Airport and by Greyhound, Short Line and other bus companies. Limousine service is available from the airport, and taxis and city buses serve the campus from the bus terminal. Hancock International Airport in Syracuse is approximately 60 miles north of Ithaca.

FIND YOUR WAY

From the New York City Area, follow Route 17 west to Binghamton and take I-81 north to Whitney Point (exit 8). Pick up Route 79 west to Ithaca. At T-intersection in Ithaca turn left onto Route 96B (Aurora St.). An alternate route of about the same distance is through Owego: Stay on Route 17 west through Binghamton to Route 96/96B in Owego. Follow 96/96B for about 25 miles. The campus will be on your right. **From Albany and New England,** follow the New York State Thruway (I-90) west to I-88 (exit 25A). Take I-88 west to Bainbridge (exit 8) and then Route 206 to Whitney Point. Pick up Route 79 west to Ithaca. At T-intersection in Ithaca turn left onto Route 96B (Aurora St.). **From Rochester and Buffalo,** follow the New York State Thruway (I-90) east to Waterloo (exit 41) and take Route 414 south to Route 318 east to Route 89 south to Ithaca. In Ithaca turn right onto Route 13 south. After passing Green St., move into the far left lane and go straight onto Route 96 B (Clinton St.). Turn right onto Aurora St. (still 96B).

STAY THE NIGHT

Holiday Inn (222 S. Cayuga St.; 607-272-1000) is only one mile from Ithaca College, and is moderately priced. It has an indoor swimming pool. See the Cornell University entry for other choices. Ithaca College is only 10 minutes away from Cornell.

AT A GLANCE

Selectivity Rating	81
Range SAT I Math	520-630
Range SAT I Verbal	530-630
Average GPA	2.8
Student to Faculty Ratio	12:1

CAMPUS TOURS

Appointment Req?	No
Dates	When school is in session
Times	Mon-Fri 9AM-3PM hourly; most Saturdays; 9AM-11AM hourly
Avg. Length	1 hour

ON-CAMPUS INTERVIEWS

Admissions

Start Date–Juniors	Any time
Appointment Req?	Yes
Advance Notice	2 weeks
Saturdays?	Yes, on selected days by appt.
Avg. Length	30 min
Info Sessions	Available only as part of day-long programs

Faculty and Coaches

Dates/Times	Year-round; subject to faculty/coach availability
Arrangements	Contact admissions office 2 weeks prior

CLASS VISITS

Dates	When classes are in session
Arrangements	Contact admissions off. 2 weeks prior

OVERNIGHT DORM STAYS

Advance Notice	At least 2 weeks
Arrangements	Contact admissions off.
Limitations	Selected Sun-Thurs while classes are in session

THE JUILLIARD SCHOOL

Admissions Office, Juilliard School, 60 Lincoln Center Plaza, New York, NY 10023-6590
(Use the main entrance when visiting) • Telephone: 212-799-5000 ext. 223 •
Web: www.juilliard.edu • Email: mgray@juilliard.edu

Hours: Monday-Friday, 9:30AM-5:30PM. Closed weekends and holidays; also closed on Friday during the summer.

The prestigious Juilliard School in New York City's Lincoln Center is perhaps the world's finest school for the performing arts. Juilliard enrolls about 750 highly diverse students and offers a variety of programs, including dance, theatre, and music. Juilliard boasts a host of famous alumni, including actor Robin Williams and musician Wynton Marsalis.

AT A GLANCE

Student to Faculty Ratio	5:1

CAMPUS TOURS

Appointment Req?	No
Dates	Year-round, excluding holidays (and Fridays in the summer)
Times	Sept-May: Mon-Fri 2:30PM. June-Aug: Mon-Thurs 2:30PM. March and May: twice a day during auditions.
Avg. Length	1 hour

ON-CAMPUS INTERVIEWS

Admissions

Start Date—Juniors	N/A
Appointment Req?	N/A
Advance Notice	N/A
Saturdays?	N/A
Avg. Length	N/A
Info Sessions	Included with tour

Faculty and Coaches

Dates/Times	N/A
Arrangements	Not generally available. Write to faculty in care of school as early as possible.

CLASS VISITS

Dates	Year-round (Mon-Fri); restrictions apply; dance students may watch dance classes; no viewing of drama classes or private lessons
Arrangements	Contact admissions off.

OVERNIGHT DORM STAYS

Advance Notice	N/A
Arrangements	Available through Admissions Hosting program
Limitations	N/A

TRANSPORTATION

La Guardia, Newark International, and Kennedy International serve the New York City area. Limousine, taxi, bus, and subway service can be combined to bring you to Lincoln Center and Juilliard. Taxi service is the most expensive means of travel. Carey bus service operates from La Guardia and Newark airports. Airport shuttles operate from Kennedy. Your airline should be able to help you plan how to get into the city. Amtrak trains and Greyhound and several other bus lines serve New York City. The closest subway to the school is the #1 subway; the closest bus stop is for the M104 bus at West 66th St.

FIND YOUR WAY

Take your favorite route into New York City (check the Barnard and Columbia entries), then head for Lincoln Center and the school near 65th and Broadway, west of Central Park.

STAY THE NIGHT

Nearby: Within walking distance is the **Alcott** (27 W. 72nd St.; 212-877-4200). Rates are moderate. In the other direction is the **Salisbury** (123 W. 57th St.; 212-246-1300). Rates here are rather expensive, but remember to ask for its musician's discount. See the Columbia University entry for other suggestions accessible to Juilliard, especially the **Empire Hotel** and the **Excelsior**, which are both within walking distance of Juilliard. (Ask the Empire for their musician's discount as well.)

A little farther: See the New York University and Eugene Lang College entries for midtown and downtown choices.

HIGHLIGHTS

ON CAMPUS
• Lila Acheson Wallace Library

OFF CAMPUS
• Central Park
• The Statue of Liberty
• American Museum of Natural History
• The Guggenheim Museum
• The World Trade Center

NEW YORK UNIVERSITY

Admissions Office, New York University, 22 Washington Square North, New York, NY 10011 • Telephone: 212-998-4500 • Web: www.nyu.edu • Email: admissions@nyu.edu

Hours: September-May: Monday-Friday, 9AM-6PM; open selected Saturdays in October and November. June-August: Monday-Friday, 9AM-5PM.

New York University offers a bevy of highly regarded and nationally competitive programs, especially in the arts and business. The hefty price tag for attending NYU still frustrates some students, but for most Greenwich Village, the heart of the social universe of young New York, helps to make it all worth it.

HIGHLIGHTS

ON CAMPUS
- The Elmer Holmes Bobst Library

OFF CAMPUS
- Central Park
- Statue of Liberty
- Museum of Modern Art
- World Trade Center
- Times Square

TRANSPORTATION

La Guardia Airport is 20 miles from campus, ordinarily a one-hour drive, but longer at rush hours. Kennedy and Newark airports also serve New York City. To get to campus from any of the airports, you can take a taxi or a bus to Grand Central Station and then take a taxi or the Lexington Ave. subway downtown to Astor Place. Long Island Railroad and Amtrak trains bring you to Pennsylvania Station; from there take the 8th Ave. subway (IND) downtown ("A" express or "C" or "E" local) to the West 4th St. stop. Metro-North trains bring you into Grand Central Station; from there take the Lexington Ave. subway (IRT) downtown (#6 local) to the Astor Pl. stop. Interstate buses come into the city's Port Authority Bus Terminal. Taxi or 8th Ave downtown to West 4th Street takes you to campus from there.

FIND YOUR WAY

From the north, take I-87 (NY State Thruway), which becomes the Major Deegan Expy. in the Bronx. From there take the F.D.R. Drive south to Houston St.; head west to La Guardia Pl. (2 blocks west of Broadway). Turn north 3 blocks to Washington Square and the university. From the west and south, take an interstate highway or the New Jersey Tpke. through the Holland Tunnel, then go north on Ave. of the Americas (6th Ave.) to W. 4th St. Take W. 4th St. east to Washington Square.

STAY THE NIGHT

New York University is in Greenwich Village, at the foot of Fifth Ave., and south of midtown. If you consult a general New York City guide, look for accommodations south of 38th St., which will put you within a 1- to 2-mile range of the school. Taxicab transportation and public transportation, of course, are readily available.

Nearby: For convenience, you cannot do better than the **Washington Square Hotel** (103 Waverly Pl.; 212-777-9515), just down the block from the admissions office. Accommodations are very modest, with rates to match. A 15-minute walk, past shops, galleries and restaurants, will bring you to the dazzlingly sophisticated, new **Soho Grand Hotel** (310 W. Broadway; 212-965-3000) in the exciting art center of Soho, where, for a moderate (for New York!) rate, you can have a unique New York experience. This is a favorite of artists and photographers. The rooms have great views, and there is valet parking. Bed-and-breakfasts are located all around town in the $80-$100 range. Two reservation agencies to call are **Abode Bed and Breakfast** (212-472-2000) and **Bed and Breakfast and Books** (212-865-8740). NYU has arranged for guests of the university to receive special rates (moderately expensive) at **Club Quarters** (52 William St.; 212-443-4700) in the heart of the Wall Street District. Slightly more expensive, but reasonably priced for New York City, is the **Gramercy Park Hotel** (2 Lexington Ave.; 212-475-4320 or 800-221-4083). It's close to the university, and the neighborhood is beautiful.

A little farther: See the Eugene Lang College and Columbia University entries for midtown and uptown suggestions. See the Juilliard School entry for suggestions near Lincoln Center.

AT A GLANCE

Selectivity Rating	89
Range SAT I Math	610-710
Average SAT I Math	660
Range SAT I Verbal	620-710
Average SAT I Verbal	664
Average GPA	3.6
Student to Faculty Ratio	13:1

CAMPUS TOURS

Appointment Req?	No
Dates	Year-round
Times	Contact admissions off.
Avg. Length	1 hour

ON-CAMPUS INTERVIEWS

Admissions

Start Date–Juniors	N/A
Appointment Req?	N/A
Advance Notice	N/A
Saturdays?	N/A
Avg. Length	N/A
Info Sessions	Year-round

Faculty and Coaches

Dates/Times	Not generally available
Arrangements	N/A

CLASS VISITS

Dates	Year-round (Mon-Fri)
Arrangements	Call 212-998-4522

OVERNIGHT DORM STAYS

Advance Notice	N/A
Arrangements	N/A
Limitations	N/A

RENSSELAER POLYTECHNIC INSTITUTE

Office of Admissions, Rensselaer Polytechnic Institute, Troy, NY 12180
(The office is in the Admissions and Financial Aid Building) • Telephone: 518-276-6216 •
Web: www.rpi.edu • Email: admissions@rpi.edu

Hours: Sept.-April: Monday-Friday, 8:30-5PM; Saturday, 9:30AM-3PM. May-Aug.: Monday-Friday, 8:30AM-5PM. Closed holidays.

Rensselaer Polytechnic Institute is a top-flight engineering school (with strong computer science and business and management departments) where mostly male students study furiously and occasionally take a road trip, go to a frat party, or watch the perennially competitive hockey team. George Ferris, inventor of the Ferris wheel, and Washington Roebling, architect of the Brooklyn Bridge, are alums.

AT A GLANCE

Selectivity Rating	82
Range SAT I Math	620-710
Average SAT I Math	659
Range SAT I Verbal	560-660
Average SAT I Verbal	607
Average ACT Composite	27
Student to Faculty Ratio	18:1

CAMPUS TOURS

Appointment Req?	No
Dates	Year-round
Times	Mon-Fri 11AM and 1PM (excluding holidays); Sat 11AM and 1PM (Sept-April)
Avg. Length	90 min

ON-CAMPUS VISIT

Admissions

Start Date–Juniors	Any time
Appointment Req?	No
Advance Notice	2-3 weeks
Saturdays?	Yes, Sept-April
Avg. Length	1 hour
Info Sessions	Year-round Mon-Fri 10AM; Sat (Sept-Apr) 1PM

Faculty and Coaches

Dates/Times	Year-round; subject to faculty/coach availability
Arrangements	Contact admissions off. 2-3 weeks prior

CLASS VISITS

Dates	Year-round (Mon-Fri)
Arrangements	Contact admissions off.

OVERNIGHT DORM STAYS

Advance Notice	N/A
Arrangements	N/A
Limitations	N/A

TRANSPORTATION

The Albany International Airport is 10 miles from campus. Taxis and rental cars are available for the ride from the airport to campus. Amtrak provides service to the Albany-Rensselaer train station; from there, take a taxi to campus. Bus service is available to Albany and to Troy; take a taxi from these terminals to campus.

FIND YOUR WAY

From north, east, south, or west, Rensselaer Polytechnic Institute is easy to reach. We are centrally located near the major highways in New York State. **From the south,** take I-87, the New York State Thruway, north to Exit 23. At Exit 23, get on I-787 N. to Rte. 7 E., Exit 9E. Disregard the sign for Rensselaer and Russell Sage College at the previous exit. Exit 9E, Rte. 7 E., provides an easier approach to campus. Follow the directions to campus given below. **From the north,** take I-87, the Adirondack Northway, south to Exit 7 E. Get on Rte. 7 headed eastbound. Follow the directions to campus given below. **From the east,** take I-90 (Massachusetts Tpke., Berkshire Spur of the New York Thruway), to Exit B1. Continue west (13.5 miles) to I-787 N. to Rte. 7 E., Exit 9E. Disregard the sign for Rensselaer and Russell Sage College at the previous exit. Exit 9E, Rte. 7 E., provides an easier approach to campus. Follow the directions to campus given below. **From the west,** take I-90, the New York State Thruway, to Exit 24. From Exit 24, take I-87 N., Exit 1N, to Exit 7 E. Follow the directions to campus given below. **Directions to Campus:** Cross the Collar City Bridge and follow signs for Rte. 7, Hoosick St. At the 4th traffic light, turn right onto 15th St. You will know you're at Rensselaer when you see the large RENSSELAER sign in granite at the intersection of 15th St. and Sage Ave. Make a left at the 3rd traffic light onto Sage Ave. The Admissions and Financial Aid Building will be directly in front of you. Bear to the left of the building onto Eaton Rd. The parking lot will be on your right, directly behind the Admissions and Financial Aid Building.

STAY THE NIGHT

We look forward to your visit to Rensselaer. Our recommended lodging accommodations are the **Albany Marriot** (189 Wolf Rd.; 518-458-8444), **Best Western** (200 Wolf Rd.; 518-458-1016), **Clarion Suites** (611 Troy-Schenectady Rd.; 518-758-5891), **Days Inn** (16 Wolf Rd.; 518-459-3600), **The Desmond** (660 Albany-Shaker Rd.; 518-869-8100), **Hampton Inn-Latham** (981 New London Rd.; 518-785-1285), **Hampton Inn-Wolf Road** (10 Ulenski Dr.; 518-438-2822), **Holiday Inn Express** (946 New London Rd.; 518-783-6161), **The Inn at the Century** (997 New London Rd.; 518-785-0931), and **Microtel-Colonie** (7 Rensselaer Ave.; 800-782-9121).

HIGHLIGHTS

ON CAMPUS
- The Approach
- The Play-house
- Mueller Fitness Center
- Houston Field House

OFF CAMPUS
- Troy Music Hall
- The Junior Museum

ROCHESTER INSTITUTE OF TECHNOLOGY

Rochester Institute of Technology, 60 Lomb Memorial Dr., Rochester, NY 14623
(The office is in the Bausch and Lomb Center) • Telephone: 716-475-6736 •
Web: www.rit.edu • Email: admissions@rit.edu

Hours: Monday-Friday, 8:30AM-4:30PM; Saturday, 10AM-noon. Closed Sundays and holidays.

If you can stand cold weather, Rochester Institute of Technology offers a demanding arts and technology school that has valuable relationships with major industries, state-of-the-art facilities, and an intense (but not cutthroat) student body. Located as it is in the hometown of Xerox, Kodak, and Bausch & Lomb, RIT provides its career-minded students with plenty of opportunities for internships.

HIGHLIGHTS

ON CAMPUS	OFF CAMPUS
• Center for Manufacturing	• Frontier Field (AAA baseball)
• Student Life Center	• International Museum of Photography
• Henry's Restaurant	• Lake Ontario
• Ritter Rice Arena	• Eastman Theatre
• Microelectronic engineering	• High Falls Entertainment

TRANSPORTATION

The Greater Rochester International Airport is approximately 5 miles from campus. Taxis and rental cars are available for the ride from the airport to campus.

FIND YOUR WAY

From I-90, take Exit 46 and proceed north on I-390 to Exit 13 (Hylan Dr.). Turn left on Hylan and continue north to Jefferson Rd., then turn left. Proceed west on Jefferson a short distance to the main campus.

STAY THE NIGHT

The **Radisson Inn** (175 Jefferson Rd.; 716-475-1910) is within walking distance. Rates are at the top end of the moderate range, and it has an indoor pool. The **Market Place Inn** (800 Jefferson Rd.; 716-475-9190) is within 5 minutes of campus. Ask for the special rate. A moderately priced **Holiday Inn** (1111 Jefferson Rd.; 716-475-1510) is also only 5 minutes away, and it has an indoor pool, restaurant, weight room, and game room.

AT A GLANCE

Selectivity Rating	84
Range SAT I Math	560-660
Range SAT I Verbal	520-620
Average GPA	3.7
Student to Faculty Ratio	13:1

CAMPUS TOURS

Appointment Req?	No
Dates	Year-round
Times	Mon-Fri 10AM, noon, and 2PM; Sat at 10AM except during summer
Avg. Length	1 hour

ON-CAMPUS INTERVIEWS

Admissions

Start Date–Juniors	Dec-May
Appointment Req?	Yes
Advance Notice	1 week
Saturdays?	Yes
Avg. Length	45 min
Info Sessions	May-Dec

Faculty and Coaches

Dates/Times	When regular classes are in session
Arrangements	Contact admissions

CLASS VISITS

Dates	Not usually permitted
Arrangements	Available as part of overnight dorm stay

OVERNIGHT DORM STAYS

Advance Notice	1 week
Arrangements	Contact admissions off.
Limitations	1-night stay

ST. JOHN'S UNIVERSITY—JAMAICA

Office of Admission St. John's University, 8000 Utopia Pkwy., Jamaica, NY 11439
(The office is in Newman Hall) • Telephone: 718-990-2000 •
Web: www.stjohns.edu • Email: admissions@stjohns.edu

Hours: Monday-Thursday, 8:30AM-4:30PM; Saturday, 9AM-noon. Closed Sundays and most holidays.

Saint John's University is a solid, very large liberal arts institution (about 18,000 students) in Queens, New York, with a strong Catholic heritage. Besides the main campus, St. John's has additional campuses on Staten Island and in Rome, Italy. Former New York governor Mario Cuomo is an alum.

AT A GLANCE

Range SAT I Math	440-560
Average SAT I Math	502
Range SAT I Verbal	430-550
Average SAT I Verbal	493
Average GPA	3.4
Student to Faculty Ratio	19:1

CAMPUS TOURS

Appointment Req?	Preferred
Dates	Year-round
Times	Mon-Sat, as needed
Avg. Length	45 min

ON-CAMPUS INTERVIEWS

Admissions

Start Date—Juniors	Spring
Appointment Req?	Preferred
Advance Notice	2 weeks
Saturdays?	Yes, by appointment
Avg. Length	30 min
Info Sessions	Yes, by appointment

Faculty and Coaches

Dates/Times	Year-round; subject to faculty/coach availability and by appointment
Arrangements	Contact Off. of Admission 718-990-2000 or 888-955-5041 for Queens campus; 718-390-4500 for Staten Island campus 2 weeks prior

CLASS VISITS

Dates	Fall/Spring by appointment (Mon-Fri)
Arrangements	Contact admissions off.

OVERNIGHT DORM STAYS

Advance Notice	N/A
Arrangements	N/A
Limitations	N/A

TRANSPORTATION

Kennedy and La Guardia Airports are 7 to 10 miles from campus. Taxi service is available from both airports. Amtrak trains and Greyhound buses serve New York City. Public transportation is available to campus: On the subway, take the E or F train to Kew Gardens; then take the Q-44A bus to Utopia Pkwy. and Union Tpke.. Or take the #7 train to Main St., Flushing; then take the Q-17 bus to Utopia Pkwy. and Long Island Expy. Transfer to the Q-30 or 31 bus to 82nd Ave. and Utopia Pkwy. From Long Island, take the Long Island Railroad to Jamaica Station; then take the Q-30 or 31 bus to 82nd Ave. and Utopia Pkwy.

FIND YOUR WAY

Take I-95 or I-80 to George Washington Bridge. Cross bridge and take the cross Bronx Expressway to I-295 to Throgs Neck Bridge. Take Throgs Neck Bridge to the Clearview Expressway, exit at Union Tpke. and make a right, follow to Utopia Pkwy. and make a left, then right onto campus. For directions to the Staten Island Campus call 718-990-2000.

STAY THE NIGHT

Nearby: The nearest accommodations are at La Guardia Airport, about 15 minutes away by car. We suggest the **Holiday Inn Crowne Plaza** (104-04 Ditmars Blvd., 94th St. exit from Grand Central Pkwy.; 718-457-6300). It has an indoor pool, health club, and sauna. Rates are expensive during the week and moderate on the weekends. Consider the **Marriott La Guardia** (102-05 Ditmars Blvd., at the 94th St. exit from Grand Central Pkwy.; 718-565-8900). If you reserve and pay for your room (nonrefundable) 21 days in advance, they offer moderate room rates. In Garden City, Long Island, about 20 minutes in the other direction from St. John's, is the fancy **Garden City Hotel** (45 7th Street, Garden City; 516-747-3000 or 800-547-0400 from out of state). It is located 5 miles south of Northern State Pkwy. (the extension of Grand Central Pkwy.) at Exit 26. This full-service hotel is quite expensive, and on weekends breakfast is included.

A little farther: A 30- to 45-minute drive will take you into Manhattan. Check the Columbia entry for suggestions in uptown Manhattan (take the Triborough Bridge from the Grand Central Pkwy.). If you would prefer to be in midtown Manhattan, check the suggestions in the NYU entry.

HIGHLIGHTS

ON CAMPUS

- 100-acre Queens campus
- Magnificent new residence halls
- Famous Alumni Hall Athletics
- Harbor views on Staten Island campus

OFF CAMPUS

- Major beaches and parklands
- Abundant shopping
- Safe residential neighborhoods
- Manhattan is just minutes away

St. Lawrence University

Admissions Office, St. Lawrence University, Canton, NY 13617
(The office is in Payson Hall) • Telephone: 315-229-5261 or 800-285-1856 •
Web: www.stlawu.edu • Email: admissions@stlawu.edu

Hours: Monday-Friday, 8AM-5PM; Saturday, 8:30AM-4:30PM by appointment. Closed Sundays and most holidays.

Students at this traditional liberal arts enclave in remote, frigid, and rural upstate New York get a good liberal arts education and have a darned good time. Good research resources and a strong placement rate throughout the Northeast Corridor are a hit with students. The Greek system is immense and SLU's competitive Division I hockey team is also very popular.

HIGHLIGHTS

ON CAMPUS
- Brush Art Gallery
- Brewer Bookstore
- ODY Library
- Athletic and recreation complex

OFF CAMPUS
- Frederic Remington Museum
- St. Lawrence Seaway
- Adirondack Park
- Ottawa
- Thousand Islands

TRANSPORTATION

The nearest major airport is in Ottawa, which is a 75-minute drive from campus. Hancock Airport in Syracuse is a 2.5-hour drive from campus. Greyhound services Canton from both downtown Syracuse and from Hancock. There are also commuter flights from Pittsburgh to Ogdensburg, which is 18 miles from campus.

FIND YOUR WAY

From Albany, take I-87 (the Adirondack Northway) north to Exit 23 (Warrensburg); then take Rte. 9 N. to Rte. 28 to Blue Mountain Lake. Follow Rte. 30 to Tupper Lake, then Rte. 3 W. to Rte. 56 N. (Sevey). Turn left on Rte. 68 to Canton. The drive takes about 4 hours. **From Syracuse**, take I-81 N. to Exit 48; then take Rte. 342 to Rte. 11 N. Follow Rte. 11 to Canton. The trip takes about 2.5 hours. **From Burlington**, VT, take I-89 N. to Swanton; then take Rte. 78 W. to U.S. Rte. 2. Take Rte. 2 N. and west to U.S. Rte. 11; then take Rte. 11 S. and west to Canton. This is a 3-hour trip.

STAY THE NIGHT

Nearby: The **Best Western University Inn** (U.S. Rte. 11; 315-386-8522), which is adjacent to campus, is a reasonably priced facility with a swimming pool, an 18-hole golf course, a driving range and putting greens.

A little farther: There are wonderful bed and breakfasts and inns throughout the North Country. Several are listed on our admissions website.

AT A GLANCE

Range SAT I Math	520-620
Average SAT I Math	567
Range SAT I Verbal	510-610
Average SAT I Verbal	564
Average ACT Composite	24
Average GPA	3.3
Student to Faculty Ratio	11:1

CAMPUS TOURS

Appointment Req?	Yes
Dates	Year-round
Times	Mon-Sat following interviews
Avg. Length	1 hour

ON-CAMPUS INTERVIEWS

Admissions

Start Date—Juniors	Any time
Appointment Req?	Yes
Advance Notice	As early as possible
Saturdays?	Yes, most Saturdays year round
Avg. Length	45-60 min
Info Sessions	N/A

Faculty and Coaches

Dates/Times	Year-round; subject to faculty/coach availability
Arrangements	Contact admissions off. as early as possible

CLASS VISITS

Dates	Academic year (Mon-Fri)
Arrangements	Contact admissions off.

OVERNIGHT DORM STAYS

Advance Notice	As early as possible
Arrangements	Contact admissions off.
Limitations	Admitted students only; limited numbers on specific nights in April

SARAH LAWRENCE COLLEGE

Office of Admission, Sarah Lawrence College, 1 Mead Way, Bronxville, NY 10708
(The office is in the Westlands Building) • Telephone: 800-888-2858 •
Web: www.slc.edu • Email: slcadmit@slc.edu

Hours: Monday-Friday, 9AM-5PM; Saturdays, October-December only, 9AM-5PM. Closed Sundays and holidays.

Sarah Lawrence College is a small and unusual school that promotes independence in its students. There are no core requirements. Barbara Walters and Brian DePalma are notable alumni.

AT A GLANCE

Selectivity Rating	89
Range SAT I Math	520-610
Average SAT I Math	570
Range SAT I Verbal	590-700
Average SAT I Verbal	640
Average ACT Composite	25
Average GPA	3.3
Student to Faculty Ratio	6:1

CAMPUS TOURS

Appointment Req?	Recommended
Dates	Year-round
Times	Mon-Fri 9AM-4PM; Sat 9AM-4PM (Oct-Dec only)
Avg. Length	1 hour

ON-CAMPUS INTERVIEWS

Admissions

Start Date–Juniors	Spring
Appointment Req?	Yes
Advance Notice	2 weeks
Saturdays?	Yes, Oct-Dec only
Avg. Length	45 min
Info Sessions	Year-round

Faculty and Coaches

Dates/Times	During academic year; subject to faculty/coach availability
Arrangements	Contact admissions off. 2 weeks prior

CLASS VISITS

Dates	Oct-April (Mon-Fri)
Arrangements	Minimum 2 weeks advance notice

OVERNIGHT DORM STAYS

Advance Notice	2 weeks
Arrangements	Contact admissions off.
Limitations	1-night stay; Mon-Thurs

TRANSPORTATION

LaGuardia Airport is 18 miles (a 25-minute drive) from campus. Taxis are available for the trip from the airport to campus. National Mountain Limousine Service provides moderately priced service directly to the College from LaGuardia Airport. You must call ahead 718-884-9400 for a reservation. Cost is $21 per person, not including tip. From the airport, you can also take a bus to Grand Central Terminal in New York City. At the Ground Transportation desk by the baggage claim, purchase tickets for Gray Line Bus Service. Tickets are $13 per person and buses depart every 20 minutes. The bus makes several stops in Manhattan, including Grand Central Terminal from which you can take a train to Bronxville. Amtrak trains and Greyhound buses serve New York City. Public transportation or taxis can take you from the Amtrak station or the Port Authority Bus Terminal to Grand Central Station. From Grand Central take the Harlem Line of the Metro North Railway to the Bronxville station. The trip takes approximately 30 minutes and trains generally leave every half-hour (check specific times at Grand Central or call 212-532-4900). Taxi service is available from the Bronxville station to the College for approximately $3 per person.

FIND YOUR WAY

Take any of the following to New York's Cross-County Pkwy.: I-87 (NY State Thruway), Henry Hudson/Saw Mill River Pkwy., Hutchinson River Pkwy., or Sprain Brook Pkwy. From the Thruway and the Henry Hudson/Saw Mill River Pkwy., head east on the Cross-County Pkwy. and exit at Kimball Ave. Turn left on Kimball to the second traffic light, then turn right on Glen Washington Rd. From the Hutchinson River and Sprain Brook Parkways, head west on the Cross-County Pkwy. to Exit 5. Make a short right on Midland Ave. to Kimball Ave.; turn left on Kimball to the first traffic light, then turn right on Glen Washington Rd.

STAY THE NIGHT

There are a number of choices within 30 minutes of the campus. The **Westchester Marriott** (670 White Plains Rd., Tarrytown; 914-631-2200) has nicely appointed rooms. There's also an indoor pool, a health club, and a disco on weekends. **Holiday Inn Crown Plaza** (66 Hale Ave., White Plains; 914-682-0050) has an indoor pool, exercise room, and running track. The **Rye Town Hilton Inn** (699 Westchester Ave., Port Chester; 914-939-6300) is set on 40 wooded acres and has indoor exercise facilities, tennis courts, and 2 restaurants. The **Royal Regency** (165 Tuckahoe Rd., Yonkers; 914-476-6200) has a fitness room, restaurant, lounge, and live entertainment, and a continental breakfast is included.

HIGHLIGHTS

ON CAMPUS
- New Cambell Sports Center
- Communitea House
- Coffee house
- Library Pillow Room
- Health food bar

OFF CAMPUS
- New York City cultural institutions and entertainment venues

SKIDMORE COLLEGE

Office of Admissions, Skidmore College, 815 N. Broadway, Saratoga Springs, NY 12866 (The office is on North Broadway, across from the main entrance to the College) • Telephone: 518-580-5570 or 800-867-6007 • Web: www.skidmore.edu • Email: admissions@skidmore.edu

Hours: Monday-Friday, 8:30AM-4:30PM; Saturday, 8:30AM-noon (academic year only). Closed Sundays and major holidays.

With over 60 degree programs, Skidmore College is a competitive liberal arts school that keeps getting better. Most students at Skidmore live on campus, which is a good thing because Skidmore's dorms are some of the most livable in the country.

HIGHLIGHTS

ON CAMPUS
- Tang Teaching Museum
- Lucy Scribner Library
- The Schick Art Gallery

OFF CAMPUS
- SPAC (Saratoga Performing Arts Center)
- National Museum of Dance
- NYRA (New York Racing Association) Race Course

TRANSPORTATION

The Albany airport is 25 miles from campus. Taxis and rental cars are available for the trip from airport to campus.

FIND YOUR WAY

From I-87, take Exit 15 and follow New York Rte. 50 S. toward Saratoga Springs. At the third set of traffic lights, turn right on East Ave.; turn right again on North Broadway and continue about a quarter of a mile to the main entrance to campus. The office is on North Broadway across from the main entrance.

STAY THE NIGHT

You have some very interesting choices in Saratoga Springs, but beware: The rates skyrocket in August with the racing season. You'll probably enjoy staying on the main drag, Broadway, where you can rub shoulders with the college students and get a good feel for the social life in Saratoga Springs. Just 5 minutes from the college is the **Inn at Saratoga** (231 Broadway; 518-583-1890), a historic Victorian structure with 34 rooms. Rates range from moderate to expensive and include continental breakfast. The **Adelphi Hotel** (365 Broadway; 518-587-4688), open from May through October (weekends only in May), ranges from moderate to very expensive. **Sheraton Hotel** (534 Broadway; 518-584-4000) is a good modern pick with an indoor pool, sauna, weight room, and tennis and golf privileges. Rates range from moderate to expensive. The **Holiday Inn** (232 Broadway; 518-584-5000) is another safe bet. One of the majestic old resort hotels, the **Gideon Putnam Hotel** (Saratoga Spa State Park; 518-584-3000) stands amidst 1,500 acres, with loads of activities including golf, swimming, tennis, cross-country skiing, and ice-skating. They even have mineral baths. Rates vary with the season, from moderate to expensive. Bed-and-breakfasts abound. **Westchester House** (102 Lincoln Ave.; 518-587-7613) has 7 guest rooms. **Eddy House** (Nelson and Crescent Aves.; 518-587-2340) has 5 rooms, with prices in the moderate to expensive range. **Six Sisters Bed and Breakfast** (149 Union Ave.; 518-583-1173) is 10 minutes from campus (as are the others), and the prices vary from moderate to expensive. Inexpensive accommodations can be found at the **Grand Union** (92 S. Broadway; 518-584-9000), about a mile from Skidmore.

AT A GLANCE

Selectivity Rating	80
Range SAT I Math	560-650
Average SAT I Math	610
Range SAT I Verbal	560-650
Average SAT I Verbal	610
Average ACT Composite	28
Student to Faculty Ratio	11:1

CAMPUS TOURS

Appointment Req?	Yes
Dates	Year-round
Times	Mon-Fri 9:45AM-4PM
Avg. Length	1 hour

ON-CAMPUS INTERVIEWS

Admissions

Start Date–Juniors	April 1
Appointment Req?	Yes
Advance Notice	1 week; but 1 month prior at peak times
Saturdays?	Yes, during academic year
Avg. Length	45 min
Info Sessions	Available only by prior arrangement for groups

Faculty and Coaches

Dates/Times	Year-round; subject to faculty/coach availability
Arrangements	Contact admissions off. 1-2 weeks prior

CLASS VISITS

Dates	Academic year (Mon-Fri)
Arrangements	Contact admissions off. for a list of classes open to visitors

OVERNIGHT DORM STAYS

Advance Notice	2 weeks
Arrangements	Contact admissions off.
Limitations	Available Mon-Thurs nights only

SUNY—BINGHAMTON UNIVERSITY

Office of Undergraduate Admissions, SUNY–Binghamton University, Vestal Pkwy. East, P.O. Box 6001, Binghamton, NY 13902-6001 (The office is located in Academic A) • Telephone: 607-777-2171 • Web: www.binghamton.edu • Email: admit@binghamton.edu

Hours: Monday-Friday, 8:30AM-5PM; Saturday, 10:30AM-1PM when tours are held. Closed Sundays and some holidays.

Binghamton University offers a top-notch education at a state-school price. Pre-professional programs, most notably in psychology, accounting, and nursing, are particularly strong here, and students say on-campus activities are varied and plentiful.

AT A GLANCE

Selectivity Rating	89
Range SAT I Math	570-660
Average SAT I Math	616
Range SAT I Verbal	540-640
Average SAT I Verbal	585
Average GPA	3.6
Student to Faculty Ratio	13:1

CAMPUS TOURS

Appointment Req?	Preferred
Dates	During fall and spring semesters and summer sessions
Times	Mon-Fri 12:30PM; Sat at noon
Avg. Length	1 hour+

ON-CAMPUS INTERVIEWS

Admissions

Start Date–Juniors	N/A
Appointment Req?	N/A
Advance Notice	N/A
Saturdays?	N/A
Avg. Length	N/A
Info Sessions	Year-round; in connection with tours

Faculty and Coaches

Dates/Times	Year-round; subject to faculty/coach availability
Arrangements	Contact dept. of interest 1-2 weeks prior

CLASS VISITS

Dates	Year-round (Mon-Fri)
Arrangements	Contact appropriate dept.

OVERNIGHT DORM STAYS

Advance Notice	N/A
Arrangements	Contact admissions off.
Limitations	N/A

TRANSPORTATION

Binghamton Regional Airport (607-763-4471) is 7 miles from campus. Taxi and airport limousine service is available to campus. Contact Broome Transit (607-778-1692) for information about the county bus. Greyhound, Chenango Valley, and Short Line buses serve the area. Buses, taxis, and limousines provide service from the bus terminals to campus.

FIND YOUR WAY

From north and south, take I-81 to NY Rte. 17 W. Pass the Binghamton exit. Take Rte. 17 W. to Exit 70 S. (Rte. 201). Follow Rte. 201 and the SUNY signs to Rte. 434 E., which runs in front of the campus. The main entrance to campus is the first right turn. **From the I-87 (NY State Thruway)**, take Exit 16 (Harriman exit), which will put you on NY Rte. 17 W. Follow the preceding directions from that point.

STAY THE NIGHT

Nearby: Accommodations closest to Binghamton University include: **Holiday Inn—SUNY** (4105 Vestal Pkwy. E., Vestal; 607-729-6371, 800-465-4329), **Howard Johnson Express Inn** (3601 Vestal Pkwy. E., Vestal; 607-729-6181, 800-446-4656), **Courtyard Marriott** (3801 Vestal Pkwy. E.; 607-644-1000), the **Hampton Inn** (3708 Vestal Pkwy.; 607-797-5000), and **Residence Inn by Marriott** (4610 Vestal Pkwy. E., Vestal; 607-770-8500). About 10 to 20 minutes from campus are: **Best Western Binghamton Regency Hotel** (1 Sarbro Sq.; 607-722-7575, 800-528-1234), **Best Western of Johnson City** (569 Harry L Drive, Johnson City; 607-729-9194, 800-528-1234), **Comfort Inn** (1156 Front Street; 607-722-5353, 800-228-5150), and **Days Inn Motel** (1000 Front Street; 607-724-3297, 800-329-7466).

A little farther: Check the Alfred University entry for suggestions in Corning, to the west of Binghamton. Check the Cornell University entry for suggestions in and around Ithaca, to the northwest of Binghamton.

HIGHLIGHTS

ON CAMPUS
- Anderson Center for the Arts
- Rosefsky Art Gallery
- Nature preserve
- Summer music festival

OFF CAMPUS
- Binghamton is the Carousel Capital of the World
- Cider Mill Playhouse
- Binghamton Mets Stadium
- Tri-Cities Opera/Binghamton Philharmonic
- Spiedie Fest and Balloon Rally

SYRACUSE UNIVERSITY

Office of Admissions, Syracuse University, 201 Tolley Administration Building, Syracuse, NY 13244 • Telephone: 315-443-3611 • Web: www.syracuse.edu • Email: orange@syr.edu

Hours: Sept.-April: Monday-Friday, 8:30AM-5PM; selected Saturdays, 9AM-noon. May-Aug.: Monday-Friday, 8AM-4:30PM. Closed holidays.

Syracuse University in upstate New York is probably best known for its outstanding school of communications, which includes one of the nation's top broadcast journalism programs (Ted Koppel is an alum). Those programs are excellent, but this large, private institution also offers many other academic opportunities and a variety of social options.

HIGHLIGHTS

ON CAMPUS
- Schine Student Center
- Lowe Art Gallery
- Archbold Athletic Complex
- Carrier Dome
- Watson Theater Complex

OFF CAMPUS
- Marshall Street shopping area
- Armory Square
- Everson Museum of Art
- Finger Lakes recreational region
- Carousel Center Mall

TRANSPORTATION

Syracuse-Hancock International Airport is 6 miles from campus. Taxis, limousines, and rental cars are available at the airport for the trip to campus. Arrangements can be made on arrival at the airport. Syracuse is served by Amtrak trains and Greyhound buses; taxis are available for the ride from the stations to campus.

FIND YOUR WAY

From I-81 (both N. and S.), take Exit 18 (Adams St. in Syracuse). Proceed up the Adams St. hill to University Ave. and turn right. At the end of that street, turn right onto Waverly Ave. and take the first left (at the light) onto Crouse Dr. This takes you to the security station at the Tolley Administration Building, where security personnel will give you parking instructions.

STAY THE NIGHT

Sheraton University Hotel (315-475-3000) is right on campus. Rates are moderate to expensive and there is an indoor pool and weight room. Two other possibilities are near campus. One is **The Genesee Inn** (1060 E. Genesee St.; 315-476-4212), about 5 blocks away. Rates here are at the high end of the moderate range. The other one is the **Hotel Syracuse, Radisson Plaza** (315-422-5121). Ten minutes north of campus (Interstate 81, exit 25) you can find several hotels and motels, including the **Hampton Inn** (315-457-9900), **Club Hotel by Doubletree** (315-457-4000), and **Ramada Inn** (315-457-8670).

AT A GLANCE

Selectivity Rating	87
Range SAT I Math	560-660
Range SAT I Verbal	540-640
Average GPA	3.5
Student to Faculty Ratio	12:1

CAMPUS TOURS

Appointment Req?	Yes
Dates	Year-round
Times	Mon-Fri, varies; selected Saturdays
Avg. Length	1 hour

ON-CAMPUS INTERVIEWS

Admissions

Start Date—Juniors	2 weeks after Labor Day of senior year
Appointment Req?	Yes
Advance Notice	2 weeks
Saturdays?	No
Avg. Length	20-30 min
Info Sessions	Year-round

Faculty and Coaches

Dates/Times	Year-round; subject to faculty/coach availability
Arrangements	Contact admissions off. 2 weeks prior

CLASS VISITS

Dates	Year-round (Mon-Fri)
Arrangements	Contact admissions off.

OVERNIGHT DORM STAYS

Advance Notice	N/A
Arrangements	N/A
Limitations	N/A

Union College

Admissions Office, Union College, Schenectady, NY 12308
(The office is located in Becker Hall) • Telephone: 518-388-6112 •
Web: www.union.edu • Email: admissions@union.edu

Hours: Monday-Friday, 8:30AM-4:30PM; Saturday, 10AM-1PM (fall only; call to confirm). Closed Sundays and holidays.

Union College provides rigorous liberal arts, science, and engineering programs that cater to the individual paths of more than 2,000 students. The campus, which is located about three hours from New York City in Schenectady, is the nation's first to be architecturally designed. Entertainment ranges from the Adventurers gaming club to an annual beach volleyball tournament.

AT A GLANCE

Selectivity Rating	91
Range SAT I Math	580-670
Average SAT I Math	630
Range SAT I Verbal	560-650
Average SAT I Verbal	600
Average GPA	3.5
Student to Faculty Ratio	11:1

CAMPUS TOURS

Appointment Req?	No
Dates	Year-round, but call to verify
Times	Mon-Fri 10AM-3PM on the hour
Avg. Length	1 hour

ON-CAMPUS INTERVIEWS

Admissions

Start Date–Juniors	May 1
Appointment Req?	Yes
Advance Notice	2 weeks
Saturdays?	Most weeks in the fall
Avg. Length	1 hour
Info Sessions	On Sat in the fall

Faculty and Coaches

Dates/Times	Year-round; subject to faculty/coach availability
Arrangements	Contact admissions off. 2 weeks prior

CLASS VISITS

Dates	Year-round (Mon-Fri)
Arrangements	Contact admissions off.

OVERNIGHT DORM STAYS

Advance Notice	2 weeks
Arrangements	Contact admissions off.
Limitations	Discouraged on weekends

TRANSPORTATION

The Albany airport is 10 miles from campus. Taxis are available at the airport for the ride to campus. The Schenectady Amtrak rail and Trailways bus stations are each a mile from campus. Taxi service is available.

FIND YOUR WAY

Coming from any direction, take Exit 24 of the New York State Thruway to Rte. 87 (The Northway). Take Rte. 87 to Exit 6 (Rte. 7 W.) and drive west toward Schenectady for approximately 6 miles. Make a right at Union St. and proceed for approximately two miles through 8 traffic lights. The college will appear on the right. Turn and follow the signs to the admissions office, which will be the 4th building on the left.

STAY THE NIGHT

There are several chain motels within walking distance. One with special inexpensive rates for Union visitors is **Days Inn** (167 Nott Terrace; 518-370-3297 or 800-325-2525). The **Ramada Inn** (450 Nott St.; 518-370-7151 or 800-272-6232) is moderately priced and has an indoor pool. The **Holiday Inn** (100 Nott Terrace; 518-393-4141 or 800-HOLIDAY), with rates in the moderate range, is the most expensive of the motels. It has an indoor pool and is 3 blocks from campus. For nearby bed-and-breakfast accommodations, call the **American Country Collection** at 518-370-4948 from 10AM-noon and 1PM-5PM, Monday through Friday, or write to them at 1353 Union St., Schenectady, NY 12309. **The Glen Sanders Mansion** (518-374-7262) offers elegant accommodations right on the Mohawk River, 3 miles from campus.

HIGHLIGHTS

ON CAMPUS
• The Nott Memorial, a national historic monument
• Schaffer Library
• Memorial Chapel
• Jackson's Garden

OFF CAMPUS
• Canali's Italian Restaurant

UNITED STATES MILITARY ACADEMY

Director of Admissions, United States Military Academy, 606 Thayer Rd., West Point, NY 10996-1797 • Telephone: 914-938-4041 • Web: www.usma.edu • Email: 8dad@exmail.usma.army.mil

Hours: Monday-Friday, 7:30AM-4PM; Saturday, 8AM-noon. Closed Sundays and holidays.

Better known as West Point, the United States Military Academy provides one of the premier educations in the arts and sciences available in nation, and students here get to use live ammunition. Training ranges from the liberal arts and engineering to mountain warfare in Vermont and winter warfare in Alaska.

HIGHLIGHTS

ON CAMPUS	OFF CAMPUS
• Cadet Chapel	• Bear Mountain State Park
• West Point Museum	• Hudson River
	• Hyde Park

TRANSPORTATION

Stewart Airport in Newburgh is 20 miles from the academy. Rental cars and taxis are available at the airport for the trip to West Point.

FIND YOUR WAY

The main highways leading to the academy are U.S. Rte. 9W and the Palisades Interstate Pkwy.; a more scenic Rte. is NY State Rte. 218. From these roads, follow direction signs to West Point and the Academy.

STAY THE NIGHT

Nearby: **Hotel Thayer** is on campus (914-446-4731) overlooking the majestic Hudson River. Rates are moderate. Within a couple of miles of West Point are the **U.S. Academy Motel** (Rte. 218, Highland Falls; 914-446-2021) and the **Best Western Palisades Motel** (Rtes. 218 and 94, Highland Falls; 914-446-9400). Both are inexpensive. By far the most interesting choice is **Bear Mountain Inn** (Bear Mountain State Park, Bear Mountain; 914-786-2731), a 1920 lodge with a lovely view of the Hudson, an outdoor pool, a gift shop, a restaurant, and hiking trails. Rates are moderate on the weekend and at the top of the inexpensive range during the week.

A little farther: Cold Spring is 20 miles from West Point. **Pig Hill Bed and Breakfast** (73 Main St.; 914-265-9247) houses 8 rooms in its 1850s brick building. Some have fireplaces and four-poster and canopy beds. Rates vary from moderate to expensive and include a full breakfast. See the Vassar College entry for another suggestion in Cold Spring and for suggestions in Poughkeepsie, about 30 miles from West Point.

AT A GLANCE

Selectivity Rating	99
Range SAT I Math	590-680
Average SAT I Math	643
Range SAT I Verbal	570-670
Average SAT I Verbal	623
Average ACT Composite	28
Average GPA	3.7
Student to Faculty Ratio	7:1

CAMPUS TOURS

Appointment Req?	Yes, 3 weeks prior
Dates	Last week of Aug to first week of May, except holidays, exams, and training periods
Times	Mon-Fri beginning 9AM
Avg. Length	4.5 hours

ON-CAMPUS INTERVIEWS

Admissions

Start Date–Juniors	Spring
Appointment Req?	Yes
Advance Notice	3 weeks
Saturdays?	Yes, generally
Avg. Length	30 min
Info Sessions	Available as part of tour

Faculty and Coaches

Dates/Times	Year-round; subject to faculty/coach availability
Arrangements	Contact admissions off. 3 weeks prior

CLASS VISITS

Dates	Year-round (Mon-Fri)
Arrangements	Contact admissions off.

OVERNIGHT DORM STAYS

Advance Notice	4 weeks
Arrangements	Contact admissions off.
Limitations	Only admissible candidates; approval must be granted by admissions officer

UNIVERSITY AT BUFFALO (SUNY)

Office of Admissions, SUNY-Buffalo, 17 Capen Hall, Box 601660,
Buffalo, NY 14260 • Telephone: 716-645-6900 • Web: www.buffalo.edu •
Email: ub-admissions@admissions.buffalo.edu

Hours: Monday-Friday, 9AM-5PM. Closed Jan. 1, Martin Luther King Day, July 4, Thanksgiving, and Christmas week.

University at Buffalo, as this SUNY school is calling itself these days, offers a great education in an abundance of fields. Engineering, business, and pre-med are the major draws, but other disciplines (especially communications and the liberal arts and sciences) also offer competitive programs, and the library, research, and recreational facilities are all very impressive.

AT A GLANCE

Selectivity Rating		81
Range SAT I Math		510-620
Average SAT I Math		564
Range SAT I Verbal		490-600
Average SAT I Verbal		543
Average ACT Composite		24
Average GPA		3.1
Student to Faculty Ratio		13:1

CAMPUS TOURS

Appointment Req?	Yes, 2 weeks prior; available as part of "Visit UB" Program
Dates	Late Sept-early Dec and early Feb-late April
Times	Mon-Fri 1PM; selected Saturdays; call for summer hours
Avg. Length	2.5 hours

ON-CAMPUS INTERVIEWS

Admissions

Start Date—Juniors	Any time
Appointment Req?	Yes
Advance Notice	2 weeks
Saturdays?	No
Avg. Length	45 min
Info Sessions	Available as part of "Visit UB" Program

Faculty and Coaches

Dates/Times	Year-round; subject to faculty/coach availability
Arrangements	Contact dept. of interest 2 weeks prior

CLASS VISITS

Arrangements	Consult list of classes in admissions office

OVERNIGHT DORM STAYS

Advance Notice	N/A
Arrangements	N/A
Limitations	N/A

TRANSPORTATION

Greater Buffalo International Airport is 20 minutes from campus. Taxis and buses are available for the trip from airport to campus. The taxis can be picked up at the airport; for bus departure times and routes call 800-231-2222. Amtrak trains and Greyhound buses provide service to Buffalo.

FIND YOUR WAY

To reach North Campus from the New York State Thruway (I-90), take Exit 50 to I-290 (Youngmann Memorial Hwy.). Take I-290 west to Exit 4 (I-990 North) and follow signs for State University (exit 1). Exit 1 will bring you to the Audubon Pkwy. Make the first U-turn (just before the traffic light), then get into the right lane. Turn right at the first exit (White Rd.). The Fronczak Lot (long-term parking, accessed through the Governors A Lot) and Hamilton Loop (short-term parking) will be on your right. The South Campus is located at the corner of State Routes 5 (Main St.) and 62 (Bailey Ave.). From the New York State Thruway (I-90), take Exit 50 to I-290, then Rte. 5 west, to Rte. 62. Available online at Web: www.buffalo.edu.

STAY THE NIGHT

University at Buffalo has 2 campuses: North and South. The admissions office and the majority of undergraduate academic departments are on the North Campus. The South Campus houses the School of Architecture and Planning, the School of Health Related Professions, and the School of Medicine and Biomedical Sciences. Because Buffalo is the second largest city in the state, there are many nationally affiliated hotels and motels in the metropolitan area, including more than 20 close to the University. Those nearest include **Marriot, Hampton Inn, Motel 6, Red Roof Inn, Residence Inn, Super 8 Motel, University Inn and Conference Center, Extended Stay America, Holiday Inn, Microtel, Sleep Inn**, and **Courtyard**. Airport-area hotels include **Comfort Suites, Days Inn, Fairfield Inn, Holiday Inn, Quality Inn, Radisson Hotel**, and **Sheraton Inn**. Popular downtown hotels are **Adam's Mark, Hyatt Regency**, and **Radisson**. To obtain a special UB discount on selected hotels, call NFT Travel at 800-633-6782 and mention the code: UB LOOK. Area maps and a list of accommodations and restaurants are available on our website: www.buffalo.edu.

HIGHLIGHTS

ON CAMPUS
- Center for the Arts
- Alumni Arena and Athletic Stadium
- Center for Computational Research
- Apartment-style student housing (new)
- The Commons (on-campus shopping)

OFF CAMPUS
- Major league sports
- Shea's Theater
- Albright-Knox Art Gallery
- Niagara Falls

UNIVERSITY OF ROCHESTER

Admissions Office, University of Rochester, Rochester, NY 14627-0251 •
Telephone: 716-275-3221 or 888-822-2256 • Web: www.rochester.edu •
Email: admit@admissions.rochester.edu

Hours: Monday-Friday, 9AM-4PM. Closed weekends and major holidays.

The University of Rochester has traditionally been known best for math and science but the school has enough diversity in its academic offerings today to change that reputation. A five-year program is available for students who find themselves unable to fit enough courses of interest into a four-year schedule.

HIGHLIGHTS

ON CAMPUS
- Eastman Theater
- Memorial Art Gallery
- Rush Rhees Library
- Interfaith Chapel
- Robert B. Goergen Athletic Center

OFF CAMPUS
- Niagara Falls
- Museum of Photography and Film
- Rochester Museum and Science Center
- Susan B. Anthony House
- Park Avenue neighborhood

TRANSPORTATION

Greater Rochester International Airport is 2 miles from campus. Taxis are available at the airport for the drive to campus. Amtrak trains and Greyhound buses serve Rochester; their stations are close to municipal bus lines that serve the university's River Campus.

FIND YOUR WAY

From the east, take I-90 to Exit 46; then take I-390 N. to Exit 17. Turn left onto Scottsville Rd., bear right onto Elmwood Ave. and cross the Genesee River bridge. Turn left onto Wilson Blvd. and proceed to the information booth for parking instructions and directions. From the south, take I-390 N. to Exit 17 and proceed as above. From the west, take the I-90 to Exit 47, then take I-490 E. to I-390 S. Leave I-390 at Exit 17 and proceed as above.

STAY THE NIGHT

One mile away is a cheerful, turn-of-the-century bed-and-breakfast that's popular with university visitors: **428 Mount Vernon** (716-271-0792). It's on the edge of Highland Park, and if you're in good shape, it's a beautiful hike to the admissions office. Other lodgings include: **Hampton Inn** (717 E. Henrietta Rd.; 716-272-7800 or 800-HAMPTON); **Days Inn** (4853 W. Henrietta Rd.; 716-334-9300 or 800-329-7466); **Courtyard by Marriott** (33 Corporate Woods; 716-292-1000); **Hyatt Regency Rochester** (125 E. Main St.; 716-546-1234 or 800-233-1234); and the **Marriott Thruway** (5257 W. Henrietta Rd.; 716-359-1800). All are within 15 minutes of campus.

AT A GLANCE

Selectivity Rating	88
Range SAT I Math	630-710
Average SAT I Math	670
Range SAT I Verbal	600-700
Average SAT I Verbal	650
Average ACT Composite	30
Average GPA	3.6
Student to Faculty Ratio	12:1

CAMPUS TOURS

Appointment Req?	Yes
Dates	Year-round
Times	Mon-Fri; call admissions for times
Avg. Length	1 hour

ON-CAMPUS INTERVIEWS

Faculty and Coaches

Dates/Times	Year-round; subject to faculty/coach availability
Arrangements	Contact admissions off. 2 weeks prior

CLASS VISITS

Dates	Academic year (Mon-Fri)
Arrangements	Contact admissions off.

OVERNIGHT DORM STAYS

Advance Notice	2 weeks
Arrangements	Contact admissions off.
Limitations	1-night maximum stay; Mon-Thurs; fall semester

VASSAR COLLEGE

Admissions Office, Vassar College, 124 Raymond Ave., Poughkeepsie, NY 12604
(The office is in the Kautz Admission House, behind the Main Building) • Telephone: 845-437-7300 •
Web: www.vassar.edu • Email: admissions@vassar.edu

Hours: Monday-Friday, 8:30AM-5PM.

There are no core requirements at Vassar College, a small liberal arts school not terribly far from New York City, and a first-year student's course work can range from ancient Chinese philosophy to an English class on the literature of the Internet. Over four years, Vassar students design their own majors and pursue interdisciplinary studies. Actress Meryl Streep is an alum.

AT A GLANCE

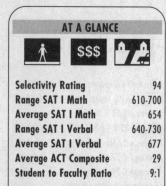

Selectivity Rating	94
Range SAT I Math	610-700
Average SAT I Math	654
Range SAT I Verbal	640-730
Average SAT I Verbal	677
Average ACT Composite	29
Student to Faculty Ratio	9:1

CAMPUS TOURS

Appointment Req?	No
Dates	Year-round
Times	Mon-Fri 11:30AM and 2PM; 9AM in summer and fall
Avg. Length	1 hour

ON-CAMPUS INTERVIEWS

Admissions

Appointment Req?	All interviews are done with local alumni representatives off campus
Info Sessions	1PM and 10AM in summer and fall

Faculty and Coaches

Dates/Times	Academic year; subject to faculty/coach availability
Arrangements	Contact dept. of interest as early as possible

CLASS VISITS

Dates	Academic year (Mon-Fri)
Arrangements	Contact admissions off.

OVERNIGHT DORM STAYS

Advance Notice	2-3 weeks
Arrangements	Contact admissions off.
Limitations	Available in the spring only

TRANSPORTATION

Stewart Airport in Newburgh is 20 miles from campus. Taxis are available for the trip from the airport to campus.

FIND YOUR WAY

From the New York State Thruway, use Exit 17 (Newburgh) and take I-84 eastbound across the Newburgh-Beacon Bridge to Route 9 north. Follow directions below.

From Route 9 northbound, drive 9.5 miles north of the intersection of I-84 and Route 9, to exit for Spackenhill Road (Route 113). The IBM main facility is on the left. Proceed about half a mile on Spackenhill Road. Turn left at the second traffic light onto Wilbur Boulevard. Turn right when Wilbur ends at Hooker Avenue. Turn left at the first traffic light onto Raymond Avenue. Enter the college through the stone archway on the right. **From Route 9 southbound**, exit at Spackenhill Road (Route 113) and follow directions above.

STAY THE NIGHT

Nearby: **Inn at the Falls** (50 Red Oaks Mill Rd.; 845-462-5770), a luxurious country place beautifully situated on the river, is about 10 minutes away. A simple motel, **Best Inn** (62 Haight Ave.; 845-454-1010), is 2 blocks away from the college. Rates are inexpensive. There is a **Sheraton Hotel** (40 Civic Center Plaza; 845-485-5300) less than a 15 minutes away, with a special rate in the moderate range for college visitors. The hotel has a well-equipped exercise room and steam room, as well as comedy club entertainment.

A little farther: Why not visit the quaint, historic town of Cold Spring? **Hudson House** (845-265-9355), the second oldest inn in New York State, is right on the river, which you can see from some of the rooms. Rates, which include a continental breakfast, vary from moderate to expensive. See the U.S. Military Academy entry for another Cold Spring suggestion.

HIGHLIGHTS

ON CAMPUS
- Library
- Shakespeare Garden
- Observatory
- Frances Lehman Loeb Art Center

OFF CAMPUS
- Franklin Roosevelt House and Museum
- Eleanor Roosevelt House
- Vanderbilt Mansion
- Rhinebeck
- Mills Mansion

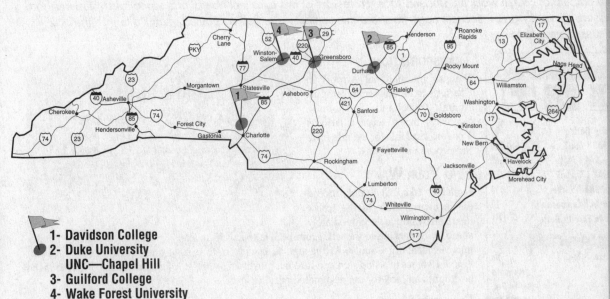

1- Davidson College
2- Duke University
   UNC—Chapel Hill
3- Guilford College
4- Wake Forest University

North Carolina	Davidson Coll.	Duke Univ.	Guilford Coll.	UNC-Chapel Hill	Wake Forest Univ.	Charlotte	Raleigh
Davidson Coll.	—	135	80	129	62	18	144
Duke Univ.	135	—	58	13	84	144	20
Guilford Coll.	80	58	—	54	25	99	74
UNC-Chapel Hill	129	13	54	—	78	142	28
Wake Forest Univ.	62	84	25	78	—	80	104
Charlotte	18	144	99	142	80	—	169
Raleigh	144	20	74	28	104	169	—

DAVIDSON COLLEGE

Admissions Office, Davidson College P.O. Box 1737, Davidson, NC 28036
(The office is in Grey House, 405 N. Main St.) • Telephone: 704-892-2230 or 800-768-0380 •
Web: www.davidson.edu • Email: admissions@davidson.edu

Hours: Monday-Friday, 8:30AM-5PM; Saturday, 8:30AM-noon (only selected Saturdays in the fall and spring).

According to students on Davidson's beautiful, wooded campus, almost every conversation touches on the massive amount of course work the students face. Professors at this excellent liberal arts school push students hard but they are generally great teachers eager to share their enthusiasm. Self-scheduled exams diminish the academic stress somewhat.

AT A GLANCE

Selectivity Rating	97
Range SAT I Math	610-700
Average SAT I Math	662
Range SAT I Verbal	610-710
Average SAT I Verbal	658
Average ACT Composite	29
Student to Faculty Ratio	11:1

CAMPUS TOURS

Appointment Req?	No
Dates	Year-round
Times	Mon-Fri 9AM, 10AM, 1PM, and 2PM
Avg. Length	1 hour

ON-CAMPUS INTERVIEWS

Admissions

Start Date–Juniors	Any time except Wed
Appointment Req?	Yes
Advance Notice	1-2 weeks
Saturdays?	Select Saturdays in fall and spring
Avg. Length	30 min
Info Sessions	Year-round

Faculty and Coaches

Dates/Times	Year-round; subject to faculty/coach availability
Arrangements	Contact coaches/ faculty directly

CLASS VISITS

Dates	Academic year (Mon-Fri)
Arrangements	Contact admissions off.

OVERNIGHT DORM STAYS

Advance Notice	2 weeks
Arrangements	Notify receptionist when making appointment to visit
Limitations	Not available during the summer, breaks, or exam periods; 1 night only; Mon-Thurs; seniors only

TRANSPORTATION

Douglas International Airport in Charlotte is 25 miles from campus. Amtrak trains and Greyhound/Trailways buses serve Charlotte. Taxis are available for the ride from the airport and stations.

FIND YOUR WAY

From I-77, take Exit 30 and proceed east a quarter mile to the traffic light. The campus is immediately ahead, with parking to the left. From I-85, take Exit 55 to Rte. 73 W. Proceed west for 8 miles into Mecklenburg County. At the sign to Davidson, turn right onto Davidson-Concord Rd. Proceed 3 miles to a stop sign and turn left into town. At the stoplight, turn right. Proceed to the next light and look for the designated parking area.

STAY THE NIGHT

Nearby: Your best bet is **Davidson College Guesthouse** (704-892-2127), an on-campus establishment that offers 8 rooms and continental breakfast at an inexpensive rate. You can use the college's sports facilities and dine on campus at the Vail Commons and Union Café. In Davidson, **The Village Inn** (704-892-8044) is a small inn that serves breakfast and afternoon tea. In Cornelius, the **Best Western** (704-896-0660) has continental breakfast, an outdoor pool, and a fitness room. Four basic choices within a 5-minute drive are the **Comfort Inn** (20740 Torrance Chapel Rd.; 704-892-3500) where the inexpensive rate (special for college visitors) includes breakfast. Some rooms even have jacuzzis, and there's a fully equipped Nautilus club across the street. **Hampton Inn** (19501 Statesville Rd.; 704-892-9900, offers a complimentary continental breakfast. **Holiday Inn** (19901 Holiday Lane, Cornelius; 704-892-9120) has an outdoor pool, jacuzzis in some of the rooms, and a Nautilus center nearby.

A little farther: There's a charming bed-and-breakfast in Charlotte: the **Home Place** (5901 Sardis Rd.; 704-365-1936), a restored Victorian with a big porch and 3 guest rooms.

DUKE UNIVERSITY

Office of Undergraduate Admissions, Duke University, 2138 Campus Dr., Box 90588, Durham, NC 27706 (The office is just off the traffic circle on Campus Dr.) • Telephone: 919-684-3214 • Web: www.duke.edu • Email: undergrad-admissions@duke.edu

Hours: Monday-Friday, 8AM-5PM; Saturday, 9AM-1PM. Closed Sundays and major holidays.

The students at prestigious and extremely competitive Duke University don't much like the way the administration is trying to emulate certain Ivies, because they wouldn't want to go to college anywhere else. Duke students continue to find release in the amazing academics and their first love, Blue Devils basketball.

HIGHLIGHTS

ON CAMPUS
- Duke Chapel
- Primate Center
- Sarah P. Duke Gardens
- Duke Forest
- Levine Science Research Center

OFF CAMPUS
- Duke Homestead
- N.C. Museum of Life and Science
- Ninth Street
- Durham Bulls Athletic Park

FIND YOUR WAY

From I-40 (from Raleigh and the airport), bear right onto Durham Freeway north (NC Rte. 147); continue into Durham and exit at Swift Ave./Duke University-East Campus. Turn left at the top of the ramp; turn right at the flashing light (Campus Dr.). Proceed for 1 mile to the admissions office; the driveway is to the right as you approach the traffic circle. **From I-85 S.**, take the exit to the left for 15-501 S. Bypass-Duke University/Chapel Hill; proceed for 2 miles and exit at the sign for NC 751/Duke University. Turn left on Rte. 751 and go 1 mile to the 4th stoplight; turn left onto Duke University Rd. and continue for 1 mile. Turn left onto Chapel Dr. at the stone pillars. At the circle, turn right onto Campus Dr.; the admissions office is the first building on the left. **From I-85 N.**, exit onto Rte. 70 E. at the sign to NC 751/Duke University. Proceed on Rte. 70 for 2 miles to the intersection with Rte. 751; turn right onto Rte. 751 for approximately 4.5 Turn left at the fifth stoplight (Duke University Rd.) and proceed for 1 mile; turn left onto Chapel Dr. at the stone pillars. At the circle, turn right onto Campus Dr.; the admissions office is the first building on the left.

STAY THE NIGHT

Nearby: The **Brownestone Inn** (2424 Erwin Rd.; 919-286-7761 or 800-367-0293) is almost on campus. The moderate price includes a continental breakfast, and there's an indoor pool and whirlpool. The **Durham Hilton** (3800 Hillsborough Rd.; 919-383-8033) is a 5-minute drive from campus. The inexpensive **Brookwood Inn** (2306 Elba St.; 919-286-3111) is across the street from the university hospital. It has a shuttle to campus, and offers a special rate for college visitors. The **Washington Duke Inn and Golf Club** (3001 Cameron Blvd.; 919-490-0999 or 800-443-3853) is convenient to campus. The inn has a golf course, with tennis and swimming facilities nearby. A complimentary shuttle service is available within the city of Durham.

A little farther: About 8 miles from the university is the delightful and hospitable **Arrowhead Inn** (106 Mason Rd., Durham; 919-477-8430). The price includes a full breakfast, refreshments in the afternoon, spa, whirlpools, and computer ports in all rooms. Chapel Hill is not far to the southwest. Check accommodations in the University of North Carolina entry.

TRANSPORTATION

The Raleigh-Durham International Airport is 18 miles from campus. Limousines, taxis, and rental cars are available at the airport. Amtrak trains serve Raleigh and Durham. You must make your own arrangements for transportation from there to campus. Greyhound bus service is available to Durham, approximately 3 miles from campus. Taxis are available at the station.

AT A GLANCE

Selectivity Rating	98
Range SAT I Math	660-760
Range SAT I Verbal	640-730
Average ACT Composite	30
Student to Faculty Ratio	11:1

CAMPUS TOURS

Appointment Req?	No
Dates	Year-round
Times	Jun-Aug: Mon-Fri 9AM, 11AM, and 3PM; Sat 11AM. Sept-Oct: Mon-Fri 11AM and 3PM; Sat 11AM. Nov-Feb: Mon-Sat 11AM. Mar-April: Mon-Fri 11AM and 3PM; Sat 11AM. May: Mon-Sat 11AM
Avg. Length	1 hour

ON-CAMPUS INTERVIEWS

Admissions

Start Date–Juniors	June 1
Appointment Req?	Yes
Advance Notice	4-6 weeks
Saturdays?	No
Avg. Length	20-30 min
Sessions	Year-round

Faculty and Coaches

Dates/Times	Year-round; subject to faculty/coach availability
Arrangements	Contact dept. of interest or particular coach 2 weeks prior

CLASS VISITS

Dates	Academic year (Mon-Fri)
Arrangements	Consult list of classes in admissions off.

OVERNIGHT DORM STAYS

Advance Notice	3 weeks
Arrangements	Contact Student Housing Off. at 919-684-3214
Limitations	1-night stay; high school seniors

GUILFORD COLLEGE

Admissions Office, Guilford College, 5800 W. Friendly Ave., Greensboro, NC 27410
(The office is in New Garden Hall) • Telephone: 800-992-7759 •
Web: www.guilford.edu • Email: admission@guilford.edu

Hours: Monday-Friday, 8:30AM-5PM (year-round); Saturday, 8:30AM-12PM (Sept-April only). Closed Sundays and holidays.

Guilford College is an intimate, Quaker-affiliated liberal arts college where students have a real say and responsibility in the running of the school. Professors and the administration receive high marks.

AT A GLANCE

Selectivity Rating	73
Range SAT I Math	510-620
Average SAT I Math	550
Range SAT I Verbal	530-660
Average SAT I Verbal	580
Average ACT Composite	23
Average GPA	3.2
Student to Faculty Ratio	15:1

CAMPUS TOURS

Appointment Req?	Preferred
Dates	Year-round
Times	Call for times
Avg. Length	1 hour

ON-CAMPUS INTERVIEWS

Admissions

Start Date—Rising Juniors	June 1
Appointment Req?	Yes
Advance Notice	1-3 weeks
Saturdays?	Yes
Avg. Length	1 hour
Info Sessions	45 min

Faculty and Coaches

Dates/Times	Year-round; subject to faculty/coach availability
Arrangements	Contact admissions off. 1 week prior

CLASS VISITS

Dates	Sept-April (Mon-Fri)
Arrangements	Contact admissions off.

OVERNIGHT DORM STAYS

Advance Notice	2 weeks
Arrangements	Contuct admissions off.
Limitations	High school seniors only; Mon-Thurs nights preferred; should arrive before 5PM on the first day of visit

TRANSPORTATION

The Triad Piedmont International Airport in Greensboro is 5 miles from campus. The admissions office will provide transportation from airport to campus if you call 1 week in advance to give them arrival time and flight information. Taxis are available at the airport if you prefer.

FIND YOUR WAY

From I-40 or I-85, exit to Holden Road N. Follow Holden Rd. to Friendly Ave., and turn left (west) to the college.

STAY THE NIGHT

It's difficult to get excited about the options very close to the college. For an inexpensive stay about 5 minutes away, try the **Innkeeper** (336-854-0090), and for a moderately priced place about 2 miles away, try the **Greensboro Courtyard by Marriott** (4400 W. Wendover Ave.; 336-294-3800). If you want to treat yourselves, however, you won't want to miss the newly opened **O. Henry Hotel**, about 10 minutes east of Guilford, near the Friendly Shopping Center. The rooms are luxuriously appointed and the service is impeccable. Be sure to ask for their "Guilford College" rate, which includes a wonderful breakfast buffet.

HIGHLIGHTS

ON CAMPUS
- The Art Gallery
- Hege Library

OFF CAMPUS
- Greensboro Historical Museum
- Emerald Pointe (water park)
- Dockside Park (theme park)

UNIVERSITY OF NORTH CAROLINA—CHAPEL HILL

Undergraduate Admissions, UNC–Chapel Hill, Jackson Hall, CB2200, Chapel Hill, NC 27599 • Telephone: 919-966-3621 • Web: www.unc.edu • Email: uadm@email.unc.edu

Hours: Monday-Friday, 8AM-5PM. Closed weekends and holidays.

With first-rate academic offerings that include great programs in business and journalism, the University of North Carolina is one of the nation's top state universities.

HIGHLIGHTS

ON CAMPUS
- Morehead Planetarium
- Coker Arboretum
- Morehead-Patterson Bell Tower
- Ackland Art Museum
- Dean Smith Center

OFF CAMPUS
- Franklin Street
- North Carolina Botanical Gardens
- Chapel Hill Museum
- Fearrington Village

TRANSPORTATION

The Raleigh-Durham International Airport is approximately 20 miles from campus. Taxis and limousines are available for the drive from airport to campus.

FIND YOUR WAY

From the east, take I-40 W. to Chapel Hill; then follow signs to campus. **From the north**, take the Rte. 15/501 S. bypass to Chapel Hill; then follow signs to campus. **From the west**, take I-85 N., then I-40 E. to Chapel Hill, then follow signs to campus. **From the south**, take Rte. 15/501 N. to Chapel Hill, then follow signs to campus.

STAY THE NIGHT

Nearby: The university has a colonial-style inn right on campus, the **Carolina Inn** (211 Pittsboro St.; 919-933-2001 or 800-962-8519). Less than a mile away is the **Best Western University Inn** (Raleigh Rd.; 919-942-4132). No surprises here, nor are there any at the **Hampton Inn** (1740 U.S. Rte. 15; 919-968-3000), 3 miles away. Its inexpensive rate includes continental breakfast. The **Omni Europa Hotel** (Europa Dr.; 919-968-4900) is a moderately priced, full-service hotel with an outdoor pool, tennis court, and nightclub, about 4 miles from the university.

A little farther: **Fearrington House** (919-542-2121), technically in Pittsboro, 8 miles south of Chapel Hill, has a charming courtyard, gardens, and a wonderful restaurant. Double rooms are expensive. Ten miles from the university is the **Inn at Bingham School** (NC Rte. 54 at Mebane Oaks Rd.; 919-563-5583), a restored headmaster's home listed on the National Register of Historic Places. This 6-bedroom inn offers rooms with a delicious southern breakfast at a moderate rate. Also check the suggestions in the entry for Duke University, not too far to the northeast.

AT A GLANCE

Selectivity Rating	90
Range SAT I Math	560-670
Average SAT I Math	630
Range SAT I Verbal	550-680
Average SAT I Verbal	620
Average GPA	4.1

CAMPUS TOURS

Appointment Req?	Preferred
Dates	When University is open
Times	Mon-Fri 10AM and 2PM
Avg. Length	1 hour

ON-CAMPUS INTERVIEWS

Admissions

Start Date–Juniors	N/A
Appointment Req?	N/A
Advance Notice	N/A
Saturdays?	N/A
Avg. Length	N/A
Info Sessions	Mon-Fri 11AM and 3PM

Faculty and Coaches

Dates/Times	Year-round; subject to faculty/coach availability
Arrangements	Contact faculty or coaches 1 week prior to visit

CLASS VISITS

Dates	Academic year (Mon-Fri)
Arrangements	Contact admissions off. 1 week prior

OVERNIGHT DORM STAYS

Advance Notice	N/A
Arrangements	N/A
Limitations	N/A

WAKE FOREST UNIVERSITY

Admissions Office, Wake Forest University, P.O. Box 7305, Winston-Salem, NC 27109
(The office is on the main drive at the Reynolda Rd. entrance) • Telephone: 336-758-5201 •
Web: www.wfu.edu • Email: admissions@wfu.edu

Hours: Monday-Friday, 8:30AM-5PM; Saturday mornings in spring and fall. Closed Sundays and holidays.

At Wake Forest University, a solid, broad-based core curriculum obligates all students to pursue a well-rounded academic program. There is tough grading and a savage workload, but social life here is reportedly excellent and the campus is gorgeous.

AT A GLANCE

Selectivity Rating	94
Range SAT I Math	610-700
Range SAT I Verbal	600-690
Student to Faculty Ratio	11:1

CAMPUS TOURS

Appointment Req?	No
Dates	When classes are in session
Times	Mon-Fri at 10AM and 3PM; call for Sat times
Avg. Length	1 hour

ON-CAMPUS INTERVIEWS

Admissions

Start Date–Juniors	During the summer
Appointment Req?	Yes
Advance Notice	Yes
Saturdays?	No
Avg. Length	30 min
Info Sessions	Year-round

Faculty and Coaches

Dates/Times	Year-round; subject to faculty/coach availability
Arrangements	Contact dept. of interest

CLASS VISITS

Dates	Year-round (Mon-Fri)
Arrangements	Obtain professor's approval prior to class

OVERNIGHT DORM STAYS

Advance Notice	2 weeks
Arrangements	Call 336-758-5239
Limitations	Available only Mon-Thurs nights

TRANSPORTATION

Piedmont Triad International Airport in Greensboro is 26 miles from campus. Call Airport Express Limousine (336-668-0164) for service to campus. The limousine leaves the baggage claim area every hour on the hour until midnight. Blue Bird Cab (336-722-7121) also provides transportation to campus. Right in Winston-Salem, 5 minutes from campus, is the Smith Reynolds Airport, a small commuter airport.

FIND YOUR WAY

From I-40 E., take the Wake Forest University/Silas Creek Pkwy. exit; proceed north on the Pkwy., which will bring you to the Reynolda Rd. entrance to the university. **From I-40 W.**, take the Cherry St. exit, which will bring you to University Pkwy. Take the Pkwy. to the university entrance. **From U.S. Rte. 52 S.**, exit to University Pkwy. and follow the Pkwy. to the university entrance. **From U.S. Rte. 52 N.**, exit to I-40 W. and follow preceding directions from there.

STAY THE NIGHT

Nearby: A very popular place to stay is the university-owned **Graylyn Inn Conference Center** (1900 Reynolda Rd.; 336-758-2600), within a mile of Wake Forest. Ask for the special rate for university visitors and advise them in advance if you would like to have meals provided. Two inexpensive choices are close to campus. The **Courtyard by Marriott** (3111 University Pl.; 336-727-1277) is 2 miles away. The other, priced slightly higher, is the **Ramada Inn** (3050 University Pkwy.; 336-723-2911), about 6 blocks away. They both offer a fitness room and pool. **Brooks Town Inn** (200 Brooks Town Ave.; 336-725-1120), 10 minutes from campus, is a restoration of an 1837 cotton mill listed on the National Register of Historic Places. The moderate price includes continental breakfast and wine and cheese in the afternoon. For a little more glitz try the **Adam's Mark Winston Plaza** (425 N. Cherry St.; 336-725-3500), a fairly expensive hotel with an indoor pool and full fitness center.

A little farther: Four or five miles south of the university, close to Old Salem (a restored 1700s Moravian village), is the **Colonel Ludlow House** (Summit and W. 5th St.; 336-777-1887). Its rates, which include breakfast, rAt a Glance

HIGHLIGHTS

ON CAMPUS
- Wake Forest Art Gallery
- Museum of Anthropology
- The Z. Smith Reynolds Library
- Wait Chapel
- The Demon Deacons Field

OFF CAMPUS
- Reynolda House
- Tanglewood Park (golf)
- Old Salem

1- Antioch College
2- Case Western Reserve University
3- Denison University
4- Hiram College
5- Kenyon College
6- Miami University (Ohio)
7- Oberlin College
8- Ohio University
9- Ohio State University
10- Ohio Wesleyan University
11- Wittenburg University
12- College of Wooster

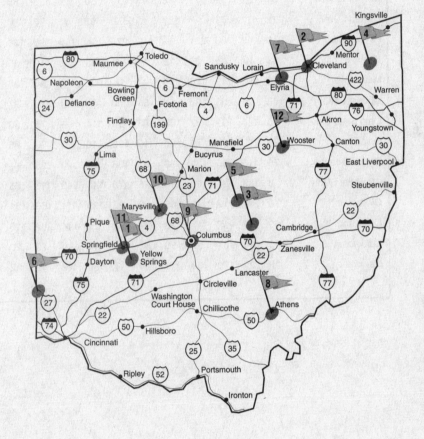

Ohio

	Antioch Coll.	Case Western	Coll. of Wooster	Denison Univ.	Hiram Coll.	Kenyon Coll.	Miami Univ.	Oberlin Coll.	Ohio State Univ.	Ohio Univ.	Ohio Wesleyan	Wittenberg Univ.	Cincinnatti	Cleveland	Columbus	Dayton
Antioch Coll.	—	190	151	78	216	103	65	162	50	125	75	9	70	190	50	20
Case Western	190	—	52	117	42	97	262	25	144	202	115	183	249	0	144	209
Coll. of Wooster	151	52	—	71	63	45	219	50	101	138	85	135	212	52	101	173
Denison Univ.	78	117	71	—	131	25	150	97	32	70	34	80	143	117	27	104
Hiram Coll.	216	42	63	131	—	112	275	58	156	195	138	196	265	35	156	228
Kenyon Coll.	103	97	45	25	112	—	171	85	52	110	35	95	163	97	52	124
Miami Univ.	65	262	219	150	275	171	—	232	118	190	138	75	33	262	118	47
Oberlin Coll.	162	25	50	97	58	85	232	—	114	216	97	145	225	26	114	186
Ohio State Univ.	50	144	101	32	156	52	118	114	—	75	20	40	111	144	0	72
Ohio Univ.	125	202	138	70	195	110	190	216	75	—	95	115	160	202	75	143
Ohio Wesleyan	75	115	85	34	138	35	138	97	20	95	—	55	131	115	20	92
Wittenberg Univ.	9	183	135	80	196	95	75	145	40	115	55	—	73	183	40	25
Cincinnatti	70	249	212	143	265	163	33	225	111	160	131	73	—	255	110	56
Cleveland	190	0	52	117	35	97	262	26	144	202	115	183	255	—	147	209
Columbus	50	144	101	27	156	52	118	114	0	75	20	40	110	147	—	72
Dayton	20	209	173	104	228	124	47	186	72	143	92	25	56	209	72	—

ANTIOCH COLLEGE

Office of Admissions and Financial Aid, 795 Livermore St., Yellow Springs, OH 45387 (The office is located in Weston Hall on President's St.) • Telephone: 800-543-9436 or 937-767-6400 (Fax: 937-754-5377) • Web: www.antioch-college.edu • Email: admissions@antioch-college.edu

Hours: Monday-Friday, 9AM-5PM. Open weekends by appointment, and closed major holidays.

The Antioch College Environmental Field Program is a major attraction of this ultra-liberal and progressive liberal arts school in southern Ohio. A somewhat notorious policy requires students to obtain verbal consent for each specific act of any sexual encounter they have with each other.

HIGHLIGHTS

ON CAMPUS
- Herndon Gallery
- Glen Hellen Nature Preserve
- Japanese Tea Garden
- Community bike shop
- Alternative Library

OFF CAMPUS
- Little Art Movie Theater
- Clifton Gorge
- Scenic trail bike path
- National Afro-American Museum and Cultural Center

TRANSPORTATION

The nearest airport to campus is in Dayton, 30 miles away, followed by airports in Columbus (72 miles) and Cincinnati (84 miles). The Dayton bus station is 25 miles away. The Admissions Office will arrange for student shuttles (cost varies by distance) between the airport or bus station and campus. Rental cars and taxis are also available at all airports.

FIND YOUR WAY

From I-70, take Exit 52 to U.S. Rte. 68 S. and follow it approximately 6 miles through Yellow Springs. Turn left at the 2nd stop light on E. Limestone St. Turn right on President St. and park at the dead end. **From the 675 bypass,** take Dayton-Yellow Springs Rd. (Exit 20) and turn right (east). Go about 6 miles. Turn right at traffic light on S. Walnut St., then turn left on Limestone St. After crossing Xenia Ave. turn right on President St. and park at the dead end. The Office of Admissions and Financial Aid is located in Weston Hall next to the Student Union.

STAY THE NIGHT

Morgan House (120 W. Limestone St.; 937-767-7509), a bed and breakfast in Yellow Springs, is a comfortable home within walking distance of campus and the downtown area. It has a limited number of rooms, shared bathrooms, a pay phone, and lots of local charm. Fairborn, about 12 miles west, has a number of hotels and motels off the 675 bypass across from Wright State University. They include **Holiday Inn** (800-HOLIDAY), **Homewood Suites** (937-429-0600), **Red Roof Inn** (800-843-7663), and **Hampton Inn** (800-HAMPTON). The **Springfield Inn** (800-234-3611) is located approximately 12 miles northeast in Springfield.

AT A GLANCE

Range SAT I Math	480-570
Average SAT I Math	495
Average SAT I Verbal	509
Average ACT Composite	24
Average GPA	3.0
Student to Faculty Ratio	11:1

CAMPUS TOURS

Appointment Req?	Yes
Dates	Year-round, except holidays
Times	Mon-Fri 10:30AM and 1PM, but other times are possible
Avg. Length	1 hour

ON-CAMPUS INTERVIEWS

Admissions

Start Date–Juniors	Any time
Appointment Req?	Yes
Advance Notice	1 week prior
Saturdays?	By appt.
Avg. Length	1 hour
Info Sessions	Mon-Fri 10AM and 11:30AM

Faculty and Coaches

Dates/Times	Year-round; subject to faculty availability
Arrangements	Contact admissions off. 1 week prior

CLASS VISITS

Dates	Year-round (Mon-Fri)
Arrangements	Obtain class schedule in admissions off.

OVERNIGHT DORM STAYS

Advance Notice	2 days
Arrangements	Contact On-Campus Coordinator
Limitations	2-night maximum stay

CASE WESTERN RESERVE UNIVERSITY

Admissions Office, Case Western Reserve University, 10900 Euclid Ave., Cleveland, OH 44106-7055 • Telephone: 216-368-4450 • Web: www.cwru.edu • Email: admission@po.cwru.edu

Hours: September-May: Monday-Friday, 8:30AM-5PM; select Saturdays. June-August: Monday-Friday, 8:30AM-5PM. Closed Sundays and national holidays.

Small classes, world-class facilities, and great professors are what you'll find at this school in Cleveland. While Case Western is widely known for churning out top-flight engineers, the students report that the liberal arts programs are excellent as well.

AT A GLANCE

Selectivity Rating	84
Range SAT I Math	630-730
Range SAT I Verbal	590-710
Student to Faculty Ratio	8:1

CAMPUS TOURS

Appointment Req?	Yes
Dates	Year-round
Times	Mon-Fri 10:30AM, 11:30AM, 1:30PM, and 2:30PM
Avg. Length	90 min

ON-CAMPUS INTERVIEWS

Admissions

Start Date–Juniors	Spring
Appointment Req?	Yes; scheduled from 9:30AM to 3:30PM
Advance Notice	2 weeks
Saturdays?	No
Info Sessions	Select Saturdays during academic year

Faculty and Coaches

Dates/Times	Year-round; subject to faculty/coach availability
Arrangements	Contact admissions off.

CLASS VISITS

Dates	Academic year (Mon-Fri)
Arrangements	Contact admissions off.

OVERNIGHT DORM STAYS

Advance Notice	2 weeks
Arrangements	Contact admissions off.
Limitations	Available when classes are in session

TRANSPORTATION

Cleveland Hopkins Airport is the closest to the university. To get to the campus, take the Regional Transit Authority (RTA) Rapid Transit from the airport terminal to University Circle; the ride takes approximately 40 minutes and is very cheap. Amtrak's Lake Shore Limited provides service to Cleveland via Toledo, Erie, and Buffalo, connecting from those cities to many other locations throughout the country. Greyhound buses also provide service to Cleveland. The Greater Cleveland Regional Transit Authority (RTA) offers extensive and economical bus and rail service throughout the metropolitan area.

FIND YOUR WAY

From I-71 and I-77, exit to I-90 in Cleveland. Take I-90 N. to U.S. 20 E. (Euclid Ave.). Proceed on Euclid Ave. to the admissions office.

STAY THE NIGHT

Nearby: A particular favorite is **Glidden House** (1901 Ford Dr.; 216-231-8900), a large, Gothic-style bed and breakfast within walking distance of campus. Prices are moderate, and a special rate is available for Case Western Reserve visitors. Also in the neighborhood is the posh **Baricelli Inn** (2203 Cornell Rd.; 216-791-6500). Somewhat smaller than Glidden House, this converted mansion is within walking distance of the school. Visitors to the university frequently stay at the **Intercontinental Suite Hotel** (8800 Euclid Ave.; 216-707-4300), a nice hotel (don't be turned off by the antiseptic name) near the campus. Special rates for Case Western Reserve visitors are at the high end of the moderate range. To get to campus, you can walk or take the convenient loop bus across the street from the hotel. There is a parking charge.

A little farther: If you want to stay downtown, try the **Stouffer Renaissance Hotel** (24 Public Sq.; 216-696-5600). This is a convenient, though pricey, place to stay. It has all the amenities of a large metropolitan hotel and the added attraction of public transportation from inside the building directly to the campus.

HIGHLIGHTS

ON CAMPUS
- Kelvin Smith Library
- Peter B. Lewis Building
- Veale Convocation Athletic Center
- Turning Point Sculpture
- Elephant steps

OFF CAMPUS
- Cleveland Museum of Art
- Cleveland Botanical Gardens
- Natural History Museum
- Cleveland Orchestra
- Crawford Auto and Aviation Museum and Historical Society

COLLEGE OF WOOSTER

Admissions Office, College of Wooster, Galpin Hall,
Wooster, OH 44691 • Telephone: 800-877-9905 • Web: www.wooster.edu •
Email: admissions@wooster.edu

Hours: September-May: Monday-Friday, 8AM-5PM; Saturday, 8AM-noon. June-August: Monday-Friday, 8AM-5PM.

This small Presbyterian liberal arts college south of Cleveland offers a wealth of interesting course titles. Recent offerings have included "Go Directly to Jail: Locking Up Minorities in America" and "The Truth About Lies."

HIGHLIGHTS

ON CAMPUS
- Severance Hall Chemistry Building
- Timken Science Library
- Physical education center/fitness center
- Ebert Art Center
- Student development center

OFF CAMPUS
- Rock and Roll Hall of Fame
- Inventure Place (inventors' hall of fame)
- Professional sports teams
- Cuyahoga Valley recreation area
- Football Hall of Fame

TRANSPORTATION

Cleveland-Hopkins Airport is 55 miles from campus. A college shuttle is available if arranged in advance through the admissions office.

FIND YOUR WAY

The college is near the intersection of U.S. Rte. 30 and Ohio Rte. 83. **From the south,** take I-71 N.; exit to U.S. 30 E. (east of Mansfield) and continue to Ohio Rte. 83 in Wooster. Or, take I-77 N. to U.S. 250 N.W. to Wooster. **From the north,** take I-71 S. to Ohio Rte. 83 S. Or, take I-77 S. to Ohio Rte. 21 S. Then take Ohio Rte. 585 S.W. to Wooster. **From the east or west,** take I-76 to Ohio Rte. 3 S. to Wooster. Or, take I-76 to Ohio Rte. 21 S.; then take Rte. 585 S.W. to Wooster.

STAY THE NIGHT

Nearby: If you fly into Cleveland—a 45-minute drive from The College of Wooster—you may be tempted to stay the night in Cleveland and push off in the morning for the campus. Don't do it! You'll miss the chance to stay at some very nice places in and around Wooster. The perfect choice for visiting the college is the **Wooster Inn** (801 E. Wayne Ave.; 330-264-2341), which is owned by the college. It's just 2 blocks from campus, and the college's athletic facilities, including a golf course, are available to guests at the inn. Rates are moderate and include a full breakfast. For a pleasant and inexpensive bed-and-breakfast within walking distance (5 blocks) of the college, try the **Gasche House** (340 North Bever Street; 330-264-8231). This is a beautifully restored 141-year-old Victorian, with four-poster beds and period furniture. The price includes a continental breakfast. If you are not a bed-and-breakfast type, but want an inexpensive place to stay in Wooster, try the **Econo Lodge** (2137 Lincoln Way East; 330-264-8883).

A little farther: Just 22 miles away is the **Inn at Honey Run** (Millersburg; 800-468-6639 in Ohio or 330-674-0011). Honey Run offers a variety of rates from moderate to expensive (continental breakfast included). The inn's earth-shelter rooms (described in the Kenyon entry) may be of interest to you. Take something other than jeans to wear in the evening—more formal attire is in order.

AT A GLANCE

Selectivity Rating	78
Range SAT I Math	540-650
Range SAT I Verbal	540-650
Average GPA	3.5
Student to Faculty Ratio	11:1

CAMPUS TOURS

Appointment Req?	Yes
Dates	See above
Times	On the hour
Avg. Length	1 hour

ON-CAMPUS INTERVIEWS

Admissions

Start Date—Juniors	Any time, usually spring or summer after junior year
Appointment Req?	Yes
Advance Notice	2 weeks
Saturdays?	Yes, during the academic year
Avg. Length	1 hour
Info Sessions	Every Mon and Fri at 11AM and 2PM; and Sat during academic year at 11AM

Faculty and Coaches

Dates/Times	Year-round; subject to faculty/coach availability
Arrangements	Contact admissions off.

CLASS VISITS

Dates	Sept-April (Mon-Fri)
Arrangements	Contact admissions off. 2 weeks prior

OVERNIGHT DORM STAYS

Advance Notice	2 weeks
Arrangements	Contact admissions off.
Limitations	Not available during vacations or in the last 2 weeks of a term

DENISON UNIVERSITY

Admissions Office, Denison University, Box H, Granville, OH 43023 •
Telephone: 800-DENISON or 740-587-6276 • Web: www.denison.edu •
Email: admissions@denison.edu

Hours: September-April: Monday-Friday, 8:30AM-4:30PM; Saturday, 8:45AM-noon. May-August: Monday-Friday, 8:30AM-4PM.
Closed Sundays and holidays.

Denison is a high-quality liberal arts school not far from Columbus, Ohio. It has been in the process of creating a more studious image for itself. Michael Eisner, CEO of Walt Disney Productions, is an alum.

AT A GLANCE

Selectivity Rating	78
Range SAT I Math	560-660
Average SAT I Math	609
Range SAT I Verbal	560-650
Average SAT I Verbal	602
Average ACT Composite	27
Average GPA	3.5
Student to Faculty Ratio	12:1

CAMPUS TOURS

Appointment Req?	No
Dates	Year-round
Times	Sept-Apr: Mon-Fri 9:30AM-3:30PM, hourly on the half hour. May-June: 2 tours daily. July-Aug: 4 tours daily.
Avg. Length	1 hour

ON-CAMPUS INTERVIEWS

Admissions

Start Date—Juniors	Spring
Appointment Req?	Yes
Advance Notice	3-4 days; 7-10 days for July, Aug, Oct, and Nov
Saturdays?	Yes, Sept-May 8:30AM-noon, except holidays
Avg. Length	30-60 min
Info Sessions	N/A

Faculty and Coaches

Dates/Times	Sept-May only
Arrangements	Contact admissions off.

CLASS VISITS

Dates	Academic Year (Mon-Fri)
Arrangements	Contact admissions off.

OVERNIGHT DORM STAYS

Advance Notice	1 week
Arrangements	Contact admissions off.
Limitations	Available Sun-Thurs nights only; bring a sleeping bag and towel

TRANSPORTATION

Port Columbus International Airport is 22 miles (a 35-minute drive) from campus. During the academic year (September-May), the Denison University Student Taxi Service provides shuttle service between the campus and the airport; call the admissions office 1 week before your visit to arrange for this shuttle. During the summer, visitors can rent a car at the airport or take a taxi to and from the campus.

FIND YOUR WAY

From I-70, exit to Ohio Rte. 37 N.; the university is near the intersection of Rte. 37 with Rtes. 16 and 661. **From the north,** take I-71 S.; exit to Ohio Rte. 13 (south of Mansfield). Take Rte. 13 S. through Mount Vernon; then make a right turn onto Rte. 661. Take Rte. 661 S. into Granville; you will pass the Denison athletic fields. The university is on Rte. 37 just west of Rte. 661.

STAY THE NIGHT

Nearby: If you have a morning visit scheduled at Denison, it's worth making the effort to spend the preceding night in Granville. The first of 2 delightful inns in this picture-postcard town (a 5-minute drive from the admissions office) is the **Buxton Inn** (313 E. Broadway; 740-587-0001). Founded in 1812, it is still operating in its original building in the middle of the village. Another gem is the **Granville Inn** (314 E. Broadway; 740-587-3333). It's also moderately priced and provides a continental breakfast. This is an English Tudor manor house with carved oak paneling and lots of character. It includes a pleasant restaurant. Just outside of Granville, another outstanding overnight and dining location is the **Cherry Valley Lodge** (2299 Cherry Valley Road; 740-788-1200).

A little farther: Check the places in the Kenyon College entry, especially **Russell-Cooper House** (in Mount Vernon, 23 miles from Denison).

HIGHLIGHTS

ON CAMPUS
- F. W. Olin Science Hall
- Mitchell Recreation and Athletics Center
- Swasey Chapel
- Biological Reserve and Polly Anderson Field Station
- Burke Hall Art Gallery

OFF CAMPUS
- Granville Historical Society Museum

HIRAM COLLEGE

Admission Office, Hiram College, Box 96, Hiram, OH 44234 •
Telephone: 800-362-5280 or 330-569 5169 • Web: www.hiram.edu •
Email: admission@hiram.edu

Hours: September-May: Monday-Friday, 9AM-4PM; Saturday, 9AM-noon. June-August: Monday-Friday, 9AM-4PM. Closed holidays.

The innovative Hiram Plan at Hiram College divides each semester into two sessions that last 3 and 12 weeks, respectively. The 3-week sessions take the form of hands-on learning experiences like study abroad, research, internships, and field trips. Also, over the past decade or so Hiram's medical school acceptance rate has been among the highest in the nation.

HIGHLIGHTS

ON CAMPUS
- James H. Barrow Field Station
- The Hiram College Library
- Kennedy Center (food court, bookstore, etc.)
- Hiram Church
- Stevens Memorial Observatory

OFF CAMPUS
- Cleveland
- The Flats
- The Science Discovery Center
- National Soccer Hall of Fame
- Orpheus Theatre

TRANSPORTATION

Cleveland-Hopkins and Akron-Canton airports are an hour's drive from the campus. The Admission Office supplies free transportation to the campus; contact the receptionist there to arrange for this service. Rental cars are also available at both airports.

FIND YOUR WAY

From the east, take I-80 to Exit 14; then take Ohio Rte. 5 E. (toward Warren). At the intersection with Rte. 82, turn left (north and west, away from Warren) and continue on Rte. 82, which merges with Rte. 700 just south of the college. The college is at the intersection of Routes 82/700 and 305. **From the west**, take I-80 to Exit 13A (S.R. 44). Take Rte 44 north 6 miles to Rte. 82. Take Rte. 82 E. to Hiram.

STAY THE NIGHT

Nearby: Located right on campus, the **Hiram Inn** (888-447-2646) offers all the modern amenities in a 19th-century setting. The 12 guest rooms, though decorated in the style of the early 1800s, come equipped with air conditioning, cable television, and access to a computer hook-up. Some rooms offer a whirlpool spa or fireplace. Ask for college visitor rates. Aurora, which is 15 to 20 minutes to the west, offers several quite respectable possibilities. Ask for college visitor rates at each. **Aurora Inn** (Ohio Rtes. 82 and 306; 330-562-6121) offers moderate prices, indoor and outdoor pools, tennis courts, and jacuzzis. The **Best Western Aurora Woodlands Inn** (800 N. Aurora Rd.; 330-562-9151) is moderately priced. It has an indoor pool with a glass dome that opens in warm weather. It also has an inexpensive Friday-night rate. For the fitness-minded, there is **Mario's International Aurora House Spa and Hotel** (35 E. Garfield Rd.; 330-562-9171). Each room has a whirlpool. Mario's is normally very expensive and would probably make sense only if you wanted to use the spa facilities, but the hotel does have a moderate visitor rate that might make this an appealing choice.

A little farther: To the east of Hiram, about a 40-minute drive away, is **Avalon Inn** (Warren-Sharon Rd., off Market St.; 330-856-1900). This is a moderately priced, modern, resort motel with indoor/outdoor lighted tennis courts, an indoor pool, and 2 golf courses. An inexpensive choice, **Knights Inn** (249 E. Highland Rd., Macedonia; 330-467-1981), offers a special rate for Hiram visitors but is a good 30-minute drive from the college. (It's just southeast of Cleveland where Rte. 271 crosses Rte. 8, a few miles north of the Ohio Tpke..)

AT A GLANCE

Selectivity Rating	78
Range SAT I Math	490-610
Average SAT I Math	560
Range SAT I Verbal	500-650
Average SAT I Verbal	580
Average ACT Composite	24
Average GPA	3.4
Student to Faculty Ratio	12:1

CAMPUS TOURS

Appointment Req?	Yes
Dates	Year-round
Times	When admissions off. is open
Avg. Length	45 min

ON-CAMPUS INTERVIEWS

Admissions

Start Date—Juniors	Any time
Appointment Req?	Yes
Advance Notice	2 weeks
Saturdays?	Yes, 9AM-11:30AM during the school year; make appt. for summer
Avg. Length	45 min
Info Sessions	N/A

Faculty and Coaches

Dates/Times	During the academic year
Arrangements	Contact Admission Off. 2 weeks prior

CLASS VISITS

Dates	Year-round (Mon-Fri)
Arrangements	Contact Admission Off.

OVERNIGHT DORM STAYS

Advance Notice	1-2 weeks
Arrangements	Contact Admission Off.
Limitations	Available to applicants only

KENYON COLLEGE

Admissions Office, Kenyon College, Gambier, OH 43022 •
Telephone: 800-848-2468 or 740-427-5776 • Web: www.kenyon.edu •
Email: admissions@kenyon.edu

Hours: September-May: Monday-Friday, 8:30AM-4:30PM; Saturday, 9AM-noon; June-August: Monday-Friday, 8:30AM-4:30PM.
Closed Sundays and holidays.

Kenyon's liberal arts-filled academic environment is quite competetive, but students are generally self-motivated and seem to really enjoy themselves.

AT A GLANCE

Selectivity Rating	90
Range SAT I Math	580-690
Average SAT I Math	634
Range SAT I Verbal	610-710
Average SAT I Verbal	666
Average ACT Composite	29
Average GPA	3.6
Student to Faculty Ratio	11:1

CAMPUS TOURS

Appointment Req?	Preferable
Dates	Year-round
Times	Mon-Fri 9:30AM-3:30PM (every hour on the half-hour, except 12:30PM); during student breaks and in the summer, call for times
Avg. Length	1 hour

ON-CAMPUS INTERVIEWS

Admissions

Start Date–Juniors	Later part of year
Appointment Req?	Yes
Advance Notice	2 weeks
Saturdays?	Yes, Sept-May 9AM-11:30AM
Avg. Length	1 hour
Info Sessions	N/A

Faculty and Coaches

Dates/Times	Year-round; subject to faculty/coach availability
Arrangements	Contact admissions off.

CLASS VISITS

Dates	Year-round (Mon-Fri)
Arrangements	Contact admissions off.

OVERNIGHT DORM STAYS

Advance Notice	2 weeks
Arrangements	Contact admissions off.
Limitations	Sun-Thurs nights only; 2 weeks after the opening of school; high school seniors only

TRANSPORTATION

Port Columbus International Airport is approximately 50 miles from campus. Call the admissions office receptionist to arrange for the college's shuttle service from the airport. (Note that this service is not free.) Rental cars are available at the airport if you prefer to drive.

FIND YOUR WAY

From U.S. Rte. 62, take Ohio Rte. 661 N. toward Mount Vernon. Rte. 661 merges with Rte. 13 S. of Mount Vernon. In Mount Vernon, look for the green Kenyon College signs. At the intersection of Rtes. 13 and 229, turn right (east) on Rte. 229 (East Gambier St.) for about 5 miles to the college.

STAY THE NIGHT

Nearby: You can roll out of bed and onto campus from the **Kenyon Inn** (740-427-2202), a pleasant colonial with rates at the low end of the moderate range. Gambier is tiny (the campus, inn, and post office make up the whole town), so you might prefer to stay in the "big city" of Mount Vernon, a short hop (10 minutes) away. The first choice in Mount Vernon is the **Russell-Cooper House** (115 E. Gambier St.; 740-397-8638), a restored Victorian mansion with rooms that are moderately priced (with breakfast). If this doesn't appeal to you, try **The Curtis** (12 Public Sq.; 800-828-7847 outside Ohio or 800-634-6835 in Ohio), a nice, simple, inexpensive motel. Also located in Mt. Vernon are **The Holiday Inn Express** (11555 Upper Gilchrist Rd.; 740-392-1900) and the **Dan Emmett House** (150 Howard St.; 740-392-6886) where local professors play the blues.

A little farther: A very special place about 11 miles away is the **White Oak Inn** (29683 Walhonding Rd., Danville; 614-599-6107). The inn is small—6 rooms and 1 suite. For recreation, it offers canoeing, fishing, and hiking; there are horseshoes, badminton, and croquet available on the grounds. Golf courses are nearby. If you prefer serenity to glamour, this is the place for you. **The Inn at Honey Run** (6920 County Rd. 203, Millersburg; 330-674-0011 or 800-468-6639 in Ohio) is a great place to stay and well worth the 40-mile drive northeast from Kenyon. Located in the Amish country, this unusual contemporary inn blends well with the wooded surroundings. You might consider staying in their Honeycombs, an earth-sheltered annex (a cave but not a cave). The rates range from moderate to expensive, depending on your room. Also in Amish country, 33 miles east of Kenyon on U.S. Rte. 36 in Coshocton, is **Roscoe Village Inn** (200 N. White Woman St.; 614-622-2222). The inn, which has a nice restaurant and a tavern, offers 50 rooms. It is moderately priced; check for AAA discounts. Denison is only 30 miles south of Gambier, so see the Denison University entry for other suggestions. You will find the usual array of hotels in Columbus, which is only about 50 miles southwest of Gambier. (Some of these are described in the Ohio State entry). Mansfield, a town 30 miles north of Gambier on Ohio Rte. 13, also has a number of standard motels.

HIGHLIGHTS

ON CAMPUS
- Olin Art Gallery
- Olin Library and Chalmers Library
- Horn Gallery
- Old Kenyon
- Erns Center

OFF CAMPUS
- Kokosing (gap walking)
- Local golf courses
- 15-mile biking/ rollerblading trail

MIAMI UNIVERSITY

Admission Office, Miami University, 301 S. Campus Ave., Oxford, OH 45056 •
Telephone: 513-529-2531• Web: www.muohio.edu •
Email: admissions@muohio.edu

Hours: Sept.-May: Monday-Friday, 8AM-5PM; Saturday, 8:30AM-noon. June-Aug.: Monday-Friday, 7:30AM-4:30PM. Closed holidays.

Miami University is widely known for offering top-rate programs in combination with state school affordability. The surrounding town of Oxford is a bit sedate, but scenic and student-friendly. Humorist P. J. O'Rourke is an alum.

HIGHLIGHTS

ON CAMPUS
- McGuffey Museum
- Center for the performing arts
- Amos Music Library

OFF CAMPUS
- The Pioneer Farm and House Museum
- Hueston Woods State Park

TRANSPORTATION

Greater Cincinnati International Airport is 55 miles south of Oxford in northern Kentucky. Dayton International Airport is 55 miles northeast of Oxford in Vandalia. Miami University Airport is quite near campus, but is suitable only for small private planes; call 513-529-2735 for information. Door-to-Door Transportation Services (513-641-0088) offers service between Oxford and the Cincinnati airport approximately every an hour and a half for less than $50; make reservations in advance. Similar fees for airport-to-campus transportation (Cincinnati or Dayton) are charged by Joan's Cab Service (513-523-2211); reservations are suggested. Rental cars are available at both major airports. Amtrak trains provide no direct service to Oxford, but make tri-weekly stops in Cincinnati (a 1-hour drive from Oxford) and Hamilton (a 30-minute drive from Oxford).

FIND YOUR WAY

From the east, take I-70 W. to I-75 S. (north of Dayton). Take I-75 S. to Ohio Rte 63 W. Take Rte. 63 W. to Ohio Rte. 4 N. From Rte. 4 N., turn west onto Ohio Rte 73. Rte. 73 joins U.S. Rte. 27 and takes you into Oxford. **From the north**, take I-75 S. and follow the preceding directions from there. **From the west**, take I-70 E. to U.S. Rte. 27 (near Richmond, IN). Take Rte. 27 S. into Oxford. **From the south**, take I-75 N. to U.S. Rte. 27 (in Cincinnati); take U.S. Rte 27 N. into Oxford.

STAY THE NIGHT

Nearby: At a moderate cost (including continental breakfast), 2 people can stay right in the university at the **Marcum Conference Center** (513-529-6911). The university advises that reservations be made 60 days ahead, but walk-ins will be accommodated if possible. You may use the university athletic facilities. In town is the **Marcum Conference Center and Inn** (100 N. Patterson Ave.; 513-529-2404), a great college-town hotel. It is somewhat more expensive, but still within the moderate range and very convenient. Another moderately priced choice in Oxford is the **Alexander House Country Inn** (22 N. College Ave.; 513-523-1200), 6 blocks from campus. Inexpensive choices, also close to campus, include the **College View Motel** (513-523-6311), a mile and a half south on Rte. 27 S.; **Cottage Inn** (513-523-6306), 2 miles northwest of Oxford on Rte. 27 N.; and **Oxford Motel** (5399 College Corner Pike; 513-523-1880).

A little farther: For a more vacation-like ambiance, try **Hueston Woods Lodge** (800-282-7275 or 513-523-6381), 5 miles north on Ohio Rte. 732 in the lovely Hueston Woods State Park. The rooms are moderately priced (ask for a cottage with kitchenette). The lodge has a pool, game room, lighted tennis facility, 18-hole golf course, boats, and private beach. If you want to stay in Hamilton, try **The Hamiltonian at Riverfront Plaza** (800-522-5570 or 513-896-6200), 25 minutes from the college. Also consider driving in from Dayton (a 1-hour drive to the northeast; see the Antioch entry) or Cincinnati (an hour drive to the southeast).

AT A GLANCE

Selectivity Rating	82
Range SAT I Math	550-660
Range SAT I Verbal	540-630
Student to Faculty Ratio	18:1

CAMPUS TOURS

Appointment Req?	Yes, call 513-529-4632
Dates	Year-round, except Sundays and holidays
Times	Mon-Fri 10AM and 2PM; Sat 11AM during the academic year only
Avg. Length	2 hours

ON-CAMPUS INTERVIEWS

Admissions

Start Date—Juniors	N/A
Appointment Req?	N/A
Advance Notice	N/A
Saturdays?	N/A
Avg. Length	N/A
Info Sessions	Weekdays and on Sat during the semester; during admissions off. hours, walk-in basis is available

Faculty and Coaches

Dates/Times	During academic year
Arrangements	Contact admissions off. 10-14 days prior

CLASS VISITS

Dates	Year-round (Mon-Fri)
Arrangements	Contact admissions off.

OVERNIGHT DORM STAYS

Advance Notice	3 weeks
Arrangements	Contact admissions off.
Limitations	1-night stay; high school seniors only; not available close to exam periods

OBERLIN COLLEGE

Admissions Office, Oberlin College, Carnegie Building, 101 N. Professor Street, Oberlin, OH 44074-1075 • Telephone: 800-622-OBIE or 216-775-8411 • Web: www.oberlin.edu • Email: college.admissions@oberlin.edu

Hours: Monday-Friday, 8:30AM-5PM; Saturday, 9AM-noon (September-May only). Closed Sundays and major holidays.

Oberlin College is an outstanding liberal arts school connected to a world-renowned conservatory of music, and has something to offer pretty much everyone. Oberlin's left-leaning undergrads say they are free thinkers who prefer political debates, concerts, and plays to drinking or playing sports.

AT A GLANCE

Selectivity Rating	90
Range SAT I Math	590-700
Average SAT I Math	637
Range SAT I Verbal	630-730
Average SAT I Verbal	671
Average ACT Composite	28
Average GPA	3.6
Student to Faculty Ratio	12:1

CAMPUS TOURS

Appointment Req?	No
Dates	Year-round, except Sun
Times	Mon-Fri 10AM, noon, 2:30PM, and 4:30PM; Sat 10AM and noon during the academic year only
Avg. Length	1 hour

ON-CAMPUS INTERVIEWS

Admissions

Start Date—Juniors	March 1
Appointment Req?	Yes
Advance Notice	3-4 weeks
Saturdays?	Yes
Avg. Length	45 min
Info Sessions	Year-round, when admissions off. is open

Faculty and Coaches

Dates/Times	Primarily during academic year
Arrangements	Contact admissions off.

CLASS VISITS

Dates	Year-round (Mon-Fri)
Arrangements	Contact admissions off.

OVERNIGHT DORM STAYS

Advance Notice	2-3 weeks
Arrangements	Contact Campus Visit Off.
Limitations	2-night maximum; not available during exam periods; not available to juniors Jan 15-May 1

TRANSPORTATION

Cleveland-Hopkins International Airport is 27 miles from the college. Relatively inexpensive limousine service is available for the ride from the airport to campus; call 216-267-8282 to arrange for this.

FIND YOUR WAY

From the east, take I-80 (the Ohio Tpke.) to Exit 9; then take Ohio Rte. 10 W. to Rte. 20 W. Take Rte. 20 to the SR 511 exit, and take Rte. 511 W. into Oberlin. **From the west**, take I-80/90 to Exit 8 (Elyria-Lorain). Do not use Exit 8A. Take Ohio Rte. 57 S. to Ohio Rte. 113; then take Rte. 113 W. to Ohio Rte. 58. Proceed south on Rte. 58 to Oberlin. **From the north**, take Rte 58 S. to Oberlin. **From the south**, take I-71 N. to the Ashland exit; take U.S. Rte. 250 E. to Ohio Rte. 89. Head north on Rte. 89 to Ohio Rte. 58, then follow Rte. 58 N. to Oberlin.

STAY THE NIGHT

Nearby: The **Oberlin College Inn** (Maine and College Sts.; across from Tappan Sq.; 216-775-1111) is convenient to the campus and moderately priced. The inn also has a decent restaurant. The Ohio Tpke. (also called I-80 and I-90) and Ohio Rte. 2 pass a few miles to the north of Oberlin, heading west from Cleveland toward Toledo. You will find the familiar chain motels located near these major highways.

A little farther: Oberlin is close to Cleveland, so check the suggestions in the Case Western Reserve University entry. If you want to stay at the Cleveland airport, try the **Sheraton-Hopkins Airport Hotel** (216-267-1500), an expensive choice (25 percent discount for AAA members). West of Cleveland, in Lakewood (about 30 minutes from campus), right off Rte. 90, is the **Captain's House** (Private Lodgings; 216-321-3213, weekdays 9AM-noon, 3PM-5PM), an attractive bed-and-breakfast with inexpensive to moderate rates. A good resort 45 minutes away is the **Aqua Marine Resort and Country Club** (216 Miller Rd., Avon Lake; 800-321-2080 in Indiana, Michigan, Pennsylvania, and New York; 216-933-2000 in other states). The resort includes an 18-hole golf course, tennis courts, indoor and outdoor pools, putting green, and exercise room. Fun for the whole family and all that. In Elyria, about 15 miles to the northeast of Oberlin, is a **Holiday Inn** (1825 Lorain Blvd.; 216-324-5411) with the usual amenities and a moderate price (10 percent discount to AAA members). Take exit 8 off the Ohio Tpke. and ask about the "great rate." Rooms reserved for Oberlin visitors are available if you mention "All roads lead to Oberlin" when you make reservations. There's also a **Knights Inn** (State Rte. 57, Elyria; 800-722-7220 or 216-324-3911) about 20 miles from Oberlin just off I-80.

HIGHLIGHTS

ON CAMPUS
- Allen Art Museum
- Memorial Arch
- Mudd Library
- Arboretum
- Observatory

OFF CAMPUS
- Rock and Roll Hall of Fame
- Cleveland Art Museum
- Cleveland Natural History Museum
- Severance Hall (concert hall)
- Downtown Cleveland

OHIO STATE UNIVERSITY—COLUMBUS

Student Visitor Center, Ohio State University, 131 Enarson Hall,
154 West 12th, Columbus, OH 43210-1390 • Telephone: 614-292-3980 •
Web: www.osu.edu • Email: oafa@fa.adm.ohio-state.edu

Hours: Monday-Friday, 9AM-5PM. Closed weekends, New Year's Day, Martin Luther King Day, Memorial Day, July 4, Labor Day, Veterans Day, Thanksgiving, and Christmas.

With over 30,000 full-time undergraduates (and another 5,000 part-timers), Ohio State University is like a small city. As an added perk, OSU is extremely affordable.

HIGHLIGHTS

ON CAMPUS
- Hale Cultural Center
- Chadwick Arboretum
- Jack Nicklaus Golf Museum
- Schottenstein Center and Value City Arena

OFF CAMPUS
- Columbus Zoo
- Wyandotte Lake
- Easton (shopping)
- MSL Columbus Crew

TRANSPORTATION

Port Columbus International Airport is a 25-minute drive from campus, depending on traffic. Taxis are available at the airport for the trip; some hotels run regular shuttles from the airport into town. Greyhound buses serve downtown Columbus; no passenger train service is available.

FIND YOUR WAY

Routes I-70, I-670, and I-71 intersect or join State Rt. 315. Exit 315 at Lane Ave. Travel east (left if you are traveling south on 315 or right if you are traveling north on 315) on Lane Ave. to Fyffe Road. Turn south (right) on Fyffe Road. to Woody Hayes Dr. Turn east (left) on Woody Hayes Dr. to College Rd. Turn south (right) on College Rd. to 12th Ave. Turn west (right) on 12th Ave. The Student Visitor Center can be followed from Lane Ave. When you check in, you will be given a parking pass.

STAY THE NIGHT

Just across the street from the university (its northern edge) is the moderately priced **Holiday Inn on the Lane** (328 W. Lane Ave.; 800-465-4329 or 614-294-4848). A free shuttle service will bring you to a hotel from the airport. The **University Plaza Hotel** (3110 Olentangy River Rd.; 877-677-5292 or 614-267-7461) is convenient and moderately priced too. An inexpensive motel 1.5 miles away is **Cross Country Inn**-OSU North (3246 Olentangy River Rd.; 800-621-1429 or 614-267-4646). Because Ohio State is located in Columbus, one of Ohio's major cities, there are a variety of places to stay. They range from the inexpensive **Red Roof Inn** (441 Ackerman Rd.; 800-843-7663 or 614-267-9941), to the **Hyatt Regency** of Columbus (350 N. High St.; 800-233-1234 or 614-463-1234) an expensive hotel with the usual amenities.

AT A GLANCE

Selectivity Rating	72
Range SAT I Math	520-640
Average SAT I Math	581
Range SAT I Verbal	500-620
Average SAT I Verbal	564
Average ACT Composite	25
Student to Faculty Ratio	14:1

CAMPUS TOURS
Appointment Req?	Yes
Dates	Call 614-292-3980 for reservation
Times	Mon-Fri 10AM and 2PM
Avg. Length	2 hours

ON-CAMPUS INTERVIEWS
Admissions
Start Date–Juniors	Any time
Appointment Req?	No
Advance Notice	None
Saturdays?	No
Avg. Length	20 min
Info Sessions	Whenever admissions off. is open

Faculty and Coaches
Dates/Times	Year-round; subject to faculty/coach availability
Arrangements	Contact dept. of interest 2 weeks prior

CLASS VISITS
Dates	Year-round; subject to availabiliy
Arrangements	Contact Nancy Brown at 614-292-3030; academic visits also available and recommended

OVERNIGHT DORM STAYS
Advance Notice	N/A
Arrangements	N/A
Limitations	N/A

OHIO UNIVERSITY—ATHENS

Admissions Office, Ohio University, 120 Chubb Hall, Athens, OH 45701-2979 • Telephone: 740-593-4100 • Web: www.ohiou.edu • Email: frshinfo@ohiou.edu

Hours: Monday-Friday, 8AM-5PM (group information sessions are scheduled from 9AM-noon and 1PM-4PM); Saturday, 10AM-noon. Closed Sundays and holidays.

Ohio University prides itself on offering a private-school-like education at a public-school-like price. The excellent honors tutorial program allows select students to work more closely with professors than is usually possible at a large university.

AT A GLANCE

Selectivity Rating	78
Range SAT I Math	490-600
Average SAT I Math	545
Range SAT I Verbal	500-600
Average SAT I Verbal	550
Average ACT Composite	23
Average GPA	3.4
Student to Faculty Ratio	21:1

CAMPUS TOURS

Appointment Req?	Yes
Dates	Year-round
Times	Mon-Fri 10AM,12PM, and 2PM; Sat noon
Avg. Length	1 hour

ON-CAMPUS INTERVIEWS

Admissions

Start Date—Juniors	N/A
Appointment Req?	Recommended, contact admissions off. 1 week in advance
Advance Notice	N/A
Saturdays?	Most
Avg. Length	1 hour
Info Sessions	Year-round

Faculty and Coaches

| Dates/Times | Year-round; subject to faculty/coach availability |
| Arrangements | Contact admissions off. 1 week prior |

CLASS VISITS

| Dates | Year-round (Mon-Fri) |
| Arrangements | Contact prof. |

OVERNIGHT DORM STAYS

Advance Notice	N/A
Arrangements	N/A
Limitations	Prospective students are permitted to stay overnight with friends or relatives

TRANSPORTATION

Port Columbus International Airport in Columbus is 75 miles (a 2-hour drive) from campus. Rental cars are available at the airport. The Ohio University Airport, which is 12 miles from campus, has a 4,200-foot lighted runway and is open to the public. Ground transportation from the airport to Athens should be arranged in advance. Bus service to and from Athens is available by calling Lakefront Trailways at 800-638-6338 ext. 162 or All Points Transportation at 740-927-9778.

FIND YOUR WAY

From U.S. Rte. 50 or U.S. Rte. 33 (which merge near Athens), take the Athens exit for Rte. 682 N. At the traffic light, turn right onto Richland Ave. Stop at the Ohio University Visitors Center (the log structure on your left at the corner of Richland Ave. and South Shafer St.) for directions to parking locations and other specific places on campus.

STAY THE NIGHT

Nearby: For convenience, you cannot beat the **Ohio University Inn and Conference Center** (331 Richland Ave.; 740-593-6661), adjacent to the campus (about a 15-minute walk to the admissions office). The prices are in the moderate range.

A little farther: If you can't get into the Ohio University Inn, call the Athens County Convention and Visitor's Bureau at 800-878-9767 for a list of other area hotels. **Lake Hope State Park** (740-596-5253), 30 minutes from campus, has inexpensive cabins available year-round (rent by the week in summer) and various types of campsites. **Burr Oak State Park** (800-282-7275), also 30 minutes away, has a lodge and 2-bedroom cabins with kitchenettes. The views are beautiful and the cost is inexpensive to moderate. Rates vary seasonally and with the day of the week. Check for special packages.

HIGHLIGHTS

ON CAMPUS
- Charles J. Ping Recreation Center
- Kennedy Museum of Art
- Templeton-Blackburn Memorial Auditorium
- Convocation Center
- Alden Library

OFF CAMPUS
- Stuart's Opera House
- Dairy Barn Cultural Arts Center
- Hocking Valley Science Railway
- Athens County Historical Society and Museum

OHIO WESLEYAN UNIVERSITY

Office of Admission, Ohio Wesleyan University, 61 S. Sandusky St., Delaware, OH 43015 • Telephone: 614-368-3020 (in OH) or 800-922-8953 • Web: www.owu.edu • Email: owuadmit@cc.owu.edu

Hours: September-April: Monday-Friday, 8:30AM-5PM. Saturday, 8:30AM-12PM. May-August: Monday-Friday, 8:30AM-4:30PM. Closed Sundays, holidays, and Saturdays during the Christmas and summer break.

The admissions office is selective at OWU, a midwestern liberal arts college with small classes and an excellent administration.

HIGHLIGHTS

ON CAMPUS
- R. W. Corns Building
- Hamilton Williams Campus Center
- Selby Stadium
- Beeghiy Library
- Sanborn Hall (music)

OFF CAMPUS
- Highbanks Nature Preserve
- The Arts Castle
- Delaware State Park
- Columbus Zoo
- Delaware County Fairgrounds

TRANSPORTATION

The Port Columbus International Airport in Columbus is a 45-minute drive from campus. Call the admissions office to arrange for transportation from the airport.

FIND YOUR WAY

The campus is located near the junction of U.S. Rtes. 23 and 36. From Rte. 36 (William St. in Delaware), head south on Sandusky St. The admissions office is near the third traffic light on Sandusky. Use the parking lot off Sandusky St. and follow signs to admissions.

STAY THE NIGHT

Numerous hotels and motels are available throughout Delaware and the northwest Columbus area. Delaware, located in the approximate center of Ohio, is 20 miles due north of downtown Columbus and 120 miles southwest of Cleveland. Worthington is a nearby north suburb of Columbus and is 15 minutes directly south of Delaware.

Nearby: Accommodations in the area include **Amerihost** (1720 Columbus Pike/Rt. 23; 740-363-3510), **Best Western Delaware Hotel** (351 S. Sandusky St.; 740-363-1262), **Hampton Inn** (171-Route 36/37; 740-363-4700), **Long View Farm B&B** (3780 Bowtown Rd.; 740-362-0387), **Super 8** (Route 23; 740-363-8869), **Travelodge** (U.S. Route 23 N.; 740-369-4421), and **Welcome Home Inn B&B** (6640 Home Rd.; 740-881-6588).

A little farther: Other options include **The Courtyard** (7411 Vantage Dr.; 800-321-2211), **Holiday Inn at Crosswoods** (175 Hutchinson; 614-885-3334), **Homewood Suites** (115 Hutchinson; 614-785-0001), **Microtel** (7500 Vantage Dr.; 800-433-3690), **Red Roof Inn** (7474 N. High St.; 800-THE-ROOF), **Sheraton Suites** (201 Hutchinson; 614-436-0004), **Travelodge** (7480 N. High St.; 614-836-2525), **Worthington Inn** (1881 Carriage House, High St. & New England; 614-885-2600), and **AmeriSuites** (Columbus/Worthington; 800-833-1516). Also, **The Frederick Fitting House** (72 Fitting Ave.; 419-886-2863) is a charming, quiet, country village bed and breakfast. Prices vary from inexpensive to moderate (including full breakfast). Nearby you will find a golf course, tennis courts, jogging trails, canoeing, shops, and skiing.

AT A GLANCE

Selectivity Rating	80
Range SAT I Math	570-660
Average SAT I Math	610
Range SAT I Verbal	550-660
Average SAT I Verbal	599
Average ACT Composite	26
Average GPA	3.3
Student to Faculty Ratio	13:1

CAMPUS TOURS

Appointment Req?	Yes
Dates	Whenever admissions off. is open
Times	Sept-April: Mon-Fri 9:45AM, noon, 2PM, and 4PM; Sat 10AM and 11AM. May-Aug: Mon-Fri 9:45AM, noon, and 2PM.
Avg. Length	1 hour

ON-CAMPUS INTERVIEWS

Admissions

Start Date—Juniors	Any time
Appointment Req?	Yes
Advance Notice	2 weeks
Saturdays?	Yes, mornings only
Avg. Length	45 min
Info Sessions	N/A

Faculty and Coaches

Dates/Times	Year-round; subject to faculty/coach availability
Arrangements	Contact admissions off.

CLASS VISITS

Dates	Sept-April (Mon-Fri)
Arrangements	Contact admissions off.

OVERNIGHT DORM STAYS

Advance Notice	2 weeks
Arrangements	Contact admissions off.
Limitations	1 night; Sun-Thurs; not available during exams

WITTENBERG UNIVERSITY

Admission Office, Ward St. & North Wittenberg Ave., P.O. Box 720, Springfield, OH 45501 (The office is in Recitation Hall) • Telephone: 800-677-7558 or 937-327-6314 • Web: www.wittenberg.edu • Email: admission@wittenberg.edu

Hours: September-May: Monday-Friday, 9AM-5PM; Saturday, 9AM-noon. June-August: Monday-Friday, 9AM-4PM. Closed Sundays and holidays.

At Wittenberg University, a unique trimester system keeps academic life interesting. The financial aid office also receives especially high praise.

AT A GLANCE

Selectivity Rating	79
Range SAT I Math	560-630
Average SAT I Math	590
Range SAT I Verbal	560-650
Average SAT I Verbal	580
Average ACT Composite	25
Average GPA	3.4
Student to Faculty Ratio	14:1

CAMPUS TOURS

Appointment Req?	Yes
Dates	Whenever admissions off. is open
Times	Every hour on the hour
Avg. Length	1 hour

ON-CAMPUS INTERVIEWS

Admissions

Start Date—Juniors	Any time
Appointment Req?	Yes
Advance Notice	7-10 days
Saturdays?	Yes, Aug-May 9AM-noon
Avg. Length	1 hour
Info Sessions	N/A

Faculty and Coaches

Dates/Times	During the academic year; subject to faculty/coach availability
Arrangements	Contact admissions off. 1 week prior

CLASS VISITS

Dates	Year-round (Mon-Fri)
Arrangements	Contact admissions off.

OVERNIGHT DORM STAYS

Advance Notice	2 weeks
Arrangements	Contact admissions off.
Limitations	Available only on Thurs and Sun nights when classes are in session; only for admissions applicants

TRANSPORTATION

Dayton International Airport is 27 miles from the campus. Car rentals are available from the airport. During the academic year, student drivers provide free shuttle service between the airport and the campus; call the Admission Office at least one week in advance to arrange for this service.

FIND YOUR WAY

From I-70, take U.S. Rte. 68 N. to Ohio Rte. 41. Proceed west for 2 miles on Rte. 41 following signs to the university.

STAY THE NIGHT

Nearby: Located conveniently on campus, Wittenberg runs its very own guest house. Not only convenient, **Benjamin Prince Guest House** is a historic landmark filled with antiques. Check with the admissions office about availability. If you are staying in Springfield, the best choice for the money is the **Springfield Inn** (100 S. Fountain Ave.; 937-322-3600). This full-service modern hotel is 1 mile from campus across from Market Place. Mention you are a guest of the Wittenberg admissions office to obtain a special rate. For a change of pace, try the **Buck Creek State Park Cottages** (1901 Buck Creek Ln.; 937-322-5284). The cottages are pretty, modern, and in a lovely setting about 4 miles from campus, with boating and fishing nearby. This is a very inexpensive choice for a family; the 2-bedroom cottages are inexpensively priced.

A little farther: Tipp City, about a half-hour west of Springfield and somewhat north of Dayton, has some charming little inns and bed-and-breakfasts. A small (4-room) bed-and-breakfast with particular charm and elegance is **Willow Tree Inn** (1900 W. State Rte. 571; 937-667-2957). Rates are inexpensive to moderate (less on weekdays than on weekends), and you will enjoy a glass of wine in the evening in addition to the continental breakfast.

HIGHLIGHTS

ON CAMPUS
- Thomas Library
- Weaver Observatory
- Chakeres Theatre
- Alumni & Visitors Center

OFF CAMPUS
- Springfield Art Center
- Kings Island
- U.S. Air Force Museum

1- Lewis & Clark College
   Reed College
2- Willamette University

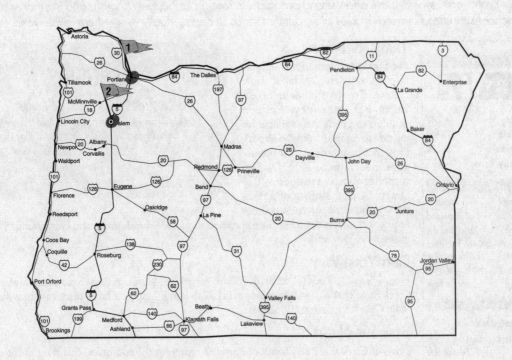

Oregon	Lewis & Clark	Reed Coll.	Willamette Univ.	Eugene	Portland
Lewis & Clark Coll.	—	5	44	114	0
Reed Coll.	5	—	49	119	0
Willamette Univ.	44	49	—	63	45
Eugene	114	119	63	—	115
Portland	0	0	45	115	—

LEWIS & CLARK COLLEGE

Office of Admissions, Lewis & Clark College, 0615 S.W. Palatine Hill Rd., Portland, OR 97219-7899 (The office is in Frank Manor) • Telephone: 800-444-4111 or 503-768-7040 • Web: www.lclark.edu • Email: admissions@lclark.edu

Hours: Monday-Friday, 8:30AM-5PM; Saturday, 9:30AM-noon, by appointment (during academic year only). Closed Sundays and major holidays.

Lewis & Clark College is a small college in Portland, Oregon, with a beautiful campus, small classes, and excellent, approachable professors. Lewis & Clark offers strong programs in foreign languages, English, and international affairs as well as a school-subsidized overseas studies program that sends students virtually everywhere in the world.

AT A GLANCE

Selectivity Rating	82
Range SAT I Math	570-660
Range SAT I Verbal	580-680
Student to Faculty Ratio	13:1

CAMPUS TOURS

Appointment Req?	Preferred
Dates	Year-round
Times	Mon, Wed, Fri 9AM and 3PM; Tue, Thurs 9:30AM and 3PM; Sat by appt. only
Avg. Length	1 hour

ON-CAMPUS INTERVIEWS

Admissions

Start Date—Juniors	Any time, except Feb and Mar
Appointment Req?	Yes
Advance Notice	1 week
Saturdays?	By appointment
Avg. Length	30 min
Info Sessions	Year-round

Faculty and Coaches

Dates/Times	Year-round; subject to faculty/coach availability
Arrangements	Contact admissions off.

CLASS VISITS

Dates	Sept-April, but not the first or last week of term
Arrangements	Contact admissions off. 1 week prior

OVERNIGHT DORM STAYS

Advance Notice	2 weeks
Arrangements	Contact admissions off.
Limitations	Available Mon-Thurs only; not the first and last 2 weeks of a term; 1 night only

TRANSPORTATION

The Portland International Airport is approximately 20 miles from campus. Tri-Met (public transportation), Raz Tranz (private airport shuttle), and taxis are available for the ride to campus from the airport; these run regularly or do not require reservations. Lake Oswego Airporter also can transport you to campus. Call the office of admissions if you want current schedules or phone numbers for these transportation services. Amtrak trains and Greyhound/Trailways buses serve Portland.

FIND YOUR WAY

From I-5, exit to Terwilliger Blvd. Follow Terwilliger south and east to campus (toward Tryon Creek State Park). The admissions office is in Frank Manor, a large brick building just inside Main Gate off Palatine Hill Road.

STAY THE NIGHT

Lewis & Clark is 6 miles south of Portland center, in the southwest quadrant of the city. For convenience to the school, the popular choice is the **Lakeshore Motor Hotel** (210 N. State St., Lake Oswego; 503-636-9679), a mile and a half away. The hotel, known as the "parents' dorm," has decks overlooking the lake that surrounds the hotel on 3 sides. All the rooms have kitchenettes. There is no dining room, but there are restaurants nearby. Rates range from inexpensive to moderate. An appealing bed-and-breakfast is **MacMaster House** (1041 S.W. Vista St.; 503-223-7362), about 15 minutes away. This is in the Washington Park area, famous for its rose gardens. Rates are in the moderate range and include breakfast served in a formal dining room. The large, 3-story colonial house is furnished with antiques, and the owners are very hospitable. Downtown options include: **Days Inn City Center**, (800-899-0248), and **Hotel Vintage Plaza** (800-243-0555), and **Portland Hilton** (800-445-8667). See the Reed College entry for other suggestions in Portland, but be aware that Reed is a 20-minute drive from Lewis & Clark. **Holiday Inn Crowne Plaza** (14811 Kinse Oaks Blvd., Lake Oswego; 800-277-6983) offers moderate pricing and free shuttle from the hotel to Lewis & Clark.

HIGHLIGHTS

ON CAMPUS
- Gallery of contemporary art
- Rose garden

OFF CAMPUS
- Portland Art Museum
- Columbia River Gorge
- Mount Hood

REED COLLEGE

Admissions Office, Reed College, 3203 S.E. Woodstock Blvd., Portland, OR 97202-8199
(The office is in Eliot Hall) • Telephone: 800-547-4750 or 503-777-7511 •
Web: www.reed.edu • Email: admission@reed.edu

Hours: Monday-Friday, 8:30AM-5PM. Closed weekends and most holidays.

Reed College is so tough. How tough is it? About half of Reed freshmen make it through all four years. This despite the fact that grades, while recorded, are neither reported nor discussed. For those intelligent and work-obsessed students who can cut the muster, this little liberal arts school is a virtual utopia.

HIGHLIGHTS

ON CAMPUS
- Thesis Tower
- Research nuclear reactor
- Crystal Springs Canyon
- Cerf Amphitheater
- The Paradox Café

OFF CAMPUS
- Powell's Bookstore
- Mount Hood
- Washington Park
- The Waterfront
- Baddad Theatre

TRANSPORTATION

The Portland Metro Airport is 20 miles from campus. Taxis, Airporter buses, public buses, and rental cars are available for the ride to campus from the airport. For taxis, call Broadway Cab at 503-227-1234 or Rose City Cab at 503-282-7707. The Blue Star Airporter bus will take you from the airport's taxi/limousine area to the campus. For an even cheaper ride, take the Tri-Met #12 bus from the taxi-limousine area; at 42nd Ave. and S.E. Halsey St. (Hollywood Transit Center), transfer to Tri-Met #75 bus going west. Get off at 39th Ave. and S.E. Woodstock Blvd. and walk west on Woodstock for 4 blocks to the college. Amtrak trains and Greyhound buses serve Portland. From the station, take a Tri-Met #1, 5, 9, or 40 bus on N.W. Broadway going south to the transit mall on S.W. 5th Ave.; transfer to bus #19, (Woodstock) which will take you to the front of the college.

FIND YOUR WAY

From the south, take I-5 N. to the Ross Island Bridge exit; then continue east on Powell Blvd. (which connects to the Ross Island Bridge). Turn right (south) on 39th Ave. and proceed a mile and a half, then turn right on Woodstock Blvd. After half a block, turn right again into the Reed parking lot. **From the north**, take I-5 S. to the Oregon City/99E exit. Stay to the far left, then after the split in the exit, stay to the right and take the Oregon City/99E off-ramp. This will put you on McLaughlin Blvd.; continue south on McLaughlin to the Holgate exit (a right-hand exit); from Holgate, turn right onto 28th Ave. and continue to the college, which will be on the left, 2 miles down.

STAY THE NIGHT

An inexpensive bed-and-breakfast is the **Portland Guest House** (1720 N.E. 15th Ave.; 503-282-1402), 15 minutes from campus and within walking distance of the Lloyd Center Mall. Also about 15 minutes away from Reed, with rooms starting at the low end of the moderate range (ask for the special rate for Reed visitors), is **Portland's White House** (1914 N.E. 22nd Ave.; 503-287-7131). None of these bed-and-breakfasts allow smoking. For other bed-and-breakfasts, call **Northwest Bed-and-Breakfast Travel Unlimited** (503-243-7616). About equidistant between Reed and Lewis & Clark is the **Riverplace Hotel** (1510 S.W. Harbor Way; 503-228-3233 or 800-227-1333). This 4-star hotel has all amenities, and the price includes a complimentary continental breakfast. You can dine overlooking the river and enjoy a jazz trio in the bar (well, your parents can). Also check out the downtown Portland accommodations in the Lewis & Clark entry.

AT A GLANCE

Selectivity Rating	88
Range SAT I Math	610-700
Average SAT I Math	653
Range SAT I Verbal	640-730
Average SAT I Verbal	690
Average ACT Composite	29
Average GPA	3.7
Student to Faculty Ratio	10:1

CAMPUS TOURS

Appointment Req?	Preferred
Dates	Year-round, except major holidays and weekends
Times	Mon-Fri, in the morning and afternoon
Avg. Length	1 hour

ON-CAMPUS INTERVIEWS

Admissions

Start Date–Juniors	Any time
Appointment Req?	Yes
Advance Notice	2 weeks
Saturdays?	No
Avg. Length	40 min
Info Sessions	Year-round, call for times

Faculty and Coaches

Dates/Times	Year-round; subject to faculty/coach availability
Arrangements	Contact dept. of interest in advance

CLASS VISITS

Dates	Sept-April, not during the first week of semester
Arrangements	Contact admission off.

OVERNIGHT DORM STAYS

Advance Notice	2 weeks
Arrangements	Contact admission off.
Limitations	First-come, first-served basis; 1-night stay

WILLAMETTE UNIVERSITY

Office of Admission, Willamette University, 900 State St., Salem, OR 97301 •
Telephone: 503-370-6303, Toll Free 877-LIB-ARTS • Web: www.willamette.edu •
Email: undergradadmission@willamette.edu

Hours: Mid-August to mid-May: Monday-Friday, 8AM-5PM. Mid-May to mid-August: Monday-Friday, 8AM-4:30PM. Closed holidays.

Methodist-affiliated Willamette University offers its students small classes, lots of individual attention, a beautiful campus, and a location that is less than an hour from Portland.

AT A GLANCE

Selectivity Rating	84
Range SAT I Math	540-650
Average SAT I Math	610
Range SAT I Verbal	540-660
Average SAT I Verbal	600
Average ACT Composite	27
Average GPA	3.6
Student to Faculty Ratio	10:1

CAMPUS TOURS

Appointment Req?	Yes
Dates	Year-round, except holidays
Times	Mon-Fri 10AM, 11:30AM, 2PM, and 3PM; Sat 10AM
Avg. Length	60 min

ON-CAMPUS INTERVIEWS

Admissions

Start Date—Juniors	Any time
Appointment Req?	Yes
Advance Notice	1 week
Saturdays?	Yes
Avg. Length	45 min
Information Sessions	At times; interviews are informational

Faculty and Coaches

Dates/Times	During academic year
Arrangements	Contact admissions off. 1 week prior

CLASS VISITS

Dates	Academic year (Mon-Fri)
Arrangements	Contact admissions off.

OVERNIGHT DORM STAYS

Advance Notice	1 week
Arrangements	Contact admissions off.
Limitations	2-night maximum stay

TRANSPORTATION

Portland International Airport is 60 miles from campus. HUT Limousine Service offers regular transportation from the Portland airport to the Willamette Campus. Amtrak offers daily north/south train service to Salem; the station is across the street from the southeast corner of the campus. Greyhound buses serve Salem from throughout the U.S.; the bus depot is 5 blocks from campus.

FIND YOUR WAY

From I-5 (N. or S.), take the Hwy. 22/Mission St. exit and travel approximately 2 miles west to the City Center/Willamette University exit. The off-ramp takes you to the southeast corner of campus. Keep to the left and proceed through the traffic signal half a block, turning right onto campus and into the University's main parking lot.

STAY THE NIGHT

Nearby: Salem hosts a variety of accommodations all within close proximity to campus. Rates range from moderate to inexpensive for university visitors depending on time of year and number of guests. The **Best Western-Mill Creek Inn** (3125 Ryan Dr. S.E.; 503-585-3332) sits 5 miles from campus and is within easy Interstate 5 access. Price includes a free breakfast at Denny's, health club privileges, pool and sauna. If a walk is what you'd like, the **Ramada Inn** (200 Commercial St. S.E.; 503-363-4123) is convenient, just minutes from shopping. Additional hotels include the **Phoenix Inn** (4310 Commercial St. SE; 503-588-9220), **Salem Inn** (1775 Freeway Ct. N.E.; 503-588-0515), and **Comfort Suites** (630 Hawthorne Ave. S.E.; 503-585-9705). Salem also boasts a number of unique and charming bed and breakfast establishments. For additional information on those, please contact the Office of Admission (503-370-6303).

A little farther: Salem is less than 50 miles from Portland. See the Lewis & Clark and Reed College entries for alternatives in Portland.

HIGHLIGHTS

ON CAMPUS	OFF CAMPUS
• Hallic Ford Museum of Art	• State Capitol (across from campus)
• Roger's Music Center	• Riverfront Park
• Sparks Sports and Recreation Center	• Silver Falls State Park
• Willamette Bistro	• Beautiful Pacific Ocean
• The Star Trees	• Bush's Pasture Park

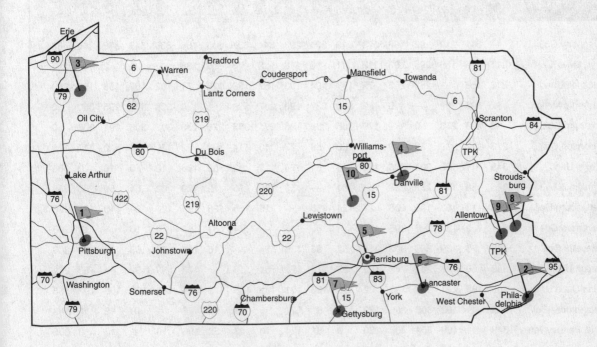

1- **PITTSBURGH AREA**
   Carnegie Mellon University
   Chatham College
2- **PHILADELPHIA AREA**
   Bryn Mawr College
   Drexel University
   Haverford College
   University of Pennsylvania
   Swarthmore College
   Villanova College
3- **Allegheny College**
4- **Bucknell University**
5- **Dickinson College**
6- **Franklin & Marshall College**
7- **Gettysburg College**
8- **Lafayette College**
9- **Lehigh College**
10- **Pennsylvania State University**

Penn.

	Allegheny Coll.	Bryn Mawr Coll.	Bucknell Univ.	Carnegie Mellon	Chatham Coll.	Dickinson Coll.	Drexel Univ.	Franklin & Marshall	Gettysburg Coll.	Haverford Coll.	Lafayette Coll.	Lehigh Univ.	Penn State Univ.	Swarthmore Coll.	Univ. Pennsylvania	Villanova Univ.	Philadelphia	Pittsburgh
Allegheny Coll.	—	341	212	92	88	273	349	325	293	344	337	345	166	339	349	336	346	88
Bryn Mawr Coll.	341	—	156	295	293	112	11	58	113	2	73	50	188	11	11	2	4	293
Bucknell Univ.	212	156	—	259	253	79	169	104	103	157	139	126	71	162	169	155	165	253
Carnegie Mellon	92	295	259	—	0	182	304	237	198	297	306	281	136	305	304	293	300	0
Chatham Coll.	88	293	253	0	—	179	306	238	196	295	303	279	133	303	306	291	308	0
Dickinson Coll.	273	112	79	182	179	—	120	59	27	113	114	103	82	120	120	110	117	179
Drexel Univ.	349	11	169	304	306	120	—	61	124	9	62	52	196	10	0	13	0	306
Franklin & Marshall	325	58	104	237	238	59	61	—	55	60	86	72	123	62	61	56	58	238
Gettysburg Coll.	293	113	103	198	196	27	124	55	—	115	135	125	131	121	124	110	121	196
Haverford Coll.	344	2	157	297	295	113	9	60	115	—	74	51	189	9	10	4	10	295
Lafayette Coll.	337	73	139	306	303	114	62	86	135	74	—	16	186	73	63	71	58	303
Lehigh Univ.	345	50	126	281	279	103	52	72	125	51	16	—	173	59	52	48	60	279
Penn State Univ.	166	188	71	136	133	82	196	123	131	189	186	173	—	186	196	186	192	133
Swarthmore Coll.	339	11	162	305	303	120	10	62	121	9	73	59	186	—	10	12	11	303
Univ. Pennsylvania	349	11	169	304	306	120	0	61	124	10	63	52	196	10	—	13	0	306
Villanova Univ.	336	2	155	293	291	110	13	56	110	4	71	48	186	12	13	—	0	291
Philadelphia	346	4	165	300	308	117	0	58	121	10	58	60	192	11	0	6	—	311
Pittsburgh	88	293	253	0	0	179	306	238	196	295	303	279	133	303	306	291	311	—

ALLEGHENY COLLEGE

Admissions Office, Allegheny College, Meadville, PA 16335 (The office is in Schultz Hall on Park Ave.) • Telephone: 800-521-5293 or 814-332-4351 • Web: www.alleg.edu • Email: admiss@alleg.edu

Hours: Monday-Friday, 8AM-5PM; Saturday, 8:30AM-noon (September-May only). Closed Sundays and holidays.

Ninety miles from Cleveland and Pittsburgh, this old-school college (founded in 1815) is located in Meadville, Pennsylvania (population 14,000), in the foothills of the Allegheny Mountains. Allegheny requires each student to complete an original senior project to demonstrate effective writing, speaking, and analysis skills and the ability to work independently.

HIGHLIGHTS

ON CAMPUS
- Rustic Bridge
- $14.5 million science complex
- $13 million sport and fitness center
- Campus Center
- Robertson Athletic Field

OFF CAMPUS
- Market House
- Academy Theatre
- French Creek
- Diamond Park
- Ernst Bike Trail

TRANSPORTATION

Erie International Airport is 40 miles from campus. The college will provide pickup service for students traveling alone if given advance notice; call the admissions office to make arrangements.

FIND YOUR WAY

To get into the city of Meadville, take I-79 to Exit 36A. You will then be traveling on Route 322 East, from which you should take the Park Ave. exit. Follow Park Avenue straight through town (6 traffic lights) to Chestnut St. and turn right. Follow the sign for Allegheny at the next light, making a left turn around Diamond Park onto North Main St. After 2 traffic lights on North Main, bear right up the hill to Allegheny. After you pass the brick gates in the center of campus (on the left), take the second left turn onto Allegheny St. At the first stop sign, turn left onto Park Ave. After passing 3 large buildings, take the first left, which leads to the admissions parking area. The admissions office is in Schultz Hall, which is the first building down the hill from the parking area.

STAY THE NIGHT

Nearby: **The Days Inn** (240 Conneaut Lake Rd.; 814-337-4264), 2 miles from campus, has a special inexpensive rate. **Super 8 Motel** (845 Conneaut Lake Rd.; 814-333-8883) is a half mile west of I-79. **Holiday Inn Express** (250 Conneaut Lake Rd.; 814-724-6012) is a half mile east of I-79. **Motel 6** (Conneaut Lake Rd.; 814-724-6366) is one-eighth of a mile west of I-79. The motels listed above offer discounted rates for families visiting Allegheny College. Mention that you are a prospective Allegheny student when you make your reservation.

A little farther: The college is in Meadville, which is 88 miles north of Pittsburgh and 92 miles east of Cleveland, Ohio. See the Carnegie Mellon and Chatham entries for suggestions in Pittsburgh and the Case Western Reserve entry for suggestions in Cleveland.

AT A GLANCE

Selectivity Rating	74
Range SAT I Math	550-650
Average SAT I Math	598
Range SAT I Verbal	540-650
Average SAT I Verbal	598
Average ACT Composite	25
Average GPA	3.6
Student to Faculty Ratio	14:1

CAMPUS TOURS

Appointment Req?	No
Dates	Year-round, except during Christmas holidays
Times	Academic year: Mon-Fri 8AM-5PM; Sat, 8:30AM-12PM
	Summer: Mon-Fri 8:30AM-4PM
Avg. Length	1 hour

ON-CAMPUS INTERVIEWS

Admissions

Start Date–Juniors	Any time
Appointment Req?	Preferred
Advance Notice	1-2 weeks
Saturdays?	Yes, during academic year only
Avg. Length	45 min
Info Sessions	N/A

Faculty and Coaches

Dates/Times	Year-round; subject to faculty/coach availability
Arrangements	Contact admissions off. 1-2 weeks prior

CLASS VISITS

Dates	Year-round (Mon-Fri)
Arrangements	Contact admissions off.

OVERNIGHT DORM STAYS

Advance Notice	1 week
Arrangements	Contact admissions off.
Limitations	Sun-Thurs

BRYN MAWR COLLEGE

Office of Admissions, Suite A, Bryn Mawr College, 101 N. Merion Ave., Bryn Mawr, PA 19010 (The office is in the Gateway Building) • Telephone: 610-526-5153 • Web: www.brynmawr.edu • Email: admissions@brynmawr.edu

Hours: Monday-Friday, 9AM-5PM; Saturday 9AM-1PM (September-January only). Closed Sundays and holidays.

The women's community at Bryn Mawr offers passionate professors, a strict core curriculum, and individualized attention. But beware, social life always comes after academics for Mawrters.

AT A GLANCE

Selectivity Rating	92
Range SAT I Math	600-680
Average SAT I Math	636
Range SAT I Verbal	610-710
Average SAT I Verbal	662
Average ACT Composite	29
Student to Faculty Ratio	10:1

CAMPUS TOURS

Appointment Req?	Yes
Dates	Year-round, except holidays and Dec 25-Jan 1
Times	Mon-Fri 10AM, 11AM, noon, 2PM, 3PM, and 4PM; Sat 10AM, 11AM, and 12PM (Sept-Jan only)
Avg. Length	1 hour

ON-CAMPUS INTERVIEWS

Admissions

Start Date–Juniors	Last 2 weeks in Mar
Appointment Req?	Yes
Advance Notice	2-3 weeks
Saturdays?	Yes, Sept-Jan mornings
Avg. Length	45 min
Info Sessions	Mon and Fri by request

Faculty and Coaches

Dates/Times	Year-round; subject to faculty/coach availability
Arrangements	Contact admissions off. 2-3 weeks prior

CLASS VISITS

Dates	Academic year (Mon-Fri)
Arrangements	Contact admissions off.

OVERNIGHT DORM STAYS

Advance Notice	2-3 weeks
Arrangements	Contact admissions off.
Limitations	1 night; Mon-Fri

TRANSPORTATION

Philadelphia International Airport is 20 miles from campus. Taxis, limousines, and trains are available. No advance arrangements are needed for a taxi. For limousine service, call Main Line Airport Service at 610-525-0513 (or 800-427-3464 in PA) for information and reservations, or use the courtesy phone at the airport (push Main Line). If you want to use the trains, take the airport shuttle from the airport (it leaves every 20 minutes) to 30th St. Station in Philadelphia. From 30th St., take the SEPTA R-5 train to Bryn Mawr (leaves approximately every half hour). Amtrak trains and Greyhound buses serve Philadelphia from all over the country. Take the Amtrak train to 30th St. Station in Philadelphia. From 30th St., take SEPTA commuter train R-5 (Paoli Local or Bryn Mawr Local, which goes from Lansdale and Doylestown to Downingtown and Paoli) to Bryn Mawr; the R-5 takes approximately 18 minutes to reach Bryn Mawr. The campus is a 5-minute walk from the station; walk straight ahead (on Morris Avenue) as you get off the train. After 2 blocks, turn left on Yarrow St.; the college stretches to your right and straight ahead. Bennett Taxi Service can be called on a direct phone line from the Bryn Mawr train station if you don't want to walk. If you want to call Bennett in advance, the number is 610-525-1770. From the Greyhound Bus terminal, walk to the Market East train station and take the SEPTA R-5 train to Bryn Mawr (see preceding directions).

FIND YOUR WAY

From the Pennsylvania Tpke., take Exit 24 (Valley Forge) and follow signs to Rte. 76 E. ("Expressway to Philadelphia"). After 3 miles, take Exit 27 (Gulph Mills and Rte. 320). Stay to the right and take Rte. 320 S. At the Spring Mill Rd. intersection, a sign indicates that 320 S. continues to the right; do not turn right here. Continue straight across the intersection; this puts you on Montgomery Ave. Continue on Montgomery for approximately 2 miles to Morris Ave (a 4-way intersection with traffic light). Turn left onto Morris and pass the first left (Yarrow St.). The entrance to the college parking lot is just beyond Yarrow on the   left. The distance from the turnpike to the college is 8 miles.

STAY THE NIGHT

On campus is the **Wyndham Alumnae House** (610-526-5236). Rates are moderate and include a continental breakfast. **Radnor Hotel** (591 E. Lancaster Ave., St. David's; 610-688-5800) is a privately owned hotel about 10 minutes from the college with an outdoor pool and a dining room. Rates are moderate. Downtown Philadelphia is a 25 minute drive to the southeast. For suggestions there see the University of Pennsylvania entry.

If a bed-and-breakfast accommodation appeals to you (even a room in a private home) contact Bed and Breakfast Connections (900-448-3619 or 610-687-3565), for reliable, personalized referrals. There is a $5 reservation fee.

HIGHLIGHTS

ON CAMPUS

- Thomas Hall (on National Historic Landmark Registry)
- Erdman Hall (designed by famed architect Louis Kahn)
- The Cloister and Great Hall
- The Labyrinth and Taft Garden
- Rhys Carpenter Library

OFF CAMPUS

- Barnes Foundation Museum
- Longwood Gardens
- Philadelphia
- Valley Forge National Park
- Shopping in Suburban Square and King of Prussia

BUCKNELL UNIVERSITY

Admissions Office, Bucknell University, Lewisburg, PA 17837
(The office is in Freas Hall) • Telephone: 570-577-1101 •
Web: www.bucknell.edu • Email: admissions@bucknell.edu

Hours: Monday-Friday, 8:30AM-4:30PM; Saturday, 8:30AM-noon. Closed Sundays and all holidays.

Bucknell University offers the best of both worlds: you have the multiplicity of majors and research opportunities offered by a huge, impersonal state school and the close-knit community and individualized education offered by a small liberal arts college.

HIGHLIGHTS

ON CAMPUS
- Weis Center for the Performing Arts
- Primate facilities
- Uptown Night Club
- Stradler Poetry Center
- Library with technology and media commons

OFF CAMPUS
- R. B. Winter State Park
- Restaurants in historic Lewisburg
- Historic movie theater
- 2 malls within 30 min. drive
- Skiing in the Poconos

TRANSPORTATION

Williamsport Airport is 25 miles from campus and Harrisburg Airport is 65 miles. The admissions office will provide transportation to campus if you make arrangements with them at least 2 weeks in advance of your arrival. Rental cars and taxis are available at the airport. Susquehanna Trailways bus lines serve the Lewisburg area.

FIND YOUR WAY

Take I-80 to its intersection with Rte. 15. Exit to Rte. 15 S. and proceed for approximately 7 miles to the university.

STAY THE NIGHT

Nearby: A few blocks from Bucknell in the restored downtown area is an antique-filled bed-and-breakfast, the **Pineapple Inn** (439 Market St.; 570-524-6200). Built in the 1850s, it has an inexpensive to moderate rate that includes a full breakfast and tea in the afternoon. You can play tennis nearby. Many inexpensive and moderate motels and hotels are located in and around Lewisburg, particularly along U.S. Rte. 15. These include: **Days Inn** (570-523-1171), only 1 mile away; **Best Western Country Cupboard Inn** (570-524-5500), about 2 miles from the university; **Comfort Inn** (570-568-8000), and **Holiday Inn Express** (570- 568-1100), 8 miles away in New Columbia at the junction of Rtes. 15 and 80; and **Hampton Inn** (570-743-2223), 10 miles south of campus on Rte. 15 in Shamokin Darn.

A little farther: If you're traveling east of the university on I-80, stop at the **Inn at Turkey Hill** (991 Central Rd., Bloomsburg; 717-387-1500) in a historic town on the Susquehanna River, 45 minutes from Bucknell (use Exit 35 from I-80). This inn is part old farmhouse and part modern wing, and its dining rooms serve a delicious dinner. If you're visiting Bucknell during the summer or early fall, consider making a little detour to the northeast (about a 75-minute drive) to the charming Victorian village of Eagles Mere, a popular resort town in the 1920s. Here you will find **Eagles Mere Inn**, a delightful country place with rates in the expensive range (but they include breakfast and dinner). From November to March, the inn is open only on weekends; from March 15 to April 15 it is completely closed. Consider also a bed-and-breakfast in Williamsport: **Reighard House** (1323 E. 3rd St.; 570-326-3593) is 2 blocks east of the Faxon Rd. exit from I-80. This Victorian home has 6 guest rooms with private baths and other modern amenities. Rates range from inexpensive to moderate.

AT A GLANCE

Selectivity Rating	89
Range SAT I Math	590-680
Average SAT I Math	637
Range SAT I Verbal	570-650
Average SAT I Verbal	614
Student to Faculty Ratio	12:1

CAMPUS TOURS

Appointment Req?	No
Dates	Year-round
Times	Mon-Fri 10:30AM, 11:15AM, 12:15PM,1:15PM, 2:15PM, and 3:30PM; Labor Day through May extra tour at 4:15PM; Sat 10:30AM, 11:15AM, and 12PM
Avg. Length	75 min

ON-CAMPUS INTERVIEWS

Admissions

Start Date—Juniors	April 15
Appointment Req?	Yes
Advance Notice	3 weeks
Saturdays?	Yes, mornings, scheduled in advance
Avg. Length	45 min
Info Sessions	Year-round

Faculty and Coaches

Dates/Times	Year-round; subject to faculty/coach availability
Arrangements	Contact admissions off. 2 weeks prior

CLASS VISITS

Dates	Year-round (Mon-Fri)
Arrangements	Contact admissions off.

OVERNIGHT DORM STAYS

Advance Notice	2 weeks
Arrangements	Contact admissions off.
Limitations	Sun-Thurs night only

CARNEGIE MELLON UNIVERSITY

Admissions Office, Carnegie Mellon University, 5000 Forbes Ave., Pittsburgh, PA 15213
(The office is in Warner Hall, Rm. 101) • Telephone: 412-268-2082 • Web: www.cmu.edu •
Email: undergraduate-admissions@andrew.cmu.edu

Hours: Monday-Friday, 8:30AM-5PM; selected Saturday mornings. Closed Sundays and holidays.

Excellent programs at Carnegie Mellon University include engineering, computer science, business, architecture, and a well-respected School of Drama with several famous alums, including Ted Danson.

AT A GLANCE

Selectivity Rating	91
Range SAT I Math	650-750
Average SAT I Math	697
Range SAT I Verbal	600-700
Average SAT I Verbal	648
Average ACT Composite	29
Average GPA	3.6
Student to Faculty Ratio	9:1

CAMPUS TOURS

Appointment Req?	No
Dates	Mid-Jan to late April, mid-May to mid-Aug; and late Sept to early Dec
Times	Mon-Fri 9:30AM, 11:30AM, 1:30PM, and 3:30PM
Avg. Length	1 hour

ON-CAMPUS INTERVIEWS

Admissions

Start Date—Juniors	First week in May
Appointment Req?	Yes
Advance Notice	2-3 weeks
Saturdays?	No
Avg. Length	45 min
Info Sessions	April, July, and Aug

Faculty and Coaches

Dates/Times	Year-round; subject to faculty/coach availability
Arrangements	Contact dept. of interest 2-3 weeks prior

CLASS VISITS

Dates	Year-round (Mon-Fri)
Arrangements	Consult course schedule upon arrival

OVERNIGHT DORM STAYS

Advance Notice	3 weeks
Arrangements	Must have invitation
Limitations	Only on specific weekends

TRANSPORTATION

Greater Pittsburgh International Airport is 25 miles from campus. Airport Limousine Service provides transportation from airport to campus; no advance reservation is necessary. Amtrak trains and Greyhound buses serve Pittsburgh. Taxis are available from the stations to campus.

FIND YOUR WAY

From the east on the Pennsylvania Tpke., take Exit 6 (Pittsburgh/Monroeville); then take I-376 W. to Exit 9 (Edgewood/Swissvale). At the end of the ramp, turn right onto Braddock Ave. and continue to the Forbes Ave. intersection (Frick Park will be on the left). Turn left onto Forbes Ave. and follow it approximately 3 miles to campus, which will be on the left. **From the west on the Pennsylvania Tpke.**, take Exit 3 (Perry Hwy.); then take I-79 S. to Exit 21 (I-279 S.). Follow I-279 S. toward Pittsburgh. As the interstate nears the city, follow signs for I-279 S. and the Fort Pitt Tunnel Bridge (left lanes). Follow signs for I-279 S./376 E. onto the bridge (right lanes). Watch carefully for signs on and after the bridge for I-376 E. (toward Monroeville). Take I-376 E. to Exit 5 (Forbes Ave. Oakland). Follow Forbes Ave. approximately a quarter mile to campus, which will be on the right.

STAY THE NIGHT

Nearby: Carnegie Mellon is about 5 miles east of downtown Pittsburgh in a section called Oakland. We could find no inexpensive motels or accommodations nearby, but several hotels offer discount rates to families visiting Carnegie Mellon. Ask about these discounts when making reservations. If you want to walk to campus, try **Holiday Inn at University Center** (100 Lytton Ave.; 412-682-6200). Rates are expensive, but there is an indoor pool, an exercise room, and jazz most evenings in the lounge. **Wyndham Garden** (3454 Forbes Ave.; 877-662-6242). Three other options are the **University Club** (123 University Place; 412-621-1890), the **Shadyside Inn** (5405 Fifth Ave.; 412-682-2300), and **The Appletree Bed and Breakfast** (703 S. Negley Ave.; 412-661-0631). The **Hampton Inn** (3315 Hamlet St.; 412-681-1000) offers a convenient shuttle to and from downtown and various shopping areas. For bed-and-breakfast accommodations, call **Pittsburgh Bed and Breakfast** (412-367-8080).

A little farther: You have some great choices 15 minutes away in downtown Pittsburgh. Across the Ninth St. Bridge over the Allegheny river is **The Priory** (614 Pressley St.; 412-231-3338). This restored 19th-century residence of Benedictine priests now houses an elegant inn. Rates, which include a continental breakfast, are in the moderate range and are less expensive on weekends than during the week. Well located near shops and restaurants, the **Sheraton at Station Square** (7 Station Sq. Dr.; 412-261-2000), is about 10 minutes away from campus. It offers rooms on weekends at a moderate rate, and on weekdays at an expensive rate. The Sheraton has an indoor pool and exercise equipment. Also about 10 minutes away is the **Double Tree Hotel** (1000 Penn Ave.; 412-281-3700). Lots of glitz here: an executive fitness club, a lap pool, a sauna, a whirlpool, an exercise room with fitness instructors, dancing, and a shopping arcade. Rates are moderate on the weekend and expensive during the week. See the Chatham College entry for other suggestions in the Pittsburgh area.

HIGHLIGHTS

ON CAMPUS
- Hunt Library
- Engineering & Science Library
- Mellon Institute Library

OFF CAMPUS
- Carnegie Museum of Art
- Andy Warhol Museum
- Pittsburgh Zoo
- Carnegie Museum of Natural History
- Carnegie Science Center

CHATHAM COLLEGE

Office of Admissions, Chatham College, Woodland Rd., Pittsburgh, PA 15232
(The office is in the Andrew Mellon Center) • Telephone: 800-837-1290 •
Web: www.chatham.edu • Email: admissions@chatham.edu

Hours: Monday-Friday, 9AM-5PM; Saturday (by appointment only). Closed Sundays, New Year's Day, Martin Luther King Day, Good Friday, July 4, Thanksgiving, and Christmas.

This tiny women's college is located in the Shadyside area of Pittsburgh, one of the safest and most livable cities in the United States. Chatham offers several unique programs, including a series interdisciplinary courses taught in exotic locales during the short January term and a year-long research project that must be completed by all seniors.

HIGHLIGHTS

ON CAMPUS
- Campus is National Arboretum
- State of the Art Science Complex
- Restored Tiffany window
- Historic Buildings

OFF CAMPUS
- Aviary
- Pittsburgh Zoo and Aquarium
- Pirates, Steelers, Penguins, and Riverhounds (sports teams)
- Festivals
- Theater, museums, and concerts

TRANSPORTATION

Greater Pittsburgh International Airport is 20 miles from campus. Buses and limousines are available for the trip from the airport to campus. Amtrak trains and Greyhound buses serve Pittsburgh. The Port Authority Transit (PAT) operates the city's public transit system (buses, subway, and rail line).

FIND YOUR WAY

From the Pennsylvania Tpke., take Exit 6 (Pittsburgh) to I-376 W. Follow I-376 (the Pkwy.) W. toward the city. Continue on the Pkwy. through the Squirrel Hill Tunnel; stay in the right lane and exit immediately after the tunnel at Squirrel Hill (Exit 8). Follow the exit ramp and make the first left onto Forward Ave. At the first traffic light, bear left on Murray Ave.; stay on Murray to the dead end. Turn right on Wilkins Ave., and within half a block turn left on Woodland Rd., which leads directly into the college. The entrance is marked on each side by a red brick wall. The distance from the Tpke.'s Exit 6 to the campus is 12 miles.

STAY THE NIGHT

Shady Side Bed-and-Breakfast (5516 Fifth Ave.; 412-683-6501) is a stone manor house built by a steel magnate at the turn of the century. It comes complete with billiard room, lots of antiques, and wood paneling and is within walking distance of the school. The **Shady Side Inn** (5405 Fifth Ave.; 412-441-4444), about a mile away, is a complex of several all-suite buildings designed for short-term apartment stays. Rates for a one-bedroom apartment, with kitchen, are moderate. See the Carnegie Mellon University entry for other suggestions. Carnegie Mellon is very close to Chatham.

AT A GLANCE

Range SAT I Math	470-580
Average SAT I Math	513
Range SAT I Verbal	500-630
Average SAT I Verbal	557
Average ACT Composite	24
Average GPA	3.3
Student to Faculty Ratio	9:1

CAMPUS TOURS

Appointment Req?	No, but recommended
Dates	Year-round
Times	Mon-Fri and scheduled weekend visitation days
Avg. Length	45 min

ON-CAMPUS INTERVIEWS

Admissions

Start Date–Juniors	Any time; summer is encouraged
Appointment Req?	No, but recommended
Advance Notice	1 week
Saturdays?	Yes, by appt. only
Avg. Length	30 min
Info Sessions	Interviews function as info sessions

Faculty and Coaches

Dates/Times	Year-round; subject to faculty/coach availability
Arrangements	Contact admissions off. 1 week prior

CLASS VISITS

Dates	Year-round (Mon-Fri)
Arrangements	Contact admissions off.

OVERNIGHT DORM STAYS

Advance Notice	1 week
Arrangements	Contact admissions off.
Limitations	Bring sleeping bag and pillow

DICKINSON COLLEGE

Office of Admissions, Dickinson College, Waidner Admissions House, P.O. Box 1773, Carlisle, PA 17013-2896 (Waidner Admissions House is at the corner of College and High Sts.) • Telephone: 800-644-1773 and 717-245-1231 • Web: www.dickinson.edu • Email: admit@dickinson.edu

Hours: Monday-Friday, 8:30AM-4:30PM; Saturday, 9AM-noon (August to mid-December and April to early May). Closed holidays.

This small liberal arts enclave is best known for its picturesque location, strong overseas education program, and the loving attention it lavishes on its undergraduates. A capable, accessible faculty motivates students to achieve their best, with the result that over half of all graduates pursue advanced academic degrees.

AT A GLANCE

Selectivity Rating	79
Range SAT I Math	550-640
Average SAT I Math	590
Range SAT I Verbal	560-650
Average SAT I Verbal	603
Average ACT Composite	27
Student to Faculty Ratio	13:1

CAMPUS TOURS

Appointment Req?	Yes
Dates	Year-round, except on college holidays
Times	Mon-Fri 9AM-4PM; some Saturday mornings
Avg. Length	1 hour

ON-CAMPUS INTERVIEWS

Admissions

Start Date—Juniors	April 1
Appointment Req?	Yes
Advance Notice	2 weeks
Saturdays?	No
Avg. Length	30 min
Info Sessions	Year-round, except on College holidays

Faculty and Coaches

Dates/Times	Year-round; subject to faculty/coach availability
Arrangements	Contact admissions off. 2 weeks prior

CLASS VISITS

Dates	Sept-Nov and Feb-April (Mon-Fri)
Arrangements	Contact admissions off. 2 weeks prior

OVERNIGHT DORM STAYS

Advance Notice	2 weeks
Arrangements	Contact admissions off.
Limitations	Sun-Thurs nights; not during college holidays and breaks

TRANSPORTATION

Harrisburg International Airport is 32 miles from campus. Taxis and airport limousines are available for the trip from the airport to campus. For airport limousine service, call 717-258-4720 to make advance arrangements. Nearby Harrisburg is served by Amtrak trains and Greyhound/Trailways buses.

FIND YOUR WAY

From the Pennsylvania Tpke., take Exit 16 (Carlisle). Take the right ramp to Rte. 11 S. Follow Rte. 11 S. into downtown Carlisle (approximately 3 miles). Turn right at the intersection of Hanover and High Streets. The Waidner Admissions House is at the corner of West High (Rte. 11) and South College Sts., with parking on the east side of the building. **From I-81 N.**, use Exit 14 (Hanover St.). Turn left at the traffic light; then turn left at the downtown intersection of Hanover and High Sts. From I-81 S., use Exit 16 (High St.). Turn right at the yield sign (Rte. 641). As you come into downtown Carlisle, you will be on High St.

STAY THE NIGHT

Hotels in the Dickinson area include **Clarion Inn and Convention Center** (1700 Carlisle Pike/Rt.11; 717-243-1717), **Comfort Suites** (10 S. Hanover St.; 717-960-1000 or 800-704-1188), **Days Inn** (101 Alexander Spring Rd.; 717-258-4147 or 800-325-2525), **Econo Lodge** (1460 Carlisle Pike; 717-249-7775), **Hampton Inn** (Carlisle Pike; 717-240-0200), **Holiday Inn-Carlisle** (1450 Carlisle Pike; 717-245-2400), **Sleep Inn** (5 East Garland Dr.; 717-249-8863), **Allenberry Resort Inn** (717-258-3211), **Harrisburg Hilton and Towers** (1 N. Second St.; 717-233-6000), **Harrisburg Marriot** (4650 Lindle Rd.; 717-564-5511), and the **Sheraton Inn** (Union Deposit Rd. and I-83; 717-561-2800).

HIGHLIGHTS

ON CAMPUS	OFF CAMPUS
• Old West, Est. 1805	• Appalachian Trail
• New math/science building	• Harrisburg (state capital)
• Observatory	• Yellow Breeches (fly fishing)
• Trout Art Gallery	• Hershey Park
• Kling Center	• Carlisle Barracks U.S. Army War College

DREXEL UNIVERSITY

Office of Enrollment and Career Management, Drexel University, 32nd and Chestnut Sts., Philadelphia, PA 19104 (The office is in the Main Building at 32nd and Chestnut Streets) • Telephone: 215-895-2400 or 800-2DREXEL • Web: www.drexel.ecu • Email: enroll@drexel.edu

Hours: Monday-Friday, 9AM-5PM; Saturdays 10AM group info sessions, 11:00AM tour. Closed Sundays and major holidays.

With its strong research orientation, Drexel University in Philadelphia has a solid record of priming undergrads for professions such as hotel management, graphic design, and, especially, engineering. A special program extends the undergraduate experience for an extra year, but it provides DU students with hands-on work experience for six months out of the year and practically guarantees a job after graduation.

HIGHLIGHTS

ON CAMPUS	OFF CAMPUS
• W. W. Hagerty Library	• Liberty Bell
• University Bookstore	• Independence Hall
• Creese Café	• Congress Hall
• Crossroads at the Handschumacher Dining Hall	• Franklin Court
	• Philadelphia Museum of Art

TRANSPORTATION

The drive from Philadelphia International Airport to campus is 20 minutes (but it could be much longer if traffic is heavy, which isn't unusual). SEPTA (the public transportation system) shuttle trains run hourly from the airport to 30th St. Station, leaving you only 2 blocks from campus. Taxis are also available. Amtrak trains from all parts of the country and SEPTA commuter trains stop at 30th St. Station, 2 blocks from campus. Greyhound bus lines serve Philadelphia from the depot in center city; from there, you can take a SEPTA bus or commuter train (from the Market East station to 30th St. Station) to campus.

FIND YOUR WAY

From Princeton, Trenton, and points north, take 95 south to 676/Central Philadelphia exit. Then take 676 west to 76 east exit. Follow 76 east exit under railroad bridge and proceed into right lane as soon as it is safe to do so. Follow the sign for exit 39 (do not continue following 76 east). Go around the 30th St. train station. **From New York and northern New Jersey**, take New Jersey Tpke. south to exit 4 (Camden/Philadelphia). Follow Rte. 73 north to Rte. 38 west. Travel 4.7 miles past Flower World and merge right onto Route 30 west. Follow 2.6 miles to the Ben Franklin Bridge. Cross bridge and stay in left lanes. Follow signs for 676 west. Follow 676 for 1 mile and take 76 east exit. Go under bridge and get into the right lane as soon as it is safe to do so and follow signs for Exit 39 (do not continue following 76 east). Go up ramp and around 30th Street Station to first light and make a right.

STAY THE NIGHT

Drexel is in the same area as the University of Pennsylvania (known as Penn), so check the Penn entry. Even though the **International House** is on the Penn campus, it is open to Drexel visitors and is within walking distance of Drexel. There's a special moderate rate at the **Sheraton University City Hotel** for Drexel visitors.

AT A GLANCE

Selectivity Rating	75
Range SAT I Math	540-640
Average SAT I Math	590
Range SAT I Verbal	520-620
Average SAT I Verbal	560
Average GPA	3.1
Student to Faculty Ratio	14:1

CAMPUS TOURS

Appointment Req?	Preferred
Dates	Year-round, except on major holidays
Times	Mon-Fri noon and 12:30PM; Sat 11AM (Sept-May only)
Avg. Length	1 hour

ON-CAMPUS INTERVIEWS

Admissions

Start Date–Juniors	All year long
Appointment Req?	Yes
Advance Notice	2 weeks
Saturdays?	No
Avg. Length	90 min
Info Sessions	All year long

Faculty and Coaches

Dates/Times	Year-round; subject to faculty/coach availability
Arrangements	Contact admissions off. 2 weeks prior

CLASS VISITS

Dates	Year-round (Mon-Fri)
Arrangements	Contact admissions off.; prof. approval may be necessary

OVERNIGHT DORM STAYS

Advance Notice	2 weeks
Arrangements	Contact admissions off.
Limitations	N/A

FRANKLIN & MARSHALL COLLEGE

Admissions Office, Franklin & Marshall College, P.O. Box 3003, Lancaster, PA 17604
(The office is in Wohlsen House at 637 College Ave.) • Telephone: 717-291-3951 •
Web: www.fandm.edu • Email: admission@fandm.edu

Hours: Monday-Friday, 8:30AM-5PM; Saturday, 9:30AM-noon (only if group information sessions are scheduled). Closed holidays.

Franklin & Marshall College is an outstanding liberal arts college about an hour from Philadelphia. Be prepared if you come here, though: the work load is demanding. Greek life consumes the social scene.

AT A GLANCE

Selectivity Rating	85
Range SAT I Math	580-690
Average SAT I Math	635
Range SAT I Verbal	570-690
Average SAT I Verbal	623
Average ACT Composite	27
Student to Faculty Ratio	11:1

CAMPUS TOURS

Appointment Req?	Yes
Dates	Year-round, except Memorial Day and Christmas week
Times	Mon-Fri, call for times
Avg. Length	1 hour

ON-CAMPUS INTERVIEWS

Admissions

Start Date–Juniors	April 1
Appointment Req?	Yes
Advance Notice	2-3 weeks
Saturdays?	No
Avg. Length	45 min
Info Sessions	Fall and spring semesters

Faculty and Coaches

Dates/Times	Year-round; subject to faculty/coach availability
Arrangements	Contact admissions off. 2 weeks prior

CLASS VISITS

Dates	Year-round (Mon-Fri)
Arrangements	Contact dept. of interest

OVERNIGHT DORM STAYS

Advance Notice	2 weeks
Arrangements	Call 717-291-4257
Limitations	Available Sun-Thurs nights only

TRANSPORTATION

Harrisburg International Airport is a 40-minute trip from campus. Lancaster Airport is a smaller airport that is a 20-minute trip from campus. Taxis and rental cars are available at the airports for the ride to campus. Amtrak trains provide regular east/west daily service to Lancaster. Continental Trailways buses also provide regular daily bus service to Lancaster.

HIGHLIGHTS

ON CAMPUS
- Mayser Athletic Facility
- Hensel Hall
- The Common Ground
- Rothman Gallery and the Dana Room

OFF CAMPUS
- Philadelphia
- Rockford Plantation and Museum
- Central Market
- The Fulton Opera House

FIND YOUR WAY

From the west, take the Pennsylvania Tpke. to Exit 19; take Rte. 283 E. (first exit after toll-booths) to the Lancaster area. Exit onto Rte. 30 W.; proceed half a mile to the Harrisburg Pike exit (also marked "Franklin and Marshall"); turn left at the end of the ramp onto Harrisburg Pike and proceed toward Lancaster. Travel approximately a mile and a half to the campus, which is on the right. **From the east**, take the Pennsylvania Tpke. to Exit 21 (Rte. 222 S. to Lancaster). Follow Rte. 222 S. to the Lancaster area and exit onto Rte. 30 W. Follow Rte. 30 W. several miles to the point where it exits from the highway you are traveling on; take the Rte. 30 W. exit. Proceed a half mile to the Harrisburg Pike exit (also marked "Franklin & Marshall"). Turn left at the end of the exit ramp onto Harrisburg Pike and proceed toward Lancaster. In approximately a mile and a half, the campus will be on your right.

STAY THE NIGHT

Nearby: Plenty of chain motel accommodations are within a 15-minute drive of campus. **Best Western Eden Inn and Resort** (222 Eden Rd.; 717-569-6444) offers an indoor pool, exercise room, electronic game room, and two restaurants. Other moderately priced choices include **Days Inn** (30 Keller Ave.; 717-299-5700), **Hotel Brunswick** (Queen and Chestnut Sts.; 717-397-4801), and **Quality Inn** (500 Center Hill Rd.; 717-898-2431). A couple of interesting bed-and-breakfast choices are within 15 or 20 minutes of the college. **Kings Cottage** (1049 E. King St.; 717-397-1017) is a Spanish-style mansion with 5 rooms, all with private baths. Rates range from moderate to expensive. The **Patchwork Inn** (2317 Old Philadelphia Pike; 717-293-9078) is about 6 miles from the college. Rates are inexpensive to moderate.

A little farther: In Ephrata, about 30 minutes from campus, is the 18th-century **Smithton Inn** (900 W. Main St.; 717-733-6094). Double rooms are priced in the moderate range during the week and become expensive on the weekends. The price includes a country breakfast. All rooms have private baths and fireplaces, and are furnished to maintain the pre-revolutionary character of the building. Also about 30 minutes away is the **Churchtown Inn Bed and Breakfast** (Rte. 23; 215-445-7794), deep in Pennsylvania Dutch country. On Saturday evening, you can go to an Amish or Mennonite home for dinner.

GETTYSBURG COLLEGE

Admissions Office, Gettysburg College, Campus Box 416, Gettysburg, PA 17325 •
Telephone: 800-431-0803 or 717-337-6100 • Web: www.gettysburg.edu •
Email: admiss@gettysburg.edu

Hours: September-May: Monday-Friday, 9PM-5PM; Saturday, 9AM-noon. June-August: Monday-Friday, 8AM-4:30PM. Closed Sundays and holidays.

An attentive administration, affable professors, and a broad set of distribution requirements covering the humanities, natural and social sciences, mathematics, foreign language, writing skills, and nonwestern civilization make small Gettysburg College a good find.

HIGHLIGHTS

ON CAMPUS
- Beautiful 200-acre campus
- Musselman Library
- Christ Chapel

OFF CAMPUS
- Gettysburg National Park
- Appalachian Trail
- Easy access to Washington, DC
- Easy access to Baltimore's Inner Harbor

TRANSPORTATION

A number of airports are within easy driving distance of Gettysburg, including Harrisburg International Airport (40 miles) and Baltimore/Washington International Airport (55 miles). Gettysburg sponsors a low-cost transportation service to and from area airports. Call Admissions: 800-431-0803 or 717-337-6100. Amtrak trains provide service to Harrisburg. Greyhound buses also serve the area; bus stops are near the admissions office.

FIND YOUR WAY

From the east, take the Pennsylvania Tpke. W. to Exit 17. Take U.S. Rte. 15 S. to the Hunterstown exit. Turn right at the end of the exit ramp. Turn left at the first intersection onto Business Rte. 15 S. Proceed approximately 4 miles. Turn left at the first traffic light (Carlisle St.). The admissions office is 1 block ahead on the right. **From the west**, take the Pennsylvania Tpke. east to Exit 16. Follow Rte. 11 to Carlisle St. Rte. 11 becomes Rte. 34 S. and is Carlisle St. in Gettysburg. The admissions office is on Carlisle. **From the north**, take I-95 and the New Jersey Tpke. S. to the Pennsylvania Tpke. From there, follow the preceding directions from the east. **From the south**, take I-95 N. to the Washington Beltway (I-495). Take the Beltway west and north to I-270. Take I-270 N. toward Frederick, MD, then take U.S. Rte. 15 N. Exit at Steinwehr Avenue (Business Rte. 15) and proceed on Steinwehr to Carlisle St. Turn left on Carlisle and continue to the admissions office.

STAY THE NIGHT

The Gettysburg Hotel (1 Lincoln Square; 717-334-6731) is an elegant choice half a mile from campus. The **College Motel** (345 Carlisle St.; 717-334-6731) is just opposite the campus. **The James Getty Hotel** (27 Chambersburg St.; 717-337-1334). **Doubleday Inn Bed-and-Breakfast** (104 Doubleday Ave.; 717-334-9119) is within a mile of the college, and has a side porch with an old-fashioned swing. **Braffeton Inn** (44 York St.; 717-337-3423) is a marvelous Colonial that features a hand-painted mural of Gettysburg in the dining room. It has an atrium, garden, and large living room, and it's only 5 blocks from the school.

AT A GLANCE

Selectivity Rating	85
Range SAT I Math	560-645
Average SAT I Math	600
Range SAT I Verbal	550-630
Average SAT I Verbal	595
Average ACT Composite	25
Student to Faculty Ratio	11:1

CAMPUS TOURS

Appointment Req?	Yes
Dates	Year-round, except from late April to late May; scheduled around interview
Times	Year-round, every hour except noon. Sept-April: Mon-Fri 9AM-4PM; Sat 10AM and 11AM. June-Aug: Mon-Fri 9AM-3PM
Avg. Length	45-60 min

ON-CAMPUS INTERVIEWS

Admissions

Start Date—Juniors	April 1
Appointment Req?	Yes
Advance Notice	2 weeks
Saturdays?	Yes, during academic year
Avg. Length	45-60 min
Info Sessions	Year-round

Faculty and Coaches

Dates/Times	Year-round; subject to faculty/coach availability
Arrangements	Contact admissions off. 2 weeks prior

CLASS VISITS

Dates	Academic year (Mon-Fri)
Arrangements	Contact admissions off.

OVERNIGHT DORM STAYS

Advance Notice	2 weeks
Arrangements	Contact admissions off.
Limitations	High school seniors only; 1 night; Sun-Thurs night

HAVERFORD COLLEGE

Admissions Office, Haverford College, 370 Lancaster Avenue, Haverford, PA 19041 (The office is in the Whitehead Campus Center) • Telephone: 610-896-1350 (Fax: 610-896-1338) • Web: www.haverford.edu • Email: admitme@haverford.edu

Hours: Monday-Friday, 9AM-5PM; Saturday, 9AM-noon (mid-September to mid-December). Closed Sundays and holidays.

With its tradition of excellence in the liberal arts, Haverford College demands intense study from its 1,100 or so students. The school's honor code is taken seriously, and students have a say in every aspect of college life. Also, we are not making this up: Dave Barry is an alum.

AT A GLANCE

Selectivity Rating	97
Range SAT I Math	630-720
Range SAT I Verbal	640-740
Student to Faculty Ratio	9:1

CAMPUS TOURS

Appointment Req?	No
Dates	March through early Dec
Times	Mon-Fri 9:45AM, 10:45AM, 11:45AM,1:45PM, 2:45PM, and 3:45PM; Sat 9:45AM,10:45AM, 11:45AM, and 12:15PM (Sept-Dec). June-Aug: Mon-Fri 9:45AM,10:45AM, 11:45AM, 1:45PM, 2:45PM, and 3:45PM.
Avg. Length	1 hour

ON-CAMPUS INTERVIEWS

Admissions

Start Date–Juniors	April 1
Appointment Req?	Yes
Advance Notice	3 weeks
Saturdays?	Yes, mid-Sept to mid-Dec
Avg. Length	45 min
Info Sessions	N/A

Faculty and Coaches

Dates/Times	Year-round; subject to faculty/coach availability
Arrangements	Contact admissions off.

CLASS VISITS

Dates	Academic year (Mon-Fri)
Arrangements	Contact admissions off.

OVERNIGHT DORM STAYS

Advance Notice	2 weeks
Arrangements	Contact admissions off.
Limitations	Available September 22 to Nov 20 and Feb 1 to Mar 25 for applying students and April 1-30 for admitted students (Mon-Thurs only)

TRANSPORTATION

Philadelphia International Airport is 20 miles from campus. Main Line Airport Limousine Service will take you directly to Stokes Hall on the Haverford campus; to call for this service, use the airport courtesy phones (push Main Line). If you want to call in advance, Main Line's number is 610-525-0513 (or 800-427-3464 in Pennsylvania). Limousines leave approximately every 45 minutes. Public transportation is also available from airport to campus. Take a SEPTA Airport Express from the airport to 30th St. Station in Philadelphia; trains run every 30 minutes and take 20 minutes to reach 30th St. From 30th St. Station, take either the R-5 Paoli Local or the Bryn Mawr Local to Haverford (not all trains stop at Haverford; check timetables available at the station). The ride from 30th St. to Haverford station takes approximately 16 minutes. The walk from Haverford station to campus takes 8 to 10 minutes: Walk down Haverford Station Road. Turn left onto Lancaster Avenue; then turn right onto campus at College Lane. If you don't want to walk, the Bennett Taxi Service can drive you from the station to campus; call 525-1770 (a local call). Amtrak trains and Greyhound buses serve Philadelphia. Amtrak takes you to 30th St. Station; to get to campus from there, use the SEPTA commuter trains as described above. From the Greyhound station, walk to the Market East SEPTA train station and take the R-5 Paoli Local or the Bryn Mawr Local as described above; the ride from Market East to Haverford takes approximately 25 minutes.

FIND YOUR WAY

From the Pennsylvania Tpke., take Exit 24 (Valley Forge Interchange) and follow signs to I-76 E. ("Expy to Philadelphia"). Take I-76 to Exit 28A for I-476 (South/Chester). Proceed south on I-476 to I-476 to exit 5: US30-St. Davids-Villanova exit. Turn east on U.S. 30 (Lancaster Ave.) and proceed for aprroximately 3.5 miles through Villanova, Rosemont, and Bryn Mawr to Haverford. After you see the Haverford Post Office on the left, turn right into the main entrance of the Haverford campus at College Lane. Follow the signs to the visitor parking lot.

STAY THE NIGHT

See the Bryn Mawr College entry for accommodations. Haverford is very close to Bryn Mawr, so all suggestions there are equally relevant to Haverford.

HIGHLIGHTS

ON CAMPUS
- Whitehead Campus Center
- Founders Hall

OFF CAMPUS
- Fringe Festival
- Philadelphia
- First Friday

LAFAYETTE COLLEGE

Admissions Office, Lafayette College, 118 Markle Hall, Easton, PA 18042-1770 • Telephone: 610-330-5100 • Web: www.lafayette.edu • Email: admissions@lafayette.edu

Hours: Monday-Friday, 9AM-5PM; Saturday, open only for information sessions. Closed Sundays and some holidays.

Lafayette College is a small liberal arts school in Pennsylvania with a nationally renowned engineering program and some of the best opportunities for research in the nation. Campus life revolves around the Greek system.

HIGHLIGHTS

ON CAMPUS
- Skillman & Kirby Libraries
- Farinon College Center
- Williams Center for the Arts

OFF CAMPUS
- Hugh Moore Park
- Lehigh Canal
- Canal Museum
- Crayola Factory
- Two Rivers Landing

TRANSPORTATION

The Lehigh Valley International Airport is a 20-minute drive from campus. Taxis are available for the trip from airport to campus.

FIND YOUR WAY

From the Northeast Extension of the Pennsylvania Tpke., take Exit 33 (Lehigh Valley) to Rte. 22 E. From Rte. 22, take the 4th St. exit (the last exit in Pennsylvania before you cross the Delaware River to go to New Jersey). At the stoplight at the end of the exit ramp make a left turn. At the next traffic light, make a left turn onto 3rd St. Go up College Hill and make the first left onto McCartney St. At the next stop sign, make another left onto High St. The admissions office is in Markle Hall, which is on the right. Parking is available on the street or on the parking deck behind Markle Hall. **From the New York area**, take the George Washington Bridge to Rte. 80 W.; then take Rte. 287 S. to I-78 W. Take I-78 to Exit 3 (Rte. 22). Proceed on I-78 to the toll bridge that connects Phillipsburg, NJ, to Easton, PA. Take the first exit labeled "Easton" (a right-hand exit). At the end of the exit ramp, make a right turn at the traffic light. Follow the preceding directions from College Hill.

STAY THE NIGHT

Nearby: The **Lafayette Inn** (525 Monroe St.; 610-253-4500) is within walking distance of campus. There is no pool or restaurant. Five minutes away, the **Holiday Inn** (Rte. 22 in Phillipsburg, NJ; 908-459-9135) has an indoor pool.

A little farther: Lafayette is about 15 minutes from Bethlehem and about a half hour from Allentown. Check the Lehigh University entry for suggestions in these towns.

AT A GLANCE

Selectivity Rating	82
Range SAT I Math	600-690
Average SAT I Math	645
Range SAT I Verbal	560-650
Average SAT I Verbal	610
Average ACT Composite	26
Student to Faculty Ratio	11:1

CAMPUS TOURS

Appointment Req?	No
Dates	Year-round
Times	Mon-Fri 10AM, 11AM, 1PM, 2PM, and 3:15PM
Avg. Length	1 hour

ON-CAMPUS INTERVIEWS

Admissions

Start Date—Juniors	May 1
Appointment Req?	Yes
Advance Notice	As much as possible
Saturdays?	Group info sessions with tour by appt. on selected Saturdays; these count as personal interviews
Avg. Length	40 min

Faculty and Coaches

Dates/Times	Sept-April; subject to faculty/coach availability
Arrangements	Contact dept. of interest in advance

CLASS VISITS

Dates	Year-round (Mon-Fri)
Arrangements	Contact admissions off.

OVERNIGHT DORM STAYS

Advance Notice	2 weeks
Arrangements	Contact admissions off.
Limitations	Available Sun-Thurs only; not during breaks or final exams

LEHIGH UNIVERSITY

Office of Admissions, Lehigh University, 27 Memorial Dr. West, Bethlehem, PA 18017 • Telephone: 610-758-3100 • Web: www.lehigh.edu • Email: inado@lehigh.edu

Hours: Monday-Friday, 8:30AM-4:45PM; open selected Saturdays in the fall. Closed Sundays and holidays.

The quality of academic programs and the facilities at Lehigh University are well worth the price. Traditionally, Lehigh has been noted for its distinguished engineering school and strong College of Business and Economics, but a push in recent years to improve the quality of the liberal arts programs—highlighted by a brand-spanking-new performing arts facility—has paid off quite handsomely. Lee Iacocca is an alum.

AT A GLANCE

Selectivity Rating	88
Range SAT I Math	598-687
Average SAT I Math	640
Range SAT I Verbal	558-654
Average SAT I Verbal	605
Student to Faculty Ratio	11:1

CAMPUS TOURS

Appointment Req?	No
Dates	Year-round, except during exam periods and from Dec 20-Jan 20
Times	Mon-Fri 10:15AM, 11:15AM, 1PM, 2PM, and 3PM
Avg. Length	1 hour

ON-CAMPUS INTERVIEWS

Admissions

Start Date—Juniors	April 1
Appointment Req?	Yes
Advance Notice	2 weeks
Saturdays?	Yes, selected days in fall
Avg. Length	45 min
Info Sessions	Daily

Faculty and Coaches

Dates/Times	Year-round; subject to faculty/coach availability
Arrangements	Contact admissions off. 2 weeks prior

CLASS VISITS

Dates	Year-round (Mon-Fri)
Arrangements	Contact admissions off.

OVERNIGHT DORM STAYS

Advance Notice	2 weeks
Arrangements	Contact admissions off.
Limitations	Oct. 13, 14, 19, 20, 26-28; Nov. 2-4, 23; Jan 31; Feb 1-3, 8-10; March 1, 2, 7-9, 14-16; April 4-6, 17, 18

TRANSPORTATION

The renamed Lehigh Valley International Airport (formerly the Allentown-Bethlehem-Easton Airport) is a 15-minute drive from campus. Taxis are available for the ride from airport to campus. A bus station is within walking distance of campus.

FIND YOUR WAY

From I-78, take the Hellertown exit; at the exit, turn left onto Rte. 412 and drive through Hellertown about 1 mile to the traffic light at Water St. (becomes Friedensville Rd.). Turn right and go half a mile to a traffic island; bear right onto Mountain Dr. South at the entrance to the Goodman Campus. Follow Mountain Dr. to the top of South Mountain (to the first stop sign), then descend on Mountain Dr. North. Keep to the right after the first stop sign. Take the second left after the next stop sign. Follow the road to the first fork and bear right. Bear right around the next curve, then at the bottom of the incline (the green-painted Taylor College is in front of you), bear left. At the stop sign at the gate, turn left; bear right at the first intersection and follow the curve around to the stop sign. Make a left; at the next stop sign turn left again. The Alumni Memorial Building is at the left. The parking lot is behind the building.

STAY THE NIGHT

The **Comfort Suites** (3rd St. and Brodhead Ave.; 610-882-9700) is within walking distance of campus and has moderate rates. A chain of **Marriotts** has recently opened (Rte. 22 and Catasauqua Rd.) 10 minutes away: **Marriott-Courtyard** (800-321-2211), **Marriott-Fairfield Inn** (800-228-2800), and **Marriott-Residence Inn** (800-331-3131). Prices vary. Another choice is **Holiday Inn-East** (Rtes 22 and 512; 610-866-5800), 15 minutes away, replete with nightclub, restaurant, and moderate rates. **The Sheraton Jetport** (3400 Airport Rd.; 610-266-1000) is located 15 minutes away in Allentown and has moderate rates. For the physically active, the **Allentown Hilton** (Hamilton Mall; 610-433-2221) is about 20 minutes away and offers an exercise room as well as an indoor pool. Several bed and breakfasts are located in the area. Five miles from campus, in Bethlehem on Old Philadelphia Pike, is the **Wydnor Hall Inn** (800-839-0020). It's a comfortable, 1820s, stone, Georgian house with 4 guest rooms. A bit more expensive, yet more convenient, the **Sayre Mansion Inn** (250 Wyandotte St.; 610-882-2100) is 5 minutes from campus. The downtown area offers the **Radisson Hotel Bethlehem** (437 Main St.; 610-867-2200).

HIGHLIGHTS

ON CAMPUS
- Athletics (division I)
- Performing Arts Center
- Greek life
- On-campus café

OFF CAMPUS
- Downtown/historic Bethlehem
- Lehigh Valley Mall
- Pocono Mountain
- Dorney Park (amusement park)
- Music Fest

PENNSYLVANIA STATE UNIVERSITY—UNIV. PARK

Undergraduate Admissions Office, The Pennsylvania State University, 201 Shields Building, Box 3000, University Park, PA 16804-3000 • Telephone: 814-865-5471 • Web: www.psu.edu • Email: admissions@psu.edu

Hours: Monday-Friday, 8AM-5PM. Closed weekends and holidays.

Penn State University is the quintessential state-sponsored university. It provides a reasonably priced education to the masses, offers studies in a mind-boggling range of areas, and maintains top departments, particularly in those fields geared toward career training.

HIGHLIGHTS

ON CAMPUS
- Mineral Museum
- Palmer Museum of Art
- Frost Entomological Museum

OFF CAMPUS
- Football Hall of Fame

TRANSPORTATION

University Park (State College-Bellefonte) Airport is 5 miles from campus. The airport is served by Air Atlantic and Allegheny Commuter airlines. Limousine or taxi service (on call) is available for all flights. Airline connections to University Park are available from the Philadelphia, Pittsburgh, and Harrisburg airports. Greyhound/Trailways buses serve State College.

FIND YOUR WAY

From I-80, exit to Pennsylvania Rte. 26 S. To reach the admissions office, exit from Rte. 26 to University Dr. west toward campus; turn left on Curtin Road to the office, which is in Shields Building. To get to the information booth and visitor parking, take Rte. 26 S. (College Avenue) to Atherton St. Turn right on Atherton to Pollock Rd.; the information booth is to the right on Pollock.

STAY THE NIGHT

On campus is the **Nittany Lion Inn** (N. Atherton St. at Park Ave.; 814-231-7500) with reasonable rates and a restaurant. One block away is a moderately priced **Days Inn** (240 Pugh St.; 814-238-8454), with an indoor pool, sauna, exercise room, restaurant, and a live band in the lounge on weekends. For inexpensive accommodations, try **Autoport** (1405 S. Atherton St.; 814-237-7666), about a mile from campus. A nice, clean motel with an outdoor pool, it has been run by the same family for over 50 years. There is also an inexpensive **Holiday Inn—Penn State** (1450 S. Atherton St.; 814-238-3001), with lighted tennis courts, an outdoor pool, a disc jockey (on weekends), and privileges at an athletic club. For bed-and-breakfasts in the area, which are generally less expensive, call **Rest and Repast** (814-238-1484). You can also stay at a Mediterranean-style resort and conference center called **Toftrees** (1 Country Club Ln.; 814-234-8000), about 10 minutes away. It boasts tennis courts, putting greens, a driving range, a golf course, an exercise room, an outdoor heated pool, and music every evening. The resort is nicely situated among rolling hills and has moderate rates.

AT A GLANCE

Selectivity Rating	85
Range SAT I Math	560-670
Average SAT I Math	617
Range SAT I Verbal	540-640
Average SAT I Verbal	593
Average GPA	3.8
Student to Faculty Ratio	19:1

CAMPUS TOURS

Appointment Req?	Yes
Dates	Year-round
Times	Mon-Fri 12:30PM (bus tour) and 3PM (walking tour); Sat 11AM and noon (walking tour)
Avg. Length	90 min

ON-CAMPUS INTERVIEWS

Admissions

Start Date—Juniors	N/A
Appointment Req?	N/A
Advance Notice	N/A
Saturdays?	N/A
Avg. Length	N/A
Info Sessions	Year-round

Faculty and Coaches

Dates/Times	Year-round; subject to faculty/coach availability
Arrangements	Contact particular faculty/coach

CLASS VISITS

Dates	Year-round (Mon-Fri)
Arrangements	Contact Registrar for class schedule; obtain prof's approval just before class

OVERNIGHT DORM STAYS

Advance Notice	N/A
Arrangements	N/A
Limitations	N/A

SWARTHMORE COLLEGE

Admissions Office, Swarthmore College, 500 College Ave., Swarthmore, PA 19081
(The office is in Parrish Hall on College Ave.) • Telephone: 610-328-8300 •
Web: www.swarthmore.edu • Email: admissions@swarthmore.edu

Hours: Monday-Friday, 8:30AM-4:30PM; Saturday, 9AM-noon (September-February only). Closed Sundays, Thanksgiving, and Christmas.

Students study with a passion at Swarthmore College, arguably the best and almost definitely the most extraordinarily rigorous small liberal arts school in the country. The dedication of the professors here is amazing and the administration runs a tight ship and stays out of the way.

AT A GLANCE

Selectivity Rating	97
Range SAT I Math	660-750
Average SAT I Math	700
Range SAT I Verbal	655-770
Average SAT I Verbal	707
Student to Faculty Ratio	9:1

CAMPUS TOURS

Appointment Req?	No
Dates	When classes are in session and on weekdays during the summer
Times	Sept-May: Mon, Wed, Fri 10:30AM and 2:30PM; Tues and Thurs 10AM and 2:30PM; Sat 10AM, 11AM, and noon (Sept-Feb only). June-Aug: Mon-Fri 10AM and 2:30PM.
Avg. Length	1 hour

ON-CAMPUS INTERVIEWS

Admissions

Start Date–Juniors	May 1
Appointment Req?	Recommended
Advance Notice	1 week
Saturdays?	Yes, Sept-Feb
Avg. Length	30 min
Info Sessions	April and selected Saturdays

Faculty and Coaches

Dates/Times	Year-round; subject to faculty/coach availability
Arrangements	Contact dept./coach 1 week prior

CLASS VISITS

Dates	Year-round (Mon-Fri)
Arrangements	Consult admissions off.

OVERNIGHT DORM STAYS

Advance Notice	2 weeks
Arrangements	Contact admissions off.
Limitations	Not during exam periods

TRANSPORTATION

Philadelphia International Airport is approximately a 20-minute drive from campus. Taxis, rental cars, or SEPTA commuter trains are available. If you are using the trains, take the airport shuttle train to 30th St. Station (in Philadelphia); then transfer to the Media Local (train number R-3) to Swarthmore. From the Swarthmore station, follow the wide walkway up the hill directly to Parrish Hall. The train trip takes an hour or more. Amtrak trains from New York and Washington arrive hourly at Philadelphia's 30th St. Station. From there, take the SEPTA Media Local (train number R-3) to Swarthmore. From the Swarthmore station, follow the wide walkway up the hill directly to Parrish Hall. Greyhound buses serve Philadelphia from many cities. From the bus station, walk to the Market East train station and take the SEPTA Media Local (train number R-3) to Swarthmore as described above.

FIND YOUR WAY

If heading east on the Pennsylvania Tpke., take Exit 24 (Valley Forge); then, take I-76 E. (Schuylkill Expressway) 2.5 miles to I-476 S. Proceed on I-476 for 13 miles to Exit 2 (Media/Swarthmore). At the bottom of the exit ramp, follow the sign for Swarthmore by turning left onto Baltimore Pike. Stay in the right lane, and in less than a quarter mile, turn right onto Rte. 320 S. Follow Rte. 320 carefully, watching turns. Proceed to the second traffic light (College Ave.) and turn right. Follow the road to visitor parking. The entrance to the admissions office is through the archway at the back of Parrish Hall. If heading west on the Pennsylvania Tpke., take Exit 25 (Norristown) and follow signs for I-476 S. Stay on I-476 for 17 miles to Exit 2 (Media/Swarthmore). Follow above directions from that point. From the New Jersey Tpke., take Exit 3 and follow signs to the Walt Whitman Bridge. After crossing the bridge, stay to the right and follow signs for I-95 S. Take I-95 S., pass the Philadelphia International Airport, and continue to Exit 7 (I-476 N./Plymouth Meeting). Take I-476 N. to Exit 2 (Media/Swarthmore). At the bottom of the exit ramp, follow the sign for Swarthmore by turning right onto Baltimore Pike. Follow above directions from that point. If heading north on I-95, pass the Chester exits and continue to Exit 7 (I-476 N./Plymouth Meeting). Take I-476 N. to Exit 2 (Media/Swarthmore). At the bottom of the exit ramp, follow the sign for Swarthmore by turning right onto Baltimore Pike. Follow above directions from that point.

STAY THE NIGHT

Fifer's Folly (3561 N. Providence Rd., Edgemont; 610-353-3366) is an interesting bed-and-breakfast about 15 minutes away. It's owned by artists and located in a lovely park. See the University of Pennsylvania and Bryn Mawr entries for more choices a little farther away. See Bryn Mawr entry for a bed and breakfast reservation service.

HIGHLIGHTS

ON CAMPUS
- McCabe Library
- Lang Performing Arts Center
- Benjamin West House
- Clothier Memoriali

UNIVERSITY OF PENNSYLVANIA

Admissions Office, University of Pennsylvania, 1 College Hall, Philadelphia, PA 19104-6367 •
Telephone: 215-898-7507 • Web: www.upenn.edu •
Email: info@admissions.ugao.upenn.edu

Hours: Monday-Friday, 9AM-5PM; Saturday, 10AM-2PM (July-November only). Closed Sundays, Memorial Day, July 4, Labor Day, Thanksgiving, and December 25 to January 2.

Each of the four schools at the Ivy League University of Pennsylvania is pretty much impeccable. Wharton, Penn's business school, is indisputably among the nation's best; both the School of Nursing and the School of Engineering and Applied Sciences are top-rate as well.

HIGHLIGHTS

ON CAMPUS
- University of Pennsylvania Museum
- Great shops and restaurants
- Annenburg Center

OFF CAMPUS
- Rodin Museum
- Philadelphia Museum of Art
- Independence Hall/Liberty Bell
- Reading Terminal
- Flyers, Phillies, Eagles

TRANSPORTATION

Philadelphia International Airport is 5 miles from campus. Airport shuttle trains take you to 30th St. Station, a 15-minute walk from campus. A train leaves approximately every half hour; no advance arrangements are needed. If you don't want to walk from 30th St. to campus, taxis are available at the station. Alternatively, you can take a shuttle bus from the airport to the Penn Tower Hotel, which is on campus; no reservations are needed, but you can phone 215-387-8333 to check the schedule for the bus. Rental cars are also available at the airport; to drive to campus, follow signs to I-76 W., the Schuylkill Expy. Take I-76 W. to Exit 40, South St. Turn left onto South St. to enter campus. Amtrak train service is available to 30th St. Station in Philadelphia, which is a 15-minute walk or short taxi ride from campus. Greyhound bus service takes you to 10th and Filbert Streets in downtown Philadelphia. A taxi will take you to campus. If you're adventurous, you can go from the bus station to the nearby Gallery Mall to take a SEPTA subway train (the Market-Frankford Line westbound) to 34th and Market Streets. The campus is 2 blocks south of Market at 34th and Walnut Streets.

FIND YOUR WAY

From the north via I-95 South, use the I-676/Center City Philadelphia Exit. Follow signs to I-676 West, the Vine Street Expressway. Take I-676 West until I-76 East, the Schuylkill Expressway. Follow I-76 East until Exit 40-South Street (a left lane exit). Turn right onto South Street to enter campus. **From the south** via I-95 North use the I-676/Center City Philadelphia Exit which is approximately 7 miles north of the airport. Follow I-676, the Vine Street Expressway, West until I-76 East, the Schuylkill Expressway. Follow I-76 East until Exit 40-South Street (a left lane exit). Turn right onto to South Street to enter campus.

STAY THE NIGHT

Nearby: The **Inn at Penn** opened in September 1999 (3600 Sansom St.; 215-222-0200).On campus is the dormitory-style **International House** (3701 Chestnut St.; 215-387-5125), with inexpensive rates. The **Sheraton University City Hotel** (36th and Chestnut Sts.; 215-387-8000) is within walking distance of campus. The Bed and Breakfast Connections (see Bryn Mawr entry) can help you find a nearby inn or private home.

A little farther: The university is about 20 blocks west of downtown Philadelphia, and public transportation is readily available. The luxurious **Four Seasons** (1 Logan Sq.; 215-963-1500) is very expensive, so ask if there are any special rates available. If you venture farther east of center city, you will come across the **Society Hill Hotel** (301 Chestnut St.; 215-925-1394). Ben Franklin used to live next door. Or try the **Shippen Way Inn** (416-418 Bainbridge Street; 215-627-7266 or 800-245-4873), around the corner from the lively South Street scene (which your teenager will definitely go for). Ask for a room on the garden. Rates are moderate.

AT A GLANCE

Selectivity Rating	98
Range SAT I Math	670-760
Average SAT I Math	709
Range SAT I Verbal	640-730
Average SAT I Verbal	681
Average ACT Composite	30
Student to Faculty Ratio	7:1

CAMPUS TOURS

Appointment Req?	No
Dates	Year-round, except Dec 25-Jan 2
Times	Jan, April-June, Sept, Dec: 2PM. Feb, March, Oct, Nov: 10AM, 11AM, 2PM, and 3PM. July and Aug: 11AM and 2PM. No weekend tours in Jan-May and Dec.
Avg. Length	1 hour

ON-CAMPUS INTERVIEWS

Admissions

Appointment Req?	N/A
Info Sessions	Jan-June, Sept-Dec 1PM; July-Aug 10AM-1PM. No weekend sessions Jan, Apr, June, Dec.

Faculty and Coaches

Dates/Times	Year-round; subject to faculty/coach availability
Arrangements	Contact admissions off. at 215-898-9683 2 weeks prior

CLASS VISITS

Dates	Academic year
Arrangements	Contact admissions off.

OVERNIGHT DORM STAYS

Advance Notice	2 weeks
Arrangements	Contact admissions off.
Limitations	1 night only; Oct, Nov, Feb

VILLANOVA UNIVERSITY

Office of University Admissions, Villanova University, 800 Lancaster Ave., Villanova, PA 19085-1672 • Telephone: 800-338-7927 (Fax: 610-519-6450) • Web: www.villanova.edu • Email: gotovu@email.villanova.edu

Hours: Monday-Friday, 9AM-5PM; select Saturdays, 9AM-1PM (while classes are in session). Closed Sundays and holidays.

A very strong honors program, great colleges of engineering and business, and all-around excellent academics all contribute to Villanova's stature. Well-attended daily masses and somewhat strict dorm policies make Villanova very Catholic.

AT A GLANCE

Selectivity Rating	82
Range SAT I Math	580-660
Average SAT I Math	620
Range SAT I Verbal	560-640
Average SAT I Verbal	600
Student to Faculty Ratio	13:1

CAMPUS TOURS

Appointment Req?	Saturday only
Dates	Academic year
Times	Mon, Wed, Fri 10:30AM, 11:30AM, 1:30PM, and 2:30PM; Tues and Thurs at 10AM, 11:30AM, 1:30PM, and 3PM; Sat at 11:30AM (follows info session)
Avg. Length	1 hour

ON-CAMPUS INTERVIEWS

Admissions

Start Date—Juniors	N/A
Appointment Req?	N/A
Advance Notice	N/A
Avg. Length	N/A
Info Sessions	N/A

Faculty and Coaches

Dates/Times	Year-round; subject to faculty/coach availability
Arrangements	Contact dept. of interest 2 weeks prior

CLASS VISITS

Dates	Year-round (Mon-Fri)
Arrangements	Contact individual academic departments

OVERNIGHT DORM STAYS

Advance Notice	N/A
Arrangements	Available only through a personal friend who is a current student
Limitations	N/A

TRANSPORTATION

Philadelphia International Airport is approximately 20 miles from campus. Bennetts Limousine Service is available for the ride from airport to campus; call it from the courtesy phone at the airport or call in advance at 610-525-0513. Public train transportation is also available: Take the SEPTA shuttle train from the airport to 30th St. Station in Philadelphia; transfer to the R-5 Paoli Local train which will take you to the Villanova station (and campus). Amtrak trains and Greyhound buses serve Philadelphia. Amtrak will bring you into 30th St. Station; from there, take the SEPTA R-5 Paoli Local train to Villanova. From the bus station, go to SEPTA's Market East station to get the R-5 Paoli Local train to Villanova.

FIND YOUR WAY

From the Pennsylvania Tpke., take Exit 24A (Midcountry Exchange Rte. 476 S.). After the tollbooths, take I-476 S. to Exit 5 (Villanova, St. David's). Bear right to Rte. 30 E. (Lancaster Ave.). Take Rte. 30 E. through 4 traffic lights; the Villanova parking lot is on the right.

STAY THE NIGHT

Nearby: Villanova refers students to the **Park Ridge Hotel** (800-337-1801) in Valley Forge. Ask for the Villanova rate when making reservations. Villanova is only 2 miles from Bryn Mawr College. For other accommodations, see the suggestions listed there, especially the **Radnor Hotel** (800-537-3000), which is 1 mile west of Villanova.

A little farther: See the University of Pennsylvania entry for downtown Philadelphia accommodations.

HIGHLIGHTS

ON CAMPUS
- Art Gallery
- Two observatories
- Arboretum
- Augustinian Historical Museum

OFF CAMPUS
- Valley Forge National Historic Park
- King of Prussia Mall
- Franklin Institute
- Philadelphia Zoo

 1- **Brown University**
   Rhode Island School of Design
2- **University of Rhode Island**

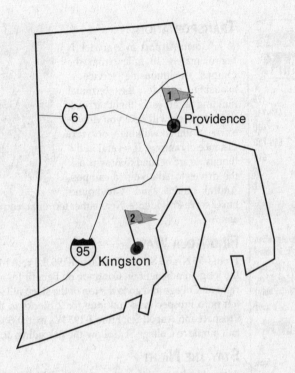

Rhode Island	Brown Univ.	Rhode Isle Design	Univ. Rhode Island	Providence
Brown Univ.	—	1	34	0
Rhode Island Design	1	—	34	0
Univ. Rhode Island	34	34	—	34
Providence	0	0	34	—

BROWN UNIVERSITY

Admissions Office, Brown University, 45 Prospect St., Providence, RI 02912 •
Telephone: 401-863-2378 • Web: www.brown.edu •
Email: admission_undergraduate@brown.edu

Hours: September-May: Monday-Friday, 8:30AM-5PM; Saturday, 9AM-noon (mid-September to mid-December only). June-August: Monday-Friday, 8AM-4PM. Closed Sundays and all holidays.

At prestigious Brown University, courses can be taken either ABC/No Credit, wherein any grade below a C does not appear on the student's transcript, or Satisfactory/No Credit, a pleasant version of Pass/Fail that leaves out the failing part.

AT A GLANCE

Selectivity Rating	98
Range SAT I Math	650-740
Average SAT I Math	690
Range SAT I Verbal	640-750
Average SAT I Verbal	690
Average ACT Composite	28
Student to Faculty Ratio	8:1

CAMPUS TOURS

Appointment Req?	No
Dates	Year-round, except when admissions off. is closed
Times	Mon-Fri at 10AM, 11AM, 1PM, 3PM, and 4PM; Sat at 10AM, 11AM, and noon (mid-Sept to mid-Dec only)
Avg. Length	1 hour

ON-CAMPUS INTERVIEWS

Admissions

Start Date–Juniors	June
Appointment Req?	Yes
Advance Notice	4 weeks
Saturdays?	No
Avg. Length	30 min
Info Sessions	Year-round

Faculty and Coaches

Dates/Times	Year-round; subject to faculty/coach availability
Arrangements	Contact faculty/coach

CLASS VISITS

Dates	When classes are in session
Arrangements	Contact admissions off.

OVERNIGHT DORM STAYS

Advance Notice	2-3 weeks
Arrangements	Contact admissions off.
Limitations	1-night stay on Sun-Thurs during the academic year; not available during holidays, vacations, or reading or exam periods

TRANSPORTATION

T. F. Green Airport in Warwick is approximately 10 miles from the campus. A limousine service is available outside the terminal building after each flight arrival; the limousine will take you downtown within walking or taxi distance of campus. If several in the limousine are headed to Brown, ask the driver to take you to campus. Amtrak trains and Greyhound buses serve Providence. Near either terminal, you can get buses to the campus or the downtown area.

FIND YOUR WAY

From I-95 N. and S., take Exit 20 to I-195 E. From I-195 E., take Exit 2 (Wickenden St.), and follow the loop onto Benefit St. Continue on Benefit for approximately half a mile to College St. Turn right on College and go to the top of the steep hill where College terminates at Prospect St. Turn left onto Prospect and continue for 2 blocks to the Admission Office on the right corner of Prospect and Angell Sts. **From I-195 W.**, exit at South Main St. and continue for approximately half a mile to College St.; follow the preceding directions from the right turn onto College.

STAY THE NIGHT

A few blocks from downtown is the **Old Court** (144 Benefit St.; 401-751-2002), a mid-19th-century mansion on historic Benefit St. It has been completely renovated and rates are expensive. For a completely different experience, you can stay at the **Omni Biltmore** (Kennedy Plaza; 401-421-0700 or 800-THE-OMNI). Built in 1922, this grand landmark hotel has nightly jazz in the lounge, and is affiliated with a health club. Rates are moderate on the weekend and in the expensive range during the week. If an indoor pool is important, try the **Marriott Inn** (Charles and Orms Sts.; 401-272-2400), 6 blocks away. Rates are moderate on the weekend and expensive during the week. The **Holiday Inn** (21 Atwells Ave.; 401-831-3900) also has an indoor pool and, in addition, a game room, weight equipment, privileges at the YMCA, a piano bar, and a restaurant. Rates are moderate. For a budget choice, drive 15 minutes to **Hi-Way Motor Inn** (1880 Hartford Ave.; 401-351-7810) at the junction of US Rte. 6 and I-295. Rates are inexpensive. Inquire about special rates at the **Days Hotel** (220 India St.; 401-272-5577), a 5-minute drive from Brown.

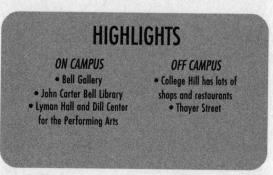

HIGHLIGHTS

ON CAMPUS
- Bell Gallery
- John Carter Bell Library
- Lyman Hall and Dill Center for the Performing Arts

OFF CAMPUS
- College Hill has lots of shops and restaurants
- Thayer Street

RHODE ISLAND SCHOOL OF DESIGN

Admissions Office, Rhode Island School of Design, 2 College St., Providence, RI 02903-2791 (The office is on the 2nd floor of the Woods Gerry Building at 62 Prospect St.) • Telephone: 401-454-6300 or 800-364-7473 • Web: www.risd.edu • Email: admissions@risd.edu

Hours: Monday-Friday, 8:30AM-4:30PM; Saturday for group information sessions and tours on selected dates. Closed Sundays and holidays.

The Rhode Island School of Design enrolls more than 2,000 students in a wide array of visual design and arts programs. The school is located in a residential section of Providence, and it's one of the few places you'll find metalsmithing and glassblowing studios. Programs of study range from animation to furniture and fashion design.

HIGHLIGHTS

ON CAMPUS
• The RISD Museum

OFF CAMPUS
• American Diner Museum
• Roger Williams National Memorial

TRANSPORTATION

T. F. Green Airport in Warwick is a 20-minute drive from campus. Taxis are available at the airport for the ride to campus. Amtrak train and Greyhound bus service is available into Providence. Taxis are available at the stations.

FIND YOUR WAY

From I-95, take Exit 20 to I-195 E. From I-195, take Exit 2 to Benefit St. Follow Benefit St. for 10 blocks to the traffic light. Turn right and go 1 block to the traffic light. Turn left on Prospect St. to the admissions office (62 Prospect St.).

STAY THE NIGHT

Rhode Island School of Design is very close to Brown University. Please see suggestions in the Brown entry, which are equally applicable to RISD. The **Marriott** is within walking distance of RISD, as is the **Westin Hotel**. The **Holiday Inn** is a mile away. The **Omni Biltmore** is about 5 minutes from RISD, the **Days Hotel** is a short drive from the campus.

AT A GLANCE

Average SAT I Math		500
Average SAT I Verbal		510
Student to Faculty Ratio		7:1

CAMPUS TOURS

Appointment Req?	Suggested
Dates	During the academic year
Times	Oct 1-Jan: Mon, Wed, Fri 2PM. Jan to early-May: Wed and Fri 2:30PM; call for additional dates
Avg. Length	90 min

ON-CAMPUS INTERVIEWS

Admissions

Start Date—Juniors	Interview not required for admission
Appointment Req?	N/A
Advance Notice	N/A
Saturdays?	N/A
Avg. Length	N/A
Info Sessions	During academic year, 1PM-2PM on tour days

Faculty and Coaches

Dates/Times	N/A
Arrangements	May be possible at graduate level

CLASS VISITS

Dates	N/A
Arrangements	Campus Tours look in on classes.

OVERNIGHT DORM STAYS

Advance Notice	N/A
Arrangements	N/A
Limitations	N/A

UNIVERSITY OF RHODE ISLAND

Undergraduate Admissions Office, University of Rhode Island, 8 Ranger Rd., Suite 1, Kingston, RI 02881-0807 • Telephone: 401-874-7000 • Web: www.uri.edu • Email: uriadmit@uri.edu

Hours: Monday-Friday, 8:30AM-4:30PM. Closed weekends and holidays.

Though fraternities and sororities still dominate social life, the party scene at the University of Rhode Island has diminished in recent years. This is a good thing, of course, for students looking to take advantage of URI's excellent pre-professional programs, reputable academics, and very affordable in-state tuition.

AT A GLANCE

Selectivity Rating	71
Range SAT I Math	480-590
Average SAT I Math	546
Range SAT I Verbal	480-590
Average SAT I Verbal	544
Average GPA	3.2
Student to Faculty Ratio	14:1

CAMPUS TOURS

Appointment Req?	No
Dates	Mid-September—end of academic year and mid-June to mid-August
Times	Mon-Fri 10AM, noon, and 2PM; Sat 10AM and 2PM
Avg. Length	75 min

ON-CAMPUS INTERVIEWS

Admissions

Start Date—Juniors	April
Appointment Req?	Yes
Advance Notice	2 weeks
Saturdays?	No
Avg. Length	30 min
Info Sessions	When classes are in session

Faculty and Coaches

Dates/Times	Year-round; subject to faculty/coach availability
Arrangements	Contact dept. of interest or particular coach 1 week prior

CLASS VISITS

Dates	Year-round (Mon-Fri)
Arrangements	Contact individual departments

OVERNIGHT DORM STAYS

Arrangements	Available only through a personal friend who is a current student

TRANSPORTATION

The T. F. Green Airport in Warwick is 20 miles from campus. The airport is serviced by the major airlines. Bus transportation and rental cars are available for the trip from the airport to campus. For information on bus transportation, contact the RI Public Transportation Authority or (RIPTA) at 401-781-9400 www.ripta.edu. Amtrak trains along the northeast corridor stop at the station in Kingston, about 2 miles from campus. Local buses (RIPTA) and taxis are available to get to campus from the station. (For train schedules, call Amtrak at 800-USA-RAIL, www.amtrack.com; for bus schedules, call RIPTA at 401-781-9400.) Bus service to Providence is provided by Bonanza Bus Lines (800-556-3815), www.bonanzabus.com; service from Providence to campus is provided by RIPTA.

FIND YOUR WAY

From the north, take I-95 S. to Exit 9, then take Rhode Island Rte. 4 S. (a left-lane exit). Follow Rte. 4 S. to Rte. 1 S., then stay on Rte. 1 S. to Rhode Island Rte. 138 W. (Note that this is just past the Holiday Inn; do not take the first 138 exit, which is 138 E.) Take Rte. 138 W. for approximately 4 miles; the university will be on the right. **From the south,** take I-95 N. to Exit 3A and Rhode Island Rte. 138 E. Proceed for approximately seven miles on Rte. 138; the university will be on the left.

STAY THE NIGHT

Nearby: About 5 minutes away is the **Holiday Inn** (3009 Tower Hill Rd., South Kingston; 401-789-1051). Rates are moderate. There is a wonderful inn in the village of Wakefield, 10 minutes south of the university. **Larchwood Inn** (521 Main St.; 401-783-5454) is a mansion with 18 guest rooms—most with private baths—situated on 3.5 acres. The inn has a restaurant that serves 3 meals a day. Rates vary with the season and are inexpensive from November through mid-May and moderate from mid-May through October. Newport, the "City by the Sea" is only about 15 miles to the east of the University and offers choices in accommodations ranging from large national hotels and motels to small bed and breakfasts at a variety of seasonal prices. Your best bet for a stay in Newport is to contact the Newport County Visitors Bureau at 800-326-6030 or 800-976-5122 of www.gonewport.com.

A little farther: Approximately 45 minutes south, in Westerly, is the **Shelter Harbor Inn** (10 Wagner Rd., 401-322-8883), with a restaurant, a rooftop deck with hot tub, flower gardens, paddle tennis courts, a shuttle to a private beach two miles away, and golf and fishing nearby. This cheerful bed-and-breakfast, with 24 rooms with private baths, has moderate prices that include a full breakfast.

HIGHLIGHTS

ON CAMPUS	OFF CAMPUS
• Athletic complex	• Newport
• Shopping emporium	• Providence
• Memorial Student Union	• Narragansett Beaches
• Multi-Cultural Center in heart of campus	• Block Island
	• South County Bike Path

1- Clemson University
2- Furman University
3- University of South Carolina

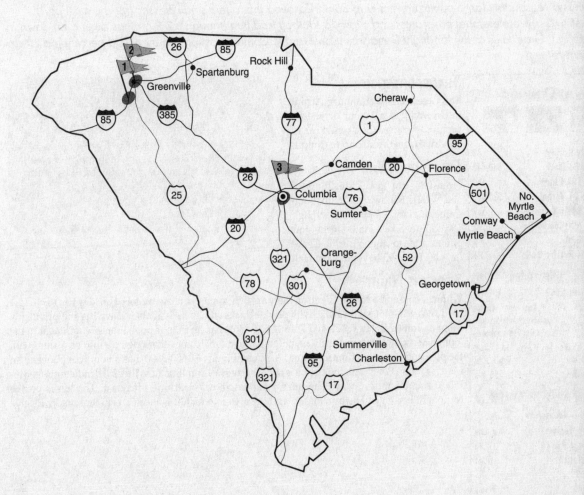

South Carolina	Clemson univ.	Furman Univ.	Univ. So. Carolina	Charleston
Clemson Univ.	—	30	118	240
Furman Univ.	30	—	101	210
Univ. So.Carolina	118	101	—	114
Charleston	240	210	114	—

CLEMSON UNIVERSITY

Admissions Office, Clemson University, 105 Sikes Hall, P.O. Box 345124,
Clemson, SC 29634-5124 (Sikes Hall is on Hwy. 93) • Telephone: 864-656-2287 •
Web: www.clemson.edu • Email: cuadmissions@clemson.edu

Hours: Monday-Friday, 8AM-4:30PM. Closed weekends and University holidays.

Clemson is a reasonably large public university in South Carolina that offers small classes (for the most part), several strong pre-professional programs, and a proud football tradition (though the team has been a bit down in recent years). Graduates of the top-flight Department of Graphic Communications enjoy a 100 percent job placement rate.

AT A GLANCE

Selectivity Rating	82
Range SAT I Math	540-640
Average SAT I Math	589
Range SAT I Verbal	520-620
Average SAT I Verbal	569
Average ACT Composite	25
Average GPA	3.5
Student to Faculty Ratio	16:1

CAMPUS TOURS

Appointment Req?	No
Dates	Year-round, except university holidays and Dec-Feb weekends
Times	Mon-Sat 9:30AM and 1:30PM; Sun 1:30PM
Avg. Length	90 min

ON-CAMPUS INTERVIEWS

Admissions

Start Date–Juniors	Any time
Appointment Req?	No
Advance Notice	None
Saturdays?	No
Avg. Length	Varies
Info Sessions	Year-round, except University holidays and Dec-Feb weekends

Faculty and Coaches

Dates/Times	Year-round; subject to faculty/coach availability
Arrangements	Contact admissions off.

CLASS VISITS

Dates	Year-round (Mon-Fri)
Arrangements	Contact Visitors Center

OVERNIGHT DORM STAYS

Advance Notice	N/A
Arrangements	N/A
Limitations	N/A

TRANSPORTATION

The Greenville-Spartanburg Airport in Greenville is a 1-hour drive from campus. Arrange for a rental car for the drive from the airport to campus.

FIND YOUR WAY

From I-85, exit to US Rte. 76 (north and west). Follow US 76 to South Carolina Hwy. 93 W. Follow Highway 93 to Sikes Hall (admissions office) and to the Visitors Center (just off Hwy. 93 beyond Sikes Hall).

STAY THE NIGHT

Within a mile and a half of Clemson there are 3 inexpensive chain motels. **Holiday Inn** (894 Tiger Blvd.; 864-654-4450) is on a lake with private docks and boats available, as well as golf privileges. **Ramada Inn** (U.S. Hwy. 123 and 76; 864-654-7501) has an indoor pool, live entertainment in the lounge Monday through Saturday, and a patio and balconies that open up into an atrium with the pool and a gazebo. **Comfort Inn** (1305 Tiger Blvd.; 864-653-3600) has an outdoor pool and an exercise room. For charm the choice is the **Liberty Hall Inn** (Business Rte. 28, Pendleton; 864-646-7500), about 6 miles away. The inn's inexpensive rates include breakfast. The inn is on the National Register of Historic Places, and the area in which it is located is exceptionally lovely.

HIGHLIGHTS

ON CAMPUS	OFF CAMPUS
• Fort Hill	• The South Carolina Botanical Garden
• Hanover House	• T. Ed Garrison Livestock Arena
• College of Architecture's Lee Gallery	• Bob Campbell Geology Museum
• Horticulture	
• Training Center	

FURMAN UNIVERSITY

Office of Admissions, Furman University, 3300 Poinsett Hwy.,
Greenville, SC 29613 • Telephone: 864-294-2034 •
Web: www.furman.edu • Email: admissions@furman.edu

Hours: Monday-Friday, 9AM-5PM. Open on selected Saturdays for tours and visitation programs. Closed Sundays and Christmas.

Furman University is a conservative liberal arts school with a caring administration, a solid core curriculum, and a well-earned reputation for rigorous academics. Furman's beautiful, well-manicured, 750-acre campus boasts tennis courts, softball fields, and an 18-hole golf course.

HIGHLIGHTS

ON CAMPUS	OFF CAMPUS
• Bell Tower	• Downtown Greenville
• Timmons Arena	• Mountains
• Tower Café	• Minor League Baseball
• 18-hole golf course	• Bi-Lo Center (concerts)
• Lakeside Amphitheater	• Peace Center for Performing Arts

TRANSPORTATION

The Greenville-Spartanburg Airport is 20 miles from campus. To arrange for limousine service to campus from the airport, call 864-879-2315; after business hours, call 864-235-1713. Amtrak trains serve Greenville; public buses or taxis are available from the station to campus. Greyhound buses stop on the east side of town; taxis are available at the terminal for the ride to campus.

FIND YOUR WAY

From Asheville, NC, and the northwest, take I-26 to Hendersonville, NC; then take U.S. 25 S. In Travelers Rest, SC, U.S. 25 South and U.S. 276 East join briefly; where highways divide, take 276 East to Furman exit. **From Charlotte, NC, and the northeast**, take I-85 to Greenville, then take I-385 into downtown. Bear right onto Highway 183, which becomes Beattie Pl. Follow Beattie Pl. (which becomes College St.) until eventually bearing right onto US 276 West. Continue 5 miles to Furman exit. **From Atlanta, GA, and the southwest**, take I-85 to Greenville, then take I-85 exit. Follow I-185 into Greenville, where it becomes Mills Ave., then Church St. Turn left from Church St. onto Beattie Pl. (which becomes College St.) until eventually bearing right onto US 276 West. Continue 5 miles to Furman exit. **From Columbia, SC, and the southeast**, take I-26 to I-385. Continue on I-385 approximately 43 miles into downtown Greenville. Bear right onto Highway 183, which becomes Beattie Pl. Follow Beattie Pl. (which becomes College St.) until eventually bearing right onto US 276 West. Continue 5 miles to Furman exit.

STAY THE NIGHT

Nearby: Your best deal for price and location is the **Comfort Inn-Executive Center** (540 N. Pleasantburg Dr.; 803-271-0060), a 15-minute drive from campus. A little more expensive and a little farther away (about 20 minutes) is **Courtyard by Marriott** (70 Orchard Park Dr.; 803-234-0300). Opened in 1991, this hotel is near downtown and shopping. Guests have privileges at the Greenville Health and Racquet Club. At the **Hyatt Regency-Greenville** (220 N. Main St.; 803-235-1234), about 15 minutes away, the rates are moderate. The Hyatt Regency also offers privileges at the Greenville Racquet Club. For bed-and-breakfasts in the area, call **Clarion Carriage House Inns** in Charleston (800-CLARION).

A little farther: A 35-minute ride to the north will take you to Flat Rock, NC, the home of author Carl Sandburg (his house is open to visitors), where you'll find the **Woodfield Inn** (Hwy. 25; 704-693-6016). Rates are moderate, but the inn is closed from January through March. Just by Flat Rock is the resort town of Hendersonville, with several reasonably priced inns. **Waverly Inn** (783 N. Main St.; 704-693-9193 or 800-537-8195) is lovely, and the price includes a full breakfast. You can dine on the premises, and tennis courts and antique shops are nearby. **Claddagh Inn** (755 N. Main St.; 704-697-7778) offers moderate prices, a full breakfast, and the benefits of being in Hendersonville.

AT A GLANCE

Selectivity Rating	81
Range SAT I Math	580-670
Average SAT I Math	626
Range SAT I Verbal	570-670
Average SAT I Verbal	622
Average ACT Composite	27
Student to Faculty Ratio	12:1

CAMPUS TOURS

Appointment Req?	Yes
Dates	Year-round, except on campus holidays, breaks, and exam periods
Times	Call for appointment
Avg. Length	45-60 min

ON-CAMPUS INTERVIEWS

Admissions

Start Date–Juniors	N/A
Appointment Req?	Yes
Advance Notice	10 days
Saturdays?	selected
Avg. Length	45-60 min
Info Sessions	Year-round, except on campus holidays, breaks, and exam periods

Faculty and Coaches

Dates/Times	Year-round; subject to faculty/coach availability
Arrangements	Contact admissions off. at least 1 week prior

CLASS VISITS

Dates	Academic year (Mon-Fri)
Arrangements	Contact admissions off.

OVERNIGHT DORM STAYS

Advance Notice	2 weeks
Arrangements	Contact admissions off.
Limitations	Available Sun-Thurs nights, for seniors only

University of South Carolina—Columbia

Visitor Center, University of South Carolina, Columbia, SC 29208 •
Telephone: 803-777-0160 or 800-922-9755 • Web: www.sc.edu •
Email: admissions-ugrad@sc.edu

Hours: Monday-Friday, 8:30AM-5PM; Saturday, 9:30AM-2:00PM (by appointment). Closed Sundays and some national holidays.

The extremely affordable University of South Carolina provides great financial aid for academic superstars and an excellent academic atmosphere. International studies and the business program are highlights among USC's multitude of majors.

AT A GLANCE

Selectivity Rating	73
Range SAT I Math	490-610
Average SAT I Math	548
Range SAT I Verbal	490-610
Average SAT I Verbal	550
Average ACT Composite	24
Average GPA	3.5

CAMPUS TOURS

Appointment Req?	Yes
Dates	Varies by season
Times	Mon-Fri 10AM and 2PM; Summer 10AM
Avg. Length	2 hours

ON-CAMPUS INTERVIEWS

Admissions

Start Date—Juniors	Any time
Appointment Req?	Preferred
Advance Notice	2 weeks
Saturdays?	No
Avg. Length	Varies
Info Sessions	N/A

Faculty and Coaches

Dates/Times	Year-round; subject to faculty/coach availability
Arrangements	Contact Visitor Center 2 weeks prior

CLASS VISITS

Dates	Year-round (Mon-Fri)
Arrangements	Contact admissions off. 2 weeks prior

OVERNIGHT DORM STAYS

Advance Notice	N/A
Arrangements	N/A
Limitations	N/A

TRANSPORTATION

The Columbia Metropolitan Airport is a 20-minute drive from campus. Taxis, limousines, and rental cars are available at the airport for the trip to campus. City bus service is also available from the airport to points near campus; this service is cheaper than other alternatives, but takes longer. Greyhound buses serve Columbia; the terminal is 6 blocks from campus.

FIND YOUR WAY

From I-20 from Florence, turn off at SC 277 (Exit 73) toward Columbia. Stay on this freeway, which becomes Bull St. Follow Bull St. until it intersects with Pendleton St. Turn right and proceed 4 blocks to Assembly St. Turn left, and the Visitor Center will be on your immediate right. **From I-20 East from Augusta**, turn off at Exit 58 (U.S. 1 toward West Columbia) and stay on this highway, which becomes Meeting St. and then becomes Gervais St. after you cross the Congaree River. Turn right onto Assembly St. at the South Carolina State Capitol. The Visitor Center will be on your right at the 2nd traffic light. **From I-26 East from Spartanburg**, follow U.S. 126/76 toward downtown Columbia and exit at Elmwood Ave. Turn right onto Assembly St. and continue for 11 blocks until you see the Visitor Center on your right just past Pendleton St. **From I-26 West from Charleston**, take the Exit 111-B (U.S. 1) and continue until you see the Congaree River. The street name changes from Meeting St. to Gervais St. Proceed several blocks. Turn right on to Assembly St., at the South Carolina Capitol. The Visitor Center will be on your right at the 2nd traffic light. **From U.S. 76/378 from Sumter**, U.S. 76/378 will change from Sumter Highway to Garners Ferry Rd. to Devine St. Devine will intersect with Harden St. at Five Points. Turn left onto Harden St. and take the next right onto Blossom St. Turn right at the 6th stoplight onto Assembly St. The Visitor Center will be 4 blocks ahead on your left. **From I-77 from Charlotte**, exit onto SC 277 toward Columbia. Stay on this freeway, which becomes Bull St. Follow Bull St. until it intersects with Pendleton St. Turn right and proceed 4 blocks to Assembly St. Turn left, and the Visitor Center will be on your immediate right.

STAY THE NIGHT

Special University of South Carolina visitor rates apply at some hotels and inns. Be sure to inquire when you make your reservation. While there are many lodging choices throughout Columbia, the following hotels are within a few blocks of the campus: **Holiday Inn Coliseum** at USC (800-HOLIDAY or 803-799-7800), the **Clarion Town House Hotel** (800-277-8711 or 803-771-8711), and **The Adam's Mark Hotel** (800-444-ADAM or 803-771-7000). Two bed-and-breakfast inns are within walking distance, **Rose Hall** (803-771-2288) and **Claussen's Inn** (800-622-3382 or 803-765-0440).

HIGHLIGHTS

ON CAMPUS
- McKussick Museum
- Confederate Relic Room
- Melton Observatory
- Williams Brice Stadium
- Historic Horseshoe

OFF CAMPUS
- Riverbanks Zoo
- South Carolina State Museum
- Robert Mills House
- Woodrow Wilson's boyhood home
- Columbia Museum of Art

 1- **Rhodes College**
2- **University of the South**
3- **Vanderbilt University**

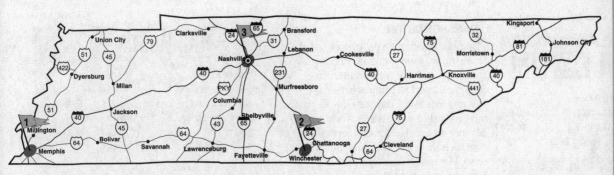

Tennessee	Rhodes Coll.	Univ. of the South	Vanderbilt Univ.	*Knoxville*	*Memphis*
Rhodes Coll.	—	260	210	387	0
Univ. of the South	260	—	96	159	260
Vanderbilt Univ.	210	96	—	178	210
Knoxville	387	159	178	—	387
Memphis	0	260	210	387	—

TENNESSEE

RHODES COLLEGE

Office of Admissions, Rhodes College, 2000 N. Pkwy., Memphis, TN 38112-1690 (The office is in Halliburton Tower in Palmer Hall) • Telephone: 901-843-3700 or 800-844-5969 • Web: www.rhodes.edu • Email: adminfo@rhodes.edu

Hours: Monday-Friday, 8:30AM-5PM; Saturday, 9AM-noon (only during the school year). Closed Sundays and holidays.

Tiny Rhodes College in Memphis offers its students the best of many worlds: a highly touted academic program, a beautiful campus, and accessibility to a major metropolis. Rhodes also boasts a highly committed faculty and a killer reputation with graduate schools; the school claims its students' acceptance rate in such programs is over 90 percent.

AT A GLANCE

Selectivity Rating	80
Range SAT I Math	600-690
Range SAT I Verbal	590-700
Student to Faculty Ratio	12:1

CAMPUS TOURS

Appointment Req?	Yes
Dates	Year-round
Times	Mon, Wed, Fri 10:20AM, 12:40PM, and 2PM; Tues and Thurs 9:40AM, 11:30AM, and 1:30PM; Sat 10AM and 11:30AM (during school year)
Avg. Length	1 hour

ON-CAMPUS INTERVIEWS

Admissions

Start Date—Juniors	Any time
Appointment Req?	Yes
Advance Notice	7 days
Saturdays?	Yes
Avg. Length	45 min
Info Sessions	Yes

Faculty and Coaches

Dates/Times	Academic year; subject to faculty/coach availability
Arrangements	Contact admissions off. 7 days prior

CLASS VISITS

Dates	Year-round (Mon-Fri)
Arrangements	Contact admissions off.

OVERNIGHT DORM STAYS

Advance Notice	7 days
Arrangements	Contact admissions off.
Limitations	1 night stay; Sun-Thurs; seniors and transfers only

TRANSPORTATION

Memphis International Airport is seven miles from campus. Rhodes students provide transportation from the airport to campus between 9AM and 9PM every day; call the admissions office at least one week in advance to arrange for this service. Amtrak trains and Greyhound buses serve Memphis. Taxis are available from the stations to campus.

HIGHLIGHTS

ON CAMPUS
- Bryan Campus Life Center
- Halliburton Tower
- Briggs Student Center
- Oak Alley
- McCoy Theater

OFF CAMPUS
- Graceland
- National Civil Rights Museum
- Beale Street
- Rendezvous BBQ
- Orpheum Theater

FIND YOUR WAY

From the north, take I-55 S. to West Memphis, AR. Exit to I-40 E. (toward Memphis). Exit at Danny Thomas Blvd. North (Exit 1B) and take the first right onto North Pkwy. Continue on North Pkwy., then turn left on University St. and continue to the Phillips Lane entrance to the campus. **From the south**, take I-55 North to Memphis and merge with I-240 North, exit Union Avenue East. Continue on Union Ave. to East Pkwy. Turn left onto East Pkwy. and continue to North Pkwy. Turn left at North Pkwy. and continue to University Street. Turn right at University to Phillips Lane Entrance. **From the east**, take I-40 W. to Memphis. Continue on Sam Cooper Blvd., which becomes Broad St. Proceed on Broad, then turn right onto East Pkwy. At the first intersection, turn left onto North Pkwy. and proceed to University St. Turn right at University to the Phillips Lane entrance. **From the west**, take I-40 E. to Memphis, then follow the directions given from the north.

STAY THE NIGHT

The Hampton Inn and Suites (175 Peabody, 901-260-4000) and **Wyndham Garden Hotel** (250 N. Main; 901-525-1800) are located near the campus. A little bit farther is the **Hampton Inn** (1180 Union Ave.; 901-276-1175), whose inexpensive rate includes continental breakfast. For a real treat, consider the famous **Peabody Hotel** (149 Union Ave.; 901-529-4000), about 10 minutes from the school. The special rate for college visitors puts it at the high end of the moderate range. Ducks march through the lobby in the afternoon. Need we say more?

UNIVERSITY OF THE SOUTH

Office of Admissions, University of the South, 735 University Ave., Sewanee, TN 37383-1000
(The office is in Fulford Hall on University Ave.) • Telephone: 931-598-1238 or 800-522-2234 •
Web: www.sewanee.edu

Hours: Monday-Friday, 8AM-4:30PM; Saturday, 8:15AM-noon (during fall and spring semesters). Closed Sundays and holidays.

The University of the South (a.k.a. Sewanee to the initiated) offers a huge Greek system and one of the best liberal arts educations in the country. The honor code here pervades every aspect of life and instills a feeling of trust on campus.

HIGHLIGHTS

ON CAMPUS
- Outdoor recreation on the 10,000-acre campus
- All Saints' Chapel
- Rebel's Rest
- Memorial Cross and University View
- University Golf and Tennis Club

OFF CAMPUS
- The Tennessee Aquarium
- Rock City
- Monteagle Assembly
- South Cumberland Recreation Area

TRANSPORTATION

The Nashville International Airport is 90 miles from campus. The Chattanooga Metropolitan Airport is 50 miles from campus. Rental cars are available at these airports and shuttle service is available from the airports for students traveling alone. Contact the Office of Admissions for details. The University has its own airport in Sewanee, a mile and a half from campus. The 3,500-foot runway is available to private planes; call 931-598-1910 for further information. The university can provide a car at the Sewanee airport for visitor use. Greyhound bus lines serve Monteagle, which is 4 miles from Sewanee. If you notify the admissions office well in advance, it will provide transportation to and from the bus station.

FIND YOUR WAY

From I-24 (between Nashville and Chattanooga), take Exit 134 (Monteagle) to Hwy. 41 N. After approximately 4 miles, pass through the stone columns and veer right onto University Ave. The admissions office is approximately 1 mile down University Ave. on the right, across from the main quadrangle and All Saints' Chapel. **If you are traveling on south Hwy. 41,** Sewanee is 6 miles east of Cowan. At the top of the mountain, turn left onto University Ave. at the small group of shops. Proceed up the hill to the heart of campus. The admissions office is on the left side of the street across from the main quadrangle and All Saints' Chapel.

STAY THE NIGHT

Nearby: For on-campus convenience, character, and fun, the **Sewanee Inn** (931-598-1686) has it all. Built from mountain stone with cathedral ceilings, the rooms include a continental breakfast. Alternatives include the **Best Western Smoke House** (Monteagle; 931-924-2091), a motel with cabins in the back and an outdoor pool; the **Monteagle Inn** (931-924-3869); or the **Edgeworth Inn** (931-924-2669), just seven miles from the university. The inn's moderate price includes a full southern breakfast with biscuits. It's fun to explore the 96 acres of this Victorian village. The inn is also great for hiking and biking. The Assembly grounds are listed on the National Register of Historic Places.

A little farther: If you're ready for a change of pace, you'll find it 11 miles west of Sewanee at **Tim's Ford State Park** (Winchester; 931-967-4457). The park has campsites and 2-bedroom housekeeping cabins with fireplaces, available from April to December. The cabins are heated, air-conditioned, and located on Tim's Ford Lake. The area has an outdoor swimming pool, bike trails, a recreation building with games and sports, and a marina with a restaurant and picnic area.

AT A GLANCE

Selectivity Rating	86
Range SAT I Math	560-660
Range SAT I Verbal	570-660
Average GPA	3.3
Student to Faculty Ratio	11:1

CAMPUS TOURS

Appointment Req?	Preferred
Dates	Year-round, except occasionally when student guides are not available
Times	Mon-Fri 10AM and 2PM; Sat 11:30AM (only when admissions off. is open)
Avg. Length	45-60 min

ON-CAMPUS INTERVIEWS

Admissions

Start Date–Juniors	Any time, but preferable to wait until second semester of junior year
Appointment Req?	Yes
Advance Notice	10 days
Saturdays?	No
Avg. Length	45 min
Info Sessions	Sat during winter

Faculty and Coaches

Dates/Times	Academic year; subject to faculty/coach availability
Arrangements	Contact admissions off. 10 days prior

CLASS VISITS

Dates	Academic year-round (Mon-Fri)
Arrangements	Contact admissions off.

OVERNIGHT DORM STAYS

Advance Notice	2 weeks
Arrangements	Contact admissions off.
Limitations	1-night stay, seniors only Sun-Thurs stay preferred

VANDERBILT UNIVERSITY

Office of Undergraduate Admissions, Vanderbilt University, 2305 West End Ave., Nashville, TN 37203-1727 • Telephone: 615-322-2561 • Web: www.vanderbilt.edu • Email: admissions@vanderbilt.edu

Hours: Monday-Friday, 8AM-5PM; Saturday mornings during the academic year. Closed Sundays, New Year's Day, July 4, Thanksgiving, and December 24-25.

Greeks dominate campus life on this beautiful laid-back campus chock full of southern hospitality, and Nashville provides plenty of social options.

AT A GLANCE

Selectivity Rating	93
Range SAT I Math	630-710
Range SAT I Verbal	610-700
Average GPA	3.6
Student to Faculty Ratio	8:1

CAMPUS TOURS

Appointment Req?	Preferred
Dates	Varies; call for schedule
Times	Varies; call for schedule
Avg. Length	1 hour

ON-CAMPUS INTERVIEWS

Admissions

Start Date–Juniors	Interviews are not offered
Appointment Req?	
Advance Notice	
Saturdays?	
Avg. Length	
Info Sessions	Year-round; 1 hour appointment preferred

Faculty and Coaches

Dates/Times	Year-round; subject to faculty/coach availability
Arrangements	Contact Athletic dept 2 weeks prior

CLASS VISITS

Dates	Academic year (Mon-Fri)
Arrangements	Consult class schedule in admissions off.

OVERNIGHT DORM STAYS

Advance Notice	2 weeks; allow more notice for April stay
Arrangements	Contact admissions off.
Limitations	1-night stay only for seniors; begins mid-Sept, April only for accepted students; not available on Sat, holidays, exam periods

TRANSPORTATION

Nashville International Airport is approximately 10 miles from campus and taxis and rental cars are available. Capitol Limousine Service offers a van limo service from the airport to any hotel or motel in the Nashville area or to any University location. They suggest that you make a reservation prior to your arrival (615-883-6777). Greyhound buses serve Nashville, and taxis to campus are available.

FIND YOUR WAY

From the north, take I-265 to I-40 E.; from I-40 take Exit 209B. Turn right on Broadway (U.S. 70 S.). Follow Broadway and veer right to West End Ave. Continue on West End to 23 Ave. Undergraduate Admissions is located on the right. **From the east or south**, take I-40 W. to Exit 209A. Turn left on Broadway and follow preceding directions from there. **From the west**, take I-40 E. to Exit 209B. Turn right on Broadway and follow preceding directions from there.

STAY THE NIGHT

Several choices are within walking distance of the university. The most expensive (the special rate for university visitors is at the high end of the moderate range) is the **Vanderbilt Plaza** (2100 West End Ave.; 615-320-1700, or 800-336-3335) which is across the street from campus. At the **Hampton Inn** (1919 West End Ave.; 615-329-1144 or 800-426-7866), you can get a cheap double room. Rates are a bit higher at the **Holiday Inn Vanderbilt** (2613 West End Ave.; 615-327-4707 or 800-663-4427), which has a pool and fitness room. We like the all-suite **Hermitage Hotel** (231 6th Ave. North; 615-244-3121 or 800-251-1908), about a 5-minute drive from the university. Built in 1910, the hotel has been beautifully restored, but rates are expensive. Another possibility, about 15 minutes away, is **Maxwell House** (2025 Metro Center Blvd.; 615-259-4343). Prices at this large hotel are expensive, but it has a fitness room, lighted tennis courts, a sauna, and a whirlpool—not to mention great food! Also about 15 minutes away is a **Courtyard by Marriott-Brentwood** (103 E. Park Dr.; 615-371-9200). Rates vary from the inexpensive to moderate range, and there's a fitness room and a pool.

HIGHLIGHTS

ON CAMPUS
- National Arboretum
- Freedom Forum First Amendment Center
- Free Electron Laser
- Robert Penn Warren Center for Humanities
- SEC Division I Athletics

OFF CAMPUS
- 2nd Avenue historic/ entertainment district
- Tennessee Performing Arts Center
- Football, hockey
- Percy Priest Lake
- The Parthenon
- The Grand Ole Opry

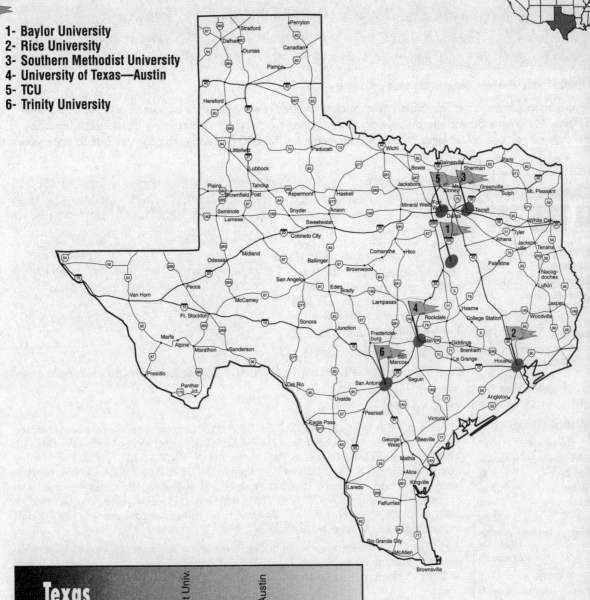

1- Baylor University
2- Rice University
3- Southern Methodist University
4- University of Texas—Austin
5- TCU
6- Trinity University

Texas

	Baylor Univ.	Rice Univ.	So. Methodist Univ.	TCU	Trinity Univ.	Univ. Texas-Austin	Dallas	Houston	San Antonio
Baylor Univ.	—	245	102	91	186	100	92	236	182
Rice Univ.	245	—	253	282	196	186	243	0	189
So. Methodist Univ.	102	253	—	35	282	195	0	240	278
TCU	91	282	35	—	273	192	31	262	269
Trinity Univ.	186	196	282	273	—	79	265	205	0
Univ. Texas-Austin	100	186	195	192	79	—	195	186	79
Dallas	92	243	0	31	265	195	—	243	272
Houston	236	0	240	262	205	186	243	—	197
San Antonio	182	189	278	269	0	79	272	197	—

BAYLOR UNIVERSITY

Admission Services Office, Baylor University, P.O. Box 97056, Waco, TX 76798-7056 (The office is in Clifton Robinson Tower, Suite 580) • Telephone: 254-710-3435 or 800-BAYLORU • Web: www.baylor.edu • Email: admissions_serv_office@baylor.edu

Hours: Monday-Friday, 8AM-5PM. Closed weekends and holidays.

This religious school in the Lone Star State has a massive Greek system and many academic and social options for Christians. The unique Baylor Interdisciplinary Core Program eats up 41 credits in various subjects, emphasizes how they all relate, and replaces normal requirements for the 200 freshman the program admits each year.

AT A GLANCE

Selectivity Rating	78
Range SAT I Math	540-650
Range SAT I Verbal	520-630
Student to Faculty Ratio	18:1

CAMPUS TOURS

Appointment Req?	Yes
Dates	Year-round, except on holidays and select weekends
Times	Mon-Fri 8:30AM-1:30PM; select Saturdays 10AM
Avg. Length	2 hours

ON-CAMPUS INTERVIEWS

Admissions

Start Date–Juniors	Spring semester
Appointment Req?	No
Advance Notice	None
Saturdays?	No
Avg. Length	30 min
Info Sessions	Year-round, except on holidays and select weekends

Faculty

Dates/Times	Year-round; subject to faculty availability
Arrangements	Contact Campus Tours at 254-710-2407 or 800-BaylorU 7 days prior

CLASS VISITS

Dates	Year-round (Mon-Fri)
Arrangements	Contact Campus Tours 7 days prior

OVERNIGHT DORM STAYS

Advance Notice	2 weeks
Arrangements	Contact Campus Tours
Limitations	Available only for seniors during the fall and spring semesters

TRANSPORTATION

Waco Regional Airport is 10 miles (a 15-minute drive) from campus. Rental cars and taxis are available at the airport for the drive to campus; call Avis at 800-331-1212 or Hertz at 800-654-3131. The Waco airport can be reached via Dallas-Fort Worth International and Houston International (George Bush) Airports.

FIND YOUR WAY

From I-35, take Exit 335B on University Parks Dr. The Campus Tours Office is 2 blocks east of I-35 in the Wiethorn Visitor's Center.

STAY THE NIGHT

Nearby: **La Quinta Inn** (1110 S. 9th St.; 254-752-9741) has an outdoor pool and a café next door. Rates are inexpensive. **Lexington Inn** (254-754-1266) is located at I-35 and University Parks Dr. Another option close to campus is the **Clarion Inn** (S. 4th St.; 254-757-2000). **The Marriott Courtyard** (University Parks Dr. and Washington; 254-752-8686) is brand-new, and, hey, you always know what to expect. **The Best Western Old Main Lodge** is across the street from campus (I-35 and 4th St.; 254-753-0316). The **Hilton Hotel** (113 S. University Parks Dr.; 254-754-8484), 1 mile from the school and near downtown, has an outdoor pool, access to a health club, a tennis court, and a restaurant and lounge.

A little farther: See the Southern Methodist University entry for suggestions in Dallas, approximately 95 miles to the north, and Texas Christian University for suggestions in Fort Worth, which is a little closer than Dallas.

HIGHLIGHTS

ON CAMPUS
- Strecker Museum
- Armstrong Browning Library

OFF CAMPUS
- Fort Fisher Park
- Texas Sports Hall of Fame

RICE UNIVERSITY

Office of Admission, Rice University, 6100 Main St., Houston, TX 77005 (The office is in Lovett Hall, Entrance C, Rm. 109, inside Door C) • Telephone: 800-527-OWLS or 713-348-RICE • Web: www.rice.edu • Email: admission@rice.edu

Hours: Monday-Friday, 8:30AM-5PM; Saturday, 9AM-noon (only during the academic year). Closed Sundays and holidays.

Rice University has a varied and challenging academic program, minus some of the intense competition that often accompanies schools of such stature.

HIGHLIGHTS

ON CAMPUS
- Rice Memorial Center
- Baker Institute for Public Policy
- Rice University Art Gallery
- Sheperd School of Music
- Rockling Park

OFF CAMPUS
- Museum of Fine Arts
- Downtown theater district
- Rothko Chapel at the
- Meril Collection
- NASA Space Center
- Museum of Natural History

TRANSPORTATION

Houston's Hobby Airport is a 30-minute (non-rush hour) drive from campus. Houston's Intercontinental Airport is a 45-minute (non-rush hour) drive from campus. Taxis, shuttles, and rental cars are available at both airports. The shuttle services pick up passengers at the baggage claim areas. The shuttle delivers passengers to the Harvey Suites substation (6700 S. Main St.). From the substation, take a taxi to campus. Amtrak trains and Greyhound buses serve Houston. The bus terminal on Main St. is a short distance from campus; taxis are available at the terminal for the ride to campus.

FIND YOUR WAY

Take I-10, I-45, or I-610 to U.S. Rte. 59 (the Southwest Freeway). Take U.S. 59 into the city to the Shepherd-Greenbriar/Rice University exit. At Greenbriar, head south to Rice Blvd. Turn left on Rice and continue to Main St. Turn right on Main St. and make an immediate right turn into the main campus gate. Lovett Hall (location of the admissions office) is at the end of the entrance driveway; visitor parking is avilable in both lots in front of Lovett Hall.

STAY THE NIGHT

The **Marriott Medical Center** (6580 Fannin St.; 713-796-0080) is within walking distance of the university. It has an indoor pool, exercise room, whirlpool, jacuzzi, and a great seafood restaurant. It's also 15 minutes from the Galleria, the big downtown shopping mall. For something special half a mile from school, we suggest **La Colombe d'Or** (3410 Montrose Blvd.; 713-524-7999), a restored 1920s mansion with 6 suites and a wonderful French restaurant. Rates are very expensive. Two other suggestions are also close to the university: **Holiday Inn Medical Center** (6701 S. Main St.; 713-797-1110), half a mile away, with an outdoor pool and a special inexpensive rate for Rice visitors and the **Park Plaza Warwick** (5701 S. Main St.; 713-526-1991), an old-fashioned hotel 5 minutes away, near the Museum of Fine Arts and a park with a jogging trail. It has an outdoor swimming pool and exercise room and a special moderate rate. Another option is **Hilton Houston Plaza** (6633 Travis St.; 713-313-4000). Rates are moderate and include a continental breakfast. Most of the rooms have shared baths.

AT A GLANCE

Selectivity Rating	97
Range SAT I Math	660-760
Range SAT I Verbal	650-760
Student to Faculty Ratio	6:1

CAMPUS TOURS

Appointment Req?	No
Dates	Year-round
Times	Mon-Fri 11AM and 3PM; Sat 10:30AM (during academic year only)
Avg. Length	1 hour

ON-CAMPUS INTERVIEWS

Admissions

Start Date–Juniors	Late May
Appointment Req?	Yes
Advance Notice	2 weeks
Saturdays?	Yes, during academic year
Avg. Length	30-45 min
Info Sessions	Year-round

Faculty and Coaches

Dates/Times	Year-round; subject to faculty/coach availability
Arrangements	Contact admissions off. 1-2 weeks prior

CLASS VISITS

Dates	Sept-April (Mon-Fri)
Arrangements	Contact admissions off.

OVERNIGHT DORM STAYS

Advance Notice	2-4 weeks
Arrangements	Contact admissions off.
Limitations	High school seniors only; 2-night maximum stay; Thurs-Sat nights recommended; only when classes are in session, but not before the third week of Sept; no Sunday nights

SOUTHERN METHODIST UNIVERSITY

Office of Undergraduate Admissions, Southern Methodist University, 6425 Boaz St., P.O. Box 750181, Dallas, TX 75275 (The office is in the Perkins Administration Building) • Telephone: 800-323-0672 or 214-768-2058 • Web: www.smu.edu • Email: ugadmission@smu.edu

Hours: Monday-Friday, 9AM-5PM; Saturday, 9AM-noon (September-December and July). Closed Sundays and holidays.

Outstanding professors and tremendous business and management programs make Southern Methodist a great choice. Students here definitely enjoy life thanks to a buzzing social scene, gorgeous campus, and easy access to metropolitan Dallas.

AT A GLANCE

Selectivity Rating	81
Range SAT I Math	520-640
Range SAT I Verbal	510-630
Average GPA	3.2
Student to Faculty Ratio	12:1

CAMPUS TOURS

Appointment Req?	Yes
Dates	Year-round
Times	Mon-Sat 10AM
Avg. Length	1 hour

ON-CAMPUS INTERVIEWS

Admissions

Start Date—Juniors	Any time
Appointment Req?	Yes
Advance Notice	2 weeks
Saturdays?	No
Avg. Length	45-60 min
Info Sessions	Year-round 1PM

Faculty and Coaches

Dates/Times	Year-round; subject to faculty/coach availability
Arrangements	Contact admissions off.

CLASS VISITS

Dates	Academic year (Mon-Fri)
Arrangements	Contact admissions off.

OVERNIGHT DORM STAYS

Advance Notice	2 weeks
Arrangements	Contact admissions off.
Limitations	Available Sun-Thurs; Sept-Nov and Jan-April; high school seniors only

TRANSPORTATION

Dallas-Fort Worth International Airport is approximately 15 miles from campus. Airport shuttle minivans are available for the ride from the airport to campus; direct-dial free phones are located near the baggage area. The minivans and taxis leave from the lower level of the airport. Love Field (served by Southwest Airlines) is approximately 4 miles from campus; airport shuttle minivans are also available at this airport. By special arrangement with SMU, American Airlines makes reduced fares available to visitors for all SMU special visitation days. For details, call the American Airlines Meeting Services Desk at 800-433-1790 and ask for Star Number S9700. Amtrak trains and Greyhound/Trailways bus lines serve Dallas.

FIND YOUR WAY

From I-30 (U.S. Routes 67/80), exit to U.S. Rte. 75 N. Exit from Rte. 75 to Mockingbird Lane West, which will take you to campus.

STAY THE NIGHT

Within walking distance is the moderately priced (ask for the special rate for SMU visitors) **Radisson** (6060 N. Central Expy.; 214-750-6060). Restaurants are just behind the hotel and theaters and shopping are nearby. The hotel has an indoor and outdoor pool, a jacuzzi, and a steam room. For luxury, consider splurging on **Mansion on Turtle Creek** (2821 Turtle Creek Blvd.; 214-559-2100). For bed-and-breakfasts, contact **Book a Bed Ahead** (312-293-8620).

HIGHLIGHTS

ON CAMPUS
- Gerald Ford Stadium
- DeGolyer Library
- Owen Fine Arts Center
- Greer Garson Theatre
- Hughes Trigg Student Center

OFF CAMPUS
- Dallas Museum of Art
- Grapevine Mills Outlet
- Mesquite Rodeo
- John F. Kennedy Memorial
- Morton H. Myerson Symphony Center

TCU

Admissions Office, TCU Box 297013, Fort Worth, TX 76129 (The office is in Rm. 112 of Sadler Hall) • Telephone: 800-TCU-FROG or 817-257-7490 • Web: www.tcu.edu • Email: frogmail@tcu.edu

Hours: Monday-Friday, 9AM-5PM; Saturday, 10AM-noon. Closed Sundays, Good Friday, July 4, Labor Day, Thanksgiving, and Christmas through New Year's Day.

Located in Fort Worth, Texas, TCU offers the nation's first academically affiliated program in ballet, but students seem more attracted to the business school; nearly 1 in 10 business majors enters an MBA program within a year of graduation. Horned Frog athletics are huge as well, and a strong Greek system rules social life.

HIGHLIGHTS

ON CAMPUS
- Amon Carter Stadium
- Monnig Meteorite Collection
- WM Lewis Collection of British literature
- Mills Glass Collection
- Tandy Film Library

OFF CAMPUS
- Kimbell Art Museum
- Billy Bob's Honkey Tonk
- Fort Worth Zoo
- Bass Performance Hall
- Downtown Sundance Square

TRANSPORTATION

Dallas-Fort Worth International Airport is 25 miles from campus. Taxis, rental cars, and the Super Shuttle (800-258-3826) are available for the trip from the airport. About 45 miles from campus, Dallas Love Field Airport serves as a base for Southwest Airlines, taxis and rental cars are available.

FIND YOUR WAY

From the east or west, take I-30 and exit at University Dr. (Signs on I-30 indicate the TCU exit.) Head south on University to the admissions office at 2800 S. University Dr. **From the north or south**, take I-35 West to I-20 West. Exit at Hulen St. (you'll see a TCU sign), then go north. Go east on Bellaire South. You will see TCU at the crest of the hill.

STAY THE NIGHT

The **Ramada Inn-Midtown** (817-228-2828), **Marriott Courtyard** (817-321-2221), **The Residence Inn** (871-870-1011), and **Fairfield Inn** (817-335-2000) are all approximately 2 miles from the TCU campus, with rates ranging from inexpensive to moderate. All are within walking distance of a 13-mile jogging trail, great restaurants, and a spectacular shopping center. The **Worthington Hotel** (817-870-1000), **Ramada Inn-Downtown** (817-335-7000), and **Radisson** (817-870-2100) are in Fort Worth's thriving downtown, which is about 4 miles from TCU. There you will find fantastic dining options, 2 movie theaters, specialty shops, coffee bars, and bookstores.

AT A GLANCE

Selectivity Rating	80
Range SAT I Math	520-640
Range SAT I Verbal	520-620
Student to Faculty Ratio	15:1

CAMPUS TOURS

Appointment Req?	Yes
Dates	Year-round
Times	Mon-Fri 9AM-3PM; Sat 10AM-noon
Avg. Length	1 hour

ON-CAMPUS INTERVIEWS

Admissions

Start Date—Juniors	Spring
Appointment Req?	Yes
Advance Notice	1 week
Saturdays?	Yes, for group sessions only
Avg. Length	45 min
Info Sessions	During Mon at TCU programs and other days

Faculty and Coaches

Dates/Times	Year-round; subject to faculty/coach availability
Arrangements	Contact admissions off. 1 week prior

CLASS VISITS

Dates	Year-round (Mon-Fri)
Arrangements	Contact admissions off.

OVERNIGHT DORM STAYS

Advance Notice	2 weeks
Arrangements	Contact admissions off.
Limitations	1-night stay only

TRINITY UNIVERSITY

Office of Admissions, Trinity University, 715 Stadium Dr., San Antonio, TX 78212
(The office is on South Campus) • Telephone: 800-TRINITY or 210-999-7207 •
Web: www.trinity.edu • Email: admissions@trinity.edu

Hours: Monday-Friday, 8AM-5PM; Saturday, 9AM-1PM. Closed Sundays and holidays; closed Saturdays during the summer.

Situated in San Antonio, Trinity University provides about 2,200 students with large school resources in a small school setting as well as a liberal arts and sciences education from excellent professors. Along with exploring San Antonio, students can relax with a variety of campus activities, including hugely popular off-the-wall intramurals like coed innertube water polo and something called flickerball.

AT A GLANCE

Selectivity Rating	83
Range SAT I Math	590-680
Average SAT I Math	635
Range SAT I Verbal	580-690
Average SAT I Verbal	636
Average ACT Composite	28
Student to Faculty Ratio	11:1

CAMPUS TOURS

Appointment Req?	Preferred
Dates	Year-round
Times	Mon-Fri 11:30AM and 3:30PM; Sat 11:30AM; summer tours at variable times
Avg. Length	1 hour

ON-CAMPUS INTERVIEWS

Admissions

Appointment Req?	Yes
Advance Notice	2 weeks
Saturdays?	Yes; information session after the tour
Avg. Length	1 hour
Info Sessions	Year-round

Faculty and Coaches

Dates/Times	Academic year; subject to faculty/coach availability
Arrangements	Contact admissions off. 2 weeks prior

CLASS VISITS

Dates	Academic year (Mon-Fri)
Arrangements	Contact admissions off. 2 weeks prior

OVERNIGHT DORM STAYS

Advance Notice	2 weeks, required
Arrangements	Contact admissions off.
Limitations	Academic year; request when making program reservations

TRANSPORTATION

San Antonio International Airport is approximately 5.5 miles from campus. SuperVan Shuttle (210-344-RIDE) and taxis are available for the ride to campus.

FIND YOUR WAY

From US 281 N. or S., exit Hildebrand. Go west on Hildebrand, then south at the first light (Devine/Stadium Drive) toward the large stadium. At the bottom of the hill, turn right toward the campus, keep going south on Stadium; the admissions office is on the right before Mulberry Ave.

STAY THE NIGHT

Affordable options include **Amerisuites** (7615 Jones-Maltsberger; 210-930-2333) and **Fairfield Inn** at the Airport (88 NE Loop 410; 210-530-9899). Ask both for their Trinity visitor's rate. You can also try the Hampton Inn near the Airport (8811 Jones-Maltsberger; 210-336-1800). **The Red Roof Inn** (333 Wolfe Rd.; 210-340-4055). **Doubletree** (37 NE Loop 410; 210-366-2424) for special Trinity rates. About 10 minutes away is the Crockett Hotel (320 Bonham St.; 210-225-6500), a historic building across the street from the Alamo. Rates vary from moderate to expensive. Right next to the Alamo is the **Menger Hotel** (204 Alamo Plaza; 210-223-4361), a landmark dating back to 1859. The Menger Hotel is about 15 minutes from Trinity and has moderate rates. The new wing to the hotel opens up onto the beautiful River Walk, which you have to see to believe. The luxurious **St. Anthony** (300 E. Travis St.; 210-227-4392 or 800-338-1338) is about 20 minutes from Trinity. The restaurant features southwestern cuisine. If you like big, lively hotels, you can't beat the **Hotel San Antonio Marriott River Center** (101 Bowie St.; 210-223-1000), about 15 minutes from Trinity. This 38-story giant with 1,000 rooms connects to the River Center Mall, which connects to the aforementioned River Walk. Needless to say, it has every amenity, including an indoor and outdoor pool, a health club, exercise room, and convention facilities. Rates are very expensive, higher than St. Anthony, and include a complimentary breakfast.

HIGHLIGHTS

ON CAMPUS
- Stiernen Theatre
- Laurie Auditorium
- Coates Library
- Bell Atlantic Center

OFF CAMPUS
- McNay Art Museum
- San Antonio Museum of Art
- River Walk
- Alamo
- Sea World

UNIVERSITY OF TEXAS—AUSTIN

Freshman Admissions Center, University of Texas–Austin, John Hargis Hall, Austin, TX 78712-1159 (The center is at Martin Luther King Blvd. and Red River) • Telephone: 512-475-7440 • Web: www.utexas.edu • Email: adfre@utxdp.dp.utexas.edu

Hours: Monday-Friday, 8:30AM-4:30PM. Closed weekends and holidays.

Tuition is so low at the extremely enormous University of Texas at Austin that some out-of-state students pay less than they would to go to public institutions in their own home states. Academics and research here are world class as well, and students love Austin, arguably the hippest small city in America and certainly one of its most vibrant bar/live music scenes.

HIGHLIGHTS

ON CAMPUS
- Texas Union
- Frank Erwin Center
- Performing Arts Center
- Athletics
- Gregory Gym/recreational sports

OFF CAMPUS
- Mount Bonnell
- Town Lake/Lake Travis
- Austin (state capital)
- 6th Street
- Museums/libraries

TRANSPORTATION

Austin-Bergstrom Airport is a 7-minute ride from campus. City buses and taxis are available for the trip from airport to campus. Amtrak trains and Greyhound buses serve Austin. City buses and taxis are available to campus.

FIND YOUR WAY

From I-35, exit to Martin Luther King Blvd. The Admissions Center is quite close to the highway, next to the Frank Erwin Special Events Center, at the corner of Martin Luther King Blvd. and Red River.

STAY THE NIGHT

The important thing in Austin is to be near 6th St., which is alive with restaurants, shops, bars, and entertainment. The **Marriott at the Capital** (701 E. 11th St.; 512-478-1111) is within walking distance of 6th St. and about a mile from campus. It has an indoor and outdoor pool, as well as an exercise room and game room. Another option is the **Doubletree Club Hotel** (1617 1H-35 N.; 512-479-4000) adjacent to the southeast corner of campus at a moderate price. Rates are expensive, but ask about special supersaver rates. The **Driskill** (604 Brazos St.; 512-474-5911 or 800-252-9367) is right in the heart of downtown near 6th St. and is our choice for character. Over 100 years old, this place will give you a nice feeling of the old Southwest. Only 10 minutes from campus, the hotel has moderate rates on the weekends and expensive ones during the week. There are also some bed-and-breakfasts not too far from the university. If you desire tranquility, consider **Brook House** (609 W. 33rd St.; 512-459-0534) or the slightly higher priced **McCallum House** (613 W. 32nd St.; 512-451-6744). The McCallum House has a full breakfast included in its moderate rate, and the Brook House offers a continental breakfast with its inexpensive rate.

AT A GLANCE

Selectivity Rating	86
Range SAT I Math	560-670
Average SAT I Math	620
Range SAT I Verbal	530-640
Average SAT I Verbal	601
Average ACT Composite	25
Student to Faculty Ratio	21:1

CAMPUS TOURS

Appointment Req?	No
Dates	Year-round
Times	May-Dec: Mon-Sat 11AM and 2PM; Sat 2PM
Avg. Length	45 min

ON-CAMPUS INTERVIEWS

Admissions

Start Date–Juniors	Any time
Appointment Req?	No
Advance Notice	None
Saturdays?	No
Avg. Length	Varies; interviews serve as info session
Info Sessions	Group sessions not available

Faculty and Coaches

Dates/Times	Year-round; subject to faculty/coach availability
Arrangements	Contact admissions off. 2 weeks prior

CLASS VISITS

Dates	Year-round (Mon-Fri)
Arrangements	Contact admissions off.

OVERNIGHT DORM STAYS

Advance Notice	N/A
Arrangements	N/A
Limitations	N/A

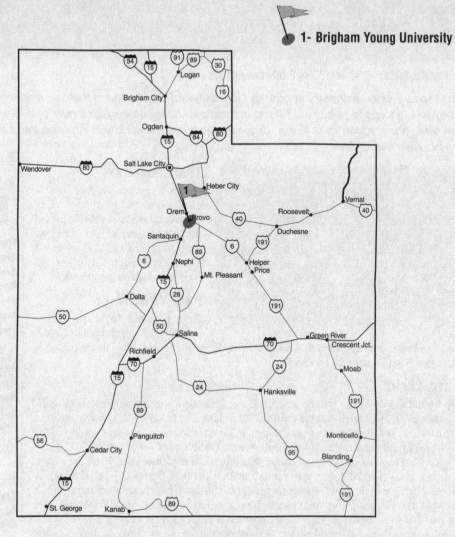

1- Brigham Young University

Utah	BYU	Provo	Salt Lake City
BYU	—	0	45
Provo	0	—	45
Salt Lake City	45	45	—

BRIGHAM YOUNG UNIVERSITY

Admissions, Brigham Young University, P.O. Box 21110, Provo, UT 84602
(The office is in the Abraham Smoot Building) • Telephone: 801-378-2507 •
Web: www.byu.edu • Email: admissions@byu.edu

Hours: Monday-Friday, 8AM-5PM. Closed weekends and holidays.

You'll find a unique experience at challenging Brigham Young University, where a whopping 99 percent of the students belong to the Mormon Church.

HIGHLIGHTS

ON CAMPUS
- Monte L. Bea Life Science Museum
- The Museum of Art
- Visitor's Center
- Harold B. Lee Library
- Wilkinson Student Center

OFF CAMPUS
- Sundance Ski Resort
- Mount Timpanogus Cave
- "Y" Mountain Hike
- Seven Peaks Resort Water Park
- Temple Square in Salt Lake City

TRANSPORTATION

Salt Lake City International Airport is fifty miles from campus. Taxis, Key Limousines, Utah Transit Authority service, and rental cars are available for the trip from the airport to campus. Arrangements can be made for these services when you arrive at the airport.

FIND YOUR WAY

Take I-15 toward Provo. **If you are coming from the north,** take Exit 272 and head east on Utah Rte. 265 (12th South St./University Parkway). Rte. 265 will intersect with U.S. 189 (University Ave.) at BYU. Turn right on University Ave. and enter campus by turning left onto 1230 North (Bulldog Ave.), which you will follow to Campus Dr. and the Administration Building. **If you are coming from the south,** take Exit 266 and head north on U.S. 189 (University Ave.) to BYU. Enter campus by turning right onto 1230 North (Bulldog Ave.), and follow it to Campus Dr. and the Administration Building.

STAY THE NIGHT

Nearby: There are 2 budget choices. **Best Value Western University Inn** (40 W. 300 South St.; 801-373-0660 or 800-500-5003) has a heated pool and is only a mile away. **Best Western Cottontree Inn** (2230 North St.; 801-373-7044), just a half-mile away, has gorgeous views of the river, a heated pool, and a jacuzzi. Rates are comparable at the **Holiday Inn** (1460 S. University Ave.; 801-374-9750), and at the **Best Inn Suites** (1555 N. Canyon Rd.; 801-374-6020). **Corn's East Bay Inn** (1292 S. University Ave.; 801-374-2500 or 800-446-4656) is 4 miles away and considerably more expensive. About 5 minutes away is the **Provo Park Hotel** (101 W. 100 North St.; 801-377-4700 or 800-777-7144), which has a shuttle to campus. For more offbeat accommodations, consider the **Pullman Bed and Breakfast** (415 S. University Ave.; 801-374-8141), about 2 miles away. Built in 1898, this beautifully restored Romanesque revival has much of the original hand-carved woodwork and stained glass. Gourmet dinners are served on Friday and Saturday (make reservations). Rates are relatively inexpensive.

A little farther: If you are willing to drive about 25 minutes, this may be your chance to stay at **Sundance** (North Fork, Provo Canyon; 801-225-4107). This is a famous ski area and winter rates are in the very expensive range, but they drop to moderate (high end) off season. In summer, try fishing here.

AT A GLANCE

Selectivity Rating	87
Average ACT Composite	27
Average GPA	3.7
Student to Faculty Ratio	16:1

CAMPUS TOURS

Appointment Req?	Yes
Dates	Year-round
Times	Mon-Fri 5 tours from 8PM to 5PM
Avg. Length	90 min

ON-CAMPUS INTERVIEWS

Admissions

Start Date–Juniors	N/A
Appointment Req?	Yes
Advance Notice	Yes
Saturdays?	No
Avg. Length	15-20 min
Info Sessions	Not given on campus; 2-hour sessions available at various places around the country

Faculty and Coaches

Dates/Times	Year-round; subject to faculty/coach availability
Arrangements	Contact dept. of interest 2 weeks prior

CLASS VISITS

Dates	Year-round (Mon-Fri)
Arrangements	While on campus, arrange through the campus tour guide

OVERNIGHT DORM STAYS

Advance Notice	N/A
Arrangements	N/A
Limitations	N/A

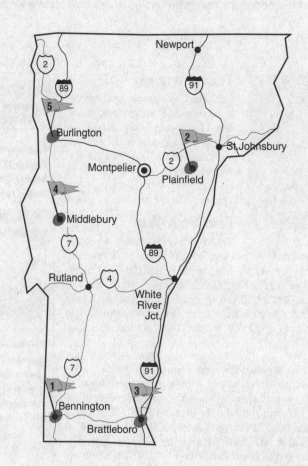

Newport

2

89

5 Burlington

Montpelier

2

Plainfield

St. Johnsbury

91

4 Middlebury

7

89

Rutland   4

White
River
Jct.

7

91

1 Bennington

3

Brattleboro

1- **Bennington College**
2- **Goddard College**
3- **Marlboro College**
4- **Middlebury College**
5- **University of Vermont**

Vermont	Bennington Coll.	Goddard Coll.	Marlboro Coll.	Middlebury Coll.	Univ. Vermont	Burlington	Rutland
Bennington Coll.	—	124	28	85	119	119	57
Goddard Coll.	124	—	120	63	43	43	71
Marlboro Coll.	28	120	—	113	150	150	80
Middlebury Coll.	85	63	113	—	34	34	30
Univ. Vermont	119	43	150	34	—	0	67
Burlington	119	43	150	34	0	—	67
Rutland	57	71	80	30	67	67	—

BENNINGTON COLLEGE

Office of Admissions & the First Year, Bennington College Rte. 67A, Bennington, VT 05201 (The office is in the "Barn," the administrative building next to the campus entrance) • Telephone: 800-833-6845 or 802-440-4312 • Web: www.bennington.edu • Email: admissions@bennington.edu

Hours: Monday-Friday, 9AM-5PM; Saturday, 9AM-noon during term. Closed Sundays and major holidays.

Bennington College is a small, progressive, very arts-oriented and "creative" liberal arts college that offers students the opportunity to put together their own programs. Classes are more akin to intimate seminars, so instead of grades and tests Benningtonians receive written evaluations of their work. Nearly weekly theme parties provide the bulk of campus entertainment.

HIGHLIGHTS

ON CAMPUS
- Edward Clark Crossett Library
- Visual & Performing Arts Center
- Hoffberger Music Library
- The Rebecca B. Stickney Observatory
- The College Farm

OFF CAMPUS
- Bennington Museum
- Old East Church
- Bennington Battle Monument
- Several local ski areas

TRANSPORTATION

The Albany, NY, airport and Albany/Rensselaer Amtrak train station are approximately 50 miles from campus. CLS transportation provides limousine service from the airport and train station; call 802-447-1609 to make arrangements.

FIND YOUR WAY

From the New York City area, take the Taconic State Parkway N. to NY Rte. 295. From Rte. 295 take NY Rte. 22 N. for about 30 miles. At the end of Rte. 22, take a left onto NY Rte. 7 E. to Vermont. (NY Rte. 7 turns to Rte. 9 in Vermont.) This brings you into the town of Bennington. At the intersection of Rte. 7 and Rte. 9 (Bennington's main 4-corner intersection), take a left onto Rte. 7 N. At the 2nd set of lights take a left onto Rte. 67A and Northside Dr. and go through 6 sets of traffic lights. The main entrance to the College is a short distance ahead on the right. At the main entrance take the College Dr. to the end, turn left to get to the visitor's parking and the red barn where the Admissions office is located.

STAY THE NIGHT

Nearby: Only 1 mile from school is the inexpensive **Best Western New Englander** (220 Northside Dr.; 802-442-6311). This facility has an outdoor pool and lawn games in the summer. Four miles from the school is the **Vermonter Motor Lodge** (West Rd.; 802-442-2529), which is open from May through December. A double room is inexpensive, and for a relatively modest rate you can enjoy mountain views. The lodge also has its own pond and cottages. About 5 miles from the school is **South Shire Bed-and-Breakfast** (124 Elm St.; 802-447-3839). This wonderful Victorian mansion has 5 rooms in the main house that are moderately expensive) and 4 (somewhat more pricey) luxurious accommodations with jacuzzis and fireplaces in the carriage house.

A little farther: You will find 2 interesting choices in Arlington, a 20-minute drive from the college. Pleasant **West Mountain Inn** (Rte. 313 and River Rd.; 802-375-6516) offers good food and rooms in the expensive range. Depending on the season, you can enjoy cross-country skiing (you're also not far from Bromley or Stratton, important Alpine centers), trout fishing, swimming, canoeing, and tubing. Tennis and golf are also available nearby. The **Arlington Inn** (Rte. A at Rte. 313; 802-375-6532) is a wonderful Greek Revival mansion with a terrific restaurant that has been featured in *New York* magazine and *Bon Appetit*. Double rooms here range from inexpensive to expensive, and the price includes a continental breakfast.

AT A GLANCE

Selectivity Rating	83
Range SAT I Math	500-610
Average SAT I Math	571
Range SAT I Verbal	560-670
Average SAT I Verbal	609
Average GPA	3.5
Student to Faculty Ratio	7:1

CAMPUS TOURS

Appointment Req?	Preferred
Dates	Year-round
Times	When needed during admissions off. hours
Avg. Length	1 hour

ON-CAMPUS INTERVIEWS

Admissions

Start Date—Juniors	Any time
Appointment Req?	Preferred
Advance Notice	Preferred
Saturdays?	Yes, 9AM-1PM during fall, winter, and spring
Avg. Length	1 hour
Info Sessions	N/A

Faculty and Coaches

Dates/Times	N/A
Arrangements	N/A

CLASS VISITS

Dates	Mon, Tues, Thurs
Arrangements	Contact admissions off.

OVERNIGHT DORM STAYS

Advance Notice	2 weeks
Arrangements	Contact admissions off.
Limitations	1-night stay; not available on weekends or holidays

GODDARD COLLEGE

Admissions Office, Goddard College, R. R. 2, Plainfield, VT 05667 (The office is in the Studies Building, Pitkin Campus) • Telephone: 800-468-4888 or 802-454-8311 • Web: www.goddard.edu • Email: admissions@earth.goddard.edu

Hours: Monday-Friday, 8AM-4:30PM. Closed on weekends and holidays.

If you loathe the idea of "traditional school," check out Goddard College, an "artsy, eccentric" school located in rural Vermont where "academic freedom" reigns supreme. Goddard's "creative, intelligent, and artistic" students "design" an individual curriculum—"a self-directed, experimental education" if you will—tailored to their own "specific needs."

AT A GLANCE

Selectivity Rating	73
Range SAT I Math	480-580
Average SAT I Math	489
Average SAT I Verbal	511
Average GPA	2.5
Student to Faculty Ratio	12:1

CAMPUS TOURS

Appointment Req?	Yes
Dates	Year-round
Times	Mon-Fri 10AM-3PM by appt. only
Avg. Length	1 hour

ON-CAMPUS INTERVIEWS

Admissions

Start Date—Juniors	Sept
Appointment Req?	Yes
Advance Notice	2 weeks
Saturdays?	Only during open houses
Avg. Length	1 hour
Info Sessions	Available only during open houses

Faculty and Coaches

Dates/Times	Year-round; subject to faculty availability
Arrangements	Contact admissions off. 3 weeks prior

CLASS VISITS

Dates	Year-round (Mon-Fri)
Arrangements	Contact admissions off.; only certain classes may be visited

OVERNIGHT DORM STAYS

Advance Notice	2 weeks
Arrangements	Contact admissions off.
Limitations	1-night stay

TRANSPORTATION

Burlington International Airport is 45 miles from campus. Buses are available from the airport to Montpelier (10 miles from campus), but not to Plainfield. Rental cars are available at the airport. The Barre-Montpelier Airport is a small commercial field only 8 miles from campus; it has daily flights to and from Boston. Contact the admissions office about transportation from this airport to campus. Taxis from both airports can be arranged in advance or summoned on arrival; call Barre Taxi Service (802-479-1985) or Norm's Taxi (802-223-5226). Amtrak has train connections to Montpelier (10 miles from campus) from Washington, DC, New York City, and Montreal. Vermont Transit, a subsidiary of Greyhound Bus Lines, serves both Barre and Montpelier. Taxis can be arranged in advance or summoned to the bus and train stations; call Barre Taxi Service or Norm's Taxi.

FIND YOUR WAY

Take I-91 or I-93 N. to I-89; then take I-89 N.W. to Exit 8 (Montpelier). Go northeast on U.S. Rte. 2 (for approximately 10 miles from Montpelier); as you enter Plainfield Village, turn left at the Goddard sign. The college is approximately one-eighth of a mile up the road on the left side.

STAY THE NIGHT

Nearby: Nearby means Montpelier, 10 miles to the west of Plainfield and a 20-minute drive from campus. Try **Montpelier Bed-and-Breakfast** (22 North St.; 802-229-0482), though there is no breakfast until May, since the owner is a congressman in the winter (try the Elm Street Café for breakfast). The moderately priced (some deluxe rooms) **Montpelier Inn** (147 Main St.; 802-223-2727) offers a game room and a comfortable living room and dining room with fireplaces, and is accessible to the shops in Montpelier. The **Capital Plaza Hotel** (802-223-5252) in downtown Montpelier is inexpensive and has an indoor swimming pool.

A little farther: Charming **Shire Inn** (802-685-3031) is about 40 minutes away in Chelsea. Chelsea, a 200-year-old town, is on the National Register of Historic Places. Built in 1832, the 6-room Shire Inn fits right in, and the meals are fabulous. The moderate prices make it a steal. In Waitsfield, about 45 minutes from campus, the 15-room **Mad River Barn** (802-496-3310) is as upbeat as can be. Off season, the rates are in the inexpensive range; in both seasons, they go down midweek. If you go in the summer, you might enjoy the swimming pool and horseback riding, as well as the theater in the area.

HIGHLIGHTS

ON CAMPUS
- Historic gardens
- Restored manor house

OFF CAMPUS
- Barre Granite Quarries
- Montpelier (state capital)

Marlboro College

Admissions Office, Marlboro College, Marlboro, VT 05344 •
Telephone: 800-343-0049 or 802-257-4333 • Web: www.marlboro.edu •
Email: admissions@marlboro.edu

Hours: Monday-Friday, 8:30AM-4:30PM. Closed weekends and most federal and state holidays.

"Intense" Marlboro College is "a dream" for academic and social self-starters, but "you have to be serious about studying" to succeed here. Under "The Plan," juniors and seniors work "one-on-one" with professors to design and pursue a self-devised curriculum, culminating in a senior research paper. The process requires "tons of writing homework" but students here unanimously agree that it's a remarkable experience.

HIGHLIGHTS

ON CAMPUS
- The Rice Library
- Whittemore Theatre
- Mac Arthur Observatory
- Drury Gallery

OFF CAMPUS
- Marlboro Music Festival
- Molly State Park

TRANSPORTATION

Bradley International Airport near Hartford, CT, is a two-hour drive from campus. Greyhound Bus Lines serves Marlboro and provides transportation from the airport to nearby Brattleboro, VT, where transportation supplied by the College is available with advance notice.

FIND YOUR WAY

Take Exit 2 off I-91 in Brattleboro. Turn right off the exit onto Rte. 9 W. through West Brattleboro into Marlboro. After passing the Marlboro Elementary School on the left, watch for signs for the College. Take a left turn as Rte. 9 makes a sweeping turn to the right. Stay on paved road through the village of Marlboro to the College (approximately 3 miles).

STAY THE NIGHT

Nearby: Convenient **Whetstone Inn** (802-254-2500), only 2 miles from campus, is right in the center of town. We might add that the "town" consists of the inn, the post office, and the church. The inn is moderately priced and offers 11 rooms, as well as breakfast. Dinner is served a few nights a week. The **Colonel Williams Inn** is located on VT Rte. 9 in Marlboro and offers fine dining and lodging. It is chef-owned and -operated.

A little farther: The college is about 20 minutes away from Brattleboro, where you'll find a couple of inexpensive motels. The **Colonial Motel** (Putney Rd.; 802-257-7733) and the **Colonial Inn** (Putney Rd.; 802-254-8701) offer indoor pools and restaurants on the premises. For charm and elegance, drive 40 minutes north of the college to Newfane, a picturesque Vermont village and the home of the **Four Columns Inn** (802-365-7713). Located on the village green, the inn is renowned in the northeast for its marvelous dining room. Rooms are in the moderate to very expensive range. The inn has a pool and is not far from the ski areas of Stratton and Mount Snow. The **Old Newfane Inn**, just across the way, is a comfortable choice. Breakfast is included. In South Newfane, on Dover Rd. about 40 minutes away from the college, is the small **Inn at South Newfane** (802-348-7191). It offers a modified American plan, providing 2 meals for an expensive rate. It's somewhat cheaper in the wintertime.

AT A GLANCE

Selectivity Rating	81
Range SAT I Math	500-620
Average SAT I Math	580
Range SAT I Verbal	580-680
Average SAT I Verbal	610
Average GPA	3.2
Student to Faculty Ratio	7:1

CAMPUS TOURS

Appointment Req?	Yes
Dates	Year-round
Times	Mon-Fri 9AM-3PM
Avg. Length	1 hour

ON-CAMPUS INTERVIEWS

Admissions

Start Date–Juniors	Spring
Appointment Req?	Yes
Advance Notice	1 week
Saturdays?	No
Avg. Length	45 min
Info Sessions	Year-round

Faculty and Coaches

Dates/Times	Year-round; subject to faculty availability
Arrangements	Contact admissions off. 2 weeks prior

CLASS VISITS

Dates	Sept-May (Mon-Fri)
Arrangements	Contact admissions off. and request a class schedule

OVERNIGHT DORM STAYS

Advance Notice	2 weeks
Arrangements	Contact admissions off.
Limitations	Available only on Mon-Thurs; no Fri night stays

MIDDLEBURY COLLEGE

Admissions Office, Middlebury College, Emma Willard House, Middlebury, VT 05753
(South Main St. is Rte. 30) • Telephone: 802-443-3000 ext. 5153 •
Web: www.middlebury.edu • Email: admissions@middlebury.edu

Hours: Monday-Friday, 8AM-5PM; Saturday, 9AM-noon (October and November only). Closed most weekends and holidays.

At Middlebury College in a remote "paradise detached from the ordeals of real life," dorms have views of the mountains and the school has its own downhill slope and lighted cross-country ski trail. In the course of completing one of the more rigorous and prestigious liberal arts curriculums in the country, students here can take advantage of a wealth of "amazing" programs, especially in writing, the world-class Language School, and theater.

AT A GLANCE

Selectivity Rating	97
Range SAT I Math	650-720
Average SAT I Math	680
Range SAT I Verbal	670-730
Average SAT I Verbal	690
Average ACT Composite	29
Student to Faculty Ratio	11:1

CAMPUS TOURS

Appointment Req?	No
Dates	Year-round, except during exam periods and vacations
Times	Mon-Fri (call for exact times)
Avg. Length	1 hour

ON-CAMPUS INTERVIEWS

Admissions

Start Date–Juniors	June 1 following junior year
Appointment Req?	Yes
Advance Notice	2-6 weeks; greatest advance notice is required in Aug, Oct, and Nov
Saturdays?	No
Avg. Length	30 min
Info Sessions	April and June-Jan

Faculty and Coaches

Dates/Times	Year-round; subject to faculty/coach availability
Arrangements	Contact admissions off. with reasonable prior notice or contact coaches directly

CLASS VISITS

Dates	Year-round (Mon-Fri)
Arrangements	Obtain a class schedule at admissions off.

OVERNIGHT DORM STAYS

Arrangements	Available only through a personal friend who is a current student

TRANSPORTATION

Burlington International Airport is 35 miles from campus. Taxi and bus service is available for the trip between the airport and campus.

FIND YOUR WAY

From New York, take I-87 N. to Exit 20 (soon after Glen Falls); take 149 E. to U.S. 4 E.; take U.S. 4 through Whitehall to the Fair Haven exit, then take Vermont Rte. 22A north to Rte. 74 E. to Rte. 30 N. to the campus. **From Boston,** take I-93 N. to I-89 (north of Manchester, NH). Take I-89 N. and west to Bethel, Vermont Rte. 107 W. Follow Rte. 107 to Rte. 100 N., then take 100 N. to Vermont Rte. 125. Take Rte. 125 W. into Middlebury.

STAY THE NIGHT

Nearby: Middlebury has some wonderful places to stay within walking distance or a very short drive from the College's campus. Travelers have a range of options, including beautifully appointed country inns, charming bed and breakfasts, and convenient and well-appointed motels. You won't go wrong with the **Swift House Inn** (25 Stewart Lane; 802-388-9925), a 15-minute walk from the school. Rooms are beautifully decorated and the grounds are lovely. The moderate-to-expensive price includes lavish continental breakfast. Even closer to campus (a 5-minute walk) is the somewhat less pricey, intimate (11 rooms), recently restored, 200-year-old **Inn on the Green** (19 S. Pleasant St.; 802-388-7512 or 888-244-7512), offering charming rooms with all amenities and continental breakfast served in your room. Around the corner, also on the green in the historic district, is the bustling, 75-room **Middlebury Inn** (14 Courthouse Sq., Rte. 7; 802-388-4961 or 800-842-4666). Rates range from moderate to expensive.

A little farther: East Middlebury offers visitors some lovely accommodations as well. For an inexpensive, small, and pleasant bed and breakfast about 4 miles from campus, try **The October Pumpkin Inn** (Rte. 125E; 802-388-9525), in East Middlebury. Rates are inexpensive to moderate and the price includes a full breakfast. Consider also the **Waybury Inn** (Rte. 125, East Middlebury; 802-388-4015), featured as the Stratford Inn on *The Bob Newhart Show*. It's a little bit farther east (6 miles from the College). Tennis courts and a golf course are also nearby. A fitness center with an indoor pool is open to inn guests at a special rate. Room prices are on the high side and include a full country breakfast. For the traveler seeking chain motels, you can enjoy a trip north on Rte. 7 to South Burlington and Burlington. There you will find many of the national chains. Please contact the Addison County Chamber of Commerce at 802-388-7951 or 800-733-8376 for more details. Log onto www.midvermont.com/ for a complete listing of area attractions, lodging, or dining.

HIGHLIGHTS

ON CAMPUS
- Bicentennial Hall (science)
- The Center for the Arts
- Athletic facilities

OFF CAMPUS
- Champlain Valley
- Skiing
- Sheldon Museum
- Lake Champlain

UNIVERSITY OF VERMONT

Office of Admissions, University of Vermont, Clement House, 194 S. Prospect St., Burlington, VT 05401-3596 • Telephone: 802-656-3370 • Web: www.uvm.edu • Email: admissions@uvm.edu

Hours: Monday-Friday, 8AM-4:30PM. Closed weekends, New Year's Day, Presidents' Day, Memorial Day, July 4, Labor Day, Thanksgiving weekend, and December 24 and 25.

The University of Vermont offers a solid overall academic reputation, accessible professors, and a great hockey team. UVM is particularly strong in animal science and health- and environment-related areas; students report that psychology, political science, and business and management are also popular majors.

HIGHLIGHTS

ON CAMPUS
- Fleming Museum
- Billings Student Center
- Campus Green
- Athletic complex/fitness cente
- Spear Street Research Farm and Equine Center

OFF CAMPUS
- Lake Champlain
- Green Mountains
- Burlington (arts, cultural events)
- UVM Morgan Horse Farm
- Shelbourne Museum

TRANSPORTATION

Burlington International Airport is several miles (a 15-minute drive) from campus. Taxis, local buses, and rental cars are available for the trip from the airport to campus. Taxis are at or can be called from the airport. Rental car agencies in the airport are open 24 hours a day. The CCTA bus line from the airport to campus runs Monday trough Friday from 6:40AM to 10:10PM and Saturday to 8:10PM.

FIND YOUR WAY

From I-89, take Exit 14W and proceed a mile west to campus. The admissions office is 1 block left on South Prospect St. From U.S. Rte. 7, enter Burlington and turn up the hill at the intersection with Main St. (Rte. 2). The campus is at the top of the hill. The admissions office is 1 block right on South Prospect St. From the east, Rte. 2 becomes Main St. in Burlington and bisects the campus. The admissions office is 1 block left on South Prospect St.

STAY THE NIGHT

Nearby: For convenience and charm, a terrific choice is **The Willard Street Inn** (349 S. Willard St.; 802-651-8710). It is a 5- to 10-minute (but uphill!) walk to UVM and offers accommodations in the grand style and a fabulous breakfast. Its rates are expensive. The **Radisson Hotel** (60 Battery St.; 802-658-6500) is 5 minutes from the University and within walking distance of Burlington's fabulous pedestrian mall. It is pricier, but still has rooms available in the moderate range (you may qualify for special rates not linked to University visitor status). The hotel has the usual amenities of a big-city hotel designed to attract the business visitor. You can also try the **Sheraton Hotel and Conference Center** (intersection 89, Exit 14W and U.S. 2; 802-655-6600 or 800-325-3535). An inexpensive choice about a mile away is the **Anchorage Inn** (108 Dorset St. South, Burlington; 802-863-7000). It provides a continental breakfast and has an indoor pool and fitness center.

A little farther: **The Inn at Shelburne Farms** (802-985-8498), about 20 minutes from the school, in Shelburne, is part of a working farm. It offers beautiful views of Lake Champlain, a tennis court, boating, and lovely walks. Wonderful food is also part of the package. Its rates are very expensive. The Inn is open from Memorial Day to mid-October.

AT A GLANCE

Selectivity Rating	76
Range SAT I Math	520-620
Average SAT I Math	566
Range SAT I Verbal	510-610
Average SAT I Verbal	562
Average ACT Composite	24
Student to Faculty Ratio	15:1

CAMPUS TOURS

Appointment Req?	No
Dates	Year-round, except during holidays, spring recess, exam periods, and occasional other weeks
Times	Mon-Fri 10AM to 2PM
Avg. Length	90 min

ON-CAMPUS INTERVIEWS

Admissions

Start Date–Juniors	Any time
Appointment Req?	Yes
Advance Notice	Several weeks
Saturdays?	No
Avg. Length	20-30 min
Info Sessions	Year-round

Faculty and Coaches

Dates/Times	Year-round; subject to faculty/coach availability
Arrangements	For faculty, contact dept. of interest; for coach, contact Off. of Athletics several weeks prior

CLASS VISITS

Dates	Academic year (Mon-Fri)
Arrangements	Contact admissions off.

OVERNIGHT DORM STAYS

Advance Notice	N/A
Arrangements	N/A
Limitations	N/A

VIRGINIA

1- Hollins College
2- Randolph-Macon Woman's College
3- Sweet Briar College
4- University of Virginia
5- Washington & Lee University
6- College of William & Mary

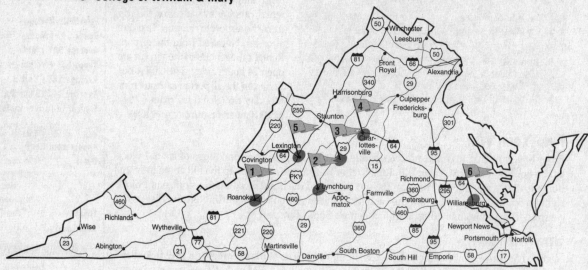

Virginia	Coll. William & Mary	Hollins Coll.	Randolph-Macon	Sweet Briar Coll.	U. of Virginia	Washington & Lee	Richmond	Roanoke
Coll. William & Mary	—	218	164	145	131	199	52	218
Hollins Coll.	218	—	52	65	115	53	185	0
Randolph-Macon	164	52	—	9	58	40	114	52
Sweet Briar Coll.	145	65	9	—	48	29	95	65
U. of Virginia	131	115	58	48	—	73	69	115
Washington & Lee	199	53	40	29	73	—	117	53
Richmond	52	185	114	95	69	117	—	185
Roanoke	218	0	52	65	115	53	185	—

COLLEGE OF WILLIAM AND MARY

Office of Admissions, College of William and Mary, P.O. Box 8795, Williamsburg, VA 23187-8795
(The office is in Blow Memorial Hall) • Telephone: 757-221-4223 •
Web: www.wm.edu • Email: admiss@facstaff.wm.edu

Hours: Monday-Friday, 8AM-5PM; Saturday, 9AM-noon (September-April only). Closed Sundays and holidays.

"The workload is obscene" at William and Mary, one of the best and most competitive public schools in the nation, where the oldest honor code in the nation allows students to take unproctored exams. W&M is probably the only school to have its social scene revolve around three "delis" across the street from campus, and a veritable catalogue of distinguished alumni includes Thomas Jefferson and Glenn Close.

HIGHLIGHTS

ON CAMPUS
- The Wren Building
- Muscarelle Museum of Art
- Lake Matoaka/College Woods recreation area
- Crim Dell Bridge
- The Sunken Garden

OFF CAMPUS
- Colonial Williamsburg
- Busch Gardens Amusement Park
- Water Country USA
- Jamestown Settlement
- Outlet shopping centers/pottery factory

TRANSPORTATION

Several airports serve the Williamsburg area: Newport News-Williamsburg International Airport in Newport News is a 20-minute drive from campus; Norfolk International Airport in Norfolk is a 90-minute drive from campus; Byrd International Airport in Richmond is a 60-minute drive from campus. The following companies offer airport limousin service: Williamsburg Limo (757-877-0279), Airport Transport (757-857-9477), and Groome Transport (757-222-7222); make arrangements one day in advance.

FIND YOUR WAY

From I-64, take Exit 238. At the second set of lights (Rte. 132), turn right. Turn right again at the next set of lights (Rte. 60 bypass). Follow Bypass Rd. to its end and its intersection with Richmond Rd. Turn left at the light onto Richmond Rd. At the third set of lights, you will see the Walter F. Zable Stadium on the right. The Office of Admission is in Blow Memorial Hall, just beyond the light on the right. Stop in Dawson Circle in front of the hall to obtain a parking permit from the Office of Admission.

STAY THE NIGHT

William and Mary is on the edge of Colonial Williamsburg. The town's restoration organization runs a number of lodging facilities, all of which are within 5 minutes of William and Mary. Of these, the least expensive is the **Governor's Inn Motel** (506 N. Henry St.; 757-229-1000). The **Motor House**, just opposite the visitors center (757-229-1000 or 800-447-8679), offers rooms in the inexpensive to moderate range. Climbing up the scale, the grand **Williamsburg Inn** (Francis St.; 757-229-1000 or 800-HISTORY) is top-of-the-line. The inn has tennis courts (with tennis pro) and a golf course. Two appealing bed-and-breakfasts are the **Applewood Colonial Bed and Breakfast** (605 Richmond Rd.; 757-229-0205), within walking distance of the college, and **Liberty Rose Bed-and-Breakfast** (1022 Jamestown Rd.; 757-253-1260), half a mile away. A romantic and charming restoration, the Liberty Rose is the more expensive of the two, with rooms in the moderate-expensive range. Basic lodgings are a stone's throw away. The **Quarter Path Inn Motel** (620 York St.; 757-220-0960) and the **Traveller's Inn** (800-336-0500) are decent, no-frills accommodations. There are many, many places to stay in the Williamsburg area. You can get a complete list from the **Williamsburg Area Convention and Visitors Bureau** (757-253-0192). This guide includes lists of campgrounds and very inexpensive private guest homes.

AT A GLANCE

Selectivity Rating	94
Range SAT I Math	610-700
Average SAT I Math	648
Range SAT I Verbal	620-710
Average SAT I Verbal	661
Average ACT Composite	31
Average GPA	3.9
Student to Faculty Ratio	12:1

CAMPUS TOURS

Appointment Req?	No
Dates	While classes are in session
Times	Following info session
Avg. Length	2 hours, includes info session

ON-CAMPUS INFORMATION SESSIONS

Admissions

Info Sessions	Mon-Fri 10AM and 2:30PM; Sat 10AM (Sept-April, except holidays)

Faculty and Coaches

Dates/Times	Year-round; subject to faculty/coach availability
Arrangements	Contact dept. of interest 3-4 weeks prior

CLASS VISITS

Dates	While classes are in session
Arrangements	Contact admissions off.

OVERNIGHT DORM STAYS

Advance Notice	2 weeks
Arrangements	Student-run program; call 757-221-3696
Limitations	Availalble only in April, and restricted to accepted students

HOLLINS UNIVERSITY

Admissions Office, Hollins University, P.O. Box 9707, Roanoke, VA 24020-1707
(The office is in the Main Building) • Telephone: 800-456-9595 or 540-362-6401 •
Web: www.hollins.edu • Email: huadm@hollins.edu

Hours: Monday-Friday, 8:30AM-4:30PM; Saturday, 9AM-noon (only during the academic year). Closed Sundays and holidays.

Tiny Hollins University is an all-women's liberal arts school with a "great creative writing program" that "encourages personal growth and discovery." Hollins boasts a "beautiful" antebellum campus, roomy and comfortable dorms, and a "wonderful community" atmosphere that is "much like your second family."

AT A GLANCE

Selectivity Rating	78
Range SAT I Math	500-580
Average SAT I Math	543
Range SAT I Verbal	530-650
Average SAT I Verbal	591
Average ACT Composite	24
Average GPA	3.4
Student to Faculty Ratio	10:1

CAMPUS TOURS

Appointment Req?	Highly recommended
Dates	Year-round
Times	Mon-Fri 9AM, 11AM, 1PM, and 3PM; Sat 9AM, 10AM, and 11AM
Avg. Length	1 hour

ON-CAMPUS INTERVIEWS

Admissions

Start Date–Juniors	Any time
Appointment Req?	Highly recommended
Advance Notice	7 days
Saturdays?	Yes, 9AM-noon during the academic year
Avg. Length	30 min
Info Sessions	Available only as part of special overnight programs

Faculty and Coaches

Dates/Times	During academic year; subject to faculty/coach availability
Arrangements	Contact admissions off. 7-10 days prior

CLASS VISITS

Dates	Academic year (Mon-Fri)
Arrangements	Contact admissions off.

OVERNIGHT DORM STAYS

Advance Notice	2 weeks
Arrangements	Contact admissions off.
Limitations	Available Sun-Thurs night

TRANSPORTATION

Roanoke Airport is 2 miles from campus. Limousine or taxi service from the airport to campus can be arranged on arrival. Call Roanoke Airport Limousine Service (540-345-7710), Star City Cab (540-366-6390), or Yellow Cab Company (540-345-7711).

FIND YOUR WAY

From I-81 (N. or S.), take Exit 146 (the Hollins exit) to the east. At the first traffic light (Williamson Rd.), make a left turn. The college is half a mile down the road on the left side.

STAY THE NIGHT

Nearby: Unfortunately, there's nothing within walking distance. The usual selection of chain hotels is approximately 10 minutes away, near the airport. One of these is the **Country Inn & Suites** (7860 Plantation Rd.; 540-366-5678 or 800-456-4000). It has an indoor pool. A little bit farther, 10 minutes from Hollins, and a tad more expensive, is the **Holiday Inn—Airport** (540-366-8861 or 800-465-4329). This facility has an outdoor pool. Farther away is the moderately priced **Clarion Hotel** (2727 Ferndale Dr.; 540-362-4500) with a heated indoor-outdoor pool, volleyball courts, lighted tennis courts, and golf privileges. There's even a horseshoe pit. Just 15 minutes away from campus, in the old Victorian section of town (a historical area on the National Registry), is the **Mary Bladon House** (381 Washington Ave. S.W.; 540-344-5361). The special rate for students visiting Hollins allows you to have 2 adjoining rooms at a moderate rate. Cheaper rooms with double beds are also available.

A little farther: An easy 45-minute drive south on the interstate will bring you to the resort area of Smith Mountain Lake and to the delightful **Manor at Taylor's Store** (Rte. 1, Wirtz; 540-721-3951), a bed-and-breakfast situated on 100 acres in a very pretty part of Virginia. There are swimming ponds and fishing ponds, movies, billiards, a guest kitchen on the property, and boating, golf, and tennis nearby. It offers a lot of fun at a moderate rate.

HIGHLIGHTS

ON CAMPUS
• Art gallery and studios
• duPont Chapel
• Wyndham Robertson Library

OFF CAMPUS
• Downtown Roanoke
• Roanoke City Market
• Tinker Mountain
• Cawins Cave

RANDOLPH-MACON WOMAN'S COLLEGE

Admissions Office, Randolph-Macon Woman's College, 2500 Rivermont Ave., Lynchburg, VA 24503 (The office is in Thoresen Building) • Telephone: 800-745-RMWC or 804-947-8100 • Web: www.rmwc.edu • Email: admissions@rmwc.edu

Hours: Monday-Friday, 9AM-5PM; Saturday, 9AM-noon. Summer: Monday-Friday: 8:30AM-4:30PM. Closed major holidays.

"I actually spend more time out of class talking to my professors than I do in class lectures," beams one of the many happy students at Randolph-Macon Woman's College, a tiny all-women's bastion in Lynchburg, Virginia. "There's little to do on campus," but the "elegant dining hall and resident halls" make students wonder if they're "living at a five-star hotel or college."

HIGHLIGHTS

ON CAMPUS
- The Maier Museum of Art
- Botanical gardens
- The Whiteside Amphitheater
- The Riding Center

OFF CAMPUS
- Point of Honor
- Blue Ridge Parkway
- Blackwater Creek Trail
- Poplar Forest

TRANSPORTATION

The Lynchburg Municipal Airport is a 20-minute drive from campus. Call the admissions office for special arranged pickup. Taxi and limousine service is available at the airport.

FIND YOUR WAY

The major north-south highway to Lynchburg is U.S. Rte. 29. The major east-west highway is U.S. Rte. 460. Both of these roads have clear signs to the college. In Lynchburg, Main St. (which is one-way) becomes Rivermont Ave. Continue on Rivermont Ave. about 2 miles to entrance of college, on the right.

STAY THE NIGHT

Some hotels in Lynchburg are, the **Days Inn** (3320 Candlers Mountain Rd.; 800-329-7466), the **Hampton Inn** (5604 Seminole Ave.; 800-426-7866), the **Lynchburg Hilton** (2900 Candlers Mountain Rd.; 800-445-8667), and the **Holiday Inn Select** (601 Main St.; 800-465-4329). Some bed and breakfasts are the **Lynchburg Mansion Inn** (405 Madison St.; 804-528-5400), the **Madison House** (413 Madison St.; 877-901-1503), **The Residence** (2460 Rivermont Ave.; 888-835-0387), and **The Federal Crest Inn** (1101 Federal St.; 800-818-6155).

AT A GLANCE

Selectivity Rating	78
Range SAT I Math	500-610
Average SAT I Math	558
Range SAT I Verbal	543-670
Average SAT I Verbal	607
Average ACT Composite	26
Average GPA	3.4
Student to Faculty Ratio	9:1

CAMPUS TOURS

Appointment Req?	Yes
Dates	Year-round
Times	Academic year: Mon-Fri 9AM-5PM; Sat 9AM-noon. Summer months: Mon-Fri 8:30AM-5PM.
Avg. Length	60 min

ON-CAMPUS INTERVIEWS

Admissions

Start Date–Juniors	Any time
Appointment Req?	Scheduled when tour is scheduled
Advance Notice	As much as possible
Saturdays?	Yes, during the academic year
Avg. Length	30-60 min
Info Sessions	N/A

Faculty and Coaches

Dates/Times	Year-round; subject to faculty/coach availability
Arrangements	Contact admissions off.

CLASS VISITS

Dates	Year-round (Mon-Fri)
Arrangements	Contact admissions off.

OVERNIGHT DORM STAYS

Advance Notice	1 week
Arrangements	Contact admissions off.
Limitations	Not available during exam periods

SWEET BRIAR COLLEGE

Office of Admissions, Sweet Briar College, Box B, Sweet Briar, VA 24595
(The office is in Hill House, the Admissions House) • Telephone: 804-381-6142 •
Web: www.sbc.edu • Email: admissions@sbc.edu

Hours: Monday-Friday, 8:30AM-5PM; Saturday, 9AM-12:30PM (only during the academic year). Closed Sundays and holidays.

The women of Sweet Briar College absolutely love the small, "fascinating," discussion-oriented classes and "accessible and enthusiastic" professors. And, to top it all off, the "beautiful" campus of SBC—complete with wooded footpaths and "bike trails out the wazoo"—is one of the "most wired" colleges in the country.

AT A GLANCE

Selectivity Rating	78
Range SAT I Math	470-580
Average SAT I Math	540
Range SAT I Verbal	520-620
Average SAT I Verbal	580
Average ACT Composite	25
Average GPA	3.4
Student to Faculty Ratio	7:1

CAMPUS TOURS

Appointment Req?	Yes
Dates	Year-round
Times	Call for times
Avg. Length	75 min

ON-CAMPUS INTERVIEWS

Admissions

Start Date—Juniors	Any time
Appointment Req?	No
Advance Notice	1 day
Saturdays?	Yes, during academic year only
Avg. Length	30 min
Info Sessions	Available only as part of prearranged group tour

Faculty and Coaches

Dates/Times	Year-round; subject to faculty/coach availability
Arrangements	Contact admissions off. as early as possible

CLASS VISITS

Dates	Year-round (Mon-Fri)
Arrangements	Contact admissions off.

OVERNIGHT DORM STAYS

Advance Notice	1 week
Arrangements	Contact admissions off.
Limitations	Not available Fri-Sat nights or during exam periods

TRANSPORTATION

The Lynchburg Municipal Airport is a 30-minute drive from campus. Taxi service is available for the trip from airport to campus. The admissions office will arrange for transportation if you request it at least 3 days prior to your visit.

FIND YOUR WAY

From Richmond, take U.S. Rte. 64 W. to U.S. Rte. 29. Head south on U.S. 29 to the college.

STAY THE NIGHT

Nearby: Right on the campus, exclusively for college visitors, is the **Florence Elston Inn** (804-381-6207). Prices are inexpensive. A lovely bed-and-breakfast, **Dulwich Manor** (Amherst; 804-946-7207), is about 5 minutes away from the college in Amherst. This 1900 English manor house in a beautiful setting surrounded by woodland can be yours—if the moderate price is right. **Winridge Bed and Breakfast** (Rte. 1, Madison Heights; 804-384-7220) about 20 minutes from campus, is a quiet southern home with a view of the Blue Hills. Its inexpensive price includes a full breakfast. Tennis courts are nearby. Other bed-and-breakfasts can be contacted through **Lamplighters B&B Hosts** (804-384-1635).

A little farther: You have several choices in Lynchburg, where Randolph-Macon Woman's College is located (this is south of Sweet Briar). Of these, the least expensive is the **Days Inn** (3320 Candlers Mountain Rd.; 804-847-8655) 16 miles south of Sweet Briar. Rooms are inexpensive and the inn is across the street from a mall. About the same distance from the college is the **Hilton Lynchburg** (2900 Candlers Mountain Rd.; 804-237-6333). The rate is moderate and the hotel has an indoor pool. Golf and tennis facilities are nearby. The **Holiday Inn** (601 Main St.; 804-528-2500) is a little closer to Sweet Briar, and it has a special inexpensive rate for college visitors.

HIGHLIGHTS

ON CAMPUS
- Monument Hill
- Rodgers Riding Center
- Boathouse

OFF CAMPUS
- Lynchburg
- Charlottesville
- Lexington
- Roanoke

UNIVERSITY OF VIRGINIA

Admissions Office, University of Virginia, P.O. Box 9017, Charlottesville, VA 22906 (The office is in Miller Hall on McCormick Road) • Telephone: 804-982-3200 • Web: www.virginia.edu • Email: undergrad-admission@virginia.edu

Hours: Monday-Friday, 8AM-5PM. Closed weekends, Memorial Day, July 4, Labor Day, Thanksgiving weekend, and much of the Christmas holiday.

The University of Virginia is one of the best and most selective state schools around. The research facilities and archives here are spectacular and "for the size of this university, UVA has a small and familiar feel." Students say classes for everybody but first-year students are surprisingly reasonable in size. Katie Couric is an alum.

HIGHLIGHTS

ON CAMPUS
- Historic Academic Village
- Bayly Art Museum
- Scott Stadium
- Outdoor amphitheater
- Observatory Hall

OFF CAMPUS
- Blue Ridge Mountains
- VA Film Festival
- Wintergreen Ski Resort
- Historic downtown mall
- James River

TRANSPORTATION

The Charlottesville-Albemarle Airport is 10 miles from campus. Taxis are available for the ride from airport to campus.

FIND YOUR WAY

From north or south, take U.S. Rte. 29 toward Charlottesville; do not take the Rte. 29 bypass around the city, but take the business route, which becomes Emmet St. and goes through campus. **From east or west** on I-64, take Exit 22B to U.S. Rte. 29 N. Follow the preceding directions from Rte. 29.

STAY THE NIGHT

Nearby: If convenience is everything, you have several choices within walking distance of the university. A special moderate rate for college visitors is offered by the **Cavalier Inn** (150 Emmet St.; 804-296-8111). Call **Guesthouses B&B** (804-979-7264) for a fantastic selection of bed-and-breakfasts, some of which are adjacent to the university. Most are moderately priced. Inexpensive accommodations can be found at the **Knights Inn** (1300 Seminole Trail; 804-973-8133), about 2 miles from the university. Even closer, with very expensive prices, is the attractive **200 South Street** (200 South St.; 804-979-0200), a 20-room inn in the downtown historic district. Rooms with whirlpool tubs, fireplaces, and canopy beds are available. If you prefer a resort with swimming pools, a tennis court, a golf course, and balloon rides (and, honestly, who doesn't?), try the university owned **Boar's Head Inn** (Ivy Rd.; 804-296-2181 or 800-476-1988). It's 5 minutes from the central campus, and you must reserve the balloon in advance. The inn has convention facilities, so you might run into a crowd.

A little farther: **Keswick Hall** (701 Country Club Dr.; 804-979-3365) offers the best opportunity to live like landed gentry for a day or so. The rooms are exquisite with prices to match, but the fall foliage views are, by themselves, almost worth the price. The gourmet will love what the renowned chefs have to offer.

AT A GLANCE

Selectivity Rating	94
Range SAT I Math	610-710
Average SAT I Math	659
Range SAT I Verbal	600-700
Average SAT I Verbal	648
Average ACT Composite	28
Average GPA	3.8
Student to Faculty Ratio	13:1

CAMPUS TOURS

Appointment Req?	No
Dates	Year-round, except during fall and spring breaks, Thanksgiving and Christmas holidays, and exam periods
Times	Mon-Sat 11AM and 2PM
Avg. Length	1 hour

ON-CAMPUS INTERVIEWS

Admissions

Start Date–Juniors	Usually June 15
Appointment Req?	Yes
Advance Notice	3-4 weeks
Saturdays?	No
Avg. Length	Varies
Info Sessions	Year-round, except some holidays

Faculty and Coaches

Dates/Times	Year-round; subject to faculty/coach availability

CLASS VISITS

Dates	Sept-April (Mon-Fri)

OVERNIGHT DORM STAYS

Advance Notice	2 weeks
Arrangements	Contact Monroe Society at 804-924-3321
Limitations	Available mid-Oct to mid-April only

WASHINGTON AND LEE UNIVERSITY

Office of Admissions, Washington and Lee University, Lexington, VA 24450
(The office is in Gilliam Admissions House on Letcher Ave.) • Telephone: 540-463-8710 •
Web: www.wlu.edu • Email: admissions@wlu.edu

Hours: Monday-Friday, 8:30AM-5PM; Saturday, 8AM-noon. Closed Sundays and holidays.

Washington and Lee is a moderately priced, traditional "liberal arts school" with a "great reputation," a "fun, wild" social scene, and a very conservative student population. The Dean of the Freshman Program "memorizes everybody's name by the first day of school," according to students, which is "both impressive and eerie." The great American author Tom Wolfe is an alum.

AT A GLANCE

Selectivity Rating	97
Range SAT I Math	640-720
Range SAT I Verbal	630-710
Average GPA	3.9
Student to Faculty Ratio	10:1

CAMPUS TOURS

Appointment Req?	Preferred
Dates	Year-round
Times	Mon-Fri 10AM-4PM; Sat 9:30AM-12:30PM, call for availability
Avg. Length	1 hour

ON-CAMPUS INTERVIEWS

Admissions

Start Date—Juniors	May
Appointment Req?	Yes
Advance Notice	2 weeks
Saturdays?	Yes, during the academic year, except Feb-March
Avg. Length	30 min
Info Sessions	June-March

Faculty and Coaches

Dates/Times	Year-round; subject to faculty/coach availability
Arrangements	Contact admissions off. for faculty. Contact coaches directly 2 weeks prior.

CLASS VISITS

Dates	Academic year (Mon-Fri)
Arrangements	Contact admissions off.

OVERNIGHT DORM STAYS

Advance Notice	N/A
Arrangements	Available only through a personal friend who is a current student
Limitations	N/A

TRANSPORTATION

The Roanoke Airport is 50 miles from campus. Taxis, limousines, and rental cars are available for the ride from airport to campus. For limousine reservations, call Shenandoah Limousine (540-464-5466) or Roanoke Airport Limousine Service (540-345-7710).

FIND YOUR WAY

From the north, take I-81 S. to the first Lexington exit and follow U.S. Rte. 11 S., which becomes Main St. in Lexington. On Rte. 11, you pass Virginia Military Institute and then enter the Washington and Lee campus, 8 miles from I-81. **From the south,** take I-81 N. to the second Lexington exit and I-64 W.; from I-64 W. follow posted directions to U.S. Rte. 11 S. Rte. 11 S. brings you onto the Washington and Lee campus, 2 miles from I-64.

STAY THE NIGHT

A popular choice and a favorite with college kids is the warm and friendly **Llewellyn Lodge** (603 S. Main St.; 540-463-3235 or 800-882-1145), within walking distance of the university. The moderate price includes a full breakfast. Tennis courts, a pool, and golf are nearby. Two interesting inns, both run by Historic Country Inns of Lexington, are only a block from campus: the **Alexander-Winthrow House** (3 W. Washington St.; 540-463-2044) and the **McCampbell Inn** (11 N. Main St.; 540-463-2044). The reasonable prices include breakfast. If you are more comfortable with the predictable chains, the **Days Inn Keydet General Motel** (U.S. Rte. 60 West; 540-463-2143) is inexpensive and has a lovely view of the Blue Ridge Mountains. The **Holiday Inn** (Rte. 11 N. and I-64; 540-463-7351) is somewhat more expensive and also has a mountain view.

HIGHLIGHTS

ON CAMPUS
- Lee Chapel
- Reeves Center
- Watson Pavillion
- Lenfest Center for the Arts

OFF CAMPUS
- Stonewall Jackson House
- George Marshall Museum at VMI
- Natural Bridge

1- Evergreen State College
2- University of Puget Sound
3- University of Washington
4- Whitman College

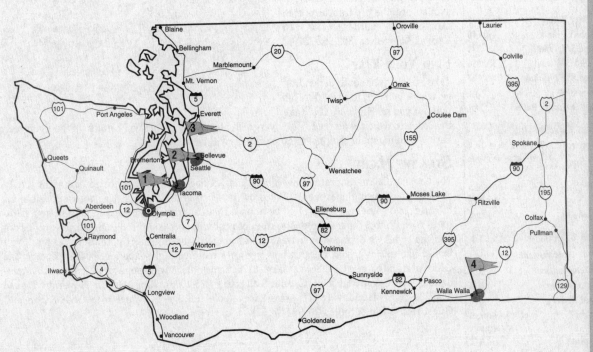

Washington	Evergreen State	Univ. Puget Sound	Univ. Washington	Whitman Coll.	Seattle	Spokane
Evergreen State	—	28	59	320	58	320
Univ. Puget Sound	28	—	30	293	30	294
Univ. Washington	59	30	—	274	0	280
Whitman Coll.	320	293	274	—	274	160
Seattle	58	30	0	274	—	280
Spokane	320	294	280	160	280	—

EVERGREEN STATE COLLEGE

Admissions Office, Evergreen State College, 2700 Evergreen Pkwy. N.W., Olympia, WA 98502 (The office is in the Library Building) • Telephone: 360-866-6000, ext. 6170 • Web: www.evergreen.edu • Email: admissions@evergreen.edu

Hours: Monday-Friday, 8AM-5PM and select Saturdays. Closed weekends and holidays.

"Alternative world views" are all the rage at Evergreen State, where "hippies, hippies, and white guys with dreadlocks" like to "think about how to change the world" and "ponder life's most mind-boggling struggles." Students design their own majors with the guidance of "highly qualified" professors throughout their academic careers. Instead of traditional grades, students receive narrative evaluations.

AT A GLANCE

Selectivity Rating	76
Range SAT I Math	490-610
Average SAT I Math	534
Range SAT I Verbal	530-660
Average SAT I Verbal	587
Average GPA	3.1
Student to Faculty Ratio	24:1

CAMPUS TOURS

Appointment Req?	Please call to check availability and times
Dates	All year
Times	Mon-Fri 10:30AM and 2:20PM
Avg. Length	1 hour

ON-CAMPUS INTERVIEWS

Admissions

Start Date–Juniors	N/A
Appointment Req?	N/A
Advance Notice	N/A
Saturdays?	Information sessions and tours only
Avg. Length	N/A
Info Sessions	All year

Faculty and Coaches

Dates/Times	Year-round; subject to faculty/coach availability
Arrangements	Contact admissions off.

CLASS VISITS

Dates	Oct-June (Mon-Fri)
Arrangements	Contact admissions off.

OVERNIGHT DORM STAYS

Advance Notice	1-2 weeks
Arrangements	Contact admissions off.
Limitations	3 male and 3 female per night; one night stay maximum

TRANSPORTATION

Seattle-Tacoma International Airport is approximately an hour from Olympia. Bus and shuttle service is available for the trip from airport to campus. For shuttle service, call Capital Aeroporter (800-962-3579).

FIND YOUR WAY

Take I-5 (north or south depending on where you are) to Exit 104. This will put you on Highway 101. Take the 3rd exit, which is marked "The Evergreen State College." Travel 2 miles on the Evergreen Parkway to the main campus entrance, which will be on your left.

STAY THE NIGHT

The Greener Guide program at Evergreen State College offers you a hosted overnight stay in our campus housing apartments. We provide a bed and all linens; you are responsible for toiletries and some meals. You will be housed in an apartment, where you may share a bathroom with up to 3 other people. The student host will take you through the different types of housing styles we offer and even treat you to a meal in the Housing Community Center. If you would like to stay in our campus housing for a real overnight experience please contact the Office of Admissions at 360-866-6000 ext. 6170. Some other suggestions for overnight accommodations are **Cavanaugh's at Capitol Lake** (800-325-4000), **Ramada Inn Governor House** (800-228-2828), **Holiday Inn Express-Lacey** (800-HOLIDAY), **Motel 6** (800-846-8356), and **Guest House Inn & Suites** (877-847-7152).

HIGHLIGHTS

ON CAMPUS
- Longhouse Cultural and Education Center
- Organic farm
- The College library

OFF CAMPUS
- State Capitol Campus
- Washington State Center for the Performing Arts
- Farmer's Market
- Tumwater Historical Park
- Washington State Capitol Museum

UNIVERSITY OF PUGET SOUND

Office of Admission, University of Puget Sound, 1500 N. Warner St., Tacoma, WA 98416-0062
(The office is in Jones Hall, Rm. 115) • Telephone: 253-879-3211 or 800-396-7191 •
Web: www.ups.edu • Email: admission@ups.edu

Hours: Monday-Friday: 8AM-5PM; Saturday mornings (August-April) by appointment only. Closed Sundays and holidays.

Students rave that professors with "a passion for their subjects" and a "stimulating, rigorous learning environment" make the very competitive University of Puget Sound "the best school in Washington." Academics are rigorous, and people "study a lot" in the "large" and "comfortable" dorm rooms on the "aesthetically beautiful" (but rainy) UPS campus.

HIGHLIGHTS

ON CAMPUS
- Three-story Pale Chihuly glass sculpture in Wyatt Hall
- Diversions Café
- Alcorn Arboretum
- Music and theater productions

OFF CAMPUS
- San Juan Islands
- Mount Rainier National Park
- Experience Music Project in Seattle
- Washington State History Museum
- Point Defiance Park, Zoo, and Aquarium

TRANSPORTATION

Seattle-Tacoma International Airport is 24 miles from campus. Capital Aeroporter provides hourly transportation from the airport to the downtown Tacoma Sheraton and, if possible, to campus. Call 800-962-3579 or 253-927-6179 (in Tacoma) or 206-838-7431 (at the airport) to arrange for this service. If the Aeroporter cannot take you to campus directly, you can take a taxi from the Sheraton. Amtrak train service is available to the station in Tacoma. From there, take a taxi or one of these public buses: #41, #400, or #500; request a transfer ticket and leave the bus at 10th and Commerce Streets. Wait there for the UPS Bus (#16A or #16B) and take it to N. 15th and Alder Sts., which is 1 block west of Wheelock Student Center. Greyhound Bus Lines also serve Tacoma. From the bus station, take the UPS Bus (#16A or #16B) at 10th and Commerce Sts. (1 block west of Pacific Ave. from the station) and follow preceding directions from there to campus.

FIND YOUR WAY

From the south, take I-5 to Exit 132 for Gig Harbor/Bremerton Hwy. (Washington Rte. 16); then take the Union Ave. exit, make a right at the light, and travel north approximately 2 miles to the campus (on your right). Continue onto N. 18th St. and turn right. Turn right again on N. Lawrence St. (at the yield sign) and continue to the stop sign. Turn right into Jones Circle. Park in the parking circle in front of Jones Hall or in the lot just south of Wheelock Student Center. **From the north**, take I-5 to Exit 133, I-705 N., City Center exit. Exit at Schuster Parkway. Continue for about a mile; stay to the left. Exit to the left, Schuster Parkway, and follow down along the water. Stay to the right and proceed approximately a mile and a half. Exit right onto North 30th. Continue through the traffic signal in Old Town and up the hill. At the top of the hill, turn left at North Alder. Continue approximately a mile to North 15th. Turn right and proceed into campus.

STAY THE NIGHT

Nearby: Just 7 blocks from campus is **Keenan House** (2610 N. Warner St.; 253-752-0702). Furnished with antiques, this Victorian home is your best bet for price and convenience. Upscale yet reasonably priced **Sheraton Tacoma Hotel** (1320 Broadway Plaza; 253-572-3200 or 800-845-9466) is about 2.5 miles from campus. **La Quinta** (1425 E. 27th St.; 253-383-0146), located approximately 4 miles from the university with a view of Mount Rainier and Commencement Bay, is more modestly priced; request the special school rate. There's also a swimming pool. Approximately 15 minutes away is affordable **Shilo Inn** (7414 S. Hosmer Rd.; 253-475-4020 or 800-334-1049), near the 77th St. exit off I-5, which offers a heated pool and a health club. Nearby **Best Western Tacoma Inn** (8726 S. Hosmer Rd.; 253-922-0080), near the 84th St. exit off I-5, has accommodations that vary from inexpensive to moderate. The inn has a pool, health club, and putting green.

A little farther: Tacoma is only 35 miles or so from Seattle. Check the University of Washington entry for suggestions there.

AT A GLANCE

Selectivity Rating	85
Range SAT I Math	580-660
Average SAT I Math	620
Range SAT I Verbal	570-670
Average SAT I Verbal	621
Average ACT Composite	27
Average GPA	3.6
Student to Faculty Ratio	12:1

CAMPUS TOURS

Appointment Req?	Preferred
Dates	Year-round
Times	Mon-Fri 9AM-4PM
Avg. Length	1 hour

ON-CAMPUS INTERVIEWS

Admissions

Start Date—Juniors	Summer before junior year
Appointment Req?	Preferred
Advance Notice	2 weeks
Saturdays?	Yes, by appt. only
Avg. Length	50 min
Info Sessions	N/A

Faculty and Coaches

Dates/Times	Year-round; subject to faculty/coach availability
Arrangements	Contact admissions off. 2 weeks prior

CLASS VISITS

Dates	Year-round (Mon-Fri)
Arrangements	Contact admissions off.

OVERNIGHT DORM STAYS

Advance Notice	2 weeks
Arrangements	Contact admissions off.
Limitations	1-night stay; Sun-Thurs night only; bring a sleeping bag and pillow

UNIVERSITY OF WASHINGTON

Office of Admissions, University of Washington, Box 355840, Seattle, WA 98195-5840
(The office is in 320 Schmitz Hall) • Telephone: 206-543-9686 •
Web: www.washington.edu • Email: askuwadm@u.washington.edu

Hours: Monday-Friday, 8AM-5PM. Closed weekends and holidays.

The University of Washington—"the premier research institution north of Berkeley and west of Minnesota"—boasts 13 colleges that offer programs for undergraduates and a picturesque and very happening Seattle location. There's a throng of "outdoorsy types" here, and fraternities and sororities are quite popular as well.

AT A GLANCE

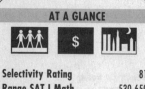

Selectivity Rating	81
Range SAT I Math	530-650
Range SAT I Verbal	510-630
Average GPA	3.6
Student to Faculty Ratio	11:1

CAMPUS TOURS

Appointment Req?	No
Dates	Year-round
Times	Mon-Fri 2:30PM, except during campus holidays
Avg. Length	90 min

ON-CAMPUS INTERVIEWS

Admissions

Start Date–Juniors	N/A
Appointment Req?	N/A
Advance Notice	N/A
Saturdays?	N/A
Avg. Length	N/A
Info Sessions	Year-round Fri at 1:30PM; call 206-543-5429

Faculty and Coaches

Dates/Times	Year-round; subject to faculty/coach availability
Arrangements	Contact admissions off. 3 weeks prior

CLASS VISITS

Dates	Year-round (Mon-Fri)
Arrangements	Contact admissions off. 3 weeks prior

TRANSPORTATION

The Seattle-Tacoma International Airport is approximately 18 miles from campus. To get to campus from the airport, take Shuttle Express, which leaves the airport on call. For Shuttle information, call 206-622-1424; no advance reservations are required. Amtrak trains and Greyhound/Trailways buses serve Seattle.

FIND YOUR WAY

From I-5 (N. and S.), take Exit 169. Proceed east on 45th St. N.E. for approximately half a mile. Turn right on 15th Ave. N.E. and head south approximately 3 blocks. The admissions office is in Schmitz Hall, at N.E. Campus Pkwy. and 15th Ave. N.E. Visitor parking is across the street.

STAY THE NIGHT

A nice range of choices can be found within walking distance of the university. **University Motel** (4731 12th St. N.E.; 206-522-4724), a small neighborhood place 6 blocks away, has great rates. All units are suites with kitchenettes. For something fancier, consider the **Meany Tower Hotel** (4507 Brooklyn Ave. N.E.; 206-634-2000), only 3 blocks from campus. There's a special moderate double-occupancy rate for university visitors. Astounding views of the mountains, lakes, and city, and a small workout room make it a good choice. The **Chambered Nautilus Bed-and-Breakfast** (5005 22nd St. N.E.; 206-522-2536), 2 blocks away, offers a tranquil retreat in the city. Prices are moderate and a gourmet breakfast is included. And who doesn't want to stay on a fully functional, exceptionally clean, restored tugboat? **The Challenger** (809 Fairview Pl. North.; 206-340-1201) has 7 guest rooms (4 with private baths), is carpeted throughout, and is furnished with nautical antiques. Rates run in the moderate range, with a full gourmet breakfast included. The tug has closed-circuit TV and videos. Five miles away is the small and lovely **Inn at the Market** (86 Pine St.; 206-443-3600), with rates that fluctuate between moderate and very expensive. Its setting is spectacular and its location is fantastic—near lively Pike Place Market. The **Silver Cloud Inn** (5036 25th NE; 206-526-5200,) is just east of campus and convenient to restaurants and shopping. **The Inn** (4140 Roosevelt Way NE; 206-632-5055) is just on the west side of the campus.

HIGHLIGHTS

ON CAMPUS
- Henry Art Gallery
- Burke Museum
- Meany Hall for Performing Arts
- Football games at Husky Stadium
- Waterfront Activities Center (WAC)

OFF CAMPUS
- The Experience Music Project (EMP)
- Safeco Field
- International District
- Seattle Art Museum/ Asian Art Museum
- Washington Park Arboretum

WHITMAN COLLEGE

Office of Admission, Whitman College, 345 Boyer Ave.,
Walla Walla, WA 99362 • Telephone: 509-527-5176 •
Web: www.whitman.edu • Email: admission@whitman.edu

Hours: Monday-Friday, 8:30AM-4:30PM; Saturday, 9AM-1PM (only during the academic year). Closed Sundays and holidays.

Whitman is "one of the best-kept secrets west of the Mississippi." This highly competitive but largely undiscovered gem of the inland Northwest has almost everything going for it: a beautiful setting, a rigorous curriculum, an "exceptionally willing" faculty, and a "helpful" administration. Whitman also boasts a phenomenal success rate among its graduates (three-quarters continue on to professional or graduate school within a year).

HIGHLIGHTS

ON CAMPUS
- Sheehan Gallery, Olin Hall Memorial Building
- Penrose Memorial Library
- Harpen Joy Theater
- Hunter Conservatory for Communication and Technology

OFF CAMPUS
- Whitman Mission National Historic Sight
- 18 local wineries
- Main Street National Historic District
- Various Lewis and Clark trail sites

TRANSPORTATION

A 10-minute drive from campus, the Walla Walla Airport is serve by Horizon Air, which offers daily flights to Walla Walla with connections through Seattle, WA. For city bus service from the airport to the campus or downtown, call Valley Transit (509-525-9140) to arrange for boarding (bus transportation from the airport Monday–Friday only). Rental cars in Walla Walla are available from Budget (509-525-8811), Hertz (509-522-3321), and Dollar (509-527-0812). For city taxi service, call A-1 Taxi (509-529-2525). Greyhound Bus Lines (509-525-9313, 800-231-2222) serves Walla Walla with daily connections from Pendleton, OR, Pasco WA, Spokane, WA, and Seattle. Delta Airlines, Alaska Airlines/Horizon Air and United Express provide additional air service with flights to Pasco (47 miles northwest of Walla Walla). Major rental car companies are on-site at the Pasco Airport.

FIND YOUR WAY

If you are traveling to Walla Walla (**from east or west**) on Highway 12, take the Clinton Street exit and proceed 6 blocks south on Clinton to Boyer Avenue. Turn right on Boyer. Penrose House (the office of admission) is 1 block ahead on the northwest corner of Boyer and Stanton. Parking is available in the driveway of Penrose House. If you are traveling **from south of Walla Walla**, Highway 11 from Pendleton, OR, becomes Highway 125 at the Washington State line, and then becomes Ninth Ave. when in enters Walla Walla. Drive north on Ninth to Main St. Turn right on Main and continue on Main until you come to a 5-way intersection. Make a soft right onto Boyer Avenue. Travel on Boyer beyond the stop sign to Penrose House on the northwest corner of Boyer and Stanton.

STAY THE NIGHT

There are several choices within walking distance of the college. The **Green Gables Inn** (922 Bonsella St.; 509-525-5501), one block north of campus, provides bed and breakfast amenities in a beautiful, 1909 Tudor-style mansion. Just across the street from the campus is the **Howard Johnson Express Inn** (325 E. Main St.; 509-529-4360, 800-446-4656), which offers a seasonal outdoor pool, jacuzzi, sauna, and exercise room. The reasonably priced **Travelodge** (421 E. Main St.; 509-529-4940, 800-578-7878) has a seasonal outdoor pool and hot tub. Just a 5-minute drive away is the **Hawthorne Suites** (520 N. 2nd St.; 509-525-2522, 800-228-5150) with inexpensive rates, a free continental breakfast, indoor pool, sauna, and spa. Nearby is Walla Walla's newest motel, the **Best Western Walla Walla Suites Inn** (7E. Oak St.; 509-525-4700) which has an indoor pool, hot tub, and fitness room. Additional guest services are available from these businesses.

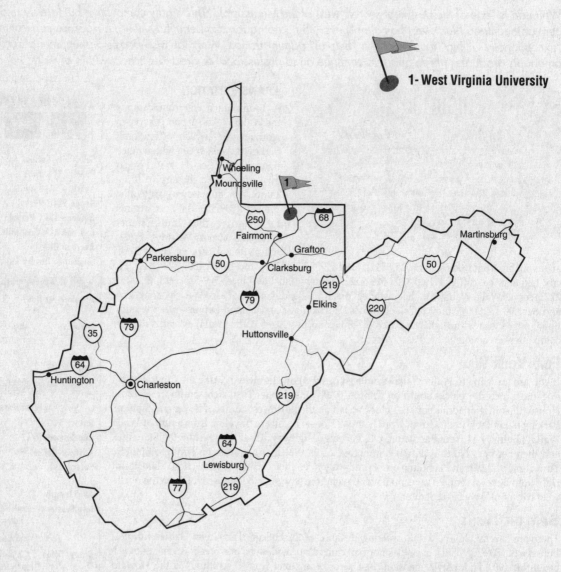

1- West Virginia University

Wheeling
Moundsville
250
Fairmont
Parkersburg
50
Grafton
Clarksburg
68
Martinsburg
50
219
79
Elkins
220
35
79
Huttonsville
64
Huntington
Charleston
219
64
Lewisburg
77
219

West Virginia		West Virginia Univ.	Charleston
West Virginia Univ.		—	153
Charleston		153	—

WEST VIRGINIA UNIVERSITY

WVU Visitors Center, P.O. Box 6690, Morgantown, WV 26506-6690 (The office is in the Communications Building off Patteson Drive) • Telephone: 800-344-WVU1 (Press 2) • Web: www.wvu.edu • Email: wvuadmissions@arc.wvu.edu

Hours: Monday-Friday, 8AM-6PM; Saturday 9AM-4PM. Closed Sundays and some holidays.

A raucous Greek scene and very popular sports programs make West Virginia University in the great college hamlet of Morgantown a fun place to go to school. Excellent programs in journalism, agriculture, engineering, and business make it a very good place to get a degree as well.

HIGHLIGHTS

ON CAMPUS	OFF CAMPUS
• WVU Visitor's Center	• Arboretum
• Mountainlair (student union)	• Cooper's Rock State Park
• Personal rapid transit	• Capeton recreational trail
• Mountaineer Field	• Downtown Morgantown
• Woodbuen Circle	• Pittsburgh (70 miles north)

TRANSPORTATION

Morgantown Airport is 2 miles from campus, available via county buses, taxi, or personal car. The Greater Pittsburgh International Airport is approximately 70 miles from campus. Flights to Pittsburgh leave Morgantown Airport daily. WVU also provides transportation to and from the Pittsburgh Airport, for a reasonable fee, during peak holiday times. Greyhound buses also run to and from Morgantown and Pittsburgh; the station is just 2 blocks from campus. Rental cars are also available.

FIND YOUR WAY

From Pittsburgh, PA, take I-79 S. to Morgantown Exit 155/Star City-WVU; make a left at bottom of ramp and bear right at first stoplight. Cross a bridge and go to the second stoplight. Turn left onto Patteson Drive; the Visitors Center will be 150 yards on your right. **From Charleston, WV,** take I-79 N. to Morgantown exit 155 Star City-WVU; make a right at the bottom of the ramp and bear right at first stoplight. Cross a bridge and go to the second stoplight. Turn left onto Patteson Dr.; the Visitors Center will be 150 yards on your right. **From Wheeling, WV,** take I-70 E. to I-79 S., then follow directions from Pittsburgh. **From Washington, DC/Northern Virginia,** take the Capital Beltway to I-270 N.; then look for I-70 W. outside Frederick, MD; take I-70 W. until you see signs for I-68 W. outside of Hancock, MD; I-68 W. will end just outside Morgantown, where you pick up I-79 N. Stay on I-79 N. for about 7 miles and get off Exit 155/Star City-WVU; then follow directions listed above. **From New York City,** take the Lincoln Tunnel and pick up I-78 W.; follow I-78 W. to I-81 S. to I-70 W. in Hagerstown, MD; Follow I-70 to I-68 W. outside of Hancock, MD; I-68 W. will end just outside Morgantown, where you pick up I-79 N. Stay on I-79 N. for about 7 miles and get off Exit 155/Star City-WVU; then follow directions listed above.

STAY THE NIGHT

Nearby: One nearby option is the **Clarion Motel Morgan** (127 High St.; 304-292-8401), just blocks from the university. Another is the **Holiday Inn** (1400 Saratoga Ave.; 304-599-1680), half a mile from the university. Five minutes away is the **Comfort Inn** (U.S. Rte. 68 and U.S. Rte. 119; 304-296-9364), which sports an outdoor pool and an exercise room. In a renovated school just 5 minutes from the university is an offbeat bed-and-breakfast called the **Chestnut Ridge Commons** (1000 Stewartstown Rd.; 304-598-9594). Fifteen minutes away is the **Lakeview Scanticon Resort** (Rte. 6; 304-594-1111), which offers a fitness center, golf courses, tennis courts, an indoor and outdoor pool, and a lake.

A little farther: If you're willing to drive an hour, the **Century Inn** (724-945-6600) in Scenery Hill, PA, is a great choice. This antique-filled, 200-year-old inn serves great fare, and its moderately priced rooms are beautiful.

AT A GLANCE

Selectivity Rating	72
Range SAT I Math	460-560
Average SAT I Math	515
Range SAT I Verbal	460-560
Average SAT I Verbal	516
Average ACT Composite	22
Average GPA	3.2
Student to Faculty Ratio	19:1

CAMPUS TOURS

Appointment Req?	Yes
Dates	Year-round, except major holidays
Times	Mon-Fri 10:30AM and 2PM; Sat 10AM and 12:30PM
Avg. Length	2 hours

ON-CAMPUS INTERVIEWS

Admissions

Start Date–Juniors	N/A
Appointment Req?	N/A
Advance Notice	N/A
Avg. Length	N/A
Info Sessions	During academic year; limited during summer

Faculty and Coaches

Dates/Times	Year-round; subject to faculty/coach availability
Arrangements	Contact Visitors Center at 800-344-WVU1 2 weeks prior

CLASS VISITS

Dates	During academic year
Arrangements	By appointment; contact Visitors Center at 800-344-WVU1 (press 2)

OVERNIGHT DORM STAYS

Advance Notice	N/A
Arrangements	N/A
Limitations	N/A

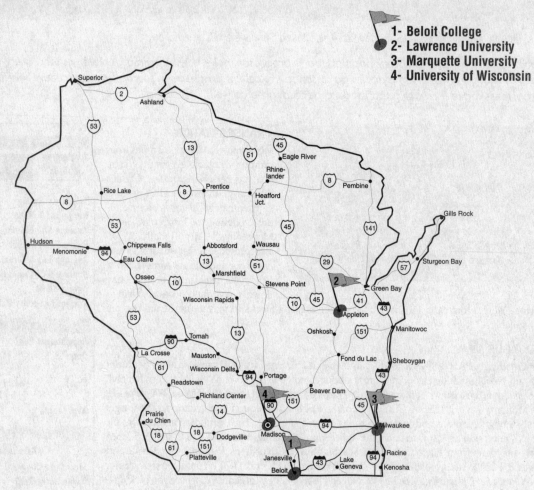

1- Beloit College
2- Lawrence University
3- Marquette University
4- University of Wisconsin

Wisconsin	Beloit Coll.	Lawrence Univ.	Marquette Univ.	U. Wisconsin-Mad.	Madison	Milwaukee
Beloit Coll.	—	148	76	56	55	70
Lawrence Univ.	148	—	102	103	103	102
Marquette Univ.	76	102	—	77	76	0
Univ. Wisconsin-Mad.	56	103	77	—	0	78
Madison	55	103	76	0	—	77
Milwaukee	70	102	0	78	77	—

BELOIT COLLEGE

Admissions Office, Beloit College, 700 College St., Beloit, WI 53511 (The office is in Middle College at the corner of College and Chapin Sts.) • Telephone: 800-356-0751 or 608-363-2500 (Fax: 608-363-2075) • Web: www.beloit.edu • Email: admiss@beloit.edu

Hours: Monday-Friday, 8AM-4:30PM; Saturday, 9AM-noon. Closed Sundays and holidays.

"Pink hair and pierced faces" are not uncommon at funky and free-thinking Beloit College, where the college motto is "Invent Yourself" and "jocks and freaks" more or less peacefully coexist in a "very demanding" and intimate academic atmosphere. Student Symposium occurs each sprin; for an entire day, students and faculty ditch classes to view student projects displayed all across campus.

HIGHLIGHTS

ON CAMPUS
- Logan Museum of Anthropology
- Wright Museum of Art
- The Poetry Garden
- Alfred S. Thompson Observatory
- Laura H. Idrich Neese Theatre Complex

OFF CAMPUS
- Angel Museum
- Wood Family Fishing Bridge
- Lincoln Center Museum
- Telfer Park and The Snappers (minor league baseball team)

TRANSPORTATION

O'Hare International Airport in Chicago is 75 miles from campus; the Van Galder Bus Company (608-752-5407 or www.vangalderbus.com/) runs hourly shuttles from the airport to Beloit.

FIND YOUR WAY

I-43, I-90, U.S. Rtes. 14 and 51, and Rtes. 2, 75, 81, and 251 lead to Beloit. Follow signs to the college.

STAY THE NIGHT

Nearby: The College has 3 guest apartments on campus in a lovely historic home that has been recently renovated. All the apartments have kitchens, though you can also use dining facilities on campus. The price is incredibly inexpensive. Call the Admissions Office at 800-356-0751 or 608-363-2500 to check on availability. Within walking distance of campus is a newly constructed boutique hotel, **The Beloit Inn** (500 Pleasant St.; 608-362-5500). Opened in November 2000, hotel services and amenities include continental breakfast and newspaper, executive fitness center, limo and airport pick-up service, business center, laundry/dry cleaning pick up and delivery, on-site wine storage, personal cigar humidor in the lounge, and meeting and catering services. Several other hotels are within 2 to 3 miles of campus. A full-service **Holiday Inn** (200 Dearborn St.; 815-389-3481) offers special rates to visitors of the College, and the **Holiday Inn Express** (2790 Milwaukee Rd.; 608-365-6000) boasts inexpensive rates, which include a full breakfast. For other lodging options, call the Admissions Office at 800-356-0751 or go to the Visit Beloit website at www.visitbeloit.com/.

A little farther: Lake Geneva is a year-round resort area about an hour's drive east of Beloit. Here you will find **The French Country Inn** (W. 41490 West End Rd., Lake Geneva, WI 53147; 262-245-5220), an unusual lakeside structure dating from the 1880s. Its wonderfully furnished guestrooms overlook the lake, and all have private bathrooms. The Inn has a lovely restaurant with creative menus—a real treat. Rates are in the moderate range during the week and expensive on the weekend. A 20-minute drive from Beloit will find you in Janesville, WI, if traveling north toward Madison, or in Rockford, IL, if traveling south toward Chicago. Both of these cities offer several accommodation options within an easy drive of Beloit.

AT A GLANCE

Selectivity Rating	79
Range SAT I Math	550-650
Average SAT I Math	600
Range SAT I Verbal	590-690
Average SAT I Verbal	640
Average ACT Composite	27
Average GPA	3.5
Student to Faculty Ratio	11:1

CAMPUS TOURS

Appointment Req?	Yes
Dates	Year-round
Times	Sept-April: Mon-Fri 11AM and 3PM; Sat 11AM. May-Aug: arranged on an individual basis.
Avg. Length	1 hour

ON-CAMPUS INTERVIEWS

Admissions

Start Date—Juniors	Fall
Appointment Req?	Yes
Advance Notice	7-10 days
Saturdays?	Yes
Avg. Length	45-60 min
Info Sessions	N/A

Faculty and Coaches

Dates/Times	Sept-April; subject to faculty/coach availability
Arrangements	Contact admissions off. 7-10 days prior

CLASS VISITS

Dates	Sept-April (Mon-Fri)
Arrangements	Contact admissions off.

OVERNIGHT DORM STAYS

Advance Notice	7-10 days
Arrangements	Contact admissions off.
Limitations	2-night maximum stay; available only Sun-Thurs

LAWRENCE UNIVERSITY

Admissions Office, Lawrence University, Appleton, WI 54912 (The office is at 706 East College Ave.) • Telephone 800-227-0982 or 920-832-6500 • Web: www.lawrence.edu • Email: excel@lawrence.edu

Hours: Monday-Friday, 8AM-5PM; Saturday, 9AM-noon (during the academic year only). Closed Sundays and holidays.

"Demanding" Lawrence University is a little liberal arts college with a slew of excellent music programs as well as a "strong" biology department and several other top-notch majors. Other characteristics include "small classes" and "dedicated" but "very tough" professors who are "always willing to help the students," and an "extremely diverse" student body given Lawrence's "small Midwestern town" location.

AT A GLANCE

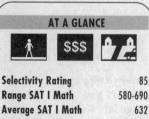

Selectivity Rating	85
Range SAT I Math	580-690
Average SAT I Math	632
Range SAT I Verbal	590-690
Average SAT I Verbal	633
Average ACT Composite	27
Average GPA	3.6
Student to Faculty Ratio	11:1

CAMPUS TOURS

Appointment Req?	Yes, contact visit coordinator at 800-448-3072
Dates	Year-round
Times	Oct-June: Mon-Fri 9AM-4PM; Sat 9AM-noon. July-Sept: Mon-Fri 9AM-4PM.
Avg. Length	75 min

ON-CAMPUS INTERVIEWS

Admissions

Start Date—Juniors	Any time
Appointment Req?	Yes
Advance Notice	3-4 days
Saturdays?	Yes, Oct-June
Avg. Length	1 hour
Info Sessions	N/A

Faculty and Coaches

Dates/Times	Year-round; subject to faculty/coach availability
Arrangements	Contact visit coordinator

CLASS VISITS

Dates	Oct-May (Mon-Fri)
Arrangements	Contact visit coordinator

OVERNIGHT DORM STAYS

Advance Notice	2 weeks
Arrangements	Contact visit coordinator
Limitations	2-night stay; Sun-Thurs nights

TRANSPORTATION

The Outagamie County Airport is approximately 5 miles from campus. Taxis are available at the airport for the ride to campus. Greyhound Bus Lines serves Appleton; the bus station is also 6 blocks from campus. Taxis are available if you don't want to walk.

FIND YOUR WAY

From U.S. Hwy. 41, exit on College Ave. Proceed east 4 miles to the admissions office (Wilson House), which is on the northeast corner of College Ave. and Lawe St. Visitor parking is located behind the office.

STAY THE NIGHT

The **Paper Valley Hotel and Conference Center** (333 W. College Ave.; 920-733-8000) is about 6 blocks away. You'll be able to keep busy without ever leaving the hotel. It has a 9-hole miniature golf course, ping-pong, shuffleboard, video games, an indoor swimming pool, a whirlpool, a sauna, a weight room, two restaurants, a shopping arcade, and entertainment. Rates are moderate. Another good bet is the **Best Western Midway Hotel** (3033 W. College Ave.; 920-731-4141), only 3 miles from the university. It has an indoor pool, a weight room, a sauna, a whirlpool, video games—all for a special moderate rate for college visitors. About 4 miles away, there's a **Holiday Inn** (150 Nicolet Rd.; 920-735-9955) with an indoor pool, exercise room, video games, tennis, and golf. Rates here are a bit higher than at the Best Western Midway during the week, but on the weekend they offer inexpensive rates. There are also 2 fine bed and breakfasts within 4 blocks off campus: **Queen Anne Bed and Breakfast** (920-831-9903) and **Franklin Street Inn** (920-993-1711), and **The Gathering Place** (920-731-4418). Other good options include **Comfort Suites** (920-730-3800), **Country Inn & Suites** (920-830-3240), **Fairfield Inn** (920-954-0202), **Hampton Inn** (920-954-9211), and **Wingate Inn** (920-933-1200).

HIGHLIGHTS

ON CAMPUS
- Wriston Art Gallery
- Music conservatory
- Main Hall
- New $18 million Science Building
- Buchanan Kiewit recreation center

OFF CAMPUS
- Numerous parks and museums
- Bjorklunden Retreat Center
- Door County, WI
- Barlow Planetarium
- Fox River Mall
- Green Bay Packers, Lambeau

MARQUETTE UNIVERSITY

Office of Undergraduate Admissions, Marquette Hall, 1217 W. Wisconsin Ave.,
Milwaukee, WI 53233 • Telephone: 800-222-6544 or 414-288-7302 •
Web: www.marquette.edu • Email: admissions@marquette.edu

Hours: Monday-Friday, 8:30AM-4:30PM; Saturday, 9AM-4:30PM. Closed Sundays and holidays.

The "Jesuit work ethic" is all the rage at Marquette University, where students say academic excellence is abundant. Distribution requirements are rigorous, including course work in mathematics, theology, science, and liberal arts. Milwaukee provides a hopping social scene.

HIGHLIGHTS

ON CAMPUS
- The Memorial and Science Library
- Law Library
- Gesu Church
- Haggerty Museum of Art
- Helfaer Theatre
- Helfaer Recreation Center

OFF CAMPUS
- Milwaukee Public Museum
- Miller Park
- The Riverwalk
- Milwaukee Art Museum
- Eisner Museum of Advertising and Design

TRANSPORTATION

General Mitchell International Airport is approximately 7 miles from campus. Taxis, limousines, rental cars, and buses run by the Milwaukee County Transit System are available for the ride from the airport to campus. Amtrak trains and Greyhound/Trailways buses serve Milwaukee. Public bus service is available from all parts of the metropolitan area.

FIND YOUR WAY

The I-94/I-43 interchange frames the south and east border of campus. Exit to W. Wisconsin Ave., which passes through the campus.

STAY THE NIGHT

Nearby: On campus **Mashuda Hall** (1926 Wisconsin Ave.; 414-288-7208) offers inexpensive rooms, though availability is limited. Breakfast is available in the cafeteria and there's access to the campus recreation center for a small fee. You can't beat this for convenience or price. The **Pfister Hotel** (424 E. Wisconsin Ave.; 414-273-8222), 1.5 miles away, is a fun off-campus choice. Known as the oldest hotel in Wisconsin, this gorgeous Victorian is modern inside, with an indoor pool, exercise equipment, and 3 restaurants. No surprises with the **Ramada Inn Downtown** (633 W. Michigan St.; 414-272-8410), 7 blocks away, or the **Holiday Inn** (611 W. Wisconsin Ave.; 414-273-2950), 6 blocks away. Both provide pleasant accommodations at extremely reasonable rates.

A little farther: If you're willing to drive 20 miles or so north to Cedarburg, you can stay in a historic mill town with many activities and attractions in the area—such as the Ozaukee Pioneer Village, the Cedar Creek Settlement, the Old Woolen Mill, and the Stone Mill Winery. The **Washington House Inn** (414-375-3550), a bed and breakfast built in 1886, is a fun place that conjures up the frontier past. Rates run the gamut.

AT A GLANCE

Selectivity Rating	77
Range SAT I Math	520-640
Average SAT I Math	580
Range SAT I Verbal	520-620
Average SAT I Verbal	571
Average ACT Composite	25
Student to Faculty Ratio	14:1

CAMPUS TOURS

Appointment Req?	No, but recommended
Dates	Year-round
Times	Mon-Sat 9AM-3PM hourly
Avg. Length	1 hour

ON-CAMPUS INTERVIEWS

Admissions

Start Date—Juniors	Any time
Appointment Req?	Yes
Advance Notice	Varies
Saturdays?	Yes
Avg. Length	1 hour
Info Sessions	Group sessions available only during open houses

Faculty and Coaches

Dates/Times	Year-round; subject to faculty/coach availability
Arrangements	Contact admissions off.

CLASS VISITS

Dates	Year-round (Mon-Fri); as part of Shadow Program
Arrangements	Contact admissions off. 3 weeks prior

OVERNIGHT DORM STAYS

Advance Notice	3 weeks
Arrangements	Contact admissions off. about the Shadow Program
Limitations	Seniors only; 2-night maximum stay

UNIVERSITY OF WISCONSIN—MADISON

Office of Admissions, University of Wisconsin–Madison, Armory and Gymnasium, 716 Langdon St., Madison, WI 53706-1400 • Telephone: 608-262-3961 (To arrange a campus visit, call the coordinator at 608-262-3318) • Web: www.wisc.edu • Email: on.wisconsin@mail.admin.wisc.edu

Hours: Monday-Friday, 8AM-4:25PM. Closed weekends and holidays.

The University of Wisconsin—Madison is a humongous institution with some of the finest academic and research facilities on the planet (including a library with a jaw-dropping 5 million bound volumes) and rock-bottom tuition rates. All undergraduate students must complete a broad and difficult assortment of distribution requirements throughout the liberal arts and sciences. Frank Lloyd Wright is an alum.

AT A GLANCE

Selectivity Rating	90
Range SAT I Math	550-670
Average SAT I Math	620
Range SAT I Verbal	520-650
Average SAT I Verbal	610
Average ACT Composite	26
Average GPA	3.7
Student to Faculty Ratio	13:1

CAMPUS TOURS

Appointment Req?	Yes, call 2 weeks prior; more if planning a visit on a day when high schools are closed
Dates	Academic year
Times	Mon-Fri, times vary
Avg. Length	2 hours

ON-CAMPUS INTERVIEWS

Admissions

Start Date—Juniors	N/A
Appointment Req?	N/A
Advance Notice	N/A
Avg. Length	N/A
Info Sessions	Available Mon-Fri as part of tour

Faculty and Coaches

Dates/Times	When school is in session; subject to faculty/coach availability
Arrangements	Contact admissions off. 2 weeks prior

CLASS VISITS

Dates	Academic year (Mon-Fri)
Arrangements	Contact tour coordinator

OVERNIGHT DORM STAYS

Arrangements	N/A
Limitations	Only commercial lodging on and near campus available

TRANSPORTATION

The Dane County Regional Airport is approximately 6 miles from campus. Taxis and limousines are available for the ride from airport to campus. Campus buses and the Madison Metro buses provide service throughout the campus and the city. The campus is also served by Greyhound, Van Galdor, and Badger bus lines.

HIGHLIGHTS

ON CAMPUS
- Allen Centennial Gardens
- Kohl Center
- Memorial Union Terrace
- Elvehjem Museum
- Badcock Hall Dairy Store

OFF CAMPUS
- State Capitol
- Monona Terrace
- Yilds Zoo
- State Street
- Arboretum

FIND YOUR WAY

From U.S. Rte. 51 and I-90, exit to U.S. Rte. 12/18 W. (Broadway). Take that to U.S. Rte. 151 N. (Park St.), which will take you to campus.

STAY THE NIGHT

The **Memorial Union** (800 Langdon St.; 608-262-1583) has double rooms at an inexpensive rate, as does **Union South** (227 N. Randall Ave.; 608-263-2600). Within walking distance is **Mansion Hill Inn** (424 N. Pinckney St.; 608-255-3999 or 800-798-9070), an 1858 Romanesque-revival mansion with an elegant, small-hotel atmosphere. Rates range from moderate to very expensive and include a continental breakfast and afternoon refreshments. Consider a prairie-style Victorian bed-and-breakfast. The **Collins House** (704 E. Gorham St.; 608-255-4230), about 1 mile from campus, is lovely. A full breakfast is included in the moderate rate. The fully equipped **Madison Concourse Hotel** (1 W. Dayton St.; 608-257-6000 or 800-356-8293, except Wisconsin) is 7 blocks from campus and has an indoor swimming pool. Rates are moderate. Another winner is also within walking distance: **Inn on the Park** (22 S. Carroll St.; 608-257-8811) with an indoor swimming pool and modest prices. On Lake Mendota, the **Edgewater Hotel** (666 Wisconsin Ave.; 608-256-9071 or 800-922-5512, outside Wisconsin) is within walking distance of the school. Rates are moderate to expensive. **Ivy Inn** (2355 University Ave.; 608-233-9717), the on-campus **Madison Inn** (601 Langdon St.; 608-257-4391), and on-campus **University Inn** (441 N. Francis St.; 608-257-4881 or 800-279-4881) are all good cheap choices. Drop a hin

APPENDIX ONE
Regional Mileage Matrices

New England

	Amherst	Bennington Coll.	Boston	Bowdoin Coll.	Colby Coll.	Dartmouth Coll.	Marlboro Coll.	Middlebury Coll.	Providence	Trinity Coll.	Univ. Maine-Orono	Univ. of New Hamp.	Univ. of Vermont	Wesleyan Univ.	Worcester	Yale Univ.
Amherst	—	70	103	215	265	102	46	166	91	47	320	141	178	63	47	85
Bennington Coll.	70	—	143	220	271	101	28	85	152	110	325	148	119	126	109	136
Boston	103	143	—	137	187	129	114	216	51	107	242	63	224	118	42	141
Bowdoin Coll.	215	220	137	—	56	177	191	267	182	229	110	94	232	244	167	267
Colby Coll.	265	271	189	56	—	144	241	285	232	280	66	144	250	294	218	317
Dartmouth Coll.	102	101	129	177	144	—	72	100	171	147	272	114	95	163	129	186
Marlboro Coll.	46	28	114	191	241	72	—	113	124	92	296	118	150	107	72	122
Middlebury Coll.	166	85	216	267	285	100	113	—	236	212	326	196	34	228	194	251
Providence	91	152	51	182	232	171	124	236	—	74	287	108	248	78	44	110
Trinity Coll.	47	110	1-7	229	280	147	92	212	74	—	334	155	224	17	66	41
Univ. Maine-Orono	320	325	242	110	66	272	296	326	287	334	—	199	291	349	272	371
Univ. of New Hamp.	141	148	63	94	144	114	118	196	108	155	199	—	199	170	93	192
Univ. of Vermont	178	119	224	232	250	95	150	34	248	224	291	199	—	240	205	263
Wesleyan Univ.	63	126	118	244	294	163	107	228	78	17	349	170	240	—	77	26
Worcester	47	109	42	167	218	129	72	194	44	66	272	93	205	77	—	100
Yale Univ.	85	136	141	267	317	186	122	251	110	41	371	192	263	26	100	—

Middle Atlantic

	Alfred Univ.	Allegheny Univ.	Bucknell Univ.	Colgate Univ.	Franklin & Marshall	Ithaca	Lehigh Univ.	New York City	Penn State Univ.	Philadelphia	Pittsburgh	Princeton Univ.	Rochester	Rutgers Univ.	St. Lawrence Univ.	Skidmore Coll.	SUNY Binghamton	SUNY Buffalo	Syracuse Univ.	Vassar Coll.
Alfred Univ.	—	198	157	187	249	99	238	311	188	292	244	285	80	287	260	299	127	109	133	277
Allegheny Univ.	198	—	212	327	325	258	345	372	166	346	88	367	205	364	401	433	292	135	284	394
Bucknell Univ.	157	212	—	201	104	143	126	178	71	165	253	169	197	171	330	282	135	236	199	201
Colgate Univ.	187	327	201	—	248	80	193	240	240	247	357	240	129	237	199	115	69	192	35	188
Franklin & Marshall	249	325	104	248	—	230	74	152	123	58	238	111	289	123	386	301	183	328	255	208
Ithaca	99	258	143	80	230	—	182	237	181	236	298	228	90	230	189	204	49	149	54	202
Lehigh Univ.	238	345	126	193	72	182	—	81	173	44	279	68	270	70	330	228	128	316	199	134
New York City	311	372	178	240	152	237	81	—	234	104	386	51	365	36	359	182	185	406	265	65
Penn State Univ.	188	166	71	240	123	181	173	234	—	192	133	225	229	226	368	337	191	208	238	257
Philadelphia	292	346	165	247	58	236	44	104	192	—	311	43	324	55	384	271	182	370	253	165
Pittsburgh	244	88	253	357	238	298	279	386	133	311	—	346	289	355	484	472	325	218	354	396
Princeton Univ.	285	367	169	240	111	228	68	51	225	43	346	—	317	18	377	239	174	363	246	123
Rochester	80	205	197	129	289	90	270	365	229	324	289	317	—	318	215	232	175	65	83	302
Rutgers Univ.	287	364	171	237	123	230	70	36	226	55	355	18	318	—	379	217	176	364	248	111
St. Lawrence Univ.	260	401	330	199	386	189	330	359	368	384	484	377	215	379	—	175	213	272	130	289
Skidmore Coll.	299	433	282	115	301	204	228	182	337	271	472	239	232	217	175	—	158	289	146	11
SUNY Binghamton	127	292	135	69	183	49	128	185	191	182	325	174	175	176	213	158	—	226	79	146
SUNY Buffalo	109	135	236	192	328	149	316	406	208	370	218	363	65	364	272	289	226	—	142	361
Syracuse Univ.	133	284	199	35	255	54	199	265	238	253	354	246	83	248	130	146	79	142	—	224
Vassar Coll.	277	394	201	188	208	202	134	75	257	165	396	123	302	111	289	115	146	361	224	—

North Middle West

	Chicago	Cincinnati	Grand Rapids	Kalamazoo Coll.	Kenyon Coll.	Indiana Univ.	Lawrence Univ.	Marquette Univ.	Oberlin Univ.	Ohio State Univ.	Ohio Univ.	Purdue Univ.	Springfield, IL	Univ. of Illinois	Univ. of Michigan	Univ. of Notre Dame	Univ. of Wisconsin
Chicago	—	290	170	134	362	229	189	90	324	358	432	121	202	135	230	89	144
Cincinnati	290	—	386	352	163	138	476	380	225	111	160	178	324	237	255	236	431
Grand Rapids	170	386	—	52	303	324	359	260	265	320	394	236	336	279	55	126	314
Kalamazoo Coll.	134	352	52	—	269	272	323	224	231	286	360	184	289	232	97	71	278
Kenyon Coll.	362	163	303	269	—	275	558	459	85	52	110	292	412	351	172	280	536
Indiana Univ.	229	138	324	272	275	—	418	319	335	230	304	105	203	151	330	198	373
Lawrence Univ.	189	476	359	323	558	418	—	102	513	547	621	310	360	324	419	278	103
Marquette Univ.	90	380	260	224	549	319	102	—	414	466	522	211	286	225	320	179	77
Oberlin Coll.	324	225	265	321	85	335	513	414	—	114	216	276	457	371	134	242	468
Ohio State Univ.	358	111	320	286	52	230	547	466	114	—	75	248	392	306	189	231	502
Ohio Univ.	432	160	394	360	110	304	621	522	216	75	—	323	467	381	264	306	577
Purdue Univ.	300	178	236	184	292	105	310	211	276	248	323	—	186	100	258	110	261
Springfield, IL	202	324	336	289	412	203	360	286	457	392	467	186	—	198	454	286	257
Univ. of Illinois	135	237	279	232	351	151	324	225	371	306	381	100	198	—	365	197	245
Univ. of Michigan	230	255	55	97	172	330	419	320	134	189	264	258	454	365	—	168	374
Univ. of Notre Dame	89	236	126	71	280	198	278	179	242	231	306	110	286	197	168	—	233
Univ. of Wisconsin	144	431	314	278	536	373	103	77	468	502	577	261	257	245	374	233	—

Middle West

	Bismark	Des Moines	Iowa State Univ.	Macalester Coll.	Northfield	Pierre	St. Louis	Univ. of Iowa	Univ. of Kansas	Univ. of Missouri	U. Nebraska-Lincoln	U. Nebraska-Omaha	Wichita
Bismark	—	689	661	438	479	209	1034	751	811	913	675	617	839
Des Moines	689	—	28	245	204	514	370	112	234	234	193	135	388
Iowa State Univ.	661	28	—	217	176	486	398	137	262	262	221	163	416
Macalester Coll.	438	245	217	—	41	424	630	291	488	484	438	380	633
Northfield	479	204	176	41	—	392	589	250	447	443	397	339	592
Pierre	209	514	486	424	392	—	808	626	595	681	441	383	630
St. Louis	1034	370	398	630	589	808	—	283	294	132	502	444	462
Univ. of Iowa	751	112	137	291	250	626	283	—	343	231	305	247	496
Univ. of Kansas	811	234	262	488	447	595	294	343	—	167	215	198	162
Univ. of Missouri	913	234	262	484	443	681	132	231	167	—	316	312	320
U. Nebraska-Lincoln	675	193	221	438	397	441	502	305	215	316	—	58	243
U. Nebraska-Omaha	617	135	163	380	339	383	444	247	198	312	58	—	301
Wichita	839	388	416	633	592	630	462	496	162	320	243	301	—

South Atlantic

	Atlanta	Baltimore	Charleston, SC	Clemson Univ.	Coll. William & Mary	Duke Univ.	Eckerd Coll.	Florida State Univ.	Orlando	Univ. of Delaware	Univ. of Florida	Univ. of Georgia	Univ. of Miami	Univ. S. Carolina	Univ. of Virginia	Wake Forest Univ.	West Virginia Univ.
Atlanta	—	654	291	117	591	374	484	267	426	796	333	66	668	215	575	350	654
Baltimore	654	—	568	609	195	296	968	895	892	58	824	615	1099	517	160	375	204
Charleston, SC	291	568	—	240	480	285	461	344	384	626	317	275	595	114	499	264	620
Clemson Univ.	117	609	240	—	478	261	561	364	517	667	418	85	747	118	395	207	566
Coll. William & Mary	591	195	480	478	—	204	899	781	822	253	755	548	1035	448	131	257	321
Duke Univ.	374	296	285	261	204	—	726	608	649	351	582	375	862	275	173	84	391
Eckerd Coll.	484	968	461	561	899	726	—	260	104	1026	166	580	278	513	899	693	1117
Florida State Univ.	267	895	344	364	781	608	260	—	254	953	158	279	494	358	728	538	936
Orlando	426	892	384	517	822	649	104	254	—	950	114	504	242	437	822	616	1040
Univ. of Delaware	796	58	626	667	253	351	1026	953	950	—	882	673	1157	575	218	433	262
Univ. of Florida	333	824	317	418	755	582	166	158	114	882	—	345	363	444	755	549	973
Univ. of Georgia	66	615	275	85	548	375	580	279	504	673	345	—	717	153	548	277	639
Univ. of Miami	688	1099	595	747	1035	862	278	494	242	1157	363	717	—	648	1035	829	1253
Univ. South Carolina	215	517	114	118	448	275	513	358	437	575	444	153	648	—	367	180	559
Univ. of Virginia	575	160	499	395	131	173	899	728	822	218	755	548	1035	367	—	190	190
Wake Forest Univ.	350	375	264	207	257	84	693	538	616	433	549	277	829	180	190	—	355
West Virginia Univ.	654	204	620	566	321	391	1117	936	1040	262	973	639	1253	559	190	355	—

Southeast

	Birmingham	Centre Coll.	Jackson, MS	Louisville	Rhodes Coll.	Tuskegee Univ.	Univ. of Alabama	Univ. of Kentucky	Univ. of Mississippi	Univ. of the South	Vanderbilt Univ.
Birmingham	—	377	245	360	249	136	49	402	175	162	188
Centre Coll.	377	—	603	92	399	514	435	36	424	241	189
Jackson, MS	245	603	—	586	213	287	187	660	157	407	414
Louisville	360	92	586	—	378	492	418	74	399	264	175
Rhodes Coll.	249	399	213	378	—	386	238	424	65	260	210
Tuskegee Univ.	136	514	287	492	386	—	149	530	312	270	325
Univ. of Alabama	49	435	187	418	238	149	—	462	163	220	246
Univ. of Kentucky	402	36	660	74	424	530	462	—	465	277	214
Univ. of Mississippi	175	424	157	399	65	312	163	465	—	274	249
Univ. of the South	162	241	407	264	260	270	220	277	274	—	96
Vanderbilt Univ.	188	189	414	175	210	325	246	214	249	96	—

South and Southwest

	Baylor Univ.	El Paso	Little Rock	LSU	New Orleans	Oklahoma City	Rice Univ.	SMU	TCU	Trinity Univ.	U. of Texas-Austin
Baylor Univ.	—	679	409	460	540	274	245	102	91	186	100
El Paso	679	—	935	1014	1095	676	742	617	595	564	575
Little Rock	409	935	—	337	417	344	434	316	344	583	520
LSU	460	1014	337	—	80	614	272	437	465	471	458
New Orleans	540	1095	417	80	—	694	352	517	545	547	538
Oklahoma City	274	676	344	614	694	—	461	209	190	477	382
Rice Univ.	245	742	434	272	352	461	—	253	282	196	186
SMU	102	617	316	437	517	209	253	—	35	282	195
TCU	91	595	344	465	545	190	282	35	—	273	192
Trinity Univ.	186	564	583	471	547	477	196	282	273	—	79
U. of Texas-Austin	100	575	520	458	538	382	186	195	192	79	—

Mountain

	Albuquerque	Arizona State Univ.	BYU	Casper	Colorado Coll.	Helena	Las Vegas	Pocatello	U. Ariz.-Tuscon	U. of Colo.-Boulder	U. of Colo.-Denver
Albuquerque	—	462	559	719	367	1213	586	706	473	463	437
Arizona State Univ.	462	—	604	1017	747	1127	291	808	103	843	817
BYU	559	604	—	447	563	523	374	204	717	524	534
Casper	719	1017	447	—	351	503	821	424	1070	280	281
Colorado Coll.	367	747	563	351	—	854	809	634	819	96	70
Helena	1213	1127	523	503	854	—	895	319	1240	779	780
Las Vegas	586	291	374	821	809	895	—	578	404	784	758
Pocatello	706	808	204	424	634	319	578	—	921	563	564
U. of Ariz.-Tucson	473	103	717	1070	819	1240	404	921	—	873	847
U. of Colo.-Boulder	463	843	524	280	96	779	784	563	873	—	26
U. of Colo.-Denver	437	817	534	281	70	780	758	564	847	26	—

Pacific and Northwest	Evergreen State U.	Los Angeles	Portland	San Diego	San Francisco	Spokane	U. Cal–Davis	U. Cal–Santa Cruz	Univ. of Redlands	Univ. of Washington	Willamette Univ.
Evergreen State U.	—	1094	124	1218	763	320	711	838	1164	59	171
Los Angeles	1094	—	968	124	387	1205	365	356	69	1134	921
Portland	124	968	—	1086	637	351	584	712	1038	174	45
San Diego	1218	124	1086	—	514	1297	611	484	117	1258	1039
San Francisco	763	387	637	514	—	879	67	75	466	810	590
Spokane	320	1205	351	1297	879	—	827	986	1274	280	396
U. Cal–Davis	711	365	584	611	67	827	—	135	470	780	539
U. Cal–Santa Cruz	838	356	712	484	75	986	135	—	425	920	699
Univ. of Redlands	1164	69	1038	117	466	1274	470	425	—	1203	993
Univ. of Washington	59	1134	174	1258	810	280	780	920	1203	—	219
Willamette Univ.	171	921	45	1039	590	396	539	699	993	219	—

APPENDIX TWO

College Calendars

School	January	February	March	April	May	June
Alabama						
AUBURN UNIVERSITY	Winter session begins 2nd week. No classes MLK Day.	Classes continue.	Exams 2nd-3rd weeks.	Spring break 1st week.	Exams 2nd week. Summer session begins 3rd week.	Classes continue.
TUSKEGEE UNIVERSITY	Spring session begins 3rd week.	Classes continue.	Spring break 2nd week. Classes resume 3rd week.	No classes Good Fri. through Easter Mon.	Exams 2nd week.	Summer session begins 2nd week.
UNIVERSITY OF ALABAMA	Spring session begins 1st week.	Classes continue.	Spring break 4th week. Exams 3rd week.	Classes resume 1st week.	Exams 1st week. Interim session begins 3rd week.	Interim session ends 1st week. Summer session begins 2nd week.
Arizona						
ARIZONA STATE UNIVERSITY	Spring session begins 3rd week. No classes MLK Day.	Classes continue.	Spring break 3rd week. Classes resume 4th week.	Classes continue.	Exams 1st-2nd weeks.	Summer session begins 1st week.
UNIVERSITY OF ARIZONA	Spring session begins 2nd week. No classes MLK Day.	Classes continue.	Spring break 2nd week. Classes resume 3rd week.	Classes continue.	Exams 1st-2nd weeks.	Summer session begins 1st week.
California						
CALIF. INST OF TECHNOLOGY	Winter session begins 2nd week.	No classes President's Day.	Exams 3rd week. Spring break 4th week.	Spring session begins 1st week.	Classes continue.	Exams 2nd week.
CLAREMONT McKENNA COLLEGE	Spring session begins 3rd or 4th week.	Classes continue.	Spring break 3rd week.	Classes continue.	Final Exams 2nd week.	No classes.
HARVEY MUDD COLLEGE	Spring session begins 3rd week.	Classes continue.	Spring break 3rd week.	Classes resume 1st week.	Exams 2nd or 3rd week.	No classes.
MILLS COLLEGE	Spring session begins 3rd week.	No classes Presidents' Day.	Spring break 4th week.	Classes resume 1st week.	Exams 2nd-3rd weeks.	No classes.
OCCIDENTAL COLLEGE	First day of classes 4th week.	Presidents' Day holiday.	Exams 2nd week. Spring break 3rd week. Spring session begins 4th week.	Classes continue.	Exams 2nd week.	Exams 1st week. Summer session begins 3rd week.
PEPPERDINE UNIVERSITY	Winter session begins 2nd week.	Classes continue.	No classes 2nd Fri.	Exams 2nd-3rd weeks. Spring break 4th week. Summer session starts 4th week or 1st week in May.	Summer session begins 1st week. No classes Memorial Day.	Classes continue.

July	August	September	October	November	December	Additional Info
No classes July 4.	Summer session ends first week. Fall session begins 3rd week.	Labor Day holiday.	Classes continue.	Break from Wed. before Thanksgiving through following Sun.	Exams 2nd week.	Campus visits are not discouraged during exam periods, but visiting on a normal class day is recommended.
No classes July 4. Summer session ends last week.	No classes.	No classes Labor Day. Classes begin 2nd week.	Classes continue.	Break from Wed. before Thanksgiving Day through the following Sun.	Exams 1st-2nd weeks.	Campus visits are not discouraged during exam periods.
No classes July 4.	Summer session ends 2nd week.	Fall session begins 2nd week.	Classes continue.	Break begins Wed. before Thanksgiving Day.		Campus visits are not discouraged during exam periods.
No classes July 4.	Summer session ends 1st week. Fall session begins 3rd or 4th week.	No classes Labor Day.	Classes continue.	Break from Thanksgiving Day through following Sun. Veterans' Day observed.	Exams 2nd-3rd weeks.	
No classes July 4.	Summer session ends 1st week. Fall session begins 3rd week.	No classes Labor Day.	Classes continue.	Break from Thanksgiving Day through the following Sun.	Exams 2nd-3rd weeks.	Residence halls unavailable during exam periods
No classes.	No classes.	Fall session begins 4th week.	Classes continue.	Break from Thanksgiving Day through following Sun.	Exams 2nd week.	Approximately 200 students are on campus conducting research during the summer.
No classes.	No classes.	Fall session begins 1st week.	Fall break 3rd week.	Break from Thanksgiving Day through following Sun.	Exams 3rd week.	Some students are on campus during the summer.
No classes.	Fall session begins 4th week.	Labor Day holiday.	No classes the 3rd Mon. and Tue.	Break from Thanksgiving Day through following Sun.	Exams 3rd week.	Approximately 80 students are on campus during the summer.
No classes.	Fall session begins last week.	Labor Day holiday.	Break mid-month.	Break from Fri. before Thanksgiving Day through Sun. following Thanksgiving.	Exams 2nd week.	
No classes July 4.	Fall session starts 3rd week.	Labor Day holiday.	Classes continue.	Break from Wed. before Thanksgiving Day through the following Sun.	Exams 2nd week.	About 100 students are on campus in the summer. Visits are not discouraged during exams, but tour/class visits are unavailable.
No classes July 4. Summer session ends last week or 1st week in August.	Summer session ends 1st week. Fall session begins last week.	Classes continue.	Classes continue.	Break from Thanksgiving Day through the following Sun.	Exams 1st-2nd weeks.	Campus visits during exam periods are not discouraged.

School	January	February	March	April	May	June
PITZER COLLEGE	Spring session begins 3rd week.	Classes continue.	Spring break 2nd week.	Classes resume 1st week.	Exams 3rd week.	No classes.
POMONA COLLEGE	Spring session begins 3rd or 4th week.	Classes continue.	Spring break 3rd or 4th week.	Classes continue.	Exams 2nd-3rd weeks.	No classes.
SANTA CLARA UNIVERSITY	Winter session begins 1st week. No classes MLK Day.	No classes Presidents' Day.	Exams 3rd week.	Spring session begins 1st week.	Classes continue.	Exams 2nd week. Summer session begins 4th week.
SCRIPPS COLLEGE	Spring session begins 4th week.	Classes continue.	Spring break 4th week.	Classes resume 1st week.	Exams 2nd-3rd weeks.	Science course offerings.
STANFORD UNIVERSITY	Winter session begins 2nd week No classes MLK Day.	No classes Presidents' Day.	Exams 3rd week. Spring session begins last week.	Classes continue.	Classes continue.	Exams 1st-2nd weeks. Summer session begins 4th week.
UNIVERSITY OF CALIFORNIA — BERKELEY	Spring session begins 3rd or 4th week. No classes MLK Day.	No classes Presidents' Day.	Spring break near end of month. Classes resume after 1 week break.	Classes continue.	Exams 2nd-3rd weeks.	Summer session begins 3rd or 4th week.
UNIVERSITY OF CALIFORNIA — DAVIS	Winter session begins 1st week. No classes MLK Day.	No classes Presidents' Day.	Exams 3rd week. Spring break 4th week. Spring session begins at end of 4th week.	Classes continue.	Classes continue.	Exams 2nd week. Summer session begins 3rd week.
UNIVERSITY OF CALIFORNIA — IRVINE	Winter session begins 1st week. No classes MLK Day.	No classes Presidents' Day.	Exams mid-month.	Spring session begins 1st week.	Classes continue.	Exams 2nd week. First summer session begins 4th week.
UNIVERSITY OF CALIFORNIA — LOS ANGELES	Winter session begins 2nd week. No classes MLK Day.	No classes Presidents' Day.	Exams 3rd week. Spring break 4th week.	Spring session begins 1st week.	Classes continue.	Exams 2nd week. Summer session begins 4th week.
UNIVERSITY OF CALIFORNIA — RIVERSIDE	Winter session begins 1st week. No classes MLK Day.	No classes Presidents' Day.	Exams 3rd week. Spring break 4th week. Spring session begins at end of 4th week.	Classes continue.	Classes continue.	Exams 2nd week. Summer session begins 4th week.
UNIVERSITY OF CALIFORNIA — SAN DIEGO	Winter session begins 1st week. No classes MLK Day.	No classes Presidents' Day.	Exams 3rd week. Spring session begins last week.	Classes continue.	No classes Memorial Day	Exams 2nd week. Summer session begins last week.

July	August	September	October	November	December	Additional Info
No classes	No classes.	Fall session begins 1st week.	Fall break from 3rd Sat. through the following Tue.	Break from Thanksgiving Day through the following Sun.	Exams 2nd week.	*Approximately 25 students are on campus during the summer.*
No classes.	No classes.	Fall session begins 1st week.	Fall break from 3rd Fri. through the following Tue.	Break from Wed. before Thanksgiving Day through the following Sun.	Exams 3rd week.	*Very few students are on campus during the summer.*
No classes July 4.	Summer session ends 1st week.	Fall session begins 4th week.	Classes continue.	Break from Wed. before Thanksgiving Day through the following Sun.	Exams 2nd week.	
Science course offerings.	No classes.	Fall session begins 1st week.	Fall break from the 3rd Fri. through the following Tue.	Break from Wed. before Thanksgiving Day through the following Sun.	Exams 3rd week.	*A very small number of students are on campus from June 1-August 20.*
Classes continue.	Summer session ends 2nd week.	Fall session begins 4th week.	Classes continue.	Break from Thanksgiving Day through the following Sun.	Exams 2nd week.	
No classes July 4.	Summer session ends 3rd week. Fall session begins last week.	No classes Labor Day.	Classes continue.	Break from Thanksgiving Day through the following Sun. Veterans' Day holiday.	Exams 2nd-3rd weeks.	*Campus visits are not discouraged during exam periods.*
No classes 4th week.	Classes continue.	Summer session ends 2nd week. Fall session begins 4th week.	Classes continue.	Break from Thanksgiving Day through the following Sun.	Exams 2nd week.	*Campus visits are not discouraged during exam periods.*
No classes July 4. First summer session ends at end of month.	Second summer session begins 1st full week.	No classes Labor Day. Second summer session ends 3rd week.	Classes continue.	Break from Thanksgiving Day through the following Sun.	Exams 2nd week.	*During the summer, fewer students are on campus, and most of them are students from other universities.*
No classes July 4.	Classes continue.	Summer session ends 2nd week. Fall session begins last week.	Classes continue.	Break from Thanksgiving Day through the following Sun.	Exams 2nd week.	*Campus visits are not discouraged during exam periods, but tours are limited at that time.*
No classes July 4.	Summer session ends 1st week.	Fall session begins 4th week.	Classes continue.	Break from Thanksgiving Day through the following Sun.	Exams 1st or 2nd week.	*Campus visits are not disacouraged during exam periods, but tours are limited during that time.*
No classes July 4.	Classes continue.	Summer session ends 2nd week. Fall session begins 3rd week.	Classes continue.	Break from Thanksgiving Day through the following Sun.	Exams 2nd week.	*Approximately 600 students are on campus during the summer.*

School	January	February	March	April	May	June
UNIVERSITY OF CALIFORNIA— SANTA BARBARA	Winter session begins 2nd week. No classes MLK Day.	No classes Presidents' Day.	Exams 2nd-3rd weeks.	Spring session begins 1st week.	No classes Memorial Day.	Exams 1st-2nd weeks. Summer session begins 4th week.
UNIVERSITY OF CALIFORNIA— SANTA CRUZ	Winter session begins 1st week. No classes MLK Day.	No classes Presidents' Day.	Exams 3rd week.	Spring session begins 1st week.	No classes Memorial Day.	Exams 2nd or 3rd week. Summer session begins 4th week.
UNIVERSITY OF REDLANDS	Winter session begins 2nd week and ends last week.	Spring session begins 2nd week.	Classes continue.	Spring break 1st week. Classes resume 2nd week.	Exams 3rd week.	No classes.
UNIVERSITY OF SAN DIEGO	Winter session: 2nd week-4th week. Spring session begins at end of month.	Classes continue.	Spring break sometime this month.	Classes continue.	Exams 3rd week.	Summer session begins 1st week.
UNIVERSITY OF SAN FRANCISCO	Winter session begins 1st week and ends 3rd week. Spring session begins last week.	No classes Presidents' Day.	Spring break last week.	Classes resume 1st week.	Exams 3rd-4th weeks. Summer session begins last week. No classes Memorial Day.	Classes continue.
UNIVERSITY OF SOUTHERN CALIFORNIA	Spring session begins 2nd week. No classes MLK Day.	No classes Presidents' Day.	Spring break 3rd week.	Classes resume 2nd week. Exams last week- 1st week in May.	Exams 1st week. Summer session begins 2nd week. No classes Memorial Day.	Classes continue.
UNIVERSITY OF THE PACIFIC	Spring session begins 3rd week.	Call regarding Presidents' Day.	Spring break mid-month.	No classes day after Easter.	Exams 2nd week. Summer session begins 3rd week. No classes Memorial Day.	Classes continue.
WHITTIER COLLEGE	Winter session begins 2nd week and ends at end of 4th week.	Spring session begins 1st week.	Spring break last week.	Classes resume 1st week.	Exams mid-month.	Limited summer term begins.
Colorado **COLORADO COLLEGE**	Spring session (5th block of academic year) begins mid-month).	Block ends 1st week. Sixth block begins 2nd week.	Spring break 1st week. Seventh block begins 3rd week.	Block ends 2nd week. Eighth block begins 3rd week.	Block ends 2nd week.	Block A begins 2nd week.
COLORADO SCHOOL OF MINES	Spring session begins 1st week.	Classes continue.	Spring break 2nd week. Classes resume 3rd week.	Classes continue.	Exams 1st week.	Summer session begins last week.
UNIVERSITY OF COLORADO— BOULDER	Spring session begins 2nd week. No classes MLK Day.	Classes continue.	Spring break last week.	Classes resume 1st week.	Exams 2nd week. Summer session begins last week.	Classes continue.

July	August	September	October	November	December	Additional Info
No classes July 4.	Summer session ends 1st week.	Fall session begins 3rd week.	Classes continue.	Break from Thanksgiving Day through the following Sun.	Exams 1st week.	
No classes July 4.	Summer session ends 4th week.	Fall session begins last week.	Classes continue.	Break from Thanksgiving Day through the following Sun.	Exams 2nd week.	*Few students are on campus during the summer.*
No classes.	No classes.	Fall session begins 2nd week.	Fall break 2nd week.	Break from Wed. before Thanksgiving Day through the following Sun.	Exams 3rd week.	*During exam periods, interviews are available, but campus tours are not.*
No classes July 4.	Summer session ends 3rd week.	Fall session begins 2nd week.	No classes 4th Fri.	Break from Thanksgiving Day through the following Sun.	Exams 3rd week.	*Campus visits are not discouraged during exams. Spring break varies from year to year.*
No classes July 4.	Summer session ends 1st week.	Fall session begins 1st week.	Classes continue.	Break from Thanksgiving Day through the following Sun.	Exams 3rd week.	
No classes July 4.	Summer session ends 2nd week. Fall session begins last week.	No classes Labor Day.	Classes continue.	Break from Thanksgiving Day through the following Sun.	Exams 2nd-3rd weeks.	*The summer population includes more international students and conference attenders than the regular student population.*
No classes July 4.	Fall semester begins last week.	No classes Labor Day.	Classes continue.	Break from Thanksgiving Day through the following Sun.	Exams 2nd week.	*Individual visits available throughout year, call for appointment*
Limited summer term.	Limited summer through August.	Classes begin 1st week.	Break from 3rd Fri. through the following Sun.	Break from Thanksgiving Day through the following Sun.	Exams 2nd week.	*Fewer than 50 students are on campus during the summer.*
Block B begins 1st week. Block C begins 3rd week.	Block C ends 3rd week.	Fall session (1st block of academic year) begins 1st week and ends last week.	Second block begins 1st week and ends 4th week.	Third block begins 1st week and ends by Thanksgiving Day, then off until Sun.	Fourth block begins 1st week and ends 4th week (before Christmas).	*The school year is divided into eight 3½-week blocks with 4½-day breaks in between. Exams are held the last 3 days of each block.*
No classes July 4.	Summer session ends 1st week. Fall session begins 3rd week.	Classes continue.	Classes continue.	Break from Thanksgiving Day through following Sun.	Exams 3rd week.	
No classes July 4.	Summer session ends 1st week. Fall session begins 3rd week.	Classes continue.	Classes continue.	Break from Thanksgiving Day through the following Sun.	Exams 2nd-3rd weeks.	*Campus visits are not discouraged during exams, but tour guides may be hard to find at these times.*

School	January	February	March	April	May	June
UNIVERSITY OF COLORADO— DENVER	Spring session begins 2nd week. No classes MLK Day.	Classes continue.	Spring break 3rd week. Classes resume 4th week.	Classes continue.	Exams 2nd week. Summer session begins last week.	Classes continue.
Connecticut						
CONNECTICUT COLLEGE	Spring session begins 3rd or 4th week.	Classes continue.	Spring break 3rd & 4th weeks.	Classes resume 1st week.	Exams 2nd-3rd weeks.	No classes.
FAIRFIELD UNIVERSITY	Spring session begins 3rd week. No classes MLK Day.	No classes Presidents' Day.	Spring break 2nd week. Break from Thu. before Easter through Easter Mon.	Break from Thu. before Easter through Easter Mon.	Exams 1st-2nd weeks. Summer session begins last week.	Summer session continues.
TRINITY COLLEGE	Spring session begins 3rd week.	Break from Sat. before Presidents' Day through Sun. after Presidents' Day.	Spring break 3rd week.	Classes continue.	Exams 1st-2nd weeks.	No classes.
UNIVERSITY OF BRIDGEPORT	Spring session begins 4th week.	Classes continue.	Spring break 2nd week. Classes resume 3rd week.	Exams last week-2nd week in May.	Exams 2nd week. First summer session begins 4th week. No classes Memorial Day.	First summer session ends last week.
UNIVERSITY OF CONNECTICUT	Spring session begins 4th week.	Classes continue.	Spring break 3rd week. Classes resume 4th week.	Classes continue.	Exams 1st-2nd weeks. First summer session begins 3rd week. No classes Memorial Day.	First summer session ends last week.
UNIVERSITY OF HARTFORD	Spring session begins 4th week.	Classes continue.	Spring break 4th week.	Classes resume 1st week.	Exams 2nd week. Summer session begins 3rd week.	Classes continue.
WESLEYAN UNIVERSITY	Spring session begins 3rd week.	Classes continue.	Spring break 2nd and 3rd weeks. Classes resume 4th week.	Classes continue.	Exams 3rd week.	No classes.
YALE UNIVERSITY	Spring session begins 2nd or 3rd week.	Classes continue.	Spring break from end of 1st week to beginning of 3rd week.	Classes continue.	Reading period and exams 1st-2nd weeks.	No classes.
Delaware						
UNIVERSITY OF DELAWARE	Winter session begins 1st week. No classes MLK Day.	Winter session ends 1st week. Spring session begins 2nd week.	Spring break last week.	Classes resume 1st week.	No classes Memorial Day. Exams last week.	Summer session begins 2nd week.
Dist. of Columbia						
AMERICAN UNIVERSITY	Spring session begins 3rd week. No classes MLK Day.	Classes continue.	Spring break 2nd week. Classes resume 3rd week.	Exams from end of month-1st week of May.	Exams continue 1st week. Summer sessions begin 3rd week. No classes Memorial Day.	Classes continue.

July	August	September	October	November	December	Additional Info
No classes July 4.	Summer session ends 1st week. Fall session begins 3rd week.	No classes Labor Day	Classes continue.	Break from Thanksgiving Day through the following Sun.	Exams 2nd week.	*Approximately 15,000 students are on campus during the summer.*
No classes.	Fall session begins last week.	Classes continue.	Fall break from 1st Thurs. through following Tues.	Break from Tues. before Thanksgiving Day through the following Sun.	Exams 3rd week.	
No classes July 4.	Summer session ends mid-month.	Fall session begins 1st week. No classes Labor Day.	Four-day Fall Break.	Break from Wed. before Thanksgiving Day through the following Sun.	Exams 2nd-3rd weeks.	*Campus visits are discouraged during exams.*
No classes.	Fall session begins last week.	Classes continue.	Fall break from Sat. before Columbus Day through Sun. after Columbus Day.	Break from Thanksgiving Day through the following Sun.	Exams 2nd-3rd weeks.	*Few students are on campus during the summer. Campus visits are discouraged during exam periods unless there is no alternative time.*
Second summer session begins 1st week. No classes July 4.	Second summer session ends 1st week.	Fall session begins 1st week.	Fall Break Sat before Columbus Day through Tue. after.	Break from Thanksgiving Day through the following Sun.	Exams 3rd week.	*During exam periods, no campus tours are offered, but interviews are available.*
Second summer session begins 1st week. No classes July 4.	Second summer session ends 1st week.	Fall session begins 1st week.	Classes continue.	Break from Wed. before Thanksgiving Day through the following Sun.	Exams 2nd-3rd weeks.	
Classes continue.	Summer session ends 2nd week.	Fall session begins 1st week.	Classes continue.	Break from Tues. before Thanksgiving Day through the following Sun.	Exams 2nd-3rd weeks.	*Summer enrollment is much smaller than winter enrollment. Campus visits are not discouraged during exams, but tours are limited.*
No classes.	No classes.	Fall session begins 1st week.	Fall break 2nd Wed. to following Mon.	Break from Wed. before Thanksgiving Day through Sun.	Exams 3rd week.	*About 200 people are on campus during the summer; they are involved in a variety of on-campus programs.*
No classes.	No classes.	Fall session begins 1st week.	Classes continue.	Break from Sat. before Thanksgiving Day through the following Sun.	Reading period and exams 2nd-3rd weeks.	
No classes July 4.	Summer session ends 2nd week.	Fall session begins 1st week. No classes Labor Day.	Classes continue.	No classes Election Day. Break from Wednesday before Thanksgiving through the following Sun.	Exams 2nd week.	
No classes July 4.	Summer sessions end 2nd week.	Fall sessions begin 1st week.	Fall break 2nd Mon. and Tues.	Break from Wed. before Thanksgiving Day through following Sun.	Exams 2nd-3rd weeks.	*About 700 students are on campus during the summer, but many are not American University students.*

School	January	February	March	April	May	June
CATHOLIC UNIVERSITY OF AMERICA	Spring session begins 2nd week. No classes MLK Day.	Classes continue.	Spring break 1st week. Classes resume 2nd week. Break from Thu. before Easter through following Mon.	Break from Thu. before Easter through following Mon. Exams last week-1st week in May.	Exams 1st week.	No classes.
GEORGE WASHINGTON UNIVERSITY	Spring session begins 3rd week. No classes MLK Day.	No classes Presidents' Day.	Spring break 3rd week.	Exams from end of month-1st week of May.	Exams 2nd week. No classes Memorial Day.	Classes continue.
GEORGETOWN UNIVERSITY	Spring session begins 3rd week. No classes MLK Day.	No classes Presidents' Day.	Spring break 1st week.	Classes continue.	Exams 2nd-3rd weeks.	No classes.
HOWARD UNIVERSITY	Spring session begins 2nd week. No classes MLK Day.	No classes Presidents' Day.	Spring break 3rd week. Classes resume 4th week.	Reading period last week.	Exams 1st-2nd weeks. Summer session begins 3rd week. No classes Memorial Day.	Classes continue.
ECKERD COLLEGE	Winter session begins 1st week and ends last week.	Spring session begins 1st week.	Spring break 4th week.	Classes resume 1st week.	Exams 3rd week.	Summer session begins 1st week.
Florida **FLORIDA INSTITUTE OF TECHNOLOGY**	Spring term begins 2nd week.	Classes continue.	Classes continue.	Classes continue.	Exams 1st week. Summer session begins 2nd week.	Classes continue.
FLORIDA INTERNATIONAL UNIVERSITY	Spring session begins 1st week. No classes MLK Day.	Classes continue.	Spring break 4th week. Classes resume 5th week.	Exams 2nd week. Classes end 3rd week.	Summers A&C start 2nd week. No classes Memorial Day.	Super Summer B starts 3rd week. Summer A ends 3rd week
FLORIDA SOUTHERN COLLEGE	Spring session begins 2nd or 3rd week.	Classes continue.	Spring break 1st or 2nd week. Classes resume 2nd or 3rd week.	Exams 4th week.	No classes. Optional May term offers classes all month in England.	Summer session begins 1st or 2nd week.
FLORIDA STATE UNIVERSITY	Spring session begins 2nd week. No classes MLK Day.	Classes continue.	Spring break 4th week.	Classes resume 1st week. Exams 4th week.	Summer session begins 2nd week. No classes Memorial Day.	Classes continue.
NEW COLLEGE OF THE UNIVERSITY OF SOUTH FLORIDA	Interim session begins 1st week. No classes MLK Day.	Spring session begins 1st week.	Spring break last week.	Classes resume 1st week.	Exams 3rd week.	No classes.
ROLLINS COLLEGE	Spring session begins 2nd week. No classes MLK Day. Winter session ends last week.	Classes continue.	Spring break 3rd week.	Classes continue.	Exams 1st-2nd weeks.	No classes.

July	August	September	October	November	December	Additional Info
No classes.	Fall session begins last week.	No classes Labor Day.	No classes Columbus Day.	Break from Thanksgiving Day through following Sun.	Exams 2nd week.	
No classes July 4.	Summer session ends 2nd week. Fall session begins last week.	No classes Labor Day.	No classes Columbus Day.	Break from Wed. before Thanksgiving Day through the following Sun.	Exams 3rd week.	
No classes.	Fall session begins last week.	No classes Labor Day.	No classes Columbus Day.	Break from Thanksgiving Day through the following Sun.	Exams 2nd-3rd weeks.	*Several hundred students are on campus during the summer.*
No classes July 4.	Summer session ends 1st week. Fall session begins last week.	No classes Labor Day.	No classes Columbus Day.	Break from Thanksgiving Day through the following Sun.	Reading period 1st week. Exams 2nd-3rd weeks.	
Summer session ends last week.	Freshman orientation term begins 2nd week.	Fall session begins 1st week.	Classes continue.	Break from Thanksgiving Day through following Sun.	Exams 2nd week.	*Only 75-100 students are on campus during the summer. Campus visits are discouraged during exam periods.*
Summer final exam 1st week.	Fall term begins last week.	Classes continue.	Classes continue.	Classes continue.	Exams 2nd week.	*Campus visits: www.fit.edu*
Classes continue. No classes July 4.	Summer sessions B and C end 2nd week. Fall session begins last week.	No classes Labor Day.	Classes continue. Midterms mid-month.	No classes Veterans' Day. Break from Thanksgiving Day through following Sun.	Exams 2nd week. Classes end 1st week.	*The campus is very active during summer sessions. Visits are not discouraged during exams, but regular session visits are preferred.*
Summer session ends last week.	No classes.	Fall session begins 1st week.	Classes continue.	Break from Wed. before Thanksgiving Day through following Sun.	Exams 2nd or 3rd week.	
No classes July 4.	Summer session ends 1st week. Fall session begins last week.	No classes Labor Day.	Classes continue.	No classes Veterans' Day. Break from Thanksgiving Day through following Sun.	Exams 2nd week.	*Information sessions and tours are available during exam periods, but the campus is very quiet at those times.*
No classes.	Fall session begins last week.	Limited class schedule on Labor Day.	Fall break 3rd week. Classes resume 4th week.	Limited class schedule on Veterans' Day. Break from Thanksgiving Day through the following Sun.	Exams 2nd week.	
No classes.	Fall session begins last week	No classes Labor day.	Classes continue.	Break from Thanksgiving Day through the following Sun.	Exams 2nd-3rd weeks.	*Campus visiting is not discouraged during exam periods.*

School	January	February	March	April	May	June
STETSON UNIVERSITY	Spring session begins 2nd week. No classes MLK day.	Classes continue.	Spring break 1st week.	No classes Good Friday.	Exams 1st week.	Summer session begins 1st week.
UNIVERSITY OF FLORIDA	Spring session begins 2nd week.	Classes continue.	Spring break 2nd week. Classes resume 3rd week.	Exams 3rd or 4th week-1st week in May.	Exams 1st week. Summer session begins 2nd or 3rd week.	Classes continue.
UNIVERSITY OF MIAMI	Spring session begins 2nd week. No classes MLK Day.	Classes continue.	Spring break 2nd week. Classes resume 3rd week.	Reading period 4th week. Exams last week-1st week in May.	Exams 1st week. Summer session begins 3rd week. No classes Memorial Day.	Classes continue.
UNIVERSITY OF SOUTH FLORIDA	Spring session begins 2nd week. No classes MLK Day.	Classes continue.	Spring break 1st week. Classes resume 2nd week.	Exams 3rd-4th weeks.	Summer session begins 1st week. No classes Memorial Day.	Classes continue.
Georgia **AGNES SCOTT COLLEGE**	Spring session begins 3rd week.	Classes continue.	Spring break 3rd week. Classes resume 4th week.	No classes Good Friday.	Reading days and exams 1st week.	No classes.
CLARK ATLANTA UNIVERSITY	Spring session begins 2nd week. No classes MLK Day.	Classes continue.	Spring break 2nd week. Classes resume 3rd week. No classes Good Friday.	No classes Good Friday.	Exams 2nd week.	Summer session begins 1st week.
EMORY UNIVERSITY	Spring session begins 3rd week. No classes MLK Day.	Classes continue.	Spring break 2nd week. Classes resume 3rd week.	Classes continue to end of month.	Reading period and exams 1st week. First summer session begins 3rd or 4th week.	First summer session ends last week.
GEORGIA INSTITUTE OF TECHNOLOGY	Winter session begins 1st week. No classes MLK Day.	Classes continue.	Exams 3rd week. Spring break 4th week.	Spring session begins 1st week.	Classes continue.	Exams 2nd week. Summer session begins 4th week.
MOREHOUSE COLLEGE	Spring session begins 2nd week. No classes MLK Day.	Classes continue.	Spring break 2nd week. Classes resume 3rd week. No classes Good Friday.	No classes Good Friday.	Exams 1st-2nd weeks.	Summer session begins 1st week.
MORRIS BROWN COLLEGE	Spring session begins 2nd week. No classes MLK Day.	Classes continue.	Spring break 1st week. Classes resume 2nd week. No classes Good Friday.	No classes Good Friday.	Reading period 1st week. Exams 1st-2nd weeks.	No classes.
OGLETHORPE UNIVERSITY	Spring session begins 3rd week. No classes MLK Day.	Classes continue.	Spring break 3rd week. Classes resume 4th week.	Classes continue.	Exams 1st week. Summer session begins 4th week. No classes Memorial Day.	Classes continue.

July	August	September	October	November	December	Additional Info
No classes July 4. Summer session ends at end of month.	Fall sessions begins last week.	No classes Labor Day.	Fall break 2nd Mon.-Tues.	Break from Thanksgiving Day through the following Sun.	Exams 2nd week.	
Classes continue.	Summer session ends 1st week. Fall session begins 3rd or 4th week.	Classes continue.	Classes continue.	Break from Thanksgiving Day through the following Sun.	Exams 3rd week.	*Campus visits are not discouraged during exam periods.*
No classes July 4.	Summer session ends 1st week. Fall session begins last week.	No classes Labor Day.	Fall break 3rd Fri.	Break from Wed. before Thanksgiving Day through the following Sun.	Reading period 2nd week. Exams 2nd-3rd weeks.	
No classes July 4.	Summer session ends 1st week. Fall session begins last week.	Classes continue.	Classes continue.	Break from Thanksgiving Day through the following Sun.	Exams 2nd week.	*About 15,000 students are on campus during the summer. Campus visits are not discouraged during exams.*
No classes.	Fall session begins last week.	No classes Labor Day.	Fall break from Friday after Columbus Day through following Sun.	Break from Wed. before Thanksgiving Day through following Sun.	Reading period 2nd week. Exams 2nd and 3rd weeks.	
No classes July 4. Summer session ends 4th week.	Fall session begins 4th week.	Classes continue.	Classes continue.	Break from Thanksgiving Day through the following Sun.	Exams 2nd week.	
Second summer session begins 1st week.	Second summer session ends 1st week. Fall session begins last week.	No classes Labor Day.	Fall break from Saturday preceding Columbus Day through following Tues.	Break from Thanksgiving Day through following Sun.	Reading period and exams 2nd-3rd weeks.	
No classes July 4.	Classes continue.	Exams 1st week. Fall session begins 4th week.	Classes continue.	Break from Thanksgiving Day through the following Sun.	Exams 2nd week.	
No classes July 4. Summer session ends last week.	Fall session begins last week.	No classes Labor Day.	Classes continue.	Break from Thanksgiving Day through the following Sun.	Exams 2nd week.	
No classes.	Fall session begins last week.	No classes Labor Day.	Classes continue.	Break from Thanksgiving Day through the following Sun.	Reading period 1st week. Exams 2nd week.	
No classes July 4.	Summer session ends 2nd week. Fall session begins last week.	Classes continue.	Classes continue.	Break from Wednesday before Thanksgiving Day through the following Sun.	Exams 2nd week.	

School	January	February	March	April	May	June
SPELMAN COLLEGE	Spring session begins 2nd week. No classes MLK Day.	Classes continue.	Spring break 2nd week. Classes resume 3rd week. No classes Good Friday.	No classes Good Friday.	Exams 1st or 2nd week.	No classes.
UNIVERSITY OF GEORGIA	Spring session begins 2nd week. No classes MLK Day.	Classes continue.	Spring break 2nd week. Classes resume 3rd week.	Classes continue.	Exams 2nd week.	Classes continue.
Idaho						
IDAHO STATE UNIVERSITY	Spring session begins 2nd week. No classes MLK Day.	No classes Presidents' Day.	Spring break 2nd week. Classes resume 3rd week.	Classes continue.	Exams 2nd week. Summer session begins 3rd week.	Classes continue.
Illinois						
ILLINOIS INSTITUTE OF TECHNOLOGY	Spring session begins 3rd week. No classes MLK Day.	Classes continue.	Spring break 3rd week. Classes resume 4th week.	Classes continue.	Exams 3rd week.	Summer session begins last week.
KNOX COLLEGE	Winter session begins 1st week.	Classes continue.	Exams end of 1st full week-following Wed. Spring session begins last week.	Classes continue.	Exams from last Fri.-1st Mon. in June.	Exams end 1st Mon.
LAKE FOREST COLLEGE	Spring session begins 3rd week.	Classes continue.	Spring break 2nd week. Classes resume 3rd week.	Exams last week-1st week in May.	Graduation 2nd week.	Summer session begins 2nd week.
NORTHWESTERN UNIVERSITY	Winter session begins 1st or 2nd week.	Classes continue.	Exams 3rd week. Spring session begins last week (or 1st week in April).	Spring session begins 1st week (or last week in March).	Classes continue.	Exams 2nd week. Summer session begins 3rd or 4th week.
UNIVERSITY OF CHICAGO	Winter session begins 2nd week.	No classes 2nd Mon.	Reading period and exams 2nd-3rd weeks.	Spring session begins 1st week.	No classes Memorial Day.	Reading period and exams 1st-2nd weeks. Summer session begins last week.
UNIVERSITY OF ILLINOIS— URBANA-CHAMPAIGN	Spring session begins 3rd week.	Classes continue.	Spring break mid-month.	Classes continue.	Exams 2nd full week. Summer session begins 3rd week.	2nd summer session begins 3rd week.
WHEATON COLLEGE	Spring session begins 2nd week. No classes MLK Day.	No classes Presidents' Day.	Spring break 2nd week. Classes resume 3rd week. No classes Good Friday.	Classes continue.	Exams first week. Summer session begins 3rd week. No classes Memorial Day.	1st Summer session ends 2nd week. 2nd session begins 3rd week.
Indiana						
DePAUW UNIVERSITY	Winter session begins 2nd week and ends last week.	Spring session begins 1st week.	Spring break last week.	Classes resume 1st week.	Exams 3rd week.	No classes.

July	August	September	October	November	December	Additional Info
No classes.	Fall session begins last week.	Classes continue.	Classes continue.	Break Thanksgiving Day through the following Sun.	Exams 2nd week.	
Classes continue.	Fall session begins 3rd week.	Classes continue. No classes Labor Day	Classes continue.	Break Thanksgiving Day through the following Sun.	Exams 2nd week.	
No classes July 4.	Summer session ends 2nd week. Fall session begins last week.	Classes continue. No classes Labor Day.	Classes continue.	Break from day before Thanksgiving Day through the following Sun.	Exams 2nd-3rd weeks.	
Classes continue.	Summer session ends at end of 2nd full week. Fall session begins last week.	Classes continue.	Classes continue.	Break from Thanksgiving Day through the following Sun.	Exams 2nd-3rd weeks.	
No classes.	No classes.	Fall session begins 2nd week.	Classes continue.	Exams from Sun.-Wed. before Thanksgiving. Optional Mini-Term begins Mon. after Thanksgiving.	Optional Mini-Term ends mid-month.	
No classes July 4. Exams last week.	Fall session begins last week.	Classes continue.	Fall break from 3rd Sat. through following Tue.	Break from Thanksgiving Day through the following Sun.	Exams 3rd week.	*Approximately 100 students are on campus during the summer.*
No classes July 4.	Summer session ends at end of 2nd week.	Fall session begins 3rd week.	Classes continue.	Break from Wed. before Thanksgiving through the following Sun.	Exams 2nd week.	*Many of the students on campus during the summer session are from other colleges and universities.*
No classes July 4.	Summer session ends 4th week.	Fall session begins last week.	Classes continue.	Break from Thanksgiving Day through the following Sun.	Reading period and exams 1st-2nd weeks.	
No classes July 4.	Summer session ends 1st week. Fall session begins last week.	Classes continue.	Classes continue.	Break from Tue. before Thanksgiving Day through the following Sun.	Exams 3rd week.	
No classes July 4. Summer session ends Friday of 2nd week.	Fall session begins last week.	No classes Labor Day.	Break 3rd Sat. through the following Tue.	Break from day before Thanksgiving Day through the following Sun.	Exams 3rd week.	
No classes.	Fall session begins last week.	Classes continue.	Classes continue.	Break from Fri. before Thanksgiving through Sun. following Thanksgiving.	Exams 3rd week.	*Fewer than 50 students are on campus during the summer. Campus visits are not discouraged during exam periods.*

School	January	February	March	April	May	June
EARLHAM COLLEGE	Spring session begins 2nd week.	Classes continue.	Spring break 3rd week. Classes resume 4th week.	Classes continue.	Exams 1st week. May term begns 2nd week.	No classes.
INDIANA UNIVERSITY	Spring session begins 2nd week.	Classes continue.	Spring break 2nd week. Classes resume 3rd week.	Exams last week-1st week in May.	Exams 1st week. Summer session begins 2nd week.	Classes continue.
PURDUE UNIVERSITY	Spring session begins 2nd week. No classes MLK Day.	Classes continue.	Spring break 2nd week. Classes resume 3rd week.	Exams last week-1st week in May.	Exams 1st week.	Summer session begins 1st week.
UNIVERSITY OF NOTRE DAME	Spring session begins 2nd or 3rd week.	Classes continue.	Spring break 2nd week. Classes resume 3rd week. Break from Good Friday—Easter Mon.	Break from Good Friday Easter Mon.	Exams 2nd week.	Summer session begins 3rd week.
Iowa						
CORNELL COLLEGE	Spring session (5th course of academic year) begins 2nd week. Course ends last week.	Sixth course begins 1st week and ends last week.	Seventh course begins 1st week and ends last week. Spring vacation begins last week.	Eighth course begins 1st week and ends last week.	Ninth course begins 1st week and ends last week.	No classes.
GRINNELL COLLEGE	Classes begin.	Classes continue.	Spring break begins 3rd week.	Classes resume 1st week.	Exams 3rd week. Spring session ends after exams.	No summer session.
IOWA STATE UNIVERSITY	Spring session begins Jan 10. Holiday Jan 17.	Classes continue.	Spring break 2nd week. Classes resume 3rd week.	Classes continue.	Exams mid-month.	Summer session begins 2nd week.
UNIVERSITY OF IOWA	Classes begin 3rd week.	Classes continue.	Spring break 3rd week. Classes resume 4th week.	Classes continue.	Exams 2nd week.	Summer session begins 2nd or 3rd week.
Kansas						
UNIVERSITY OF KANSAS	Spring session begins 3rd week.	Classes continue.	Spring break 3rd week. Classes resume 4th week.	Classes continue.	Exams 2nd-3rd week.	Summer session begins 1st week.
Kentucky						
CENTRE COLLEGE	Winter session begins 1st week.	Winter session ends 2nd week. Spring session begins 3rd week.	Spring break end of month-1st week in April.	Spring break 1st week. Classes resume 2nd week.	Exams 4th week.	No classes.
UNIVERSITY OF KENTUCKY	Spring session begins 2nd week. No classes MLK Day.	Classes continue.	Spring break 2nd week. Classes resume 3rd week.	Exams last week-1st week in May.	Exams 1st week. Summer session begins 2nd week. No classes Memorial Day.	Classes continue.

July	August	September	October	November	December	Additional Info
No classes.	Fall session starts last week.	Classes continue.	Break Fri.-Sun. at end of 2nd week.	Break from Wed before Thanksgiving Day through the following Sun.	Exams 3rd week.	
Classes continue.	Summer session ends 1st week.	Fall session begins 1st week.	Classes continue.	Break from Tue. before Thanksgiving Day through the following Sun.	Exams 3rd week.	*Campus visits are not discouraged during exam periods.*
No classes July 4. Summer session ends last week.	Fall session begins 3rd week.	No classes Labor Day.	Fall break 2nd Mon.-Tue.	Break from Wed. before Thanksgiving Day through the following Sun.	Exams 2nd week.	
Classes continue.	Summer session ends 1st week. Fall session begins last week.	Classes continue.	Fall break 3rd week. Classes resume 4th week.	Break from Thanksgiving Day through the following Sun.	Exams 3rd week.	
No classes.	No classes.	Fall session (1st course of academic year) begins 1st week and ends last week.	Second course begins 1st week and ends last week.	3rd course begins 1st wk. and ends by Thanksgiving. Break: Wed. before Thanksgiving thru Sun.	Fourth course begins 1st week and ends by Christmas.	
No summer session.	Fall session begins 4th week.	Classes continue.	Fall break 3rd week.	Break from Wednesday before Thanksgiving Day through the following Sun.	Exams 3rd week. Fall session ends after exams.	
No classes July 4. Summer session 1 ends July 7.	Summer session ends 1st week. Commencement Aug 5. Fall session begins last week.	Classes continue.	Classes continue.	Break from Sat. before Thanksgiving Day through Sun. following Thanksgiving.	Exams 2nd week. Holiday Dec. 25-26.	
No classes July 4.	Summer session ends 1st week. Fall session begins last week.	No classes Labor Day.	Classes continue.	Break from Tue. before Thanksgiving Day through the following Sun.	Exams 3rd week.	
No classes July 4. Summer session ends last week.	Fall session begins last week. First day of classes is Aug 19.	Classes continue.	Classes continue.	Break from Wed. before Thanksgiving Day through the following Sun.	Exams 2nd-3rd weeks.	
No classes.	No classes.	Fall session begins 2nd week.	Classes continue.	Break from Wed. before Thanksgiving Day through the following Sun.	Exams 2nd week.	*Only 30-40 students are on campus during the summer.*
No classes July 4. Summer session ends last week.	Fall session begins last week.	No classes Labor Day.	Oct. 6 academic holiday	Break from Thanksgiving Day through the following Sun. Election Day holiday.	Exams 2nd week.	*Many students are on campus during the summer.*

School	January	February	March	April	May	June
Louisiana						
LOUISIANA STATE UNIVERSITY	Spring session begins 2nd week. No classes MLK Day.	No classes from Mon. before Ash Wednesday through 12:30 PM Ash Wednesday.	Spring break last week.	Classes resume 1st week.	Exams 2nd week.	Summer session begins 2nd week.
LOYOLA UNIVERSITY	Spring session begins 3rd week. No classes MLK Day.	No classes Mardi Gras week, Feb. 26 to Mar. 4.	No classes from Wed. before Easter to the following Tue.	No classes from Wed. before Easter to the following Tue.	Exams 2nd-3rd weeks.	No classes.
TULANE UNIVERSITY	Spring session begins 2nd week. No classes MLK Day.	No classes the Mon. and Tue. of Mardi Gras (before Ash Wednesday).	Classes continue.	Classes resume 1st week. Exams last week-1st week in May. Easter break.	Exams 1st week. Summer session begins 3rd week.	Classes continue.
Maine						
BATES COLLEGE	Winter session begins 2nd week. No classes MLK Day.	Break from end of 2nd week to beginning of 4th week.	Classes continue.	Reading period 1st week. Exams 2nd week. Short term begins 4th week.	Short term ends last week.	No classes.
BOWDOIN COLLEGE	Spring session begins 3rd week.	Classes continue.	Spring break 3rd-4th weeks.	Classes resume 1st week.	Exams 3rd week.	No classes.
COLBY COLLEGE	Winter session begins 1st week and ends last week.	Spring session begins 1st week.	Spring break 3rd week.	Classes continue.	Exams 2nd week.	No classes.
UNIVERSITY OF MAINE-ORONO	Spring session begins 3rd week.	Classes continue.	Spring break 2nd-3rd weeks. Classes resume 4th week.	Classes continue.	Exams 1st-2nd weeks. Summer sessions begin 3rd week.	Classes continue.
UNIVERSITY OF NEW ENGLAND	Winter session begins 3rd week and ends last week.	Spring session begins 1st week.	Spring break 4th week.	Classes resume 1st week.	Exams 2nd week. Summer session begins 3rd week. No classes Memorial Day.	Classes continue.
UNIVERSITY OF SOUTHERN MAINE	Spring session begins 3rd week. No classes MLK Day.	Break from Sat. before Presidents' Day through Sun. after Presidents' Day.	Spring break last week.	Classes resume 1st week.	Exams 1st-2nd weeks. Summer session begins 2nd or 3rd week.	Classes continue.
Maryland						
COLLEGE OF NOTRE DAME— MARYLAND	Winter session begins 2nd week and ends 4th week. Spring session begins at end of month.	Classes continue.	Spring break from week before Easter to week after Easter.	Spring break from week before Easter to week after Easter.	Exams 2nd-3rd weeks. Summer session begins last week.	Classes continue.
GOUCHER COLLEGE	Spring session begins 4th week.	Classes continue.	Spring break 3rd week. Classes resume 4th week.	Classes continue.	Exams 1st week.	No classes.

July	August	September	October	November	December	Additional Info
No classes July 4. Summer session ends last week.	Fall session begins 3rd week.	No classes Labor Day.	Classes continue 2nd week. Fall holiday last week.	Break from Thanksgiving Day through the following Sun.	Exams 1st week.	
No classes.	Fall session begins 3rd week.	No classes Labor Day.	No classes Loyola Day.	No classes All Saints Day. Break from Wed. before Thanksgiving Day through Sun.	Exams from end of 1st week-2nd week.	
No classes July 4.	Summer session ends 3rd week. Fall session begins last week.	No classes Labor Day. No classes Yom Kippur.	Classes continue.	Break from Wed. before Thanksgiving Day through the following Sun.	Exams 3rd week.	
No classes.	No classes.	Fall session begins 2nd week.	Fall break 3rd week. Classes resume 4th week.	Break from Fri. before Thanksgiving Day through Sun. after Thanksgiving Day.	Reading period 1st week. Exams 2nd-3rd weeks.	Campus visits are not discouraged during exam periods.
No classes.	Fall session begins last week.	No classes Labor Day.	Fall break last week.	Classes resume 1st week. Break from Thanksgiving Day through the following Sun.	Exams 2nd-3rd weeks.	About 150 students are on campus during the summer. Visits are permitted during exams, but interviews are limited.
No classes.	No classes.	Fall session begins 2nd week.	Fall break from Sat. before Columbus Day through the following Tue.	Break from Wed. before Thanksgiving Day through the following Sun.	Exams 2nd-3rd weeks.	Approximately 60 students are on campus during the summer.
Classes continue.	Summer session ends last week.	Fall session begins 1st week. No classes Labor Day.	Fall break from Fri. before Columbus Day through the following Tue.	Break from Wed. before Thanksgiving Day through the following Sun.	Exams 3rd week.	
No classes July 4. Summer session ends 4th week.	No classes.	Fall session begins 2nd week.	No classes Columbus Day.	Break from Wed. before Thanksgiving Day through the following Sun.	Exams 2nd-3rd weeks.	Approximately 80 students are on campus from mid-June through August.
No classes July 4.	Summer session ends 2nd week.	Fall session begins 1st week.	Classes continue.	Break from Tue. before Thanksgiving Day through the following Sun.	Exams 3rd week.	Call ahead for tour availability. Many students on campus during summer.
No classes July 4. Summer session ends last week.	No classes.	Fall session begins 1st week.	No classes 3rd Fri.	Break from Wed. before Thanksgiving Day through the following Sun.	Exams 3rd week.	Very few College of Notre Dame students are on campus during the summer session.
No classes.	No classes.	Fall session begins 1st week.	No classes 3rd Mon. & Tue.	Break from Wed. before Thanksgiving Day through the following Sun.	Exams 3rd week.	Visits are permitted during exams, but student-led tours are not guaranteed. About 25 students are on campus during the summer.

School	January	February	March	April	May	June
Hood College	Spring session begins 4th week. No classes MLK Day.	Classes continue.	Spring break 2nd week. Classes resume 3rd week.	Easter break from Fri. before Easter through the following Mon.	Exams 2nd week.	No classes.
Johns Hopkins University	Winter session: 1st–3rd wks No classes MLK Day. Spring session begins 4th week.	No classes Presidents' Day.	Spring break 3rd week. Classes resume 4th week.	Classes continue.	No classes 1st week (reading period). Exams 2nd week.	No classes.
Loyola College	Spring session begins 3rd week. No classes MLK Day.	No classes Presidents' Day.	Spring break 1st week. Classes resume 2nd week. Break from Thurs. before Easter through the following Mon.	Break from Thurs. before Easter through the following Mon.	Exams 1st week.	Summer session begins 1st week.
Morgan State University	Spring session begins 4th week.	Classes continue.	No classes Good Friday Spring break last week.	Classes resume 1st week. No classes Good Friday.	Exams 2nd-3rd weeks.	Summer session begins 2nd week.
Towson University	Winter session begins 1st week and ends 4th week. Spring session begins at end of month.	Classes continue.	Spring break 3rd week. Classes resume 4th week.	Classes continue.	Exams 3rd week.	Summer session begins 2nd week.
United States Naval Academy	Winter session begins 2nd week. No classes MLK Day.	No classes Presidents' Day.	Spring break 2nd week. Classes resume 3rd week.	Classes continue.	Exams 1st-2nd weeks.	Summer session begins 1st week.
University of Maryland— College Park	Spring session begins 4th week. No classes MLK Day.	Classes continue.	Spring break 3rd or 4th week.	Classes resume 1st week.	Exams 3rd week.	Summer session begins 1st week.
Washington College	Spring session begins 3rd week.	Classes continue.	Spring break 2nd week. Classes resume 3rd week.	Classes continue.	Exams 2nd week.	No classes.
Western Maryland College	Winter session begins 1st week and ends 4th week. Spring session begins at end of month.	Classes continue.	Spring break 3rd week. Classes resume 4th week.	Classes continue.	Exams 1st-2nd weeks.	Summer session begins 4th week.
Massachusetts **Amherst College**	Winter session begins 1st week and ends 3rd week. Spring session begins at end of 3rd week.	Classes continue.	Spring break begins at end of 2nd week. Classes resume last week.	Classes continue.	Exams 2nd week.	No classes; some students work on campus.
Babson College	Winter session 2nd-4th week. Spring session begins 4th week. No classes MLK Day.	No classes Presidents' Day.	Spring break 3rd week. Classes resume 4th week.	Classes continue. No classes Patriot Day.	Exams 2nd weeks. First summer session begins 4th week. No classes Memorial Day	Classes continue.

July	August	September	October	November	December	Additional Info
No classes July 4.	Fall session begins last week.	Classes continue. No classes Labor Day.	October break mid-month.	Break from Wed. before Thanksgiving Day through the following Sun.	Exams 3rd week.	*Hood offers 3 summer terms with classes in three-, five- and six-week sessions.*
No classes.	No classes.	Fall session begins 1st week.	No classes 2nd Mon.	Break from Thanksgiving Day through the following Sun.	No classes 2nd week (reading period). Exams from end of 2nd -3rd weeks.	*A limited number of students are on campus during Winter; only a few undergrads during Summer. Visits are not discouraged during exams.*
No classes July 4.	Summer session ends 3rd week.	Fall session begins 1st week. No classes Labor Day.	No classes 3rd Fri.	Break from Wed. before Thanksgiving Day through the following Sun.	Exams 2nd-3rd weeks.	*Summer classes are held in the evening; there are daytime programs, but very few college students are around during the day.*
No classes July 4. Summer session ends last week.	Classes begin.	No classes Labor Day.	Classes continue.	Break from Thanksgiving Day through the following Sun.	Exams mid-month.	
Classes continue.	Summer session ends 3rd week.	Fall session begins 1st week. No classes Labor Day.	Classes continue.	Break from Thanksgiving Day through the following Sun.	Exams 2nd-3rd weeks.	
No classes July 4.	Summer session ends and Fall session begins at end of month.	No classes Labor Day.	No classes Columbus Day.	Break from Thanksgiving Day through the following Sun.	Exams 2nd-3rd weeks.	*About 2,000 midshipmen are at the Academy during the summer (except June). Visits are not discouraged at any time.*
No classes July 4.	Summer session ends 3rd week.	Fall session begins 1st week.	Classes continue.	Break from Thanksgiving Day through the following Sun.	Exams 2nd-3rd weeks.	*Campus visits encouraged any time except Spring Break and Dec 25-Jan 1.*
No classes.	Fall session begins last week.	Classes continue.	Break from 2nd Fri. through the following Sun.	Break from Wed. before Thanksgiving Day through the following Sun.	Exams 2nd-3rd weeks.	
Classes continue.	Summer session ends 3rd week.	Fall session begins 1st week.	Break from 3rd Fri. through the following Tue.	Break from Tue. before Thanksgiving Day through the following Sun.	Exams 2nd week.	*Campus visits are not discouraged during exam periods.*
No classes.	No classes.	Fall session begins Tue. after Labor Day.	Break from end of 2nd week through Mon. & Tue. of 3rd week.	Break from Sat. before Thanksgiving Day through following Sun.	Exams from end of 2nd week through Wed. of 3rd week.	
No classes July 4. First summer session ends 1st week. Second summer session begins 2nd week.	Second summer session ends 3rd week.	Fall session begins 1st week. No classes Labor Day	No classes Columbus Day.	Break from Sat. before Thanksgiving Day through the following Sun.	Exams 3rd week.	

School	January	February	March	April	May	June
BENTLEY COLLEGE	Spring session begins 2nd week. No classes MLK Day.	No classes Presidents' Day.	Spring break 2nd week. Classes resume 3rd week.	No classes Patriots' Day.	Exams 1st-2nd weeks. First summer session begins 3rd week.	First summer session ends last week.
BOSTON COLLEGE	Classes begin 3rd week. No classes MLK Day.	No classes Presidents' Day.	Spring break 1st week. Classes resume 2nd week. No classes Thu.-Fri. before Easter.	No classes Thu.-Fri. before Easter.	Exams 1st 2nd weeks. Summer session begins late May. No classes Memorial Day.	Classes continue.
BOSTON UNIVERSITY	Spring session begins 2nd week. No classes MLK Day.	No classes Presidents' Day.	Spring break 1st week. Classes resume 2nd week.	Classes continue.	Summer session begins 3rd week. No classes Memorial Day. Exams 2nd week.	Classes continue.
BRANDEIS UNIVERSITY	Spring session begins 4th week.	Spring recess 1st week.	Classes continue.	No classes Passover week.	Exams 1st-2nd weeks.	Limited summer classes.
CLARK UNIVERSITY	Spring session begins 3rd week.	Classes continue.	Spring break 1st week. Classes resume 2nd week.	Classes continue.	Exams 1st week. First summer session begins 3rd week. No classes Memorial Day.	First summer session ends last week.
COLLEGE OF THE HOLY CROSS	Spring session begins 3rd week.	Classes continue.	Spring break 1st week. Classes resume 2nd week. Break from Wed. before Easter through the following Mon.	Break from Wed. before Easter through the following Mon.	Reading period 1st week. Exams 2nd week.	No classes.
CURRY COLLEGE	Spring session begins 4th week.	No classes Presidents' Day.	Spring break 2nd week. Classes resume 3rd week.	No classes Patriots' Day.	Exams 2nd-3rd weeks.	Summer session begins 2nd week.
EMERSON COLLEGE	Spring session begins 3rd week.	No classes Presidents' Day.	Spring break 2nd week. Classes resume 3rd week.	No classes Patriots' Day.	Exams 1st week. First summer session begins last week.	Classes continue.
HAMPSHIRE COLLEGE	Winter session begins 1st week and continues for 3 weeks. Spring session begins last week. No classes MLK Day.	Classes continue.	No classes on Exam Day during 2nd week. Spring break: 3rd–4th weeks.	No classes on Advising/Exam Day during 2nd week.	Exams 2nd week.	No classes.
HARVARD AND RADCLIFFE COLLEGES	Fall reading period 1st and 2nd weeks. Fall session exams 3rd-4th weeks.	Spring session begins 1st week. No classes Presidents' Day.	Spring break last week.	Classes resume 1st week.	Exams 2nd-3rd weeks.	Summer session begins last week.
MASSACHUSETTS INSTITUTE OF TECHNOLOGY	Winter session begins 1st week and ends last week. No classes MLK Day.	Spring session begins 1st week. No classes Presidents' Day.	Break 3rd week. Classes resume last week.	Classes resume 1st week.	Exams 3rd week.	Summer session begins 2nd week.

July	August	September	October	November	December	Additional Info
Second summer session begins 1st week. No classes July 4.	Second summer session ends 2nd week.	Fall session begins 1st week.	No classes Columbus Day.	Sat. classes held on Veterans' Day. Break Wed. before Thanksgiving Day through following Sun.	Exams 2nd-3rd weeks.	*Campus visits are not discouraged during exam periods.*
No classes July 4.	Summer session ends early August.	Classes begin Wed. after Labor Day.	No classes Columbus Day.	Break from Wed. before Thanksgiving Day through the following Sun.	Exams 2nd-3rd weeks.	
No classes July 4.	Summer session ends 2nd week.	Fall session begins 1st week.	No classes Columbus Day.	Break from Wed. before Thanksgiving Day through the following Sun.	Exams 2nd-3rd week.	*Campus visits are not discouraged during exam periods.*
Limited summer classes.	Limited summer classes. Fall session begins last week.	No classes Labor Day, Rosh Hashanah, Yom Kippur, and Succoth.	Classes continue.	Break from Wed. before Thanksgiving Day through the following Sun.	Exams 2nd week.	*Campus visits are not discouraged during exam periods.*
Second summer session begins 1st week. No classes July 4.	Second summer session ends 1st week. Fall session begins last week.	No classes Labor Day.	Fall break from 3rd Fri. through the following Tue.	Break from Tue. before Thanksgiving Day through the following Sun.	Exams 2nd-3rd weeks.	*Approximately 200 students are on campus for summer sessions.*
No classes.	Classes begin last Wed. or 1st Wed. of September.	Classes begin 1st Wed. (or last Wed. of August).	No classes Columbus Day and Tue. following it.	Break from Wed. before Thanksgiving Day through the following Sun.	Reading period 1st or 2nd week. Exams 2nd or 3rd week.	*Few students are on campus during the summer. Campus visits are not discouraged during exams, but tours are unavailable.*
No classes July 4. Summer session ends at end of month.	Summer break all month.	Fall session begins 1st week.	No classes Columbus Day.	No classes Veterans' Day. Break from Wed. before Thanksgiving Day through the following Sun.	Exams 3rd week.	*Approximately 250 students are on campus for summer sessions. During exams, interviews are available; tours are discouraged.*
First summer session ends 1st week. No classes July 4. Second summer session begins 2nd week.	Second summer session ends 2nd week.	Fall session begins 2nd week.	No classes Columbus Day.	No classes Veterans' Day. Break from Wed. before Thanksgiving Day through the following Sun.	Exams 3rd week.	
No classes.	No classes.	Fall session begins 1st week.	Break 3rd Mon.-Tue. No classes on Advising/Exam Day during last week.	No classes Exam Day during 2nd week. Break from Wed. pre-Thanksgiving Day to Sun.	Exams 2nd week.	*Campus visits are not discouraged during exam periods.*
No classes July 4.	Summer session ends after 2nd week.	Fall session begins 3rd week.	No classes Columbus Day.	No classes Veterans' Day. Break from Thanksgiving Day through the following Sun.	Break from end of 3rd week to 1st week after New Year. (Fall exams are 3rd-4th weeks of Jan.)	*Fall classes are held Sept.–Dec. Visits are not discouraged during exams, but there are no classes, and overnight visits are not allowed.*
No classes July 4.	Summer session ends 3rd week.	Fall session begins 1st week.	No classes Columbus Day.	Break from Thanksgiving Day through the following Sun. No classes Veteran's Day.	Exams 3rd week.	

School	January	February	March	April	May	June
MERRIMACK COLLEGE	Spring session begins 3rd week. No classes MLK Day.	No classes Presidents' Day.	No classes Thu.-Fri. before Easter. Spring break 3rd week.	Classes resume 1st week. No classes Thu.-Fri. before Easter.	Exams 1st-2nd weeks. Summer session begins 3rd week.	Classes continue.
MOUNT HOLYOKE COLLEGE	Winter session begins 1st week and ends 4th week. Spring session begins at end of month.	Classes continue.	Spring break 3rd week. Classes resume 4th week.	Classes continue.	Exams 2nd-3rd weeks.	No classes.
NORTHEASTERN UNIVERSITY	Winter session begins 1st week. No classes MLK Day.	Classes continue	Exams 3rd week. Break 4th week.	Spring session begins 1st week.	No classes Memorial Day.	Exams 2nd week. Summer session begins 4th week.
SIMMONS COLLEGE	Spring session begins 4th week. No classes MLK Day.	No classes Presidents' Day.	Spring break 2nd week. Classes resume 3rd week.	No classes Patriots' Day.	Exams 2nd week.	No classes.
SMITH COLLEGE	Winter session lasts 2nd week through 4th week. Spring session begins at end of month.	Classes continue.	Spring break 3rd week. Classes resume 4th week.	Classes continue.	Exams 1st-2nd weeks.	No classes.
TUFTS UNIVERSITY	Spring session begins 3rd week. No classes MLK Day.	No classes Presidents' Day.	Spring break 3rd week. Classes resume 4th week.	Classes end 4th week.	Exams 1st - 2nd weeks. Summer session begins 3rd week.	Classes continue.
UNIVERSITY OF MASSACHUSETTS —AMHERST	Winter session begins 1st week and ends 4th week. Spring session begins last week.	No classes Presidents' Day.	Spring break 3rd week. Classes resume 4th week.	Classes continue.	Exams 3rd week.	Summer session begins 1st week.
WELLESLEY COLLEGE	Winter session: 2nd week–last week. Spring session begins last week. No classes MLK Day.	No classes Presidents' Day.	Spring break 4th week.	No classes Patriots' Day. (3rd Mon)	Exams 3rd week.	No classes.
WHEATON COLLEGE	Spring session begins last week.	Classes continue.	Spring break 3rd week. Classes resume 4th week.	Classes continue.	Exams 2nd week.	No classes.
WILLIAMS COLLEGE	Winter session begins 1st week and ends 4th week. Spring session begins at end of month.	No classes Fri. of Presidents' weekend (Winter Carnival).	Spring break from end of 2nd or 3rd week to end of month.	Classes resume beginning of month.	Exams 2nd-3rd weeks.	No classes.
WORCESTER POLYTECHNIC INSTITUTE	Winter session (Term C) begins 2nd week.	No classes on Advising Day. Winter session (Term C) ends at end of month.	Break 1st-2nd weeks. Spring session (Term D) begins 3rd week.	Classes continue.	Spring sess. (Term D) ends 1st week. Summer sess. (Term E) begins end of month.	Summer classes continue.

July	August	September	October	November	December	Additional Info
No classes July 4.	Summer session ends 3rd week.	Fall session begins 1st week.	No classes Columbus Day.	Break from Wed. before Thanksgiving Day through the following Sun.	Exams 2nd-3rd weeks.	
No classes.	No classes.	Fall session begins 1st week.	Fall break from Sat. before Columbus Day through the following Tue.	Break from Wed. before Thanksgiving Day through the following Sun.	Exams 3rd week.	*Daytime campus visits are not discouraged during exams; tours are available, but overnight dorm visits are discouraged.*
No classes July 4.	Classes continue.	No classes Labor Day. Summer exams 1st week. Fall session begins 4th week.	No classes Columbus Day.	Break from Thanksgiving Day through the following Sun. No classes Veterans' Day.	Exams 2nd week.	*Campus visits are not discouraged during exam periods.*
No classes.	Classes begin last week.	No classes Labor Day.	No classes Columbus Day and Tue. following it.	Break from Wed. before Thanksgiving Day through the following Sun.	Exams 2nd-3rd weeks.	
No classes.	No classes.	Fall session begins 1st week.	Fall break from Sat. before Columbus Day through the following Tue.	Break from Wed. before Thanksgiving Day through the following Sun.	Reading period end of 2nd-3rd weeks. Exams 3rd week.	*Very few students are on campus during the summer.*
No classes July 4.	Summer session ends 1st week.	Fall session begins 1st week.	No classes Columbus Day.	Break from Wed. before Thanksgiving Day through the following Sun.	Exams 2nd-3rd weeks.	*The summer session offers courses to about 2,000 degree and non-degree students; many of them are not regular Tufts students.*
No classes July 4.	Summer session ends 3rd week.	Fall session begins 2nd week.	No classes Columbus Day.	Break from Wed before Thanksgiving Day through the following Sun.	Exams 3rd week.	
No classes.	No classes.	Fall session begins 1st week.	Fall break from Sat. before Columbus Day through the following Tue.	Break from Wed. before Thanksgiving Day through following Sun.	Exams 3rd week.	*When classes are not in session (including exam periods), tours are subject to the availability of student guides.*
No classes.	No classes.	Fall session begins 1st week.	Fall break from Sat. before Columbus Day through the following Tue.	Break from Wed. before Thanksgiving Day through the following Sun.	Exams 2nd-3rd weeks.	*About 30 students are on campus during the summer. Campus visits are not discouraged during exam periods.*
No classes.	No classes.	Fall session begins 1st week.	Break mid-month Mon.-Tue.	Break from Wed. before Thanksgiving Day through the following Sun.	Exams 2nd week.	*About 90 students involved in faculty-sponsored research are on campus for the summer.*
No classes July 3-5. Summer session (Term E) ends 3rd week.	Fall session (Term A) begins at end of month.	No classes Labor Day.	Term A ends 3rd week. Break 2nd-4th weeks. Term B begins end of 4th week.	Break from Wed. before Thanksgiving Day through the following Sun.	Second Fall session (Term B) ends 3rd week.	

School	January	February	March	April	May	June
Michigan **KALAMAZOO COLLEGE**	Winter session begins 1st week.	No classes Fri. of Presidents' Day weekend.	Exams 3rd week. Winter session ends at end of 3rd week. Spring break from end of 3rd week through last week.	Spring session begins 1st week.	Classes continue. No classes Memorial Day.	Exams 2nd week. Summer session begins last week.
UNIVERSITY OF MICHIGAN	Winter session begins 1st week. No classes MLK Day.	Spring break last week.	Classes resume 1st week.	Reading period and exams last 2 weeks in May.	Spring session begins 1st week. No classes Memorial Day.	Reading period and exams 3rd week.
Minnesota **CARLETON COLLEGE**	Winter session begins 2nd week.	Midterm break over 1st or 2nd weekend.	Spring break 3rd or 4th week. Spring session begins at end of month.	Last weekend break.	Classes continue.	Reading period and exams 1st-2nd weeks.
MACALESTER COLLEGE	No classes.	Spring session begins 1st week.	Spring break last week.	Classes resume 1st week. No classes Good Friday.	Exams 2nd week.	No classes.
ST. OLAF COLLEGE	Winter session begins 1st week and ends last week.	Spring session begins 1st week.	Spring break 4th week.	Classes resume 1st week.	Exams 2nd-3rd weeks.	Summer session begins 1st week.
UNIVERSITY OF MINNESOTA — TWIN CITIES	Winter session begins 1st week. No classes MLK Day.	Classes continue.	Exams mid-2nd-beginning of 3rd weeks. Spring break 3rd week.	Spring session begins last week.	Classes continue. No classes Memorial Day.	Exams 2nd week. Summer session begins 3rd week.
Mississipi **UNIVERSITY OF MISSISSIPPI**	Spring session begins 2nd week.	Classes continue.	Spring break 2nd week. Classes resume 3rd week. No classes Good Friday—Easter Monday.	No classes Good Friday through Easter Monday.	Exams 2nd week. Summer session begins last week.	Classes continue.
Missouri **ST. LOUIS UNIVERSITY**	Spring session begins 3rd week. No classes MLK day.	Classes continue.	Spring break 2nd week. Classes resume 3rd week. Spring session begins 3rd week.	Classes continue.	Exams 2nd week.	Summer session begins 1st week.
UNIVERSITY OF MISSOURI	Winter session begins 2nd week. No classes MLK Day.	Classes continue.	Spring break 3rd week. Classes resume 4th week.	Easter Break.	Exams 1st-2nd weeks.	Summer session begins 2nd week.
WASHINGTON UNIVERSITY	Spring session begins 3rd week. No classes MLK Day.	Classes continue.	Spring break 2nd week. Classes resume 3rd week.	Classes continue.	Exams 1st-2nd weeks. Summer session begins 3rd week.	Classes continue.
Nebraska **UNIVERSITY OF NEBRASKA — LINCOLN**	Spring session begins 3rd week.	Classes continue.	Spring break 2nd week.	Classes continue.	Exams 1st-2nd weeks. Summer session begins 3rd or 4th week. No classes Memorial Day.	Classes continue.

July	August	September	October	November	December	Additional Info
No classes July 4.	Exams last week.	No classes Labor Day. Summer session ends 1st week. Fall session begins 2nd week.	Classes continue.	Break from Thanksgiving Day through the following Sun.	Exams 2nd week.	
Summer session begins 1st week. No classes July 4.	Reading period and exams 3rd week.	Fall session begins 2nd week.	Classes continue.	Break from Wed. before Thanksgiving Day through the following Sun.	Reading period and exams 3rd week.	
No classes.	No classes.	Fall session begins 2nd week.	Midterm break over 2nd weekend.	Reading period and exams week before Thanksgiving Day. Winter break begins Wed. before Thanksgiving Day.	No classes.	Approximately 125 students are on campus during the summer.
No classes.	No classes.	Fall session begins 2nd week.	Break last Thu. through Sun. at end of month.	Break from Thanksgiving Day through the following Sun.	Exams 3rd week.	
Classes continue.	Summer session ends 3rd week.	Fall session begins 1st week.	Fall break last Mon.-Tue.	Break from Thanksgiving Day through the following Sun.	Exams 3rd week.	Approximately 70 regular students are on campus during the summer.
No classes July 4.	Summer session ends 3rd week.	Fall session begins 1st week.	Classes continue.	Break from Thanksgiving Day through the following Sun.	Exams from mid-1st week to mid-2nd week.	Campus visits are not discouraged during exam periods.
Classes continue.	Summer session ends 1st week. Fall session begins 4th week.	No classes Labor Day.	Fall break mid-month.	Break from Wed. before Thanksgiving Day through the following Sun.	Exams 2nd week.	Approximately 3,000 students are on campus during the summer sessions.
No classes July 4. Summer session ends last week.	Fall session begins last week.	Classes continue.	Fall break 2nd week. Classes resume 3rd week.	Break from Thanksgiving Day through the following Sun.	Exams 3rd week.	During summer session, no students live on campus; many visiting students are enrolled in the classes.
No classes July 4.	Summer session ends 1st week. Fall session begins last week.	Classes continue.	Fall break mid-month.	Break from Tue. before Thanksgiving Day through the following Sun.	Exams 3rd week.	Campus visits are not discouraged during exam periods.
No classes July 4.	Summer session ends 2nd week. Fall session begins last week.	No classes Labor Day.	Classes continue.	Break from Wed. before Thanksgiving Day through the following Sun.	Exams 2nd-3rd weeks.	
No classes July 4.	Summer session ends 2nd week. Fall session begins last week.	Labor Day holiday.	Mid-month Fall Break.	Break from Wed. before Thanksgiving Day through the following Sun.	Exams 3rd week.	

School	January	February	March	April	May	June
UNIVERSITY OF NEBRASKA— OMAHA	Spring session begins 2nd week. No classes MLK day.	Classes continue.	Spring break 2nd week.	Classes continue.	Exams 1st week. Summer session begins 2nd week.	Classes continue.
New Hampshire **DARTMOUTH COLLEGE**	Winter session begins 1st week.	Classes continue.	Exams 2nd-3rd weeks. Spring session begins last week.	Classes continue.	Exams last week-1st week of June.	Exams 1st week. Summer session begins 3rd week.
UNIVERSITY OF NEW HAMPSHIRE	Spring semester begins 4th week. No classes MLK day.	Classes continue.	Spring break 3rd week. Classes resume 4th week.	Classes continue.	Exams 3rd week. Summer session begins last week.	Classes continue.
New Jersey **DREW UNIVERSITY**	Winter session begins 1st week and ends 4th week. Spring session begins at end of month.	Classes continue.	Spring break 3rd week. Classes resume 4th week. No classes Good Friday	No classes Good Friday	Exams 2nd-3rd weeks. Summer session begins end of month.	Classes continue.
PRINCETON UNIVERSITY	Fall session reading period 2nd-3rd weeks. Fall session exams 3rd-4th weeks.	Spring session begins 1st week.	Midterm exams 2nd week. Spring break 3rd week. Classes resume 4th week.	Classes continue.	Reading period 2nd-3rd weeks. Exams 3rd week-end of month.	No classes.
RUTGERS UNIVERSITY	Spring session begins 3rd week.	Classes continue.	Spring break begins end of 2nd week. Classes resume 4th week.	Classes continue.	Exams 2nd week. Summer session begins after Memorial Day.	Classes continue.
New York **ALFRED UNIVERSITY**	Spring session begins Tue. of 3rd week.	Classes continue.	Spring break 1st or 2nd weeks. Classes resume on 2nd or 3rd week.	Classes continue.	Exams 2nd week. Summer session begins 3rd week.	1st summer session ends 3rd week. 2nd summer session starts 4th week.
BARD COLLEGE	Winter session begins 1st week and ends 4th week. Spring session begins last week.	Classes continue.	Reading period 3rd week. Spring break last week.	Classes resume 1st week.	Spring session ends 3rd week.	No classes.
BARNARD COLLEGE OF COLUMBIA	Spring session begins 3rd week. No classes MLK Day.	Classes continue.	Spring break 2nd week. Classes resume 4th week.	Classes continue.	Exams 1st-2nd weeks.	No classes.
CLARKSON UNIVERSITY	Spring session begins 3rd week.	Classes continue.	Spring break from March 10-20.	Classes continue.	Exams 1st week. First summer session begins last Mon. of month.	First summer session ends last Sat. of month.
COLGATE UNIVERSITY	Spring session begins 3rd week.	Classes continue.	Spring break 3rd week. Classes resume 4th week. No classes Good Friday.	No classes Good Friday.	Exams 2nd week.	No classes.

July	August	September	October	November	December	Additional Info
No classes July 4.	Summer session ends 2nd week. Fall session begins last week.	Classes continue. No classes Labor Day.	Fall Break on Mon. and Tue. of the 3rd week.	Break from Wed. before Thanksgiving Day through the following Sun.	Exams 3rd week.	*Campus visiting is not discouraged during exams.*
No classes July 4.	Exams 4th week.	Fall session begins 3rd week.	Classes continue.	Break from Thanksgiving Day through the following Sun.	Exams 1st week.	
No classes July 4.	Summer session ends 2nd week. Fall semester begins last week.	No classes Labor Day.	Classes continue.	No classes Veterans' Day. Break from Thanksgiving Day through the following Sun.	Exams 3rd week.	*About 4,500 students are on campus during the summer. Campus visits are welcome during exams.*
No classes July 4. Summer session ends 4th week.	No classes.	Fall session begins 1st week.	No classes the 9th and 10th.	Break from Wed. before Thanksgiving Day through following Sun.	Exams 2nd-3rd weeks.	*Visits are not discouraged during exams, but overnight visits are discouraged then. About 300 students are on campus during the summer.*
No classes.	No classes.	Fall session begins 2nd week.	Midterm exams 3rd week. Fall break end of month-1st week of November.	Classes resume 1st week. Break from Wed. before Thanksgiving Day through the following Sun.	Winter break from 2nd-3rd week of January.	*Campus visits are not discouraged during reading and exam weeks, but classes cannot be visited during those times.*
Classes continue.	2nd Summer session ends mid-month.	Fall session begins 1st week.	Classes continue.	Break from Thanksgiving Day through the following Sun.	Exams 2nd-3rd weeks.	
Classes continue.	2nd Summer session ends 1st week. Fall session begins last week.	Classes continue.	Midsemester break, 2nd or 3rd Mon. and Tues.	Break from Wed. before Thanksgiving Day through the following Sun.	Exams 2nd-3rd weeks.	*Campus visits are strongly encouraged all year long.*
No classes.	Freshman workshop begins 2nd week and ends last week.	Fall session begins 1st week.	Reading period 3rd week.	Break from Wed. before Thanksgiving Day through the following Sun.	Fall session ends 3rd week.	*Reading periods in Mar. and Oct. precede exams, and students may leave campus. Exams are held the final week of each session.*
No classes.	No classes.	Fall session begins 1st week.	Classes continue.	Break from Tue. before Thanksgiving Day through the following Sun.	Exams 3rd week.	*Approximately 200 high school and freshmen students are on campus during the summer for pre-college programs.*
Second summer session begins 1st week.	Second summer session ends 1st week. Fall session begins last week.	Classes continue.	Fall break from Sat. before Columbus Day through the following Tue.	Break from Tue. before Thanksgiving Day through the following Sun.	Exams 3rd week.	*Interviews are not discouraged during exams, but it can be difficult to get tours at those times.*
No classes.	Fall session begins 4th week.	Classes continue.	Fall break from 3rd or 4th Thurs. through the following Sun.	Break from Wed. before Thanksgiving Day through the following Sun.	Exams 2nd-3rd weeks.	*Very few students are on campus during the summer.*

School	January	February	March	April	May	June
COLUMBIA UNIVERSITY	Spring session begins 3rd week. No classes MLK Day.	Classes continue.	Spring break 3rd week. Classes resume 4th week.	Reading period last week-1st week in May.	Exams 1st-2nd weeks.	No classes.
CORNELL UNIVERSITY	Spring session begins 3rd week.	Classes continue.	Spring break 3rd week. Classes resume 4th week.	Classes continue.	Exams 2nd-3rd weeks.	Summer session begins 1st week.
EUGENE LANG COLLEGE	Spring session begins 3rd or 4th week. No classes MLK Day.	Classes continue.	Spring break 2nd week. Classes resume 3rd week.	Classes continue.	Exams 2nd week.	No classes.
FORDHAM UNIVERSITY	Spring session begins 3rd week. No classes MLK Day.	No classes Presidents' Day.	Spring break 2nd week. Classes resume 3rd week. No classes Holy Thu. & Good Fri.	No classes Holy Thu. & Good Fri.	Exams 2nd week.	Summer session begins 1st week.
HAMILTON COLLEGE	Spring session begins 3rd week.	Classes continue.	Spring break 2nd and 3rd weeks. Classes resume 4th week.	Classes continue.	Exams 2nd week.	No classes.
HARTWICK COLLEGE	January session begins 2nd week and ends 4 weeks later.	Spring session begins 2nd week.	Spring break last week.	Classes resume 1st week.	Exams 3rd-4th week.	No classes.
HOBART & WILLIAM SMITH COLLEGES	Spring session begins 3rd week.	Classes continue.	Spring break.	Classes continue.	Exams 2nd week.	Exams 1st week.
ITHACA COLLEGE	Spring session begins 3rd week.	Classes continue.	Spring break 2nd week. Classes resume 2nd or 3rd week.	Classes continue.	Exams 1st week. Summer session begins last week.	Classes continue. Session I ends last week. Session II begins last week.
THE JUILLIARD SCHOOL	Spring session begins 2nd week. No classes MLK Day.	Classes continue.	Spring break 1st week. Classes resume 3rd week. No classes Good Friday.	No classes Good Friday. Only dance and drama classes from last week-1st week in May.	Only dance and drama classes 1st week. Exams 2nd week.	No classes.
NEW YORK UNIVERSITY	Spring session begins 3rd or 4th week. No classes MLK Day.	No classes Presidents' Day.	Spring break 2nd week. Classes resume 3rd week.	Classes continue.	Exams 1st-2nd weeks. Summer session begins 3rd week. No classes Memorial Day.	Classes continue.
RENSSELAER POLYTECHNIC INSTITUTE	Spring session begins 2nd week. No classes MLK Day.	No classes Presidents' Day.	Spring break 2nd week. Classes resume 3rd week.	Classes continue.	Exams 1st week. First summer session begins 3rd week.	First summer session ends last week.

July	August	September	October	November	December	Additional Info
No classes.	No classes.	Fall term begins 1st week.	Classes continue.	No classes Election Day and Mon. preceding it. Break from Thanksgiving Day through the following Sun.	Reading period and exams 2nd-3rd weeks.	*Summer session offered*
Classes continue.	Summer session ends 2nd week. Fall session begins last week.	Classes continue.	Fall break from Sat. before Columbus Day through the following Tue.	Break from Wed. before Thanksgiving Day through the following Sun.	Exams 2nd-3rd weeks.	*Campus visits are not discouraged during exam periods.*
No classes.	No classes.	Fall session begins 1st week.	Classes continue.	Break from Thanksgiving Day through the following Sun.	Exams 3rd week.	
No classes July 4.	Summer session ends 2nd week.	No classes Labor Day. Fall session begins 1st week.	No classes Columbus Day.	Break from Wed. before Thanksgiving Day through the following Sun.	Exams 3rd week.	
No classes.	Fall session begins last week.	Classes continue.	Fall break from Fri. before Columbus Day through the following Tue.	Break from Tue. before Thanksgiving Day through the following Sun.	Exams 3rd week.	*Approximately 50 students are on campus during the summer. Campus visits are not discouraged during exam periods.*
No classes	No classes.	Fall session begins Labor Day.	Fall break from 3rd Sat. through the following Tues.	Break Wed. before Thanksgiving Day through the following Sun.	Exams 3rd week.	*During the summer, the campus is host to extensive programs for high school students.*
No classes.	Classes begin last week.	Classes continue.	Fall break 2nd week.	Thanksgiving break Wed.-Sun.	Exams 2nd week.	
No classes July 4. Session II classes continue.	Summer session ends 1st week. Fall session begins last week.	No classes Labor Day.	Fall break 2nd or 3rd week.	Break from Sat. before Thanksgiving Day through following Sun.	Exams 3rd week.	
No classes.	No classes.	No classes Labor Day, Rosh Hashanah, and Yom Kippur.	No classes Rosh Hashanah and Yom Kippur.	Break from Thanksgiving Day through the following Sun.	Exams 3rd week.	*At press time, Juilliard was considering forming a summer session. At present, some students are on campus during the summer.*
No classes July 4.	Summer session ends 2nd week.	Fall session begins 1st week. No classes Labor Day.	Classes continue.	Break from Thanksgiving Day through the following Sun.	Exams 2nd-3rd weeks.	*Campus visits are discouraged during exam periods if other visiting days are available.*
Second summer session begins 2nd week.	Second summer session ends 2nd week. Fall session begins last week.	No classes Labor Day.	Fall break from Sat. before Columbus Day through the following Tue.	Break from Wed. before Thanksgiving Day through the following Sun.	Exams 3rd week.	*Campus visits are discouraged, but available, during breaks.*

School	January	February	March	April	May	June
ROCHESTER INSTITUTE OF TECHNOLOGY	Winter session continues 1st week.	Exams last week. Spring break from end of month-1st week in March.	Spring break 1st week. Spring session begins 2nd week.	Classes continue.	Exams 4th week.	Summer session begins 1st week.
ST. JOHN'S UNIVERSITY	Spring session begins 3rd week. No classes MLK Day.	No classes Presidents' Day.	Spring Break 2nd week.	Easter recess from Holy Thurs. to Easter Mon.	Exams 1st week.	First summer session begins.
ST. LAWRENCE UNIVERSITY	Spring session begins 4th week	Classes continue.	Spring break 3rd week. Classes resume 4th week.	Classes continue.	Reading period and exams 1st-2nd weeks. Summer session begins last week.	Classes continue.
SARAH LAWRENCE COLLEGE	Spring session begins 3rd or 4th week.	Classes continue.	Spring break 3rd-4th weeks.	Classes resume 1st week.	Spring session ends 3rd week.	No classes.
SKIDMORE COLLEGE	Spring session begins 3rd week.	Classes continue.	Spring break 2nd-3rd weeks. Classes resume 4th week.	Classes continue.	Exams 1st week. First summer session begins 3rd week or 4th week.	First summer session ends last week.
SUNY BINGHAMTON	Spring session begins 4th week. No classes MLK Day.	Classes continue.	No classes 1st or 2nd Thu.-Fri. Spring break last week-1st week in April.	Classes resume 2nd week.	Exams 3rd week.	First summer session begins 1st week.
SUNY BUFFALO	Spring session begins 3rd week.	Classes continue.	Spring break 2nd week.	Classes continue.	Exams 2nd-3rd weeks. Summer session begins last week.	Summer classes continue.
SYRACUSE UNIVERSITY	Spring session begins 2nd week. No classes MLK Day.	Classes continue.	Spring break 1st week (varies slightly each year). Classes resume 2nd week. No classes Good Friday.	No classes Good Friday. Exams last week-1st week in May.	Exams 1st week. Summer session begins 2nd or 3rd week.	Summer break last week.
UNION COLLEGE	Winter session begins 1st week.	Classes continue.	Exams 2nd-3rd weeks. Spring break 4th week.	Spring session begins 1st week.	Classes continue.	Exams 2nd week. Optional summer session begins 3rd week.
UNITED STATES MILITARY ACADEMY	Spring session begins 3rd week. No classes MLK weekend.	No classes Presidents' weekend.	Spring break 3rd week. Classes resume 4th week.	Classes continue.	Exams 3rd week.	Military training exercises.
UNIVERSITY OF ROCHESTER	Spring session begins 3rd week.	Classes continue.	Spring break 1st week. Classes resume 2nd week.	Classes continue.	Reading period and exams 2nd-3rd wks. No classes Memorial Day. Summer session begins last week.	Classes continue.

July	August	September	October	November	December	Additional Info
No classes July 4.	Summer session ends 2nd week.	Fall session begins 1st week.	Classes continue.	Exams 3rd-4th weeks. Break after exams through end of month.	Winter session begins 1st week. Break from Sat. before Christmas–January 3.	A fairly large number of students are on campus for summer session. Campus visits are not discouraged during exam periods.
Summer session I ends before July 4. Summer session II begins 2nd week.	Summer session II ends at end of 1st week.	Fall session begins 1st week.	No classes Columbus Day.	Break from Thanksgiving Day through the following Sun. No classes All Saints' Day.	Exams 2nd-3rd weeks. No classes December 8.	Campus visits are not discouraged during exam periods.
Classes continue.	Summer session ends 1st week. Fall session begins last week.	Classes continue.	Fall break from 3rd Thu. through the following Sun.	Break from Sat. before Thanksgiving Day through the following Sun.	Reading period and exams 2nd-3rd weeks.	Campus visits are not discouraged during exam periods.
No classes.	No classes.	Fall session begins 2nd week.	Classes continue.	Break from Wed. before Thanksgiving Day through the following Sun.	Fall session ends 2nd week.	Only a few students are on campus during the summer.
Second summer session begins 1st week.	Second summer session ends 2nd week.	Fall session begins 2nd week.	No classes Fri. mid-month.	Break from Wed. before Thanksgiving Day through the following Sun.	Exams 3rd week.	Campus visits are not discouraged during exams, but visits at other times are preferred. About 700 students are on campus each summer.
First Summer session ends 1st week. Second summer session begins 2nd week.	Second summer session ends 1st week. Fall session begins last week.	No classes Labor Day.	No classes Rosh Hashanah and Yom Kippur.	Break from Wed. before Thanksgiving Day through the following Sun.	Exams 3rd week.	Check with the Admissions Office before visiting during exam periods. Visits should be scheduled at least a week in advance.
No classes July 5.	Summer session ends 2nd week. Fall session begins last week.	No classes Labor Day. No classes Yom Kippur.	Classes continue.	Break from Wed. before Thanksgiving Day through the following Sun.	Exams 2nd-3rd weeks.	During exam periods, information sessions and tours are not scheduled, but interviews are available.
Classes resume 1st week.	Summer session ends approximately 1st week. Fall session begins last week.	No classes Labor Day. No classes Yom Kippur.	No classes Yom Kippur. Fall break mid-month (long weekend).	Break from Wed. before Thanksgiving Day through the following Sun.	Exams 2nd-3rd weeks.	Campus visits are not discouraged during exam periods.
No classes July 4.	Summer session ends 1st week.	Fall session begins 2nd week.	Classes continue.	Exams just before Thanksgiving.	No classes.	Campus visits are encouraged throughout the year.
Military training exercises.	Fall session begins 3rd week.	Classes continue.	Fall break 3rd Sat. through the following Mon.	Break from Thanksgiving Day through the following Sun.	Fall session ends 3rd week.	In summer, cadets receive training that does not allow interaction with visitors. Summer holidays vary with individual and class.
No classes July 4.	Summer session ends 2nd week.	No classes Labor Day. Fall session begins 1st week.	Fall break from Fri. before Columbus Day through the following Tue.	Break from Fri. before Thanksgiving Day through following Sun.	Reading period and exams 2nd-3rd weeks.	

School	January	February	March	April	May	June
VASSAR COLLEGE	Spring session begins 3rd week.	Classes continue.	Spring break 2nd week. Classes resume 4th week.	Classes continue.	Exams 2nd-3rd weeks.	No classes.
North Carolina **DAVIDSON COLLEGE**	Spring session begins 2nd week.	Classes continue.	Spring break 1st week.	Easter break Thurs. before to Sun.	Exams 1st-2nd weeks.	No classes.
DUKE UNIVERSITY	Spring session begins 2nd week. No classes MLK Day.	Classes continue.	Spring break from end of 2nd week to beginning of 4th week.	Exams last week-1st week in May.	Exams 1st week. Summer session begins 3rd week.	Classes continue.
GUILFORD COLLEGE	Spring session begins 2nd week. No classes MLK Day.	Classes continue.	Spring break from 1st weekend through following weekend.	Exams from end of month-1st week in May.	Exams continue 1st week. Summer session begins mid-month.	Classes continue.
UNIVERSITY OF NORTH CAROLINA— CHAPEL HILL	Spring session begins 2nd week. No classes MLK Day.	Classes continue.	Spring break begins end of 1st full week. Classes resume 3rd full week. No classes Good Friday.	No classes Good Friday. Exams last week-1st week of May.	Exams 1st week. Summer session begins 3rd full week. No classes Memorial Day.	Classes continue.
WAKE FOREST UNIVERSITY	Spring session begins 3rd week. No classes MLK Day.	Classes continue.	Spring break 2nd week. Classes resume 3rd week.	Classes continue.	Exams 2nd-3rd weeks. Summer session begins last week.	Classes continue.
o h i o **ANTIOCH COLLEGE**	Classes begin 2nd week.	Classes continue.	Exams during 3rd week. Spring break last week.	Classes resume 1st week.	Classes continue.	Exams during 3rd week. Summer break begins last week.
CASE WESTERN RESERVE UNIVERSITY	Classes begin 3rd week. MLK holiday.	Classes continue.	Spring break 2nd week. Classes resume 3rd week.	Exams begin last week.	Exams continue 1st week. Summer break 2nd week.	Summer session begins.
COLLEGE OF WOOSTER	Spring session begins 2nd week.	Classes continue.	Spring break 2nd week. Classes resume last week.	Classes continue.	Exams begin 2nd week. Summer break 3rd week.	Summer session-small number of students on campus.
DENISON UNIVERSITY	Spring session begins 3rd week. MLK holiday.	Classes continue.	Spring break at end of 2nd week. Classes resume 4th week.	Classes continue.	Exams 1st week. Summer break begins 3rd week.	No classes.
HIRAM COLLEGE	Spring-12 session begins 2nd week.	Classes continue.	Spring Break at end of 2nd week	Spring-12 exams in 2nd week. Spring-3 classes begin in 3rd week.	Spring-3 exams in 2nd week, followed by summer break.	Limited summer classes.

July	August	September	October	November	December	Additional Info
No classes.	No classes.	Fall session begins 1st week.	Fall break 3rd or 4th week; classes resume last week or 1st week in November.	Break from Wed. before Thanksgiving Day through the following Sun.	Exams 3rd week.	
No classes.	Fall session begins 3rd week.	Classes continue.	Break from middle of 1st week-beginning of 2nd week.	Break from Tue. before Thanksgiving Day through following Sun.	Exams 2nd-3rd weeks.	*Campus visits are allowed during exams; overnight stays and class visits are not. About 30 students are on campus in the summer.*
Classes continue.	Summer session ends at end of 2nd week.	Fall session begins 1st week.	Break from end of 2nd week to Wed. of following week.	Break from Wed. before Thanksgiving Day through following Sun.	Exams 2nd week.	*Campus visits are not discouraged during exams, but visitors at these times will not get a good sense of the school.*
No classes July 4. Summer session ends at end of 3rd week.	Fall session begins 4th week.	Classes continue.	Break from end of 3rd week through following week.	Break from Wed. before Thanksgiving through the following Sun.	Exams 3rd week.	*Approximately 300 students are on campus for summer session.*
No classes July 4. Summer session ends last week.	Fall session begins 3rd week.	No classes Labor Day.	Break Mon.-Tue. of 2nd week.	Break from Wed. before Thanksgiving Day through the following Sun.	Exams 2nd week.	
No classes July 4 weekend.	Summer session ends 2nd week. Fall session begins last week.	Classes continue.	No classes Columbus Day.	Break from Wed. before Thanksgiving Day through the following Sun.	Exams 2nd week.	*Campus visits are not discouraged during exams, but no tours are available. Instead information sessions can be scheduled.*
No students on campus.	No students on campus.	Classes begin during 3rd week.	Classes continue.	Exams during week before Thanksgiving. Classes continue after Thanksgiving.	Winter break begins mid-December.	*Antioch discourages visits during first and last weeks of every quarter.*
Summer session ends. July 4th holiday.	No students on campus until last week. Fall session begins last week.	Classes continue.	October break from end of 2nd week to middle of 3rd week.	Break from Thanksgiving Day through following Sun.	Exams middle of 2nd week-3rd week.	
Summer session continues to end of month.	Classes begin last week.	Fall break begins 4th week.	Classes continue.	Break from Thanksgiving Day through following Sun.	Exams 2nd-3rd weeks.	
No classes.	Classes begin last week.	Classes continue.	Fall break 3rd week.	Break from Thanksgiving Day through following Mon.	Exams 3rd week.	
Limited summer classes.	Fall-12 classes begin last week.	No classes Labor Day.	Fall break 2nd weekend.	Fall-12 exams week before Thanksgiving, followed by session break.	Fall-3 classes.	*Hirams calendar consists of 2 semesters, each with a 12-week and a 3 week session. 50-100 studentts are on campus during the summer.*

School	January	February	March	April	May	June
KENYON COLLEGE	Spring session starts 3rd week.	Classes continue.	Spring break 1st week. Classes resume 3rd week.	Classes continue.	Exams 2nd week. Summer break begins 3rd week.	No classes.
MIAMI UNIVERSITY	Spring session begins 2nd week. No classes on MLK Day.	No classes Presidents' Day.	Spring break 3rd week. Classes resume 4th week.	Classes continue.	Exams 1st week. Break 3rd week. Summer session begins 4th week.	Classes continue. Only a limited number of students are on campus.
OBERLIN COLLEGE	Winter session begins 1st week and ends last week.	Spring session begins 1st week.	Spring break last week.	Classes resume 1st week.	Reading period and exams 2nd-3rd weeks. Summer break begins last week.	No classes.
OHIO STATE UNIVERSITY	Winter session begins 1st week. No classes MLK Day.	Classes continue.	Exams 3rd week. Spring break 3rd week. Spring Session begins last week.	Classes continue.	No classes Memorial Day.	Exams 1st week. Break 2nd week. Summer session begins 3rd week.
OHIO UNIVERSITY	Winter session begins 1st week. No classes MLK Day, offices are closed.	Classes continue.	Exams 2nd week. Spring break 3rd week. Spring session begins 4th week.	Classes continue.	No classes Memorial Day and offices are closed.	Exams 1st week. Summer session begins 2nd week.
OHIO WESLEYAN UNIVERSITY	Spring session begins 3rd week.	Classes continue.	Spring break 2nd week. Classes resume 3rd week.	Classes continue.	Exams 1st-2nd weeks. Spring session ends 2nd week.	Summer session begins 1st week and ends last week.
WITTENBERG UNIVERSITY	Winter session begins 2nd week.	Classes continue.	Exams 1st week. Break 2nd week. Spring session begins 4th week. No classes Good Friday.	Classes continue.	Classes continue.	Exams 1st week. Summer session begins late June.
Oregon **LEWIS & CLARK COLLEGE**	Spring session begins 2nd week.	Classes continue.	Spring break 3rd-4th week.	Classes continue. Final exams last week.	Summer sessions begin.	Summer sessions continue.
REED COLLEGE	Spring session begins 3rd or 4th week.	Classes continue.	Spring break 2nd week. Classes resume 3rd week.	Reading period last week-1st week in May.	Reading period 1st week. Exams 2nd week.	No classes.
WILLAMETTE UNIVERSITY	Spring session begins 3rd week.	Classes continue.	Spring break 4th week. Classes resume 5th week.	Exams last week-1st week in May.	Exams 1st week.	No classes.
Pennsylvania **ALLEGHENY COLLEGE**	Spring session begins 3rd week.	Classes continue.	Spring break 3rd week. Classes resume 4th week.	Classes continue.	Exams 1st-2nd weeks.	No classes.

July	August	September	October	November	December	Additional Info
No classes.	Fall session begins last week.	Classes continue.	Reading Days Oct. 9-10.	Break from Sat. before Thanksgiving through the following Sun.	Exams 3rd week.	
Classes continue. Only a limited number of students are on campus.	Summer session ends 3rd week. Fall session begins 4th week.	No classes Labor Day.	Break 2nd Fri.- following Sun.	Break from Tue. evening before Thanksgiving Day through the following Sun.	Exams 3rd week.	
No classes.	No classes.	Classes begin last week. No classes Labor Day.	Break 3rd week. Classes resume mid-4th week.	Break from Thanksgiving Day through the following Sun.	Reading period 2nd week. Exams 3rd week.	
No classes July 4.	Summer session ends last week.	Fall session begins 3rd week.	Classes continue.	No classes Veterans' Day. Break from Thanksgiving Day through the following Sun.	Exams 1st week. Winter break begins 2nd week.	On Martin Luther King Day, Memorial Day, July 4, and Veterans' Day the campus is closed.
No classes July 4 and offices are closed.	Summer break begins 3rd week.	Fall session begins 2nd week.	Classes continue.	Exams begin 5 days before Thanksgiving. Winter break begins Thanksgiving Day.	No classes.	
No classes.	Fall session begins last week.	Classes continue.	Classes continue.	Break from Sat. before Thanksgiving Day through the following Sun.	Exams begin at end of 2nd week. Winter break begins at end of 3rd week.	Only a small number of students are on campus during the summer session.
Classes continue.	Fall session begins 4th week.	Classes continue.	Classes continue.	Exams week before Thanksgiving. Winter break begins at Thanksgiving.	No classes.	Wittenberg's academic year consists of 3 trimesters and a summer term.
Summer sessions end.	No classes.	Fall session begins after Labor Day.	Fall break 2nd week.	Exams immediately precede Thanksgiving Day.	Classes end Dec 13. Exams Dec 15-20.	Campus visits are not discouraged during exams, but overnight dorm stays and class visits are not possible.
No classes.	Fall session begins last week.	No classes Labor Day.	Fall break 3rd week. Classes resume 4th week.	Break from Thanksgiving Day through the following Sun.	Reading period 1st week. Exams 2nd week.	Campus visits are not discouraged during exams but overnight and dorm stays are not possible.
No classes.	No classes.	Fall session begins 1st week.	No classes 4th Fri.	Break from Wed. before Thanksgiving Day through the following Sun.	Exams 3rd week.	Very few students are on campus during the summer.
No classes.	Fall semester begins 4th week.	Classes continue.	Classes continue. Fall break 2nd week.	Break from Wed. before Thanksgiving Day through the following Sun.	Exams 3rd week.	Approximately 100 students are on campus during the summer.

School	January	February	March	April	May	June
BRYN MAWR COLLEGE	Spring session begins 3rd or 4th Mon.	Classes continue.	Spring break 1st week. Classes resume 2nd week.	Classes continue.	Exams 1st-2nd weeks.	No classes.
BUCKNELL UNIVERSITY	Spring session begins 3rd week.	Classes continue.	Spring break 2nd week.	Exams last week.	Exams 1st week.	Summer session begins 3rd week.
CARNEGIE MELLON UNIVERSITY	Spring session begins 3rd week.	Classes continue.	No classes 1st Mon. Spring break last week.	Classes resume 1st week.	Exams 2nd-3rd weeks. Summer session begins 3rd week. No classes Memorial Day.	Classes continue.
CHATHAM COLLEGE	Winter session begins 2nd week and ends last week. No classes MLK Day.	Break beginning of 1st week. Spring session begins 1st week.	Spring break last week.	Classes resume 1st week.	Exams end of 2nd-3rd week.	Summer session begins 1st week.
DICKINSON COLLEGE	Spring session begins 4th week.	Classes continue.	Spring break from end of 2nd week to beginning of 4th week.	Classes continue.	Exams 2nd-3rd weeks. Summer session begins last week.	Classes continue.
DREXEL UNIVERSITY	Winter session begins 2nd week. No classes MLK Day.	No classes Presidents' Day.	Exams 3rd week. No classes Good Friday.	Spring session begins 1st week. No classes Good Friday.	No classes Memorial Day.	Exams 2nd week. Summer session begins 4th week.
FRANKLIN & MARSHALL COLLEGE	Spring session begins 3rd week.	Classes continue.	Spring break begins at end of 2nd week. Classes resume middle of last week.	Classes continue.	Reading days and exams 1st-2nd weeks.	Summer session begins 1st week.
GETTYSBURG COLLEGE	Spring session begins 3rd week.	Classes continue.	Spring break 3rd week. Classes resume 4th week.	Classes continue.	Exams 1st-2nd weeks.	No classes.
HAVERFORD COLLEGE	Spring session begins 3rd week.	Classes continue.	Spring break 2nd full week.	Classes continue.	Reading period/ exams 2nd-3rd weeks.	No classes.
LAFAYETTE COLLEGE	Winter session begins 1st week and ends 4th week. Spring session begins last week.	Classes continue.	Spring break 3rd week.	Classes continue.	Exams 2nd week.	Summer session begins 1st week.
LEHIGH UNIVERSITY	Winter/Spring session begins 3rd week.	Break Thu.-Fri. of Presidents' weekend.	Spring break 3rd or 4th wk. Classes resume after 1 wk. Break from Thu. before Easter through following Tue.	Break from Thu. before Easter through following Tue.	Exams 2nd-3rd weeks. Summer session begins last week. No classes Memorial Day.	Classes continue.

July	August	September	October	November	December	Additional Info
No classes.	No classes.	Fall session begins 1st week.	Break from end of 2nd week to middle of 3rd week.	Break from Wed. before Thanksgiving Day through the following Sun.	Exams from end of 2nd week to end of 3rd week.	
Summer session ends 3rd week.	Fall session begins 4th week.	Classes continue.	Fall break from 2nd Sat. through the following Tue.	Break from Wed. before Thanksgiving Day through the following Sun.	Exams 2nd and 3rd week.	*Except for 50 students engaged in research, very few students are on campus during August.*
No classes July 4.	Summer session ends at end of 1st week. Fall session begins last week.	Classes continue.	No classes Columbus Day.	Break from Wed. before Thanksgiving through following Sun.	Exams 2nd-3rd weeks.	
Summer session ends 3rd week.	No classes.	Fall session begins 1st week.	Break Thu.-Fri. of 3rd week.	Break from Wed. before Thanksgiving Day through the following Sun.	Exams from end of 2nd week-beginning of 3rd week.	*Campus visits are not discouraged during exam periods.*
No classes July 4.	Summer session ends at end of 2nd week.	Fall session begins 1st week.	Break Thu.-Fri. of last week.	Break from Tue. before Thanksgiving Day through the following Sun.	Exams 3rd week.	
No classes July 4.	Classes continue.	No classes Labor Day. Exams 1st week. Fall session begins 3rd week.	No classes Columbus Day.	Break from Wed. before Thanksgiving Day through the following Sun.	Exams 1st week.	*Campus visits are not discouraged during exam periods.*
Classes continue.	Summer session ends mid-month.	Fall session begins 1st week.	Break from end of 2nd week to middle of the following week.	Break from Tue. before Thanksgiving Day through the following Sun.	Reading days and exams from end of 1st week-middle of 3rd week.	*About 250 students are on campus in the summer. Campus visits are not discouraged during exams.*
No classes.	Fall session begins last week.	Classes continue.	No classes 2nd Mon. and Tue. (reading days).	Break from Wed. before Thanksgiving Day through the following Sun.	Exams 3rd week.	
No classes.	No classes.	Fall session begins on Labor Day.	Break Mon.-Tue. of 3rd week.	Break from Thanksgiving Day through the following Sun.	Reading period/exams 2nd-3rd weeks.	*Approximately 50 students work on campus from June 1-August 15.*
Classes continue.	Summer session ends last week. Fall session begins last week.	Classes continue.	Break 1st Mon. and Tue.	Break from Wed. before Thanksgiving Day through the following Sun.	Exams 2nd-3rd weeks.	
Exams 1st week. No classes July 4. Second summer session begins 2nd week.	Summer session ends at end of 2nd week. Fall session begins end of month or early September.	Fall session begins 1st week (or end of August).	Break from Sat. before Columbus Day through the following Tue.	Break from Thanksgiving Day through the following Sun.	Exams 2nd & 3rd weeks.	

School	January	February	March	April	May	June
PENNSYLVANIA STATE UNIVERSITY	Spring session begins 2nd week.	Classes continue.	Spring break 1st week. Classes resume 2nd week.	Classes continue.	Reading period 1st week. Exams 2nd week. Intersession begins 3rd week. No classes Memorial Day.	Intersession ends 1st week. Summer session begins 2nd week.
SWARTHMORE COLLEGE	Classes begin 3rd or 4th week.	Classes continue.	Spring break 2nd week. Classes resume 3rd week.	Classes continue.	Exams 1st-2nd weeks.	No classes.
UNIVERSITY OF PENNSYLVANIA	Spring session begins 3rd week.	Classes continue.	Spring break 2nd week. Classes resume 3rd week.	Classes continue.	Exams 1st-2nd weeks. Summer session begins 4th week.	Classes continue.
VILLANOVA UNIVERSITY	Spring session begins 3rd week.	Classes continue.	Break 1st full week. Break from Thu. before Easter through the following Mon.	Break from Thu. before Easter through the following Mon. Reading days and exams last week-1st week in May.	Exams 1st week. Summer session begins last week.	Classes continue.
Rhode Island **BROWN UNIVERSITY**	Spring session begins during 3rd full week.	Break from Sat. before Presidents' Day through the following Tue.	Spring break last week.	Classes resume 1st week. Reading period begins end of month.	Exams 2nd-3rd weeks.	No classes.
RHODE ISLAND SCHOOL OF DESIGN	Winter session begins 2nd week. No classes MLK Day.	Winter session ends 2nd week. Spring session begins 3rd week.	Spring break 4th week.	Classes resume 1st week.	Exams 3rd-4th weeks.	Summer session begins 3rd week.
UNIVERSITY OF RHODE ISLAND	Spring session begins 3rd week. No classes MLK Day.	Classes continue.	Spring break 2nd week. Classes resume 3rd week.	Classes continue.	Exams 1st-2nd weeks. Summer session begins 4th week.	Summer session I ends 3rd week. Summer session II begins 4th week.
South Carolina **CLEMSON UNIVERSITY**	Spring session begins 2nd week.	Classes continue.	Spring break 3rd week. Classes resume 4th week.	Exams from last week-1st week in May.	Exams 1st week. Summer session begins 3rd week.	Classes continue.
FURMAN UNIVERSITY	Winter session begins 1st week.	Exams 3rd-4th weeks. Spring break 4th week-1st week in March.	Spring session begins 1st or 2nd week. No classes Good Friday or Mon. after Easter.	No classes Good Friday or Mon. after Easter.	Exams last week.	First summer session begins 2nd week and lasts 6 weeks.
UNIVERSITY OF SOUTH CAROLINA	Spring session begins 3rd week.	Classes continue.	Spring break 2nd week. Classes resume 3rd week. No classes Easter Monday.	No classes Easter Monday. Exams last week-1st week in May.	Exams 1st week.	Summer session begins 1st week.
Tennessee **RHODES COLLEGE**	Spring session begins 2nd week. No classes MLK Day.	Classes continue.	Spring break 2nd week. Easter break from Wed. before Easter to following Mon.	Classes end last week.	No classes after exams in 1st week.	No classes.

July	August	September	October	November	December	Additional Info
No classes July 4.	Summer session ends 1st week. Fall session begins 3rd week.	No classes Labor Day.	Classes continue.	Break from Thanksgiving Day through the following Sun.	Exams 2nd week.	
No classes.	No classes.	Fall session begins Labor Day.	Break from end of 2nd week through end of 3rd week.	Break from Thanksgiving Day through the following Sun.	Exams from end of 2nd week–end of 3rd week.	*Interviews can be scheduled during exam periods.*
Classes continue.	Summer session ends 1st week.	Fall session begins 1st week.	Fall break mid-month.	Break from Wed. before Thanksgiving Day through the following Sun.	Exams 2nd–3rd weeks.	
No classes July 4. Summer sessions end last week.	Fall session begins last week.	Fall session begins 1st week. No classes Labor Day.	1-week break scheduled 2nd, 3rd, or 4th week.	Break from Wed. before Thanksgiving Day through the following Sun.	Reading days and exams from end of 2nd–3rd week.	*Campus visits are not discouraged during exam periods.*
No classes.	No classes.	Fall session begins 1st week.	No classes Columbus Day.	Break from Wed. before Thanksgiving Day through the following Sun.	Reading period begins end of 1st week. Exams 2nd–3rd weeks.	
Summer session ends last week.	No classes.	Fall session begins 2nd week.	No classes Columbus Day.	Break from Wed. before Thanksgiving Day through the following Sun.	Exams 2nd week.	*The summer session is only for transfer students; no other students are on campus at that time.*
No classes July 4. Summer sesion II ends 4th week.	No classes.	Fall session begins 1st week.	No classes Columbus Day.	Break from Thanksgiving Day through the following Sun.	Exams 2nd–3rd weeks.	
No classes July 4. Summer session II ends 4th week.	Classes begin 3rd week.	Classes continue.	Classes continue.	Fall break 1st week. Break from Thanksgiving Day through the following Sun.	Exams 2nd week.	*Campus visits are not discouraged during exam periods.*
Second summer session begins 4th week.	Second summer session ends mid-month.	Fall session begins 2nd week.	No classes last Fri. of month (Fall Weekend).	Break from Sat. before Thanksgiving Day through the following Sun.	Exams 1st–2nd weeks.	*Approximately 300 students are on campus for summer sessions.*
Exams 1st week. No classes July 4. Summer session continues 2nd week.	Summer session ends 2nd week. Fall session begins last week.	No classes Labor Day.	Fall break Mon.-Tue. mid-month.	No classes Election Day. Break from Wed. before Thanksgiving Day through the following Sun.	Exams 2nd–3rd weeks.	*Campus visits are not discouraged during exam periods.*
No classes.	Fall session begins last week.	Classes continue.	Break 3rd Mon.-Tue.	Break from Wed. before Thanksgiving Day through the following Sun.	Exams from end of 2nd–3rd weeks.	*Approximately 30 students are on campus during the summer.*

School	January	February	March	April	May	June
UNIVERSITY OF THE SOUTH	Spring session begins 2nd week.	Classes continue.	Spring break from mid-2nd week-end of 3rd week. Classes resume 4th week.	Classes continue.	Exams 1st-2nd weeks.	Summer session begins 2nd week.
VANDERBILT UNIVERSITY	Spring session begins 2nd week.	Classes continue.	Spring break 1st week. Classes resume 2nd week.	Exams last week-1st week in May.	Exams continue 1st week. May session.	Summer session begins 1st week.
Texas **BAYLOR UNIVERSITY**	Spring session begins 2nd week.	Classes continue.	Spring break 2nd week. Classes resume 3rd week. Break from Good Friday-Easter Monday.	Break from Good Friday-Easter Monday.	Exams 2nd-3rd weeks. Summer session begins Wed. after Memorial Day.	Classes continue.
RICE UNIVERSITY	Spring session begins 2nd week.	Classes continue.	Spring break 1st week. Classes resume 2nd week. No classes Thurs.-Fri. before Easter.	No classes Thurs.-Fri. before Easter. Reading period 3rd week. Exams 4th week.	No classes.	No classes.
SOUTHERN METHODIST UNIVERSITY	Inter-term classes to mid-month. Spring session begins 3rd week. No classes MLK Day.	Classes continue.	Spring break 2nd week. Classes resume 3rd week. No classes Good Friday.	No classes Good Friday.	Exams 2nd week. Summer session begins 3rd or 4th week. No classes Memorial Day.	Classes continue.
TCU	Spring session begins 3rd week.	Classes continue.	Spring break 3rd week. Classes resume 4th week. No classes Good Friday.	No classes Good Friday.	Exams 2nd week. Summer session begins 3rd week.	Classes continue.
TRINITY UNIVERSITY	Spring session begins 3rd week.	Classes continue.	Spring break 2nd week. Classes resume 3rd week. No classes Good Friday.	No classes Good Friday.	Reading period 1st week. Exams 1st-2nd weeks. Summer session begins last week.	Classes continue.
UNIVERSITY OF TEXAS—AUSTIN	Spring session begins 2nd or 3rd week. No classes MLK Day.	Classes continue.	Spring break 2nd or 3rd week. Classes resume 3rd or 4th week.	Classes continue.	Exams 2nd week.	Summer session begins 1st week.
Utah **BRIGHAM YOUNG UNIVERSITY**	Winter session begins 2nd week. No classes MLK Day.	No classes Presidents' Day.	Classes continue.	Exams 4th week.	Spring session begins 1st week.	Exams 3rd week. Summer session begins 4th week.
Vermont **BENNINGTON COLLEGE**	No classes: winter term is a fieldwork term.	No classes.	Spring session begins 1st week.	Spring break last weekend.	Exams last week-2nd week of June.	Exams continue into 2nd week.
GODDARD COLLEGE	No classes.	Spring session begins 1st week.	Spring break 3rd week.	Classes continue.	Evaluation week last week.	No classes.

July	August	September	October	November	December	Additional Info
Summer session ends at end of 3rd week.	Fall session begins last week.	Classes continue.	Break from end of 2nd week-middle of 3rd week.	Break from Wed. before Thanksgiving Day through the following Sun.	Exams 2nd-3rd weeks.	*About 110 students are on campus in the summer for music and writing programs. During exams, interviews are available; tours are not.*
No classes July 4 (in most cases).	Summer session ends 2nd week. Fall session begins last week.	Classes continue.	Classes continue.	Break from Sat. before Thanksgiving Day through the following Sun.	Exams 2nd-3rd weeks.	
No classes July 4.	Summer session ends 2nd week. Fall session begins last week.	Classes continue.	Classes continue.	Break Wed before Thanksgiving Day through the following Sun.	Exams 2nd week.	
No classes.	Fall session begins last week.	No classes Labor Day.	No classes Mon.-Tues. mid-month.	Break from Thanksgiving Day through the following Sun.	Reading period 2nd week. Exams 2nd-3rd weeks.	
No classes July 4.	Summer session ends 1st week. Fall session begins last week.	Classes continue.	Classes continue. Fall break 11-12.	Break from Thanksgiving Day through the following Sun.	Exams 2nd week.	
No classes July 4.	Summer session ends 1st week. Fall session begins last week.	Classes continue.	Break (1-day) mid-month.	Break from Wed. before Thanksgiving Day through the following Sun.	Exam 3rd week.	
No classes July 4. Summer session ends 2nd week.	Fall session begins last week.	No classes Labor Day.	No classes 3rd Fri.	Break from Thanksgiving Day through the following Sun.	Reading period 1st or 2nd week. Exams 2nd-3rd weeks.	*Campus visits are not discouraged during exam periods.*
No classes July 4.	Exams 2nd-3rd weeks. Fall session begins last week.	No classes Labor Day.	Classes continue.	Break from Thanksgiving Day through the following Sun.	Exams 2nd-3rd weeks.	*About 10,000 students are on campus during the summer. Visitors are welcome during exams, but it's best to visit another time.*
No classes July 4.	Summer session ends 2nd week.	Fall session begins 1st week.	Classes continue.	Break from Thanksgiving Day through following Sun.	Exams 3rd week.	
No classes.	No classes.	Fall session begins 1st week.	Break 3rd-4th weeks.	Break from Wed. before Thanksgiving through following Sun.	Exams 1st and 2nd weeks.	*Tours and interviews are available during exam periods.*
No classes.	No classes.	Fall session begins 1st week.	Classes continue.	Break from Wed. before Thanksgiving Day through the following Sun.	Evaluation week 3rd week.	*Campus visiting is discouraged during evaluation weeks.*

School	January	February	March	April	May	June
MARLBORO COLLEGE	Spring session begins 3rd week.	Classes continue.	Spring break from end of 2nd week to end of month.	Classes resume 1st week.	Exams end of 2nd-3rd weeks.	No classes.
MIDDLEBURY COLLEGE	Winter session begins 2nd week and ends last week.	Spring session begins 2nd week. No classes from 3rd Wed. through following Sun.	Spring break last week.	Classes resume 1st week.	Exams 2nd-3rd weeks.	No classes.
UNIVERSITY OF VERMONT	Spring session begins 3rd week. No classes MLK Day.	No classes Presidents' Day.	Spring break 3rd week. Classes resume 4th week.	Classes continue.	Exams 2nd week. Summer session begins 4th week. No classes Memorial Day.	Classes continue.
Virginia **COLLEGE OF WILLIAM AND MARY**	Spring session begins 3rd week.	Classes continue.	Spring break 1st full week. Classes resume 2nd week.	Classes continue to end of month.	Exams 1st-2nd weeks.	Summer session begins 1st week.
HOLLINS UNIVERSITY	Winter session begins during 1st week and ends at end of month.	Spring session begins 1st week.	Spring break last week.	Classes resume 1st week.	Exams end of 2nd-3rd weeks.	No undergraduate classes.
RANDOLPH MACON WOMAN'S COLLEGE	Spring session begins 3rd week.	Classes continue.	Spring break 1st week. Classes resume 2nd full week.	Exams last Sat.-1st week in May.	Exams 1st week.	No classes
SWEET BRIAR COLLEGE	Spring session begins 2nd or 3rd week.	Classes continue.	Spring break 1st week.	Exams last week.	No classes.	No classes.
UNIVERSITY OF VIRGINIA	Spring session begins 3rd week.	Classes continue.	Spring break from end of 1st full week to Mon. of 3rd week.	Classes continue to end of month.	Exams end of 1st week-2nd week.	No classes.
WASHINGTON AND LEE UNIVERSITY	Winter term begins 2nd week.	Break from end of 2nd week to beginning of last week.	Classes continue.	Exams 2nd wk. Break from end of 2nd week to beginning of 4th week. Spring term begins 4th week.	Classes continue.	Exams and graduation 1st week.
Washington **EVERGREEN STATE COLLEGE**	Winter session begins 2nd week. No classes MLK Day.	No classes Presidents' Day.	Exams and end of winter session 3rd week.	Spring session begins 1st week.	No classes Memorial Day.	Exams 2nd week. Summer session begins last week.
UNIVERSITY OF PUGET SOUND	Spring session begins 4th week.	Classes continue.	Spring break 3rd week. Classes resume 4th week.	Classes continue.	Exams 2nd week. Summer session begins 3rd week.	Classes continue.

July	August	September	October	November	December	Additional Info
No classes.	No classes.	Fall session begins 1st week.	Classes continue.	Break from Tue. before Thanksgiving Day through the following Sun.	Exams 2nd week.	*Campus visits are not discouraged during exams.*
No classes.	No classes.	Fall session begins 2nd week.	Break from 3rd Sat. through following Tue.	Break from Tue. before Thanksgiving Day through the following Sun.	Exams 2nd-3rd weeks.	*Very few regular college students are on campus during the summer.*
No classes July 4.	Summer session ends at end of 1st week. Fall session begins last week.	Classes continue.	No classes Columbus Day.	Break from Wed. before Thanksgiving Day through the following Sun.	Exams 2nd week.	*Interviews with counselors, but not tours, are available during exam periods.*
Classes continue.	Summer session ends at end of 1st full week. Fall session begins last week.	Classes continue.	Break from end of 2nd week to Wed. of the following week.	Break from Wed. before Thanksgiving through the following Sun.	Exams from end of 1st week through 3rd week.	*Campus visits are not discouraged during exam periods.*
No undergraduate classes.	No undergraduate classes.	Fall session begins 1st week.	Classes continue.	Break from Sat. before Thanksgiving Day through the following Sun.	Exams 2nd-3rd weeks.	
No classes.	Fall session begins last week.	Classes continue.	Fall break from 3rd Sat. through following Tues.	Break from Wed. before Thanksgiving Day through the following Sun.	Exams 2nd-3rd weeks.	
No classes.	Fall session begins last week.	Classes continue.	Classes continue.	Break from Tue. before Thanksgiving Day through the following Sun.	Exams 2nd-3rd weeks.	
No classes.	Fall session begins last week.	Classes continue.	Break from end of 3rd week through the following Tue.	Break from Wed. before Thanksgiving Day through the following Sun.	Exams 2nd week.	
No classes.	No classes.	Fall term begins 2nd week.	No classes for 2 reading days mid-month.	Break from Fri. before Thanksgiving Day through the following Sun.	Exams from end of 2nd week through 3rd week.	
No classes July 4. Summer session ends last week.	No classes.	Fall session begins 4th week.	Classes continue.	Break from Sat. before Thanksgiving Day through the following Sun.	Exams 2nd week.	*Only limited visits are available during the summer. Make arrangements 2-3 weeks in advance.*
Classes continue.	Summer session ends 2nd week.	Fall session begins 1st week.	Classes continue.	Break from Thanksgiving Day through the following Sun.	Exams 3rd week.	*Only 350 students are on campus in the summer. Campus visits are allowed during exams, but class visits and overnight stays are not.*

School	January	February	March	April	May	June
UNIVERSITY OF WASHINGTON	Winter session begins 1st week. No classes MLK Day.	No classes Presidents' Day.	Exams 2nd or 3rd week. Spring break 3rd or 4th week. Spring session begins at end of month.	Classes continue.	Classes continue. No classes Memorial Day.	Exams 2nd week. Summer session begins last week.
WHITMAN COLLEGE	Spring session begins 3rd week. No classes MLK Day.	No classes Presidents' Day.	Spring break 2nd-3rd weeks. Classes resume last week.	Classes continue.	Exams 2nd week.	No classes.
West Virginia **WEST VIRGINIA UNIVERSITY**	Spring session begins 2nd week. No classes MLK Day.	Classes continue.	Spring break 3rd week. Classes resume 4th week.	Exams last week-1st week in May.	Exams 1st week. Summer session begins 3rd week. No classes Memorial Day.	Classes continue.
Wisconsin **BELOIT COLLEGE**	Spring session begins 3rd week.	Classes continue.	Spring break 1st full week. Classes resume 2nd full week.	Classes continue.	Exams from end of 1st week-2nd week.	No classes.
LAWRENCE UNIVERSITY	Winter session begins 2nd week.	No classes 1st Fri.-Sat.	Exams 2nd or 3rd week.	Spring session begins last week.	No classes Memorial Day.	Exams 1st or 2nd week.
MARQUETTE UNIVERSITY	Spring session begins 3rd week.	Classes continue.	Spring break 2nd week. Classes resume 3rd week.	No classes from Holy Thursday through the following Mon. (Easter Break).	Exams 2nd week. Summer session begins 3rd or 4th week. No classes Memorial Day.	Classes continue.
UNIVERSITY OF WISCONSIN— MADISON	Spring session begins 4th week.	Classes continue.	Spring break 2nd or 3rd week. No classes Good Friday.	Classes resume 1st week. No classes Good Friday.	Exams 2nd-3rd weeks. Summer session begins last week.	Classes continue.

July	August	September	October	November	December	Additional Info
No classes July 4.	Summer session ends 3rd week.	No classes Labor Day. Fall session begins last week.	Classes continue.	No classes Veterans' Day. Break from Thanksgiving Day through the following Sun.	Exams 2nd-3rd weeks.	*Approximately 13,000 students are on campus during the summer session.*
No classes.	No classes.	Fall session begins 1st week.	No classes Columbus Day.	Break from Sat. before Thanksgiving Day through the following Sun.	Exams 2nd week.	
No classes July 4.	Summer session ends 1st week. Fall session begins 3rd week.	Classes continue.	Classes continue.	Break from Sat. before Thanksgiving Day through Sun. following Thanksgiving.	Exams 3rd week.	*About 7,000 students are on campus during the summer session.*
No classes.	Fall session begins last week.	Classes continue.	Break from end of 2nd week to beginning of 4th week.	Break from Thanksgiving Day through following Sun.	Exams 3rd week.	*About 100 students are on campus in the summer, but no classes are scheduled. Campus visits are not permitted during exams.*
No classes.	No classes.	Fall session begins 4th week.	Classes continue.	Break from Thanksgiving Day through the following Sun.	Exams 1st-2nd weeks.	*Some students are on campus in the summer, but no classes are scheduled. Visits can be arranged during exams, but no overnight stays or class visits.*
No classes July 4.	Summer session ends 2nd week. Fall session begins last week.	No classes Labor Day.	No classes 4th Fri.	No classes Nov 1. Break from Wed. before Thanksgiving through the following Sun.	Exams 3rd week.	
No classes July 4.	Summer session ends at end of 1st full week.	Fall session begins 1st week.	Classes continue.	Break from Thanksgiving Day through the following Sun.	Exams from end of 2nd full week-3rd week.	

ALPHABETICAL SCHOOL INDEX

ALPHABETICAL STATE INDEX

ABOUT THE AUTHORS

JANET SPENCER is a professor of law and the mother of two children with whom she visited 30 schools. She lives in New York City.

SANDRA MALESON is a technical writer and editor and has toured many colleges with her two children. She lives in Elkins Park, PA.

NOTES

NOTES

NOTES

NOTES

NOTES

NOTES

NOTES

NOTES

NOTES

NOTES

www.review.com

Expert Advice

Talk About It

www.review.com

Pop Surveys

Paying for it

www.review.com

THE PRINCETON REVIEW

www.review.com

Getting in

Word du Jour

www.review.com

Find-O-Rama School & Career Search

www.review.com

Best Schools

Finding it

www.review.com

The Princeton Review

Find the Right School

**BEST 331 COLLEGES
2002 EDITION**
The Smart Buyer's Guide to College
0-375-76201-9 • $20.00

**COMPLETE BOOK OF COLLEGES
2002 EDITION**
0-375-76202-7 • $26.95

**COMPLETE BOOK OF
DISTANCE LEARNING SCHOOLS**
0-375-76204-3 • $21.00

**POCKET GUIDE TO COLLEGES
2002 EDITION**
0-375-76203-5 • $9.95

**AFRICAN AMERICAN STUDENT'S
GUIDE TO COLLEGE**
Making the Most of College:
Getting In, Staying In, and
Graduating
0-679-77878-0 • $17.95

Get in

**CRACKING THE SAT & PSAT/NMSQT
2002 EDITION**
0-375-76207-8 • $18.00

**CRACKING THE SAT & PSAT/NMSQT
WITH SAMPLE TESTS ON CD-ROM
2002 EDITION**
0-375-76192-6 • $29.95

**SAT MATH WORKOUT
2ND EDITION**
0-375-76177-7 • $14.95

**SAT VERBAL WORKOUT
2ND EDITION**
0-375-76176-4 • $14.95

**CRACKING THE ACT WITH
SAMPLE TESTS ON CD-ROM
2001 EDITION**
0-375-76180-2 • $29.95

**CRACKING THE ACT
2001 EDITION**
0-375-76179-9 • $18.00

CRASH COURSE FOR THE ACT
10 Easy Steps to Higher Score
0-375-75376-5 • $9.95

CRASH COURSE FOR THE SAT
10 Easy Steps to Higher Score
0-375-75324-9 • $9.95

Get Help Paying for it

DOLLARS & SENSE FOR COLLEGE STUDENTS
How Not to Run Out of Money by Midterms
0-375-75206-4 • $10.95

**PAYING FOR COLLEGE WITHOUT GOING BROKE
2001 EDITION**
Insider Strategies to Maximize Financial Aid
and Minimize College Costs
0-375-76156-X • $18.00

**THE SCHOLARSHIP ADVISOR
2001 EDITION**
0-375-76160-8 • $25.00

Make the Grade with Study Guides for the AP and SAT II Exams

AP Exams

CRACKING THE AP BIOLOGY 2000-2001 EDITION
0-375-75495-4 • $17.00

CRACKING THE AP CALCULUS AB & BC 2000-2001 EDITION
0-375-75499-7 • $18.00

CRACKING THE AP CHEMISTRY 2000-2001 EDITION
0-375-75497-0 • $17.00

CRACKING THE AP ECONOMICS (MACRO & MICRO) 2000-2001 EDITION
0-375-75507-1 • $17.00

CRACKING THE AP ENGLISH LITERATURE 2000-2001 EDITION
0-375-75493-8 • $17.00

CRACKING THE AP EUROPEAN HISTORY 2000-2001 EDITION
0-375-75498-9 • $17.00

CRACKING THE AP PHYSICS 2000-2001 EDITION
0-375-75492-X • $19.00

CRACKING THE AP PSYCHOLOGY 2000-2001 EDITION
0-375-75480-6 • $17.00

CRACKING THE AP SPANISH 2000-2001 EDITION
0-375-75481-4 • $17.00

CRACKING THE AP U.S. GOVERNMENT AND POLITICS 2000-2001 EDITION
0-375-75496-2 • $17.00

CRACKING THE AP U.S. HISTORY 2000-2001 EDITION
0-375-75494-6 • $17.00

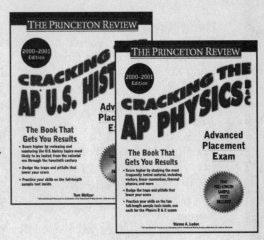

SAT II Exams

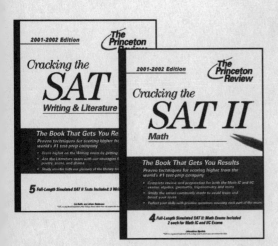

CRACKING THE SAT II: BIOLOGY 2001-2002 EDITION
0-375-76181-0 • $17.00

CRACKING THE SAT II: CHEMISTRY 2001-2002 EDITION
0-375-76182-9 • $17.00

CRACKING THE SAT II: FRENCH 2001-2002 EDITION
0-375-76184-5 • $17.00

CRACKING THE SAT II: LITERATURE & WRITING 2001-2002 EDITION
0-375-76183-7 • $17.00

CRACKING THE SAT II: MATH 2001-2002 EDITION
0-375-76186-1 • $18.00

CRACKING THE SAT II: PHYSICS 2001-2002 EDITION
0-375-76187-X • $17.00

CRACKING THE SAT II: SPANISH 2001-2002 EDITION
0-375-76188-8 • $17.00

CRACKING THE SAT II: U.S. & WORLD HISTORY 2001-2002 EDITION
0-375-76185-3 • $17.00

Available at Bookstores Everywhere.
www.review.com

FIND US...

International

Hong Kong
4/F Sun Hung Kai Centre
30 Harbour Road, Wan Chai,
Hong Kong
Tel: (011)85-2-517-3016

Japan
Fuji Building 40, 15-14
Sakuragaokacho, Shibuya Ku,
Tokyo 150, Japan
Tel: (011)81-3-3463-1343

Korea
Tae Young Bldg, 944-24,
Daechi- Dong, Kangnam-Ku
The Princeton Review—ANC
Seoul, Korea 135-280,
South Korea
Tel: (011)82-2-554-7763

Mexico City
PR Mex S De RL De Cv
Guanajuato 228 Col. Roma
06700 Mexico D.F., Mexico
Tel: 525-564-9468

Montreal
666 Sherbrooke St.
West, Suite 202
Montreal, QC H3A 1E7 Canada
Tel: 514-499-0870

Pakistan
1 Bawa Park - 90 Upper Mall
Lahore, Pakistan
Tel: (011)92-42-571-2315

Spain
Pza. Castilla, 3 - 5º A, 28046
Madrid, Spain
Tel: (011)341-323-4212

Taiwan
155 Chung Hsiao East Road
Section 4 - 4th Floor,
Taipei R.O.C., Taiwan
Tel: (011)886-2-751-1243

Thailand
Building One, 99 Wireless Road
Bangkok, Thailand 10330
Tel: 662-256-7080

Toronto
1240 Bay Street, Suite 300
Toronto M5R 2A7 Canada
Tel: 800-495-7737
Tel: 716-839-4391

Vancouver
4212 University Way NE,
Suite 204
Seattle, WA 98105
Tel: 206-548-1100

locations

National (U.S.)
We have more than 60 offices around the U.S. and
run courses at over 400 sites. For courses and locations
within the U.S. call 1-800-2-Review and you will be
routed to the nearest office.